FIFTY MORE CONTEMPORARY
ONE-ACT PLAYS

Fifty More Contemporary One-Act Plays

Selected and Edited
BY
FRANK SHAY

D. APPLETON AND COMPANY
NEW YORK :: :: MCMXXXII

PRINTED IN THE UNITED STATES OF AMERICA

INTRODUCTION

This volume, like its predecessor, contains some fifty one-act plays by authors of various nationalities. Like the previous collection the selection entailed great labor and an enormous amount of reading in the works of contemporary writers. The result, to a very great extent, is practically the same.

The editor of such a collection of plays stands, somewhat unwillingly, as a sort of a playreader in extraordinary to the little theatres of America. He is, in the manner of speaking, the first reader. The very fact that he includes a given play in his book indicates his belief that the play is one that little theatres will approve. Whether the play in question is actually suitable will always remain a matter for the decision of the final playreader and the director of the individual group. The chief difficulty is what group or type of organization is he to select plays for? Manifestly a group of intelligent adults will not be content with a play that might find great favor with a group of school children. Yet both these groups will repair to the editor's work to find the play they are seeking. That both groups must find what they are seeking is the single duty of the editor.

There seems to be an opinion prevalent in some circles that the one-act play has been finally thrown into the discard. To give their statements a semblance of strength these detractors point to the great number of independent producing groups confining their efforts to full-length plays. In the days of the Washington Square Players, the early days of the Provincetown and Neighborhood groups the short play was preëminent. Diminutive dramas echoed up and down the continent and were considered the entire stock-in-trade of the so-called little theatre. One could see longer plays in the routine theatres and it would have been ruinous for the younger groups to attempt such an effort. Even the playwrights whose work was shown by these groups confined their work to the shorter form. And, to-day, those very groups who would not attempt a long play are confining all their activities to full-length plays.

There is a modicum of truth in these conclusions. The shorter form served both the playwright and the producing group as a vehicle to get where they were going. It was a means to an end: they found their wings or cut their eye-teeth on the dwarfed drama and went on to greater heights. Now, after many years of experience they have large theatres where they produce the long plays of those writers who formerly wrote short plays.

For all this there are a greater number of little theatre and amateur groups using short plays than ever before. Those who lease plays to these groups report a constantly growing clientele and an ever-increasing demand for short plays of distinction. Is it too much to suppose that these consumers of short plays will not, in time, become sufficiently experienced to engage and sustain the longer rôles?

This collection then is dedicated to those younger players and groups who, realizing their limitations, are trying to find their wings, who are using the short play as means to this end.

I wish to acknowledge the valuable assistance given me by the late Arnold Daly, Mr. Barrett H. Clark and Miss Paula Holladay. Thanks are also due those authors and publishers who have so kindly permitted me to reprint their plays.

F. S.

CONTENTS

vii

LIARS

A Comedy

By Sholem Aleichem

Adapted and Translated from the Yiddish by Etta Block

CHARACTERS

A KALOMAIER.
A RUSSIAN.

LIARS

A Comedy   By Sholem Aleichem

[*The dialogue takes place on board the train en route to Kalomai between a Kalomaier on his way home and a Russian who has just boarded the train.*]

THE RUSSIAN. You're going to Kalomai, I believe.

THE KALOMAIER. How did you know I was going to Kalomai?

THE RUSSIAN. I heard you talking to the conductor. A real Kalomaier or just going there?

THE KALOMAIER. Really a Kalomaier. What of it?

THE RUSSIAN. Nothing. Just so. I just ask. A nice town, Kalomai?

THE KALOMAIER. What do you call a nice town? A town like all other towns in Galicia, a fine town, a very fine town.

THE RUSSIAN. I mean have you nice people there, rich men?

THE KALOMAIER. There are all kinds. There are rich, there are poor; naturally more poor than rich.

THE RUSSIAN. The same as with us; to one rich man, no Evil Eye, a thousand poor. In Kalomai there should be living one Finkelstein, a very rich man.

THE KALOMAIER. There is a rich Finkelstein. What of it, you know him?

THE RUSSIAN. I do not know him but I've heard tell of him. Isn't he called Reb Shiah?

THE KALOMAIER. Reb Shiah. What of it?

THE RUSSIAN. Nothing, just so. I just ask. Is he really as rich as they say, this Reb Shiah?

THE KALOMAIER. Do I know? I haven't counted his money. Why do you inquire so after him? Has it to do with credit, perhaps?

THE RUSSIAN. No, just so. He has, it is said, a daughter.

THE KALOMAIER. He has three daughters. Aha! about a match, maybe?

How much do they say does he give with her, his daughter?

THE RUSSIAN. It's not a question of dowry here, understand me. We're talking about his house, we are. What sort of house does he have, this Reb Shiah Finkelstein? What sort of home does he run, I mean?

THE KALOMAIER. What kind of home should it be? A home like all homes, a Jewish house, a fine house, a *Schedische*, a very fine house. They do say, though, that as regards Jewishness of late . . . but it's a lie!

THE RUSSIAN. *What* is a lie?

THE KALOMAIER. Whatever they may say is a lie. Kalomai, you should know, is a *town* of liars!

THE RUSSIAN. It would be interesting anyhow to hear what they do say of his house.

THE KALOMAIER. What they say is, that it isn't any more what it used to be. For instance, formerly they used to celebrate the Passover according to ritual—strict! He, himself, even used to make a pilgrimage to the Rebbe twice a year—but nowadays—nowadays, it isn't the same any more.

THE RUSSIAN. And that's all?

THE KALOMAIER. What did you expect to hear? That he had already cast off his earlocks and beard and eats pig meat openly?

THE RUSSIAN. You say "they say" so I thought goodness only knows what they say. But the main thing after all is, is the man himself *a man*. What I mean, is *he*—this Reb Shiah Finkelstein I mean—a fine man, reputable, highly respectable? That's what I mean.

THE KALOMAIER. What do you call a fine man? He's a man like other men. Well, how shall I put it? Yes, a really fine person. Though at home they talk —that he *is* a bit of a . . . But it's a lie!

3

THE RUSSIAN. What is a lie?

THE KALOMAIER. Everything they say about him is a lie. Kalomai is such a town. They like to talk about one another so I don't care to repeat it because you know such talk is already an evil.

THE RUSSIAN. As long as you know it's not so, it is quite harmless to repeat it.

THE KALOMAIER. Well, they say he is—somewhat of a—swindler.

THE RUSSIAN. A swindler? Every man is a bit of a swindler. Men swindle. And you don't swindle sometimes?

THE KALOMAIER. There's a difference between swindling and swindling, too. Of him they say, you understand me . . . but it's a lie!

THE RUSSIAN. What, for instance, do they say about him?

THE KALOMAIER. But I'm telling you it's a lie.

THE RUSSIAN. I should like to hear the lie though.

THE KALOMAIER. They say that he has already bankrupted three times, but it's a lie! I know of only once.

THE RUSSIAN. And that's all? Where have you ever seen a merchant who has not bankrupted? A man, if he stays long enough in business, bankrupts. One trades so long until one overreaches himself. If a man in business dies without having failed it is a sign that he died before his time. What, not so?

THE KALOMAIER. Everything he calls bankrupt. They say his was a nasty failure—simply pocketed the money and showed the world—a fig! You understand?

THE RUSSIAN. No fool apparently. No, and nothing else?

THE KALOMAIER. What more do you want? he should commit a crime, commit murder? There is a story going around among us though—a rather ugly tale—but it's a lie!

THE RUSSIAN. What kind of tale?

THE KALOMAIER. An affair with a Poretz—not a word of truth to it!

THE RUSSIAN. What kind of an affair was it with the Poretz?

THE KALOMAIER. Some sort of a Poretz out there—notes—do I know what Kalomai can make up? A lie! I know it's a lie!

THE RUSSIAN. But if you know it's a lie it can't hurt him any.

THE KALOMAIER. It is said he did business with a Poretz, a very rich Poretz, who made much of him—very much. In the meantime the Poretz goes and dies. What does Finkelstein do? He presents a couple of notes against the Poretz. The town commenced to boil, I can tell you. How does he come to have notes against the Poretz when he was known never to have signed a paper in his whole life? Kalomai, you should know, is a town that takes note of things.

THE RUSSIAN. Well?

THE KALOMAIER. Well, he had a load on his back, I tell you.

THE RUSSIAN. And is that all? Every Jew carries a load on his back. Ever see a Jew without his load to pack?

THE KALOMAIER. But of him they said he was carrying not one but three loads!

THE RUSSIAN. Three? What else do they say of him?

THE KALOMAIER. That he had something to do with a mill. But that is plainly a lie.

THE RUSSIAN. So the mill burned down, I suppose, and they said that he set fire to it himself, because the mill was an old one anyway, and he had her well insured so that he could afterwards erect a new one.

THE KALOMAIER. But how did you know that that's how it was?

THE RUSSIAN. Know it, I didn't, but I just guessed that that's how it must have been.

THE KALOMAIER. And that's how we gossip in Kalomai, but it's a lie. I could take an oath on it—it's a lie.

THE RUSSIAN. It doesn't bother me —if it be true. What other pack was he carrying on him did you say?

THE KALOMAIER. I said? The town says. But that surely is a false charge!

THE RUSSIAN. A false charge—accusation? Counterfeiting, perhaps?

THE KALOMAIER. Worse!

THE RUSSIAN. What can be worse?

THE KALOMAIER. It's a disgrace— upon my word. Empty heads—idlers —and, perhaps, it is just plain blackmail so they can wring money from him. You know how it is, a small town— and a rich man has enemies.

THE RUSSIAN. I suppose he had to do with the servant girl.

THE KALOMAIER. Now, how did *you* know? You've already been told?

THE RUSSIAN. No, I've not been told, but it isn't hard to guess. I suppose it must have cost him a few kreutzer, this little matter of the servant girl, now?

THE KALOMAIER. May each of us hope to earn it every week, and I wish you no ill, what this cost him, though he was perfectly innocent. A small town—a wealthy man—it goes well with him. They begrudge it to him! They actually begrudge him! . . .

THE RUSSIAN. Possibly. He has nice children? Three daughters, I think, you said he had.

THE KALOMAIER. Three. Two married and one still a girl. Fine children, very fine children. They say of the eldest, however . . . but it's a lie!

THE RUSSIAN. What do they say of her?

THE KALOMAIER. But I tell you that it's a lie.

THE RUSSIAN. I *know* it's a lie, but I would like to hear the lie just the same.

THE KALOMAIER. If you were a mind to listen to all the lies that go around in Kalomai you would need three days and three nights. Of the oldest they say that she goes about with her own hair and I can bear witness that that's a lie, because she isn't such an educated lady at all she should wear her own hair.* And of the second daughter they actually invented a tale that as a girl she . . . but what Kalomai can't make up! It's a lie!

* Without the customary wig (*shaitel*) which a woman is enjoined to wear after marriage so that the locks of maidenhood are not exposed.

THE RUSSIAN. I am really curious to hear what Kalomai *can* make up.

THE KALOMAIER. I am telling you that Kalomai is a town of liars and gossips and scandalmongers and long tongues! Don't you know in a small town if a girl goes walking alone at night on the street in the dark with a young man, there is at once a great *tara-ram*. . . . What business has a young girl to go about in Kalomai at night all alone with a young druggist?

THE RUSSIAN. And so that's all?

THE KALOMAIER. What else did you want? She should run away with him in the middle of Yom Kippur to Czernowitz, just as they tell of the little trick the youngest girl played?

THE RUSSIAN. What trick did the youngest one play?

THE KALOMAIER. As I live, it's not worth repeating all the *klatcherei* going about among us in Kalomai, and I *do* hate to repeat a lie. . . .

THE RUSSIAN. You've already repeated so many lies, you can tell one more.

THE KALOMAIER. I'm not telling my own lies, Reb Yüd! I told the lies of others. And anyway I don't understand why you inquire so after each particular person separately like a prosecuting attorney. It seems to me you're a man who loves to worm out of the other fellow—to draw out the marrow of his very bones and all the while you're afraid to drop a word yourself. . . . Don't be offended that I speak so plain. It seems to me you're a Russian and the Russians have in them the ugly habit—they like to crawl into another's heart, boots and all. And the Russians, I see, are no small gossips themselves! Aha, we are nearly there and I must get my things together. I wish you a good. . . .

[*Exit.*]

[*Curtain.*]

MARTHE

A Play

By Noel Armstrong

CHARACTERS

MARTHE RIGNEY [*an aged Irishwoman*].
MARY DAVIS [*an elderly neighbor*].
FANNY WASHBURN [*another neighbor*].
DAVID LELAND [*a peddler of eggs and butter*].
LUCIE OLIVER [*a young school-teacher*].
JOHN DAVIS [*a young man*].

MARTHE

A PLAY

By NOEL ARMSTRONG

[*The* SCENE *is a large square room with four windows, the kind of room that in an eastern farmhouse is used for both living room and kitchen. The walls are wainscoted elbow-high with unpainted hardwood that has turned brown with age. Above the wainscoting, the walls are hung with a striped wall paper. The floor is of wide smooth boards, scrubbed a glistening white. On the floor are faded braided and hooked rag rugs. At the back of the room on the right is a door that leads into a bedroom. This door is open and one sees a high four-poster bed covered with a blue and white woolen counterpane. At the back of the room on the left a door with upper panels of glass opens into a woodshed. On the left side of the room another door opens into a pantry. On the wall near the pantry door is a shelf of wood, unpainted and brown with age and the smoke of many fires. On the shelf are old blue china cups and saucers and plates, a sugar bowl, a cheap clock and a kerosene lamp. In the middle of the room is an old-fashioned stove with a high oven and doors in front of the fire box that may be flung open to give the effect of a fireplace. On the right side of the room is a plain table with folding leaves covered with a blue and white checked spread. On the walls are two crayon portraits in hideous tawdry gilt frames. One is the likeness of a plain-featured young Irishwoman, the other is that of a handsome young Irish lad leaning on a stick. Both have apparently been copied from daguerreotypes. A tawdry bright-colored calendar of the current year—1890—hangs over the table and a yellow almanac hangs under the clock shelf suspended from a peg by a loop of string.*

On the high oven of the stove are old-fashioned flatirons with bright patchwork covers on their handles. Behind the stove is a wood box covered with the same striped paper that decorates the walls. Four unpainted wooden chairs are ranged stiffly against the three walls. A chair similar to those against the walls is on the right of the stove well out toward the middle of the room. Mary Davis sits in this chair knitting. She is an old woman in her seventies, sprightly, modern-minded, and energetic. She wears a shabby but decent black silk dress made with a basque and a full gathered skirt. She has a bit of old lawn pinned about her throat with an oval gold brooch. Her one bit of flair is a pair of antique earrings that match the brooch.

On the left of the stove but toward the side wall, Fanny Washburn is sitting. She is slightly younger than Mary Davis, a simple, kindly, credulous soul. Her dress is a faded wine-colored cashmere made with a polonaise and a plain skirt with a flounce. She has yellowish mull ruches in her high straight collar and in the edges of her tight cuffs. She is gentle, subdued, and resigned in manner. Her hands are folded on her lap.

Near the stove on the left, ranged so that the three women make an arc of a circle, Marthe Rigney is sitting in a wide, deep, wooden armchair cushioned in red calico. She is a hard-minded old woman. Her face is Irish, squarish, masculine and grim, her eyes bright. When she speaks her voice will have the note of time and her hard nature— a dry irritating rasp. She wears skirts of faded blue calico and a light lemon-colored basque. A large plain, white, cotton handkerchief is pinned around her throat, fichu fashion. Her stockings are white and wrinkled around her ankles and her coarse leather pumps have been made by cutting off the tops of a pair of congress gaiters. She wears a cap

9

of fluted yellowish muslin with strings that dangle on either side of her face. Her hair is scanty, but not white. It has been black and is a grizzled gray. She is smoking a blackened clay pipe which she fills from time to time from a pocket in her skirt. Near her chair on the left is a small semicircular green plant stand. On the plant stand is a paper of smoking tobacco. The women wear dresses ten years behind the styles of the period because fashions did not change in the remote mountain hamlet where they lived. Dresses were cherished possessions and lasted many years.]

MARTHE. And what do folks say about me, Fanny Washburn? Mary is always hinting that they have something to say.

FANNY. I'm not one to be carrying tales, Marthe. What does their talk matter? We all have to live our own lives. Your way ain't their way.

MARTHE. But I want to know . . . what do they say?

MARY. I'll tell you what they say, Marthe. No use to ask Fanny. She's too chicken-hearted to tell you. They say . . . you're *hard as nails.*

MARTHE. Hard as nails. . . . [*She chuckles.*] I don't mind that. What else do they say?

MARY. Oh, a lot of things. They ain't forgot how you drove off that handsome Michael Callahan that wanted to marry you when you was young and broke his heart, and they ain't forgot you married your hired man—just in name—to keep him on the farm to do your work; and they ain't forgot the hard bargains you've drove. . . .

FANNY. Mary . . . we've always been friends, you and I and Marthe. Let's forget that old talk. It's nigh dead and buried. We're too old to be carrying scandal. Besides you'll hurt Marthe's feelings.

MARTHE [*motioning her to be silent*]. No, she won't hurt my feelings. According to most folks round here, I haven't got feelings. I don't remember having any myself. You're better off without 'em. I've lived just as I wanted to and I ain't sorry. You tell folks they won't gain nothing talking about me.

I've always had my own way and what folks said didn't matter.

FANNY [*trying to change the subject*]. Let sleeping dogs lie—that's what I think. . . . Marthe, why don't you have some house plants? You've got that nice stand to have them set on.

MARTHE. I never had no time for flowers. I don't know one kind from another. I had enough to do raising corn and rye and buckwheat without fussing with flowers. [*To Mary.*] Where's that pesky butter and egg man, Dave Leland? Why don't he come fer my eggs? Go and look out the door and see if his wagon is up the road.

[*Mary Davis goes to the window.*]

MARY. He's here. He's coming round to the woodshed door. [*Knocking. She calls.*] Come in, come in.

MARTHE. Go and get the eggs.

[*Mary Davis goes into the pantry. Dave Leland comes in through the woodshed door. He is a roughly-dressed farmer, with high boots and a soft felt hat.*]

DAVE. How de do, how de do, Mis' Rigney. How de do, Mis' Washburn.

MARTHE. You're late, Dave.

DAVE. Yes, I've been up on Pride's Hill gathering up eggs and butter. The road's bad up there. I had to drive slow. One of my horses is lame.

MARTHE. Dave, you've known me a long time, ain't ye?

DAVE. Why, yes, Mis' Rigney.

MARTHE. Do you ever hear folks talking about me?

[*Mary Davis comes out of the pantry with a basket of eggs. She stands holding the eggs.*]

DAVE. Talking about you . . . what do you mean, Mis' Rigney? I reckon the best of us gets talked about.

MARTHE. Do they say I'm a *hard* woman? Oh, you needn't be touchy about telling me. . . . You tell me what they say.

DAVE. Well, seeing as you've asked it and no offense, they say you ain't got no heart, Mis' Rigney.

MARTHE. Is that so? Well, you tell 'em it's true—I ain't; and what's more, I don't want one either. I've lived my life and worked my farm myself and I'm not beholden to anybody. I'll live as I please and die as I please and it's none of folks' business.

MARY [to Marthe]. Are you going to get through this nonsense and count these eggs? Put out your pipe. I never saw such a woman as you are—smoking, smoking all the time. The house smells like a shanty from your dirty old pipe. Put it on the hearth and count the eggs while I go and get the sticks. [She goes to the woodshed to get the sticks.]

MARTHE [to Fanny]. You never wanted to smoke, did ye, Fanny?

FANNY [scandalized]. Me? No, I never did. Me! smoking before my children and grandchildren!

MARTHE. Well, I never had no children or grandchildren so I can smoke. [Counts the eggs.] One, two, three, four, one, two, three, four, one, two, three, four, one dozen, one, two, three, four, one, two, three, four, one, two, three, four, two dozen, one, two, three, four, one, two, three, four, one, two, three, four, three dozen. [To Dave.] You can have 'em for fifty cents a dozen, Dave.

DAVE. I ain't paying but forty-five, Mis' Rigney. Eggs has gone down.

MARTHE. Trying to rob a poor woman, ain't ye?

[Mary Davis returns with the sticks.]

MARTHE. Where is the knife?

MARY. Here is your knife. Now cut the notches for the eggs. Why didn't you ever learn to read and write?

MARTHE. One, two, three—three dozen to sell to-day. [She runs her hand over the old notches.] I tell ye, I've got the hens for laying eggs. [Recollecting herself.] Why didn't I learn to read? Well, I learned to count if I didn't learn to read, and that's something you've never had much need of with your spendthrift ways. That's about all I had time to learn, Mary Davis. What do you know about working land and making a living —you, who have sons and daughters to keep you in silk?

DAVE. Well, well, I must be getting on with my load. Are you taking the forty-five for the eggs, Mis' Rigney?

MARTHE. I suppose I'll have to. Put the money in the blue teacup on the shelf. Count it out to me first. [He counts out the sum.] Now here they are. [Hands the basket to him.] And see that ye put the basket back in the woodshed after ye empty it.

DAVE [takes the basket, counts the money in her hand, then puts it in the blue teacup on the shelf]. Good-by, Mis' Rigney; good-by, Mis' Davis; good-by, Mis' Washburn. See you next week.

[Dave Leland goes.]

FANNY [looking at the clock]. Land! I must be getting home. [She goes into the bedroom and puts on a wrap and a bonnet; then goes up to Marthe and gives her a pat on the shoulder.] Don't you be caring what folks say. Good-by, Mary. Come down to see me when you can. Good-by, Marthe.

[She goes out the woodshed door.]

MARY [sitting down in her chair]. Well, you've found out what folks say about you. I could 'a' told you any time for forty years back.

MARTHE. Yes, I found out what kind of a neighborhood I live in. Folks that'll spend their time talking about a poor old woman with no children to stand up fer her or any kin this side the water.

MARY. Well, you might o' had some! Why didn't you marry when you were young and have a family to keep you in silk? I know why you didn't. You thought too much of your land and the money you'd saved. I remember you said once that you didn't know but children would be wasting what you had and anyway you couldn't tell how children might turn out. Always thinking of yourself when you might have been doing what other folks did and having what they had—always thinking of yourself and your land.

MARTHE. Why didn't I marry when I was young? Well, there was a gossoon running here and trying to be courting me when I was young. He was a well-favored lad, but he had nothing, nothing I tell you, not even a cow, and I thought what a fool I'd be, making off from my pa and ma and the land, and trying my luck with a stranger. He was always singing a song, an Irish song—you wouldn't know it—"Pastheen Finn" is the name, and he was that tall y'd think a tree came walking down the road when y'd see him coming. You'd thought I was a queen to hear his tongue, Mary Davis. The things he said were like burning coals; I remember them yet. But I was young and hard and I sent him away. I never knew whether I wanted him or whether I didn't, but I knew

I did want the land. And as fer thinking o' myself, as you say, and the land
. . . maybe I did. Who worked the land
and got a living after my pa and ma were
old? You never plowed all day with
horses or oxen, tugging through green-
sward with the plow catching on roots!
Did you ever sow and reap and burn off
fallow land and be out toiling from sunrise to dark? No, you never did, and
that's why you don't know what *land*
means and why I liked to sit here when
I had my eyes looking over the fields
and thinking about nothing else. [*Smokes
again.*] And as for children, they're for
soft women who can wear silk like you,
Mary Davis. They mightn't o' been children I'd like—and I might 'a' been leaving them alone after a few years. Put
these sticks back in the shed.

[*Mary Davis trots out to the shed
and hangs the sticks on their peg.
She comes back with another armful of wood which she puts in a
wood box that stands at the back
of the stove. She stands by the
stove brushing the wood dust from
her apron. The stove is red with
fire, although it is a warm day in
early autumn.*]

MARY. Land! But it's hot in here.
You *do* feel the least bit of chill in the
air! Shall I make tea and start supper
now?

MARTHE. You can make some biscuits. There's flour and lard and milk in
the pantry. And you can make some tea.
Put it on and let it boil. I don't like tea
unless it's boiled half an hour.

[*She empties her pipe by knocking
it out on the hearth and lays it
down. Then she walks with difficulty to the window and peers out.
Mary Davis, who has gone into the
pantry, comes back with a teapot
in her hand. She pours water into
the teapot from the teakettle
steaming on the stove and sits
down again in the rocker.*]

MARY. I don't see how you keep your
health drinking tea that's boiled and
strong as lye. But you can stand more
than most folks. You went on hounding
that good-for-nothing hired man you
married until I should have thought
'twould have worn you out.

MARTHE [*groping back from the window*]. The good-fur-nothing I married to

keep on the place! Well, the ceremony
was all he had and that was more than
he deserved. He gave me a bad time. He
wouldn't stick to *his* bargain. 'Twas
agreed that if I married him he would
stay here and work the farm for sake o'
having the land when—when I wouldn't
want it any more. He was flighty, and
when I'd gone to town and married him,
he was never satisfied and kept sulking
around and wouldn't work, and begun
buying everything and having store debts
charged to me. I was near ruined with
the debts, so I drove him off. I never
heard from him but once.

MARY. That was when he fell off a
load of logs and was killed, wasn't it?

MARTHE. Yes. He never knew anything after he fell and when they got
him up here there wasn't a mite of breath
left in him. I buried him up in the orchard. 'Twasn't my place to take him
out to the church burying ground and
spend money for a grave plot. *He wasn't
my folks.* I only *married* him. I was
trying to get some one to work the land.
I was glad when it was all over. I've
had better luck hiring—and cheaper.
Besides, he spoiled the land.

MARY. I get tired of hearing you talk
about the *land*, Marthe. One would
think that your land was the only land
in the world and that all the rest of the
earth was water. You've slaved and dug.
And all for the *land*. And your pa and
ma slaved and dug and 'twas for the
land. And what did they get out of it
more than a living? And what have you
got out of it more than a living?

MARTHE [*rises and points to the fields
outside the window with a trembling finger. Her voice crackles with anger and
passion*]. I expect you wouldn't know—
you and your folks have always had land.
Your folks had it in the old country and
you've had it here. My pa and ma came
over from County Moynihan years back
when I was a little thing in arms. They
came over steerage with all they had on
their backs and a bundle or two besides.
In the old country they'd never had land
or anything but black poverty and curses.
And they came over here—and old Thur-
man Barnes had the selling of this township and he brought them up here and
put them on a bit of wild land where
there was an old log shanty the lumber-
man had left. But it looked like a pal-

ace to my ma and pa. And the land—sure, now, you couldn't find a prettier field than that one beyond the brook, and the wood lot, sure they're fine trees, and there's the swale below the barn. It's a fine place for grass. Well, my pa and ma took the land and they bound over their work for a bit until they could get seed and get started farming. And they prospered and paid for the land. There was a lot to do then—logging and clearing the fields and picking up the stone and raising crops and sheep and cattle. I never had time to learn much except how to work in the fields, and I grew up loving the land just as my ma and pa loved it. We never wanted to leave it. And after a while my pa built this frame house and a frame barn and all the neighbors helped at the "raising." And he built a cowshed out of the old logs—and the place came on—and we had a living and never saw black poverty this side of the water. [*Standing up and speaking fiercely.*] Haven't I wood in my shed, Mary Davis, and pork in my cellar, and a barrel of flour and sugar, and dried cod, and all a body could want? And don't my hens lay me eggs to buy all I'm wanting at the store? And haven't I a good bit laid by? And you say I've had *just a living.* Sure, there's many that have had fine and plenty and had no more than I. [*A knocking is heard at the door.*] Who's that? Hide the tea, Mary Davis. I've no mind to be asking the neighbors to eat. Shut the pantry and go to the door.

> [*She sits down. Mary opens the door. In the doorway with one foot on the sill a young man of about twenty-one years is standing. Slightly behind him is a girl perhaps a year or two younger. The boy is olive-skinned with smoothly brushed dark hair and bright dark blue eyes. He has the look of a young eagle. The girl is bareheaded with heavy golden hair half clouding her eyes. Her skin is tanned to a golden shade. They look radiantly happy.*]

MARY. It's only my John and Lucie.

MARTHE. Your John? Put the tea back on the stove. Will ye come in and sit down and bring the young lady in. We'll have tea and some biscuits that yer gran is going to make and I've a comb of honey on the shelf. Come in.

> [*Mary Davis pulls out two of the stiff-backed chairs from their places against the wall and dusts them with her apron. The boy and girl sit down.*]

JOHN. Hello, Gran! Well, aren't you going to speak to Lucie?

MARY. Of course I am! [*Shakes hands.*] How do you do, Lucie? I'm glad to see you. How is your mother?

LUCIE. She's very much better.

MARY. You had the new doctor from Warrensburg, didn't you?

LUCIE. Yes, and he gave her something that helped her very much.

MARTHE [*querulously*]. Mary Davis, why don't you tell me who the young lady is? I don't know her voice. You forget I haven't my eyes. You needn't be thinking I don't *want* to see.

MARY. I'm sorry, Marthe. I thought you knew Lucie. This is Lucie Oliver, our new school-teacher.

MARTHE. The one whose folks 'moved down here out of Canada?

MARY. Yes. She's been teaching over in the Spruce Mountain District and now she's hired out to our trustee and she's going to teach here in this district.

LUCIE [*rising and going over to Marthe*]. How do you do, Mrs. Rigney? I'm glad to come and see you.

MARTHE. How de do? How de do? I don't see many young folks—they don't come often to see an old lady—and when they do come, I can't see 'em plain unless the sun shines right in their faces. Then I can see a little. Won't ye stay and have some biscuits and honey? [*A ray of sunlight from the window lights up Lucie's hair.*] The sun is around your head! Miss Lucie. Lucie—I like that name. And you're teaching school—teaching school. You must know a lot. Be ye John's girl?

JOHN. Now, Mis' Rigney—

MARTHE. Nothing to be ashamed of, is there? You can tell *me.* Be ye courting?

MARY. Marthe Rigney, have you lost your manners? May be they *are* courting, but you and I ain't. Let them alone.

JOHN [*holding out a paper bag*]. I came to bring you something, Mis' Rigney—oranges. [*He empties the bag into her lap.*] I got them when I was "down below"—in Albany. They're big ones.

MARTHE [*feeling one*]. I never had such big ones before. Ye got them in Albany?

MARY. Yes, Marthe, John's been down to Albany to work and he's going back next week. He's been offered a good position down there. Did you ever see such oranges?

MARTHE. No, I never did. [*Marthe lifts one of the oranges until it catches a ray of light and shines like a ball of gold. She lifts it to her nose and sniffs a little.*] Thank ye, thank ye. It's good of ye, John, to remember an old blind woman. I remember the first time I ever set eyes on an orange. My pa was drawn on a jury and he went off to the county seat. And he drove away in the new buggy with our brown mare and it was a fortnight before he came back. And I watched for him every day up the road, and after a while one day I saw the mare come trotting up the valley road, and I hid behind the dooryard gate, but my pa saw me and when he drove past the gate to put the horse up in the barn he threw me something yellow and round that looked like the moon. And it rolled in the grass and I ran after it and picked it up and ran to show my ma what my pa had brought me. And my ma said it was an orange. I had never seen anything like it before.

LUCIE. Did you like it when you tasted it?

MARTHE. I never tasted an orange for many a day after that. I couldn't bear to cut it or take the peel off; it was so pretty and I kept it in the cupboard and took it out and looked at it every day until it was rotten. And my ma planted the seeds and they came up little smooth green trees with sweet smelling leaves and I thought they would grow but the frost killed them—[*slowly*] I remember that first orange—I thought it was the moon.

JOHN. Well, these are not moons and you are to eat them right away and not put them in the cupboard. [*To Lucie.*] We must be going, Lucie, if I'm to get down to the post office before six o'clock.

MARTHE. Now John and Miss Lucie, I thought ye were going to stay and have supper with an old blind woman.

LUCIE. Thank you so much. I'd love to stay but John has to get to the post

office before it closes. He expects a letter from Albany.

MARTHE. Perhaps you'll go down to Albany with him some time, eh?

LUCIE [*smiling*]. Perhaps—some time.

JOHN [*taking her arm*]. Perhaps soon, Mis' Rigney. Will you come to our wedding? [*To Lucie.*] Now, don't mind, Lucie. Gran would tell her to-morrow anyway. It's nicer to tell her ourselves.

MARTHE [*at the word wedding rises out of her chair. Her features work with excitement, the wrinkles gathering into knots and then loosening again. The ghost of her youth glooms in her eyes*]. So ye're courting. I felt it when ye came in. And ye're going to be married soon—a wedding—a wedding. Come here, both of ye. Come close. Don't be afraid of an old blind woman. I want to touch yer faces. I want to see with my hands. [*John and Lucie come close to her and half kneel by her side. The sun catches them all in its dying splendor. Marthe runs her right hand lightly over John's face.*] Why, ye're not a boy any longer—ye're a man grown, John. And I'm not too blind to see that ye're tall and wide at the shoulders and that yer eyes are shining. Miss Lucie, may I touch yer face?

LUCIE. Of course you may. I'm so sorry you don't see well.

MARTHE. Soft and young and yer hair is soft and yer going to have a wedding.

JOHN. There, there, take it easy, Mis' Rigney. You'll come to our wedding, won't you?

MARTHE [*does not listen*]. A wedding —soft and young—

[*She strokes the air.*]

LUCIE. There, there, you *will* come, Mis' Rigney, won't you? I'm so happy that I want everybody to come to my wedding and be as happy as I am.

JOHN. Gran, we must go or we'll find the post office closed. We'll stop in on the way back and take you home with us.

MARY. Stop if you see a light. If I've gone home there won't be a light.

JOHN. Good-by, Mis' Rigney. Good-by, Gran.

[*They go. Mary Davis starts for the pantry. Halfway there she comes back and opens the doors of the old-fashioned stove and puts in two fresh sticks through the griddle in the top. The burned coals*] *make a glow in the room. The sun's light is fading; twilight begins to darken the shadows.*]

MARTHE. I'm thinking I can't eat biscuits, so you've no need to make them. And you needn't cut the comb of honey. I'm not hungry. You can put on a pot of tea and have a cup yourself. But perhaps you'd like biscuits.

MARY [*startled by Marthe's unwonted solicitude*]. I don't want biscuits and I've honey at home. I'll slick up a bit and make the tea and then I'll go home and get supper for John. He'll be wanting something to eat when he gets back from the post office. And perhaps Lucie'll stop and have a bite with us. I'll make the tea now.

[*Mary lights the kerosene lamp on the shelf and sets it on the plant stand. Then she puts the tea back on the stove and goes into the pantry. She brings two old-fashioned blue teacups without handles, and sets them down on the hearth. She takes a blue china sugar bowl from the shelf by the clock and carefully measures a teaspoonful of sugar into each cup. She puts the sugar bowl back on the shelf and then pours the tea into the cups. She replaces the pot on the stove and hands Marthe a cup of tea. Then she takes the other and sits down in the rocker with the cup of tea in her lap. The firelight plays on their old faces, giving them the look of sibyls.*]

MARTHE. Did ye put the sugar in?

MARY. Yes, I put the sugar in. Why don't you stir your tea?

MARTHE. I went to Albany once—where your John's been. I went as far as Rome. We went up from Albany on the packet boat on the Erie Canal. I remember sitting up on top of the boat all day long in my starched skirts with the green fields sliding past me. I never went anywhere else though.

MARY. That was your own fault if you didn't, Marthe. You've had money to go where you liked; and you had it long before your sight failed. You could 'a' gone anywhere you'd a mind to go—Albany or New York—or even back to the old country—you could 'a' gone.

MARTHE. I could 'a' gone with my feet, Mary, but I couldn't 'a' gone with my head, because my head couldn't see that I ought to go. My eyes were looking always at my bit of land, the cow yard and the pasture, and I was seeing that the pasture fence needed mending and thinking what I'd plant in the fallow lot in the spring. Now that I can't see much, I do see that I ought to have gone many places. But now it's too late to go, Mary. I should have gone more places than you know—more than you'll ever know.

MARY. You always were a blow-hard, Marthe. What places could you go that I couldn't know about?

MARTHE. Places I could see in my head in the dark before the lamp was lit. I can see them now in the fire. But I never went to see them—and I never did anything but stay at home and work. I never did anything I should 'a' done. I'm thinking now that I might 'a' married that fine young man, Michael Callahan, when I was young, not waiting until I was forty past to drive a bargain with a hired man to keep him on the land. I might have had a grandson like your John—and his wedding coming on. I might have had a lad to stroke my face when I was young and give me lovin'. I know all I might have had better than you know it. And the land out there took it all from me. Now when I'm sitting alone looking at it I'm thinking if it can give me back smooth cheeks and soft hair and a fine lad and days and nights to be courting together.

MARY. You're in your dotage, Marthe Rigney. You—to be talking of smooth cheeks and loving at your age.

MARTHE. You don't know my age.

MARY. To be sure I don't—but I can see your face. I'm going home to get supper for John.

MARTHE [*gets up with sudden energy and screams*]. And I'm going to *die.*

MARY [*shaking Marthe by the shoulder*]. Stop blaspheming! You'll die when your time comes—not before—although you're stubborn enough to defy the Almighty and have your own way. You've always had it—ever since you were born.

MARTHE. Help me into the bedroom. I've a queer feeling in here [*puts hand over her heart*] and I tell you I'm going to die. I've found out that there's loving in the world—going on all the time—passing me by.

[*She almost screams the last sentence.*]

MARY [*helping her to the bedroom door*]. The Lord will punish you.

MARTHE [*pushing her hands off*]. I'm going to die!

MARY [*comes back, leaving the door open*]. I'll come down in the morning.

MARTHE [*standing in the doorway*]. I'll go to sleep for a while. I'm terrible sleepy. [*In a louder voice.*] I'll die when I've a mind to, Mary Davis.

[*She disappears in the bedroom. Mary Davis puts wood on the fire, closes the pantry door, and hangs her apron on a peg by the pantry door, also her coat which has hung under the hat. She tiptoes to the bedroom door and peers inside. Then she blows out the kerosene lamp and goes.*

The glow from the fire lights the room and fills it with flickering shadows. As the fresh wood burns the glow from the hearth becomes brighter.

A knock comes at the door. It is repeated. Then the door opens and John and Lucie come in. They are carrying packages and Lucie has a bouquet of late roses and sweet scented pinks.]

JOHN. Gran's gone home, I guess.

LUCIE. Where's Mis' Rigney?

JOHN. Look in her bedroom. [*Lucie tiptoes to the door and comes back with her finger to her lips.*] She's asleep. We'll leave the things here for her. Let us put them on the stand and move it up beside her chair. She'll see them the first thing in the morning. [*John moves the plant stand up beside the armchair. Lucie unwraps a small jar of bright-colored candies and puts it on the stand. She opens another parcel and takes out a white china hen.*] Where are you going to put that?

LUCIE. We'll put it right here beside the candy. She'll like it on account of her hens. Can you get me a vase for the flowers?

JOHN. A vase! A vase in Marthe Rigney's house! She wouldn't know a vase if she saw one. I'll get a tumbler out of the pantry. [*He comes back empty-handed.*] I can't find anything but teacups.

LUCIE. Oh, I know. [*Looks at clock shelf.*] I'll put them in that lovely blue sugar bowl.

JOHN. Will that do? It's full of sugar.

LUCIE. Empty the sugar into a teacup and put some water in it. That's lovely for the flowers. It's awfully old, isn't it? [*Examining it and arranging the flowers.*] There—that's pretty!

[*Sets them on the plant stand.*]

JOHN. But she can't see them.

LUCIE. She can touch them and smell them, can't she? Anyway, I'm so happy I wanted to bring her something—a little happiness. Now suppose I were blind. [*Closes her eyes.*] I would put my hands over the flowers like this— [*touches them*] and smell them—so—

[*Lifts them to her face. John has come behind her. He puts his arm around her and kisses her.*]

JOHN. And—not hear me coming—and I'd kiss you—so—

LUCIE. Sh-h-h. She might wake up.

JOHN. She won't. Besides, she's a little deaf. Lucie!

[*Kisses her.*]

LUCIE. John!

JOHN [*holding Lucie in his arms, but a little way apart from him so that he can look at her*]. Lucie, I can't tell you. I never can tell you. I see your face everywhere I look. I want to come and touch your sleeve or the hem of your skirt, and I want to pick you up and carry you off and tell you things I can't even think about yet. About places we've never been. And yet where it seems we've always been—white water and waves tumbling and great ships—and some place where we've been hundreds of years ago and lived together and died. And a place where there is a great wood. I can see you coming to me out of the wood with the sun shining on your hair.

LUCIE. I know, John. I know. I think those things too. [*She runs her hands over his face, over his lips, neck, arms, sliding them down to his waist.*] I can see with my fingers like old Marthe. I could find you if I were blind. John, don't you ever think you have been some one else—perhaps some one who *was* blind—and loved me when you were that some one else?

JOHN. I've always loved you—and I'm frightened for fear of losing you. Why, I wake up at night and for a minute I can't remember where you are and I feel that you have gone away—that I've lost you—and I'm nearly crazy. And then I get my senses and know you are alive and that you love me and it's like coming home again after being lost. Say we shall always be together, Lucie. Say it. I can't bear to think of things ever coming to an end.

LUCIE. We shall always be together, John—always—

JOHN. Always.

LUCIE. John, suppose *she* had had a lover when she was young, would he have been like you?

JOHN. No. He would have been an Irish boy—one that came over from County Moynihan where her folks came from—not a bit like me.

LUCIE. What would *he* have said to her? I wonder.

JOHN [*backing towards the door*]. I'll tell you; I've read it in books. [*He swaggers toward her.*] He'd say—

LUCIE. Well, what would he say?

JOHN. Well, first tell me what she would say.

LUCIE. That's not hard. I've read a book too. [*She tucks up her skirt in imitation of an Irish colleen and winds her neck scarf about her head. She assumes an Irish accent.*] And it's a great lad ye are to be coming over seas a-dazzling a poor girl like me wid yer tongue a-saying words that shine like the stars themselves. There's a doubt in me that says I'm dreaming, but if I'm not, why, I'll say I knew the first time my eyes fell on ye, that you were the lad I'd be loving. It's you and I will be having great days loving and long nights sitting by the fire.

JOHN [*assuming a strong Irish accent and swaggering*]. Sure, and it's from far off that I've come to ye, Marthe Rigney, and it's long I've been waiting for this time and searching ye out, Rose o' the World, that ye are. And now I've found you, it's blinded I know I was in my long wandering. For I had not the thought that yer two eyes were like the stars and yer lips the color o' the berries o' the rowan tree. An' now it's half blinded I am again at the sight of ye and it's many a lad will go envying me the length of his days. And if ye love me,

it's I that will be walking humble all me life—knowing it's I that'll be taking the honey of your lips, and it's I that would come back to you from the wild waters of the Seven Seas and the four corners of the earth—and you might be old, Marthe Rigney, but I'd always see you young and I'd sing to ye always. [*He sings.*]

PASTHEEN FINN

Love of my heart, my fair Pastheen;
Her cheeks are red as the rose's sheen.
Like apple blossoms her bosom is white
And her neck is a swan's on a March
morn bright.

[*At the beginning of John's speech Marthe appears in the bedroom door. She clutches the sill and peers out, listening. After he sings she leans a bit heavily against the door. It creaks and startles Lucie.*]

LUCIE. Sh-h-h. She's awake. [*Takes John by the arm.*] Come, now, we must go.

[*They fly out by the woodshed door, shutting it softly behind them. They do not see Marthe. A pause.*]

MARTHE [*in her bewilderment listening to John she believes that Michael Callahan has come back.*] Michael [*softly*]. Michael [*again softly*]. Michael [*raising her voice*], have you come back at last? Your voice is still young, young as it was when ye sang that song to me years ago. [*She advances, groping with her hand and her cane.*] Michael, I can't be seeing so well now. Where are you? Let me touch your hand, my fingers are my eyes now. Are you bearded, Michael, or smooth? You must let me touch your face. [*The silence begins to sift down heavily.*] Michael [*poignantly*], why don't you speak? I'll take back all the bitter words I said. I've been a hard woman, Michael, but it's all past now. Something in me wasn't awake, wasn't born when you left me. I think it was my heart. But it's born now, Michael. I had to wait to be old to have my heart born. It's alive now. [*Puts her hand to her heart.*] It hurts me, Michael. It's been hurting a long time. [*A pause. She becomes suspicious.*] Why don't you answer me? Don't be holding anger. We're both too old to be foolish. I've just thought that you were old too, Michael. Some way I always thought you'd never be old—like me. [*She creeps out and searches the room with her hands and cane. Her face tells the story of her final realization that the room is empty. She gropes to her armchair, clutches it and sits down. The light of the fire plays over her face. She feels for the plant stand and finds the china hen. She examines it and puts it back. Then she discovers the flowers. She seems to sense for the first time the fragrance of a flower. She sinks back in the chair.*] Michael—Michael—[*Her voice is strange.*] I sent him away—Michael, that's a fine name—loving going on—going on—loving I never had—[*She sinks back in her chair holding the flower.*] I'm tired—Michael—tired—loving going on all the time—[*The firelight flares up for a moment and in its glow she seems to see her lover. She tries to rise but her strength is going. She half rises and whispers.*] Michael—

   [*She tries to lift the flower but collapses and falls back in the chair dead. The light of the fire illumines her face for a moment and then dies down, leaving the stage in darkness.*]

[*Curtain.*]

FAITHFUL ADMIRER
A Comedy

By Elizabeth Baker

CHARACTERS

KITTY MAGGS [*known professionally as "the Daisy"*].
GEORGE MAGGS [*her husband*].
ANDREW HOSKINS.

TIME: *The Present.*

FAITHFUL ADMIRER

A COMEDY   BY ELIZABETH BAKER

[SCENE: *Dressing room of "the Daisy" at the Clapham Bush Palace of Varieties.*

A small apartment with furniture that has been showy in its day but is now rather dingy. But it hardly shows for it is littered with various items of the Daisy's wardrobe—straw hats of ample size and wreathed with artificial flowers of gay color, and all suggesting the countryside—buttercups, wild roses, big daisies, etc., two or three of the Daisy's simple but not inexpensive frocks, colored silk stockings, bright-hued shoes, etc. Her "turn" is that of the artless country girl and her clothes are of the idealized stage milkmaid variety.

Door down right, another up left. A settee stands down left. A small table is right, just beyond door. A showy dressing table is up center, with a full-length mirror beside it.

It is evening, just at the close of the Daisy's turn.

Stage empty as curtain rises. Then George Maggs comes in right. He is a man of middle age. In addition to being the Daisy's husband he is her maid and general attendant. He is now carrying a bouquet which he puts on table right, and also a large box of confectionery which he puts beside the flowers. As he puts these down the telephone rings. He sits at table and replies in loud confident tones.]

GEORGE. Yes? . . . Put 'em on, Barrett. . . . Is that Skinner and Isaacs? . . . No, the Daisy's husband, Maggs. . . . You can't speak to her, she's on. . . . No, she can't see you, she's booked for an important supper directly she's off. But I'm her agent, so push on. . . . Where? . . . Napoo, old chap, she hasn't got a vacant date till next year. . . . What? Holiday engagement?

Nothing doing, sorry, old man, ring up again next year. Good-by. . . .

[*As he is speaking the final words the door up left opens with a flourish and Kitty runs in. She looks a delectable milkmaid and at a distant view is not older than twenty. She is very fair with a babyish pink and white face and curling fair hair beneath a sunbonnet. She is humming the refrain of her last song.*]

GEORGE [*looking round*]. Thought you were never coming off. Haven't been giving 'em another, have you?

[*Kitty breaks off her song. She flings the sunbonnet on to settee and crosses to table right.*]

KITTY [*carelessly*]. What do you take me for?

GEORGE. A soft-hearted little fool, sometimes.

[*He pulls her on to his knee and kisses her. She takes it complacently.*]

KITTY. Silly ass, you'll cover yourself with powder. [*Takes his cigarette case from his inner pocket and lights a cigarette for herself.*] You can bet I don't give anything for nothing any time, least of all to this show. They can afford to pay.

[*Rises and goes above table, where she pauses and begins to look over the bouquet, boxes, etc.*]

GEORGE. You bet, old Solly with his millions. [*Rises and goes left, where he begins to collect her wardrobe, props, etc.*] How many calls?

KITTY [*sniffing flowers*]. Six.

GEORGE. You don't say.

KITTY. They kept shouting for another song, but old Sol was waiting in the wings. So I didn't give it.

GEORGE. He wouldn't have paid you another tenner for it.

21

KITTY. Not him. [*Opening box of chocolates and beginning to eat some.*] My bond and nothing but my bond. That's all I'm giving. Where's that come from? Shakespeare? I'd like to play Juliet before I die.

GEORGE. Juliet hadn't anything to do with a bond. That's Shylock.

KITTY. Did I say she had? I know Shakespeare all right. "Romeo, Romeo, where art thou, Romeo?" Who sent these chocs?

GEORGE. Teddy. Didn't you see his billee-do? It's there somewhere.

KITTY. Here. What a fist he's got! You'd never think he'd been to Oxford.

GEORGE. They don't go there to learn readin', writin', and 'rithmetic.

KITTY [*reading note carelessly*]. What do they go for?

GEORGE. Search me!

KITTY. Did you read this?

GEORGE. No. Anything new?

KITTY [*reading*]. "Darling Daisy: Sweets to the sweet."

GEORGE. Fathead.

KITTY. The box gets bigger every time. Aren't you jealous?

GEORGE. I've seen him. I'd be sorry to get jealous of a tailor's dummy. I'll be jealous proper when a man blows along. Aren't you going to change or are you going out to supper in that get-up?

KITTY. Plenty of time, old bean. Solly can't be ready yet. He wants us to wait.

GEORGE. Where's he going to take us?

KITTY. Didn't say.

GEORGE. Anyway it's sure to be a good supper.

KITTY. Bet you he wants to renew the contract.

GEORGE. Of course, that's what the supper's for, isn't it?

KITTY. Who are the flowers from?

GEORGE. Bertie Rackstaff.

KITTY. Moldy lot—and him with enough cash to buy a greenhouse.

GEORGE. Skinner and Isaacs rang up.

KITTY [*hunting among contents of table*]. What did they want?

GEORGE. Give you any terms they like for a week's show any time before July.

KITTY [*complacently*]. I daresay. You ticked them off properly, I hope.

GEORGE [*equally complacent*]. You

bet, and us going out to supper with Solly.

KITTY. Remember what they offered me only two years ago?

GEORGE. Don't I!

KITTY. Now we give them the lemon —and get our own back a bit.

GEORGE. You bet. [*She is still searching among contents of table.*] What are you looking for?

KITTY [*evidently surprised and a little chagrined*]. Isn't there anything from the "Faithful"?

GEORGE [*suddenly morose*]. No.

KITTY [*incredulous.*] Go on! [*Suddenly.*] You've hidden it.

GEORGE [*indignant*]. I haven't. What should I do that for?

KITTY [*ignoring his indignation*]. But he always sends.

GEORGE. He's come to his senses at last, that's what it is.

KITTY. He hasn't missed a Saturday before. He's followed me all round London. And what do you mean, he's come to his senses?

GEORGE [*grumpily*]. What I say.

KITTY. He'll send yet, I bet. It isn't too late.

[*George says nothing. Kitty goes to her dressing table and sitting down begins to make her complexion rather more suitable for a restaurant. Maggs walks about finishing the packing up.*]

KITTY. Where's the grease?

GEORGE [*still grumpy*]. There—right in front of you. But what are you taking off your complexion for? Have you forgotten we're going—

KITTY. You think me a fool, don't you?

GEORGE. When you get thinking about that—that idiot of a Faithful you'd forget anything.

KITTY. It's you who go off your head when his name's mentioned. You wouldn't have me go out with Solly with lips like these, would you? "Oh, cherry lips! Oh, ruddy nose!" Oh, I do wish I could play Juliet. Don't tell me Juliet didn't say that. I know where it comes from, all right. [*Looking round.*] Sulky beast—you are a jealous old owl!

GEORGE [*hurt and indignant*]. I like that. Have I ever said a word about the Teddies and the Berties and all the rest of them? I've got some sense, I hope, and it's all in the way of advertisement. A few minutes ago you were ragging me because I wasn't jealous and now I'm too jealous.

[*Shakes one of her skirts viciously.*]

KITTY [*watching him*]. Steady on, old sport—you'll tear it, and it isn't insured. [*Comes down to him and takes dress.*] I know when you're jealous and when you're not.

GEORGE. You'd never get any other husband to put up with what I do without shooting somebody.

KITTY. You're jealous of Faithful Admirer.

GEORGE. I'm not.

KITTY. You are.

[*Pause. Kitty folds dress and puts it on settee. George goes to back of settee where he stands sulkily smoking a cigar.*]

GEORGE. What gets me is why the fool skulks behind a fool name like that. Faithful Admirer!

[*Snorts contemptuously.*]

KITTY [*suddenly flaming out*]. It's lovely—and that's why I like it, owl. Anybody can send fat bouquets made up at the swell shops and boxes of chocs and sign themselves "Yours ever" and their card inside and an address which they hope you're going to without your husband. But when somebody got a brain wave to send lovely little nosegays without trying to push himself forward and only signs himself Faithful Admirer, why, it gets me, and I tell you flat.

GEORGE. D'ye think he doesn't know it? He gets you thinking about him. He isn't the little gray dove you like to pretend. He's an artful cuss. When he thinks he's got you all right, then he'll come out. I'd like to meet him, that's all. If he's honest, let him come out and show himself. [*Kitty turns away and he stares after her.*] I believe you know who he is.

KITTY. I don't.

GEORGE [*following her*]. You've got a notion. You do know.

KITTY. I don't, I tell you.

[*But she smiles to herself.*]

GEORGE. What are you looking so pleased about?

KITTY. I've told you. I like the way the Faithful does it. What else are you driving at?

GEORGE. It's something else. You've got some one in your mind. Out with it.

KITTY. What did Barrett say he was like?

GEORGE. Barrett? He hasn't set eyes on him. Nobody has.

KITTY. I mean the chap who brings the flowers.

GEORGE. What's that got to do with it?

KITTY. Thin, isn't he?

GEORGE. Yes, and shabby and wears specs.

KITTY. And got a thin little voice?

GEORGE. Like a frightened chicken, Barrett says. But what—

[*Kitty suddenly turns on George with a certain triumph.*]

KITTY. That's just like Lord Dalston.

GEORGE [*taken aback*]. Who?

KITTY. Lord Dalston.

GEORGE. But that's only the messenger, the chap who—

KITTY. How do we know that?

GEORGE. You mean to say you think it's—? But why should he come looking like a bally butler?

KITTY. Butler! Try again. Why, a butler looks more like a lord than a real lord does.

GEORGE. Well, why should a bally old lord come creeping round looking like a broken-down railway porter?

KITTY [*impatiently—not wishing to give up her dream*]. How do I know what lords will do? Anyhow, it sounds more like old Dalston than anybody else I've heard of.

GEORGE. How do you know what he's like?

KITTY. I've seen him at Jess Horrock's flat.

GEORGE. Well, if he's after her—

KITTY [*meaningly*]. He was—once.

GEORGE. So he is now by all accounts.

KITTY. Who says so?

GEORGE. Everybody.

KITTY. Everybody is sometimes wrong.

GEORGE. You mean he's given Jess up?

KITTY. I know he has.

GEORGE. And now he's coming round after you?

[*Kitty moves away, humming a little and glancing carelessly back at George.*]

KITTY. We shall never get packed at this rate.

[*George follows her.*]

GEORGE. Look here, Kit, you don't tell me if it's that infernal old sinner you're proud of it.

KITTY. I didn't say I was proud of it. I've met lots of lords.

GEORGE. No, you haven't—and I don't see you doing it either. [*Kitty moves still farther from him, tossing her head.*] So that's why you're always so bucked by these tuppenny-ha'penny bunches of violets and things. You think they come from old Dalston. I never thought you'd come down to that sort of thing, Kit.

KITTY. What d'ye mean? I haven't come down to anything. I merely remarked that Faithful Admirer might be Lord Dalston. That's all.

GEORGE. And I say if it does turn out to be him you ought to throw his stuff back in his wicked old face.

KITTY [*flashing round*]. And I say that if he is an old sinner he's got the loveliest ways of doing things when he likes. There's not many lords would dream of sending those ducky little nosegays and sign himself just Faithful Admirer, week after week, and never trying to get anything back for it.

GEORGE. Oh, come off it, Kit. If you didn't think they came from a bally old lord you'd chuck 'em away.

KITTY. I shouldn't.

GEORGE. You would.

[*Pause. Kitty flings herself on to settee and prepares to change shoes and stockings for some more suited to her evening gown.*]

KITTY. Where are my others? [*George brings her stockings and satin shoes over to her.*] Got my dress?

[*Kitty has removed one shoe. George stoops to remove the other. He is very grumpy. She pulls his ear but he takes no notice. She tweaks his hair, but he goes on with his work without looking up. Suddenly she puts her hand under his chin and forces him to look at her.*]

KITTY. You great, stupid, jealous, old elephant. A nice life it's going to be if you go on like this.

GEORGE. It's all that Faithful—

KITTY. Oh, drop him.

GEORGE. I don't care how many Teddies and Berties you have hanging round, but that wicked old—

[*Kitty suddenly springs up, sending George sprawling.*]

KITTY. I've had enough of this. I'm going to find out just who it is and have done with it.

[*She goes to telephone.*]

GEORGE [*from floor, staring after her*]. What're you going to do?

KITTY. Have him up. [*At telephone.*] Hi-hi—you there?

GEORGE. He hasn't come to-night.

KITTY. There's time yet. He sometimes sends at the last minute. Hi—that you, Barrett? . . . I say, if that shabby old thing with the bunch of flowers blows along, hold on to him. . . . What? . . . [*Turning.*] George, George, quick—fly down, he's just coming in. Barrett says he always runs off sharp. Catch him— [*George jumps up and hurries out.*] Hi, there, Barrett, hold on to him, George is just coming.

[*Rings off. Kitty goes back to settee and hurriedly finishes changing her shoes and stockings but is still in her milkmaid costume. She goes to mirror, pirouettes before it, humming one of her famous songs, and turns to face door as it is opened.*

Andrew Hoskins comes in, followed by George, who towers over him, barring any exit.

Hoskins is thin and shabby and looks very much, as he has been described, like a frightened chicken. His clothes hang badly, he crushes his old felt hat nervously in his hands. His age is uncertain. His hair is thin and graying, and he blinks timidly through spectacles. In one hand is a bunch of flowers.]

GEORGE [*breezily*]. Here he is.

[*Kitty is taken aback by the apparition of Hoskins. Even the most romantic imagination cannot pretend that he suggests a noble lord in masquerade.*

Hoskins says nothing, but stands meekly silent, eyes cast down, looking like a naughty boy caught in his naughtiness.]

KITTY [*puzzled*]. Who are you?

[*George is surprised by her tone and relieved. He glances at Hoskins, then moves up right. Kitty comes slowly down center as she speaks and Hoskins raises his eyes to her, his whole attitude suggesting the most humble devotion.*]

HOSKINS [*to Kitty*]. I—I beg your pardon—I shouldn't have intruded—I didn't mean—
[*Stops.*]

KITTY [*coming up to him and holding out her hand for flowers*]. Are those for me?

HOSKINS. Yes— Oh, yes—if you don't mind—I—
[*Stops.*]

KITTY. There's nothing to be afraid of. How sweet these flowers are! I do so want to know where they come from. You don't mind coming up, do you?

HOSKINS. Oh, no—thank you—
[*His eyes on the flowers as she puts them to her lips a moment.*]

KITTY. You see, I don't like to take presents from people I don't know.
[*George up stage looks over at her quickly and gives a hasty little cough.*]

HOSKINS. I—I beg your pardon—I didn't know—

KITTY. It's not your fault, is it— you can't help it. You have to do as you're told. Now, tell me who sent the flowers and then it'll be all right.

HOSKINS [*startled more than ever*]. Er—who?

KITTY [*reassuringly, easily*]. Yes— where do you come from?

HOSKINS. Peckham.

KITTY [*taken aback*]. Peckham? Oh, yes—you mean that's where you live yourself. But tell me, who sent you?

HOSKINS. Sent me?

KITTY [*with some impatience*]. Yes, yes—who sent you with these lovely flowers?

HOSKINS. Nobody.

KITTY. Nobody?
[*George is intensely interested and comes more down center. Kitty is taken aback again.*]

HOSKINS. Oh, please—I beg your pardon—it was very presumptuous of me—

KITTY. Nobody sent you? Then where do the flowers come from?

HOSKINS. Me.

KITTY. You! Then who are you?

HOSKINS. A—a barber.

KITTY. A what?

HOSKINS. A hairdresser.

KITTY. A—barber! What is your name?

HOSKINS. Hoskins, Andrew Hoskins.

KITTY. Andrew Hoskins—of Peckham —a barber!
[*She stares at him, surprised, disillusioned. Her tone suggests it and Hoskins interprets it as annoyance, anger. Wringing his hat in both hands he makes a step forward.*]

HOSKINS. Please don't be angry. I beg your pardon, I do indeed. I know it wasn't for one like me to do such things, but—you are so beautiful, like a dream of the country and the green fields I used to know when I was a boy. That's why I did it. I know I'm nobody and I never meant you to know only— and now I'll go—I—
[*He turns and goes quickly, but stumblingly, to door.*]

KITTY [*just as he reaches it and has his hand on the handle*]. Stop!
[*He pauses. George comes down to him.*]

GEORGE. She wants you.
[*Hoskins turns slowly, ignores George, and looks only at Kitty, who has sat down on settee, the flowers beside her.*]

KITTY. Come here. [*He comes forward timidly. George near him.*] Give him a pew, George. [*George brings forward a chair. Hoskins sits on the extreme edge. To Hoskins.*] Now, tell me all about it. You're Mr. Hoskins?

HOSKINS. Yes, miss.

KITTY. And you live at Peckham?

HOSKINS. Yes, miss.

KITTY. And you work in a shop?

HOSKINS. Yes, miss.

KITTY. Then how can you afford to go round spending a lot of money on hothouse flowers? I know what they cost.

HOSKINS. It's all I earn it for—to buy flowers for you.

KITTY. You'll ruin yourself.

HOSKINS. I get enough, miss—I don't want to spend it on anything else.

KITTY. But you can't— Aren't you married?

HOSKINS. No, miss.

KITTY. You'll want to some day and then you'll have spent all your money.
[*Putting her hand earnestly on his*

knee.] I can't let you go on doing it, Mr. Hoskins.

HOSKINS [*rising, agitated*]. But I want to. Oh, don't stop me— It's all I live for—Saturday, miss, when I can come and see you.

KITTY. Do you mean to say you follow me all round the halls?

HOSKINS. Yes, miss, when it isn't too far out. I've seen you sixty-eight times as Polly Petlington, miss, and fifty-nine times as Peggy the Milkmaid and forty-five times as Dolly from Devon.

KITTY [*graciously*]. And which do you like best?

HOSKINS [*fervently*]. I don't know, miss—you are always so beautiful.

KITTY. How nice you are, Mr. Hoskins. Where do you sit?

HOSKINS. Only in the pit, though sometimes I treat myself to a pit stall so that I can see you better.

KITTY. I'll send you tickets. Let me have your address—

HOSKINS. Oh, no, miss, please don't say that. I don't want you to do anything for me. It's me that wants to do things for you.

[*She picks up the flowers again.*]

KITTY. That's very sweet of you, Mr. Hoskins, but—

HOSKINS [*his eyes on the flowers held at her lips*]. If—if I was rich I'd bring you all the most beautiful things in the world and lay them at your feet. I wouldn't want a word from you—it'd be all I want to know I could give them to you—

[*Kitty stares at him an instant, as if fascinated, then rises abruptly.*]

KITTY. Mr. Hoskins—

[*Her voice is sharp, but he disregards her.*]

HOSKINS. You're the spirit of spring to me—wild roses and thrushes singing in the hedgerows and hay fields and woods full of bluebells like I used to see when I was a little chap—

KITTY. Hoskins—did you hear me? [*Hoskins comes to a sudden dismayed stop.*] Stop talking all this sort of thing. I can't have it—

HOSKINS [*disconcerted, then humbled, moves slowly right*]. I—I beg your pardon—I—I know I didn't ought—

KITTY. It's not you—it's me. I'm not what you think I am.

HOSKINS [*pausing and looking at her*]

adoringly]. It's like you to say that—but you're the spirit of spring—

KITTY. I'm not—I'm not the spirit of anything. Look here, come down to earth. You mustn't go up in the air about anybody like that. It's—it's awful. It isn't healthy. You'll never have a cent if you go on like that. I can't let you do it. Now, look here, believe me, I'm just an ordinary woman—do you get that? Ask George. [*She waves her hand towards George. Her tone is very matter of fact. Hoskins' gaze for the first time acknowledges the presence of George. But he only glances at him.*] He's my husband. I'm married.

HOSKINS. Married!

KITTY. Rather—aren't I, George?

GEORGE. You are.

KITTY. And a mother—aren't I? George?

GEORGE. Mother of three—eldest nine.

KITTY. And when I'm at home my name isn't as pretty as the Daisy. I'm Kitty Maggs—aren't I, George?

HOSKINS. Maggs!

GEORGE [*explanatorily*]. My name—she's my wife.

KITTY. And I can't be a spirit of anything because I'm—I'm thirty-one—aren't I, George?

GEORGE [*startled*]. Thirty-fi—one. [*Coughs.*] Yes, you are.

HOSKINS. But you look—like spring itself.

KITTY. That's easy enough [*turns to toilet table, picks up lipstick and powder puff*] with this sort of thing.

[*Dabs powder on and touches her lips. Hoskins' eyes are fixed on her, puzzled, incredulous, but still humbly adoring. Suddenly she whips off her golden wig, disclosing bobbed brown hair. Nothing can make her unattractive, but she certainly is no longer the Daisy.*]

KITTY. There's nothing much now of the spirit of spring, is there?

HOSKINS. I can't believe it hardly— [*Suddenly turns.*] I wish you hadn't told me.

[*Goes out right. Kitty and George stare after him. Kitty throws wig on settee.*]

KITTY. Well!

GEORGE. Balmy, that's what he is. [*Looks at watch and crosses to get*

Kitty's evening gown.] Time we got a move on. Solly's car'll be round soon.

[*But Kitty still stands staring at door. George brings the gown.*]

KITTY [*clutching his arm*]. Oh, George, I wish I hadn't told him all that.

GEORGE [*patting her reassuringly*]. He won't give you away. He's not the sort.

KITTY [*pushing him away*]. I didn't mean that, you owl. Of course he won't. I know that. But, oh, George, he was so disappointed.

GEORGE. Poor old chap. Come on, get into this.

[*But Kitty sinks on to settee.*]

KITTY. I wish I hadn't made him come.

GEORGE. Better for him, anyhow.

KITTY. No, it isn't. He was so happy before. If I hadn't been such a fool about that bally old lord—

GEORGE. I was a silly ass to be jealous. Well, the little chap'll save his money now, anyway.

KITTY. That's what I felt, George— I couldn't let him go on wasting it like that.

[*Telephone rings. George goes. Kitty sits pensive*].

GEORGE. Yes? . . . Car round? All right. . . . [*Rings off.*] Here, hop it, old girl. It's time.

[*But Kitty refuses to hurry. She rises slowly and begins to unfasten her gown.*]

KITTY [*wistfully*]. The spirit of the country—and spring—and all! [*George suddenly pauses and looks over at door right, then crosses right.*] And now he won't think it any more!

[*Sighs. George opens door. Kitty looks after him. George stares out.*]

GEORGE. Thought I heard something or somebody—

[*Stares down, picks up a scrap of paper, then comes in.*]

KITTY. What is it?

GEORGE. For you—but who the devil—

[*Kitty takes paper, turns it over, and then reads.*]

KITTY. From him, George.

GEORGE. Who?

KITTY. Listen. [*Reads aloud.*] "Thank you for all you did and for telling me which I know you meant for my good, but if you please, don't be angry, for it can't make any difference. You will always be the spirit of spring for me. Faithful Admirer."

KITTY [*clasping George's arm*]. Oh, George!

[*Curtain.*]

A MORALITY PLAY FOR THE LEISURED CLASS
A Satire

By John L. Balderston

CHARACTERS

SOUL.
THE PRESENCE.

A MORALITY PLAY FOR THE LEISURED CLASS

A SATIRE   BY JOHN L. BALDERSTON

[SCENE I. *From a dark mist a voice is heard in plaintive soliloquy.*]

VOICE. This can't be Hell, they've put me in a nice, soft chair. I don't believe in Purgatory. [*Doubtfully.*] But a fog like this in Heaven. . . . I wish it would clear up. Is anybody there?

[*The mist dissipates as a shining Presence, wearing white robes, with the wings of the "Nike" in the Louvre and the head of the "Hermes" at Olympia, appears before a morris chair, that stands in the middle of a large but otherwise bare drawing-room. The Soul is sitting in the chair. His form is that of a young man, with well-cut brown business suit, a straw hat on his knees.*]

SOUL [*exclaiming in relief*]. Thank goodness you're here! [*Rises deferentially*]. I was afraid they'd sent me to the wrong address. Are you an archangel—er—Your Highness?

PRESENCE. Oh no, sir. Merely your servant, sir. I am to carry out your commands forever. [*Soul sits down.*] I have anticipated one wish, sir.

SOUL. What's that?

PRESENCE. Eternal youth! I've taken thirty years from your back.

SOUL. I'm twenty-eight again?

PRESENCE. Forever, sir.

SOUL. That's fine. And you—you are to take orders from me?

PRESENCE. Not only take them, sir. Execute them.

SOUL. I see. You're part of my reward. Do you mind if I call you Clarkson? My old butler, you know. I'd feel more at home. [*The Presence bows.*] Queer place. Not what I expected. What about the halos and the harps?

PRESENCE. They often ask about them at first, sir, before they quite understand.

[*Steps forward, makes a circle above the Soul's head. A ring of gold now shimmers there, and a harp appears beside the morris chair. The Soul looks at the harp, then uncomfortably upwards at the halo.*]

SOUL. Just as advertised. But I don't know how to play this thing. I suppose I've got to learn?

PRESENCE. Not at all, sir. You've got to do nothing here, sir, excepting whatever you please.

[*The harp vanishes.*]

SOUL. That's great. Is this my celestial mansion? Seems a bit bare, Clarkson.

PRESENCE. Whatever furnishings, pictures, hangings you desire shall be installed at once.

SOUL. I can have whatever I like? [*The Presence assents.*] Regardless of expense?

PRESENCE. In this, as in all things, you speak and I obey.

SOUL [*excitedly*]. I can have everything I want? Absolutely everything?

PRESENCE. Subject only, sir, to restrictions imposed by the nature of this place.

SOUL. What are they?

PRESENCE. You must wish for nothing unpleasant or painful for yourself or others. Pain, suffering, struggle, cannot exist on our plane.

SOUL. Just as advertised.

PRESENCE. About furnishings, sir?

SOUL. Well, I like the French style. I'll take the best you can give me; Louis Quinze furniture, some pictures and statues—same period, of course—and the right tapestries and what not.

PRESENCE [*bowing*]. We'll do the dining room afterwards, and the rest of the house while you lunch, sir.

SOUL [*jumping up*]. Lunch! That's talking. I'm hungry as the devil.

31

Presence [*after slight shudder*]. Of course, sir, after your long journey. What will you have, sir?

Soul. Leave it to you. Something filling. Can I smoke up here?

Presence. A Corona Corona, sir.

Soul [*brightening; then gloomily*]. That's something. But, of course, the place is dry.

Presence. Will you try some Veuve Cliquot 1906? And before that a Chateare Lafitte '74? And a chartreuse (pre-Dissolution) with your coffee, sir?

Soul [*joyfully*]. Well, I'm damned!

Presence [*in tones of respectful reproof.*] These expletives, sir—in this place, sir—

Soul. I beg your pardon. I should say, I'm blessed. I never expected to get a drink if I were saved.

Presence. Luncheon is served, sir.

[*They move towards the door, the Soul looking up wearily at the halo, which follows him.*]

Soul. Clarkson, take this thing away, will you?

[*Halo vanishes.*]

[*Curtain.*]

[Scene II: *The Soul and the Presence pause on entering the doorway of the same room, now transfigured as foreshadowed in the previous conversation.*]

Soul. Best lunch I ever ate. Great stuff, that ambrosia, or was it manna? Hello! No time wasted here.

[*Looks about.*]

Presence. Ceiling by Fragonard. Pictures on that wall Watteaus. A Boucher, there behind you. Tapestries Gobelin. That commode is Boulle work, designs by Bérain. The desk in the corner was made for Louis Quinze. The terra cotta group, Clodion.

Soul [*sinking, replete, on couch*]. This is what I call life!

Presence. Eternity, sir.

Soul. Are these things originals?

Presence. Oh, yes, sir. Watteau's "Embarquement" there and the "Bureau du Roi" are in the Louvre.

Soul. Then how can these be genuine?

Presence. We keep the archetypes of works of art. The artist on earth only copies archetypes that we, and our friends in the Other Place, possess.

Soul. There is art in Hell, then, too?

Presence. Both places of abode possess archetypes, but the bulk of them are here. We have all the sacred art.

Soul. I don't quite make you out, but if you say these things are originals, it's all right. How much is the stuff in this room worth?

Presence. There is nothing to buy here, sir, since you have only to ask to receive. So we can't speak of things here in terms of money.

Soul [*disappointed*]. Of course, that would be true. Then all these masterpieces aren't worth a dollar? Anybody can have things just as good?

Presence. Yes, sir. But if you'd like money, I can bring you any number of millions, in gold or notes as you prefer.

Soul. What good is it, if it won't buy anything?

Presence. Oh, none, sir, but still some gentlemen when they first come like to finger it, so we give it to them as we give jewels to a lady.

Soul. But every other woman can have stones just as fine?

Presence. Yes, sir, and she soon gets tired of queens' necklaces.

Soul [*turning it over*]. Yes, I can see she would. . . . Do you have movies and theaters?

Presence. The archetypes of all plays, films, and music are here; performances take place whenever you wish; you select the programs yourself.

Soul [*pleased*]. It's better than the advertisements promised. I've always been too tired in the evenings to enjoy a show. I'll make up for it here.

Presence. You'll have plenty of time to do that, sir. And, now, your costume? French of the period, sir?

Soul. What's the matter with these?

Presence. To match the background, sir.

Soul [*firmly*]. Nonsense, Clarkson. People don't dress to match their furniture.

Presence. As you wish, sir.

Soul. Look here, I suppose I can see my friends?

Presence. Any that are here, sir. Some are in the Other Place.

Soul [*complacently*]. Yes, poor devils. Why couldn't they lead decent, that is reasonably decent, lives?

PRESENCE. I ought to warn you, sir, before you see any one, that we don't discuss the Other Place here. We never mention it at all.

SOUL. Very considerate of you. Shows fine feeling, I'm sure. I'll remember. [*With hesitation.*] My wife is here, of course?

PRESENCE. Shall I take you to her, sir?

SOUL [*downcast*]. I suppose I have to go?

PRESENCE. That's as you please.

SOUL. But I want to do the right thing.

PRESENCE. You are still confused by earthly scruples, sir. There is no right or wrong; you have no duties, no restrictions; in this existence you are beyond good and evil. Besides, sir, I don't think your wife will be anxious to see *you*, unless she knows that you don't want to see *her*.

SOUL [*confidentially*]. We didn't get along very well, Clarkson.

PRESENCE. Quite so, sir.

SOUL [*hesitating*]. "Beyond good and evil," you said? I always thought you must be very moral, here.

PRESENCE. Morality is for men on earth. Elsewhere the concept does not exist.

SOUL. Indeed. [*Pause.*] "There shall be neither marriage nor giving in marriage." So I suppose there's no such thing as bigamy?

PRESENCE. You need have no fears, sir. I understand, sir. I will collect a harem this afternoon. Your specifications, sir?

SOUL [*shocked*]. Come, Clarkson, I'm a good Christian. Nothing like that.

PRESENCE. Just as you wish, sir. But remember you are not a sultan for nothing.

SOUL. But if you could introduce me to some nice girls, just in a quiet, friendly way, you know—

PRESENCE. Certainly, sir. So stupid of me, sir, I had forgotten you were Anglo-Saxon.

SOUL. Mohammed knew a thing or two about Paradise that our preachers miss.

PRESENCE. What do you wish to do now, sir?

SOUL. See the sights, Clarkson. I've not been outside my mansion yet, you know. I want to look over your town, or country, or whatever it is.

PRESENCE. It is the archetype of cities, sir.

SOUL. The New Jerusalem?

PRESENCE. You shall see the great Palaces of the Thrones, Powers, Principalities, the Temples of jasper and emerald, the streets of gold and the gates of pearl.

SOUL [*awed*]. I thought they were figures of speech.

PRESENCE. Oh, no, not here, sir.

SOUL [*eagerly*]. Come along and show me! [*As they move towards the door.*] And, Clarkson, since you've got all those archetypes, and no labor troubles, you might clear out all this French junk. Let's have some Italian old masters, and fittings to match. Only double-star goods, mind you.

PRESENCE. Which school do you prefer, sir?

SOUL. I don't know one school from the other. Get me the best, from all schools.

PRESENCE. As you would say on earth, sir, the most expensive?

SOUL. That's it. Market price sets the value. [*Puzzled.*] But all the stuff up here has no price. That's what beats me.

PRESENCE. Beyond price, sir.

[*Holds door open.*]

SOUL [*drawing long breath*]. What you are going to show me will bowl me over, eh, Clarkson?

PRESENCE [*as they go out*]. All our guests are very much impressed, sir—for the first few days.

[*Curtain.*]

[SCENE III: *Some time has elapsed. The furniture now is Italian, the room hung with sixteenth-century masterpieces familiar to everybody, while beneath the Leonardos, Raphaels, Correggios, and Titians stand a marble group by Michelangelo and two Donatello bronzes. The ceiling is the one done for the Sistine Chapel, but its colors are fresh as painted, and there are no cracks. The Soul is reclining on a heavily gilded Venetian couch, his feet cocked up on two crouching cupids at its feet. He wearily throws a copy of "The Saturday Evening Post" on the floor.*]

SOUL. Clarkson, I wish you were here. [*The Presence reappears as before.*]
PRESENCE. You wished for me, sir?
SOUL [*sighing*]. Clarkson, I dare say what you do for me is no more than I deserve, or you wouldn't do it.
PRESENCE. Quite true, sir.
SOUL. But all the same, I appreciate it.
PRESENCE. Thank you, sir.
[*Pause.*]
SOUL. Eternity must be a long time.
PRESENCE. I have found it so, sir.
[*Another pause.*]
SOUL. These ladies I meet are getting on my nerves, Clarkson. Too stunning, too clever, too charming, too obliging. What are their names, again?
PRESENCE. Helen, Laïs, Cleopatra, Theodora, Madame Du Barry, Lady Hamilton.
SOUL. I'd read about two of them. What made you pick 'em out for me?
PRESENCE. You gave me no directions, sir, so I applied what you said about your interior decorating.
SOUL. What are you talking about?
PRESENCE. The best from all schools —and the most expensive.
SOUL. Well, this evening I want to meet some ordinary women. This everlasting perfection palls, Clarkson. It palls.
PRESENCE. Very good, sir.
SOUL. I'm tired of the shows and the movies. The plots are all alike. Why don't some of your supernatural people give us something new?
PRESENCE. We're not allowed to do that, sir. The only archetypes available for exhibition are those of earthly productions.
SOUL. And I've had enough sight-seeing. [*Yawns.*] It's all too infernally beautiful. What I'd really like is some work.
PRESENCE. What kind shall I provide?
SOUL. How can I work, here? What is work?
PRESENCE. In this case, something to amuse you, sir.
SOUL [*rising and emphasizing his points by platform gesticulations*]. Then it isn't work. Work is trying to

do or reach or get something you want. I used to work for money. But whether it's money, a woman, a bird, or a mountain top you're after, you must want what you work for. Now, when I want anything here I get it at once. Therefore, I can't work for it. Nothing to work for, no work. So I must loaf, through eternity.
PRESENCE. Oh, very well reasoned, sir. That's how the philosophers talk, for the first ten years or so after they come.
SOUL [*sitting down*]. What do they do after that?
PRESENCE. What the rest do, sir. Exist.
SOUL. Do people in—in the Other Place have too hot a time to be bored?
PRESENCE. I don't know, sir. I've not been there, since the souls began to arrive.
SOUL [*surprised*]. You *have* been there, then?
PRESENCE. Not for forty thousand years, sir And then I left in a hurry.
SOUL. I've been thinking a lot about the Other Place, Clarkson, since I met my wife.
PRESENCE. Indeed, sir? Your meeting was pleasant?
SOUL [*mournfully*]. You very well know it had to be. After it was over, she admitted she was glad to see *me*, for the same reason that made me look *her* up. Said she hoped when she saw me I'd make her angry and perfectly miserable.
PRESENCE. Impossible, sir. We have no such emotions.
SOUL. So I've found out. That's where this getting whatever I want breaks down. When I wish anything unpleasant to happen to me, just for variety or contrast, it doesn't.
PRESENCE. The nature of the place, sir. There can be nothing unpleasant here. Sometimes it seems to me you hardly realize where you are.
SOUL. What makes you think so?
PRESENCE. Just your attitude, **sir.** You seem aggrieved, yet surely things here are much more tolerable than you were led on earth to expect.
SOUL. It's better than the orthodox expectation, yes.
PRESENCE. And you were confused, when you first came, you know.
SOUL. Oh, you mean that fog. It had

me going for a minute. But when I saw you, I knew at once. [*Sighing.*] No use my getting rid of this Dago museum, I suppose? There's nothing better, is there?

PRESENCE. You might try the Greek style, sir. [*Glances at "The Saturday Evening Post."*] Tired of reading already, sir? Too bad you didn't take to classics, on earth.

SOUL. Why?

PRESENCE. We had a Greek professor who cried for joy when he got a roll of Sappho's poems that had been lost in your world for centuries. Then we gave him forty or fifty plays, histories, and what not, missing since the Dark Ages, and the stuff kept him perfectly happy for twenty years.

SOUL. What did he do after that?

PRESENCE. Went on existing, sir. About the Greeks, sir—shall I furnish your house with hangings, paintings, vases of the best period, with famous paintings and statues destroyed by the barbarians? We have their archetypes. We'll take the Florence "David" out of your entrance hall, and put the "Zeus" of Phideas from Olympia there.

SOUL [*stifling a yawn*]. All right, go ahead. [*Sits up with animation.*] There's one thing left that really would pick me up.

PRESENCE. Only one, sir, already?

SOUL. I'd like to see the world again. I couldn't go back, just for a visit?

PRESENCE. The only thing you can't do here, sir, is leave. But these will serve just as well. [*Produces from under robe a pair of binoculars.*] With these you can see the world. [*Soul makes gesture of impatience.*] They are very remarkable glasses, sir, especially designed to gratify the strongest human passion.

SOUL. And what is that?

PRESENCE. Curiosity. You can pick out the star Earth, then look at a continent, then focus down to a city, then to a house, and then see right through the walls, and into every room. Many arrivals here are amused for years with these, sir.

SOUL [*pleased*]. Give them here. I knew a lot of people down there whose private lives I'd like to probe, as my paper used to say.

[*They go out.*]

[*Curtain.*]

[SCENE IV: *More time has passed. The room is now a Greek hall; on the walls two frescoes correspond to description by ancient writers of the works of Polygnotus in the Poikile, and a painting opposite appears to be the "Aphrodite Anadyomene" of Apelles. Several statues in marble and bronze, it is clear from debased copies in European galleries, must be the originals of the "Cnidian Aphrodite" by Praxiteles. Myron's heifer from the Agora, and perished examples of Lysippus and Scopas.*

The Soul walking impatiently back and forth on the marble pavement.]

SOUL. Clarkson, I want you.

[*The Presence enters, looking more at home against the classic background.*]

SOUL. Clarkson, I'm bored. Bored to extinction.

PRESENCE. Not extinction, sir. Not here.

SOUL. I'm sick to death of this eternal life.

PRESENCE. That paradox has escaped you before, sir.

SOUL [*accusingly*]. I've always worked at something. By giving me whatever I want you prevent me from working for it—

PRESENCE [*interrupting*]. You made that clear, before, sir. It can't be helped.

SOUL. Well, what am I to do to-day? I'm tired of everything!

PRESENCE. Of watching the world, sir, so soon?

SOUL [*explosively*]. Those cursed binoculars! Clarkson, I never thought myself a saint, down there. But what I've seen since you gave me those glasses! Things seem all right, when you look at a crowd in the street, at the outside of things. But when you see inside! [*Gesture of disgust.*] Well, why don't you suggest something? Is this my reward, to be bored to the end of time?

PRESENCE. Strictly speaking, sir, there is no end to time. The phrase we use here is "from everlasting to everlasting."

SOUL. Everlasting fiddlesticks! I want you to tell me what to do.

PRESENCE. Are you tired of reading, sir?

SOUL. How can I read the nonsense people down there think about life? I know the truth about it now.

PRESENCE. You seemed so pleased to meet your friends, sir.

SOUL. What is there left to talk about? I heard on earth most of what they had to say. I've heard it all now a dozen times. Why, I can't even play cards with them. There's nothing in cards without a little something on the game.

PRESENCE. There's no objection to gambling.

SOUL. Same old trouble. There's nothing to gamble *with*. Anything you win, you could get by asking for it, and if I lose my shirt, I have only to wish for another.

PRESENCE. You will get used to our different economic system, sir. But the ladies are the same as on the earth.

SOUL. There's nothing in that, either, when you only have to *wish*.

PRESENCE. But any uncertainty would mean you mightn't get what you want, and what you desire, that you must have.

SOUL. Why must I?

PRESENCE. Orders, sir [*bowing slightly*], from General Headquarters.

SOUL. I call it rotten. It's driven me to drink, that's what it has. And there's no fun in that, up here.

PRESENCE. If your vintages pall, sir, there's our own nectar. There's nothing better in Heaven.

SOUL. I've tried that. It is *some* drink. But the trouble is, I can't get drunk.

PRESENCE. If you were drunk, you would be ill afterwards. You would have headaches. .

SOUL. But I want to be ill, I want headaches!

PRESENCE. There can be no illness, no aches, sir, as I made clear when you came.

SOUL. Well, what is there left? What are you standing there for like one of these frozen heathen statues? Suggest something!

PRESENCE. Please don't be angry with me, sir. I carry out my orders, sir; my orders are to do the very best for you I can. I'm in the same boat myself, sir.

SOUL [*surprised*]. Then you're bored here, too?

PRESENCE. Infinitely, sir.

SOUL. Shake. [*They do so.*] You don't show it.

PRESENCE. I believe I did, sir, for my first few thousand years.

SOUL. Good God!

PRESENCE [*shocked*]. You mustn't say that here!

SOUL. There must be something left for me to do!

PRESENCE. Why not have your house done over, sir?

SOUL [*wearily*]. Again? What else is there?

PRESENCE. The future.

SOUL. We'll deal with that when we come to it.

PRESENCE. Why not now, sir?

SOUL. I'll bite. What's the answer?

PRESENCE. We have the archetypes not only of art existing and extinct, but of art that will be. In about three hundred years another great period is coming at Bokhara, the world metropolis of that time. "The Asian Naissance." Let me do you up in that.

SOUL [*angrily*]. I'm sick of your periods and your art. I care no more for your future than your past. What good is any of it? No standard of value, no comparison. My stuff no better than any moth-eaten fellow has in the next street. What's it all *worth*? [*Contemptuously.*] A wish!

PRESENCE [*looking at his master's brown suit, now very shabby, and at his battered and spotted straw hat*]. You yourself, sir, might experiment to find more appropriate clothes. We offer an infinity of backgrounds. They often amuse our lady visitors for several years; you might be diverted for a time, sir.

SOUL [*more angrily*]. How often have I told you that I won't wear wings or nightgowns? This suit and this hat are all I have to remind me of life, where I sweated and was kicked about and was happy even if I didn't know it, not having your fiendish spyglasses, and going about the world as innocent as I thought down there the girls in boarding schools were. And what's more, when these wear out, you've got to replace them!

PRESENCE [*resignedly*]. Very good, sir.

SOUL. Why, I was wearing this suit when that fellow's motor ran over me. And you ask me to give it up! My last real experience! My last thrill! [*With rapture.*] You can't imagine what agony

I felt from my crushed thigh, before I fainted. My last pain!

PRESENCE [*turning away, discouraged, to go*]. I don't know what to propose, sir. But when there's anything you want—

SOUL [*excitedly*]. There is! Pain, that's it! I want to suffer!

PRESENCE. I'm afraid you can't do that here, sir.

SOUL. I'm sick of Heaven!

PRESENCE [*puzzled*]. Sick of Heaven, sir?

SOUL [*shouts*]. I want to want things I can't have!

PRESENCE [*patiently*]. A contradiction in terms, sir.

SOUL [*more loudly*]. I can't stand this damned everlasting bliss!

PRESENCE [*mildly*]. We all have to stand it, sir.

SOUL [*howls*]. Whatever the devils do to me can't be so bad as this. [*Screams.*] I want to go to Hell!

PRESENCE [*stepping back and looking at him in astonishment*]. And wherever do you think you *are*, sir?

[*The Soul stares in horror as the truth breaks upon him. The Demon, first to recover from their common surprise, respectfully and sympathetically shrugs his wings.*]

[*Curtain.*]

WINTER'S NIGHT
A Play
By Neith Boyce

CHARACTERS

RACHEL WESTCOTT.
JACOB WESTCOTT.
SARAH [*a neighbor*].

WINTER'S NIGHT

A PLAY   BY NEITH BOYCE

[SCENE: *A room in the Westcott farm-house. Through the two large windows at the back moonlight streams in. The curtains are drawn back, and without, ground and trees covered with snow can be seen.*

At one side of the room is a stove, with fire glowing dimly in it, and a teakettle singing on top. A large grandfather's chair stands beside stove. A sofa under one window, under the other a sewing machine with a basket piled with stuff. On the other side of room, cupboards with glass doors. Center, a round table with lamp. Tall clock in one corner, and near it a mirror. Over the mirror hangs a shotgun.

Sleigh bells heard off stage, stopping before the house. A man's voice.]

VOICE. Whoa, boys! Steady now, steady!

[*Sound of key turning in lock. Door center back opens. Enter Rachel. She turns and calls out.*]

RACHEL. Better blanket the team, Jacob. It'll be down to zero before morning.

JACOB [*off*]. Yes, yes, I'll tend to it. Don't hold the door open.

[*Rachel closes door, throws off heavy cloak, goes to lamp and lights it, looks at key. She has the door key, with note tied to it, in her hand. She is a woman of middle age, dressed in black, with a widow's bonnet and long crape veil hanging over her shoulders. She sits down in rocking chair beside table, reads the note, then looks absently about the room. In the light it is very attractive—the woodwork painted white, the curtains, couch cover and table covers of scarlet, several red and blue rugs on the floor, gay china showing in the cupboards, and some*]

flowering plants on the window-sills. *After a moment Rachel takes off her bonnet, holds it in her hand, shaking out the crape veil, looks at it fixedly, and lays it on table. She smooths her thick gray-black hair, rocks back and forth, then, clasping her hands, sits motionless, looking before her.*

Stamping of feet, off left. Enter Jacob, in heavy ulster and fur cap, carrying an armful of wood and a lighted lantern. He blows out lantern, hangs it by the door, goes to stove, and puts down the wood, then takes off his coat and cap. He is dressed in stiff black clothes. A lean man, gray, carefully shaved. He glances at Rachel, who does not look at him; then makes up the fire, and stands warming his hands and staring at Rachel.]

JACOB. You must want something to eat, don't you, Rachel?

RACHEL [*absently*]. No. I don't want anything.

JACOB. It was a long drive, and cold. You'll have a cup of tea, anyway?

RACHEL. No—yes—I don't care. Sarah left a note, Jacob—she says she'll be over to stay the night.

JACOB. That so?

[*He goes to cupboard, takes out tea-pot, cup and saucer, sugar bowl, canister, makes tea, and brings it on small tray, puts it beside Rachel on the table. She does not notice him, but sits folding and refolding her black-bordered hand-kerchief.*]

JACOB [*gently*]. Drink your tea, Rachel. You must be mortal cold and tired.

RACHEL [*turning suddenly*]. No—[*She stirs sugar in the tea and drinks it slowly.*] It's queer—but I don't feel tired—nor anything. I didn't feel the

41

cold so much, coming home. The wind was behind us. But going over— [*She shivers.*] It was a long journey—

JACOB [*moving chair and sitting down at the other side of the table*]. Perhaps you'd better have stayed at the minister's to-night, after all. When they asked you, after the funeral, I thought—

RACHEL. Why? I didn't want to stay at the minister's.

JACOB. Well—I only thought it would seem so lonely to you, coming back here—

RACHEL. Lonely? It does seem strange to be here—without him—don't it, Jacob? It does seem strange—you and me alone here—without Daniel. I can hardly realize he's gone—

[*Jacob gets up hastily and goes right, opens a door, and takes down brown coat, changes his black coat for the brown. Takes pipe from pocket and fills it. Goes to cupboard for matches.*]

RACHEL. Death's a strange thing, Jacob. It changes everything, Daniel's going.

JACOB [*huskily*]. Yes.

[*Rachel sighs, turns to look at Jacob and starts.*]

RACHEL. Oh, you've taken off your black already!

JACOB. Well—it's too tight for me, you see, the black coat is— You don't mind, do you—Rachel?

RACHEL. No—I don't know as I do. Though I suppose you'll wear the black, when you go out, for awhile. That's no more than right, seeing Daniel was your brother—

JACOB [*hastily*]. Oh, of course, of course—

RACHEL [*firmly*]. I shall wear my crape a year for him, though heaven knows I've always hated black. But I always did my duty by my husband, and I shall now.

JACOB [*moving about restlessly*]. Yes —of course—

RACHEL. And you did your duty by him, too, Jacob.

JACOB. I—hope so—

RACHEL [*taking up bonnet and smoothing strings*]. Yes, you were a good brother to him, all these years he's been ill. And you've been a good brother to me. I don't know how I could have got on without you— [*She sighs.*]

[*Jacob goes to window and looks out.*

Knocks over small flower pot, which falls and breaks.*]

RACHEL [*getting up*]. Mercy, what's that? It's one of my begonias! [*Jacob stoops to pick up flower pot. Drops his pipe.*] Mercy, what ails you, Jacob? Now you've broken your pipe, too! I never knew you to be so clumsy! [*Going toward him.*] Why, you're as pale as a sheet! I know what's the matter; you want your supper—

JACOB. No, Rachel, no—I don't want any supper—

RACHEL [*firmly*]. Yes, you do. You need it, whether you want it or not. People have to eat, Jacob, as long as they're alive, whether there's death in the house or not— [*Sighs. She takes an apron out of a drawer in cupboard and ties it on. It is trimmed with lace and has a red bow in one corner. Jacob stands with his broken pipe in his hand, watching her. She moves briskly from cupboard to table.*] There—there's some bread and cheese and apple pie. Sit down, Jacob. I don't believe you've eaten a morsel all day.

JACOB [*sitting at table*]. I don't want it, Rachel.

RACHEL. You feel it a great deal, Jacob—Daniel's going. I never thought you would feel it so much. But you've got deep feelings, though you're so quiet. You thought a lot of Daniel. I never heard a harsh word from you to him in all these years, though goodness knows he was unreasonable enough sometimes, poor man, with his pains. Well [*sighing*], it's a mercy he's at rest at last. These four years past were nothing but suffering for him— Aren't you going to eat anything, Jacob?

JACOB. I don't seem to want it, Rachel. It chokes me, somehow—

[*He pushes his chair back a little, looking up at her as she stands beside him. His eyes rest on the red bow on her apron; she notices it for the first time, and pulls off the ribbon.*]

RACHEL. Pshaw! I never thought—

JACOB [*putting out his hand*]. Give it to me, Rachel.

RACHEL. The ribbon? Whatever do you want of it?

JACOB. I don't know—I like the color. I always did like red.

RACHEL [*giving him the bow*]. Well,

there, then. It's my favorite color, too
—bright red, scarlet—though I like purple, too, deep purple— Well, I mustn't
think of such things now. [*Sighs.*] It's
foolish, come to think of it—

[*She moves about, taking things
from table and putting them back
in cupboard.*]

JACOB. No! It isn't foolish! It's
wonderful, liking colors, the way you do,
and fixing things up to look pretty. You
made a wonderful difference in this old
house, Rachel. Before you come into it,
it was all gray and dull. You made it
seem like a different place, all bright
and cheerful, with flowers, too, even in
winter— That reminds me. [*He gets
up and goes to window.*] I came near
forgetting your plants. They'd surely
freeze there to-night; it's going to be
mighty cold before morning. [*He moves
the flower pots to table.*] I'm sorry I
broke the begonia—

RACHEL. Oh, it doesn't matter. [*She
looks out the window.*] It does look cold!
I don't believe Sarah'll come over after all.

JACOB. Oh, I guess she'll come. She
said she didn't think you'd ought to be
alone to-night.

RACHEL. Well, it's kind of her—
though I don't know as I need her. I
don't feel much like talking. I'd rather
be alone with my own thoughts— Draw
the curtains, Jacob—it does look so mortal cold outside in the moonlight!

[*Jacob draws the red curtains over
the two windows. Rachel moves
rocker to stove and sits down.*]

RACHEL. I wish I had some work to
do—I never could bear to sit idle.
There's that dress of Mrs. Gray's—but
I suppose it would seem terrible heart-
less of me to sit sewing to-night, and
Daniel hardly in his grave—

JACOB. I don't think so, Rachel! It's
got nothing to do with your feelings.
Shall I bring you the dress?

RACHEL. I don't know—yes, just hand
me the basket there—I guess everything's just where I left it when Daniel
was took so bad a week ago—but Sarah
mustn't see me sewing; it'd be all over
the neighborhood—

[*Jacob brings the basket from the
sewing machine.*]

JACOB. Oh, we'll hear her, time
enough, when she comes.

[*Rachel shakes out the dress, a purple cloth.*]

RACHEL. It's a nice color, but the
stuff is cheap. I never would have
cheap stuff.

[*She begins to sew. Jacob wanders
about the room. He takes down
the shotgun from its hooks, draws
up a chair near Rachel, and looks
the gun over carefully, loading it.*]

JACOB. I reckon I'll get that fox yet,
one of these nights. I found his tracks
again this morning and I think he got
another of the white pullets.

RACHEL [*absently*]. That so? [*Pause.*]
I was thinking, Jacob—it's twenty-seven
years since I came to this house. It
don't seem possible.

JACOB. No.

[*He finishes loading the gun and
lays it across his knees.*]

RACHEL. It was June, though—when
I married Daniel—twenty-eight years
ago come next June. He was twenty-
three and I was twenty. And you—let's
see, you was four years older'n Daniel,
wasn't you?

JACOB. Five years.

RACHEL. Well, you seemed more than
that—always so queer, you were, and
quiet. It's too bad, Jacob, you never
married—you wouldn't be alone now.

[*Jacob gets up and goes to put the
gun back on its hooks.*]

JACOB. I'm not alone—so long as
you're here.

RACHEL. No—but I don't suppose I'll
be here forever.— [*Jacob drops the gun.
Rachel jumps up, the basket falling from
her lap.*] For goodness' sake, Jacob,
what does ail you? Ain't that gun
loaded?

JACOB [*huskily*]. Yes—it's loaded.

[*He picks up gun and stands looking at it.*]

RACHEL. Well, I declare! I could almost think you'd been drinking—you
haven't been and broke your promise to
me, have you—

JACOB. No. I haven't touched liquor
for ten years, and you know it, Rachel.

RACHEL. Well, for goodness' sake, put
up that gun. I think you'd better go to
bed, Jacob. You must be tired out, the
way you act.

[*She picks up her basket and sits
down again.*]

JACOB. No, I'm not tired. It isn't

that. [*He hangs up gun.*] It was only—

RACHEL. Only what? [*He stands up with his back to her, his head bent.*] Only *what?* You've got one of your queer streaks again, Jacob. I declare there's times when I can't make you out, no more than the man in the moon—for all we've lived side by side for twenty-seven years!

JACOB. Side by side! Yes— It was what you said, Rachel, about my being alone. [*He turns suddenly and comes toward her.*] You said—"Perhaps I won't be here forever"—

RACHEL. Did I? Well—yes—I've been thinking—

JACOB. Thinking what, Rachel?

RACHEL. Thinking I've spent enough of my life here, Jacob. I never meant to stay here forever. [*She threads her needle and goes on, without looking at him.*] I've had my ambitions, Jacob, and for all I'm forty-seven I can't feel that my life's over yet. You know yourself, Jacob, there isn't enough here to keep me busy. If I'd had children now, it might've been different. But just looking after you two men, and with you taking all the care of the farm off me—no, it wasn't enough. 'Twas for that, you know, that I took up dressmaking. Not that I needed the money. But I like the work. And for years I've had a plan, only it was no use speaking of it—it would only have worried Daniel. I want to go into business—dressmaking—in some big town, Bridgeport, perhaps. I've got a little capital, even without my share of the farm. And I'm free now. [*She drops her sewing in her lap and looks eagerly round at Jacob, who stands rigid.*] I can have what I've always wanted—more life, something going on, and a business of my own—and, Jacob, you don't know how, all my life, I've loved colors and stuffs! What I want is to make clothes for people that are well off and can have nice things. Just to handle the velvets and silks and the rich colors would make me happy! I can't say why it is—it seems foolish—but a color I like—some of these deep reds or purples, why, it'll almost bring tears to my eyes, looking at it, I enjoy it so! Why, Jacob—

JACOB [*harshly*]. And how about me? [*Rachel stops and looks at him in astonishment.*] How about me, I say? You're just planning to go off and leave me, then, as if—as if—

RACHEL. Why, Jacob! I never thought of your taking it that way! Why, surely—

JACOB. You never thought a thing about me. [*He walks up and down the room, in excitement.*] You just planned to leave me here, to go and leave me—when all my life's been spent for you—

RACHEL.. For me! Jacob!

JACOB. Yes—for you! Why else do you think I've stayed here? Wasn't there other things I might have done? Do you think I haven't had my ambitions, too? Haven't I got a man's heart in me? Why do you think I've lived lonely here beside you?— Don't you know, Rachel?

RACHEL [*getting up, dropping things from her lap*]. Jacob!

JACOB. Don't you know I've loved you all my life?

RACHEL [*gasping*]. Jacob! And your brother hardly cold in his grave!

JACOB. Oh, Rachel! I loved you before he did! I thought you knew—I thought you knew! [*He comes slowly toward her. She moves away. He stops near her.*] I loved you before he ever saw you. All my life—all my life. Do you mean to say you never knew?

RACHEL [*harshly*]. You're crazy.

JACOB. Am I, Rachel? Perhaps— To hear you say, so cold, that it was too bad I never married, so I wouldn't be alone now— Alone! Haven't I always been alone? How could I think of another woman after you? Yes, I know this wasn't the time to speak to you—but I couldn't help it— When you said that about going away, my heart seemed to burst. Rachel—oh, Rachel!

RACHEL. Jacob, you are stark, staring crazy. You're an old man, and I'm an old woman. It's awful, that's what it is—it's awful! Even if I hadn't just buried your brother—

JACOB. Oh, Rachel, that doesn't count. He had his life. But I've never had mine! And no more have you had yours— Rachel, you never rightly loved Daniel.

RACHEL. And you say that to me! Me that was a faithful and dutiful wife to your brother all his years! I won't talk to you!

[*Trembling, she takes off her apron and folds it and moves toward the door.*]

JACOB. Rachel, for God's sake, don't be angry. Try to understand.

RACHEL. I don't want to understand anything you say. You've gone plumb out of your head, that's what it is.

JACOB [barring her way to the door]. Rachel, you must listen to me now, after all these years I've kept silent. You wouldn't believe all I've had in my heart for you—you can't ever know how I would have loved you! And it's never changed, Rachel—it's just the same to me now—I can't feel I'm old—I can't feel you are. There's no age to feelings. Don't throw away my love for you now, Rachel—don't scorn it. Let me go with you, wherever you're going, if you won't stay here with me! Take me with you, Rachel! I can't live without you.

RACHEL. Move out of my way, Jacob.

JACOB. No! Why do you act like this? Do you think it's wrong of me to love you? There's no law against our marrying, if—

RACHEL. Marrying! You're stark crazy!

JACOB. Yes, marrying. Why not? It's lawful. And I thought it would come natural enough us living so long under the same roof and you being used to me— Of course I know you don't feel as I do to you. But yet you was always fond of me—

RACHEL. I was fond of you as a brother, but now—

JACOB. Now what, Rachel?

RACHEL. Now it's best for us to part, as quickly as may be.

JACOB. No! I can't part from you. If I could've gone, years ago, I would. But I couldn't. And I stayed. And you never thought anything against my staying. And you took the work of my hands and the love of my heart—yes, even if you say you didn't know it, you took it! And now you owe me something, Rachel!

RACHEL. You have your half of the farm, Jacob. And if you want more, you can have all of it—

[Jacob seizes her by the arms.]

JACOB. No, you don't speak like that to me! That's too heartless—you know better. Oh, I know you're heartless, right enough! I haven't lived near you and watched you, and not know that, for all you're kind and do your duty! There's no love in your duty! But you

can't speak so to me. You owe me some kindness, anyhow—

RACHEL. Let me go! I'm afraid to be here with you. I always knew there was something crazy about you— First you know, you'll be in the asylum—

JACOB [releasing her and staggering away]. Yes, that's a true word you say. You can drive me to it. If you leave me—

RACHEL. Jacob, listen to me. I don't want to part with you like this, after all our years together. You've done for me, and I've done for you too, and we've lived peaceful. Years ago you'd have drunk yourself to death, if it hadn't been for me, and you know it.

JACOB. Better if I had

RACHEL. Better to lie in a drunkard's grave! I saved you from that—and you've lived decent. Maybe you've had some crazy ideas, but you had sense enough to keep them to yourself. And you have sense enough now, Jacob, to see things must change. You must see I can't stay here— You take the farm and run it, or we'll sell it, just as you like—

JACOB. So you mean to go?

RACHEL. Why, of course I mean to go! I'm in prison here, I have been for years!

JACOB [huskily]. Rachel, take me with you. I'll go wherever you want. I'll work for you—

RACHEL [shrinking away]. Jacob, I can't do that. I'll just have a room somewhere at first, till I get started—

JACOB. I could be somewhere near you—

RACHEL [bursting out]. No! Can't you see after what you've said it can't be? I wouldn't have an easy minute. Anybody that could have such an idea— you and me marrying—

[She laughs nervously.]

JACOB [starting]. Don't laugh, Rachel!

RACHEL [placatingly]. Well, it did sound so foolish—but I guess you were just scared of being left alone—you didn't really mean it, and now we'll forget all about that—

JACOB [dully]. We'll forget—all—

RACHEL [increasingly nervous]. That's right, Jacob, and we'll part good friends.

Two old people like us, we can't be thinking of such things—

[*She laughs a little, hysterically.*]

JACOB [*turning on her, seizing her*].
Don't laugh.

RACHEL.   Oh, my God, he's crazy!
Help! help!

[*She breaks from him, rushes to
door.*]

JACOB [*staggering, grasps back of
chair, panting*]. Rachel—I wouldn't
hurt you—don't be frightened—my dear,
my dear—I'd never hurt you—I'll never
say any more— We'll just forget—forget—

[*Stumbles, sinks into chair by table,
buries his head on his arms.*]

[*Knock at door.*]

RACHEL.   Oh, thank God!   Sarah!
[*Pulls door open and throws herself into
Sarah's arms.*] Oh, I thought you'd
never come—

SARAH [*pushing Rachel gently from
door and closing it*]. Why, of course I
wouldn't leave you alone this night, you
want a woman with you. And Jacob—
ah, poor man, he's feeling it too—

RACHEL [*hurriedly*]. Yes, Jacob's feeling bad.   Take off your things, Sarah,
come and warm yourself, it's so cold.
[*Shivers, takes Sarah's cloak and hood
and lays them aside, both women stand
by stove.*] Oh, Sarah, I'm so thankful
you came—

SARAH.   I know, I've been through it
too, Rachel. [*Sighs.*] It's so lonesome
at first, it seems as if you can't stand
it— [*Jacob rises slowly without looking
at the women, moves stiffly, takes gun
and goes out door back.   Rachel starts
and looks after him.*] But we have to
live on, Rachel. You must bear up best
you can. Poor Jacob! he seems to feel
it terrible. No wonder, fond of Daniel as
he was.   A lonely man like him, it's

hard to see changes.   It's lucky for
him he could have a home here with
you all these years. There's not many
would've put up with his queer ways,
for all he was so faithful, working year
in, year out. You couldn't've kept up
the farm without him, Rachel, Daniel being laid up the way he was— But now
it's to be hoped you'll have a good rest,
and a little peace and quiet, and well
you've earned it— [*Report of a gun
outside.   Both the women spring up.*]
What's that?

RACHEL.   It's Jacob—he went out—
look, he's taken the shotgun—

SARAH.   What on earth is he doing
with the shotgun?

RACHEL.   It must be the fox—he was
talking to-night about getting the fox—
we've lost a lot of chickens lately—
[*She goes to the window and pulls aside
the curtains.*] I can't see him, Sarah!

SARAH.   What's the matter, Rachel?
Why, you're all trembling! Whatever is
the matter?

RACHEL.   I'm going out—

SARAH.   What are you thinking of?
Why, you're shaking so you can hardly
stand!   Here—let me go—

[*Catches up her cloak.   Rachel
comes forward, catches back of
chair, and leans on it.   Exit Sarah,
left.   Rachel leans heavily on
chair, gasping.*

*A cry outside, repeated nearer.   Sa-
rah rushes in, dropping her
cloak.*]

SARAH [*shrieking*]. Down by the barn
his head all blown to pieces—Rachel!
Rachel!

[*She falls, catching Rachel round
the knees.   Rachel pulls away
from her, clapping her hands to
her ears.*]

[*Curtain.*]

DEATH SAYS IT ISN'T SO
A Satire

By Heywood Broun

CHARACTERS

THE DOCTOR.
THE NURSE.
THE SICK MAN.
THE FAT MAN.

DEATH SAYS IT ISN'T SO

A SATIRE   BY HEYWOOD BROUN

[*The SCENE is a sick room. It is probably in a hospital, for the walls are plain and all the corners are eliminated in that peculiar circular construction which is supposed to annoy germs. The shades are down and the room is almost dark. A doctor who has been examining the Sick Man turns to go. The Nurse at his side looks at him questioningly.*]

THE DOCTOR [*briskly*]. I don't believe he'll last out the day. If he wakes or seems unusually restless, let me know. There's nothing to do.
  [*He goes out quietly, but quickly, for there is another man down at the end of the corridor who is almost as sick. The nurse potters about the room for a moment or two, arranging whatever things it is that nurses arrange. She exits left center, or, in other words, goes out the door. There is just a short pause in the dark, quiet room shut out from all outside noises and most outside light. When the steam pipes are not clanking only the slow breathing of the man on the bed can be heard. Suddenly a strange thing happens.*
  The door does not open or the windows, but there is unquestionably another man in the room. It couldn't have been the chimney, because there isn't any. Possibly it is an optical illusion, but the newcomer seems just a bit indistinct for a moment or so in the darkened room. Quickly he raises both the window shades, and in the rush of bright sunlight he is definite enough in appearance. Upon better acquaintance it becomes evident that it couldn't have been the chimney, even if

there had been one. The visitor is undeniably bulky, although extraordinarily brisk in his movements. He has a trick which will develop later in the scene of blushing on the slightest provocation. At that his color is habitually high. But this round, red, little man, peculiarly enough, has thin white hands and long tapering fingers, like an artist or a newspaper cartoonist. Very possibly his touch would be lighter than that of the nurse herself. At any rate, it is evident that he walks much more quietly. This is strange, for he does not rise on his toes, but puts his feet squarely on the ground. They are large feet, shod in heavy hobnail boots. No one but a golfer or a day laborer would wear such shoes.
  The hands of the little, round, red man preclude the idea that he is a laborer. The impression that he is a golfer is heightened by the fact that he is dressed loudly in very bad taste. In fact, he wears a plaid vest of the sort which was brought over from Scotland in the days when clubs were called sticks. The man in the gaudy vest surveys the sunshine with great satisfaction. It reaches every corner of the room, or rather it would but for the fact that the corners have been turned into curves. A stray beam falls across the eyes of the sick man on the bed. He wakes, and, rubbing his eyes an instant, slowly sits up in bed and looks severely at the fat little man.*]

THE SICK MAN [*feebly, but vehemently*]. No, you don't. I won't stand for any male nurse. I want Miss Bluchblauer.

49

THE FAT MAN. I'm not a nurse, exactly.

THE SICK MAN. Who are you?

THE FAT MAN [*cheerfully and in a matter of fact tone*]. I'm Death.

THE SICK MAN [*sinking back on the bed*]. That rotten fever's up again. I'm seeing things.

THE FAT MAN [*almost plaintively*]. Don't you believe I'm Death? Honest, I am. I wouldn't fool you. [*He fumbles in his pockets and produces in rapid succession a golf ball, a baseball pass, a G string, a large lump of gold, a receipted bill, two theater tickets, and a white mass of sticky confection which looks as though it might be a combination of honey and something—milk perhaps.*] I've gone and left that card case again, but I'm Death, all right.

THE SICK MAN. What nonsense! If you really were I'd be frightened. I'd have cold shivers up and down my spine. My hair would stand on end like the fretful porcupine. I'm not afraid of you. Why, when Sadie Bluchblauer starts to argue about the War she scares me more than you do.

THE FAT MAN [*very much relieved and visibly brighter*]. That's fine. I'm glad you're not scared. Now we can sit down and talk things over like friends.

THE SICK MAN. I don't mind talking, but remember I know you're not Death. You're just some trick my hot head's playing on me. Don't get the idea you're putting anything over.

THE FAT MAN. But what makes you so sure I'm not Death?

THE SICK MAN. Go on! Where's your black cloak? Where's your sickle? Where's your skeleton? Why don't you rattle when you walk?

THE FAT MAN [*horrified and distressed*]. Why should I rattle? What do I want with a black overcoat or a skeleton? I'm not fooling you. I'm Death, all right.

THE SICK MAN. Don't tell me that. I've seen Death a thousand times in the war cartoons. And I've seen him on the stage—Maeterlinck, you know, with green lights and moaning, and that Russian fellow, Andreyeff, with no light at all, and hollering. And I've seen other plays with Death—lots of them. I'm one of the sceneshifters with the Washington Square Players. This isn't regular, at all. There's more light in here right now than any day since I've been sick.

THE FAT MAN. I always come in the light. Be a good fellow and believe me. You'll see I'm right later on. I wouldn't fool anybody. It's mean.

THE SICK MAN [*laughing out loud*]. Mean! What's meaner than Death? You're not Death. You're as soft and smooth-talking as a press agent. Why, you could go on a picnic in that make-up.

THE FAT MAN [*almost soberly*]. I've been on picnics.

THE SICK MAN. You're open and above board. Death's a sneak. You've got a nice face. Yes; you've got a mighty nice face. You'd stop to help a bum in the street or a kid that was crying.

THE FAT MAN. I have stopped for beggars and children.

THE SICK MAN. There, you see; I told you. You're kind and considerate. Death's the cruelest thing in the world.

THE FAT MAN [*very much agitated*]. Oh, please don't say that! It isn't true. I'm kind; that's my business. When things get too rotten I'm the only one that can help. They've got to have me. You should hear them sometimes before I come. I'm the one that takes them off battlefields and out of slums and all terribly tired people. I whisper a joke in their ears, and we go away, laughing. We always go away laughing. Everybody sees my joke, it's so good.

THE SICK MAN. What's the joke?

THE FAT MAN. I'll tell it to you later.

[*Enter the Nurse. She almost runs into the Fat Man, but goes right past without paying any attention. It almost seems as if she cannot see him. She goes to the bedside of the patient.*]

THE NURSE. So, you're awake. You feel any more comfortable?

[*The Sick Man continues to stare at the Fat Man, but that worthy animated pantomime indicates that he shall say nothing of his being there. While this is on, the Nurse takes the patient's temperature. She looks at it, seems surprised, and then shakes the thermometer.*]

THE SICK MAN [*eagerly*]. I suppose

my temperature's way up again, hey? I've been seeing things this afternoon and talking to myself.

THE NURSE. No; your temperature is almost normal.

THE SICK MAN [*incredulously*]. Almost normal?

THE NURSE. Yes; under a hundred.

[*She goes out quickly and quietly. The Sick Man turns to his fat friend.*]

THE SICK MAN. What do you make of that? Less than a hundred. That oughtn't to make me see things; do you think so?

THE FAT MAN. Well, I'd just as soon not be called a thing. Up there I'm called good old Death. Some of the fellows call me Bill. Maybe that's because I'm always due.

THE SICK MAN. Rats! Is that the joke you promised me?

THE FAT MAN [*pained beyond measure*]. Oh, that was just a little unofficial joke. The joke's not like that. I didn't make up the real one. It wasn't made up at all. It's been growing for years and years. A whole lot of people have had a hand in fixing it up—Aristophanes and Chaucer and Shakespeare, and Mark Twain and Rabelais—

THE SICK MAN. Did that fellow Rabelais get in—up there?

THE FAT MAN. Well, not exactly, but he lives in one of the most accessible parts of the suburb, and we have him up quite often. He's popular on account of his after-dinner stories. What I might call his physical humor is delightfully reminiscent and archaic.

THE SICK MAN. There won't be any bodies, then?

THE FAT MAN. Oh, yes, brand new ones. No tonsils or appendixes, of course. That is, not as a rule. We have to bring in a few tonsils every year to amuse our doctors.

THE SICK MAN. Any shows?

THE FAT MAN. I should say so. Lots of 'em, and all hits. In fact, we've never had a failure. [*Provocatively.*] Now, what do you think is the best show you ever saw?

THE SICK MAN [*reminiscently*]. Well, just about the best show I ever saw was a piece called "Fair and Warmer," but, of course, you wouldn't have that.

THE FAT MAN. Of course, we have.

The fellow before last wanted that.

THE SICK MAN [*truculently*]. I'll bet you haven't got the original company.

THE FAT MAN [*apologetically*]. No, but we expect to get most of them by and by. Nell Gwyn does pretty well in the lead just now.

THE SICK MAN [*shocked*]. Did she get in?

THE FAT MAN. No, but Rabelais sees her home after the show. We don't think so much of "Fair and Warmer." That might be a good show for New York, but it doesn't class with us. It isn't funny enough.

THE SICK MAN [*with rising interest*]. Do you mean to say you've got funnier shows than "Fair and Warmer"?

THE FAT MAN. We certainly have. Why, it can't begin to touch that thing of Shaw's called "Ah, There, Annie!"

THE SICK MAN. What Shaw's that?

THE FAT MAN. Regular Shaw.

THE SICK MAN. A lot of things must have been happening since I got sick. I hadn't heard he was dead. At that I always thought that vegetable truck was unhealthy.

THE FAT MAN. He isn't dead.

THE SICK MAN. Well, how about this "Ah, There, Annie!"? He never wrote that show down here.

THE FAT MAN. But he will.

THE SICK MAN [*enormously impressed*]. Do you get shows there before we have them in New York?

THE FAT MAN. I tell you we get them before they're written.

THE SICK MAN [*indignantly*]. How can you do that?

THE FAT MAN. I wish you wouldn't ask me. The answer's awfully complicated. You've got to know a lot of higher math. Wait and ask Euclid about it. We don't have any past and future, you know. None of that nuisance about keeping shall and will straight.

THE SICK MAN. Well, I must say that's quite a stunt. You get shows before they're written.

THE FAT MAN. More than that. We get some that never do get written. Take that one of Ibsen's now, "Merry Christmas"—

THE SICK MAN [*fretfully*]. Ibsen?

THE FAT MAN. Yes, it's a beautiful, sentimental little fairy story with a ghost for the hero. Ibsen just thought about it and never had the nerve to go through with it. He was scared people would kid him, but thinking things makes them so with us.

THE SICK MAN. Then I'd think a sixty-six round Van Cortlandt for myself.

THE FAT MAN. You could do that. But why Van Cortlandt? We've got much better greens on our course. It's a beauty. Seven thousand yards long and I've made it in fifty-four.

THE SICK MAN [*suspiciously*]. Did you hole out on every green or just estimate?

THE FAT MAN [*stiffly*]. The score is duly attested. I might add that it was possible because I drove more than four hundred yards on nine of the eighteen holes.

THE SICK MAN. More than four hundred yards? How did you do that?

THE FAT MAN. It must have been the climate, or [*thoughtfully*] it may be because I wanted so much to drive over four hundred yards on those holes.

THE SICK MAN [*with just a shade of scorn*]. So that's the trick. I guess nobody'd ever beat me on that course; I'd just want the ball in the hole in one every time.

THE FAT MAN [*in gentle reproof*]. No, you wouldn't. Where you and I are going pretty soon we're all true sportsmen and nobody there would take an unfair advantage of an opponent.

THE SICK MAN. Before I go I want to know something. There's a fellow in 125th Street's been awful decent to me. Is there any coming back to see people here?

[*A pause.*]

THE FAT MAN. I can't explain to you yet, but it's difficult to arrange that. Still, I wouldn't say that there never were any slumming parties from beyond the grave.

THE SICK MAN [*shivering*]. The grave! I'd forgotten about that.

THE FAT MAN. Oh, you won't go there, and, what's more, you won't be at the funeral, either. I wish I could keep away from them. I hate funerals. They make me mad. You know, they say "Oh, Death, where is thy sting?" just as if they had a pretty good hunch I had one around me some place after all. And you know that other—"My friends, this is not a sad occasion," but they don't mean it. They keep it sad. They simply won't learn any better. I suppose they'd be a little surprised to know that you were sitting watching Radbourne pitch to Ed Delehanty with the bases full and three balls and two strikes called. Two runs to win and one to tie.

THE SICK MAN. Will Radbourne pitch?

THE FAT MAN. Sure thing.

THE SICK MAN. And, say, will Delehanty bust that ball?

THE FAT MAN. Make it even money and bet me either way.

THE SICK MAN. I don't want to wait any longer. Tell me that joke of yours and let's go.

[*The light softens a little. The room is almost rose color now. It might be from the sunset. The Fat Man gently pushes the head of the Sick Man back on the pillow. Leaning over, he whispers in his ear briefly and the Sick Man roars with laughter. As his laughter slackens a little The Fat Man says, "I'll meet you in the press box," and then before you know it he's gone. The Sick Man is still laughing, but less loudly. People who did not know might think it was gasping. The Nurse opens the door and is frightened. She loudly calls "Doctor! Doctor!" and runs down the corridor. The Sick Man gives one more chuckle and is silent. The curtains at one of the windows sway slightly. Of course, it's the breeze.*]

[*Curtain.*]

ORLANDO FURIOSO
A Marionette

By Remo Bufano

CHARACTERS

MALIGIGI [*the magician*].
DODO [*the devil*].
ORLANDO FURIOSO.
THE FAYRE LADY.
FIRST ROBBER.
SECOND ROBBER.
POLIDORO.
AMOROSO [*the dragon*].

ORLANDO FURIOSO

A MARIONETTE

By REMO BUFANO

[SCENE I: *A vast amount of space which is the tabernacle of the magician Maligigi. Maligigi is discovered making many gyrations and mumbling magic words. The scene is dimly lighted. A continuous noise of rolling thunder and of whistling wind is heard. This noise rises and falls with the varying importance of the magic words. Maligigi seems to be conducting an invisible band.*]

MALIGIGI. I am Maligigi, the magician. My rule unbroken and unending weighs everywhere over the powers of the Prince of Darkness. The knights of Charlemagne I have made my especial charges, to shield them from the machinations of the evil enchanters. I am troubled to-night. The omens presage great danger to Orlando, Charlemagne's most valiant champion. [*Noise increases violently.*] Ha, a spirit is trying to reach my ears. [*What seems to be the wind is heard wailing.*]
Presently, presently I will aid thy approach.
Mara mara brak
cut cut round the circle
stud the girdle with
a tack tack tack
wind and water
sea and wind
mix mix mix
from the tree in the styx
gather six six six
peal them across it
flail and nail
white cerulean fly to dawn
cock a doodle doo.
> [*At the last magic word the light changes, the noise becomes deafening and then the devil appears. During the scene between Maligigi and the Devil, the noise is heard throughout as an accompanying background, now soft and now*

loud, depending on the tenseness of the movement.]
DEVIL. M-a-a-a-s-ter. Orlando is in great danger though he knows it not.
MALIGIGI. Where is he now?
DEVIL. In the forest of Roncevalle, the lair of evil spirits, evil men, and evil beasts. Death with fiery breath and brazen claws hovers near him.
MALIGIGI. Who dares to threaten Orlando, the bravest knight and the sweetest singer of Charlemagne's court?
DEVIL. Fate! She has directed his steps to the realm of Polidoro, the bandit chief. His lusty cutthroats and his fearsome dragon Amoroso will soon fall upon Orlando.
MALIGIGI. Has he not his good sword Durandel with him? It has served him in many a desperate fight.
DEVIL. Aye, M-a-a-a-s-ter. But it will not avail him against the poisonous breath of the dragon. Without your aid Orlando is undone, and at sundown he will be but a memory.
MALIGIGI. Then bear me swiftly to him. I will surround him with a benefic aura.
DEVIL. Aye, M-a-a-a-s-ter.
> [*The Devil stoops. Maligigi mounts upon his back like a rider and they fly off through the air at an eye-blinking speed followed by the loudest clash of noise which gradually dies in the distance.*]

[*Curtain.*]

[SCENE II: *In the forest of Roncevalle. Enter Orlando Furioso.*]

ORLANDO FURIOSO [*singing*]. They call me Orlando the Furious
Furioso is more to my *gout*
Though the knights of the court
Think it curious

The ladies adore it *beaucoup.*
It rings with a high
Sky-high mad sigh
On the hearts of the ladies I woo
On the hearts of the ladies I woo.

FAYRE LADY [*off stage and in the distance*]. Help! Help!

ORLANDO FURIOSO. What noise was that? Methought I heard a feminine voice calling for aid. [*Listens.*] No. My ears deceive me. It was a trick of the rapscallion wind in the trees. [*Sings.*]
It rings with a high
Sky-high mad sigh
On the hearts of the ladies I woo.

FAYRE LADY [*a little nearer*]. Help! Help! Help!

ORLANDO FURIOSO. Again the same sweet voice. No deception surely this time. I must bestir me. [*He bestirs himself very violently.*] No damsel in distress ever calls on the great-hearted Orlando in vain.

FAYRE LADY [*quite near*]. Help me! Help! Help!

ORLANDO FURIOSO. A lady runneth this way. Two armed ruffians pursue her closely. Ho there! Milady, come this way! Have no fear! How fortunate for the age that Orlando exists to rescue its womanhood. How beautifully disorganized are those golden tresses as she runneth against the wind.

FAYRE LADY [*runs into Orlando's arms*]. Help! Help!

ORLANDO FUROSIO. Courage! Courage, fayre lady!

FAYRE LADY. Oh, help me, sir knight. I am dead with fright and fatigue. Save me! Save me!

ORLANDO FURIOSO. Have no fear, fayre damozel, I will take care of those scaramuffians.

FAYRE LADY. They are robbers, my lord.

ORLANDO FURIOSO. Good.

FAYRE LADY. They are cutthroats, my lord.

ORLANDO FURIOSO. Very good.

FAYRE LADY. They are assassins, my lord.

ORLANDO FURIOSO. Excellent. Go hide behind yon tree until this little affair is over.

FAYRE LADY. I fear for you, gentle knight.

ORLANDO FURIOSO. I never fear for me, gentle lady.

FAYRE LADY. Let us both run away before it is too late.

ORLANDO FURIOSO. And turn our backs to the enemy? To adventure? Ha, ha, ha! Damozel, you are ignorant of the rules of chivalry. [*He sees the pursuers approaching.*] Quick. Get behind yon tree!

FAYRE LADY. O-o-o-h.

[*She disappears behind a tree. Orlando takes a firm stand. The First Robber advances. He eyes Orlando up and down and salutes him.*]

FIRST ROBBER. Sir knight, you are an ill-bred, insolent rooster to interfere in our affair. For the sake of your new shining armor, we will allow you to proceed unscathed, if you will give up the lady.

ORLANDO FURIOSO. My good friend, I am unable to accede to your wishes. I am very stubborn.

FIRST ROBBER. But your new shining armor, think of that.

ORLANDO FURIOSO. There are many ladies at court whose greatest pleasure it would be to brighten up the dull spots in my armor; think also of that.

FIRST ROBBER. Too bad. Then you must d-i-e.
[*With an ominous tremolo.*]

ORLANDO FURIOSO. Then go before me and see that my new abode is made ready.

BOTH. To arms!
[*The two engage in a combat. It gets very hot. The Robber falls several times.*]

BOTH. To arms!
[*The Second Robber appears stealthily through the trees behind Orlando. He gets ready to attack when*]

FAYRE LADY [*screams*]. Orlando! Turn!
[*Orlando turns and engages both the Robbers, striking fiercely to right and to left. Both Robbers are badly beaten. At the first chance the Second Robber withdraws and runs off the scene and the First Robber is beheaded.*]

ORLANDO FURIOSO. Idiot. Thou hast bluffed thyself to perdition. Get into the ditch. [*He pushes the body into the ditch and then calls.*] Fayre lady, come forth! [*The Lady comes out of her hiding place.*] See, my good sword Durandel hath sent this knave to his judgment. The other scamudgeon runneth away. We must follow him to his cavernous *palazzo.*

FAYRE LADY. Oh, no, gallant knight. That would mean certain death. He is one of the band of Polidoro, the bandit king. His servitors are strong and cruel. His dragon Amoroso is unconquerable by man. Scores of knights and ladies lie imprisoned in Polidoro's power. Each day Amoroso eats one of them for his midday meal.

ORLANDO FURIOSO. Sayest thou so? Ha, ha, a fresh exploit to add to my triumphs! My song, fayre lady, is no idle boast. They call me Orlando the Furious in no mocking vein. Point me the way to the lair of this knave Polidoro and his hungry dragon.

FAYRE LADY. I beseech you, fayre sir, do not go. Mortal man thou need not fear, I know, but Amoroso will surely overcome you.

ORLANDO FURIOSO. If the Fates have destined me for Amoroso's belly, I shall not balk them. My purpose is firm. You, fayre lady, remain here, hidden in these sylvan recesses. Tell me the way and await my return.

FAYRE LADY. Then follow that path and turn to the right at the twin oaks.
[*She points the way to Orlando who contemplates it with several serious nods of the head.*]

ORLANDO FURIOSO. Good. And now, fayre damozel, before I go forth to meet the dragon, will you tell me that the hope that your beauty and graciousness have raised in me is not in vain? If I conquer the dragon, will you go with me to Charlemagne's court as my lady?

FAYRE LADY. Sir knight, you honor me with your suit. You have my dearest prayers and wishes.

ORLANDO FURIOSO. And may I have your heart?

FAYRE LADY. You may have the hope of that, gallant knight.
[*He kneels knight-errantly and kisses the Lady's hand which is held out for him—twice. He rises, salutes, and strides off with a determined step. The Lady is*

left alone looking in the direction of the hero as

The Curtain Falls.]

[SCENE III: *The Robbers' Cave. A villainous and rocky formation in blacks, blues, and reds. It is dimly lighted. The colored forms give the appearance of luminous and ugly gargoyles closing in on the scene.*]

POLIDORO [*appearing with a huge curved sword in his hand*]. I am I, Polidoro. I rule all things my eyes perceive, for I am I, Polidoro. Oh, where are those lazy rogues? I am impatient. These arms are hungering for the damsel.
[*Noise is heard off stage. Various guards are heard relaying a password. The Second Robber rushes in.*]

SECOND ROBBER. Master, master.

POLIDORO. Ha, ha! Bring the damsel here.

SECOND ROBBER. She is not here, master.

POLIDORO. What! Darest thou come back without the damsel?

SECOND ROBBER. Aye, master. And without my companion.

POLIDORO. What!

SECOND ROBBER. As we were chasing the lady. . . .

POLIDORO. Yes!

SECOND ROBBER. She ran into a knight in full armor.

POLIDORO. Yes.

SECOND ROBBER. My companion came upon him first.

POLIDORO. Yes.

SECOND ROBBER. And fought with the knight.

POLIDORO. Good.

SECOND ROBBER. No. With two blows, master, he cut him into three parts.

POLIDORO. Ha, ha! In three parts.

SECOND ROBBER. Yes, in three parts.

POLIDORO. And how did the knight look in three parts?

SECOND ROBBER. Master?

POLIDORO. How did he look? You said he cut the knight in three parts.

SECOND ROBBER. Oh, master, master. My companion was cut into three parts.

POLIDORO. Oh! [*He deals the Second*

Robber a terrific blow with his sword which sends him to the ground.] Thou art a coward. Didst thou stand by and look on idly?

SECOND ROBBER. Only for a moment. Then my legs counseled me to be prudent so they ran here that I might tell your lordship of the affair.

POLIDORO [*repeats the blow*]. A fine affair. Did I not tell you to bring back the lady at all costs?

SECOND ROBBER. But my life would have cost you nothing, master.

POLIDORO [*repeats the blow*]. Thou art an impudent coward.

SECOND ROBBER. The knight is terrible. He made short work of my comrade. He is coming here. His name is Orlando.

POLIDORO. Let him come. Be he more mighty than all of Charlemagne's knights he shall see that I am I, Polidoro. Out of my sight and come to me at the first sign of Orlando's approach.

SECOND ROBBER. Aye, master.

[*Exit.*]

POLIDORO. Amoroso will dine well tonight. Amoroso. Amoroso. [*He whistles and Amoroso answers with a distant whine.*] Dainty Amoroso. [*Amoroso's head appears.*] Ha, ha! My pet, approach. [*The dragon's form slowly reveals itself with many turns and twists and with affectionate croonings of his brass voice. When all his long body and its curves have been dragged on, he settles at Polidoro's feet.*] There is a treat in store for you to-night.

AMOROSO. Ra?

POLIDORO. Are you pleased?

AMOROSO. Ra-a-a-a-a-a!

POLIDORO. You should be.

AMOROSO. Rr.

POLIDORO. Are you not my pet?

AMOROSO. R-ra.

POLIDORO. Are you not my puppy?

AMOROSO. Rar. Rar. Rar.

POLIDORO. Are you not my Amoroso?

AMOROSO. R-r-o-o-r-r-o-o.

[*He writhes very coquettishly, almost standing on his tail, and ends up by rubbing the long of his back against Polidoro's legs.*]

POLIDORO. For dessert to-night you shall have a delicious dish of fried knight's legs. [*During these last lines Amoroso purrs with delight. He finally rears and coils himself about Polidoro*

and licks and paws him to show his appreciation.] Down! Down! Down! [*Amoroso eventually downs.*] Come let me ride upon your back.

AMOROSO. Ra-a-a-a. [*He flattens himself on the ground. Polidoro straddles him horse fashion.*] Ra-ra-ra-ra.

[*Makes a few gallops and leaps through the air.*]

POLIDORO. Do you like me to ride upon your back?

AMOROSO. Ra.

POLIDORO. Good. [*Amoroso repeats the gallops and leaps.*] Do you like your master?

AMOROSO. Ra. Ra.

POLIDORO. Very good. [*Amoroso repeats business again.*] Would you give your life for your master?

[*A moment of silence and then—*]

AMOROSO. Ar?

POLIDORO. No? [*Amoroso quietly slips from under him and disappears.*] Um. Not so good.

SECOND ROBBER [*appearing at the door trembling.*] Master, master, master!

POLIDORO. Well! What's the matter now?

SECOND ROBBER. I see Orlando's armor shining through the leaves. What shall we do?

POLIDORO. Do? Wait for the knight. I shall summon the others. Out! [*Exit the Second Robber.*] Don Chiaro!

FIRST VOICE [*rather weak and frightened*]. Here!

POLIDORO. Good. Don Drico!

SECOND VOICE [*same as First Voice*]. Here!

POLIDORO. Good. Don Corbeau!

THIRD VOICE [*same as First Voice*]. Here!

POLIDORO. Good. Let every man go to his post within the circle of the door. Do you hear? [*He is answered by a deep silence.*] Do you hear?

THREE VOICES [*very unwilling and with intermissions between.*] Here. Here. Here.

POLIDORO. Um. Not so good. Not so good. Amoroso.

AMOROSO [*just his head appears. Quite weak*]. Ar.

POLIDORO. To the vanguard. Go swallow up the knight—arms, legs, head—everything. Go!

AMOROSO. Ar.

[*Disappears.*]

POLIDORO. Now men. [*No answer from the men.*] Men!

FIRST VOICE [*weak*]. Ah.

SECOND VOICE [*weaker*]. Oh.

THIRD VOICE [*weakest*]. Eh.

POLIDORO. Um. [*Pause.*] If the knight should escape Amoroso you must join the attack and fall on him. Do you hear? [*They do not.*] Do you hear?

THREE VOICES. Ya— Ye— Yea.

POLIDORO. Um. Not so good. Not so good. As for me, I shall retire to my sanctum sanctorum until this little affair is over. Have no fear, beloved men, for I shall be perfectly safe in my *palazzo* of rock. Fight well, men, for I am I, Polidoro.

[*Rumbling is heard. Polidoro disappears. The rumbling continues and Maligigi appears on the back of the Devil.*]

MALIGIGI. Dodo, go into Polidoro's sanctuary and scare him into the open for I want him to meet Orlando.

DEVIL. Aye, master.

[*Exits. Clashing of swords, shrieks, and other noises are heard off stage.*]

MALIGIGI. Orlando has reached the outer door. They can't hold him long.

[*Drops out of sight. Noises off stage increases. Crashing, smashing, howling, swearing—and altogether it sounds as if a piece of hell had been let loose. Then all of a sudden all is quiet.*]

ORLANDO FURIOSO [*still off stage*]. Ha —ha—ha. [*He appears quite undamaged.*] So much for them. Now for their master. [*Another queer noise is heard in the direction of Polidoro's sanctuary.*] That must be my man.

POLIDORO [*dashes in howling and runs blindly into Orlando's sword*]. Oh-o-o-f. Who are you? Are you a magician? Why did you send the fiend to me?

ORLANDO FURIOSO. There is no fiend here but myself. Prepare, dog, to die. I am Orlando, slayer of all vile things like you.

POLIDORO. What? [*tremolo*] O—R—LANDO. Amoroso. Amoroso. [*Orlando forces him to combat.*] Amoroso. Amoroso. Oh, where is that lazy beast?

ORLANDO FURIOSO. You will find him with the rest of your thievish band.

[*Duel continues and gets very hot though very one-sided. Polidoro*

falls a number of times and becomes more helpless each time.*]

POLIDORO. Amoroso. Amoroso. Amor—

[*In the middle of the last "Amoroso," Orlando sticks him through the pit of the stomach so he is unable to finish it.*]

ORLANDO [*finishes the word for Polidoro*]. Oso. Too bad you couldn't finish it yourself. [*Goes into song.*]
And it rings with a high
Sky-high mad sigh
On the hearts of the ladies I woo.
On the hearts of the ladies I woo.

MALIGIGI [*appears*]. Cousin.

ORLANDO FURIOSO. Who are you?

MALIGIGI. Your labor is but half done. The lady you left in the forest has taken refuge in a tree. She is besieged by the terrible dragon.

ORLANDO FURIOSO. Farewell then. I go.

MALIGIGI. Wait! Without the protection of my magic circle you go in vain. Let me surround you with the charm.

ORLANDO FURIOSO. Not for me. I fight with my own strength alone, for they call me Orlando the Furious. Furioso is more to my *gout.* . . .

[*He disappears singing his song.*]

MALIGIGI. Rash youth! Rash youth!

[*As he performs his incantations*

The Curtain Falls.]

[SCENE IV: *Forest same as Scene II. When the curtain rises the Fayre Lady is perched up in a tree screaming for help. The dragon is coyly frisking around the tree as though he were coaxing her to come down.*]

FAYRE LADY. Help! Heip! Help! Help! Go away! Go away, you ugly monster!

AMOROSO. No-o-o.

FAYRE LADY. I'm not good to eat. I'm really very thin.

AMOROSO. Um—Um—Um.

FAYRE LADY. Nice dragon, kind little dragon, please, please, go away.

AMOROSO. No—o—o.

FAYRE LADY. Shoo! Shoo!

AMOROSO. Ar—ar—ar.

[*He makes great leaps and curves in*

the air and all but snatches the Lady out of the tree.]

FAYRE LADY. Oh! Oh! Oh! Orlando, come save me! Save me!

ORLANDO FURIOSO [*off stage*]. Take heart, fayre lady, I'll be there anon! [*The dragon continues to lash about the tree. Orlando appears and leaps upon him. Amoroso catches Orlando's sword in his mouth and shakes it. Orlando, however, hangs on.*] Aye, my Amoroso, see how you can eat Durandel.

[*Discouraged, the dragon releases the sword and goes back to the tree snorting.*]

FAYRE LADY. I smell something terrible. I am going to faint.

ORLANDO FURIOSO. Don't faint, dear lady. You will fall right in the monster's mouth. Wait! [*Orlando attacks the dragon again and there is a tumbling and tossing about for a moment during which Orlando advises the lady—*] Now climb down quickly and run away. Now, my pernicious fiend of the scoriac valley, let me see thy teeth.

AMOROSO [*shows teeth*]. Ps-s-s.

ORLANDO FURIOSO. Ha! Thou hast them. Thou art well equipped. [*The opponents eye each other quietly for a few seconds. The dragon springs. Orlando steps aside, then leaps on him, and straddles him, beating him with his sword. The dragon rages about. He finally succeeds in turning and the two end up embracing each other quite fiercely. They roll about, first this way, then back again.*] Do thy work more quickly, Durandel. Remember the monster of the Black Valley. Thou didst not fail me then, do as well this time. [*During the rolling about the dragon succeeds in getting Orlando's head between his jaws.*

This is a terrible moment for Orlando. He pulls and tugs and beats with great rapidity at the dragon with both sword and shield until the monster is actually scared into opening his jaw.] Father, direct this arm that is always raised against the spoilers of thy good works! [*He rushes at the dragon and thrusts his sword down the monster's throat, pinning its head to the ground.*] Ah! Splendid, Durandel. Now dig for the monster's heart! [*The dragon goes through many convulsions but cannot free himself. He lashes at Orlando with his tail, wraps it around the knight, but Orlando continues to dig deeper in his throat. Gradually the dragon's movements become weaker and weaker—and weaker. Then he dies.*] Now the trees and the flowers of the forest may bloom again without fear of being poisoned. [*He calls.*] Fayre lady!

FAYRE LADY. Hoo!

ORLANDO FURIOSO. Come forth! The pestiferous poodle hath perished!

FAYRE LADY [*enters very cautiously*]. Oh, great prince Orlando, I know not what to say to you. Knights like you should live forever in song and story.

ORLANDO FURIOSO. Perhaps I shall, for—[*song*]
They call me Orlando Furioso
And the ladies adore it *beaucoup.*

And now, sweet lady, now that the dragon is dead, will you go back with me to Charlemagne's court?

FAYRE LADY. I will gladly go, sir knight.

ORLANDO FURIOSO. And be my lady.

FAYRE LADY. And be your lady.

[*They embrace.*]

[*Curtain.*]

THE DUCHESS SAYS HER PRAYERS
A PLAY

BY MARY CASS CANFIELD

FOR CECILIA

CHARACTERS

MADONNA CECILIA GALLERANI.
LODOVICO SFORZA [*Duke of Bari, Regent of Milan*].
BEATRICE D'ESTE [*his wife*].

TIME: *A March evening in the year 1491.*

THE DUCHESS SAYS HER PRAYERS was first presented at the Belasco Theater, New York, January 31, 1926, with the following cast:

CECILIA GALLERANI . . . . *Marion Waring-Manley.*
LODOVICO SFORZA . . . . *Ernest Glendenning.*
BEATRICE D'ESTE . . . . *Helen Chandler.*

Directed by Arnold Daly.

THE DUCHESS SAYS HER PRAYERS

A PLAY   BY MARY CASS CANFIELD

[SCENE: *A chapel in the Duomo at Milan. A corner of the cathedral. Long, lighted tapers stain the incense-laden air. At the back, an altar. On the right, an elaborate carved niche with steps leading up to it, bare of its statue. On the left, a bench. In center, an upholstered prie-dieu.*

At the rise of the curtain the scene is empty. An organ is sounding softly in the distance. Enter, from the left, Cecilia Gallerani, a lady of the Milanese court, tall, palely beautiful, about thirty years old. Upon her heels, Lodovico Sforza, Duke of Bari, a handsome man of thirty-nine, at the height of his faculties and magnetism. Both are sumptuously dressed.]

CECILIA. Why did you follow me to church, my lord duke?

LODOVICO [*smiling*]. Why does the needle turn to the pole?

[*He kisses her hand lightly.*]

CECILIA. It was imprudent.

LODOVICO. It was a necessity.

CECILIA. A necessity?

LODOVICO. I mean, to my nature.

CECILIA. Very pretty. But we may be seen. The people are coming in to vespers.

LODOVICO. Not likely. This chapel is remote. Besides I had to talk to you.

[*He approaches her but she turns away. The organ music ceases.*]

CECILIA. What means that empty shrine?

LODOVICO. It means that Bramante is obtaining for me from Florence a most excellent and curious statue of the Blessed Virgin, molded in colored wax by no less a master than Rossellino. She should be almost as lovely as you, Cecilia.

CECILIA. Signor Lodovico—

LODOVICO. Signor Lodovico—why so formal, my beautiful? It is only since my marriage that you give me this Signor.

CECILIA [*shrugging*]. Marriage alters many things.

LODOVICO. I know a man who paints tender Madonnas, smiling a benediction on the Holy Child. But in his sketch books, there are drawings of the most cruel monsters. When he first came to Milan, he brought me a lute, fashioned as a silver horse's head, from which divine music might be drawn. He also constructs engines of war, capable of blowing a town to pieces and thousands of souls into hell.

CECILIA. You mean Leonardo da Vinci?

LODOVICO. Yes.

CECILIA. Well, what of it?

LODOVICO. Only that Leonardo's cannon are as perfect as his Virgins. Only that man is various, of myriad aspirations. Only that life is brief and we should follow every spark which will kindle our spirits into flame.

CECILIA [*smiling*]. Only that you have acquired a wife and want to keep your mistress.

LODOVICO [*gayly*]. Others have done so before.

CECILIA. And what says your Beatrice?

LODOVICO. Beatrice is a child. I love her as a child. I love you differently.

CECILIA. Is that an excuse?

LODOVICO. Besides, she knows nothing. She need never know.

CECILIA. She may be informed. There are a hundred ways. Do you trust Bellincioni, that poetaster, who writes to order and may be bought by any one? Do you trust Diodato, your wife's fool, who adores her like a faithful dog and is keen beneath his folly?

LODOVICO. Life itself is danger. But I am in love with both.

[*He laughs.*]

CECILIA [*sighing*]. Ah, yes. I think that is why I am in love with you; if I am in love with you.

LODOVICO. You seem doubtful. Do you dare to be?

CECILIA. I have felt so many things for you. I have admired your mind and your power. I have loved your laughter and your bold ways. I have hated your conduct, so often.

LODOVICO. Beloved. The only wisdom in this world is to take people as they are.

CECILIA. Yes. If we can do that we are wise—and lonely forever.

LODOVICO. Why should you be lonely? I shall always be there.

CECILIA. Always is a word I distrust. It is an idea strayed down to us from the infinite, too big for human beings. When stars drop to earth, they are just stones.

LODOVICO. Ah, Cecilia. Now you are being metaphysical!

CECILIA. Poor Lodovico! I shall keep my metaphysics and my philosophy to myself. With you I shall talk of other things: whether the Marchioness of Mantua should have stolen her sister Beatrice's design for a velvet cape lined with peacock feathers—or whether—

LODOVICO. By the way. I have been sent from Venice two golden robes embroidered with aquamarines. You shall have one.

CECILIA [*smiling*]. And Madonna Beatrice the other, I suppose?

LODOVICO. Quite. I have already given it to her.

CECILIA. Ah.

LODOVICO. Cecilia, listen. I have told you once already. The little princess is a happy child. She is sweet and gay like a singing bird in the spring. My marriage was a political necessity; I pray she may give me an heir. I shall not pretend I am displeased with my wife. Still I do not love her as I love you.

CECILIA. And how exactly do you love me, my lord duke of Bari?

LODOVICO [*smiling*]. That I shall never tell you.

CECILIA. Clever man. Sometimes we do not want to be too clear with ourselves, do we? [*She laughs.*] But tell me about this Madonna. Is she standing or sitting? How does she hold her Babe?

LODOVICO [*as if not hearing her*]. To-night, after the pageant given for the Papal legate, I shall come to you, Cecilia. [*A pause.*] Will you be there?

CECILIA [*thoughtfully*]. Rossellino—exquisite talent, turning stone into flesh and flesh into spirit, with the eternal passion and purity of the artist.

LODOVICO. Will you be there, Madonna?

CECILIA [*facing him abruptly*]. Yes.

LODOVICO [*bending over her hand*]. Cecilia!

CECILIA. I shall never let you go. Never. Never— [*Changing her tone and going towards the shrine.*] But tell me, how is she, this Virgin?

LODOVICO. A strange fancy of Rossellino's. She is without a Child and in her heart there are seven swords.

CECILIA. Ah. [*A silence.*] The aspect of a statue in colored wax must be surprising.

LODOVICO. Most lifelike. The magnificent Lorenzo himself has written me about it.

CECILIA. So she will seem almost like a human being?

LODOVICO. Yes. [*He is struck with an idea.*] Cecilia!

CECILIA. What?

LODOVICO [*glancing off stage*]. No one about. Yes. Look you. Let me see what the effect of the statue will be. Go, stand in the niche.

CECILIA. I?

LODOVICO. Why not? [*He laughs.*] You need not fear the priests. They fear the Duke of Bari. Let me help you up, I beg you.

CECILIA. Well then—for a moment. If it amuses you.

[*With a bow, he hands her up the steps and she stands in the shrine.*]

LODOVICO. Enchanting! Your head bent a little more. There. Perfect! Why, in this light, you are almost made of wax. I have not seen you more beautiful. I shall be saying my prayers to you in a moment! [*He laughs.*] You lack nothing—except the seven swords.

CECILIA [*pensively*]. The seven swords— [*A trumpet blast peals outside, very near.*] What is that?

LODOVICO. It sounds like— [*He crosses towards the right and looks off stage.*] Yes. By the bones of St. Anselm, it is—

CECILIA. What?

LODOVICO. My wife's escort. She is alighting at the west portal. She must pass through here. Friday was ever my unlucky day. By St. Mercurial, this is terrible.

CECILIA. Well, if you would help me down instead of talking, we might be able to escape.

LODOVICO. We should be observed in the cathedral. There is no time. We are lost!

[*The organ begins once again.*]

CECILIA [*calmly*]. Lodovico.

LODOVICO. What?

CECILIA. Listen to me. Go, be found at your devotions before the high altar. I shall stay just where I am.

LODOVICO [*stupefied*]. Stay there?

CECILIA. Yes. I shall be unnoticed. Be off! Hurry! [*Stamping.*] Do as I tell you. Go!

[*Lodovico rushes off stage to the right. There is an interval during which Cecilia remains motionless. In the twinkling light of the tapers, her figure assumes a statue-like appearance. From the left enters slowly and pensively Beatrice d'Este, Duchess of Bari. She is a girl of fifteen, dark, with an intelligent, eager face, at present veiled with melancholy. Her heavy brocade dress weighs down her youthful form. She advances towards the center of the stage and only glances at the figure in the shrine, before going to the prie-dieu and sinking to her knees. Abruptly she buries her face in her hands and her shoulders shake. Cecilia cannot restrain a gesture of surprise, but she remembers her rôle and resumes her attitude. A pause, broken only by Beatrice's sobs.*]

BEATRICE. O Madonna, Mother of God, you who bend over the sufferings of the whole world, incline to me and listen, for I bring you a broken heart. Listen, Blessed Virgin, have mercy and ask God the Father, to give me back—to give me back my happiness. You are forever pure, but I think you have divine pity on the passions of men. O Madonna, be to me a mother, since my mother is no longer by my side. [*She weeps.*] I am alone, Holy One, and must hold my head very high for I am wedded to the greatest lord in Italy. I act my part, but often I am frightened and weary because I have become sad. Those things that I loved, I love no longer, and when I ride over the hills at dawn, I do not cry for joy at the sight of the hounds and there is no singing in my heart. [*Confidentially.*] Mother of God, would you believe that the Gonzaga lately sent me a monkey from Arabia, besides a Spanish dwarf from the palace of the Borgias; and I could not even look at them, out of the dreadful heaviness in my soul. [*Shaking.*] I will confess—I must confess to you that I have done evil. I have resorted to magic and incantations. The old witch, Simonia, has given me a potion made of powdered bats' wings distilled with the blood of an adder, which I have drunk at the young quarter of the moon—so that Lodovico might find me beautiful and love me and me only. [*She weeps.*] It tasted very nasty, Blessed One, and I was sick and only looked ugly the next day. [*She weeps.*] Holy Virgin, my husband is strong and clever, he is magnificent and of great courtesy—and I dreamed of him all my youth. When he came at last, I thought the sun had risen for the first time. I loved him, his laugh and the toss of his head—his will over men. If he had been a beggar on the road, I would have followed where he went. He was kindly, he called me his child—his little flower—and I thought he loved me. [*She rises. The organ stops.*] And then, and then—they came and told me —[*pause*] Blessed Virgin, I have not seen her, and I do not want to see her! But they say she is lovely and when he married me, he belonged to her all the time. Holy One, I do not know if she loves him, this Cecilia. But he is her very servant, for she is witty and a student, proud and beautiful—a lady of most diverse enchantments. [*Throwing herself on her knees.*] I do not understand the ways of God. How can Lodovico love us both? Listen. He has given me a golden garment, one of two sent him by the Signory of Venice—the other he will give to Cecilia. This was reported to me. [*With fury.*]. I will never wear that dress. I will tear it into bits and throw them in his face! [*Sobbing.*] No, no. I dare not —I am afraid to anger him. O Blessed One, you are fortunate to be in heaven with the saints in glory, for the loves of earth are dark with uncertainty and the blindness of our souls. [*Still weeping, she rises.*] Mother of God, I must go. For to-night, there is a ball—and I must be there and smile and be the Duchess of Bari. [*Her voice breaks.*] But it is not I who am his wife—it is that other woman. [*Kneeling on the steps of the shrine.*] Mother of Christ, there is a child growing within me. He does not know. Once I was glad, but now—it is a sin to tell you—I hope the child will never be born. Blessed One, pray for me to God, that he may change the heart of my husband. For I cannot be so miserable and live.

[*She rises with difficulty, turns away, and goes out to the left, Cecilia lifts her head, which she has kept inclined and follows her with her eyes. She remains where she is, lost in thought. Lodovico enters cautiously from the right. A silence.*]

LODOVICO. Cecilia! Merciful heaven! I saw that she stayed here. What took place? Has she really gone?

CECILIA [*slowly*]. Yes. She has gone.

LODOVICO. What happened?

CECILIA. Much happened.

LODOVICO. In God's name what?

CECILIA [*with irony*]. You are quite safe, my lord.

LODOVICO. She did not notice you?

CECILIA. Yes. She noticed me.

LODOVICO. But then?

CECILIA. She thought me the Madonna in wax.

LODOVICO. No? Really? The saints protected us!

CECILIA. Yes. Well, perhaps now you will help me down from my exalted station?

LODOVICO. To be sure. You are a trifle pale. It must have been a strain. What did she do?

CECILIA. The duchess said her prayers.

LODOVICO. Really?

CECILIA. She said them to me.

LODOVICO. Amazing! Did she say them aloud?

CECILIA. Yes.

LODOVICO. Jupiter! What an escape! [*A silence. Cecilia sits down.*]

CECILIA. For that gold dress from Venice that you spoke of, I do not want it.

LODOVICO. No?

CECILIA. You will be kind enough to present it to your wife.

LODOVICO. To my wife? But she has one already.

CECILIA. She will like the second one better than the first.

LODOVICO. What do you mean?

[*A pause.*]

CECILIA [*in the same tone*]. You are acquainted with Count Bergamini?

LODOVICO. Yes. A worthy nobleman, though a trifle ponderous. Why?

CECILIA. He has asked for my hand in marriage.

LODOVICO. What impertinence!

CECILIA. I take it rather as an honor, my lord, the circumstances being what they are.

LODOVICO. I could horsewhip him with pleasure.

CECILIA. And I shall wed him.

LODOVICO. What?

CECILIA. I will send him his answer to-night.

LODOVICO. Are you mad?

CECILIA. No, I have come to my reason at last.

LODOVICO. Cecilia. Do not jest with me. The subject is too serious.

CECILIA. I do not jest.

LODOVICO. In God's name, what has come over you? [*A silence.*] Ah, another of your moods. I have in some way displeased you and you are trying to make me suffer. Like the time you forsook me for the shores of the Adriatic and stayed away a whole year for no reason at all.

CECILIA. For no reason?

LODOVICO [*shrugging*]. A wretched intrigue with a courtesan who meant nothing to me. You should understand the value of such things; they are no more than straws in the wind.

CECILIA. I never told you what I did at Rimini.

LODOVICO. Ah. I dare say you were unfaithful to me.

CECILIA. I sat long hours by the sea, with a volume of Virgil in my hand, where the pines bend over the quiet waves. My soul was wounded and I think the sun, the calm, the gentle winds, healed it once more. I have not much faith in the mysteries of the Church; these are sweet legends to hush the spirits of men, who in this world are like children crying in the dark. But I have faith in the mysteries of nature. For in the line of hills against the sky there is strength and in sudden flowers among the rocks there is wonder and in the splendor of sunset over darkening seas there is a great promise of some unthinkable peace. As I played with the shining sand pebbles and listened to the cries of fishermen folding their sails at evening, wisdom flowed into my heart. And I knew that the two sins we must not commit or forgive in this life, are cruelty and deceit.

LODOVICO. Well?

CECILIA. You had deceived me and that was cruel. We are deceiving your wife—or at least trying to, which is the same thing.

LODOVICO. Trying to? You mean that she is not deceived? That she knows?

CECILIA. I listened to your wife's prayers. Her heart is breaking.

LODOVICO. On account of you?

CECILIA. Yes.

LODOVICO. Ah! What are we to do?

CECILIA. I have told you.

LODOVICO. No! No! [He goes to her and seizes her in his arms.] Cecilia. I cherish Beatrice. I feel for her. But I cannot lose you. That is incredible.

CECILIA. You must learn to believe it.

LODOVICO. Ah. Now, it is you who are cruel.

CECILIA. Cruel to Beatrice?

LODOVICO. You can think of her, but you cannot think of me.

CECILIA. Does it seem I am thinking of myself?

LODOVICO. Oh. Women will sacrifice a whole existence for a becoming moment.

CECILIA [rising]. That is unfair. Let me pass, my lord.

LODOVICO [intercepting her]. Cecilia!

CECILIA. I am going.

LODOVICO [seizing her wrists]. So. You can say, "I am going"—like that, calmly. Have these years left no mark on you?

CECILIA [faintly]. Let me go, Lodovico.

LODOVICO. My love! My love! Without you, I am lost. You have been a flame leading me. You have been a sword in my hand.

CECILIA. Have pity. Have pity. Do not say those things to me now.

LODOVICO. Have you any pity! Cecilia! My troubled spirit has found its rest in you. You have been my hope and my peace.

CECILIA. Sometimes God grants us absolute beauty. We cannot always keep it. But, in our memory, we have its essence forever.

LODOVICO. We have shared every breath and every thought. You belong to me. No one else. [Violently.] I am a despot here. I can prevent your marriage and I will.

[He paces up and down.]

CECILIA [quietly]. My lord duke, your wife is to give you a child.

LODOVICO [struck still with emotion]. What do you say? A child?

CECILIA. But a moment since, she prayed aloud that the child might never be born.

LODOVICO. God in heaven!

[With a groan, he sinks onto the bench and buries his face in his hands. Cecilia crosses swiftly and kneels at his feet.]

CECILIA [tenderly]. Come. We cannot run away from life. It is only how we meet it that matters.

LODOVICO [rebelliously]. I have always had the will to conquer life.

CECILIA. You have been too arrogant. God is jealous of such pride.

LODOVICO [brokenly]. I fear your resolution. You were always unbreakable.

CECILIA [gently]. Let it be your resolution too.

LODOVICO. Never! Never!

[A silence. She takes his hand.]

CECILIA. If I have guided you before, let me be a light to you now.

LODOVICO [lifting his head at last]. Do as you will. I shall not act against your marriage. But I shall not see you again. [Half bitterly, dropping her hand.] After all, perhaps you are prudent to turn your eyes towards safety.

CECILIA [rising, proudly]. I am not seeking refuge in this marriage. I am only making the chasm between yourself and myself so deep that no one can mistake it—not even Beatrice d'Este.

LODOVICO [also rising]. Ah. The

house of Este is costing me dear!

CECILIA. The motto of the house of Este is "Diamante." The soldiers of Ferrara go to their death with that cry. But this Beatrice is not hard, like a diamond. Take care of her. *She* is not unbreakable. Keep her happy—so that she may dance and ride her horses, sing, order silks and pearls and perfumes, talk with artists, and jest with the lords at her side. Smile at her pranks, her whims, her mischief—for gayety is blessed and you have already made her acquainted with tears. [*Suddenly the bells in the campanile of Milan begin to toll the sunset hour. Their sweet, sonorous disharmony is melancholy yet thrilling.*] And now, I must go.

LODOVICO. Then I cannot see you again?

CECILIA. The evening bells are ringing. Listen. They sound like the hopes of men, sending up cries into a heaven which is perhaps empty! [*A pause.*] Do not be afraid of pain, my lord, for it will teach you pity. In the end, when we are stripped of everything, we have lost nothing if we can trust our own charity. [*A silence.*] To-night you can bring happiness like a great gift in your hand. For now your palace is being lit with a thousand torches and the stage is being set for this evening's masque. [*Pause.*] Tell Beatrice d'Este to wear her bright costume embroidered with stones, blue and mysterious as the canals of Venice. Tell her that Cecilia Gallerani is to be married. Tell her I am only a memory to you now. She will smile. She will play with her new monkey and tease the little twisted dwarf from the court of Cæsar Borgia. She will mimic her Mistress of the Robes, behind her back. She will tell brave stories of the chase and dance until the morning sun turns to pink the distant Alps and the Lombardy plain changes from flat darkness to immense green gardens, rich as your own fortune. You will see.

LODOVICO [*falling to his knees*]. Cecilia! My love! Where shall we find the courage for this?

CECILIA. We must seek until we find it. I will pray for us all, my lord.

[*Slowly, she goes out to the left. Lodovico, with a broken gesture, prostrates himself before the altar. Now all the bells are pealing and the candles burn steadily before the empty shrine.*]

[*Curtain.*]

ACROSS THE BORDER
A Play
By Colin Clements

CHARACTERS

MRS. HOPPER.
ED HOPPER.
FRANK HENDERSON.

ACROSS THE BORDER

A PLAY   BY COLIN CLEMENTS

[SCENE: *The main room of an adobe ranch house somewhere north of El Paso, Texas. The only bit of color in this somber, low-ceilinged room is the homespun curtains which are drawn over the small window at the back—a feminine touch in a masculine world. At the left of the audience is a heavy door opening into the patio; in the right wall is a square hole, from which a short ladder is hung, opening into the sleeping loft.*

Near the center of the room stands a heavy table. A lighted lantern, hung on a wire from a rafter above, throws a circle of yellow light on the table and catches part of a kitchen chair which is pushed up close to it. The rest of the room is in shadow. Against the wall at the left is a rough Spanish cupboard, the lower part of which has swinging doors, kept in place by a heavy lock.

During the action of the play there is the suggestion of howling wind and the sound of fine sand blown against the window at the back.

When the curtain rises, Mrs. Hopper is seated in the chair near the table. She is a woman of thirty-six or seven. Although her body is slight, there is in her quick nervous movements a suggestion of underlying reserve power. Her large eyes have a haunted look; her face is drawn.

The wind outside becomes louder, then gradually dies away. The howl of a distant coyote is heard, a clock in the loft at the right strikes twelve.

Mrs. Hopper starts suddenly, moves to the window, pushes back the curtain, and stands for a moment looking out into the night; slowly she shakes her head, goes to the door, left, makes sure the bolt is in place, then turns and walks back to the chair near the table. She looks toward the sleeping loft at the right, half smiles, then sinks down wearily into the chair.

There is a soft rap at the door. Mrs. Hopper lifts her head and waits. The rap is repeated. She rises and moves to the door.]

MRS. HOPPER [*softly*]. Who's there?
ED [*from outside*]. It's me! Ed.
MRS. HOPPER. Say it louder.
ED [*outside; impatiently*]. Oh, hell, open the door! It's Ed, I tell you! Can't you recognize your own husband's voice when you hear it? Open the door!
MRS. HOPPER [*a catch of happiness in her breath*]. I am! I am!
[*She pushes back the heavy bolt.*]
ED [*stands in the doorway for a moment bewildered, as if the light blinded him*]. For God's sake, woman! [*He turns and bolts the door, then turns toward his wife and stands brushing the thick yellow dust from his clothes as he speaks.*] Did y' want me to stand out there all night!
[*He walks toward the table, into the light. Ed Hopper is a tall, thin man with shifting eyes and a narrow, weak face. He is unshaven and dirty.*]
MRS. HOPPER [*following him*]. Ed! You're back! You can't know how glad I am to see you. And Jackie hasn't slept for nights—just waitin' for his daddy to get back. [*She holds up her arms but he brushes her aside and moves closer to the table.*]. What is it, Ed? What's the matter? I'll make you a hot cup of coffee. Are you sick?
ED [*unbuckles his belt and holster, throws them down on the table*]. There ain't anything the matter . . . and I ain't sick, either.
MRS. HOPPER [*taking several steps closer to her husband*]. Ed, you've brought back the cattle they stole from us? [*He does not answer.*] You've brought 'em back, ain't you?
ED. Aw, don't stand there askin'

71

damn fool questions. Can't y' see I don't feel like talkin'?

MRS. HOPPER. Oh . . . then I'll make you some coffee, Ed. Won't take a minute.

ED. Don't want any coffee.

MRS. HOPPER. Warm you up. Always cold ridin' at night this time of year.

ED. I said I don't want no coffee.

MRS. HOPPER [*stands looking at her husband several minutes before she speaks*]. Ed, what is it? What's the matter with y'? You been down there in Mexico for five days and naturally I want to know about things. Five days is a long time without a man in the house.

ED [*slowly*]. Only five days? That's all I been gone? Five damn long years it seems to me.

MRS. HOPPER. You caught the thieves? [*He does not answer.*] You caught 'em?

ED. What?

MRS. HOPPER. Y' wouldn't come back till you'd caught 'em, I know.

ED [*indignantly*]. That's where you're damn wrong.

MRS. HOPPER [*sinks down into the chair near the table*]. Y' haven't brought 'em back . . . you haven't brought back our cattle, Ed?

ED [*mockingly*]. No; we ain't brung back your cattle. At least, I didn't.

MRS. HOPPER [*lifts her eyes pleadingly, hopelessly*]. What'll we do now, I wonder?

ED [*turns; frenziedly*]. Just like you . . . like you. What about me, eh? Why don't y' ask about me? Hell of a lot you care, don't y'? Think more of a few damned head of steers than y' do your own husband.

MRS. HOPPER. You know better than that, Ed. It's just . . . just . . . I . . . what'll we do?

ED [*straightens*]. I don't know what you're plannin' on doin' 'n' what's more I don't give a damn. [*He leans across the table.*] But I can tell you right now I know damn well what I'm going to do. [*He takes out his watch*]. What time is it? M' watch is stopped . . . every damned thing's stopped. Sand! Sand! Sand! I can even feel it between my teeth. Sand! What time is it? D' y' hear what I'm askin' y'? What time is it?

MRS. HOPPER [*whose thoughts have been wandering*]. It's a little after midnight, Ed.

ED [*looking at his watch disgustedly*]. There. Guess that's done for, too. Plugged with sand. I'll leave that turnip behind for you.

[*He flings the watch across the room.*]

MRS. HOPPER [*slowly*]. Did Henderson . . . and the other ranchers . . . come back with you?

ED. What? Come back with me? I don't know what they've done 'n' let me tell y' I don't care. I don't give a damn, if that's any consolation to y'.

MRS. HOPPER [*rises slowly*]. But you wouldn't come back and let them go on without you!

ED. Oh, wouldn't I? What do y' think this is standin' here talkin' to y'? A ghost?

MRS. HOPPER. You couldn't let them go on alone, Ed.

ED [*leers at his wife; laughs*]. Well, that's just what I *did* do. I gave 'em the slip.

MRS. HOPPER. Ed!

ED. Sure, gave 'em the slip. And what's you or anybody else goin' to do about it? A man don't have to go on lookin' for cattle thieves all his life 'less he's a mind to.

MRS. HOPPER [*stands looking across the table at her husband; the lines of her tired face harden; she pauses a moment before she speaks*]. I'm ashamed of you. I'm . . . ashamed of you, Ed. I . . . .

ED [*interrupting quickly*]. I don't give a whoop in hell if you are . . . or if you ain't. One way or 'nother is the same to me. It's not my game, this ridin' across the desert for days, ridin' across hell after a gang of dirty greasers. Shootin' 'em down like dogs because they happen to rustle a few head of cattle. It's not my game, I tell y'! And, by God I can't stand it. . . . I can't stand it. This life down here in this God-forsaken hole is drivin' me crazy. I can't go through with it. [*He raises his voice.*] I can't go through with it!

[*Mrs. Hopper takes several steps toward the sleeping loft at the right, then turns back.*]

MRS. HOPPER [*in a calm, even tone*].

We've got to get back what those Mexicans have stolen from us, Ed.

ED. That ain't so easy.

MRS. HOPPER [*moving toward her husband*]. If we can get back the cattle they've taken from us, another two years will see us clear, Ed. Clear, with our heads above water. Clear, with a little money in the bank and a sure future. Clear, with a chance of making good in a big way . . . all the chance in the world. But if we don't get back those cattle, Ed, we'll have to start all over again. We'll be right back where we were eight years ago.

ED. Not me! I ain't droppin' no more sweat into this here desert. Not me! I'm through!

MRS. HOPPER. There's no other way out . . . just hard work.

ED. That may be your way of lookin' at things.

MRS. HOPPER. I tell you, Ed, there's no other way of lookin' at them.

ED. Oh, ain't there? I'm not so sure about that as you seem to be. [*His mouth curls into a sneer.*] You're always so damned sure about *everything*. [*He straightens.*] Look here, Martha, I might as well tell y' straight. I'm clearin' out. D' y' hear? I'm clearin' out.

MRS. HOPPER. What do y' mean, Ed?

ED. Just what I said. I'm leavin'. You know how I hate ranchin'. Hated it to begin with . . . every year I've hated it worse 'n' worse until . . . well, the last couple of years have been hell on earth. I hate this life. Hate it! Now do you understand?

MRS. HOPPER [*intent*]. Hate it? Who hasn't hated it at times? But when y' start a thing you've got to go on to the finish. You and I have got to see this thing through. When we ride out of El Paso it's got to be with our heads up. I tell you—

ED [*shrugging his shoulders*]. Maybe that's your way . . . I guess it is. I wish y' luck. You always was so damned superior. Comes from readin' books 'n' things, I s'pose. Well, you can do as you like. I'm goin' . . . I'm clearin' out the quickest 'n' shortest way. I'm through.

MRS. HOPPER [*hesitating a moment*]. Then you mean this place of ours is for sale? You're selling out, is that it?

ED. Don't ask so damned many questions.

MRS. HOPPER. I've got a right to know. Why shouldn't I ask questions?

ED. 'Cause I don't want y' to. I'll tend to my affairs in my own way.

MRS. HOPPER [*with hatred growing in her face*]. I'm your wife, Ed.

ED [*lifts his hand; mockingly*]. Wife, hell! You've been the man of this ranch ever since I can remember. Always nagging at me to do this . . . nagging at me to do that till I'm damn near out of my head.

MRS. HOPPER. That's a lie! I've never nagged you!

ED [*weakening a little*]. Well, maybe not *nagged* me. Leastwise y' ain't done it like other women do . . . but your damned coldness . . . that's what gets me. Hell! To you this old adobe shanty 'n' a few head of cattle is everything there is in life.

MRS. HOPPER [*turns and looks at the ladder, right; shakes her head*]. No; not everything. He's everything. This is just a beginning . . . a beginning. Look here, Ed, you know why we come out here and—

ED. You've been throwing that up in my face ever since I can remember. You're damned right I know why we come out here. But I guess by this time my lungs is about as good as anybody else's, if that's what y' mean. Anyhow, what's lungs compared to a lot of other things in life, eh? What's the use livin' if you got t' just keep on grubbin' . . . slavin' out your heart 'n' soul in a rotten place like this? I won't stand it, I tell you!

MRS. HOPPER [*moves over and lays her hand on his shoulder*]. You'd best turn in and get some rest, Ed. You're tired out . . . that's the trouble. You're talkin' wild to-night, but after a good rest you'll feel better about things.

ED [*grumbling*]. Bah! That's always your attitude. Always know better than anybody else about things. So damned high 'n' 'mighty.

MRS. HOPPER. Ed, I'll do anything within reason. [*There is a tense pause.*] What is it, Ed? Tell me what's the matter.

ED [*with a sneer*]. I s'pose if I was a steer you'd call me locoed. Well, I ain't.

I know what I'm sayin' 'n' why I'm sayin' it.

MRS. HOPPER [*wearily*]. Ed, we've had other nights like this. We've gone through all this a hundred times before. I tell you, Ed, we've got to stick here. There's no other way out right now. Sometime . . . somehow, we'll be on top. [*She holds out her hand.*] I'm still your partner, Ed.

ED [*ignoring his wife's hand*]. Partner, hell! Yes; maybe we have been through all this before . . . and I've heard all this talk of yours before, too. I've heard it so often that it's gettin' funny.

MRS. HOPPER. Then what are we going to do? What do you want us to do?

ED. I told you before what I'm goin' to do. [*He pounds on the table with his fist.*] Martha—

MRS. HOPPER [*starting toward the right*]. Sh-h-h. You'll wake up Jackie!

ED. I know damn well what I'm goin' to do. [*His voice drops.*] Eight years ago, or something like that, we come out here to Texas . . . a couple of greenhorns. Just like kids. Everything was fine . . . everything was an adventure. But, my God, we've paid for that adventure ten times over. We've paid for it! Why, I'm an old man and you—you—

MRS. HOPPER [*a woman again*]. What . . . what am I, Ed?

ED. Y' was purty once, Martha.

MRS. HOPPER. Ain't I any more?

ED [*shaking his head*]. Just a slave to a piece of grazin' land. Just a chunk of gumbo . . . mud . . . like everybody else down here. That's what soil does to you . . . drags y' down till you're just like it. I tell y', there's more in life than this 'n' I'm goin' to find it.

[*He moves to the window at the back, takes down a heavy key from a nail, walks to the cupboard, left, and throws open the lower doors. He takes out a battered tin box, moves to the table, and, under the light of the hanging lantern, fills a small bag with gold pieces.*

MRS. HOPPER [*who has been looking on with astonishment*]. Money?

ED [*shaking the bag in his wife's face*]. See that? See that? I'm goin' out where it can buy things. . . . I'm goin' out 'n' see if there ain't somethin' left in

life but drudgery 'n' backaches 'n'—well, I'm takin' a fling.

MRS. HOPPER. Ed, where'd you get that money?

ED. Like to know? Well, I ain't tellin'.

MRS. HOPPER. Where did you get that money? [*He does not answer.*] Where did you get it?

ED. Who wants to know?

MRS. HOPPER. I do, Ed . . . I do.

ED. Well, it's like this. . . . Where I got this money ain't none of your business, Martha. See?

MRS. HOPPER. It is!

ED. I reckon y' thought you was the only clever one around the ranch, eh? Well, you've got another think comin'. I can pull a deal off once in a while myself.

MRS. HOPPER. Tell me, Ed. Where did you get that money?

ED [*casually*]. The ranch is sold, in a manner o' speakin'. Sold, see? Jim Marston, they call him Texas Jim around here, is movin' in to-morrow. Now you know.

MRS. HOPPER [*speaking with tremendous difficulty*]. You mean we don't own this place any more? You mean, you've sold us out?

ED. That's it. Yes; out from under. [*He puts the money into an inside pocket.*] Plumb clean. I'm ridin' the pinto pony over to the depot 'n' takin' the early train for 'Frisco.

MRS. HOPPER. You're ridin' over to-night?

ED. Heard me, didn't y'?

MRS. HOPPER. You mean . . . you're going alone?

ED. Yes; damn it . . . alone.

MRS. HOPPER. Y' can't do it, Ed. You can't just go out like this without—

ED. Eh?

MRS. HOPPER. Y' can't do it! Y' can't leave us like this—me and Jackie. What is it? What's happened, Ed? What are you holding back on me? What makes you like this? Tell me. There's something you're keeping from me.

ED. I tell y', Martha, this country has got me . . . it's got under my skin. I'm gettin' out of it. . . . I'm gettin' out of it fast.

MRS. HOPPER. You've done something, Ed. You ain't tellin' me the whole truth. [*She rushes to the door, left, and stands before it.*] You ain't leavin' us. You ain't goin' out alone, either.

ED. Alone? Aw, hell, what kind of a woman have you been to me? Tell y', Martha, if you want to know, there's a dame up in 'Frisco who—

MRS. HOPPER. So that's it?

ED. What of it?

MRS. HOPPER. Just leavin' us flat.

ED. You'll get along. I ain't worryin' my head none about you. You've got the guts to make anything go. I'll say that for you. I ain't worryin' about how you'll make out . . . and I ain't holdin' anything against y', Martha. It's just that you 'n' me don't pull together in the same harness.

MRS. HOPPER. I ain't thinking about me, Ed. I'm thinking about our boy. What about Jackie—what about him?

ED [*almost violently*]. Aw, you're his mother, ain't y'? What's the brat to me?

MRS. HOPPER [*shuddering involuntarily*]. Ed!

ED. He's nothin' to me—nothin'.

MRS. HOPPER. He's yours and mine together. He's the one thing we've got that's worth going on for—

ED. He's your kid, not mine. Dead spittin' image of y'. He speaks your language, not mine—gets more like y' every day. What's he t' me? Nothin'. We ain't got a damn thing in common—not a thing. [*He shrugs his shoulders.*] Aw, hell, what's the use standin' here arguin' all night? I'm off.

MRS. HOPPER [*defiantly*]. No, y' ain't neither, Ed.

ED. You ain't stoppin' me.

MRS. HOPPER. Y' can't, Ed, y' can't go!

ED. Get out of my way.

MRS. HOPPER. You can't just go away and leave me alone with the kid like this— You can't do it, I tell y'.

ED. Get out of my way or by God— Get out of my way, woman.

[*He grabs his wife's arm, twists it until she winces with pain, then he throws her back into the room. He reaches for the heavy bar and is about to lift it. There is a sharp rap. In surprise and fear Ed backs away. The rap is repeated. He turns towards the window at the back and makes sure the curtains are drawn. There is a*

frightened, haunted look in his eyes as he glances hopelessly around the room for some means of escape.]

MRS. HOPPER. It's somebody.

ED [*speaking in a hoarse whisper*]. There's somebody out there in the patio.

MRS. HOPPER. I'll see who it is.

ED. Wait!

MRS. HOPPER [*shaking her head*]. No; I'm opening the door, Ed!

ED. Wait, damn y'! [*He points to the cupboard.*] If it's any one to see me, y' don't know nothin' about me. See? Y' don't know where I am— Y' ain't seen me since I started out with the others to look for the cattle thieves. See? [*His voice falters.*] Martha, what you said a little while ago about us bein' partners goes with me. We're stickin' together in everything. You've got to see me through —I'm your husband, ain't I? You're stickin' by me, ain't you? [*He grabs his wife by the arm.*] An', by God, if y' don't stick by me I'm puttin' both you 'n' the kid in hell—in hell, understand? I'm speakin' plain, Martha. [*He points to the cupboard again.*] I'm goin' in there. [*His face close to Martha's.*] You hold the key.

[*The rap at the door is repeated and voices are heard. Ed moves quickly across the room and crawls into the lower part of the cupboard. Mrs. Hopper, nursing her bruised arm, follows him, hesitates a moment, turns the key in the heavy lock, and moves slowly toward the door, left. Again the knock is repeated, louder this time.*]

MRS. HOPPER [*now at the door*]. Who's there?

HENDERSON [*outside*]. It's me, Martha—Frank Henderson.

MRS. HOPPER [*brushes back her hair, glances quickly around the room, then opens the door slowly*]. Come in, Frank.

[*Henderson steps into the room. He is a tall, gaunt, angular man, slightly bow-legged and pigeon-toed. His hair is iron gray; his face is thin and hard lined, but his blue eyes are kind.*]

HENDERSON [*speaking with a drawl*]. 'Evenin', Martha. [*He laughs.*] More'n likely it's mornin', though.

MRS. HOPPER [*trying to smile*]. Yes; it's way past midnight.

HENDERSON [*his hand reaches for his gun*]. Hate t' bother y' thisaway. S'pose y' was in bed, sleepin'?

MRS. HOPPER. No; I was sitting up.

HENDERSON [*kindly*]. That's like womin folks. [*He looks about the room.*] Always a stayin' up while their men is away.

MRS. HOPPER [*nodding toward the chair*]. Won't y' sit down, Frank?

HENDERSON. No; I ain't stoppin' but a jiffy, Martha. Got t' git over 'n' see how my woman is makin' out. Ain't seen her for a spell now.

MRS. HOPPER [*glances at the cupboard then quickly turns her head*]. How'd y' happen to get back before the others?

HENDERSON. Did I? I thought mebbe—

MRS. HOPPER [*interrupting quickly*]. How about the cattle?

HENDERSON. Got 'em back—most of 'em.

MRS. HOPPER [*with a little catch in her breath*]. Thank God! [*She straightens.*] I mean Ed's back then too, ain't he?

HENDERSON. That's what I come here to find out.

MRS. HOPPER. He's back then?

HENDERSON [*looks at her a moment*]. Ain't he?

MRS. HOPPER. Is—he—why do you ask me like that, Frank?

HENDERSON. Well, Martha, it's like this— I'm sorry t' put y' out but I thought mebbe—I had a 'spicion mebbe—

MRS. HOPPER. What is it, Frank? I've been waiting here alone, except with Jackie, for the men to get back.

HENDERSON. Yea; I know.

[*There is an awkward pause.*]

MRS. HOPPER. You said the cattle were back safe?

HENDERSON [*watching Mrs. Hopper closely*]. Yea; most of 'em.

MRS. HOPPER [*firmly*]. Why did you come here first—I mean before you went to your own ranch? You said you hadn't seen your wife yet. Frank, is there something you want to tell me?

HENDERSON [*pulling himself together*]. See here, Martha. I always play square.

MRS. HOPPER [*backing toward the window*]. I know you do, Frank. Yes; you do play square, Frank.

HENDERSON. I always had an idea you was on the square, too, Martha.

MRS. HOPPER [*visibly weakening*]. Ain't I?

HENDERSON. Are you?

MRS. HOPPER [*becoming hysterical*]. Ain't I— Ain't I? Oh, God—what are you men trying to do to me—trying to do to me? You all go away and leave me alone for days and nights—nights—nights and when you come back—back, y' stand askin' me questions and— [*She suddenly realizes what she is saying.*] I tell you I am on the square. I am, Frank. Maybe my way of seeing things ain't your way, but it's just as square as your way is. I tell you I am square, Frank.

HENDERSON [*now near the table*]. I don't want to press y', Martha, but if you're as square as y' say y' are, then— then what's this gun doin' here?

MRS. HOPPER [*throws back her head; takes a step forward*]. I told you I've been alone here for five days—just me and Jackie. [*She nods toward the sleeping loft.*] We've been here alone and—

HENDERSON. I see. Y' might of had need for a gun, eh?

MRS. HOPPER. You never can tell what might happen down here when none of your own men are on the ranch.

HENDERSON [*suddenly*]. You're a good woman, Martha.

MRS. HOPPER. What did you say, Frank?

HENDERSON [*moving toward the door at the left*]. I said you're too good for the man y' got—too good. I ain't one t' step between a man 'n' his woman, but just the same I'm tellin' y' what I think.

MRS. HOPPER. He's my man—yet.

HENDERSON [*turns at the door*]. Yea; I s'pose he is, Martha. I s'pose when a woman loves a man she's just dumb blind about him till something opens her eyes.

MRS. HOPPER. He's the father of my boy, ain't he?

HENDERSON. Yea; y' know all of us down here have always liked y' a heap. We've liked y' ever since the day y' moved in—liked the way you've stuck it out— plucky like. But I don't have t' tell y' none of us ever trusted Ed Hopper any too much. Y' know that as well as I do.

MRS. HOPPER. I s'pose I do. I know how all you old-timers have felt about him. I'm sorry—I'm sorry. I guess it's just his way of not fitting in with most other people.

HENDERSON [*hesitates a moment; awkwardly*]. I s'pose I've got to tell y' —the truth straight out, Martha. 'Tain't any too easy but you'll find it out purty soon.

MRS. HOPPER. What have you got to tell me, Frank?

HENDERSON. I told y' the cattle was back.

MRS. HOPPER. Yes.

HENDERSON. We didn't kill no greasers t' get 'em back nuther. Them cattle warn't stole out 'n' out. No. They was sold. Yea; sold. We was double-crossed by a certain party that lives on our side of the river. Yea; a bunch of Mexicans paid for them cattle before they drove 'em down into old Mexico.

MRS. HOPPER. Y' don't mean my husband—

HENDERSON. I'm sorry, Martha, but that's what I do mean.

MRS. HOPPER [*moves away to the table; throws back her head*]. And that's the man who called my boy a—a—

HENDERSON—What's that you're sayin', Martha?

MRS. HOPPER. Nothing—nothing.

HENDERSON [*scratching his head*]. We'd 'a' got back sooner with them cattle, but we was damn fools enough to let Ed act as guide for the outfit 'n' of course he kep' puttin' us off the track. 'Course he knowed where them cattle was all the time. Soon's we'd hit the right trail he turned his ho'se 'n' cleared out—gave us the slip. I'm mighty sorry, Martha, for you 'n' the kid. I ain't aimin' t' stir up no trouble, but I calc'late the boys'll want to see Ed Hopper. He'll have t' answer t' them for a thing or two.

MRS. HOPPER [*who has been listening to Henderson intently*]. You'll come over first thing in the morning? Maybe he'll be here then.

HENDERSON. Yea; I'll be over early. I s'pose some of the boys'll want to hang around outside to give Ed a rousin' welcome if he shows up. Two of 'em's ridin' over t' put up a sign in the post office at El Paso.

MRS. HOPPER. You mean—

HENDERSON [*nodding his head*]. Dead or alive. Y' know as well as I do, Martha, what stealin' ho'ses 'n' cattle means

down in this part of the country.

MRS. HOPPER [*in a strange state of terror; she speaks with passionate earnestness*]. Don't let them do it, Frank —don't let them put up that sign! Talk to them. They'll listen to you—they'll do whatever you say, Frank! Oh, for God's sake, don't let them put it up. Think of my boy—think of Jackie! It ain't right, Frank—no; it ain't right.

HENDERSON [*firmly but with a certain rough tenderness*]. But y' know what the laws out in this country is, Martha. I mean the laws that all of us hold to.

MRS. HOPPER. There's also a law out here that every man gets a square start. My kid can't start life straight with a blot like that against his name, Frank. He can't, I tell you! Nobody could.

HENDERSON. Laws is laws. I reckon it's up to you t' give the boy a new start. Leastwise, it looks thataway. I ain't aimin' t' be stubborn, but cattle thieves is cattle thieves, 'n' there's only one way of dealin' with 'em. [*With true feeling*]. But I just want t' say this, Martha, if you 'n' the kid have any need for it, why me 'n' the Missus'll help y' out any way we can. Y' can ask us anything y' got a mind to.

MRS. HOPPER. Then I'm askin' you now, Frank. Don't let that sign go up in the post office over in El Paso. [*She looks up into his face searchingly; grimly.*] I'll turn your thief over to you in the morning.

HENDERSON. You'll turn him over? Y' know what it means? Hangin' ain't a purty word t' say t' any man's wife, but that's what it means, Martha.

MRS. HOPPER [*takes a step toward Henderson*]. I said I'd turn your cattle thief over to you in the morning, Frank.

HENDERSON. You will?

MRS. HOPPER [*throws back her head and looks Henderson straight in the eye*]. I promise you.

HENDERSON [*squaring his shoulders*]. I believe y', Martha. I'll send one of the boys over t' see that that sign don't go up. You're a brave little woman, Martha. We've knowed y' for some years now. You're like one of our own kind. I've seen y' havin' some purty hard ridin' 'n' I'll say y' sure don't pull leather.

MRS. HOPPER [*who has not heard what*

he is saying]. Thanks, Frank, about the sign.

HENDERSON. Well, I'd best be movin'. [*He offers her his hand.*] 'Night, Martha.

MRS. HOPPER. Want a lantern t' light your way?

HENDERSON. No; the sun'll be streakin' over the desert soon. Near time for it, I guess.

MRS. HOPPER. Good night.

[*She closes the door after him, pushes the bolt into place, stands there for a moment, then turns and starts toward the table. Her mouth is set with grim determination. There is a sound from the cupboard at the left. Mrs. Hopper turns like a startled deer. She remembers her bruised arm and begins to nurse it. The soft rap from the cupboard is repeated.*]

MRS. HOPPER [*laughing softly, hysterically*]. Now you're locked up— For eight years you've kept me that way—locked up—locked up—workin' for you night and day—drudgin' for you—starvin' and eatin' my heart out for you—locked up inside myself. [*Ed's voice is heard from the cupboard.*] Then you steal and try to run away—steal all we've worked for and try to run away with it all for some woman in 'Frisco, leavin' us behind to starve—leavin' us behind to bear the shame of it—the shame of it. [*Slowly she takes the key out of her pocket and looks at it.*] Now it's you that's locked up! Bringin' shame on your own kid and then runnin' away from him! [*She*

beats on the cupboard with her fists.*] But you can't do it, Ed. You can't do it! You can't! You can't! [*Ed's voice is heard inside. Mrs. Hopper nursing her arm moves back around the table.*] Stealin'—callin' your kid a brat—hurtin' me—killin' me. Killin'—Killin'— [*She has reached the table as she says these words and her eyes look down upon Ed's gun.*] Killin'—They hang cattle thieves—hang 'em by the neck. They'll say my kid's father was hung for stealin' cattle. They'll say—no—no. I won't let 'em say that—I won't let 'em. D' hear me, Ed, nobody's ever goin' to say you was hung for stealin' cattle.

[*Calmly she removes the revolver from its holster. Her hand is steady now. She raises the gun slowly, points it toward the cupboard, and fires. There is a long pause. A child's voice is heard from the loft, right.*]

JACKIE [*from the loft*]. Mother, are you there? Mother, do you want me?

MRS. HOPPER [*lets the gun slip from her hand to the table. She straightens. Her tired face is changed, the hard lines have disappeared, there is the light of freedom in her eyes; her face is almost radiant as she brushes the hair back from her eyes*]. I'm coming, son. I'm coming up to rest now.

[*She takes down the lantern and starts toward the ladder of the loft. The room is left in shadow with only the sound of the wind outside and of fine sand blown against the window.*]

[*Curtain.*]

MOUNTAIN LAUREL

A Comedy

By Curtis Cooksey

CHARACTERS

JIM BOLTON.
SAIRY BOLTON [*Jim's daughter*].
YOUNG JIM MARTIN [*in love with Sairy*].

TIME: *When the laurel blooms.*

PLACE: *On a mountain top.*

MOUNTAIN LAUREL

A COMEDY   BY CURTIS COOKSEY

[*In the home of Jim Bolton, who
lives in the hills. The house is made of
peeled logs, checked with yellow clay.
The furniture is homemade; everything
is solid and substantial.*

*There is a fireplace, built of badly cut
rock, on the left side of the room, and
a door on the right, which leads to the
outdoors. A door on the right, which
opens into an adjoining room. In the
center of the back wall, there is a window. A few "hands" of tobacco hang on
the wall. An old hand-woven carpet
covers the floor.*

*Jim Bolton, dressed in rough "hick-
ory" shirt and washed-out blue jeans,
is greasing his boots. His coarse gray
socks are pulled up over the legs of his
jeans.*]

SAIRY [*enters. Sairy is fair, her hair
hangs in a plait. She wears a much-
washed gingham dress. On one arm she
carries a lighted lantern, on the other a
pail, which she takes into the adjoining
room, and returns at once with the lantern*]. Milkin's done, Paw.

JIM [*pulling on his boot*]. All right,
honey. Is the old Jersey doin' any better?

SAIRY. I kain't tell. 'Tain't reached
the ring on the gallon bucket yit
though.

JIM. I'd git rid o' her, but yer Maw
allus liked her so well. Seems a shame
to sell 'er now. Guess I'll keep 'er now
till she dies.

SAIRY. Yes, maw thought a right
smart o' her.

[*Unseen by Jim, she swings the
lantern twice across the window,
then lifts the chimney to put out
the light.*]

JIM [*hearing the rattle of the lantern*]. Don't put that out yit. I ain't
fed the hosses.

[*Pulling on the other boot, he
takes the lantern and goes out.
Sairy waits a moment to make
sure he is gone, then goes quickly
to the chest near the window, and
takes out an old-fashioned valise,
which she drops out the window.
Gets her best hat from the chest,
hurriedly puts it on, and starts
toward the door, then stops, hesitating, undecided what to do,
when*]

YOUNG JIM MARTIN [*appears at the
window. He wears rough clothes and
an old slouch hat. His speech is soft,
and he is much in love with Sairy*].
Are you ready, honey?

SAIRY [*startled*]. Oh! Ye scaired
me!

YOUNG JIM MARTIN. Hadn't ye better hurry a bit?

SAIRY. Oh! I'm a little afeard!

YOUNG JIM MARTIN. No! You're
not afeard. Ye' air goin' with me!

SAIRY. You s'pect I'm doin' right?

YOUNG JIM MARTIN. Why, yes,
honey. Hain't I told ye? It's the only
way!

SAIRY. Mebbe I better wait, till he
goes to bed, and then sneak out.

YOUNG JIM MARTIN. No, don't! It'll
be nine o'clock 'fore we reach the valley,
now.

SAIRY. My! How'll paw git along
'ithout me?

YOUNG JIM MARTIN. He's big 'nough
to take keer o' his self.

SAIRY. He's got a powerful temper,
Jim. He'll try to shoot ye shore!

YOUNG JIM MARTIN. We'll think
'bout that, after it's over. [*Jim Bolton's steps are heard.*] I'll be waitin'
for ye!

[*He disappears from the window.*]

JIM [*entering, notices Sairy's hat*].
What are ye doin' with yer hat, Sairy?

SAIRY. Why—I— I wuz aimin' to go to the dance—over at Hallard's.

JIM. Who's goin' with ye?

SAIRY. Th—th—the Beaty girls are goin' to drive by fer me, I—I—I'm to wait fer 'em down by the big gate. [*Starts to go.*]

JIM. Wait a minute, honey. [*She stops, Jim takes time to blow out the light, and hang the lantern in the corner, then he speaks kindly.*] I didn't hear ye say anything 'bout goin' to a dance to-night.

SAIRY. N—no— I didn't say anything—I—

JIM. Well, ye generally tell me, when ye're goin' some place at night, don't you?

SAIRY. Y—es—gener'ly—but—

JIM. Huh—h?

SAIRY. I reckon I—d-didn't think about it. [*Starts again.*]

JIM. Sairy—

SAIRY [*stops and waits*]. Yes, Paw.

JIM. Come here a minute. [*Sairy slowly walks over to him, and stands waiting. He looks down into her lifted face, and speaks gently.*] Where wuz ye goin', Sairy?

SAIRY. Why, Paw—I told ye—to the dance.

JIM. I know ye did. But ther' ain't no dance to-night.

SAIRY. Ev-ev'lyn Beaty told me—that—

JIM. No, ye better not tell me, Sairy. I don't want ye to tell me something that ain't right. Now look here, honey—I ain't a-goin' a be hard on ye, and keep ye home all the time, away from the young folks—'cause I don't think that's right. But last Tuesday ye went to a dance, with the Beaty girls, and left an hour afore they did.

SAIRY. Why, Paw! How do—

JIM. Didn't ye?

SAIRY. Yes, I did—but I'm gettin' old enough to have a feller! Maw told me she was goin' with you, when she wuz younger'n I am now.

JIM. 'Tain't yer havin' a feller I care about, Sairy. But when you left Tuesday night, it warn't but a few minutes till Young Jim Martin left too!

SAIRY [*frightened*]. Oh!

JIM. Now, I ain't accusin' ye o' comin' home with Young Jim Martin,

and I don't want to think you did. But I'm just a askin' ye—did ye?

SAIRY. I don't think ye ought to ask me anything like that, Paw—because—

JIM. You did! Didn't ye?

SAIRY. Yes.

JIM. Sairy! I didn't think ye'd do it! Damn his soul! I'll git him for that! I'll show him he cain't steal my girl!

SAIRY. Paw! He ain't tryin' to steal me! Honest he ain't!

JIM. I ain't a-blamin' you! I'm a-blamin' him! He knows I ain't got no use fer him, ner none o' his breed. I'll git 'im—just like I got 'is uncle! I'll git 'im to-morrow! Yes—I'll git 'im if I have to go on his own ground fer 'im!

SAIRY. H'it ain't his fault, Paw! Any more'n 'tis mine! Ye don't know him, Paw! You don't know what kind of a boy he is! He wuzn't tryin' to steal me! He wouldn't do no one any harm!

JIM. You a-holdin' up fer him! Fer Young Jim Martin! Why, Sairy! Don't ye know his uncle killed your brother!

SAIRY. I know 'e did. But you got even by gittin' one o' his kin fer it.

JIM. Yes! And on to-morrow, there'll be another Martin less, on these hills!

SAIRY. But not Jim, Paw! Please not Jim!

JIM. Sairy! What air ye talkin' about!

SAIRY. I don't want you to hurt Jim.

JIM. Why! Tell me why!

SAIRY. Because—we—I—oh, it's my fault, Paw! Honest it is!

JIM. You! Sairy! You've been seein' 'im right along!

SAIRY. Yes, and he likes me—and we—we air aimin' to marry!

JIM. Ah! Sairy! The young dog! Oh! Sairy! I—I—don't know what to do with ye! Go up to bed! [*He grabs his gun.*] I won't wait! I'll do it to-night!

[*Young Jim Martin appears at the window.*]

SAIRY. No! Paw! Don't do it! Wait till I tell ye—the whole thing—

JIM. No, take your hands off o' me! Leave me alone! I'll git 'im to-night!

YOUNG JIM MARTIN [*speaks without*

any excitement]. Don't turn round with that gun p'inted at me, or I'll lay you low!

JIM. You! You dirty whelp!

[*Starts to raise his gun.*]

SAIRY [*screams*]. Oh!

YOUNG JIM MARTIN. Put 'er down, Jim! I ain't foolin'! I know it ain't a fair way, to git a man in his own house—

JIM. Nobody but a sneakin' Martin'd do it! Go into the other room, Sairy, 'fore he hurts ye!

YOUNG JIM MARTIN. I ain't a-goin' to bother her!

SAIRY. Course he won't hurt me, Paw, 'cause he—

JIM. Course he would! He's a Martin! Airy one of 'em 'ud rob a bird's nest, and then bust the eggs!

SAIRY. I'd rather stay, Paw!

JIM. Did ye hear what I said!

SAIRY. Yes.

JIM. Then do it!

[*Sairy exits. Young Jim Martin climbs into room.*]

JIM. It's a damned queer way ye got a-comin' into my house! But somebody'll be sorry fer—you mark my words!

YOUNG JIM MARTIN. I ain't a-arguin' that p'int with ye, but they ain't no other way uf us two a-meetin' athout some one bein' badly hurt.

JIM. What do you mean a-comin' on my ground thisaway? What do ye want?

YOUNG JIM MARTIN. I heerd what ye said 'bout me just now.

JIM. Then ye heard what I think of you and all yer fambly.

YOUNG JIM MARTIN. I ought to know what each side think o' t'other, after all that's happened a'tween us, the last eighty year.

JIM. And they's goin' a be some more happen!

YOUNG JIM MARTIN. No, they ain't. To-night's goin' a end it.

JIM. They ain't no way this fight can end but one! One side has got to go clean out! And it looks pretty bad fer the Boltons, with you a holdin' that gun on me, 'cause I'm the last one left. But that ain't 'cause your people air any better on the trigger—

YOUNG JIM MARTIN. It's 'cause they's more uv us, an' we could spare more. Ye might 'uv figgered, we'd get the best 'uv ye in the end.

JIM. Ye wouldn't, ef ye hadn't a done the way ye're doin' now!

YOUNG JIM MARTIN. I ain't a goin' a take any advantage of ye, Jim. And I ain't a goin' to shoot, unless ye make me. I'm goin' a ask ye to let up on this, an' be friends. Now what do ye say to that?

JIM. You—Young Jim Martin, say a thing like that to a Bolton! I thought ye had better stuff in ye! I thought ye had more spunk!

YOUNG JIM MARTIN. I got the stuff all right—er I couldn't a figgered a way to come to ye, and say what I have. They ain't no use a goin' on the way we have. They's been good men, on both sides, put under the trees, over thar' on the hill, jest 'cause a couple o' ol' fools had a fight about a hawg.

JIM. Well—my granpaw was right! Yer granpaw ought o' kep' his hawg on 'is own ground!

YOUNG JIM MARTIN. Your granpaw shouldn't o' been so quick-tempered. He ought o' druv' the pig back.

JIM. He did drive 'im off! But your granpaw didn't keep 'is fence up, an' the pig come back—and when my granpaw shot that hawg, he done right!

YOUNG JIM MARTIN. I won't argie that p'int with ye neither. Ye see I want to patch it up, and start all over. They ain't no use uf us bein' bad friends, jes' 'cause our granpaws fit over a hawg.

JIM. Yes, they is! If ye're granpaw'd a kep' 'is hawg at home—

YOUNG JIM MARTIN. Well, the pig's dead now, Jim! Let 'im rest! An' let's join the fambly hands, and—

JIM. Join the fambly hands! I don't think I know jest what you mean.

YOUNG JIM MARTIN. Yes, ye do. Sairy an' me want to get married—

JIM. You! Marry my girl! I'd jest as soon see her dead!

YOUNG JIM MARTIN. Well, we're goin' a do it whether you say so er not.

JIM. No! Sairy— No! I won't let you! Git out o' my house! I'll make you!

[*Reaches for gun.*]

YOUNG JIM MARTIN. Leave 'er alone, Jim!

JIM. Ye're doin' a mighty low trick, Young Martin! A-slippin' up on me like this! None o' the rest o' your folks 'ud do it! Fer all the shootin' that's been done a'tween us, nary one o' your folks er mine, has ever been shot in the back.

YOUNG JIM MARTIN. Don't think I'm goin' a begin it. There'll never be any more shootin' a'tween us, 'lessin' it's about Sairy.

JIM. That's the only way you'll ever git my gal! I'll tell ye that right now. And if my gal wants to marry a man, that can't figger a better way to git 'er than to come and kill 'er dad in 'is own house—let 'er do it.

YOUNG JIM MARTIN. Well, she ain't a-goin' a do that. [*Still keeping Jim covered, he crosses to him and takes his gun.*] Sairy an' me's talked this over, many an evenin' comin' down the ol' cowpath. We love each other, Jim, an' we couldn't figger out why somethin' that happened eighty year ago should stop us.

JIM. So! That's what made her late ever' evenin', bringin' home the cows!

YOUNG JIM MARTIN. I guess that's what it was, 'cause we used to sit out there on the railin' to that ol' footbridge—

JIM. I wisht I'd a know'd it!

YOUNG JIM MARTIN. I'm glad ye didn't—'cause each day I wuz a-workin' on a little cabin, over there on Cedar Hill. An' it's made fer Sairy an' me—an' we're gonna invite you over—to stay as long as you like—that is, the first time ye feel ye can leave your gun at home.

JIM. Why! Ye think Sairy'll marry you!

YOUNG JIM MARTIN. Course I do. [*Calls*] Sairy! Oh, Sairy! Come on in! [*Sairy enters.*] Air ye ready, honey?

SAIRY [*a little breathless*]. Yes, Jim, I'm ready.

YOUNG JIM MARTIN. Come on then.

[*She starts toward Young Jim.*]

JIM. Sairy! Honey! Air ye gonna go back on yer paw, like that!

[*Sairy looks appealingly to Young Jim.*]

YOUNG JIM MARTIN. Go on—kiss 'im good-by.

SAIRY [*goes to her father, almost crying*]. Oh—I'm so sorry, Paw! But—I —like Jim so—that—that—an' if you get lonesome, here—you can come an' live with us! Oh-h-h-h! Paw!

[*Throws her arms around his neck.*]

YOUNG JIM MARTIN. Come on, honey. It's gittin' late.

[*Sairy starts.*]

JIM. No! By God! I tell ye! I won't have it!

YOUNG JIM MARTIN [*as he holds the gun on him*]. We're gonna do it, jest as sure as pie! But remember, Jim, there's a standin' invite to come an' see yer son and daughter, over on Cedar Hill.

[*Young Jim and Sairy exit, slamming the door. Jim stands amazed, then makes a bolt after them. Just as he reaches the door, the young people pass the window, at the back, and Jim's gun is thrown in on to the cabin floor. Jim runs and snatches it up. As he raises it to take aim out the window, the sharp clatter of horses' hoofs is heard, galloping down the mountain road. Jim slowly lowers his rifle, comes down by the fireplace, and, after a few seconds, he breaks the gun and removes the cartridges.*

He looks speculatively at the pegs, high in the wall over the fireplace, then hangs his gun thereon. Lighting his pipe, he sits in the big hickory chair before the fire, then stretching comfortably, takes a good draw at his pipe, and blows the smoke toward the ceiling.]

JIM. Oh, well! The dawggoned hawg kain't be no deader!

[*Curtain.*]

A LADY AND THE LAW
A PLAY

BY GEORGE W. CRONYN

CHARACTERS

THE LADY.
THE OUTLAW.
THE SHERIFF.

A LADY AND THE LAW

A PLAY   By GEORGE W. CRONYN

[*The* SCENE *is laid in upper New Mexico at the present time. It is the evening of Thanksgiving Day. The scene shows the interior of an adobe house in the Cañon Del Oro, near the Sangre de Cristo Mountains. It is one of several shacks which are all that remain of Nuggetville, once a thriving mining town, now utterly deserted.*

The room is square. Back left an open door through which a glimpse can be had of a whitewashed cell containing a single cot and a box which serves as a dressing table, with a small cheap mirror above it, a little square window with a bit of muslin tacked up for curtain. The few toilet articles are feminine.

Down left the main wall of the room is cut by a door outside. Center of left wall another cot covered with a figured quilt. The rear wall at the center has one window, without curtain, through which can be seen, in sharp moonlight, a deserted street backed by the vast bulk of a snow peak. Snow has fallen, the first of the year. In front of the window is a dilapidated rocker occupied by a woman. Her head is thrown back as though she slept, and an Indian blanket is drawn up over her knees.

In the upper right corner a crude adobe fireplace gives out a feeble flicker of light from piñon logs, and considerable smoke. On one side of the fireplace is a wood box, on the other a handmade stool. A door to a lean-to kitchen opens in the right wall toward the center. Down right a handmade bench against the wall faces a square heavy table, set with food, for two, and lighted by a candle. A plain chair on the other side of the table. Another candle rests on a bracket between the window and fireplace.

The woman stirs restlessly, raises her

head, adjusts the blanket about her with a listless movement, glances through the window as though fascinated by the intense solitude and desolation outside, and then lets her head fall back wearily. The handle of the outside door turns, the door is thrust open quickly, and a man steps half in. For a second he blinks at the light in astonishment, then with guarded care, his right hand at the holster of a gun, advances cautiously, peering intently into the dim interior. He wears corduroy trousers tucked into heavy boots, a worn mackinaw, a thick woolen plaid shirt, a battered Stetson, and a beard which scarcely conceals the vigorous youthfulness of his face. Catching sight of the woman apparently asleep, his hand drops from the holster and he stands awkwardly quiet, embarrassed and hesitant, finally clearing his throat resolutely.*]

THE LADY [*without raising her head*]. Back so soon, Jim? Didn't expect you before midnight. The venison's hardly done—that damned oven, you know—[*Conscious of something strange, she sits up, staring at the stranger. A flicker of apprehension passes into a tone casual and level as she says*]: Well? What do you want?

[*The Man starts, pulls himself together and answers her harshly.*]

THE MAN.   Food!

THE LADY [*without changing her attitude*]. Help yourself. I couldn't stop you if I wanted to. I'm alone, as you see. [*The Man strides to the table, cuts himself a large slice of bread and begins to devour it voraciously. Lady still cold and indifferent.*] There's venison grease in the kitchen—for butter—and a can of jam.

THE MAN [*looking up, his mouth full*]. I don't want none.

THE LADY [*a shade less disinterested*]. You might like coffee. The pot's on the stove. Canned milk on the shelf.

THE MAN [*surly*]. Don't want none.

THE LADY [*ironic*]. Perhaps you expect me to wait on you?

THE MAN [*roughly*]. I don't expect nothing. [*He walks into the kitchen and returns with a large pot of coffee, pours coffee into a thick china cup, and swallows it in several gulps. Man coughs as the liquid burns.*] Hot as hell!

THE LADY [*slightly amused*]. You wouldn't take my suggestion about the milk.

THE MAN. I ain't askin' advice.

THE LADY [*coldly*]. Cheerful guest!

[*The Man abruptly reënters the kitchen, returning with a can of milk, one of jam, and another one. He starts to place the three cans on the table, drops the third which spills its contents of sugar over the floor. For a moment he is overcome with dismay, then he turns with sullen irritation.*]

THE MAN. S'pose that's all the sweetenin' you got?

THE LADY [*with asperity*]. It is!

THE MAN [*after a pause during which he nervously pours himself another cup*]. Didn't aim to dump it.

[*The Lady says nothing and he suddenly takes a spoon and kneeling begins clumsily to scrape up the sugar into the can.*]

THE MAN [*on his knees*]. I reckon sugar's pretty scarce up in these parts.

THE LADY. Your observation is correct.

THE MAN [*annoyed by her manner and conscious of being in the wrong*]. But there's plenty a folks don't taste it from one year's end to the next. [*Puts can on table and looks into it.*] They's specks in it. [*Refusing to weaken.*] But they'd be glad to git it, specks or no specks!

THE LADY [*coldly*]. Would they? I've heard that *some* people don't object to maggots in their meat.

THE MAN [*defensively*]. I've et it that way and been damn glad to! [*The Lady throws back the blanket and rises, as though with an effort, crosses to the fireplace, picks up a brushbroom and a piece of cardboard from the box, then comes down to the spilled sugar where she begins to sweep up the remnants. Man approaches sheepishly.*] Let me hold it. Them crumbs scatter. [*She gives him the improvised dustpan and he holds it while she sweeps. The Man, looking up, sees the effort in her movements.*] You don't seem any too vig'rous fer housework, lady. You'd best set.

THE LADY [*haughtily*]. I don't recall asking your advice.

THE MAN. No'm, you didn't, but I give it, free, like you done to me. [*He holds the cardboard helplessly.*] Where'd I best dump it?

THE LADY [*ironic again*]. It probably wouldn't put the fire out.

THE MAN [*moving sheepishly toward the fireplace*]. You sure got a tart way of speaking, miss.

THE LADY. Missus.

THE MAN [*on his way back*]. I heerd you say the venison was comin' along slow. Mebbe I might stir the fire a bit?

THE LADY. Don't trouble yourself.

[*She goes into the kitchen. There is the sound of wood being poked into a stove, and the opening of an oven door. The Man looks irresolute. Suddenly a heavy thump makes him dart through the kitchen door. A moment later he returns, holding her in his arms, limp. On his face an expression of terrified dismay. He looks wildly about the room, then carries her to the cot where he lays her down, and returns quickly to the kitchen.*]

THE MAN [*in passing, mutters*]. Christ A'mighty! Passed out! [*Comes back with a cup of water which he brings to her, raises her head awkwardly, holding the cup to her lips. Almost gently.*] There now, swaller this here and you'll be all right in two shakes! [*Her eyes remain closed. He takes out a bandanna, pours water on it, and bathes her forehead. She slightly opens her eyes. As though remembering something he reaches into his left hip pocket and brings out a flask, uncorks it, and raises it to her lips. She sips, and coughs.*] White Mule, ma'am, hundred proof, but it'll set you up quicker'n a wink. [*Pours a small quantity of the liquor into the cup of water and offers it to her.*] Now you jest gargle a little of that fer the next five minutes and you'll feel as chipper as a hawk on a telegraph pole!

[*After a few swallows the Lady sits up, holding the cup and drinking from time to time.*]

THE LADY. How stupid of me! I don't often faint that way. It was the hot air from the oven, I guess.

THE MAN. Lucky there was some un around to tote you. [*A thought occurs to him.*] Hev you ever done it when you was here alone?

THE LADY. Two or three times.

THE MAN [*curiously*]. And what happened?

THE LADY. Nothing. I just lay on the floor a few hours until I came to. Once I lay for a whole day and night—when my husband was away.

THE MAN. I reckon he was plumb distracted when he come back, uh?

THE LADY. No. He was drunk. He threw a pail of water on me and I got up.

THE MAN [*explosively*]. Son of a gun!

THE LADY [*without emotion*]. Oh, no. Just irresponsible. He's that way when he's drunk. He can't help it.

THE MAN. And how often is he sober?

THE LADY [*after a pause*]. I am not accustomed to discussing private matters with strangers.

THE MAN [*ashamed*]. Excuse me, ma'am, but—I jest couldn't picture *any* man throwin' water on you, and lettin' you—[*chokes*] git up yourself.

THE LADY [*lightly*]. Oh, that was good for me. It taught me a lesson. I had been pitying myself before that, and I got over it. Self-pity, you know, is one of three deadly sins.

THE MAN. And what's the other two?

THE LADY. Spiritual dependence and humility.

[*The Man goes thoughtfully toward the table, and brings back the chair which he places beside the cot.*]

THE MAN [*pondering, as he sits down*]. What about murder?

THE LADY [*looking at him with interest for the first time*]. Murder is a crime, according to law. There have been times when it was a necessity. In war, for instance. My grandfather shot his brother during the Civil War; they

were on opposite sides, of course. It was a pardonable mistake.

THE MAN. And did your granddad have it on his mind all his life?

THE LADY. Yes. . . . We can't escape from our fatal mistakes. But there are worse murders than that of brother by brother. [*With intensity.*] When one person slowly, over a period of months or years, murders the being who is closest to him—or her. When a wife, for instance, kills all that is fine in her husband. Or when a husband poisons with his jealousy and hate, all imagination, all gayety, all passion in the woman he took for his wife. That sort of murder is unpardonable. Horrible.

THE MAN [*slowly, trying to grasp this*]. I don't know nothing about that kind of thing. You see, I run away when I was eighteen, and I've never owned kith nor kin—so fer as livin' with 'em went—from that day till now. Fact is, I hain't even seed hide nor hair of 'em until—lately.

THE LADY. You haven't ever been in love?

THE MAN. Ye-es. Kinda. I've had sweethearts, of course, and sech like, but not what you'd call bein' in love. Mex girls mostly. Dark and pretty, and good enough to dance with and hug. But not real, honest-to-God love. [*Emphatically.*] No! But even if I *had* had anybody around continuous, I wouldn't have let myself in fer the sort of murderin' business you speak of. Would you? [*The Lady does not answer. Instead she places her feet on the floor.*] Y'ain't goin' to git up, are you?

THE LADY. Yes. I hate this feeling of dependence that lying down gives one. If you will be kind enough to bring that rocker over near the table, we can talk while you finish eating. [*The Man goes to the chair, starts to lift its sagging bulk.*] Be careful! It's an antique.

THE MAN [*takes the chair carefully and holds it a moment as he glances out into the deserted street*]. Reckon this here piece o' furniture was val'ible when this ghost town was alive. When they fu'st hit gold up the Cañon Del Oro the hull territory went wild as mavericks. Thought they was goin' to live in marble palaces and eat off'n gold plate! Then the vein petered out, they scratched and dug till they went flat one by one. And now it's a town of tombstones! [*Brings the chair over, still speaking.*] Now you could buy all the cañon fer the price of a drink! [*Grins.*]   White Mule, too!

THE LADY. We paid five thousand for it.

THE MAN [*dropping the chair in amazement*]. You folks *bought* this collection of rock and 'dobe?

THE LADY. My husband was led to believe that it was a rich claim.

THE MAN. He sure must be irresponsible! Why, there aint enough gold left in this cañon to plate a silver nickel! [*Mutters.*] So that's the kind you're tied to! [*She starts to walk across the room, unsteadily. He hastens to her side and helps her into the chair.*] No'm. You hadn't ought to *try* it!

THE LADY [*faintly*]. It's silly to be so weak.

THE MAN [*arranging the blanket about her*]. Sometimes it's jest nateral. [*Looks at her.*] Lungs?

THE LADY. Heart.

THE MAN. T'ain't so good fer a hearter —at eight thousand feet. What brung you here?

[*He sits down opposite and cuts another slice of bread and covers it with jam. Then pours more coffee.*]

THE LADY [*faintly humorous*]. The gold mine. Our cañon!

THE MAN [*stopping, open-mouthed*]. Good God! And what keeps you?

THE LADY. Poverty—and hope.

THE MAN. You better put your hope away in moth balls, ma'am. Hope died a long time ago in Cañon Del Oro. And you'd better sell out to another sucker. [*Offering her a cup of coffee.*] Milk? and speckled sugar?

THE LADY [*stirs her cup*]. I haven't asked you what brought *you* here.

THE MAN [*stops eating and leans forward*]. Do you want fact or fancy?

THE LADY. I'm pretty well hardened to fact.

THE MAN [*clearly and steadily*]. Last night I killed my brother.

[*There is a pause. Then she says quietly*]:

THE LADY. You don't look like a murderer.

THE MAN. You can't always tell by looks.

THE LADY. Can you talk about it?

THE MAN [*a bit desperately*]. I *want* to—I *got* to talk about it! [*Leans forward on his elbows, looking into space, as though visualizing some occurrence.*] Y'see, I been thinkin' some about this thing that happened, stedyin' it and figgerin' about it fer the last twenty-four hours—ever since I jumped through the window of the Bonita Dance Hall and made my get-away with the sheriff blazin' away at me all the way out of town.

THE LADY [*with some excitement*]. But then, if it's known, they must be after you!

THE MAN [*grimly*]. They are! But if I ain't mistook, I left 'em a cold scent. The snow last night saved me. I rid like hell out a town ten miles into the bresh where I knowed a greaser by the name of Montoya. Come the snow and buried my tracks. This mornin' Montoya brung me into the hills in a windbroken Ford truck under a load of hay, which he was feedin' to some steers. When I got to the Cañon Del Oro trail he dumps me out and here I am, after eight miles of climb—free to go on over the pass to Taos, Santa Fe, Mexico!

THE LADY. But the killing. How did that happen?

THE MAN. We was twins, Jim and me.

THE LADY [*excitedly*]. Jim!

THE MAN. Yes'm. Jim. That's his name. No need to tell you the last of it. Was quite a fancy name back where we come from. Jim and me is—or was— as like as two peas—outside. And as onlike as day and night under the skin. Ever since we was big enough to heave rocks we hated each other like p'isen. Brother love! He tried to brain me with an ax onct, and I near had the extreme satisfaction of stranglin' him jest before I left home, when he messed up a little girl I was goin' with. . . . Anyway, it's been our good luck to stay apart the last ten years or so till we met last night. Seems he'd found out I had a nice little sheep ranch up in the hills. Fu'st thing I knowed of his bein' alive was a letter beggin' me to let him have a thousand dollars. He had T.B., goiter, hernia, and five or six other things wrong with him, so it says, needed three operations and was flat broke. Well, family feelin' [*ironic*] or mebbe the hope of gittin' rid of him once and fer all, induced me to come down to see him, with seven hundred iron men in my saddle bags. I reckon the cuss wasn't countin' on my appearin' quite so sudden because when I come on that invalid he was cuttin' up all kinds of high jinks on the dance floor of the Bonita at Rossville. Course he didn't recernize me [*strokes his beard*] in this disguise and I found out a few things about him. What I heard was [*leans forward looking intently at the Lady*] that he'd married a woman with a lot of money and had sort of spread it all over the landscape, playin' races and other women, and that his last big investment was a gold-brick mine.

THE LADY [*faintly*]. Could I trouble you for another drink—straight?

THE MAN. You sure can, ma'am!

[*He pours a drink for her, and one for himself.*]

THE LADY [*composed again*]. Go on! I find it terribly interesting!

THE MAN [*leans back now, not looking at her*]. Well! I begun to savvy that mebbe my little stake warn't so badly needed after all, except as a card and booze endowment. At first I thinks I'll jest sneak back to my sheep without sp'ilin' the evenin' by conversin' with the skunk. But blood's thicker'n bootleg and after a couple of drinks I couldn't resist the temptation to tell that hound what color his hide was. [*Pause.*] Which I done. And damned if he didn't come back with another argiment. Seems this lady he'd married had run off with another feller. And the two of 'em had cleaned him out, mine and all.

[*She suddenly stiffens, clenching her fist.*]

THE LADY. Oh! the beastly liar! [*Recovers.*] That is, I suppose that's what you told him?

THE MAN [*slowly*]. I told him I had never believed a word he'd said since he could talk, but I'd like fer him to prove to me he wasn't gittin' ready to run off with pretty little Paulita Ferrera, the wench he'd been runnin' with the last six weeks.

THE LADY [*with intensity*]. How did you find *that* out?

THE MAN [*grinning sardonically*]. I happened to have knowed Paulita *some* time. It was her favorite sport, stringin' a sucker along, fakin' an elopement, and cleanin' up his stake. She almost

throwed me fer a loop onct. *And* she spilled the beans. She was tight, and told me she had the handsome señor Jeem on the hook. Pretty humorous, ain't it?

THE LADY [*with compressed lips*]. Very! . . . And then?

THE MAN. Things happened all at onct and very quick. We was both pretty well tanked. All I remember is watchin' his hand travel toward his hip jest after I called him what it ain't necessary to repeat and at that same second pressin' the trigger of my gun. It was a hip shot aimed at his shoulder but it made a bull's eye of his heart. If I hadn't been drunk I'd jest have laid him out fer a *real* hospital bill, and been glad to pay it. As it was, it ended in an inquest. And they got me dead to rights because he hadn't had time to touch his own gun. If it was twenty years ago they'd jest pass it up as shootin' and let it go at that, but now it means a jury trial.

THE LADY [*earnestly*]. Why don't **you** stand trial?

THE MAN. What! in Rossville? Why, ma'am, that's a cattle town, and I'm a sheep man. They wouldn't want nothin' better in this county than to git me sent up, fer life. Besides, I got a record from when I was considerable younger that I been livin' down. I don't aim to spend the rest of my days behind bars, so long as I got legs—and a gun.

[*There is a long pause. The wind moves about the house. After a time she whispers:*]

THE LADY. Dead! Jim!

THE MAN [*leans forward and says softly*]. Did you *love* him, ma'am?

THE LADY [*low*]. For quite a long while. [*She gets up. He makes as though to help her but she waves him off.*] No! I feel quite strong, just now. [*She walks to the window and looks up the bleak street toward snow-hung heights. Turning.*] How did you know I was his wife?

THE MAN. I didn't till jest a minute ago, then, all at once, it struck me . . . you'd be jest the kind he'd grab, some un with class—some un different from our family, which was only *folks*. Jim allus was a snob—at other people's expense! I s'pose you think I hadn't ought to talk about a brother that way, 'specially after havin' killed him . . . but, ma'am, that's the way I feel, and you might as well hear the truth, even if you do think me a low-down, ornery, cold-blooded son of a gun!

THE LADY [*quietly*]. I don't. I think that here if anywhere the truth may be told. Up here in Cañon Del Oro, cut off from the world, outside of life, separated from all the easy lies of crowds and conventions, we can speak facts to each other. [*Her voice rises to greater intensity.*] Jim, you know, always shied away from facing facts, about himself and about me. You ask me if I loved him, and I say, yes, for a long time. I loved the man he would never let himself be. And then, after a while, I got tired . . . and I stopped loving . . . and just kept on suffering a little, and later, that stopped, too, so that for months, while I've been living up here, mostly alone, I haven't felt anything. I've been . . . [*low and tense*] as dead as that street out there, and those houses. So dead that I cannot even regret his death. I'm only sorry it had to be through you . . . sorry because of you!

THE MAN [*rising*]. You needn't feel sorry about me. I can take care of myself. But what about you, ma'am?

THE LADY [*looking out of the window*]. I can take care of myself, too. I've had to learn to do that. Perhaps that's the one thing for which I'm grateful to him. [*Something in the landscape catches her attention. She leans forward, rubbing the windowpane clean. She turns back, her voice clear and sharp.*] Are you ready?

THE MAN [*startled*]. What?

THE LADY. There's a party of men coming down the cañon! [*He leaps from behind the table and starts toward the window.*] Don't! Keep away from the window.

[*He slides along the wall past the fireplace and peers out.*]

THE MAN. They've picked up my trail! [*Laughs with high good humor.*] That Sheriff at Rossville is—a wiz! I take off my hat to him fer bein' a prize bloodhound! Well, ma'am, I sure hev enjoyed your hospitality and talk! Wisht I could see you out of *your* mess, but I reckon [*examines his gun, filling the chambers*] it can't be done! [*Looks out again.*] Six of 'em, and lordie, I bet he's got the best shots in the county!

THE LADY. What are you going to do?

THE MAN. Clear out of here. Locate a shack with one little window and wait fer the barrage! I got jest about ten minutes. They're a good half mile away and comin' slow and careful! [*With enthusiasm.*] Ma'am, this sure is goin' to be one fine little shindig! [*Anxiously.*] Only, you best lie down on that there cot till it's over. A stray bullet might wander in this way and upset you.

THE LADY [*rapidly*]. You mustn't leave this house! They can see you at once because it stands out from the others. Besides, it's the only one that will stand a siege. The rest are only thin shells. They'd have you at the first volley.

THE MAN [*soberly*]. No, ma'am, not right at fu'st, they won't. They'll be too narvous. As fer stoppin' here, thanks jest the same, but I guess I won't let you in fer a shootin' affair. Your heart mightn't quite stand it.

THE LADY [*thinking with energy*]. Does the sheriff know you?

THE MAN [*wondering*]. Not too well. I hain't made a practice of visitin' Rossville. Springer's where I allus go fer supplies. Sheriff he knows me as much as you could know a jackrabbit you was shootin' at and him streakin' it fer the brush!

THE LADY. Then listen! There's a better chance than fighting. You're going to be Jim, see?

THE MAN. Jim! Your husband. But he's *dead!*

THE LADY. You're going to be Jim. You must cut off your beard and put on Jim's clothes. Then when the sheriff comes, you've got to play Jim!

THE MAN. I don't quite git you, ma'am. How'm *I* goin' to be my brother, if I shot him?

THE LADY. You didn't shoot him. You don't know anything about him. He's an impostor, *was* an impostor who looked like you . . . don't you see? Passed himself off as you. Borrowed money, as you. A bunco man. Buncoed a wild sheep-herder, who killed him. You don't know all this. You've been here, all the time, with *me?* See?

THE MAN [*slowly, with admiration*]. You sure hev brains, ma'am . . . but will they believe me?

THE LADY. They'll believe *me!* Now go in the kitchen. Take the scissors on the shelf over the stove and cut your beard as close as possible. I'll get you some clothes. [*The Man goes into the kitchen. The Lady enters the bedroom. In a moment she returns with a soft white shirt, a pair of dirty duck trousers, and a dressing gown, comb, and brush, which she hands through the door.*] Wet your hair and comb it back from your forehead. There's a sack of flour under the table; put a little on your face to whiten it. You must look pretty sick. You've got T.B., understand? You'll have to cough once or twice. You'll sit here in this rocking chair with the blanket over you. Don't talk much and try not to say "sure" too often. Can't you imitate a dude's voice?

THE MAN [*in kitchen*]. I'll sure— I'll certainly try my best, ma'am!

THE LADY. And remember, you're Jim. *My* Jim. My *dear* husband! And I'm Jane. *Your* Jane. Jane dear! Try it!

THE MAN [*coughing*]. Jane dear!

THE LADY. Yes, dear Jim!

THE MAN. Is the bawth prepahed?

THE LADY. Don't exaggerate. Bath. Prepared.

THE MAN [*still within*]. By the way, how about the tracks?

THE LADY. You were out hunting deer. We've been out of venison. You shot your deer. The venison is now in the oven. We'll even offer the sheriff some. Leave all that to me. They're pretty close, Jim dear!

THE MAN. I'm as close to the skin as I can get. Now for the dude outfit. Where do I hang my duds?

THE LADY. Roll them up tight and lay them behind the wood box. I hope you're a good actor!

[*The Man steps out, transformed. Close-clipped, hair brushed, he is good-looking in spite of his artificial pallor. He lounges toward the chair with assumed graceful indolence.*]

THE MAN. Allus—always did want to try the stage! Well, if this act don't— doesn't git—get over, there'll be no encore!

[*Sits down, holding a gun casually in his lap.*]

THE LADY [*seeing the gun*]. You mustn't have that around!

THE MAN [*draws the blanket up over it*]. Just fer—for an emergency. Case our argiments don't go down.

THE LADY [*glancing into kitchen*]. Where's the beard?

THE MAN. In the stove. Comb and brush in the breadbox. All set! Curtain! [*He turns the chair toward the table, so that he is back to the door. She sits on the bench. He studies her.*] Ma'am, how come—how did it happen you weren't skeered—scared to death when I come—came rompin'—entered this here—this establishment?

THE LADY. You didn't, somehow, seem as dangerous as you acted. After the first few minutes I felt I wasn't in danger. And then I began to get interested. And pretty soon I began to—like you—

THE MAN [*incredulous*]. You—like *me*?

THE LADY [*candidly*]. Why not?

THE MAN. I dunno. Don't know, except that—[*gradually speaks more clearly*] I never would have thought a real lady would look twice at me.

THE LADY. Why shouldn't a real lady look twice or maybe—a number of times at a *real* man? After so many years of looking—at the opposite? And, after all, the lady is only a woman, a real woman, Jim dear! [*He reaches forward as though to lay his hand upon hers. There is an imperative knock at the door. He leans back, limp. She rises and goes to the door. Opens. The Sheriff enters. He is rather stout, and when not on business, wears an expression of habitual good humor. At the moment his face is grim and set. He keeps his right hand at his hip. Lady showing surprise*]. How do you do? Come in!

THE SHERIFF [*sardonically*]. I hev, ma'am! Sheriff Willetts, of Rossville, travelin' on business.

THE LADY. Let me take your hat, Mr. Willetts.

THE SHERIFF. Thanks, no!

[*He looks quickly and suspiciously around the room, and at the seated figure.*]

THE LADY. Jim dear, this is Sheriff Willetts of Rossville.

["*Jim*" *swings about, feebly, coughing*].

"JIM." Hello, Sheriff. Glad to see you. We don't have many visitors up in these dig—in these parts.

THE SHERIFF [*staring at him dumfounded*]. By the Lord A-mighty! A live ghost in a ghost town!

THE LADY. My husband, Jim Devine, Mr. Willetts. You'll excuse his not rising. My husband is—an invalid, and very foolishly went off on a long hunting excursion—yesterday. We were out of meat, you see. His horse went lame at—where was the place, Jim dear?

"JIM." Montoya's ranch. He brought me back to-day as far as his Ford could go, then I walked the rest of the way. It *was* pretty stiff goin'—going for a lunger, but, thank God, I ain't—I'm not ready for the undertaker yet!

[*Coughs.*]

THE SHERIFF [*suspiciously*]. Oh!— And did you *git* your meat?

THE LADY. A whole side of venison, Sheriff! Montoya gave it to us because of some favors we had done him. We helped out when they had their last child. By the way, that roast must be nearly done. If it is, I'll expect you to sit right down and have some. We were just about to eat our Thanksgiving dinner!

THE SHERIFF. Thanks, ma'am, but don't bother. I et hearty just an hour ago, and hev got to be travelin' back so soon as I git some things straightened up.

THE LADY. You'll pardon me, if I look at my roast.

[*Exit. The Sheriff walks close to "Jim," staring fixedly at him.*]

"JIM." Well, Sheriff, what's troubling you?

THE SHERIFF. What's troublin' me? Nuthin'—except that last night a coroner's jury sat on yore corpse and pronounced you dead at the hands of a party unknown, and now I see you settin' here playin' with yore knife and fork, as nat'ur'l as life!

"JIM." Mr. Willetts, you surprise me!

THE SHERIFF. Yore surprise ain't a patch to mine.

"JIM." So you came up here to verify the reports as to my passin'—as to my death?

THE SHERIFF. No, sir! I come up here with five depities, which is now planted all about this shack, to take inter custody the murderer of Jim Devine!

[*The Lady reënters, with a platter of meat.*]

THE LADY. Do sit down and have a bit, Sheriff. I'm sure you must be hungry.

[*Sheriff sits gingerly on the chair near the cot, eyeing the sick man closely. She goes out and reenters with a bottle and three glasses. Pours into them and carries a glass to the Sheriff.*]

THE SHERIFF. I ain't got any stumick fer grub, but I reckon a little taste of likker ud hearten me considerable.

THE LADY. It's sherry, Mr. Willetts. Jim and I have been saving it for this occasion. You see, it's our wedding anniversary.

[*Sheriff drinks it down with relish, rises and holds out his hand.*]

THE SHERIFF. Well, congratulations, ma'am!

THE LADY. Thank you! What did you say about some one being murdered?

THE SHERIFF. It's been my impression, ma'am, that yore husband was killed by some wild sheep herder from the hills last night at the Bonita Dance Hall at Rossville, but I 'pear to be mistook!

[*The Lady laughs.*]

THE LADY. What an extraordinary impression! [*Goes to "Jim," puts her arms about his neck, and leans over his chair.*] Just think, Jim dear, Mr. Willetts thinks you were killed last night at Rossville! [*Kisses him.*] Thank goodness, you weren't! I'd be left all alone in Cañon Del Oro!

"JIM" [*facing about*]. Mr. Willetts, this story of yours must be based on facts. I recollect now, that there was a man hanging around Rossville who pretended to be me, at least, he was able to get some money under false pretenses by makin' out to be a mine owner using my name. They say he even looks some'at like me. The way I come—came to hear about this game was that a man named Barnes wrote me, sayin' as how—saying that I had given him a mortgage on this mine property for five thousand dollars. Of course, that was all the bunk because I only paid five thousand for the whole works—the whole property, myself. If this bunco-steerer has been shot by one of his victims, all I can say is, it served him right! And if I was you, I'd figure the county was saved money by having one no-account rattler bumped off.

THE SHERIFF [*draining his glass*]. Well, sir, that sounds pretty reasonable. Mebbe yo're right about the county bein' saved the expense of prosecutin' this Slippery Dick fer fraud. Don't know as I blame the pore sheep wrangler fer puttin' out his light ef he lost a stake by the cuss. Only I hate to lose a chance to send up one o' them no-account sheepraisers. They jest naturally oughtn't to be let loose to run nohow! [*Rises*.] Well, ma'am, I reckon I'll be pullin' freight as me and my posse has to make twenty-seven miles back to Rossville tonight before moon-set. [*Stares again at "Jim."*] Never in all my born days have I seen *sech* a likeness! They might be twins, and that's a fact!

THE LADY. Mr. Willetts, I wish you would stay. Perhaps your men would like to come in and warm up.

THE SHERIFF [*twinkling now*]. No, ma'am, I wouldn't trust 'em. If that crew got a good look at you, ma'am, I wouldn't git 'em out o' here before midnight! Let well enough be, says I. Yore husband looks like he couldn't stand any too much goin's-on, and besides [*with a broad wink*] seein' as how it's yore anniversary night—[*Chuckles, moving down toward "Jim."*] Glad to hev met the *real* Jim Devine!

[*Holds out his hand. "Jim" takes out his left and shakes.*]

"JIM." Pardon my left, Sheriff. It's neuritis.

THE LADY [*holding out her hand*]. Awfully glad you stopped in, Mr. Willetts. Perhaps Jim and I will see you soon. We're going to California, and we may pass through Rossville.

THE SHERIFF [*shaking hands vigorously*]. If you come down my way, drop in on us and stop as long as you can.

"JIM." By the way, Sheriff, I feel sort of responsible for this killing, because of the likeness. I'll be glad to stand the expenses of the man's funeral.

THE SHERIFF. His funeral cost jest seventy-two cents. We had a nice pine coffin that didn't fit the man it was ordered fer, so we donated it to this purpose. The seventy-two cents was fer coffin nails! And we all figgered it was wu'th it, jest to keep up Rossville's repitation fer bein' a he-town whar shootin' was *shootin'!* [*He backs toward the door.*] Well, good night, folks! Thanks fer the entertainment and good luck and long life to ye both, and a happy anniversary!

THE LADY AND "JIM." Good night! Good night, Sheriff!

[*He goes out. For a moment after the door closes there is utter silence in the room. The Lady, standing toward the center, sways as though about to fall. "Jim" seems about to spring to his feet, but she motions him to keep still.*]

THE LADY. I'm all right, Jim. It was just for a second. Stay where you are. They might be looking in the window. In fact, I'm sure some one *is* watching! [*She walks steadily toward him.*] Take me in your arms, and hold me. You *must!* They're watching! [*He holds out his arms and she sinks down. He holds her gently.*] Now kiss me, Jim dear. *Pretend* you love me!

[*He kisses her, at first with restraint, then with sudden passion.*]

"JIM" [*fiercely*]. God! as if I'd have to pretend! [*She relaxes, goes limp. Contritely.*] I'm sorry—I overplayed my part—

THE LADY [*softly and contentedly*]. You haven't, Jim dear. You won't *ever!*

[*Their heads are close together as The Curtain Falls.*]

THE WEATHER BREEDER
A PLAY
BY MERRIL DENISON

CHARACTERS

OLD JOHN [*a backwoods farmer*].
LIZE [*his daughter*].
JIM
LEVI } [*two helpers*].
MURL [*a boat owner*].

THE WEATHER BREEDER

A PLAY   BY MERRIL DENISON

[*The* SCENE *is in a back-country shack, situated on a lake farm and inaccessible except by water. The room has the appearance of a camp rather than that of a permanent abode, for it is used only when John is working his lake farm. There are two doors; one at the rear leading into another room and one at the right leading outside. Two chairs have been placed in front of the window at the left. One faces the window while the second one is sideways to it as if it had been used as a support for someone's foot. Beside the door, on a low bench, are a pail of water and a tin dipper. Sunshine pours through the window, flooding the far end of the kitchen table with light.*

Lize, a woman of twenty, enters at the rear door and begins arranging the piled up dishes on the table. A moment later Jim, a gay, happy fellow of twenty-three, comes through the other door and turns to the water pail. He is hot and sweaty and has been working hard, evidently, for he pays no attention to Lize until he has finished drinking. When he does turn to her, she retreats behind the table. They move around the table with cautious quietness as if they were both afraid of disturbing some one in the back room.

Jim soon tires of trying to catch her and stops dead, assuming a hurt, pleading air which is more successful. Lize relents but before edging cautiously around the table she warns him to keep quiet and, after kissing him quickly, shoves him away.]

LIZE. No, Jim, no! Paw might come in any minute. He's awful sour this afternoon. Besides you ought to be gettin' on with that grain and gettin' it down to the shore.

JIM [*peevishly*]. What's he got to be sour about? We ain't got but thirty bags to carry down. Levi and me has most two hundred on the shore now and

the motor boat ain't around the head of the bay yet. Can't see what he's got to be sour for. He ain't done nothin' but set. Sour?

LIZE. Yes, he's sourer'n I've ever seen him before.

JIM. It's his leg.

LIZE [*shaking her head in a slow, mystified way*]. No, it ain't his leg. He'll jest sot hisself down in that chair and set and set and kinda keep mumblin' to hisself. Swearin', soft and low, like he wasn't happy.

JIM [*worried*]. It ain't loud swearin', eh?

LIZE [*hopeless*]. No, Jim, it's awful gentle. I get to wishin', when I'm here alone with him sometimes, and you carryin' them bags down to the shore, that he'd curse like he used to and break the stove or somethun. He ain't like hisself. And Jim, he ain't gettin' any more kindly towards you and me.

JIM [*indignantly*]. What's he got agin me? Ain't I done my share of the work, all summer'n' fall . . . 'n' last spring?

LIZE [*anxiously*]. Jim, don't talk so loud. He'll hear you.

JIM. I don't care if he does. [*But he lowers his voice and leans across the table to speak.*] Ain't I helped him plow'n' seed and done most of the reapin'? Ain't I run the threshing engine'n' ain't I been luggin' grain about half a mile down to the shore fer two days? Ain't I? It ain't my fault he's got his foot caught in the belt of the thresher.

LIZE. He ain't said it is. [*Sighing.*] He's jest sour.

JIM. What's makin' him sour? Did you ast him?

LIZE. I ain't ast him but I've kinda hinted he weren't any cheerfuller'n he had to be. He just growled.

JIM. It ain't the crop. We's the best one they's been in years. He oughta make quite a bit outen the farm even

99

though it is ten miles from the village and there ain't a road you can get to it on. Seems kinda queer. [*He looks out the window and the sight of the fall sunlight restores his gayety.*] Look! Feelin' sour and a sun like that. Lookout, Lize.

[*Lize turns and looks out the window with a touch of wistfulness. Jim creeps around the table behind her but she turns just before he takes her in his arms and tries to evade him.*]

LIZE [*watching the door at the rear*]. Jim, it ain't right. Paw'll hear you and come out. And besides, you ought to be gettin' them bags down.

JIM [*turning away, disgustedly*]. Aw! It ain't no wonder your paw's sour.

LIZE. I jest seen Levi go past. He's workin'.

JIM. Ain't I been workin'? I been carryin' two to his one all day. And I come in fer a minute . . . to get a drink and you're tryin' to histe me outen the door. Levi was here for a good half hour this mornin'. You didn't try to histe him out.

LIZE. He was talkin' to paw.

JIM. It seems like you didn't want me hangin' around, to my way of thinkin'.

LIZE. Jim!

JIM. And it ain't as if you hadn't promised me. If I hadn't been shinin' up to you. . . .

LIZE [*wearily*]. Don't be foolish, Jim. You know we can't go agin paw, not when he's sour, anyways. You ain't got a thing to get married on till your shares of the crop. Not a thing. I wished you had but you ain't. And paw's gettin' sourer'n' sourer every day we stay up here.

JIM [*moving toward the door, disgruntled*]. Well, I'll be gettin' sourer myself. I got a right to be gettin' sour, he ain't. All he does is sit there and watch us work. Why don't he sit outside in the sun instead of stickin' around here?

LIZE. He don't seem to like it outside. Every time he goes to the door he seems to get worse'n' sourer. Jim, I wish you'd go back to work . . . afore he comes.

JIM [*with a "you'll be sorry when I'm dead" sort of air*]. All right, I'll go. I'll go.

LIZE [*relenting a little*]. Jim.

JIM. I ain't goin' to be Jimmed. 'N'

lookut! I'm goin' to see your paw and I'll say to him, I'll say, "lookut. You ain't the only one around here that's gettin' sour."

[*He turns toward the door and opens it quickly and angrily and takes a step to go out but runs into Levi who is coming in. Levi, a young back country lad, is hot and tired as Jim was and immensely cheerful.*]

LEVI. Look out, Jim. Holy, old Lincoln, but she's a great day, ain't she? I never seen such weather. [*He turns to the bucket.*] There ain't been a cloud in the sky for three weeks'n' she's getting on for the middle of October. The hardwoods is hardly turned yet.

JIM. How many bags is down?

LEVI. I brung down six more.

JIM. Where'd you put 'em?

LEVI. Right on the shore with the rest.

LIZE. Levi, did you see the motor boat in the bay? Paw says he might try and get down to-night.

LEVI. I thought he was figgerin' on a hunt for a couple of days. Them back fields is full of birds.

JIM. Lize, he ain't goin' down right away?

LIZE. It's hard to tell what he'll do, he's so sour. [*She moves toward the door and listens.*] Sh! He's comin'. [*Anxiously.*] Go on to work, afore he comes. Hurry. It'll only make him sourer if he sees you here.

[*The two young men start to move quietly toward the outer door but, before they have taken more than a step or two, the rear door opens and Old John appears. He stands there looking at the boys, the picture of complete and absolute gloom. As Lize has remarked, he is sour.*]

JOHN. Gerhh!

LEVI. Har . . . harye, Mr. Hawley?

JIM. We jest been gettin' a drink. Kinda hot, eh? Fine day.

JOHN. Gerhh!

LEVI. Great day for workin'.

JOHN. Why don't you work then?

LIZE. Come and sit in your chair, Paw, where you can see outside. Over here in the sun.

JOHN [*an even more vicious growl*]. Gerhhh! Sun? Gerhhh!

[*John hobbles over toward the chair, assisted by Lize, who is most tender and solicitous. The two boys are too embarrassed to leave and wait, awkwardly.*]

LEVI. Shame you can't get out and around these days, Mr. Hawley. They's never been such a fall. You'd feel better. It'd get your mind off'n that lame foot.

JOHN [*easing himself into the chair*]. My mind ain't on my foot. Look out there, Lize! Watch how you move that leg. It ain't cordwood. Lift her up. Easy! There. [*He cranes his neck so that he may look out.*] Look at that sun pourin' in. Can't you move this here chair so's I can see somethun? [*Jim takes the chair and moves it the wrong way.*] No! No! The other way. Can't you see I can't see out where you're movin' it?

JIM. I thought you wanted to get outen the sun.

LEVI. We might rig a paper or somethun over the window, there. Might kinda kill the glare.

JOHN. What'd I want to kill the glare for? It'd be still there, wouldn't it? What's it like out?

LIZE. Oh, Paw, it's lovely. It couldn't be nicer. There ain't a cloud in the sky.

JIM [*doing his best to cheer John up*]. Ain't never been such a month. Jest one day follerin' another like this. Warm and sunshiny with a little haze on the hills. There ain't been a cloud. . . .

JOHN [*in a perfect fury*]. You're fools, the pack of you.

LIZE. Paw!

JOHN. Fools. Don't you know nuthin'?

LEVI. I know we've got most of the grain down. There ain't but thirty bags left.

JOHN. They'll all be spoilt.

LIZE. I can't see what you're so crabbed and sour about, Paw. It seems to me you're gettin' sourer'n' sourer'n'; there ain't a thing we do'll ever please you. [*She begins to cry.*]

JIM. Yes, Lize is right. You done nothin' but grumble since we come up here and there ain't been a thing wrong. There ain't been a day we've had to stop work. Lookut to-day and you're kickin' about the weather. What do you want? The sun to shine all night?

JOHN. They's weather breeders, I tell you. We ain't had a day since we come up here that wasn't a weather breeder. Jest one damn day like this after another. All weather breeders. [*Trying to rise from his chair, angrily.*] And we'll pay for it. It ain't natural to have three weeks without a storm and the longer she waits the worse she'll be. We'll have to pay for it.

JIM. You been sayin' that every day that comes along that ain't near zero or they ain't a cloudburst. Just let the sun poke out from behind a cloud and you says it's a weather breeder. To my way of thinkin' you're gettin' so sour you can't tell a good day when you see it. You're sick!

JOHN. I ain't sick. I ain't sour. It's them damn weather breeders get on a feller's nerves.

LEVI. Well, what if they is weather breeders? Ain't most of the grain piled on the shore and Murl'll be here any time with the boats.

LIZE. He said he'd make four or five trips to-night because there'll be a full moon. What do you see, Paw?

JOHN [*who has been leaning forward, disappointedly*]. Ain't nothin'. I thought fer a minute I seen a cloud, but it ain't. What did you pile them bags on the shore for?

LEVI. It's the easiest place to load 'em into the boats.

JOHN. Why didn't you put 'em into the shack, like I said.

JIM. Weren't no sense makin' a double haul. There ain't no danger where they is.

JOHN. What if it storms . . . like it will?

LEVI [*laughing*]. It ain't goin' to storm, Mr. Hawley. Keepin' in the house is kinda makin' you heavy.

JOHN. I ain't heavy. What if a west wind blows up . . . which it will.

JIM. There ain't been a wind for a month.

LIZE. Paw, perhaps you'd like some tea.

JOHN. No, I wouldn't like some tea.

LIZE. Why don't you light your pipe, Paw?

JOHN. Because I ain't got it.

LIZE [*very patiently*]. Where did you leave it, Paw?

JOHN. I don't know where I left it.

I don't care where I left it, neither.
Gerhh! Look at that sky!

JIM. See if you can see any signs of
Murl and the boat yet, Levi.

[*Levi goes out the door at the side.*]

JOHN. Gerhhh! That infernal motor
boat. Somethun'll get intul her in the
middle of the lake like it always does.
Fool notion to drag a couple of tons of
grain around the big lake with them
there squalls that come up.

LIZE [*wearily*]. Paw, there ain't been
a wind for a month. Can't you stop
grumblin' for a little? It ain't our fault
the weather's been so good.

JOHN. I ain't sayin' it is, am I? But
that's no excuse for you three enjoyin' it
the way you do. The trouble with you
is you don't know nothin'. We ought to
had a storm when the moon turned. You
think it's all right not to have a storm
with the moon, don't you? Ain't got
enough sense to know better. [*Lize and
Jim have been carrying on a surrepti-
tious flirtation behind his back.*] You
think . . . . Are you listenin'?

LIZE. Why, Paw, why shouldn't we
be listenin'?

JOHN. There ain't been an equalnoxial
gale this year. Not an equalnoxial oncet.
Do you know what that means?

JIM. Kinda lucky we missed her for
oncet, eh?

JOHN. Gerh! We ain't missed her.
She's savin' herself up. Lookut it.
[*Waving toward the window.*] Same
haze they's been on the hills for a month.
Not a breath of air movin'. Nothin' but
weather breeders. Lize!

LIZE [*jumping away from Jim*]. What
is it, Paw?

JOHN. What are you doin' there?

LIZE. Nothin', Paw, just listenin' to
you. What do you want?

JOHN. I want my pipe. [*Hearing no
movement behind him.*] Lize!

LIZE. Yes, Paw. [*Motioning Jim to
leave.*]

JOHN. My pipe, Lize! What are you
doin' anyway? Still listenin'? [*Looking around.*] You still hangin' around,
Jim? Why don't you get them bags
down?

JIM. There ain't no hurry. The boat
ain't here yet and there'll be a full moon
to-night.

[*Lize goes into the other room.*]

JOHN. You're nothin' but a fool with

as much brains intul your head as a loon
that's lost her mate. You're carcallatin'
this'll keep up forever just because they
was a moon last night and they's goin'
to be one to-night.

JIM [*defensively*]. You couldn't ask
for a better day.

JOHN [*indignantly*]. Ain't that what
I been tellin' you for three weeks? Every
day for three weeks you say it's the best
day you ever seen and what did I say,
eh? Tell me that?

JIM. Every day you says it was a
weather breeder.

JOHN. And I was right and the storm
she's breedin'll drown us when it comes.

JIM. Aw, you're actin' like a cow in
fly time. You old lads always figger you
can tell about the weather and I ain't
never seen one of yous ever get it right
yet. Last fall, when you found that
milt in the hog we butchered, you says
it was goin' to be an open winter without
snow. It was the worst we seen in years.
You said so yourself, when it was over.
There ain't goin' to be no storm.

JOHN [*almost speechless with indignant rage*]. Get out of here. Get them
bags down. [*As Jim hesitates.*] What
are you hangin' around for?

JIM. I was goin' to ast you somethun.

JOHN. About Lize, I spose, eh? Comin' around whinin' to marry the girl and
you ain't got nothin' in the world to call
your own but them shares in that grain
and it's all down on the beach and goin'
to get spoiled. Don't come around here
throwin' that pig's milt up in my face
and then ast me to give a thanks offerin'
of Lize. Lize!

[*Lize appears at the rear door and
motions Jim, frantically, to go.
Jim, very disgruntled, goes to the
door and opens it as if to go out
but immediately his attitude
changes to one of anxious surprise.*]

LIZE. I can't find it, Paw.

JOHN. Gerhhh!

[*The old man struggles out of his
chair and hobbles past Lize, who is
standing in the doorway. She is
watching Jim anxiously and goes
to him as soon as her father has
departed.*]

LIZE [*anxiously*]. Jim, perhaps paw's
right, after all.

JIM [*seriously, but shaking off his*

air of worry]. No he ain't. That ain't nothin' at all. Just some smoke from them fires north of Mallory Lake, lyin' low down. Here's Levi. He'll say it's the fires.

[*Levi comes in.*]

LEVI. He's just passed little Doe Island, with the little boat and towin' two row boats. Let's get them bags down and have supper and leave afterwards.

JIM. Levi, look over there back of you? What do you make of that? Smoke, ain't it?

[*The two men stand looking out the open door.*]

LEVI [*puzzled*]. Don't look like smoke. Lookut over there, Jim. Just beyond that swale. Lookut them birches.

JIM [*a little more anxiously, but being very careful not to draw John's attention*]. See that swirl of sand by the fence corner? There!

LEVI. Don't seem to be no wind, neither. That smoke's coming fast, Jim. Look! There's another. Kinda funny you can't hear the motor boat engine at all.

JIM. He's close in, too. See that, Levi?

LEVI. Perhaps the old lad's right after all. Look! That ain't smoke, beyond the big rock. And look! Look! Over there. [*In an awed tone.*] Jim, she's a comin'.

JIM [*with forced indifference*]. No, it ain't nothin'. You're gettin' as bad as the old lad.

LIZE. It don't seem right to me. [*Turning to the window.*] See what it's like out here. [*She and Jim go to the window and Jim peers out.*]

LEVI. They won't be nothin' in the north. She's a comin' from the east.

JIM. You see there ain't a thing. Clear as crystal.

LEVI [*from the door*]. Here's Murl comin'. He's beached the boats.

JIM. Ain't no need of that. No sea on there.

LEVI. They's whitecaps out beyond Big Bay point, Jim.

[*John returns from the other room.*]

JOHN [*from the door*]. Ain't you two started workin' yet?

JIM. We was gettin' a drink.

JOHN. Aw, you've drunk enough now to founder a team of horses. Get on with you. What're you lookin' at, any-

ways? Admirin' the sunset, I suppose, eh?

LEVI. We was waitin' for Murl. He's just beachin' his boats. Jim, come here. Look! Out beyond that knoll. In the Dyer Lake hardwoods.

JOHN [*starts to limp toward the door but is diverted by Lize.*] What're you lookin' at there?

LIZE. Hadn't you better sit down and rest, Paw?

[*A low rumble like distant thunder is heard.*]

JOHN. What's that? Murl beachin' a boat? It's so still you can hear most a mile.

LEVI [*to Jim*]. Thunder?

JIM [*nodding his head*]. Yes.

LIZE. Sit down, Paw. It won't do that leg no good walkin' around on it. Sit down and let me put it up on the chair.

LEVI. Jim, Murl's callin' for us to come down.

[*The two men go out hurriedly and Lize closes the door after them, while John looks out the window. The sunlight has been growing gradually less strong.*]

JOHN. Ain't it gettin' late awful early, Lize? Sun ain't gone down, surely.

LIZE. No, Paw, it's kindo hazy out, that's all. They's smoke from the Mallory Lakes fires driftin' west.

JOHN [*disgustedly*]. It's these damn weather breeders. If we'd had anythin' but this sunshine them fires'd been out long ago. [*The sunlight is hardly perceptible. Another low rumble is heard.*] How many boats has he got up anyways? That's about the third he's pulled up.

LIZE [*at the door again*]. Paw, what would happen if they was a storm come?

JOHN. We'd lose all them oats down on the shore. A couple of hundred bags and about half of the year's crop. They'd get soaked.

LIZE. Couldn't they be dried afterwards?

JOHN. Wouldn't be worth the trouble. But it's all their fault. I told 'em. That smoke seems to be gettin' thicker.

[*While he is looking out of the window Murl comes in. He is a summer camper, about the same age as the other two young men, and like them is very cheerful, in contrast to John.*]

MURL. Hello, Lize. Hello, Mr. Hawley. How are you? Fine weather we've been having, isn't it? I've never seen such a fall in my life. Beautiful. Wonderful, mellow sunshine every day. Now, if you only had autumns like this every year, eh? Perfect.

JOHN [*very, very sourly*]. Perfect? They's nuthin' but weather breeders. Enough to take the heart outen a man.

MURL. Why, what's the trouble, Mr. Hawley? You're not like yourself at all. You're usually working around, cheerful and whistling and having a great time. Enjoying life. Is that foot bothering you as much as all that? It must have been a nasty accident.

JOHN [*disagreeably*]. Got nothin' to do with the foot. It's this damn weather. Look out there.

MURL. Beautiful, isn't it? Almost think it was August instead of this late in the year. I noticed that it is looking pretty dark over toward the east.

JOHN. Smoke! Beautiful! You don't know what you're talking about. What's beautiful about it? Why, we've had three solid weeks of sunshine. That ain't right. Not an equalnoxial gale yet. Do you know what that means?

MURL [*laughing*]. Oh, you're a confirmed pessimist, Mr. Hawley.

LIZE. Paw's been sittin' at the window ever since he got his leg hurt grumblin' about how fine the weather is.

MURL. Well, by the looks of things I wouldn't be surprised if we had a change any time now.

JOHN [*with a glint of enthusiasm*]. That's what I been sayin' for the last two weeks.

MURL. The sky is beginning to look very threatening over toward the east. But I don't think it will break.

JOHN [*excitedly*]. Was it? Was it? Where? [*Looking out the window.*] The sun's gone down already. Is it that late?

[*Lize goes outdoors unnoticed by the two men.*]

MURL. I don't think so. No, it's only half past four. That's funny. [*The low rumble is heard again.*] Listen, what's that?

JOHN. I figgered it was you drawin' your boats up.

MURL. I didn't draw them up. That's thunder.

JOHN [*as if this were too good to be true*]. It ain't thunder, is it? [*Anxiously.*] Do you think it's really thunder?

MURL. Sounds mighty like it.

JOHN [*beginning to cheer up*]. I told 'em it was a weather breeder. [*Chuckles.*] I told 'em it was. Let me look.

[*He starts to get up and Murl opens the door and turns with a look of consternation.*]

MURL. Why, good Lord! Look at that, would you. The whole sky's black, right across. It looks like an awful storm.

JOHN [*gloating with glee*]. Let me see it. Let me see it.

MURL. Why, that'll be terrible, Mr. Hawley. All that grain down on the beach will be completely ruined, won't it?

JOHN. Sure it will. Every last kernel of it. Look at her come.

MURL. But can't we do something? Haven't you got a tarpaulin or an old tent or something we can put over it?

JOHN [*with complete satisfaction*]. There ain't a thing. Anyways, the boys ain't got time to do a thing before she breaks. Look at them clouds. They's as black as ink. They'll be more'n one house get struck by that storm. Oh, she's ararin'.

MURL. But, Mr. Hawley, your whole summer's work will go for nothing. The terrible labor you three have put in on this farm, plowing that hard clay and . . . .

JOHN. Here comes the wind. I wonder where Jim is. I'd like to see his face when she breaks. Tellin' me they wasn't weather breeders.

MURL. Why, it's awful to think of you losing everything, Mr. Hawley. I can remember you passing my camp every day during the summer. It's an eight mile row up here, isn't it?

JOHN. Ten, each way.

MURL. It seems a damn shame to lose it all this way. Are you insured?

JOHN [*with the utmost cheer*]. Not a cent. Listen to her. [*The sound of the wind is becoming audible and the window has darkened to a dull gray*]. Holy old Lincoln, watch her come!

MURL. Jove, it's getting dark. Where did Lize go? She'll be getting all wet.

JOHN. Serves her right. She said they wasn't weather breeders.

MURL. Why didn't you put them in that shack instead of out on the beach?

JOHN [*ignoring him*]. I knew she'd be a hell bender when she come. I knew. Look at her, Murl. She's past the Buck Lake Ridge.

MURL. Perhaps it will blow over all right. It mightn't rain a drop. It might pass to the south.

JOHN [*indignantly*]. What? Not rain a drop? Why, Murl. She's goin' to be a cloudburst. Nothin' short of it'n' she's headed straight for us. Ain't no doubt of that.

[*He hobbles back to the chair, turns it and sits down and puts his feet on the stove. He is a new man, cheerful and exultant. The approaching storm has been gathering in volume; the sunlight has been gone for some time and the interior of the shack is quite dark.*]

JOHN. Have a smoke, Murl. There's nothin' to do but sit down and enjoy her, now she's come. She might be the equalnoxial.

[*Lize comes in.*]

MURL. No, thanks. I'm going to see where the boys are.

[*Murl goes out and John sits by the stove enjoying his pipe and his storm.*]

LIZE [*in a frightened tone*]. Oh, Paw, it's goin' to be an awful storm. Somethun terribul. Ain't there nothin' we can do?

JOHN. Nothin' but sit here and watch her. She ought to be a rip tail snorter.

LIZE [*almost frenzied*]. But, Paw, all them bags down on the beach. They'll be soaked through.

JOHN. They won't be worth a red cent when this rain gets at 'em. Might as well throw 'em away.

LIZE. It don't seem fair. All Jim's work gone for nothin'. It means we'll never be able to get married, at all.

[*She breaks down and weeps, John goes on smoking.*]

JOHN. I says every day for the last three weeks that she was a weather breeder and none of you would listen to me. No, you says, ain't it a fine day, Paw? And you said I was sour and didn't know what I was talkin' about and

tried to blame my foot. You thought you three young ones knowed more about the signs than I did. Ha! There ain't been a day I ain't said it was a weather breeder. Not a day. And I was right, wasn't I? Lize? Quit your cryin' and tell me. I was right, wasn't I?

LIZE [*crying quite lustily*]. Oh, keep quiet, Paw. Keep quiet. It's too hard. A whole summer's work.

JOHN. I told them they ought to put that grain in the shack. I knowed it'd never last till the new moon. [*Laughs.*] Can't fool me on a weather breeder. I seen too many of 'em. These days that is too good to be true, they's the kind to watch out for. And no equalnoxial gale, Lize, that makes her worse. These days all fall that didn't have a thing wrong with 'em, that a feller couldn't find a thing to find fault with, not a thing, they's weather breeders and when they come that's the time to sit tight and pray for the best. [*The wind has dropped to absolute silence.*] Listen! There ain't a sound. She's about here.

LIZE. You'd think it didn't matter at all the way you're talkin'.

JOHN. Matter? Ain't I been tellin you it mattered? That's just what I been sayin' for three weeks. I wish the boys'd come so's I could see their faces. Throwin' that milt that come outen a half starved pig up in my face. But I got 'm now. Listen, Lize! Ain't that the rain? Lize, look outen the door and see if she's broke.

LIZE. Oh, shut up.

JOHN [*surprised and hurt*]. Why, Lize, what a way to talk to your old paw. You ungrateful girl.

[*Lize gets up and opens the door. There is a rush of rain on the roof and through the door as Lize opens it. She closes it with difficulty.*]

JOHN. Open the door, Lize. Let's see the rain. It sounds like the whole sky was droppin' buckets.

[*The door opens and Jim and Levi burst in, both wet.*]

JIM. Shut the door. By the livin' twist she's goin' to pour.

LEVI. I never seen a storm come up so quick. Half an hour ago they wasn't a cloud in the sky. It's a good job we left them thirty bags in the barn.

[*Murl comes in.*]

MURL. It looks as if it would be a terrible storm. About as bad as I've ever seen. And right on the heels of that perfect weather, too.

JIM [*sitting down, dejectedly*]. Seems kinda funny it couldn't 've held off another day till we got that grain down.

LEVI [*despondently*]. Sort of shoots our whole summer's work to hell, don't it? Think of the times we've rowed up here and back in the day, ten miles each way, and worked this hard clay. This is just about give me enough of farmin'. Listen to her pour. This roof won't stand an awful lot with them loose shingles.

LIZE. Oh, Jim. You won't make a cent outen the whole summer, will you?

JIM. Not a cent, Lize, except from what's left in the barn.

JOHN [*cheerfully*]. And it's mine.

MURL. It seems a hang shame after all the work you've put in on the farm this year. The bitter thanklessness of it. You know, I'm awfully sorry. [*To John.*] If there's anything I can do. . . .

JIM. Yes, that's so. And you done as much work as anybody till you got hurt.

[*There is complete silence for an instant. Levi and Jim sit dejectedly. Murl is very sympathetic and Lize is weeping softly. Old John is listening ecstatically to the storm and finally breaks into a cheerful peal of laughter.*]

MURL [*anxiously*]. Why, what's the matter, Mr. Hawley? What's the matter? Don't let your loss get the better of you. Keep hold of yourself. Your friends will help you, you know.

JIM. I don't see what you got to feel so infernal cheerful over.

LIZE. Paw, stop that awful laughin'.

JOHN. Ha, ha, ha! Listen to her. Comin' down like the whole Mishinog Lake was turned upside down. By God, she's good to hear. She was atunin' a minute ago. You lads look good and mournful now, don't you, eh? And feel kinda mournful. Didn't I tell you all them good days was nothin' but weather breeders? Didn't I say they'd breed a storm like this? Didn't I say we'd missed the equalnoxials and we'd pay for it? Eh? Didn't I, Jim?

JIM [*who has moved over to comfort Lize*]. Yes. You've made life miserable for everybody in camp for most a month with your cheerless prophesyin'. You'd get a day from heaven, made by all the angels for God hisself, and you'd get sour and say it was a weather breeder. I hope you're happy, now, anyways. There, Lize, your paw's havin' a good time, anyways.

LIZE. Oh!

JOHN. Didn't I? I ask you, now, didn't I?

JIM. Oh, damn it. Yes. Yes. If it'll please you any. Ten times a day you said it.

JOHN. You see. I knew. I said all along they was weather breeders. I told yous. You can't fool me on them days when they don't seem to be a thing you could ask for to make 'em better. When you lads have farmed, like I have, for forty years, you won't be so cheerful when they's a fine day.

MURL. But, Mr. Hawley, you don't seem to appreciate your own loss. You're going crazy, man.

JOHN. Oh, no, I ain't. And even if I was I'll wager none of you lads'll ever tell me I don't know what kind of a day it is again.

LEVI [*looking out the window*]. It's lettin' up a bit.

JOHN. Oh, no, it ain't. Don't you fool yourselves. She'll pour most of the night. She's just takin' a new breath. I was right, wasn't I? Eh, Jim? Eh, Levi? I knew a thing or two.

LEVI. Oh, keep quiet. Ain't it bad enough to lose the whole summer's work without you chatterin' like a jay bird?

JIM [*viciously, so that his unpopularity begins to penetrate the old man's head*]. Yes. Shut up. Can't you see Lize is bawlin' her eyes out? You may think a cloudburst's a fine thing, but you're the only one that does.

JOHN. Why, Lize, what's the matter? Come here.

LIZE. I won't.

JOHN. Why . . . what's the trouble, Lize?

JIM. You give us all a pain sittin' there sour'n last year's milk for three weeks not able to enjoy a day and then comes along a cloudburst and you act like somebody's give you a free trip and your board to the Toronto fair. How'd you like to be figgerin' on gettin' married and waitin' till you got a stake and then seen it wiped clean in twenty minutes, eh?

LEVI. It's a damn shame, that's what it is, Jim.

MURL. I don't blame you feeling as you do, Jim.

LIZE. And you laughin' there like you didn't care at all, Paw. It's cruel.

JOHN [*persistently*]. But I was right, wasn't I? Wasn't I right?

JIM [*his temper breaking*]. Christ, YES! You was right. Once and for all, you was right. If you'll only keep that trap of your'n closed, you was always right.

LIZE. But that don't help me and Jim none.

MURL [*who has opened the door*]. Levi, come here.

[*The two men step out and it is noticed, through the open door, that the outside is much brighter again.*]

JOHN. How don't it help you and Jim?

LIZE. How can we get married now when you said you wouldn't let us till Jim'd sold his shares in the grain? There ain't any grain to sell, now. It'll be another six months at least.

JIM. But that don't matter, of course, Lize. Your paw's havin' such a good time outen this here storm. You oughta be happy he's cheered up. He'd been hell to live with all winter if they hadn't come some sort of a calamity. [*Through the window comes a glint of sunshine which shows on the far wall. None of the three see it.*] I got a mind to marry you anyways. Will you, Lize?

LIZE. Jim, I want to, but you know I promised maw I'd always ask paw before I done anythin' and I don't care nothin' about him, but I don't want to break a promise to her.

JOHN [*rising*]. Why, Lize, there ain't no need to take on this way.

JIM. Don't you touch her. Go and enjoy your storm. Be cheerful while it lasts. It may be a good day to-morrow and you won't be fit to live in the same township with.

[*Again the momentary flash of sunlight appears.*]

JOHN [*quite humbled*]. Now, Lize, don't take on this way and rob your old paw outen all the fun he's got this fall. Lize, I didn't know you wanted to get married that bad. There ain't no reason you and Jim can't get married.

JIM. With all the summer's crop down there on the beach soakin' wet because of your weather breedin'. How can we get married?

JOHN. You could live down at the house. Lize's got to look after one of us and she might as well look after both.

LIZE [*excitedly*]. Then we can, Paw, we can!

JOHN [*a little ashamed*]. There ain't nothin' to stop it, to my way of thinkin'.

LIZE. Paw!

[*She runs to him and the old man awkwardly takes her in his arms. Levi bursts in the door in tremendous excitement.*]

LEVI. Jim! Jim! There ain't nothin' but the top layer of the bags a bit wet, Jim. It ain't hardly rained a drop.

JOHN [*turning from Lize's embrace, the horror of a great disappointment on his face*]. What? It ain't stormed? We heard it. There on the roof.

LEVI. Must a been them loose shingles you heard, rattlin' in the wind.

JOHN. The grain ain't spoilt?

[*Murl comes in.*]

MURL. It's going to be a perfectly wonderful sunset. The storm has passed off to the west. Take a look outside.

[*Levi, Jim, Lize and Murl look out the door. John is standing in the center of the room, a broken-hearted figure.*]

JOHN. Murl, it ain't right. You don't mean it ain't rained buckets?

MURL. The storm passed to the south of here. Only a bad wind storm here.

JOHN. I don't believe it.

MURL [*pointing to the rear wall, which is bathed in soft sunlight*]. Look behind you, then.

[*John turns, sees the sunlight on the wall, creeps back to his chair and sits down, sour, disappointed and disgusted. Jim stands with his arm about Lize's shoulders, looking out.*]

JOHN [*with a vicious kick at the stove*]. Gerhhh! More of them damn weather breeders.

[*Curtain.*]

WHOSE MONEY?

A Farce

By Lee Dickson and Leslie M. Hickson

CHARACTERS

HENRY DELL.
ISABEL DELL.
A BURGLAR.

WHOSE MONEY?

A FARCE   By LEE DICKSON AND LESLIE M. HICKSON

[SCENE: *The living room of the Dells' house. In the rear is a door leading to a hallway. On the right are windows, and on the left a fireplace. Near the fireplace is a large table, backed by a lounge. There is a telephone on the table. There are several chairs, tables and so forth about the room. The walls are paneled.*

AT RISE: *The stage is empty. In a moment Henry Dell enters and walks cautiously to the center of the room. He stands there a moment, looking at the ceiling and apparently listening for any sound upstairs. Then he returns to the entrance in the rear, looks out in hallway and listens again. Apparently satisfied he takes off his hat and coat and hastens to the rear wall on the right, where he slides back a panel behind which is concealed a small safe. He starts turning the knob.*]

HENRY. Three to the left to thirty and four to the right to forty-five and two to the left to fifteen. . . . [*He counts this off slowly as he turns the knob and then gives it an expectant pull. It does not open.*] Confound it! [*He works at it again, this time even more deliberately.*] Three to the left to thirty and four to the right to . . . .

[*Isabel Dell appears in the rear doorway, carrying a large pasteboard box. She starts on seeing Henry, then recognizes him.*]

ISABEL [*angrily*]. Henry!

HENRY [*jumping away from the safe*]. Izzie!

ISABEL [*looking at him severely*]. What are you doing there?

HENRY. Why . . . er . . . exercising the safe. . . .

ISABEL. You can save yourself the trouble! I had the combination changed the last time I caught you there.

HENRY. Oh! You did!

ISABEL. Yes! And I must say! Any man who would rob his own safe. . . .

HENRY.. It's better than robbing somebody else's! [*Angrily.*] Besides! If you'd give me the money I need I wouldn't have to stoop to these . . . undignified proceedings!

ISABEL [*putting her box on the large table*]. Did it ever occur to you, Henry, there's another way you might get the money to pay your debts?

HENRY [*eagerly*]. No! How?

ISABEL. Go out and work for it!

HENRY [*angry and disappointed*]. Izzie! How do you get those ideas?

ISABEL. I've heard of men working just because they liked it!

HENRY. Say! Some birds may get their pleasure out of work . . . I get mine dodging it! Besides! Why should *I* work? I've got an independent income! Or I had one before I married you! Now you've got it!

ISABEL. Yes! And that's better than having your gambling friends take it away from you!

HENRY. All right! I admit it! I realize I don't know how to handle money and that I did the right thing in putting all mine in your name! [*Indignantly.*] But I didn't expect to be treated like a child after I did it! [*Earnestly.*] It's only a hundred dollars I want, Izzie, and I've simply *got* to have it right away!

ISABEL. So you've been telling me all the week! I'll give it to you, Henry, just as soon as you tell me what it's for.

HENRY. I've told you! It's to pay a debt . . .

ISABEL [*angrily*]. A poker debt!

HENRY. No! It's not a poker debt!

ISABEL. You know it is!

HENRY. Now listen, Izzie. . . .

ISABEL. Stop calling me Izzie!

HENRY. Well Isabel. . . . [*The telephone starts ringing. Henry looks at it apprehensively*]. Good Lord!

111

ISABEL [*as Henry makes no effort to answer the phone*]. Well! Aren't you going to answer the phone?

HENRY [*nervously*]. Izzie! You answer it!

ISABEL. Henry! Answer the phone!

HENRY. But listen, dearie. . . .

ISABEL [*severely*]. Answer the phone, Henry! *You're* the master of this house!

HENRY [*sorely*]. Aw, Izzie! Quit your kidding! [*He takes up the phone angrily and shouts into it.*] Hello! . . . What? Is this the National Peace League? No! It's the local war office! Yes! You've got the wrong number. . . . I can't tell you. I can't tell you. I don't know anything about peace. I've been married three years. [*He hangs up the receiver, annoyed.*] We must be the only wrong number in town! [*In the meantime Isabel has opened her cardboard box. She now takes out of it a crown of jewels and several magnificent jeweled ornaments. When Henry sees them his eyes pop.*] Say! Have you been buying out Tiffany's?

ISABEL. Don't be silly! They'e just a lot of glass. I'm going to play the Queen of Sheba in the Charity League Revue.

HENRY. The Queen of Sheba! Huh! They gave you the wrong part to play. You ought to be Shylock!

ISABEL [*ignoring Henry's remark and carrying the paste jewels over toward the safe.*] I'm going to put them in the safe, however. If the servants saw them, they might ask me to raise their wages!

[*She starts turning the knob of the safe.*]

HENRY [*looking over her shoulder*]. What's that? Thirty-*five* to the left!

ISABEL [*looking up angrily*]. Henry! Stop it!

HENRY. All right! But confound it! I ought to know how to open my own safe!

ISABEL. It's *our* safe!

HENRY. No, it's not *your* safe! It's *my* safe! [*Looking into it as Isabel puts the paste jewels away.*] Say! You've got a lot of money in there! [*Isabel bangs the safe closed.*] Izzie! You've closed up without getting my hundred!

ISABEL. But you're not going to get your hundred! How many times must I tell you that I've paid the last of your poker debts, Henry!

HENRY. But it's *not* a poker debt!

ISABEL. What *is* it then?

[*The phone starts ringing again. Henry starts nervously.*]

HENRY. Confound that phone! [*He takes up the receiver nervously.*] Hello! [*Making an attempt at cheerfulness.*] Oh hello, Baker old man! I was *expecting* to hear from you! [*His face takes on a pained expression.*] What! [*He listens for a moment, apparently to some unpleasant conversation. Then he breaks in angrily.*] Say! Wait a minute! Don't get sore! Sure! I know I promised to give it to you this afternoon, but I couldn't get around to the club! No! [*looking at Isabel nervously*] my . . . my wife's sick! Yes! No! Nothing serious, but I didn't want to leave her! You know! [*Nodding his head emphatically.*] Sure! Sure! I've got the hundred in my pocket for you now! Sure! You know me, old man! I always pay my card debts! [*He glances at Isabel, frightened at his break.*] What? Sure! I'll meet you at the club first thing in the morning! Sure! We'll make it early! Say about noon! What? Nine o'clock! All right! Nine o'clock! Sure I'll be there! Can I get up that early! I don't know! I never tried! All right, old man! And don't worry, will you! I've got it in my pocket for you right now! Yes! Yes! Good-by!

[*He puts down the receiver and looks sheepishly at Isabel.*]

ISABEL. So! You didn't want that money to pay a poker debt, Henry! [*Angrily.*] How *can* you lie to me the way you do!

HENRY [*unhappily*]. Izzie! This time I'm going to tell you the truth. . . .

ISABEL. Yes! After I've discovered it! That's like a husband!

HENRY. I . . . I lost a hundred dollars to Baker a couple of weeks ago. And, Izzie, you heard what I just said on the phone. I've simply got to pay him to-morrow *now!*

ISABEL [*decidedly*]. Well, Henry! You're not going to get the money from me!

HENRY. But . . . but Izzie! I've told Baker I've got it in my pocket for him! If I don't show up with it to-morrow, what'll he *think?*

ISABEL. He'll probably think you're an awful liar, and he'll be quite right'

HENRY. Confound it, Izzie! Don't try to be funny! This is a serious matter! It's terrible! I've been putting Baker off all week and he's sore as a boil about it now!

ISABEL. Why don't you borrow the money to pay him from one of your *gambling* friends?

HENRY. Fat chance of any one lending *me* a hundred dollars! Everybody knows my allowance from you is twenty-five dollars a week! [*Beseechingly.*] Izzie! Give me a hundred dollars and I'll never play poker again!

ISABEL. I've heard that before!

HENRY [*desperately*]. But Izzie! This time I swear. . . .

ISABEL [*angrily*]. No! No! No! You'll not get a cent out of me! And stop nagging me about it, Henry, when you know I'm not well!

HENRY. Not well?

ISABEL. Yes! Isn't your wife *sick?*

HENRY. Aw Izzie! Quit your kidding, will you? [*Beseechingly again.*] Now listen, dearie. . . .

ISABEL [*starting for the door in the rear*]. No!

HENRY [*desperately*]. But think of my reputation! Think of what my friends will say! After I've absolutely *promised* him. . . .

ISABEL [*scornfully*]. Your friends!

HENRY [*horrified at the thought*]. Think of what Baker will say! My God! I won't be able to show my face at the club!

ISABEL [*at the door*]. Well, Henry! I think that will be a very good thing! [*She exits.*]

HENRY [*bitterly, after she is gone*]. Oh, hell! [*He walks about unhappily.*] I've got to get that money some way! [*His eyes return to the safe. He hastens over to it and starts turning the knob.*] Three to the left to thirty-*five* and four to the right to forty and two to the left to fifteen. . . . [*He pulls at it, but it does not open.*] Confound it! [*The telephone rings again. Henry starts, looks at it dubiously, then answers it, angrily.*] Hello! [*His voice takes on an anxious tone again.*] Oh, hello, Baker, old man! What? You want the hundred now! But . . . but listen, boy! I'll give it to you first thing in the morning! What? They're getting up a big game at the club to-night and you need it

right away! But . . . but old man! I told you my wife's sick. I can't get over there! [*In a frightened voice.*] What? You're coming over here! When? Right away! My God! Don't do that! Hello! Hello! [*Working the receiver hook up and down desperately.*] Hello, central! Hello! You've cut me off! Hello! Hello! [*In a trembling voice.*] Is this the Cosmopolitan Club I . . . I was speaking to Mr. Baker. Let me have him again, please! Yes! Hurry! Hurry! [*He waits impatiently.*] Hello! What? [*A look of consternation coming over his face.*] What? You . . . you say Mr. Baker's just gone out! [*Gulping over his words.*] Did he . . . did he say where? Yes! This is Mr. Dell! Oh! He . . . he's on his way over to see me! I . . . I see! Thanks! [*He hangs up the receiver.*] Oh, my God! [*He starts walking about and pulling at his hair.*] What am I going to do? What am I going to do? [*He stops and stares at the safe. A look of great determination comes over his face.*] I've got to get that safe open! That's all. . . .

[*He hastens out the door in the rear. When he is gone a window on the right opens and a rough looking face with a cap pulled down over the eyes peers in. Then a burglar comes over the sill and into the room. He is roughly dressed and carries a kit-bag. He starts on seeing the safe exposed in the rear wall. He is about to go back to it, when he stops suddenly and looks in the direction of the door in the rear. He hastens over to it and looks out into the hallway. Then he comes down quickly to the sofa on the left and conceals himself behind it.*

Henry reënters with a hammer and a chisel in his hands. He is too engrossed in his business to notice the open window. He goes to the safe with a very determined expression on his face, puts the chisel against it and aims a blow at it with his hammer. He misses the chisel and hits his finger. He drops the chisel and hammer and jumps about in pain. He puts his finger in his mouth and starts sucking it. As he is doing so he notices the open window. An ex-

pression of surprise comes over his face, his mouth opens and he forgets about the injured hand. He goes over to the window, a mystified expression on his face, sticks his head out and looks around. As he does so the burglar takes a blackjack from his pocket and creeps up stealthily behind him. As Henry turns from the window he sees the burglar aiming a blow at his head. Henry dodges it and grapples with him. They fall to the floor. Henry gets on top of the burglar, grabs his hammer and aims a blow at the burglar's head. misses him and hits the floor. The burglar squirms loose and draws a pistol from his pocket, but Henry seizes his hand before he can turn it on him. There is another scuffle during which Henry gets the pistol away from the burglar and from which he finally emerges, gasping and triumphant, sitting on the burglar's back.

Then the light of a brilliant idea flashes over Henry's face.]

HENRY. Say! You're just the bird I'm looking for!

THE BURGLAR [*his face buried in the carpet*]. Huh?

HENRY [*springing to his feet, the pistol in his hand*]. Get up! [*The burglar gets unsteadily to his feet. Henry goes to the door in the rear and looks anxiously in the hallway. Then he returns to the burglar.*] Look here! Can you open a safe without knowing the combination to it?

THE BURGLAR [*indignantly*]. Say! Are you tryin' to insult me?

HENRY [*gladly*]. Of course! That's your business, isn't it? Fine! Fine! [*Then waving the pistol at him threateningly.*] Now! I don't suppose you want me to turn you over to the police!

THE BURGLAR. Don't do that, boss! I got an old mother at home, and God! A burglar's life is hard enough without gettin' arrested!

HENRY. Don't worry! I'm not going to waste you on the police! I've got a job for you! [*Pointing to the safe.*] Do you see that safe over there?

THE BURGLAR. Sure! I ain't blind!

HENRY [*excitedly*]. Well! I want you to open it for me and get me a hun-

dred dollars out of it! Do that and . . . and I'll let you go!

THE BURGLAR. Say! Are you kidding me?

HENRY [*impatiently*]. Confound it! No! I never was more serious in my life!

THE BURGLAR [*confusedly*]. But . . . but what's the big idea?

HENRY [*angrily*]. Never mind! Will you open the safe and get me a hundred dollars or do you want me to telephone for the police?

THE BURGLAR. Nix! Nix, boss! [*Hastily picking up his kit-bag.*] I'll do it and no questions asked!

[*He goes over to the safe and drops his kit-bag on the floor. Henry starts nervously.*]

HENRY. Sh! My wife'll hear you! Not so much noise!

[*He hastens to the door in the rear and looks into the hallway.*]

THE BURGLAR [*grinning at him*]. Say! I get the idea now, boss! I was married wonst myself!

HENRY [*turning to the burglar impatiently*]. Stop talking, will you? And hurry up with your job!

THE BURGLAR. Sure! Sure! Keep your shirt on!

[*He works over the safe. Henry watches him anxiously.*]

HENRY [*after a moment*]. Can you . . . open it all right?

THE BURGLAR [*contemptuously*]. This here tin box? I could open it with a toothpick!

HENRY. Huh! I never thought the blame thing was any good! *She* bought it! [*Startled.*] My God! What's that? [*He hastens to the door in the rear and looks into the hallway. Then he turns to the burglar, reassured.*] It's all right! I thought I heard the wife!

THE BURGLAR. Boss! There's no mistakin' it! She's got you well trained all right!

HENRY [*angrily*]. Say! Never mind discussing my family affairs! Open that safe!

THE BURGLAR. Sure! Keep your shirt on, boss! I'm about through with this baby now!

[*He hits the safe a resounding blow with one of his tools.*]

HENRY [*walking about nervously*]. Say! Say! Not so much noise!

[*He trips over his hammer, falls against a table and makes a great racket himself. As he is struggling to his feet, a loud humming noise is heard from upstairs. The burglar gets to his feet, startled.*]

THE BURGLAR. What's that?

HENRY [*listening for a moment frightened, then an expression of delight coming over his face*]. It's the wife! Taking a bath!

[*The burglar turns to the safe again and hits it another blow. Then he pulls it open.*]

THE BURGLAR. There! [*As the safe opens the imitation jewels are revealed.*] Holy Tripe! Some swag!

HENRY. Pooh! They're fakes! Imitations of the jewels the Queen of Sheba wore! Get the hundred, will you?

THE BURGLAR. And she's got the real stuff, heh? You don't know where that dame lives, do you?

HENRY. The Queen of Sheba? She's dead!

THE BURGLAR. Well! Who's her heirs?

HENRY. Say! Get the hundred, will you? And shut up!

THE BURGLAR. Sure! Sure! [*He picks up a large pile of bills.*] Boss! There's some bunch of change here! [*Running his fingers through the bills.*] All hundred dollar notes! Holy Tripe!

HENRY [*warningly*]. Yes! But just take one of them, you know!

THE BURGLAR. Sure, boss! Just as you say! [*There is a look of cupidity on his face. Suddenly he looks in the direction of the door in the rear and exclaims in a low voice.*] What's that?

HENRY [*frightened*]. Where? [*He hastens to the door in the rear and looks out into the hallway. As he does so the burglar stuffs all the bills but one into his kit-bag and bangs the safe closed. Henry turns to him angrily.*] Say! What's the idea anyway? There's no one there!

THE BURGLAR [*grinning at him apologetically*]. I thought I heard some one comin'! [*Handing him the bill.*] Here's your change, boss!

HENRY. Thanks! Fine! [*He puts the bill in his pocket, slaps it and looks at the burglar with great satisfaction.*] Well! I don't mind telling you I'm mighty glad you dropped in!

THE BURGLAR. You ain't got nothing on me! This is the softest job I ever had!

HENRY. Yes, sir! I don't know what I'd have done without you! And just to show my appreciation . . . [*He takes out a flask.*] Here! Have a drink!

THE BURGLAR [*putting up his hand*]. Thanks! Never drink durin' business hours!

HENRY. Well! You've got the right idea! Neither do I! But I haven't got any business! [*He takes a long swig and then replaces the flask in his pocket.*] And now! You'd better run along! The wife'll be down soon, and I don't suppose you're anxious to meet her!

THE BURGLAR. Not for me, boss! [*Grinning at Henry innocently.*] But before I go . . . can I have my persuader back?

HENRY. Your revolver? I think *I'd* better keep that!

THE BURGLAR. Better not! It's against the law to have a gun!

HENRY. Ha! Ha! I suppose you've got a permit!

THE BURGLAR. Sure! From the president of our union!

HENRY [*amused*]. You have! Well then! Here it is!

[*He gives the burglar his gun.*]

THE BURGLAR. Thanks! You've forgot somethin' else, ain't you?

HENRY [*surprised*]. Something else?

THE BURGLAR. Yea! That hundred berries I just gave you! [*Sticking the gun in Henry's stomach.*] Hand it over, young fella!

HENRY [*reproachfully*]. Is that a nice thing to do? I ask you! Is that a nice thing to do?

THE BURGLAR. Huh! I ain't in a nice business! And I'm lettin' you off easy at that after you threatenin' me with a gun!

HENRY [*indicating the revolver*]. Look here! You don't think I'm scared of that toy, do you?

THE BURGLAR. You was when I came in!

HENRY. It was loaded then!

THE BURGLAR [*taking the gun from Henry's stomach and looking at it*]. Huh?

HENRY. If you hadn't been so interested in the contents of my safe, you might have noticed me taking the cartridges out a while ago!

THE BURGLAR [*pocketing the revolver*]. Well! You're a pretty smooth young fella, ain't you?

HENRY [*chestily*]. Yes! You'll have to get up earlier in the morning if you want to put anything over on me!

THE BURGLAR [*slyly*]. Yea! You must get up pretty early, boss! About twelve o'clock! Ha! Ha! [*Holding up his wrist and looking at a wrist watch.*] Well! I got some calls to make yet and I hate to keep people waitin'! [*He starts for the window.*] So long!

HENRY. So long! Drop in again some time! I may need you!

THE BURGLAR [*as he goes out the window*]. I may do that, boss . . . sooner than you expect!

[*He disappears. When he is gone, Henry hastens over to the window and calls out after him.*]

HENRY. Say! You big simp! Take another look at that gun! It's still loaded. [*He closes the window and chuckles to himself. Then he goes to the center of the room, his expression changing to a troubled one. He stands for a moment as though he were thinking hard what to do next. Finally he hurries to the hallway in the rear, where he gets a piece of rope. He returns and seats himself on a chair. He takes a handkerchief from his pocket and gags himself with it. Then with the rope he binds himself loosely to the chair. Having done this he starts stamping on the floor and cries out as loudly as he can through his gag*]: Izzie! Izzie!

[*After a moment Isabel, in a wrapping gown, enters hastily from the rear. She sees Henry with a cry and rushes over to him.*]

ISABEL. Good Heavens! Henry darling! What's happened? [*She starts releasing him.*]

HENRY [*feigning excitement*]. Oh, Izzie! There's been a burglar here!

ISABEL. A burglar!

HENRY. Yes! He . . . he pointed a big gun at me, bound me up and robbed the safe!

ISABEL [*hastening over to the safe*]. Oh! My Heavens! The safe!

HENRY [*as Isabel opens the safe*]. But . . . but he only took one bill, darling!

You . . . you see, my stamping on the floor scared him away!

ISABEL [*looking in the safe*]. Only one bill, Henry?

HENRY [*glibly*]. Yes! That's all he had time to take!

ISABEL [*looking at Henry impatiently*]. He took them all!

HENRY [*springing to his feet*]. What!

ISABEL [*looking about in the safe*]. There's not a bill left in the safe!

HENRY [*thunderstruck*]. My God! That burglar must have been a crook! [*Desperately to Isabel.*] I didn't see him take them, Izzie! Honest I didn't! How . . . how many bills were there?

ISABEL. About a hundred. . . .

HENRY [*horrified*]. About a hundred! Ten thousand dollars! Oh, by God! Now I'll have to go to work!

[*He falls into a chair.*]

ISABEL [*in a relieved tone*]. Thank goodness he didn't take the jewels! It was such a trouble having them made. . . . [*She gives a final look about the safe.*] And my papers all seem to be here. . . . [*She closes the safe and hastens to the table on the left. She pulls open a drawer and looks into it. She seems very much relieved, closes the drawer and turns to Henry.*] Did he take anything else?

HENRY [*springing to his feet again*]. Anything *else*? Isn't that enough! [*Walking about angrily.*] I must say, Izzie, you don't seem very worried over my loss!

ISABEL [*starting to laugh*]. I'm not! Really, it's funny, you know. . . .

HENRY [*looking at her in astonishment*]. Funny?

ISABEL. Yes! You see, Henry! Those bills were the stage money we were going to use in the Charity League Revue!

HENRY [*dumfounded*]. What!

ISABEL. Certainly! Do you think I'd keep any real money in the safe with you around?

HENRY. Izzie! There . . . there wasn't any *real* money in there at all?

ISABEL. Not a cent! [*Observing Henry, who is staggering.*] What's the matter with you, Henry! You look positively sick!

HENRY [*falling into a chair again*]. I am sick!

ISABEL [*impatiently*]. For Heaven's sake! Just because a burglar has held you up! I could understand it if he had gotten anything!

HENRY. That's just it! I mean. . . .

ISABEL [*anxiously*]. Did he take anything from you?

HENRY. From me! Ha! Ha! Don't make me laugh!

ISABEL. Then all he got was that worthless paper money! [*With a laugh.*] Really! It's a good joke on him, I think!

HENRY. Oh, yes! It's a great joke on the *burglar!* Ha! Ha! Ha!

ISABEL. And can you imagine his feelings when he finds out how he's been fooled?

HENRY. You bet I can! I wonder what *he'll* do with it!

ISABEL. Well! If he's clever enough, I suppose he'll get it all changed at different stores. . . .

HENRY [*startled*]. Say! Do you think he could?

ISABEL. I wouldn't be surprised! Those bills were very good imitations, you know. . . .

HENRY [*getting to his feet suddenly*]. Izzie! If you don't mind, I think I'll just put on my hat and run down to the corner drug store!

ISABEL. What for?

HENRY. I want to get a bill changed! A . . . a hundred dollar bill!

ISABEL [*astonished*]. Henry Dell! Where did you get a hundred dollar bill?

HENRY. I . . . I saved it up!

ISABEL. You've been saving money! What's the matter with you?

HENRY [*getting an inspiration*]. Izzie! Can't you guess?

ISABEL [*surprise and pleasure on her face*]. Henry! It's not. . . .

HENRY. Yes, darling! For your birthday!

ISABEL [*putting her arms around him and kissing him*]. Oh! You dear sweet boy! [*Then with a reproving look.*] But Henry! You shouldn't carry all your savings around in one big bill!

HENRY. I know, dearie! [*taking out the bill*] that's why I'm going down to the drug store to get this changed right now!

ISABEL [*starting to protest*]. But Henry. . . .

HENRY [*putting the bill back in his pocket and hastily picking up his hat and coat*]. I won't be a minute, Izzie!

And if anybody calls, tell them to wait!

ISABEL. Oh, very well!

[*Henry starts for the door. When he reaches it he hesitates for a moment, then turns to Isabel.*]

HENRY [*anxiously*]. Look here, Izzie! Have you any idea how long a term the burglar would get if they caught him passing that money?

ISABEL. Oh, I don't know . . . ten or twenty years!

HENRY [*dropping his hat and coat on a chair in dismay*]. Ten or twenty years?

ISABEL. How long did you think he'd get?

HENRY. Well, I was willing to take a chance on six months!

ISABEL. Six months? For passing counterfeit money? My dear boy! [*Observing Henry, who is pacing about agitatedly.*] Aren't you going to the drug store?

HENRY [*unhappily*]. No! I've changed my mind!

ISABEL [*looking at him impatiently*]. Well! I'm going to get dressed!

[*She goes to the table on the left, opens the drawer and takes a large purse out of it. Henry sees her take out the purse with astonishment.*]

HENRY [*his mouth opening*]. Say! Was your purse there all the time that I . . . I mean the burglar. . . .

ISABEL [*smiling at Henry*]. Yes! It's lucky he didn't think of looking there, wasn't it?

HENRY. Wa . . . was there much money in it?

ISABEL. Several hundred dollars!

HENRY [*astounded*]. Well, I'll be. . . .

[*He walks about, shaking his head.*]

ISABEL [*starting for the door in the rear*]. You see, I wanted to hide it away from you while I was out this afternoon, and I knew *you'd* never think of looking for it there, you stupid old thing!

HENRY [*walking about angrily*]. Oh, boy! Stupid is right! [*Isabel exits. As she does so Henry suddenly stops walking about. His eyes gleam with another idea. He hastens to the door in the rear and calls after Isabel.*] Oh, Izzie! Just a minute, will you?

ISABEL [*returning*]. What is it?

HENRY [*taking the bill out of his pocket again*]. Look here, Izzie! I . . .

I haven't felt comfortable since I've had this bill in my pocket and known that . . . that I ought to get it changed! Now, I don't want to ask the druggist to change it . . . he's a friend of mine! I mean I wouldn't like to ask him to change such a big bill! You know! [*Brightly.*] So I've got an idea, dearie! Since you've got all that money in your purse why can't *you* change it for me?

ISABEL. I?

HENRY [*looking at her askance*]. Sure! Why not? Huh?

ISABEL [*after a moment*]. Why certainly! I'll change it for you, Henry, if I can. . . .

HENRY [*triumphantly, while trying to look unconcerned about it*]. Will you, Izzie? Say! That's fine!

> [*Isabel opens her purse, takes out a roll of bills and starts counting them. Henry walks about, his eyes gleaming happily as he watches her*].

ISABEL [*looking up at Henry*]. Yes! I can change it, dear, easily! Give me your bill!

HENRY [*handing her the bill with an innocent smile*]. There you are! Darling!

ISABEL [*starting to hand Henry a lot of bills*]. I think there's a hundred dollars there. . . . [*Henry is about to take them when Isabel draws back her hand and looks at him suspiciously*]. Henry! you're not going to give this money to Mr. Baker!

HENRY [*earnestly*]. I should say not, dearie! Absolutely not!

ISABEL. You promise me?

HENRY. Izzie! Did I ever lie to you?

ISABEL [*handing him the bills*]. Oh, well! Here you are!

HENRY. Thanks, Izzie! Thanks. [*He counts the bills happily*]. And gosh! You don't know what a favor you're doing me!

ISABEL [*giving him a fond look*]. And Henry! Just because you remembered my birthday . . . I think *this* time I'll give you the money to pay Mr. Baker, too!

HENRY [*turning to her delightedly*]. Oh, Izzie! Honest! Will you?

ISABEL. Yes! [*She hands him back his bill.*] So you can keep your hundred-dollar bill!

HENRY [*taking the bill with a stung expression*]. But dearie! Don't you. . . don't you think I ought to have that in small bills, too? [*Handing her back the bill.*] Because I don't think Baker cares for bills like that either!

ISABEL [*counting out more bills and handing them to Henry*]. Very well! There you are!

HENRY [*taking them happily*]. Thanks, Izzie! Thanks!

ISABEL [*closing her purse*]. And now, Henry! You won't go and gamble that money all away, dear. . . .

HENRY. Not me! It was too hard to get!

ISABEL. And remember! You've promised me! You won't ever play poker again!

HENRY [*holding up his hand*]. Never again!

ISABEL [*happily*]. That's a dear boy! [*Kissing him tenderly.*] And it *was* sweet of you to think of my birthday!

HENRY [*shaking his head*]. I'll say it was! [*Isabel goes to the door in the rear, smiling at Henry in a pleased way as she does so, and exits. When she is gone Henry puts the money in his pocket and starts walking about, whistling cheerfully. Then the telephone rings again. Henry looks at it in surprise, goes over and takes up the receiver.*] Hello! Who? [*In a tone of surprise.*] Say! I thought you were on your way over here! What? You changed your mind? [*Disgustedly.*] Well, my God! What? Oh, nothing! Nothing! Never mind! You'll see me in the morning, will you? [*In a decided voice.*] You will not! Say! I'll be over at the club in ten minutes! And listen, Baker, old man! Hold a place open for me! I'm playing in that game!

> [*He hangs up the receiver, picks up his hat and coat and hastens for the door.*]

> [*Curtain.*]

WINNERS ALL

A Farce

By Ida Lublenski Ehrlich

CHARACTERS

GRACE. *Mary Motsinger*
FRED. *Bill Young*
STELLA. *Betty Jane Bagby*
ANDY. *Ed Bean*

WINNERS ALL

A FARCE   By IDA LUBLENSKI EHRLICH

[*Grace and Fred have come to spend a week-end with Stella and Andy.*

As the curtain rises Grace and Stella are discovered sitting on a sofa. Stella is knitting. Grace is weeping.]

STELLA [*with a cynical smile*]. You'll be needing glasses soon if you don't stop that everlasting crying.

GRACE. I can't help it. It breaks my heart.

STELLA. Something to break your heart over! A quarrel with your husband! Why, if every woman's heart broke every time she quarreled with her husband this world would be "Heart-Break House" indeed. With apologies to Bernard Shaw.

GRACE. But why should we quarrel so much when we love each other so dearly?

STELLA. That's the trouble. You love each other too much. Love is very jealous and very selfish. We demand everything from those we love—and rightly so. Give all, get all. People who don't love each other are not so particular.

GRACE. To hear you talk one would think that you didn't love your husband.

STELLA [*calmly*]. I don't.

GRACE [*aghast*]. You don't? You mean to say you don't love Andy?

STELLA. No. I do not love Andy any more.

GRACE. Good God! Since when? What has happened?

STELLA. It's a long time now. I used to love him so that I demanded perfection on every little point. Since Andy was no angel we quarreled continually. Life was unbearable. More than once I wanted to leave him.

GRACE. To leave him!

STELLA. I couldn't do that. But I felt the quarreling had to stop. So I began to use tact. I let him have his own way and maneuvered so that I had mine in the end. He thought he was

keeping me in my place when all the time he was dancing to my tune. I began to despise him for letting me play with him in that way and finally I ceased to love him altogether. You know when tact comes in the door, love flies out of the window.

GRACE. How horrible!

STELLA [*shrugging her shoulders*]. I admit it isn't love's young dream, but it is peaceful.

GRACE. But you seem so devoted, so affectionate. No one would believe that you didn't love him. Andy doesn't know it, does he?

STELLA. Andy least of all.

GRACE. How can you be such a hypocrite!

STELLA. It's a self-preservation, my dear. I'd be dead and gone now if I had kept up that quarreling these ten years. As it is, I look positively younger than I did five years ago.

GRACE. You really do, and I've often wondered how you managed it.

STELLA. Peace! that's my secret. And let me tell you, you've aged five years in this one year of your married life.

GRACE [*horrified*]. I have?

STELLA [*emphatically*]. Yes, you have. What with your red eyes, your swollen nose from constant crying, your gloomy face—you'll be an old woman in no time.

GRACE. Oh, my God!

STELLA. I advise you to take a leaf out of my book. Learn to manage your husband as I manage Andy. If he doesn't want you to have the dress, say you don't want it. You'll get it in the end if you do as I do. Last week we saw a fur coat. It was a thousand dollars, a beauty. I knew that we could afford it so I told Andy that I wanted it. Did he say yes? Of course not. There was another one for five hundred and he said that that was good enough. Did I argue

121

about it with him? Of course not. But I'll get the coat, you wait and see. Deep down in his heart Andy really wants me to have it. Men like their wives to have what they want, but when a woman asks for it there's something in a man that makes him say "NO."

GRACE. I believe you're right.

STELLA. Of course I'm right. Now you come along with me and put some powder on your nose. I wouldn't be seen with such a nose, love or no love.

[*They go out. Fred and Andy come in.*]

ANDY. Well, old man, you certainly look as though hard times hit your way. What's the matter now?

FRED [*gloomily*]. The same old thing. Quarrel—quarrel—quarrel. It's a dog's life.

ANDY. You're a fool. You don't know how to manage your wife. Grace is a dear little thing. They're all dear little things, but if you'll let them they'll walk over you rough-shod. You've got to hold them down. They'll love you all the more for it. I've had experience. I know.

FRED. It's easy for you to talk. You have a perfect wife.

ANDY. You think so? [*Chuckling.*] Well, that's my doing. Stella is as good as gold. But she wasn't always like that, I assure you. We used to quarrel all the time. If I refused her anything she would fly into a rage. But that's all changed now. I put a stop to that.

FRED. How did you put a stop to it?

ANDY [*with the assurance of victory*]. I wouldn't stand for it, that's all. If I said "NO," it was "NO" and that's all there was to it. And she loves me just the same, more, I think. Sometimes I positively think she is sweeter to me now than she used to be.

FRED. You're lucky.

ANDY. Why, only last week we saw a fur coat—a thousand dollars. A nice coat, I admit, but a lot of money. Of course I've been making plenty. There's no reason why she can't have it. In fact, she looked stunning in it. I liked to see it on her. But when she asked for it I said "NO." Did she make a fuss? Not a bit of it. In former years she'd have chewed my ears off. [*Laughs.*] And because she was so sweet about it I have a surprise for her. Hush! Here she comes. [*Grace and Stella come in.*] Hello, Grace.

GRACE. How do you do, Andy?

[*She does not notice Fred, but passes him and stands stiffly at the other end of the room.*]

STELLA [*runs to Andy affectionately*]. Good evening, dearie.

[*Kisses him.*]

ANDY [*throws a wink to Fred*]. Good evening, girlie.

STELLA. Good evening, Fred.

FRED. Good evening.

STELLA [*anxiously to Andy*]. How is your head? Does it still ache?

ANDY. Not a bit. It is all better.

STELLA. I'm so glad. [*Kisses him again.*] Here, give me that. [*She takes his hat.*] I made something you like for dinner.

ANDY. Yum—yum—

STELLA. And, darling, I ran down to that store again and told them to send that five-hundred-dollar coat. It really is a beauty. I'm glad you decided not to get the other. A thousand dollars is a ridiculous price for a coat. I like the cheaper one just as well.

ANDY. Well, you can call them up again and tell them not to send it.

STELLA [*meekly*]. Why, do you think that's too expensive also, dear?

ANDY [*grandly*]. No, I don't, but the fact is, I've already bought the thousand-dollar one.

STELLA [*feigning stunned surprise*]. You bought the thousand-dollar coat!

ANDY [*thoroughly pleased with the effect he has created*]. I thought you looked rather sweet in it.

STELLA [*still breathless with surprise, to Grace*]. A thousand-dollar coat. What do you think of Andy?

GRACE. He's a dear.

STELLA [*to Andy*]. You're sure it isn't too expensive, dear?

ANDY [*pinching her cheek*]. Nothing is too expensive for you.

STELLA. And you've actually bought it?

ANDY. It's bought and paid for. They'll send it up in the morning.

STELLA. You are a darling! [*She gives him a hug. As they embrace Stella winks broadly to Grace who is behind Andy. Andy winks to Fred who is behind Stella.*] Well, I'll telephone about the coat. I don't want them to send both. Come, dear.

[*Stella and Andy go out, leaving Grace and Fred standing at opposite ends of the room. There is a moment's silence. Then after a struggle with herself, Grace completely changes her manner.*]

GRACE [*cordially*]. Wasn't it nice of Stella to want to get the cheaper coat?

FRED [*surprised that she talks to him, and in such cordial tones*]. Yes—yes—

GRACE. It's lovely how she gives in to him—willing to do without when he says "NO" and ready to take when he says "YES." I'm going to try to be like her.

FRED [*delighted*]. Really? You see how pleasant it makes things.

GRACE [*smiling*]. Very well, dear. We'll not quarrel again.

FRED [*rushing to embrace her*]. Sweetheart.

GRACE [*coldly—holding him away*]. Hold on.

FRED. What's the matter? Can't I kiss you?

GRACE. No.

FRED. Can't I kiss you when we've made up?

GRACE. I said we wouldn't quarrel again. I didn't say anything about kissing. [*Pause.*] You might as well know. I won't be a hypocrite like Stella. I don't love you any more.

FRED [*thunderstruck*]. You don't love me any more?

GRACE. No.

FRED. But a little while ago—since when?

GRACE. Our quarreling, your constantly opposing me, has killed my love for you. Hereafter I'll be an obedient wife but not a loving one. About that dress, we'll consider the matter closed. I don't want it. The victory is yours.

FRED. But if you don't love me. . . . It's a hell of a victory!

GRACE [*shrugging her shoulders*]. You can't eat your cake and have it too.

FRED [*amazed at her coldness*]. And you tell me this so calmly?

GRACE. I'm not going to grieve. I'm learning from Stella.

FRED. What has Stella to do with this?

GRACE. Stella has taught me how to be happy though married. Let your husband have his own way even if you must stop loving him to do it.

FRED. But Stella loves Andy.

GRACE. She doesn't.

FRED. She doesn't love Andy? How do you know?

GRACE. She told me herself.

FRED. I don't believe it. I never saw a sweeter, more loving wife than Stella.

GRACE. Camouflage, that's what it is, to cover her indifference to him—to keep things sailing smoothly. And it's good business. She gets her own way, too.

FRED. But Andy thinks. . . .

GRACE [*scornfully*]. Andy thinks! Andy is as blind as a bat. He thinks he is the winner. If he only knew.

FRED. I would never have believed it of Stella—to be such a hypocrite.

GRACE. Why not? If Andy doesn't know the gold from the dross.

FRED. And that's how you're going to live with me?

GRACE. I can't be such a hypocrite. I can't disguise my feelings to such an extent. I'll be above board with you. I don't love you. [*Putting on a sweet smile.*] But I'll be sweet and lovely to you. I'll obey you in everything. [*Andy appears in the doorway and hears the last words.*] I'm going to Stella. I'll be with you in a moment—[*with mocking emphasis*]—darling!

[*She sails out leaving Fred crestfallen. Andy comes forward with a pleasant smile.*]

ANDY [*slapping Fred on the back*]. Congratulations, old man. You certainly managed it quickly. You're a winner!

FRED. Some winner!

ANDY. Say, you don't seem to be very happy about it.

FRED. What's there to be happy about? I don't want her obedience without her love.

ANDY. What do you mean without her love?

FRED. Grace doesn't love me any more.

ANDY. Who says so?

FRED. Grace said so herself and I believe what she says.

ANDY. Nonsense! She's just saying it to tease you. Look at me.

FRED [*irritated by his boasting*]. You needn't be so cocky about yourself. You're not such a winner either. Stella obeys you but she doesn't love you.

ANDY. What's this? Your little joke?

FRED. It's no joke. Grace told me just now. Stella told Grace that she stopped loving you long ago.

ANDY [*blankly*]. Stella stopped loving me? But that's impossible. You saw for yourself her way with me.

FRED. All put on — hypocrisy — woman's guile to delude the trusting male.

ANDY. I don't believe it.

[*Grace comes in.*]

GRACE. Oh, have you disillusioned him, Fred?

FRED. He won't believe it.

GRACE [*to Andy*]. You can believe it, I assure you.

ANDY. But why? Why does she have to play the hypocrite with me?

GRACE. So that she can have peace. Formerly when she wanted her way she had to quarrel all the time. She loved you and it hurt her to think of your opposing her. But now she lets you do as you please. She doesn't quarrel with you.

ANDY. We haven't quarreled for years.

GRACE. You couldn't get her to quarrel with you. She doesn't love you.

ANDY [*positively limp at the thought*]. Good God!

FRED [*maliciously*]. You're the winner.

ANDY [*piteously*]. But she's so sweet. I can't believe it's hypocrisy. She does everything I want so pleasantly.

GRACE. That's tact. Formerly her straightforward demands led to constant quarreling. Now she uses tact and gets what she wants in peace.

ANDY. We certainly have had peace. But who wants peace at such a price?

GRACE. Well, she'll never quarrel with you.

ANDY [*desperately*]. I'll make her. I'll make her quarrel with me.

[*Stella comes in smiling.*]

STELLA. Oh, you're here, dear. I called up the store. I'm all impatience to see that coat.

[*There is a strained pause for a moment.*]

GRACE [*to Fred*]. Come, dear, I want to show you that picture. [*As Stella raises an inquiring eyebrow at her tone, Grace whispers to her.*] I'm taking your advice.

FRED. I'm coming.

STELLA. Don't be long. Dinner will be ready in five minutes. [*Grace and Fred go out. Andy fumbles nervously with his watch chain. Stella sits down and knits. She smiles to herself.*] I'm so excited about that coat. You're a dear. I'm so glad that I made your favorite pie for dinner.

ANDY [*with a growl*]. Hang dinner.

STELLA. Aren't you hungry, dear? Huckleberry pie will tempt you.

ANDY [*brutally*]. Your pies aren't any good.

STELLA. No? Why, I thought you liked them. You always seemed to enjoy them.

ANDY. One wants to be polite.

[*Waits for her to flare up.*]

STELLA [*sweetly*]. How considerate you are, darling!

ANDY [*bites his lip and tries again*]. You're not much of a cook, you know.

STELLA [*meekly*]. And I try so hard. I'm sorry, dear.

ANDY. That dress you're wearing— it's about time you shed it.

STELLA. Why, dearie, don't you like it?

ANDY. It makes you look like the last rose of summer.

STELLA [*agreeably*]. I'll go and change directly. It won't take me a minute.

ANDY. And while we're on the subject, I would suggest, your hair—

STELLA. Yes?

ANDY. I think it would be more proper if you wore it a little less—[*He hangs fire.*]—a little less—er—girlish.

STELLA. Why, I thought you liked it that way.

ANDY. I did, when we were married. But that was ten years ago. No, so simply done, it looks as though you were trying to look younger than you are.

STELLA [*reflectively*]. Um—I had thought of changing it—of piling it high on my head. Yes, I think you're right, dear.

[*She continues to knit, occasionally she smiles to herself. Andy watches her, furious that he cannot ruffle her good-natured way of receiving his criticism.*]

ANDY. Stella, do you love me?

STELLA [*absently*]. Yes, dear?

ANDY. You're not listening.

STELLA. Excuse me, dear. I was counting my stitches. What did you say?

ANDY. Do you love me?

STELLA. Of course I do, darling.

ANDY [*bursting out*]. Stella. . . .

STELLA [*solicitously*]. I'm sure something has upset you. I must get that powder for your nerves, or you'll not be able to eat a bite of dinner.

[*She gets up, gives him a kiss on the forehead and goes out of the room. Andy remains standing staring after her. Grace and Fred come in. They are reconciled and happy.*]

FRED. We've made up, old man. [*Seeing his dejection.*] Why, what's the matter?

ANDY. She wouldn't quarrel with me.

GRACE. You see? It's just as I said.

ANDY. I criticized her cooking, her dress, her hair—

GRACE. Well, what did she say?

ANDY. Never batted an eyelash.

FRED. There must be something that will rouse her.

ANDY. The things I said to her—another woman would have killed me outright. All she said was [*He imitates her sweet manner.*] "Yes, dear."

GRACE. Then there's only one thing left—that last resort. Jealousy. You must make her jealous.

ANDY. What is there for her to be jealous of?

GRACE. Another woman.

ANDY. But there isn't any other woman.

GRACE. You must pretend there is.

ANDY [*with extreme distaste*]. None of that! I draw the line there. I won't have anything to do with "another woman" business.

GRACE. It's your only chance of finding out whether there is a spark of affection left in her heart for you. If you love her—

ANDY. Of course I love her.

FRED. Then play the game. [*With a touch of Andy's former manner.*] You may win out after all.

ANDY [*with a gleam of hope*]. Do you think so?

GRACE. Many a woman thought she had ceased to care for her husband until she discovered that he had stopped loving her.

ANDY. I'll do anything you say.

GRACE. You go with Fred and get all spruced up for going out.

ANDY. But I'm not going out.

GRACE [*impatiently*]. You're just pretending to go out.

FRED. Make believe you have a date with a peach. [*Slaps him on the back.*] Cheer up—look like a sport—like a gay dog.

ANDY [*gloomily*]. I feel like a dog all right, but not like a gay one. What am I to say? What must I do?

FRED. I'll give you a few points. Come on.

GRACE. I'll stay here and prepare Stella. And remember, don't weaken, until she says positively that she loves you.

[*Andy and Fred go out of the room. Stella comes in with the powder.*]

STELLA. Where's Andy? I have a powder for him. [*She sees the angry and disgusted expression which Grace has assumed.*] Why, what's the matter?

GRACE. The beast!

STELLA. Who's a beast?

GRACE. I never would have believed it. Not of Andy.

STELLA. What's the matter with Andy?

GRACE. Disgusting! That's what I call it.

STELLA. What are you talking about? What's disgusting?

GRACE. Well, it's a good thing you don't love him any more.

STELLA. Why is it a good thing?

GRACE. The sly fox. Buys you a coat for a thousand dollars when all the time —conscience salve, I call it.

STELLA. Conscience salve? Will you tell me what you're talking about?

GRACE. I just overheard a little talk between Fred and Andy.

STELLA. Yes.

GRACE. Andy's carrying on with another woman.

STELLA. What?

GRACE. Disgusting, isn't it?

STELLA. I don't believe it.

GRACE. It's true enough. I heard what he said. And when I spoke to Fred—

STELLA [*breathlessly*]. What did he say?

GRACE. At first he wouldn't say anything. You know how men stick by on another. But I finally wormed it out of him. Oh, it's true enough.

STELLA [*sinks into a chair*]. Good Lord!

GRACE. It's a mercy that you don't love him any more. At least you are spared the pain of being betrayed by one you love. But I never would have believed it of Andy.

STELLA. The hypocrite! Pretending all the time that he loved me so.

GRACE. Surprising you with an expensive coat.

STELLA. I don't see how he's managed to go philandering. He's always at home after business hours.

GRACE. When men want to do such things they find time. They're devils.

STELLA. So Andy is going to the Primrose Path. [*Pause.*] Well, he won't get away with it.

GRACE. What do you care? You don't love him. [*Stella does not answer immediately.*] Do you?

STELLA [*mechanically*]. No, I don't love him. But I won't let him get away with it just the same. [*Viciously.*] I won't let him imagine that he can fool me.

GRACE. Are you going to make a scene? Hush! Here he comes. I'd better go.

[*She goes out left as Andy comes in right. He is in evening dress, and is fussing with his tie. He hums "Just a little love—" Stella pretends to be engrossed in her knitting.*]

STELLA. I brought your powder, dear.

ANDY. I don't need it. I feel fine. [*Struggling with his tie.*] Can you help me with this?

STELLA. Why, you're in evening dress. I wasn't expecting to have to dress up for dinner to-night.

ANDY. I won't be home for dinner.

STELLA. Why, where are you going?

ANDY. Out.

[*Hums the love ditty.*]

STELLA. But Grace and Fred?

ANDY. They're old friends. They won't mind.

STELLA. But dinner—

ANDY [*smiling to himself*]. Don't want dinner.

STELLA. I made huckleberry pie especially for you.

ANDY. You eat my portion.

[*Pause.*]

STELLA. I suppose you must go?

ANDY. Yes.

STELLA. Business?

ANDY. No.

[*Smiles as he hums.*]

STELLA [*fighting to keep her rising anger down*]. Where did you say you were going?

ANDY. I didn't say.

[*Stella bites her lips. Her needles click angrily.*]

STELLA [*suddenly*]. Andy, where are you going?

ANDY. I told you—out.

STELLA. Can't you tell me where you're going?

ANDY. I can, but you don't want me to.

STELLA [*bursting out*]. Andy, you're going to meet another woman.

ANDY. Well, suppose I am.

STELLA. You don't deny it?

ANDY. Why should I deny it?

STELLA [*covers her face with her hands*]. OH, oh!

ANDY [*smiles for an instant, then as she uncovers her face he frowns*]. What's the matter with you? I haven't seen you so upset for years.

STELLA. I didn't know that you went with other women.

ANDY. Didn't know that your Andy was a gay dog.

STELLA. I thought you loved me. You made me believe that you loved me. How could you be such a hypocrite?

ANDY. When it comes to hypocrisy you can hold your own very well.

STELLA. What do you mean?

ANDY. What about your pretending to be a loving wife when you stopped loving me long ago?

STELLA [*gasps*]. You know? How do you know?

ANDY. Do you think I'm blind? Don't you think I saw right through you? Well, I did, my dear.

STELLA. But you never said anything.

ANDY. What was there to say? Did you think I was going to beg you to love me? You played your game and I played mine. [*Smiles.*] Oh, indeed, I saw through you, with your sweet obedience, your tact. . . .

STELLA. But I never went with anybody else. I never looked at another man.

ANDY. I wouldn't have cared if you had. Look at a hundred if you like.

STELLA. It's nothing to you?

ANDY [*lying bravely*]. Not a darn.

STELLA [*weakly*]. Oh!

ANDY [*fussing with his tie*]. So that's that!

[*Hums.*]

STELLA [*furious at his composure*]. You ought to be ashamed of yourself, Andrew Clemens—

ANDY [*laughing*]. That sounds like the days of yore. Andrew Clemens! Whenever we quarreled you called me Andrew Clemens.

STELLA [*loudly*]. I repeat, you ought to be ashamed of yourself.

[*Grace and Fred come in.*]

GRACE. What's the matter?

FRED. What's happened?

ANDY. I do believe Stella is jealous.

GRACE. Jealous?

ANDY [*whispers to her*]. It's going fine.

GRACE [*whispers*]. Keep it up.

FRED [*to Stella*]. What are you jealous about?

STELLA. Andy is going out to meet another woman. He admits he's been going with another woman.

GRACE. Why, Stella, I thought. . . .

STELLA. Pshaw! What you thought!

ANDY. You're a dog in the manger, Stella. I get no love from you, but you don't want me to go elsewhere.

STELLA. If I did love you would you be willing not to go with that other woman?

ANDY [*delighted at the promise in her question.*] Why, if. . . .

GRACE [*pulling his sleeve, whispers*]. Don't weaken.

ANDY. What's the use of talking "Ifs."

[*He slips his coat on.*]

STELLA. Don't go, Andy. Maybe. . . .

ANDY. Maybe what? [*Waits for her to speak. Looks at his watch.*] Heavens! I'll be late.

STELLA. You're not going, Andy.

ANDY. What's to prevent me?

STELLA. I will. I won't let you go.

[*Grace and Fred are delighted at Stella's anger. Behind Stella's back Grace waves to Andy to continue with a bold front.*]

ANDY. Now, Stella, don't be foolish. [*He makes for the door. She quickly gets there first and stands with her back to it.*] Over my dead body.

ANDY. Well, I declare. Any one would think that you still cared for me.

[*Stella suddenly sinks into a chair and covers her face with her hands to hide her tears. The other three exchange delighted smiles. Andy takes a step toward Stella. Grace pulls him back.*]

STELLA. Andy, dear—

ANDY. Yes?

STELLA. I'm sorry—I—[*With a fresh outburst.*] Oh, Andy dear—

[*Andy is ready to rush toward her, but Grace still holds him back.*]

ANDY [*in a whisper*]. Say, what more do you want?

GRACE [*whispers*]. She must say that she loves you.

STELLA. I'm sorry that you don't love me any more.

ANDY. Why should you be sorry?

STELLA. Because—because—

ANDY. Because what?

STELLA. I love you, Andy.

ANDY [*overjoyed*]. Do you really?

GRACE. Oh, Stella. After what you said to me, you must be mistaken.

STELLA. I'm not mistaken. And dear, if you leave me you'll break my heart. Please forgive me and love me again.

ANDY. Oh, my darling! [*He embraces her.*] Sweetheart! I've never loved any one but you.

STELLA. And all this?

ANDY. Grace's scheme to find out whether you still loved me. It was a fine trap and you were well caught. I'm sure of you now.

[*Kisses her again.*]

STELLA. Well, let's go in to dinner. Oh, by the way, Andy, I saw a lovely hat that will go wonderfully well with that coat. It's only twenty-five dollars.

ANDY. Only twenty-five dollars. . . .

FRED [*laughing*]. There it goes again!

GRACE [*turning on him*]. What are you laughing at? Is it a joke to want a pretty hat? I suppose when I ask for one. . . .

STELLA [*to Andy*]. Are you going to begin to fuss again every time I want something?

FRED [*to Grace*]. But I thought you said. . . .

ANDY. You know I don't like. . . .

[*Both couples quarrel.*]

[*Curtain.*]

TWO PASSENGERS FOR CHELSEA

A COMEDY

BY OSCAR W. FIRKINS

CHARACTERS

MR. WILLIAM BINGHAM BARING
    [*heir to the Ashburton peerage*].
LADY HARRIET BARING [*his wife*].
JANE WELSH CARLYLE.
THOMAS CARLYLE.
GIUSEPPE MAZZINI.
ALFRED TENNYSON.
RICHARD MONCKTON MILNES.
TRAVERS MILDMAN.
CHARLES BULLER.
FOOTMAN.

Reprinted from *The Cornhill Magazine*, London, by special permission of the author.

TWO PASSENGERS FOR CHELSEA

A COMEDY

By OSCAR W. FIRKINS

[*The action takes place at Addiscombe Farm, a Baring estate in the Croydon suburb of London, between ten and half-past eleven of a bright May morning in the year 1847. The morning room at Addiscombe Farm, on which the curtain rises, is large and long, furnished in dark oak, with pictures and bronzes. The middle section, which is frowned upon by a huge old fireplace and chimneypiece in the back wall, is somber enough to be just perceptibly avoided by the guests, but the two ends of the room are very cheerful. That at the spectator's right looks out from the deep recesses of a sixteenth-century bow window upon a broad sweep of undulating landscape, while the view to the left is stopped by garden trees and shrubs in the luxuriance of bright leaf and early blossom. The entrances are in the back wall near the corners, right and left. At the left entrance Jane Carlyle appears, followed by Thomas.*]

JANE CARLYLE. Thomas, you shouldn't have eaten that cherry tart.

CARLYLE. At great houses, my dear, one eats the wrong thing while one waits for the right one. At the moment nothing was in sight but cherry tart. The edible universe was reduced for the time being to cherry tart and I—I was hungry.

[*He takes easy chair, left.*]

JANE CARLYLE [*at the window, left, looking out*]. Thomas, save the universe for Cheyne Row. I am thinking of your stomach.

CARLYLE. I was thinking of my hunger.

JANE CARLYLE. That is unimportant. With Cerberus in a man's inside—

CARLYLE. They fed honey cakes, you know, to Cerberus.

JANE CARLYLE. I know—when they wanted to go down into hell.

CARLYLE. Ye know the classics—to their depths, Jane.

JANE CARLYLE. As for visiting hell, Thomas, I need no help from the classics. I can go down there in my own person —or in yours.

CARLYLE [*not ungenially*]. We have had our travels, Jeannie—in all quarters.

JANE CARLYLE [*hands on chair-back, facing Thomas*]. And I have to leave you here to contend all by yourself with the enticements of cherry tart and—

CARLYLE. And what?

JANE CARLYLE [*repressing an impulse to specify*]. Nothing else. Cherry tart is quite enough for a feeble man like you to contend with. [*With a slightly noticeable carelessness.*] You *are* staying?

CARLYLE. Perhaps. She wishes it.

JANE CARLYLE [*with pointed innocence*]. She?

CARLYLE [*falling, as often, into voluntary dialect*]. Dinna play the fool, Jane. It's a part Nature has not qualified ye for.

JANE CARLYLE [*very urbanely*]. I understand, my dear. There is a time in a man's relations with a woman when "She" becomes a proper name. But I didn't know you'd quite reached that point with Lady Harriet.

CARLYLE. As for that, there's a point in a man's relations with a woman when the pronoun "She" becomes a coronet. Ye should know that yourself.

[*He speaks bluffly, as if to excuse the blandness of the words.*]

JANE CARLYLE. Thank you, Thomas. I begin to think cherry tart agrees with you.

CARLYLE. She wants *you* to stay, too.

JANE CARLYLE. She? [*Feigning to bethink herself.*] Oh, yes. But I really must go back to Chelsea, that is, if I can find a carriage, or a dogcart, or a wheelbarrow to take me to the station. One can trust to nothing in a house like this. They put heliotropes in your bedroom and forget the soap.

CARLYLE. Ay, ay, giddypates, feather-heads, all of them.

[*Enters Footman, right, with the "Times."*]

FOOTMAN [*offering paper to Jane Carlyle*]. Times, Madam?

[*He goes out.*]

JANE CARLYLE. Will you have the *Times*, Thomas?

CARLYLE [*reaching for it*]. Why not?

JANE CARLYLE. Because you never read it at Chelsea—in the morning.

CARLYLE. A man's mornings in his own house are serious, Jane, but here! —the *Times* fits like a knicknack on an *étagère*. Besides, it shuts out the company. Is that somebody coming?

[*He hastily screens his face with the unfolded "Times."*]

JANE CARLYLE [*seating herself near Thomas, and speaking low*]. It is Mr. Travers Mildmay.

[*Carlyle mutters something between a grunt and a moan. Enter, at right, Mr. Travers Mildmay, young, scrupulously dressed, sometimes tongue-tied, sometimes blunt.*]

TRAVERS MILDMAY. Good morning, Mrs. Carlyle. [*Jane Carlyle bows graciously*]. Good morning, sir. [*Carlyle growls an inarticulate response.*] A fine day.

CARLYLE. Fire-new from the old mint.

TRAVERS MILDMAY [*at a loss*]. Sir?

CARLYLE. The morning's a coin, I say, sterling metal, with the king's head stamped on it.

TRAVERS MILDMAY [*still at a loss*]. I suppose so.

JANE CARLYLE. You must excuse my husband, Mr. Mildmay. It isn't insanity; it's cherry tart. He has had too good a breakfast.

TRAVERS MILDMAY. Does that make him. . . .

JANE CARLYLE. Yes, it makes him lyrical. Let us hope that poetry will be the only consequence. At home, now, where he eats bread and butter, he is fairly rational.

TRAVERS MILDMAY. I should enjoy talking to literary men—if they'd only talk like other people.

JANE CARLYLE. Try him before breakfast, Mr. Mildmay.

TRAVERS MILDMAY. The breakfasts here are very irregular.

JANE CARLYLE. There is system under it, Mr. Mildmay. Each rank breakfasts at its own hour. The peasantry break their fast at nine.

CARLYLE [*not to Mildmay, but dispersedly to the walls and furniture*]. That's for me. She's a doctor's lass.

JANE CARLYLE. The commoners breakfast at half-past nine; the minor gentry at a quarter-past ten; and the earls and marquises at eleven. The earliest arrivals in England come last to the breakfast room. [*Demurely.*] Have you breakfasted, Mr. Mildmay?

TRAVERS MILDMAY. Half an hour ago.

CARLYLE [*in a moment's truce with Travers Mildmay*]. That puts ye down with us.

TRAVERS MILDMAY [*with an air of achievement*]. That's high enough.

CARLYLE [*again putting up the "Times" as a breastwork*]. Humph!

TRAVERS MILDMAY [*glancing out of the window*]. Mr. Tennyson is coming in.

JANE CARLYLE. Is Mr. Tennyson up?

TRAVERS MILDMAY. Yes. He breakfasted with me.

CARLYLE. Another peasant, Jane.

JANE CARLYLE. Oh, we can't hold Mr. Tennyson to any rule. Poets are the most simple-hearted creatures. For them morning begins at daybreak.

[*Enter, at left, Alfred Tennyson, thirty-eight years old, large, a little stooping, lazily majestic, good-humoredly saturnine, with a lounging stateliness of gait. He comes over to Jane Carlyle and Mildmay, exchanging nods of succinct cordiality with Carlyle.*]

ALFRED TENNYSON [*to Jane Carlyle*]. Good morning.

JANE CARLYLE. Good morning, Mr. Tennyson. You come from the garden, I see. Have you been teaching the thrushes music?

ALFRED TENNYSON. No. [*Pause.*] I should as soon think of teaching—felicity—to Mrs. Carlyle.

[*He has, in the slow utterance of this compliment, the effect of a half-skilled navigator bringing to port*] *a heavy cargo through a choppy sea.*]

JANE CARLYLE. You are turning courtier, too?

CARLYLE [*sunk in his chair and in the "Times."*] His pension has corrupted him.

ALFRED TENNYSON [*who has seated himself, while Mildmay, feeling a little neglected, moves off to the other end of the room*]. You know who got me that pension?

CARLYLE. How should I know who gives pensions?

ALFRED TENNYSON [*in his ruminative bass*]. You know Richard Milnes, don't you?

CARLYLE [*the "Times" on his knees*]. Ay, I know Milnes, God forgive me for including such a popinjay in my acquaintance.

ALFRED TENNYSON [*fixing his eyes on Carlyle*]. Who spoke to Milnes?

CARLYLE [*letting the paper fall to the ground*]. Who spoke to Milnes? Heavens, man, do you think I keep a register of all the simpletons in the British Isles under my forehead?

JANE CARLYLE. Don't mind him, Mr. Tennyson. That is just his way of saying that Milnes is a very decent fellow, and so he is.

[*Enter, at left, Richard Milnes, well dressed, smiling, with a social ease that finds vent alternately in stingless cynicism and unfeigned kindness.*]

RICHARD MILNES. Who is that saying that I am a very decent fellow?

CARLYLE. Not me, Richard, God be praised! I ha'ena that load upon my conscience.

RICHARD MILNES. It wasn't your voice, I think, Tennyson.

ALFRED TENNYSON [*sincerely.*] It wasn't my voice, Milnes; though it expressed my feeling.

RICHARD MILNES. Then it comes home to you, Mrs. Carlyle.

JANE CARLYLE. I was just explaining to Mr. Tennyson that my husband has his own way of expressing fondness. When he says: "The devil damn thee black, thou cream-faced loon" all he means is: "Sit down, my dear fellow, and have another pipe."

CARLYLE. D'ye hear what comes frae the creature? And men marry the jades,

knowing all the while that they have tongues!

[*He resumes the "Times" as if in renunciation of human society from that time forward.*]

JANE CARLYLE. Sit down, Mr. Milnes, unless you want to go into the garden. Mr. Tennyson has been out already listening to the thrushes.

ALFRED TENNYSON [*simply*]. I went out to smoke.

JANE CARLYLE [*with a disdainful gesture*]. Ah, these poets! Their trade is disenchantment.

RICHARD MILNES. I know Lady Harriet is inexorable on tobacco. But I will sit down, Mrs. Carlyle, since I don't feel any great need either of smoke or thrushes at this moment.

[*He takes a chair.*]

JANE CARLYLE. You look ridiculously cheerful. I believe you slept last night.

RICHARD MILNES. I did. My sleep is masterly.

JANE CARLYLE [*with velvety satire*]. Each of us has his accomplishment, Mr. Milnes.

RICHARD MILNES. Thank you. Are you learning the art of paying compliments from your husband?

[*They both glance at the "Times" behind which Carlyle is ambushed.*]

JANE CARLYLE. No, my wickedness is all original, a poor thing, but mine own. [*She observes the "Times" narrowly.*] My dear, you are reading that paper upside down.

CARLYLE. It's every bit as sensible that way as the ither.

JANE CARLYLE [*surprised into familiarity.*] Milnes, I verily believe he put that paper down and took it up wrong side first for the express purpose of making that remark.

[*They wait for a retort, but Carlyle is, or seems, oblivious.*]

RICHARD MILNES [*after a pause, in a low tone, which escapes the confidential*]. Don't you think that Mr. Carlyle reads the world much as he is now reading the *Times?* He holds it upside down and finds it nonsense.

JANE CARLYLE. Exactly. And Mr. Carlyle means to turn the world upside down and find the sense in it.

RICHARD MILNES. The rest of us find it fairly sensible as it is.

JANE CARLYLE. That is because you

are standing on your heads to read it. You don't expect Mr. Carlyle to stand on his head, do you?

RICHARD MILNES [*laughing*]. No, we don't expect that.

[*Enter, at right, Lady Harriet Baring, a regal woman, with a fine, dashing geniality, convertible at the shortest notice into authority or disdain.*]

LADY HARRIET [*speaking to persons without*]. Where is Charles Buller? Such a man! When Charles Buller is wanted for Addiscombe, he is almost undiscoverable, and when we have him at Addiscombe, he simply cannot be discovered at all.

VOICE OFF STAGE. Mr. Buller has gone for a ride, Lady Harriet.

LADY HARRIET. He leaves us for our horses. I always said he could discriminate. Come in, both of you. [*Giuseppe Mazzini, melancholy and brooding enthusiast, enters the room, followed by Mr. Baring. Mildmay is already on his feet; Milnes and Tennyson have risen on Lady Harriet's entrance; Carlyle pointedly keeps his seat. Lady Harriet includes the whole company in a bright nod, then turns to whisper an aside to Mr. Baring.*] That young Mildmay is sulking in a corner. He mustn't be allowed to get peevish. Go to him, William. Convince him that he is somebody. Two minutes will do it. [*Mr. Baring moves toward Mildmay, whom he engages in a quiet conversation, while Mazzini, following Lady Harriet at a rather cautious distance, crosses to left stage. Lady Harriet continues.*] Mr. Milnes, you are blooming as usual. Mr. Tennyson, we saw you from our upper windows in the garden at a legendary hour. Mr. Carlyle, I'm sorry I can't thank you for rising to greet your hostess when she enters her morning room after breakfast, but I am glad that you appreciate my chairs.

CARLYLE [*getting up in a perfectly deliberate and unembarrassed fashion*]. I am on my feet, not for the lady, but—

LADY HARRIET [*peremptorily*]. For what, then?

CARLYLE. For the woman.

LADY HARRIET. That deserves any reward—even a chair. Sit down, Mr. Carlyle, Mr. Milnes, Mr. Tennyson, Mr. Mazzini. I hate to see a man idle on his feet. [*The men seat themselves, while Lady Harriet approaches Jane Carlyle.*] Let us look at this woman.

JANE CARLYLE. Am I to get up, too?

LADY HARRIET. If you please, my dear. I can't inspect you in that retirement. [*Jane Carlyle rises with mock dudgeon, and offers herself to Lady Harriet's imperious scrutiny.*] Mrs. Carlyle, you outshine us all. With that color in your face you will not venture to tell me that you have not slept.

JANE CARLYLE. I'm sure the color is much obliged to you.

LADY HARRIET. You have slept, then?

JANE CARLYLE. I slept—in particles.

LADY HARRIET [*to the men*]. I believe the woman falls asleep and dreams that she is awake and reports her dreams as history the next morning.

RICHARD MILNES. In other words, her sleeplessness is a nightmare.

LADY HARRIET. You put the case with masculine brutality, Mr. Milnes, but you say what I mean.

JANE CARLYLE. Men utter the brutalities that women only think; that is why women are so fond of their company.

LADY HARRIET [*to Jane Carlyle*]. The only really sleepless thing about you is your wit. Its wakefulness is scandalous.

JANE CARLYLE [*her eyes traversing Lady Harriet's person from foot to forehead.*] It caught the disease at Addiscombe.

LADY HARRIET [*graciously masterful*]. Mrs. Carlyle, you will have the kindness to remember that I hate flattery.

JANE CARLYLE. I have observed that there are no persons whom it is safer to flatter than those who hate flattery.

LADY HARRIET [*to the company*]. Isn't it provoking that this person has gone and married herself to Mr. Carlyle, and has made it indiscreet for me to box her ears.

JANE CARLYLE [*with affected gravity*]. I shouldn't advise you to do that, Lady Harriet, in my husband's presence.

CARLYLE. Eh, Jane, why not?

LADY HARRIET. You think he would defend you?

JANE CARLYLE [*meekly*]. He would defend his prerogatives.

[*This requires some seconds to sink in, but finally scores a general laugh, in which Carlyle's bass outvoices all the rest.*]

LADY HARRIET. We will give you one more chance to better your record. If you sleep to-night we may possibly forgive you.

[*She sits down, and Jane Carlyle, obeying her signal, sits down by Mazzini.*]

JANE CARLYLE. I can't sleep here to-night. I am going home by the half-past eleven.

LADY HARRIET. To Chelsea?

JANE CARLYLE. Yes. [*Pause.*] Our villa in the Riviera isn't open.

LADY HARRIET. I ignore your levity. Don't you know that Mr. Carlyle is here?

JANE CARLYLE. Yes, I know that my husband is here, but my house is in Chelsea.

LADY HARRIET. It won't run off, I suppose?

JANE CARLYLE. No, Lady Harriet, but it runs down. A house like ours has to be painted and papered and subjected to various other tortures from time to time, and I—I am the grand inquisitor.

LADY HARRIET. But Mr. Carlyle tells me that all this doesn't begin till Tuesday.

JANE CARLYLE [*with a peculiar look at her husband*]. Mr. Carlyle is most communicative. It doesn't begin till Tuesday, Lady Harriet, but—I have to break the news to the house.

LADY HARRIET. She thinks her very house has nerves.

JANE CARLYLE. It has.

ALFRED TENNYSON [*with a certain robust shyness*]. Hasn't it some excuse for nervousness?

[*He stops.*]

LADY HARRIET [*with mock severity*]. Proceed, Mr. Tennyson.

ALFRED TENNYSON. It has sucked in —a French Revolution.

JANE CARLYLE [*smiling at Tennyson*]. Not to mention little Reigns of Terror which it sets up on its own account.

LADY HARRIET [*affecting the Titaness*]. Mr. Tennyson, if you are here to abet Mrs. Carlyle—

ALFRED TENNYSON [*with unexpected courage*]. I can't imagine any better reason for being anywhere.

JANE CARLYLE. Alfred, if I do not kiss you for that, it is only in order not to scandalize Lady Harriet.

LADY HARRIET. Mr. Carlyle, I think she should go home.

CARLYLE. Nay, she's but a flighty lass. She would kiss the postman if he brought her a letter she wanted.

RICHARD MILNES. You trust her, then, Mr. Carlyle?

CARLYLE. Divil a bit. I trust Alfred.

LADY HARRIET [*changing the subject with a tactician's quick perception of a check*]. With your nerves, Mrs. Carlyle, I somehow can't see you in a household maelstrom.

JANE CARLYLE. Ah, you see, if one has a hurricane in one's nerves, it is thankful for a little company.

LADY HARRIET [*with entire geniality*]. Then you are quite sure that you want to go and that you don't need Mr. Carlyle's help?

JANE CARLYLE. Lady Harriet, my husband in a domestic squall is about as helpful as a seasick passenger in the cabin is to the skipper in the storm on deck.

CARLYLE [*to Lady Harriet*]. She should have gone home yesterday.

LADY HARRIET. When Mrs. Carlyle points out the delinquencies in her husband, she reminds me of the woman that swept cobwebs out of the sky.

JANE CARLYLE. Thank you for forgetting that she was on *old* woman, Lady Harriet. No, Mr. Carlyle is literature, and literature at the proper time and place is highly captivating; but literature groaning because its inkstand is in the coalscuttle, literature fuming because its nightgown is in the garret or its toothbrush in the paintpot, is quite another matter. No, it is best that literature stay at Addiscombe and be taken care of by Lady Harriet. I have already made that suggestion to literature, and literature has listened with the most beautiful docility.

LADY HARRIET [*to Carlyle*]. Then it is all settled—you will stay?

CARLYLE [*in his large way*]. We shall see, we shall see.

[*Enter, from the right, Charles Buller, over forty, six feet three, flushed with riding, athletic, unabashed, and carelessly good-natured.*]

LADY HARRIET. Charles Buller at last. [*Buller advances toward his hostess with a stride modulated, as it were, to the drawing-room, and kisses her hand with brusque deference.*] Your tardiness has cost you dear, Charles. You have missed some delightful exposures of Mr. Carlyle by his wife and some particularly sharp things that I have been at the pains to tell the company about you.

CHARLES BULLER [*who has been scattering nods and handshakes in all directions*]. As to the first loss, Lady Harriet, I am sorry to have missed any abuse of my old tutor [*he nods toward Carlyle*] or any scintillations from his wife. For the second loss I hope to be compensated in the near future.

LADY HARRIET. You read my intentions perfectly, Charles. It appears that you find our horses interesting.

CHARLES BULLER. Engrossingly so.

LADY HARRIET. We have noticed that. Mr. Baring and I are very grateful to our horses. They keep several desirable friends on our visiting list.

CHARLES BULLER. Lady Harriet, I will not undervalue your horses even to flatter the first woman in England. Keep your stables, and my heart is yours.

LADY HARRIET. You must come and show yourself to Mr. Baring. You can spare a minute for the lower animals? Come, all of you. [*In the responsive movement which follows, Jane Carlyle and Mazzini are a little slower than the rest, and Lady Harriet gives emphasis, gives, as it were, conclusiveness, to this backwardness by her swift remark.*] You two want to stay behind? Please yourselves, by all means.

[*The party moves to the right. Jane Carlyle reseats herself beside Mazzini.*]

JANE CARLYLE [*tranquilly*]. They have left us to ourselves, Mazzini.

MAZZINI [*simply*]. I am glad to be alone with you.

JANE CARLYLE [*faintly indicating Lady Harriet*]. You like her, don't you?

MAZZINI. Very much. She is a great lady.

JANE CARLYLE. She is more than that, Mazzini. She is a fine creature.

MAZZINI. That is what Mr. Carlyle likes, I think—the fine creature.

JANE CARLYLE. True, my dear. It is the fine creature that he likes. [*She pauses.*] But he likes *to be liked* by the great lady.

MAZZINI. You English are hard on each other.

JANE CARLYLE. Are we?

MAZZINI. I sometimes think you do not deserve your liberty. You are hard and greedy—and you are free. And the races that throb and aspire—they are chained.

JANE CARLYLE. That is true, and you know why, don't you? We English have liberty because we can content ourselves with its prose. You Italians want its poetry, and so—

MAZZINI [*bitterly*]. We do not even get its prose.

JANE CARLYLE. Quite so. Some day you will learn prose from us. Then, perhaps, you will get your Italy.

MAZZINI. It is hard to get what one has never had.

JANE CARLYLE. There is a thing still harder, Mazzini: *to get what one has.*

[*Her eyes wander toward Carlyle, now talking keenly with Lady Harriet.*]

MAZZINI. I do not understand that.

JANE CARLYLE. To get back what one has never lost! But that is foolishness. [*She changes the subject resolutely.*] When do you expect your Italy will wake, Mazzini?

MAZZINI. Who knows? The sleep is drugged; that is the trouble. But I have hope; sometimes I say to myself, next year.

JANE CARLYLE. Have you never feared that Italy's waking might be like—

[*She pauses half repentingly.*]

MAZZINI. Like what?

JANE CARLYLE. Like the waking of Juliet—*in the tomb?*

MAZZINI [*wincing*]. Ah, you are cruel.

JANE CARLYLE. Forgive me. I was thoughtless. I meant nothing. [*There is a burst of laughter from the other group.*] We are quite on the edge of things, Mazzini.

MAZZINI [*trying to smile*]. I am used to exile.

JANE CARLYLE [*reaching for his hand*]. Ah! [*Pause.*] Well, let her exile us, if she chooses. She is a queenly woman.

MAZZINI. I am glad she is not a queen.

JANE CARLYLE [*looking at him curiously*]. Why?

MAZZINI [*simply*]. She would make it hard to be a revolutionist.

JANE CARLYLE [*with a faint edge in*

her voice]. You feel that way about her?

MAZZINI. Yes, don't you? You called her a fine creature just now.

JANE CARLYLE. Oh yes, that. It is easy to offer praise, Mazzini. The hard thing is to agree to it.

MAZZINI [*very simply indeed*]. I do not understand women.

JANE CARLYLE. Neither do I. [*She looks toward the other group.*] Is that Mr. Travers Mildmay actually detaching himself from Lady Harriet? I believe he is coming to us.

TRAVERS MILDMAY [*slightly fatigued and discontented*]. May I sit down here, Mrs. Carlyle?

JANE CARLYLE. By all means. In this out-of-the-way district we are pining for dispatches from the capital.

TRAVERS MILDMAY [*perfectly blank, but seating himself*]. Ah!

JANE CARLYLE. What are our friends talking about?

TRAVERS MILDMAY. They are talking about the Corn Laws.

JANE CARLYLE. Is Lady Harriet talking about the Corn Laws?

TRAVERS MILDMAY [*ingenuously*]. She is talking more than any one else.

JANE CARLYLE. Is she really? That must be looked into. You don't care for the Corn Laws, I judge, Mr. Mildmay?

TRAVERS MILDMAY. They may be all right. I don't know. It's hard to feed everybody.

JANE CARLYLE. Mr. Carlyle would begin with the poor.

TRAVERS MILDMAY. It's simpler not to begin.

JANE CARLYLE. Was Lady Harriet supporting the Corn Laws?

TRAVERS MILDMAY. Yes. She let no one else speak.

JANE CARLYLE. I'm afraid you're not fond of women, Mr. Mildmay.

TRAVERS MILDMAY. I like them well enough—if they'd let a man speak.

JANE CARLYLE. We have another recruit, Mazzini. [*Charles Buller is crossing to the group at left.*] Mr. Buller, you surprise us. Have you been sent to Coventry?

CHARLES BULLER [*seating himself easily*]. No, I've fled to Coventry—if this is Coventry. Coventry appears to be a very habitable place. Do you happen to be contemplating any experiments in the line of Lady Godiva?

JANE CARLYLE. Mr. Buller, please speak low. I am nearly ruined in Lady Harriet's esteem already. The one thing needed to complete my fall would be the mention of my name in connection with Lady Godiva.

CHARLES BULLER [*easily*]. I fancy Lady Harriet would like to play the part of Lady Godiva herself.

JANE CARLYLE. I fancy she would, but I don't think she would like to see the chance of doing it first snapped up by any other woman. The only proper indecorums are those which begin with the aristocracy.

CHARLES BULLER [*with absolute unconcern*]. Lady Harriet's a. nice woman.

JANE CARLYLE. You seem to fight with her a good deal.

CHARLES BULLER. Oh yes, a standing fight is the easiest way to handle such a woman. It saves a man from the sillier sort of nonsense, and it keeps the woman occupied; it keeps her from asking the man to treat her seriously.

JANE CARLYLE. You don't like serious women?

CHARLES BULLER. No, women are bad enough when they are frivolous.

JANE CARLYLE. I believe you are trying to get up a standing fight with me.

CHARLES BULLER. I should enjoy it of all things.

JANE CARLYLE. No, if that is your attitude, it would be sinful to oblige you. I shall leave you no excuse for not treating me seriously—unless, indeed, you want to try me with the sillier sort of nonsense.

CHARLES BULLER [*with a something that might or might not be seriousness.*] Carlyle is a lucky man.

JANE CARLYLE. Tell him so, Mr. Buller, tell him so.

[*Richard Milnes leaves the group at the right and crosses to Mrs. Carlyle and her companions. From this time on the liveliness transfers itself to the group at left.*]

CHARLES BULLER. Hello, Milnes. Are you an emigrant, too?

JANE CARLYLE [*looking at Lady Harriet*]. I should call him a refugee.

RICHARD MILNES [*taking a chair*]. Why not a pioneer?

JANE CARLYLE. We hope you'll find the climate bearable. We were very few at first, only Mazzini and I, but we grow, Mr. Milnes, we grow like an American state. [*She looks again at Lady Harriet.*] We shall brave the mother country some day.

RICHARD MILNES. The Americas have some delightful products.

JANE CARLYLE. You are thinking of Mr. Emerson. That man is so good a picture that it is a pity he is a man. I always wanted to frame him and set him up above the mantelpiece.

MAZZINI. It would be an altarpiece then.

JANE CARLYLE. That is better than my husband's phrase. Carlyle says of him that he sheds light.

CHARLES BULLER. Where did he get his light?

RICHARD MILNES. You aren't looking for any, are you, Buller?

CHARLES BULLER. Not just that kind. It wouldn't help the gloom of Parliament. But where did he get his light? I have always fancied that he filled that pretty agate lamp of his from an overflowing oil well at Craigenputtock. You know about that, Mrs. Carlyle?

JANE CARLYLE. He borrowed the oil, perhaps, but I think the fragrance is his own.

RICHARD MILNES. That is it—the fragrance. You feel somehow that incense is always arising from him.

JANE CARLYLE [*after an appreciative pause*]. Richard Milnes, there are times when I forgive people for thinking you intelligent.

RICHARD MILNES. We all rise above ourselves now and then. Mrs. Carlyle is sometimes charitable.

JANE CARLYLE [*satirical again*]. When I rise above myself, Mr. Milnes, I have the grace to relapse. But when you are chidden for wit, you repeat the offence—indelicately.

RICHARD MILNES. Indelicately? I don't see that.

JANE CARLYLE. It is always indelicate to outshine one's neighbors.

RICHARD MILNES [*unguardedly eager*]. I am not the only one.

[*The company laugh.*]

JANE CARLYLE. Confession at last.

LADY HARRIET [*from across the room*]. What are you people laughing at?

JANE CARLYLE. Mr. Milnes has begun to confess his superiorities. We shall have occupation for the whole day.

LADY HARRIET. I advise you to stop at once, Mr. Milnes. Those are the only confessions for which your friends will never absolve you.

RICHARD MILNES. Mrs. Carlyle has made that quite clear.

JANE CARLYLE. Never mind. Mr. Milnes. I am off by the half-past eleven. I go and leave my character behind me.

RICHARD MILNES. You leave a husband behind you to defend it.

JANE CARLYLE. You remind me of an interesting fact. I have a husband. A husband always defends the wife who has gone away. Out of mere gratitude —were there nothing else.

[*The company recognize a phrase of Carlyle's and the laughter is general.*]

CARLYLE [*who has heard imperfectly*]. Woman! Woman!

JANE CARLYLE [*feigning to whisper*]. What names he calls me!

CARLYLE. Jeannie, woman!

JANE CARLYLE [*mimicking a corrected housemaid*]. Sir!

CARLYLE [*quite beaten by the laughter which ensues*]. Gang your gait, hizzie. Ye hae too many abettors in your wickedness. It's nae guid, marryin' 'em. It's like holdin' Ireland. The mair ye have her, the less she minds ye.

[*Alfred Tennyson rises with an incidental air and strolls over to the group on the left.*]

JANE CARLYLE. Mr. Tennyson, you are a loiterer. You should have come to us in our destitution.

ALFRED TENNYSON. I wanted to come.

JANE CARLYLE. You are punished for your delay. The only seat now available is this one beside me, which Mr. Milnes and Mr. Buller and Mr. Mildmay have carefully avoided. Mazzini is on my other side, but he's a revolutionist and likes adventure.

ALFRED TENNYSON [*seating himself*]. I like adventure, too.

JANE CARLYLE [*looking at the other group*]. There's only one person left to capture. I should like to annex Mr. Baring. Mr. Carlyle, of course, doesn't count.

RICHARD MILNES. Why doesn't Mr. Carlyle count?

JANE CARLYLE. A husband is not amenable to capture. If he were—
[*She leaves the sentence unfinished.*]
RICHARD MILNES. I suppose he'd be the supreme conquest.
JANE CARLYLE. Yes, the supreme conquest, Mr. Milnes—the conquest of impossibility. The least attractive woman in the company—to say nothing of the Lady Harriets—can hold the husband against the wife.
ALFRED TENNYSON. Are you sure of that?
JANE CARLYLE. Sure of it? The proof of it is that at this very moment Mr. Baring is getting up and coming over to talk to me. I say "Me" because I refuse to believe that so sane a gentleman is coming over to talk to Mr. Buller.
CHARLES BULLER. He's sane enough to follow my example.
[*Mrs. Carlyle rises to greet Mr. Baring, a grave and courtly man of middle age, essentially modest, but with a slight pomp of station beneath which his inherent modesty is uncomfortable.*]
MR. BARING. Mrs. Carlyle, Lady Harriet and I are very sorry that you insist upon leaving us this morning.
JANE CARLYLE. You are most kind, Mr. Baring, and I am very sorry to go. But Cheyne Row is insistent—even more so than Addiscombe. I am leaving my husband behind to tell you how sorry I am that I cannot stay too.
MR. BARING. That does not console Lady Harriet and me for your departure, glad as we are to keep Mr. Carlyle.
JANE CARLYLE [*taking the seat which Mr. Baring, by a courtly gesture, has invited her to resume, and speaking with much apparent sincerity*]. I am very glad to leave Mr. Carlyle in such excellent and friendly hands. There are very few places where his contentment is even probable. Addiscombe is one.
MR. BARING. We are sorry that you will not add to his contentment and ours—our happiness, I would say [*he is unduly troubled by the trifling inadvertence*]—by staying with us.
JANE CARLYLE. You are both very kind.
CHARLES BULLER [*who has fetched another chair*]. Sit down, Baring. You shan't miss the last minutes of Mrs. Carlyle's society. Go on, Mrs. Carlyle. Give Mr. Baring some of those little stabs you've been showering on Milnes and me. The only decent thing you can do now is to prove that your malignity is impartial.
[*The action in this quarter is carried on for some minutes in dumb show, while the center of interest shifts to the other end of the room, where Lady Harriet and Carlyle are left in somewhat obvious intimacy in the farthest recess of the bow window.*]
LADY HARRIET [*impetuously*]. Your wife is a superb woman.
CARLYLE [*tranquilly*]. Men have fared worse in this tickle gear of matrimony.
LADY HARRIET. I could not find a fault in her, except that I dream sometimes that she has lost a little—a very little—of the first edge of her appreciation of you.
CARLYLE. There's edge enough.
LADY HARRIET. That is your admirable comedy. Nothing will ever convince me that your married life is not radiant—consummate.
CARLYLE. There's nae question of convincing. If it weren't—what was that braw word ye used?—consummate, ye'd have to find that out for yourself. Oh, I don't doubt that ye could. Ye're sharp enough.
[*A burst of laughter from the other end of the room draws the eyes of both momentarily to Jane Carlyle.*]
LADY HARRIET. She holds them all.
CARLYLE. The lass has a spike at the end of her tongue. [*He pauses.*] I wouldna have the spike removed. I should miss the glint on it.
LADY HARRIET. That is what I envy you. You understand each other perfectly.
CARLYLE. Fairly weel, fairly weel. Barrin' the fact that she is a woman, which is a sore disadvantage, and that I am a man, which is a sorer, and that the kind God put a bit of the devil into both of us—doubtless for the furtherance of our mutual understanding—Jeannie and I get on cannily enough. From year's end to year's end it works out not so badly. [*He pauses, then adds.*] There's room for many things in a year.

LADY HARRIET. There's room for reality in your year—not in mine.

CARLYLE [*disobligingly*]. Like enough.

LADY HARRIET. I want reality, Mr. Carlyle.

CARLYLE [*whose eyes have been passingly drawn to his wife by another burst of merriment in the distance*]. Jane would say, "Don't you wish you may get it?"

LADY HARRIET [*imperiously*]. Never mind what Jane would say.

CARLYLE [*with sudden energy*]. Mind what I say, then. Realities are no stuff for you. You are a noble seeming, set aloft, majestical, like Artemis on a frieze, worthy of all men's eyes. But for the doing and the being, for the bread-baking and the bairn-bearing, the first hard-knuckled lass in Dumfries that can barely spell her own name is worth scores of ye. Stay on your frieze, woman, beautiful to men's sight, and let the poor old world's eyes get what good they may of your grace and queenliness. Let that content you, if there's strength in you to be content and, if that be not granted ye, be dumb.

LADY HARRIET [*a little shaken, but on the whole more pleased at having evoked the cataract than startled by its vehemence*]. Mr. Carlyle, you are the first of men, but I will not be thrust out of my rights as a human being, because I am a peer's daughter and may be a peer's wife some day. I hold my own with any milkmaid.

CARLYLE [*grimly*]. Except in the milking.

LADY HARRIET [*with great good-humor*]. Come, you shall talk to me, you masterful farmer's son. Tell me what will put meaning, substance, into my life.

CARLYLE [*abruptly concise*]. Study German.

LADY HARRIET. I have told you already that I have no time for learning languages.

CARLYLE. No—only time for putting substance into your life. Ye'll do that while ye're putting on your gloves nae doubt.

LADY HARRIET. That is a petty gibe, sir. Let me tell you that it takes a long time to do nothing.

CARLYLE [*dryly*]. I have observed that.

LADY HARRIET. The hardest drudgery is drudging at frivolities.

CARLYLE. It's hard work—digging with a feather. I grant ye that.

LADY HARRIET. A man like you doesn't realize the extent to which a life can be empty—and yet crowded.

CARLYLE. And why can I not? Any dolt can see that an empty box—or an empty head, for that matter—takes up as much room as a full one.

LADY HARRIET. You shall not escape me. I don't want metaphors—not even *your* metaphors. I want counsel, definite counsel.

CARLYLE [*abruptly concise again*]. Keep a diary.

LADY HARRIET. A diary?

CARLYLE [*his eye attracted to his wife by renewed laughter in the distance*]. You know all the spangles, all the nobodies. Keep a diary. Some day the historian of human folly will be thankful to ye.

LADY HARRIET. I see your drift. You want provender for another Carlyle. There will be no other.

CARLYLE. I do not know that. There might be one honest man in the twentieth century.

LADY HARRIET [*with a deprecatory gesture*]. I can't pin life to a page. I am too impatient.

CARLYLE. Like enough.

LADY HARRIET [*a little sharply*]. Give me some advice that I can take.

CARLYLE. There are only two sorts of advice for a fine woman: the advice that is good for nothing and the advice that she will not take.

LADY HARRIET. Mr. Carlyle, I am a very long-suffering woman; I wish sometimes that I were back in the feudal ages, when a woman in my position could have ordered forty lashes for a man in yours.

CARLYLE. Ye would have been a great lady at any time; but [*he looks at her curiously*] I doubt if I should have cared to see the backs of your bondsmen.

LADY HARRIET. Churl!

[*She stamps her foot, then laughs, then holds out her hand.*]

CARLYLE [*taking the hand warmly*]. There are times when I'm nae so sure that ye are na' a great woman, too.

[*Lady Harriet and Carlyle converse for some minutes in dumb show.*]

JANE CARLYLE. Oh, these differences between husband and wife are much exaggerated. A wife is a convenience; a husband is an inconvenience; it is only the difference of a prefix.

RICHARD MILNES. You should be the last person to say that, Mrs. Carlyle.

JANE CARLYLE. And why, Mr. Milnes?

RICHARD MILNES. You have married into the firmament, so to speak!

JANE CARLYLE. Into the firmament! How delightful! [*In a stage whisper to Tennyson.*] Is he thinking of the Great Bear?

MR. BARING [*seriously*]. It seems strange that any one should know Carlyle well enough to say that.

JANE CARLYLE [*respectfully*]. Use and wont, Mr. Baring—it works marvels.

RICHARD MILNES. Even at a distance the thought of use and wont in relation to genius seems almost paradoxical, and when one thinks of living like Mrs. Carlyle day after day with the paradox at one's elbow—

[*He pauses to measure the idea.*]

JANE CARLYLE. Oh, one takes the genius in sections, Mr. Milnes. He takes himself in sections. That's his recipe for living.

RICHARD MILNES. I suppose in a less degree there's the same confusion in all of us. It's a long road from our tooth-picks to our prayer books.

CHARLES BULLER. Yes, if we read our prayer books. Tennyson, how do you reconcile the Muses to your pipe?

ALFRED TENNYSON. They seem to like it.

RICHARD MILNES. Considering the fact that the Muses are ladies and that they were brought up in Greece, where nobody smoked, they have an astonishing indulgence for tobacco.

JANE CARLYLE. That reminds me that, since Mr. Tennyson has been sitting by me, I have been visited by hallucinations in my nose. I have dreamt of odors from the spicy shore of Araby the Blest—or what shore is it, Mr. Tennyson? If Lady Harriet's eye were not upon me, I should certainly investigate the contents of this pocket next me.

ALFRED TENNYSON. The pocket would be grateful.

JANE CARLYLE. No, Mr. Tennyson, Lady Harriet would not approve. I renounce the satisfaction of my curiosity—unless, indeed, Mr. Buller—

CHARLES BULLER. By all means.

[*He reaches across and draws from Tennyson's pocket a well-browned meerschaum pipe.*]

JANE CARLYLE [*much interested*]. Is that all?

CHARLES BULLER. There's his tobacco-pouch.

JANE CARLYLE. Give them to me, Mr. Buller. [*She takes the pipe and pouch with affected daintiness.*] It's really too tempting—all the necessities in one's hands at once.

[*She begins to fill the pipe.*]

CHARLES BULLER. Shan't I do that for you?

JANE CARLYLE. Thank you, I know how to fill pipes. Though I have married into the firmament, as Mr. Milnes so charmingly suggests, it is a London firmament and very smoky. [*She surveys the filled bowl.*] It lacks something. Mr. Buller, have you a match? I was sure you had. [*She applies to the tobacco the match which Buller has lighted and put into her hand.*] Look at that smoke. I can almost see little wisps of the *Day-Dream* and rings from the *Lyrical Monologue* floating in it. Open your mouth, Mr. Tennyson.

[*She puts the pipe into Tennyson's mouth. Murmurs of amusement in the group alternate with cautious glances toward Lady Harriet.*]

LADY HARRIET [*sniffing*]. Who is smoking? Mr. Tennyson, you surprise me. Poets are kings at Addiscombe, but even kings obey the law of the house. You might, at least, have respected Mrs. Carlyle's presence.

[*At this everybody laughs.*]

ALFRED TENNYSON [*removing the pipe from his mouth*]. The woman tempted me and I did—smoke.

JANE CARLYLE. The man was in Paradise. You can see that by his excuses.

LADY HARRIET [*severely*]. Mrs. Carlyle!

JANE CARLYLE. Yes, Lady Harriet.

LADY HARRIET. You are fairly riotous this morning.

JANE CARLYLE. I belong to the mob, you know.

LADY HARRIET. Mr. Tennyson, you are forgiven—that is, if you don't repeat the offense. When the persuasions of tobacco are added to the seductions of woman, man is helpless between two sirens.

ALFRED TENNYSON. If you please, Lady Harriet—

LADY HARRIET. Well?

ALFRED TENNYSON. I should like to keep all the blame to myself—if you don't mind.

LADY HARRIET. Keep it by all means. We grudge you nothing, Mr. Tennyson, in our house.

JANE CARLYLE. No, I will not be absolved at Mr. Tennyson's expense. Alfred, give me that pipe.

[*She takes the unextinguished pipe from Tennyson's hand and deliberately applies her mouth to the stem. Sensation.*]

LADY HARRIET [*this time almost genuinely angry*]. Mr. Baring, you are the master in this house. Will you ask Mrs. Carlyle to put aside that pipe?

MR. BARING. I beg your pardon, my dear, but it seems to me that my being the master of the house should make me the servant of its guests.

LADY HARRIET. Is his name Baring or forbearing? Mr. Carlyle, will you discipline your wife?

CARLYLE [*who has hugely enjoyed the pipe episode*]. Ask the possible, Madam.

LADY HARRIET [*still resourceful*]. Mr. Tennyson, at my earnest entreaty, you will have the goodness to remove your pipe from the mouth of Mrs. Carlyle.

ALFRED TENNYSON. Lady Harriet, I don't quite see myself snatching any article of mine from a friend who is using it.

JANE CARLYLE. What shall he do with it, Lady Harriet, if he takes it from me?

LADY HARRIET. Anything he likes.

JANE CARLYLE. Mr. Tennyson, smoke your own pipe.

ALFRED TENNYSON [*taking the pipe*]. I have your permission, Lady Harriet?

LADY HARRIET. Do anything except return the pipe to Mrs. Carlyle.

ALFRED TENNYSON [*in apology to the company*]. I smoke in the drawing-room at Cheyne Row.

LADY HARRIET [*resenting the comparison*]. You are at Addiscombe, Mr. Tennyson.

RICHARD MILNES [*glancing at Jane Carlyle*]. Cheyne Row is powerful even here.

LADY HARRIET [*with a leonine glance at Jane Carlyle*]. Powerful, Richard Milnes? You mean *sovereign*.

[*Footman enters, right, and approaches Lady Harriet.*]

FOOTMAN. The housekeeper asks to see you, my lady.

LADY HARRIET [*instantly resuming her regal suavity*]. Excuse me for a moment. [*To Carlyle, whom she evidently wishes to detain in the bow window.*] I will be back instantly, Mr. Carlyle.

[*She goes out, right.*]

JANE CARLYLE [*whose chair is so placed that she cannot see Carlyle, whispering to Mazzini*]. Is he stirring, Mazzini?

MAZZINI. Who?

JANE CARLYLE. Carlyle.

MAZZINI. No.

JANE CARLYLE. Immovable. I knew it. He is waiting for her to come back.

RICHARD MILNES. Mrs. Carlyle, you have defended poetry against power. Tennyson should write you a lyric.

JANE CARLYLE. Impossible, Mr. Milnes. Tennyson was not foreseen when I was born, and my parents had the heartlessness to name me Jane.

CHARLES BULLER. Jane is a good name.

TRAVERS MILDMAY. Better than most. A man can spell it.

JANE CARLYLE. Oh, Jane is good cobblestone, Mr. Mildmay, but it doesn't fit into Mr. Tennyson's mosaic.

MAZZINI [*to Jane Carlyle*]. He is getting up.

JANE CARLYLE. We shall win yet, Mazzini. [*Carlyle has risen, and slowly makes his way toward the group at the left. The impulse that brings Jane Carlyle to her feet is reflected in the entire company, who form instinctively a kind of lane through which Carlyle, with whimsical deliberation, advances toward his wife.*]

CARLYLE. Well, Jeannie.

JANE CARLYLE. Yes, Thomas.

CARLYLE. The de'il's been in you this morning.

JANE CARLYLE. Yes, Thomas. He likes the places he is used to.

CARLYLE. Ay, ay, the places where he is made much of. Is it from him that ye get your damnable proclivity for smoke?

JANE CARLYLE. From him, Thomas, I think—or from some of his associates.

[*She looks meaningly at her husband.*]

LADY HARRIET [*entering right and approaching Jane Carlyle*]. Mrs. Carlyle, I am very sorry to see the end of a visit which Mr. Baring and I have thoroughly enjoyed, but the carriage is at the door, and I fear that no time is to be lost if you insist upon leaving by the half-past eleven.

JANE CARLYLE. Lady Harriet, the happiest visits must come to an end, and I have the most urgent reasons for getting back to Chelsea.

[*Various salutations.*]

LADY HARRIET. If you would like to say good-by to Mr. Carlyle in your own room—

JANE CARLYLE. No, no, the front steps will do perfectly well. We shall edify all the lady's-maids by the sobriety of our endearments.

CARLYLE [*quietly*]. I'm going with you, Jane.

LADY HARRIET [*thunderstruck*]. But, Mr. Carlyle, you were to stay with us.

CARLYLE [*genially*]. Some other time, some other time. Don't you see that the creature's clean daft and not fit to be trusted in the street by herself? She'd be run over by the first omnibus in Soho, and, mad as the queen is, I shauld miss her.

[*Jane Carlyle, glancing through her dropped eyelashes at Lady Harriet's face, bends her head in a pose of meek surprise and deprecating humility. Lady Harriet, shaken by the blow, recovers herself gallantly and speaks in the tone of royalty at bay.*]

LADY HARRIET.. Any reasons which grow out of concern for Mrs. Carlyle are conclusive for Mr. Baring and myself. We are grateful beyond words for all that you have given us.

[*Curtain.*]

THE HOME FOR THE FRIENDLY

A Comedy

By Florence Kiper Frank

CHARACTERS

JOHN AUBREY.
WILLARD HENDRICKS.
RUTH DUDEBY [*a widow*].
WITHERSTINE [*a man of the fashionable world*].
AN OLD GENTLEMAN.
A POETESS.
ANNIE, A MAID.

TIME: *The Present.*

THE HOME FOR THE FRIENDLY

A COMEDY   By FLORENCE KIPER FRANK

[*The* SCENE *is a large old-fashioned sitting room with marble mantel and ample lace-curtained windows—a room that is rather proud of being old-fashioned and makes no pretensions to modernity. A grand piano occupies one corner, big doors open onto the hall at back. The large and heavy furniture is plush-covered, but not in the atrocious mid-Victorian taste. The large prints are for the most part reproductions of famous paintings. The room in fact evidences 1880 done over by a person of discrimination.*

The stage is for a moment empty, and then John Aubrey enters, a well-set-up, engaging chap not yet thirty, well groomed and likable. He is followed by Annie, the maid, not neatly attired in black dress and white cap and apron. She has a wide and slack mouth wreathed in smiles.]

MAID. Your hat, sir!

AUBREY. Thank you!

MAID. Shall I help you off with your coat, sir?

AUBREY. No! I can manage that nicely myself.

MAID. Do let me! [*She tugs at his coat as he is taking it off.*] There!! It is such a comfort to be of help to folks, isn't it?

AUBREY [*staring at her*]. Yes! Quite so!

MAID [*seating herself and beaming*]. Lovely weather we're having! These constant steady rains in the spring always do make the flowers grow in June so—don't you think so?

AUBREY [*with a significant jerk toward his card which she is holding in her hand*]. Isn't Mr. Hendricks at home?

MAID [*leisurely and with expansive interest examining the card*]. Yes! I mean no! I think he's out for a walk with one of the pash—with one of the ladies. [*Looks at card again intently.*] Elegant name, Aubrey! But wouldn't it be better if Aubrey was the first name now and John the last? "Aubrey John," I mean, instead of "John Aubrey." [*With a shake of the head and a sigh.*] But there! I suppose it's no use talking about it now, is it? Having had it that way so long you natcherly wouldn't care about changing. [*Reflectively.*] Aubrey John! John Aubrey! Aubrey John! John Aubrey! Aubrey—

AUBREY. Is Mr. Hendricks expecting me?

MAID [*confidentially and again beaming*]. I don't know! He hasn't been quite so confiding-like lately with me as usual. [*Rising and patting his shoulder.*] But there—you just sit there and make yourself comfortable. I'm sure he'll be in any minute now. Ta-ta!

[*She goes off, waving her hand to Aubrey. He sits there, shaking his head in bewilderment. Several times he pulls out his watch and looks at it impatiently.*

Enter a small, very cheerful, very red-cheeked little old gentleman, quite Dickensesque and Cheeryble brotherly in appearance, who goes up to Aubrey and shakes hands with him energetically. Aubrey returns the handshake with perplexed cordiality.]

OLD GENTLEMAN. Ah, how-do-you-do, sir! How-do-you-do! Friend of Mr. Hendricks, I take it.

AUBREY. Yes. An old friend of Mr. Hendricks.

OLD GENTLEMAN. We're all friends of his here. All friends. All very friendly to him—very devoted to him—very!!

AUBREY. Aah!

OLD GENTLEMAN. You've known Mr. Hendricks for some time, I take it?

147

AUBREY. Chums at college, sir. Have been abroad and haven't seen him since then, however.

OLD GENTLEMAN. He's been occupied since then!

AUBREY [*somewhat delicately*]. You know him—well, do you?

OLD GENTLEMAN. Oh yes, yes! Very well indeed! Very friendly with him. Ah, yes—indeed, yes—very!

AUBREY [*with a glance around room*]. Could I trouble you to tell me in what manner my friend Hendricks has been occupying himself?

OLD GENTLEMAN. A bit difficult to explain. Difficult to explain. Yes—very! I'll leave it to him, I think, to explain things. He has such a—such a pleasant method of explaining things. Indeed yes—yes indeed! He'll explain things. Oh yes!

AUBREY. Not a relative of his, are you, sir? I can't remember that he said anything—

OLD GENTLEMAN. No, no, just a friend of his—just a friend! [*Is silent for a moment, rubbing his hands in gleeful contemplation.*] In fact, we're none of us related to him—none of us. That makes it all the more charming of him, doesn't it?

AUBREY [*with a stare and a sympathetic shake of the head*]. Ah, yes, I suppose so!

[*Enter a tall, loose-jointed, rather bony female of uncertain age. She has a pad and pencil and is occupied with composition. She comes in reading aloud, oblivious of the presence of the others.*]

POETESS. *There once was a man who of beer full*
So thoroughly was, he was cheerful.
Though much inebriety
Leads to satiety—
It won't come right! Started well enough, but it won't come right, now.
[*Dreamily.*]
There once was a man who—
[*Energetically.*]
There once was a man who—
[*Despondently.*]
There once was a man who—
No, it won't come right at all.

OLD GENTLEMAN. Sounds very good, however. Very good indeed to me, I must say.

POETESS [*turning suddenly to Aubrey, whom she has not noticed before and who is consequently much startled, says intensely*]. Ah, but what does it mean? That's what I'd like to know.

AUBREY. I—I—I didn't hear, really. [*Tentatively.*] You might repeat it, however.

POETESS. Oh, don't apologize! Please don't. Don't think of apologizing. I'll read it over to you any number of times. *There once was a man who of beer full So thoroughly was, he was cheerful.*
Though much inebriety
Leads to satiety—
[*She ends on a puzzled frown.*]

OLD GENTLEMAN [*enthusiastically*]. Splendid! Splendid! Couldn't be better!

POETESS [*wildly, to Aubrey*]. But do you think the first line—the one ending on "beer full"—do you think that entirely explicable?

AUBREY. No, frankly, I don't. Rather rot, I think, to tell the truth.

POETESS [*sobbing*]. I knew it! I felt it from the beginning.

OLD GENTLEMAN [*rising and patting Aubrey genially*]. You shouldn't speak so to her. Shouldn't speak so! [*Goes over to Poetess and pats her on the shoulder much as he has patted Aubrey.*] There, now, my dear, come and play me something soothing and gentle. Something harmonious and cheerful, that shall smooth out all the wrinkles.

[*They move over to the piano, where she seats herself and plays a popular fox-trot legato and with much expression. The old gentleman is greatly delighted. Aubrey manifests much uneasiness—pulls out his watch several times again—moves about restlessly. Annie, the Maid, enters, all smiles.*]

MAID. Now don't go! I'm sure he'll return if you'll have just a bit of patience.

[*The bell rings loudly, and the Maid rushes off. There is first a sound of talking in the hall, and then Willard Hendricks enters, an interesting and individual looking man of about twenty-eight years. The two young men shake hands cordially, Annie meanwhile looking on in the greatest delight and nodding approval. In the corner the playing goes on softly.*]

HENDRICKS [*heartily*]. Glad to see you, old chap. Awf'lly good of you to run down. you know, immediately.

AUBREY. Don't mention it! Been eager for a sight of you, Hendricks— [*looking about with intention*]—a sight of *you!*

·HENDRICKS [*nodding his comprehension*]. Ah! [*To Old Gentleman.*] Mr. Steffens, don't you think you might take Miss Oglebay out for a walk? The air's delightful.

OLD –GENTLEMAN. So pleased! So pleased!—if she'll give me the honor.

POETESS. Oh, Mr. Steffens! The spring always makes me feel so—so— [*with a burst*] I could do anything!

[*And they go off together. Annie, however, still stands there, staring and smiling. Aubrey indicates her to Hendricks with a jerk of his thumb.*]

HENDRICKS. Annie! Mrs. Dudeby has just come in from her walk, and is dying, I think, for a little chat with someone. Don't you want to go up and ask her if you can help her with her wraps?

MAID. I'd just love to, Mr. Hendricks —and J do so admire your tac'!

[*This with rather an aggressive glance at Aubrey. She goes out.*]

HENDRICKS [*genially*]. Well?

AUBREY [*looking about and exploding on a sigh of relief*]. Well!

HENDRICKS. Now sit right down, old man, and tell me all about yourself and everything.

AUBREY [*wildly*]. I? I shan't utter another word in this place until I've found out where I am and what you are doing here. What sort of an institution is this? Who are these—these individuals? Are you perhaps crazy—or [*excitedly*] maybe it's I—maybe it's I!

HENDRICKS [*laughing*]. My home! Yes, in a way it is an institution. Although Witherstine, poor fellow, is the only one who—[*taps forehead*] Witherstine—you haven't met him yet. [*Thoughtfully.*] But the others—

AUBREY [*solemnly*]. Let me know the worst at once!

HENDRICKS. Nothing to be alarmed about, old fellow. This place—this "Institution" of mine as you are pleased to call it—is a little idea of my own. I am convinced that it is based on principles of sound social psychology. It's name is The Home for the Friendly.

AUBREY [*shouting*]. The—what!

HENDRICKS. The Home for the Friendly. The meeting place of those overamiable and genial souls who are a pest to society. The abode of the hypersaccharine. The domicile of those too thoroughgoing exponents of the golden rule, who are literally bursting with benevolence. One knows the kind. One meets them. One avoids them. Theoretically one approves; actually one rushes away. And yet doesn't a bit of analysis show that they are the logical results of our accepted moral training? But the normal man doesn't want the logical results of his accepted moral training. A primitive, healthy instinct has kept the normal man largely egoistic, sufficiently anti-social.

What are these poor benevolent creatures to do with themselves! They ask so little of life, the dears—merely a bit of gratitude, of sunshine and appreciation.

I gave the subject much thought—I went in, you know, for reform, sociology, that sort of thing, even at college. Then the brilliant idea came to me—a Home for the Friendly. Homes for the Friendless there are—multitudinous. But a Home for the Friendly—one which would not only accomplish the purpose of protecting society at large, but by segregating these altruistic individuals would thus in simple fashion furnish them each other as willing victims—ah there, said I, is something worth the doing—a scheme of novel humanitarianism. [*Beaming.*] Well, what do you think of us now!

AUBREY [*who has been attempting, during the preceding speech, to get a word in edgeways*]. Really—to tell the truth—I'm just a bit dazed yet.

HENDRICKS. Take your time, old top. Think it over!

[*Enter Maid.*]

MAID. Mrs. Dudeby is rested now, and she says she's coming down to the sitting room.

HENDRICKS. Very good, Annie. See that tea is served at once.

MAID. Yes, sir. Thank you, sir.

[*She leaves.*]

HENDRICKS [*appreciatively*]. Good maid, Annie! [*Aubrey makes a grimace of distaste not seen by Hendricks.*] I must tell you about this Mrs. Dudeby, John. A widow, remarkably charming woman. Her story has affected me deeply. In fact, it has made my blood boil. The perfidy of men, Aubrey. This—this husband of hers that just died wasn't her first love-affair by any means. No, indeed. She'd been engaged, will you believe it, to three men—one at a time, of course—before her marriage—three men! And each of the three—Oh, it makes me rage to say it—each of the three, without any excuse whatsoever, had jilted her. The last scoundrel, without a word of explanation, suddenly disappeared into the thick of the World War. That was the man who broke her heart. She married the deceased one, as consolation.

AUBREY [*grasping at Hendricks' arm*]. Would you mind telling me the name of this—Mrs. Dudeby—before she was married!

HENDRICKS [*in surprise*]. Her name was—let me see!—Williston—yes, that's it—Ruth Williston.

AUBREY [*grabbing for his cane and hat*]. My God, Willard, I was the man that went into the war-zone.

[*He tries to make his escape, but it is too late. Ruth Dudeby is already entering. She is pretty indeed, a well-rounded, curvy little creature, with tendrils of hair curling about her face in appealing feminine fashion.*]

RUTH. I haven't kept you waiting, Mr. Hendricks? John!! Mr. Aubrey! [*There is a painful and disconcerting pause. Then Ruth, all sweetness, goes up to Aubrey and takes his hand.*] I forgive you!

AUBREY [*limply*]. Thanks awfully!

[*Annie at this moment brings in the tea things and Ruth seats herself behind the tea table to do the honors. The two men sit, awkward and uncomfortable, one at either side of the table. Ruth is the only one of the three who preserves her savoir faire.*]

RUTH [*to Hendricks*]. Sugar?

HENDRICKS. Two.

RUTH [*to Aubrey*]. Sugar?

AUBREY [*growls*]. None whatsoever.

RUTH. Of course! I remember!

[*Her manner is sweetness itself, but she is using her handkerchief surreptitiously to mop the tears. Hendricks is observing this.*]

RUTH [*affably*]. And was it pleasant in the war-zone?

AUBREY [*jerks out*]. Oh—very!

[*There is another pause, during which she is smiling bravely whenever they look at her, but Hendricks observes her wiping her eyes when they are not. He is growing more and more uncomfortable. Finally he bursts out.*]

HENDRICKS. This is pathetic. It's too damned pathetic! Are you going to continue acting the scoundrel to this noble woman? You're a fine fellow at heart, John. There is only one way in which you can make reparation. Will you marry her or won't you?

[*Ruth leans forward eagerly to hear the answer. Aubrey jumps up precipitately, overturning his chair.*]

AUBREY [*vehemently*]. I'll be dashed if I will!

RUTH [*sinking back*]. Oh!

HENDRICKS [*sadly and nobly*]. Then will you marry me, Mrs. Dudeby?

[*At this moment there enters in a frock-suit, Witherstine, an immaculately dressed, slim, middle-aged man, hair slightly gray, his manner conventional and distinguished. He is bowing from side to side as if there were a large number of people in the room.*]

HENDRICKS [*with finger to lips*]. S-sh!

[*Witherstine proceeds down the room, stopping every few moments as if he were speaking to some one, and then going on down the line to the next. His manner is dignified urbanity.*]

WITHERSTINE. Yes, Mrs. Willoughby, delightful weather. And your flowers—the arrangement—so very lovely! The opera—Garden, yes—no voice, but that acting!—Oh, how-do-you-do, Mrs. Alden! Yes, aren't the flowers charming! Yes, quite so—the popular impression notwithstanding. Her vocalization undoubtedly as superb as her histrionic powers. Aah, Garden, Garden!—Yes, Mrs. Stuart, aren't the flowers well done, unusually—

[*And on he goes, bowing and smiling, his voice becoming a murmur.*]

HENDRICKS. Poor fellow! Too many afternoon teas, Aubrey. When he sees the table laid it always sets him off in this way.

AUBREY [*gloomily*]. He's happier than the most of us.

RUTH [*very charmingly, toward Witherstine*]. Tea, Mr. Witherstine?

[*She takes care of him with tea and cakes. He accepts them from her with graciousness, goes to corner and sits there sipping his tea, talking and smiling first to one side and then to the other.*

This leaves the situation among the three of them much as it was at Witherstine's entrance. They look at each other in some dismay. Then Ruth leans toward Hendricks.]

RUTH [*very softly and sweetly*]. I have decided to accept you—Willard.

[*She lingers shyly on the "Willard."*]

HENDRICKS [*rising*]. Thanks.

[*Overcome with emotion, he grasps her hand and starts to speak. His words choke in his throat, however; he pulls out a big pocket-handkerchief, blows his nose loudly, and rushes from the room.*

Aubrey reaches stealthily for his hat, intending to "beat it," but Ruth, with a gently outstretched hand, arrests him.]

RUTH. Don't go yet, John. [*He sinks back, miserable.*] Because you and I must have a long, long talk about the past and all that is still unexplained between us.

[*Witherstine in the meantime is continuing in the corner with his tea conversation, phrases of which occasionally drift out to them.*]

AUBREY. Do you think this advisable?

RUTH [*sweetly but decisively*]. I think so. [*There is a pause between them, John fidgeting. Then Ruth says firmly.*] Now tell me, John, why you broke my heart?

AUBREY [*uncomfortably*]. Did I— break your heart?

RUTH. Yes. It would be pleasanter to tell you that you didn't, but I am constrained to say that you did.

AUBREY [*defensively*]. You married soon enough after.

RUTH. For his sake, poor dear Dude-by. Because he needed a woman's tenderness and her unceasing attentions. And I gave them him, John. I am proud to say that I didn't leave him to himself for a moment. I poured out on Dudeby the fullest treasures of my care and my affection. Though I carried about with me a broken heart, I failed not for an instant. Never did my sweetness falter.

AUBREY. Very touching of you, Ruth. What did he die of?

RUTH [*with a faint melancholy*]. That they were never able to determine.

AUBREY. Ah!

RUTH. He merely faded away and withered.

AUBREY. Poor chap!

RUTH. With a smile I soothed his dying pillow. I was with him to the last. No, I have no least thing with which to reproach myself in the case of Dudeby.

AUBREY. No, of course, not.

RUTH. Can you say the same for yourself, John?

AUBREY [*startled*]. Me? I never met the fellow.

RUTH [*laughingly*]. No, not self-reproach for Dudeby, John. [*Gravely.*] But for no other have you felt the merited pangs of self-chiding?

AUBREY. Aah, can't we let bygones be bygones?

RUTH. For your soul's sake I am speaking. Do you think I am thinking of myself? Little do you know me. For your own sake I urge confession. Why did you throw me over?

AUBREY. Don't use those words. They're—uncomfortable.

RUTH. In the ears of a gentleman— yes.

AUBREY. This is beyond endurance.

RUTH. I shall endure, John, until the end. I shall endure—

AUBREY [*stamping foot*]. Don't look so pretty!

RUTH [*wiping her eyes*]. Don't flatter!

AUBREY. When a man's with you he can't—you seem so helpless—no wonder Hendricks—

RUTH [*into handkerchief*]. I shall marry him, but I do not love him.

AUBREY. Then don't—

RUTH. Neither did I love Dudeby. But my sacrifice was not in vain.

AUBREY. Then you really mean to sacrifice Hendricks—yourself, I mean—?

RUTH. I shall give him devotion, but you are the only man I love! Why—why—did you jilt me?

AUBREY [*perplexed and backing away*]. I don't know. There was no reason. You are all that is good and sweet—

RUTH [*eagerly nodding*]. Yes, I am, John—aren't I?

AUBREY. All that is womanly and tender—

RUTH [*nodding*]. Yes, I am, John!

AUBREY. And so I can't understand—

RUTH. That's what the others said.

AUBREY. The others?

RUTH. The other two that threw me over.

AUBREY. The brutes!

RUTH [*softly*]. Don't you think you could learn to love me again, John?

AUBREY [*wavering*]. I—

RUTH [*arms outstretched*]. You're in love with me now this very instant.

[*He is overcome. He crushes her to him. Hendricks enters. They spring apart.*]

HENDRICKS. I don't understand, quite!

RUTH [*very sweetly*]. John has just urged me to marry him. You don't mind, do you?

HENDRICKS. Perhaps it is as well this way!

[*Aubrey has been pacing rapidly, in an agitated manner. Bursts out explosively.*]

AUBREY. No, I can't do it, Ruth! I can't!

RUTH AND HENDRICKS. You can't!

AUBREY. It's a life and death matter! Some instinct—

HENDRICKS. But after you said—

AUBREY. No! no, it's impossible. She's too good for me. I couldn't bear it.

[*There is a miserable pause during which Witherstine in the corner says—"And those little cakes! so delicious! Where did you get them?" Ruth stands by the tea table, one hand resting on it, back to the audience.*]

HENDRICKS [*lukewarmly*]. Then I guess you'll have to marry me—

RUTH. Oh!

HENDRICKS [*tamely*]. I'm sure we shall be very happy.

[*At this Ruth turns, and the men fall back astonished, for she is in a perfect passion, eyes flashing, lips curling in scorn. She blazes out at them.*]

RUTH. Happy! You can go to the devil!

[*The two men can scarcely credit their senses. She now tears up and down, a vixen. Instinctively the men pace up and down after her.*]

RUTH [*gesticulating like a windmill*]. I mean it! Go to the devil! Go to the devil! [*Stamping vigorously.*] Hell! Hell! Hell! [*Like a schoolboy breaking loose.*] You are cads, both of you. I despise you! Oh, that I could think of either of you for a moment! No! No, don't come near me. I'll tear your eyes out!

[*Aubrey has recovered from the shock of her change. He is now full of glee, and wildly enthusiastic.*]

AUBREY. Do you hear, Hendricks? Do you hear her? Just listen!

RUTH. I can't abide you. Either one of you! Moonheads! Cowards! Pig-faced imbeciles!

AUBREY. She means it, Hendricks! By George, she means it!

RUTH. Mean it! Of course I mean it. Damn!

[*She chokes on her emotions.*]

AUBREY. Would *you* have imagined it! She's the woman for me, all right! Beauty with spirit! Don't you see she's the ideal mate for me?

HENDRICKS [*with patronizing patience*]. But she's definitely turned you down, old chap. She's jilted you, Aubrey. You've jilted him, of course you have, haven't you, Mrs. Dudeby? [*Fatuously.*] Dear Ruthie!

RUTH. Jilted him! I should say so! That—

AUBREY. There! She begins again! Isn't she great! Isn't she ripping! It's the real thing all right. She's so mad she could bite our heads off.

HENDRICKS [*quite pleased with himself*]. And you've jilted her, old boy! He jilted you, didn't he, Mrs. Dudeby?

RUTH. Oh! Oh! Just let me tell him what I think of him!

HENDRICKS. I've never behaved as he has, so undoubtedly I'm the one who—

AUBREY [*interposing*]. By George, that's nervy of you!

HENDRICKS [*with beaming confidence*]. You'll marry me of course, Ruth, won't you?

AUBREY [*excitedly*]. Don't listen to him! Don't listen to the scoundrel!

HENDRICKS. Ruth, you can see he's a double-dyed villain.

AUBREY. Please have me, Ruth! You said you were madly in love with me!

HENDRICKS. No one but a cad would refer to such a confession.

AUBREY. Don't listen to him!

HENDRICKS. Don't hear what he's saying!

AUBREY. Take me, Ruth!

HENDRICKS. Oh, please marry me!

[*They are both now on their knees. She brushes between them, knocking them both over, and paces the length of the room.*]

RUTH. No! No! No! And again no!

[*Her pacing has now brought her to Witherstine, standing by the table.*]

WITHERSTINE [*in very courtly fashion*]. Would you do me the honor to marry me, Mrs. Dudeby?

RUTH [*standing in deep thought*]. Do you know—I've half a mind to!

[*This novel idea transfixes all of them but Witherstine. Dead silence. Outside, a dreadful altercation is heard. Presently the Poetess enters in high dudgeon followed by the Old Gentleman, and Annie, who is much interested in the fracas.*]

POETESS [*wildly*]. He said he didn't like the shape of my bonnet!

OLD GENTLEMAN. I said—

POETESS [*more wildly*]. He said he didn't like the shape of my bonnet!

OLD GENTLEMAN. I only said—

POETESS [*giving Old Gentleman a ripping slap*]. There!!

OLD GENTLEMAN [*holding cheek and speaking with whiteheat asperity*]. I consider your poetry in the most execrable taste.

MAID [*vindictively*]. I do too, and I'm just glad of the chance to say so.

[*The Poetess here slaps Annie, who returns the attack with vigor. The two are finally separated by Hendricks. Hendricks is overcome, totters weakly and sits in chair.*]

HENDRICKS. I give up! You're too much for me! My life's scheme is dissolving before my eyes. The fair fabric of my Home for the Friendly is tumbling about my head. My work is a failure. My love is a failure. I'm a failure! Go, Aubrey! Go, leave me among the ruins of my hopes.

[*He hands Aubrey his hat. Aubrey goes sadly towards the door. Mrs. Dudeby, seeing that he is really going, starts toward him.*]

RUTH. You're not going, John?

AUBREY [*sepulchrally*]. Yes!

RUTH [*smiling*]. I—oh—I wouldn't if I were you, Johnny.

[*She holds out her arms to him. He springs toward them.*]

AUBREY. Ruth! Loved one!

[*This picture as a culmination to his misfortune is too much for Hendricks. He sobs. Aubrey, with Ruth clasped tightly in his arms, turns to him.*]

AUBREY. Hendricks, old chap, you're not a failure. Can't you see that you have succeeded beyond your dreams? You're a winner! Isn't the whole object of modern sociological reform, to reform the object of its reform? Isn't the whole tendency of modern sociological methods to do away with the subject of its tendency? You've accomplished this! You've abolished your own institution. You've attained the farthest goal of the true reformer. I congratulate you, old man, I congratulate you!

HENDRICKS [*whose face has been lighting, accepts his outstretched hand with enthusiasm*]. You're right, John Aubrey!

[*Annie, the maid, has her cheek affectionately against that of Hendricks. Ruth and Aubrey are in each other's arms. The Poetess and the Old Gentleman are making faces at each other. Witherstine is gobbling cakes from the tea table.*]

WITHERSTINE. Really—where did you get such cakes—they are a credit to—

[*Curtain.*]

BUMBO THE CLOWN
A Fantasy

By Lawrence Gibson

CHARACTERS

JIMMY WESTON [*a sick boy*].
MRS. WESTON [*his mother*].
DOCTOR HOLLADAY [*a physician*].
BUMBO THE CLOWN.

TIME: *Night.*

BUMBO THE CLOWN is fully protected by copyright and no performance may be given without the consent of the author or his representative, LAURA WILCK, 226 WEST 42ND ST., NEW YORK CITY.

BUMBO THE CLOWN

A FANTASY   By LAWRENCE GIBSON

[SCENE: *A bedroom in the house of Mrs. Weston. The room is tastefully furnished, with bed at right, and table, bearing lamp and telephone, in center. Door at back leads to hall, door at right leads to rest of apartment. Window at left.*

As the curtain rises, little Jimmy is seen in bed. His mother is bending over him anxiously. He moans from time to time. Doctor Holladay is examining a thermometer under the lamp. The room is also lighted by an electrolier.]

MRS. WESTON [*to the Doctor, anxiously*]. Well, Doctor, what do you think?

DOCTOR [*shaking his head gravely*]. If he lives through the night, there may be a chance.

MRS. WESTON [*fearfully*]. You don't mean—?

DOCTOR [*sincerely*]. I'm sorry, Mrs. Weston.

[*Mrs. Weston begins to cry.*]

JIMMY [*moaning*]. Bumbo—Bumbo— why don't you come?

MRS. WESTON [*wringing her hands*]. Isn't there something you can do, Doctor?

DOCTOR [*sorrowfully*]. I am afraid I have done all I can, Mrs. Weston.

JIMMY [*tossing on the pillow*]. I want you, Bumbo. Don't you hear me?

DOCTOR. What is he saying?

MRS. WESTON. He's calling for that clown, Bumbo—he saw him at the theater. He keeps calling for him all the time.

DOCTOR. Oh, yes, Bumbo. He works in the theater where I am house physician—or, rather, he *did*—

JIMMY [*crying*]. Bumbo, I'll be mad at you if you don't come pretty quick.

MRS. WESTON [*suddenly*]. Doctor—

DOCTOR. Well?

MRS. WESTON. I—I was just thinking —couldn't we get that clown to come here? It's silly, I suppose—he probably wouldn't do any good—but there's just a chance—he might cheer my boy up.

DOCTOR [*shaking his head sadly*]. Bumbo is through with cheering people up. He has made them laugh for the last time.

MRS. WESTON. What do you mean?

DOCTOR. He is dying—been dying for a week. I never saw a case of such remarkable vitality—the man laughs at death.

MRS. WESTON [*kneeling at the boy's bedside*]. Oh, my boy—my boy!

DOCTOR [*going toward door*]. I'm going to see him now, but I'll be back.

[*He goes out.*]

JIMMY [*after a pause*]. Mamma—

MRS. WESTON. Yes, dear?

JIMMY. Why don't Bumbo come?

MRS. WESTON. He can't, dear. He's going to Heaven to see God.

JIMMY. Is God anything like Bumbo?

MRS. WESTON. I don't know, darling. Why do you ask?

JIMMY. Oh, I was just thinkin'—if God is like Bumbo, I shouldn't mind going up there.

MRS. WESTON [*crying*]. Oh, don't talk like that, dear—please—please—

JIMMY [*after a pause*]. Mamma— won't you sing for me?

MRS. WESTON. I'll try, dear. What shall I sing?

JIMMY. Sing the Clown Song—the one Bumbo sings.

MRS. WESTON. I'll try, dear, but you must go to sleep. I'll put out the light.

[*She switches off the electrolier, leaving only the table lamp. Then she sings in a quavering voice the words of the foolish little song.*]

I'm Bumbo, brave Bumbo, the Clown;
I'm a man of undoubted renown;
I'm mad as a hatter,

157

But what does it matter?
I'm brimful of folly,
I'm awfully jolly,
I'm Bumbo, brave Bumbo, the Clown.

I laugh when my heart is breaking,
I dance when—

[*She breaks down and cannot go on.*
Jimmy is very still. She bends
over him anxiously, then goes
softly into the other room. When
she is gone, Jimmy lifts his head
cautiously, then creeps out of bed,
goes to the table, climbs up on a
chair, so that he may reach the
telephone.]

JIMMY [*at the phone*]. Hello! . . .
I want God's house, if you please. . . .
What is it? . . . But I don't want a
number. I want Mr. God. . . . I want
to speak to Bumbo—Bumbo the Clown.
. . . Is that you, Bumbo? . . . This is
Jimmy—Jimmy Weston. I'm sick.
Won't you come and see me? . . . Oh,
isn't that Bumbo? . . . Oh, shucks!
Well, will you tell him to call me up
when he comes?

[*He hangs up the receiver and is*
about to get back into bed when he
sees the tall figure of a man who
has entered noiselessly by the win-
dow and stands silently in the
fringe of the lamplight. He wears
a long black cloak and hood, which
conceal his face and figure.]

JIMMY [*startled*]. Who are you—a
burglar? [*The man slowly shakes his*
head]. What did you come for? For
me? [*The figure slowly nods his head.*]
Who are you? Not—not Mr. Death?

THE STRANGER. I'm Death—I'm Life
—I'm Nothing—I'm Everything—I'm the
Spirit of Joy—I'm the Essence of Youth
—I'm Happiness—I'm Bumbo the Clown!

[*He throws off his cloak and reveals*
his motley; then he crosses over
and switches on the lights.]

JIMMY [*clapping his hands*]. Well, if
it ain't Bumbo!

BUMBO. Don't say "ain't"—it ain't
grammatical.

JIMMY [*correcting himself*]. I mean,
if it isn't Bumbo! I just telephoned you.

BUMBO. Yes, I know.

JIMMY. How did you know?

BUMBO. Oh, I was perched on a telegraph pole. I was on my way up there.

[*He points toward the ceiling.*] I had
stopped to light a cigarette when I heard
your message coming over the wire, so I
just hopped on a passing snowflake and
drifted down to the window.

JIMMY. I thought you were dead.

BUMBO. The body may die, but the
spirit of Bumbo will live forever in the
hearts of little children.

JIMMY. Why aren't you at the theater, making 'em laugh?

BUMBO [*a little wistfully*]. Bumbo
will make 'em laugh no longer. He has
laughed his last laugh. He has made
people laugh and grow young again, but
he can't grow young himself.

JIMMY [*disappointed*]. Aren't you
going to play in the theater any more?

BUMBO. No. To-night I go to play for
the angels in heaven.

JIMMY. Gee! I bet they'll be glad to
see you. And won't they just laugh
themselves sick! Do you think you'll
see God?

BUMBO. Of course. But, what is more
important, God will see me. Ah, now,
there is a chap that will appreciate me;
for God is the Greatest Humorist of us
all. It is He that puts happiness in the
hearts of little children before they are
born.

JIMMY. It must be awful crowded up
there. Are you sure He'll let you in?

BUMBO. Why shouldn't He? I've
helped to put joy into the lives of men.
What more can any one ask than that?

JIMMY. It's a long way off. How are
you going to get there?

BUMBO. Up the Rainbow, of course.
How did you think?

JIMMY [*looking around*]. But where
is the Rainbow?

BUMBO [*pointing toward the window*].
Out there. It leads from over here to
over there—into the Somewhere. It's a
flower-bedecked pathway, gay with blossoms of many hues. I change at the
Moon, you know—I take the boat there
and sail down the Milky Way. It's all
very simple when you're used to traveling.

JIMMY. But there isn't any Rainbow
now.

BUMBO. Oh, yes, there is, only you
can't see it. You see, the flowers grow
so close to the sun that they are wilted
most of the time. It's only when it rains
that they lift their heads and you can

see all their many colors. The Rainbow is God's Ladder of Flowers.

JIMMY. I see—sort of a fire-escape.

BUMBO [*wistfully*]. Yes, that's it. And it's always there waiting for us—waiting—waiting. [*He turns to the boy.*] I can't stay very long. I came because you were sick. [*Reaching into his pocket.*] Guess I'll have to take your temperature.

JIMMY [*making a face*]. I hate those mouth thermometers. You can't talk.

BUMBO. You won't hate mine. Look! [*Takes something from his pocket and holds it up.*]

JIMMY [*clapping his hands*]. A stick of candy!

BUMBO. A proper kind of thermometer—the more you suck on it, the less there is to read. Open your mouth.

[*Jimmy opens his mouth, and Bumbo inserts the stick of candy. Then he takes out a pair of huge spectacles and puts them on, at the same time assuming a profoundly professional air.*]

JIMMY [*with the candy in his mouth*]. Why do you wear glasses?

BUMBO [*his finger to his lips*]. 'Sh! [*Impressively.*] To make people think I'm wise. I'm a fool, but I'm a wise fool.

JIMMY. Our doctor wears glasses, too.

BUMBO. For the same reason, I think. Doctors don't know anything. But these glasses are different from your doctor's. His magnify the vision; these minimize it. If you're looking for trouble, you'll find it—so why look for it? When I look at you through these glasses, I can see hardly anything wrong with you. Now let me read your temperature. .[*He reads it and frowns.*] Ahem! Serious —very serious.

JIMMY [*alarmed*]. What's the matter?

BUMBO [*impressively*]. I'm afraid you won't live more than a hundred years.

JIMMY [*relieved*]. Oh, but that's a long time.

BUMBO. No, it isn't. It's only a second in the life of the Universe.

JIMMY. Anyway, I'm glad I ain't going to die soon.

BUMBO. Don't say "ain't." If you must die, at least, you can die grammatically. Now let me see your tongue. [*Jimmy sticks out his tongue.*] Ahem! Bad—very bad.

JIMMY. Now what's the matter?

BUMBO. You've got your tongue twisted round your eye-tooth so you can't see what you're saying. [*He takes rolls and rolls of multicolored paper out of the little fellow's mouth.*] No wonder you're sick, with such a load on your stomach!

JIMMY [*laughing and clapping his hands*]. I know—you're playing tricks on me.

BUMBO. Why shouldn't I? I'm the doctor, and all doctors are tricksters. The only difference between a physician and a magician is in the first syllable.

JIMMY. I like you better than our doctor. I'm sure you can make me well.

BUMBO. You still look a little pale, but I'll soon fix that. Let me pinch your cheeks. There—that's better. Now you have cheek enough for anything. [*Bumbo has on his thumbs some grease-paint which he applies to Jimmy's cheeks.*] Now your cheeks are bright and rosy. Oh, Bumbo is a wonderful doctor!

JIMMY. Do some more tricks.

BUMBO. Open your mouth. [*He takes out silk flags of all nations, tied together.*] I'm not at all surprised that you're ill, with all this *foreign* substance on your stomach. All the nations in the world are fighting inside of you. Why, you're a regular battlefield!

JIMMY. But where is the American flag?

BUMBO [*raising a finger*]. Ah, that's the point. That's the only flag that agreed with you—that's the only one you were able to assimilate. The American flag is in your blood—in your brain. Look! [*He takes an American flag from Jimmy's ear.*] Now, that's what I call an earful.

JIMMY [*laughing with glee*]. Gee! but you're funny!

BUMBO. Now, I wonder what else is wrong with you. Let me turn you upside down. If there's anything bad in you, it will come out. [*He turns the child upside down, and coins fall on the floor.*] Ha, ha! Evidently you aspire to be a banker. You're a regular savings bank.

JIMMY [*with wide open eyes*]. I didn't know there was so much money in the world—there's enough to buy ice cream sodas for the rest of my life.

BUMBO [*laughing*]. You didn't know when you were well off, did you? But, seriously, don't you think that doctors are stupid? I bet they never thought of upsetting a man when his stomach is upset. But, then, doctors are old fogies—they're too old to understand the young.

JIMMY. But aren't you old?

BUMBO [shocked]. I? How dare you! I'm as young as the morning. I was born yesterday. I'll be born again tomorrow. There's a fool born every minute. . . . How do you feel?

JIMMY [gratefully]. Oh, much better, thank you. Won't you sing for me?

BUMBO. Of course. That's what I came for. What shall I sing?

JIMMY. Sing the Clown's Song—that one about yourself.

BUMBO. I always sing about myself. I can think of nothing more important to sing about.

[He sings the song "Bumbo the Brave."]

I'm Bumbo, brave Bumbo, the Clown;
I'm a man of undoubted renown;
I'm as mad as a hatter,
But what does it matter?
I'm brimful of folly,
I'm awfully jolly,
I'm Bumbo, brave Bumbo, the Clown.

Chorus

I laugh when my heart is breaking;
I dance when my feet are aching;
I sing when I ought to be sighing;
I play when I ought to be dying;
I'm Bumbo, brave Bumbo, the Clown.

I'm Bumbo, brave Bumbo, the Clown;
I'm the talk of each village and town;
I'm a little bit hazy,
Some think I am crazy;
I'd rather be loony
Or mad than be gloomy.
I'm Bumbo, brave Bumbo, the Clown.

JIMMY [when the song is finished]. Oh, that's great! I feel a lot better. I think you're better than medicine.

BUMBO. Which reminds me—I think you ought to have some medicine.

JIMMY. [making a face]. I hate the nasty stuff.

BUMBO. Ah, but I'll give you a bit of my own medicine. I make it myself. [He goes over to the lamp and apparently takes from the top of it a dish of something, which he brings to Jimmy.] Now, how do you like that?

JIMMY [tasting it, delighted]. Why, it's ice cream! [He eats greedily, then pauses.] But you got it off the lamp—why isn't it melted?

BUMBO. I got it from the sun—it's so hot up there that the lamp is cool by comparison. I made it myself out of snow and a Little Dipper of milk from the Milky Way. I had an angel smile into it to make it sweet.

JIMMY. But what if you wanted chocolate ice cream?

BUMBO. Then, I'd get a little darky angel to smile into it.

JIMMY [laughing]. What a funny old fool you are!

BUMBO. Yes, I am a fool. I wear a fool's cap—but on fool's cap wise men write their wise thoughts. I wear a ruff—but I'm never ruffled. I wear a fool's face—but I'll face any fool and beat him at a quip or a jest. I have the look of a clown—but a laugh of silver. I'm an ugly old toad—but I have a jewel in my head. I'm a black spider—but I weave a web of gold. I'm a bat—but my wings are of the richest velvet. Watch me, and I'll make you bat your eyes with wonder.

[He dances the Dance of the Bat, to Jimmy's delight.]

JIMMY [clapping his hands when it is finished]. Oh, I think you're awfully jolly. You're the funniest man I ever met. Do it some more.

BUMBO [picking up his bag]. I haven't time. I really must be going now.

JIMMY [noting the bag]. Oh—you have a black bag just like our doctor's.

BUMBO. Of course. All doctors have black bags. That's what they bring the babies in.

JIMMY. Have you got a baby in there?

BUMBO. Lots of babies—you shall see. [He opens the bag.] Baby rabbits—baby ducks—baby pigeons!

[He takes some oranges out of the bag and begins to juggle them.]

JIMMY. My goodness! What a lot of things you've got in that bag! Oranges, too?

BUMBO. Oranges nothing. They're a couple of stars and a baby moon. Watch me juggle the moon and the stars. Oh, I'm a great astronomer, I am!

JIMMY [admiringly]. There's no limit to you, is there? I could watch you all night long.

BUMBO [*stops and looks at his watch*]. Whew! I had no idea it was so late. I'm afraid I've missed my connections. Think I'll send a telegram to St. Peter and tell him I'll take the next boat.

[*He catches a white pigeon, writes a message on one of its wing feathers, takes the pigeon to the window and releases it.*]

There—that'll reach him all right.

JIMMY [*wonderingly*]. Will he fly straight up to heaven?

BUMBO. Of course—but then he isn't a real pigeon, you know.

JIMMY. I thought he was.

BUMBO. Oh, no! He's only the ghost of a pigeon. Didn't you notice how white he was?

JIMMY [*thoughtfully*]. He did look kind of pale.

BUMBO. He was shot in the Great War while carrying a message at the front.

JIMMY [*sympathetically*]. Poor little pigeon!

BUMBO. Poor nothing! He's happy now—he's probably singing on his way to Heaven's Gate.

JIMMY. But pigeons don't sing.

BUMBO. Of course they do—after they die. What's the use of dying if you can't sing? Oh, yes, they all sing—all but the ducks, and they whistle. [*He stops suddenly and listens at the open window.*] Do you hear anything?

JIMMY [*listening*]. No. What is it?

BUMBO [*listening, his face strangely aglow from a light off stage*]. The Music of the Spheres. The stars are singing in unison. They want me to join them.

JIMMY. Do the stars sing, too?

BUMBO. Naturally. The stars sing to the birds at night—a song too fine for mortal ears to hear; a song that even the birds may hear only in dreams. And then the birds, when breaks the morning light, attempt to sing the song the stars have sung o'ernight.

JIMMY. I never knew that before.

BUMBO. Of course the birds make a rotten job of it; but, then, the poor things can't afford a vocal teacher. [*He listens again. Then he resumes.*] Ah, if the birds could but sing the Song of the Stars! If they could sound but one chord of that sweet symphony of sound, the whole dissonant world would then vibrate in unison and be in tune again.

JIMMY [*yawning*]. I don't know what it's all about—but I do know I'm getting sleepy.

BUMBO. Yes—let me put you to bed before I go.

JIMMY. But you will come back again, won't you?

BUMBO. Yes; I'll come back to you many times—in dreams.

JIMMY. Well, if you don't, I'll get sick again—and then you'll just have to come back.

[*He is about to climb into bed.*]

BUMBO. Haven't you forgotten something?

JIMMY [*making a face*]. Oh, yes. What a nuisance! [*He comes and kneels at the knees of Bumbo and in a hurried voice.*] Now I lay me down to sleep, I pray the Lord my soul to keep. God bless papa and—

BUMBO [*interrupting*]. You're cheating.

JIMMY. I forgot.

BUMBO [*in an impressive voice*]. If I should die before I wake, I pray the Lord my soul to take.

JIMMY [*hurriedly*]. God bless papa and mamma—and *Bumbo*, and make me a good little boy, for Jesus' sake. Amen. [*He climbs into bed.*] Won't you tell me a story before I go to sleep?

BUMBO. All right. I'll turn off the lights first. [*He switches off the electrolier, leaving only the night lamp. As he sits by the bed, telling the story, the strange light from the window still shines on his face.*] Once upon a time there was an old fool who had a big heart—for even fools have hearts. And this fool's heart was big as a house, but as cold as a barn.

JIMMY [*sleepily*]. What made it cold?

BUMBO. Well, you see, the steam heat hadn't been turned on yet. But a little boy found his way into the heart of the old fool, and curled up to go to sleep. There was lots of room—I guess there was room enough for all the children in the world. And still space enough for some grown-ups. And it didn't matter about the steam heat any longer, for the little boy warmed the heart of the fool. And as the little boy slept, he dreamed—and dreamed that the old fool was dead.

[*Jimmy is asleep. Bumbo bends over him tenderly and kisses him; then he goes silently over to the window, the strange light envelops*] *him, and he vanishes into the night.*

Mrs. Weston enters from the other room. She watches her boy anxiously, and listens to his regular breathing. Then she picks up a glass from the table and is about to leave the room, when Jimmy calls.]

JIMMY. Bumbo!

MRS. WESTON [*turning*]. What is it, dear?

JIMMY. Oh! I thought it was Bumbo.

MRS. WESTON. Do you feel better, darling?

JIMMY. Oh, I feel much better! I've just had the most scrumptious time.

[*The Doctor enters from the door at back. He approaches his patient quietly and examines him. The mother watches anxiously.]*

DOCTOR [*surprised*]. He's stronger. His pulse is firmer and more regular.

MRS. WESTON [*eagerly*]. You mean— he's going to get better?

DOCTOR. I see no reason why he shouldn't.

MRS. WESTON [*kneeling at his bedside and crying*]. Oh, thank God!—thank God!

JIMMY. Mamma, Bumbo was here.

MRS. WESTON. You were dreaming, dear.

JIMMY. No, I wasn't. He was here in this very room.

DOCTOR. But that's impossible, Jimmy. [*To Mrs. Weston, aside.*] Bumbo is dead.

JIMMY [*positively*]. I tell you, he was here. He went out that window.

[*He points. Mrs. Weston gives a start of surprise.]*

MRS. WESTON. Look! The window is open! I'm sure I closed it.

JIMMY [*triumphantly*]. There! I told you so.

DOCTOR. The wind, perhaps.

JIMMY. Wind nothin'. I guess I know. Look out, Mamma, and see if you can see him.

MRS. WESTON [*looking out*]. I see nothing, dear.

JIMMY. Are you sure? Look again.

MRS. WESTON [*humoring him*]. Nothing—nothing but a shooting star.

JIMMY [*with satisfaction*]. That's Bumbo. He's turning somersaults in the sky!

MRS. WESTON [*to the Doctor, anxiously*]. Are you sure he's out of danger?

DOCTOR. Quite. A little feverish still, but it will pass.

[*The orchestra plays softly the music of "Bumbo the Brave."*]

JIMMY [*listening gleefully*]. Listen! Bumbo is singing to the stars.

[*The telephone suddenly begins to ring. Mrs. Weston answers it.]*

MRS. WESTON [*at phone*]. Hello! Hello! . . . I don't want a number. You called mine. . . . There must be some mistake.

[*She hangs up the receiver.]*

JIMMY [*smiling*]. There ain't any mistake. It's Bumbo. I left word to have him call me up when he got there.

MRS. WESTON [*to the Doctor*]. What are these strange fancies?

DOCTOR [*gravely*]. How should I know? We doctors know little enough about the living. We know nothing at all about the dead. Little Jimmy was pretty close to death to-night. Who knows? Perhaps Bumbo was here.

JIMMY. Doctor, tell Bumbo I'm all right now—and tell him to give my regards to God.

DOCTOR [*hesitating, then picking up the phone, as if to humor the boy—but speaking as if he meant it*]. Jimmy is all right now. We thank you, Bumbo. And give our regards to God.

[*Curtain.*]

THE VANISHING PRINCESS
A Magical Play

By John Golden

CHARACTERS

Mr. I-Say.
Miss Cindy.
Matinka.
The King.

THE VANISHING PRINCESS

A MAGICAL PLAY   **BY JOHN GOLDEN**

[SCENE: *We are in the quaint, misty, musty magic-shop of Matinka, the once-famous Master Magician.*

Youth and Magic go together, but when gray hairs come Old Age resorts to tricks to simulate Youth, and Matinka has descended from the brewing of true magic to the business of selling tricks.

If you care to know how to make a rabbit jump out of a little boy's ear, or the secret recipe by which you can scramble eggs in a gentleman's silk hat and still remain a gentleman, you may—for an absurdly small sum—learn from Matinka just how these things may be done.

Alas and alack! Business is none too brisk, for what with the radio and other bewildering inventions the Practical Public is fast losing faith in fairy-things.

However, there is a very happy, very old story of magic-romance in this place if you have the eyes to see it.

The shop is stuffed with many grand and gaudy mysteries, made by the deft hands of poor Matinka when the magic was still in his fingers.

Here are grinning masks and care-free dummies—some have happy faces—some have wistful faces—and some have no faces at all. Mysterious sawed-off hands try to clutch you from the corners—a crocodile eyes you hungrily from the ceiling—playing cards hang on invisible wires—magic wands—brass and silver gew-gaws—giant dice—skulls on plate glass—and in the very center of it all is a curtained cabinet in which there stands an empty chair. This is Matinka's Great Vanishing Act.

Through the windows of the little shop you can see the street and the snow and the houses on the other side all huddled together to keep warm.

And there can't be snow at this magic season without chimes—so there are chimes, soft and delicate as a mother's memories.

Later you will see a lighted candle warming a window here and there in the houses across the way.

Between the shop windows there hangs on great black hinges the Blue Door from the street. Fastened to it is the Yellow Bell which rings politely when you enter.

In one corner there is an old fireplace with a pot hanging on a crane.

A broken down counter, a few hopeless chairs, a workbench and a kit of shiny tools are about the room.

In another corner there is a little tired door. It is open just now, so that with one glance you may see who and how Matinka lives.

Outside the snow is softly falling, but you cannot see clearly. Evening is coming on.

Occasionally a pedestrian hurries by, coat collar turned up, with an armful of bundles, for this is Christmas Eve.

The shop is empty, but in a moment or two the Blue Door is rudely opened, the Yellow Bell jangling a complaint at such treatment, and there before us is Mr. I-Say, the most disagreeable looking man you ever saw, and obviously the sort of person to whom one owes money.

He stands there slapping the snow from his great fur overcoat, grunting his disapproval of everything as he glares about the place.

He bangs his stick upon the floor, but as no one answers he bawls.]

MR. I-SAY. Is anybody in? [*Stomp-stomp-stomp.*] I say, is anybody here?

[*He looks in through the little tired door in the corner and, determining to investigate further, goes into the other room. Once more the street door opens, but this time the bell tinkles gently a welcome to a friend. It is Miss Cindy, staggering under the weight of a large bundle of sticks and a package wrapped in butcher's paper. She is tired, ragged and lovely. Of course you realize that she is none other than Cinderella herself. She places her parcel upon the counter and throws the sticks down on the hearth. She swings her arms to warm them and blows upon her poor red hands; then she places a few sticks in the fireplace and as she sets a match to them she burns her fingers.*]

CINDY. Holey Swiss Cheese! [*She sucks her fingers and jumps about as Mr. I-Say quietly enters and frowns at her. Then, looking at her finger, Cindy speaks again.*] You big idiot!

MR. I-SAY. Are you speaking to me?

CINDY. I was speaking to my own finger and it was private, and you had no right to be listening. You'll get big ears snoopin' around like that!

MR. I-SAY. You're very rude. I say, you're very rough.

CINDY. I'm so tough—where I come from the canary birds sing bass!

MR. I-SAY. Tct! Tct! Such language —I say, such language from little children.

CINDY. I'm no little children—I'm a grown-up young lady. [*She points with pride to a knot at the back of her head.*] Pipe!

MR. I-SAY. Are you Matinka's daughter?

CINDY. No.

MR. I-SAY. Then who are you? I say, where are you from?

CINDY. I am Cindy. I was born in a carrousel and I'm still dizzy.

MR. I-SAY. You work for Matinka?

CINDY. Sure, I work for him. We sell tricks—don't you want to buy this? [*She has taken from the counter a dagger and, much to the surprise of Mr. I-Say, perhaps even to yours—unless you know how it is done—and very likely you do—she plunges it through her arm.*]

MR. I-SAY. Good heavens! I say, good heavens, don't do that!

CINDY [*loosening the dagger and showing it to Mr. I-Say*]. Ain't it a good one? Only seventy-five cents.

MR. I-SAY. I don't want it. I say, I don't like it. I shouldn't think anybody would want to buy things like that.

CINDY. Business *is* terrible. We ain't made enough in the last month to buy a blanket for a horsefly.

MR. I-SAY. Then you're poor.

CINDY. We're so broke we rattle.

MR. I-SAY. I thought so. I want to see Matinka—I want to see him at once.

CINDY. You can't do that because he ain't here—he went out a little while ago and I don't know when he'll be back. Say, Mister, don't you want to take home one of these things around here? I'll sell it to you awful cheap.

MR. I-SAY. No, thank you. I say, thanks no.

CINDY. I heard you the first time. But, look! [*From the counter she takes something that is meant to look like a rose.*] Here's a thing you can have a barrel of fun with. Just smell it and I'll show you what it does. A hundred dollars' worth of fun for a dime—a thin, round dime!

MR. I-SAY. I don't need a rose. I say, I don't need a rose.

CINDY. You don't know whether you need this one or not. You don't know what it'll do—it's a trick—smell it!

MR. I-SAY. I tell you I don't want one. I want to see Matinka. Do you know how long it's been since he's paid his rent? I say, do you know how long it's been—

CINDY. Say, I'm so far ahead of you I'm lonesome. I got you now! You're the new landlord!

MR. I-SAY. Yes, I am. I've taken over this property. The man who had it before was an old fool. I say, he was an old fool. From now on I propose to conduct matters in a businesslike way. Business is business is what I always says—I say, business is business—brass tacks—brass tacks!

CINDY. Oh, buy a fiddle and rest your chin!

MR. I-SAY. I shall leave here at once! I say, I shall leave here at once!

CINDY. You mean you're not going to stay.

MR. I-SAY. That's it exactly. And you can tell Matinka that he will have to pay before the end of the year or get out of here.

CINDY. Get out of here? Why, where will we go?

MR. I-SAY. That's no concern of mine. I'm a business man. I pride myself that when I'm talking business I talk business. Oh, don't get the idea that I'm not charitable. I do lots of things for a great many people—well, when I say a great many—I do things for some people. Charity begins at home, I always say. I say, charity begins at home. But charity is one thing and business is another. You tell Matinka he's got to pay. He can't skin me. I say, Matinka can't skin me.

CINDY. Aw, he wouldn't skin a banana. If you'll just wait a little while maybe we'll have some money.

MR. I-SAY. Maybe, eh? I've heard that kind of talk before.

CINDY. No, but maybe it's true! There's a great man that I know—and he's a King—and he said he might come and buy the disappearing act.

MR. I-SAY. What are you talking about—a King—I say, a King and a disappearing act!

CINDY. Yes. [She shows Mr. I-Say the chair that Matinka has made for the Vanishing Act.] This is Matinka's very best trick—and the King has said he might buy it.

MR. I-SAY. You're a lunatic. I say, you're crazy. I'll listen to no more of your nonsense. I believe in laying my cards on the table. I say, I lay my cards on the table—

CINDY [quickly taking a pack of cards from the counter, throws them into the air and catches them. Of course, you know that there is a string through them]. Well, here's a trick pack that you can lay on the table, and I'll let you have them for twenty cents.

MR. I-SAY [starting toward the door and making a great deal of unnecessary noise with his stick]. Good night, young lady. I say, good night.

CINDY. Wait, please! Here—take them —you can have them for nothing. [Mr. I-Say grabs the cards and puts them in his pocket.] But, please, Mister—please don't make me tell Matinka he's got to leave—not to-night. It's Christmas Eve and it would be an awful dirty deal if the only thing he got for Christmas was a notice to get t'blazes out of here. I don't have to tell him to-night, do I?

MR. I-SAY. Now, really, young lady, a spade's a spade. I say, a spade's a spade —brass tacks—brass tacks!

CINDY. Look! I'll give you this rose, too. We've got a lot of 'em and nobody's buyin' 'em anyway. You can have stacks of fun if you take it home and make somebody you don't like smell it. Don't you know somebody you don't like?

MR. I-SAY. Of course I do!

CINDY. Well, now, you smell this flower and you'll see what I mean.

[Mr. I-Say reluctantly puts his nose to the flower and a stream of water shoots into his face. Cindy laughs heartily but stops suddenly for there is a murderous gleam in his eye. Before she realizes it he has given her a push that sends her spinning to the floor.]

MR. I-SAY. You miserable, ill-bred little wretch! I say, you ill-bred, miserable little wretch!

CINDY. Say, who are you pushing?

MR. I-SAY. Now you tell Matinka that I was going to give him a day or two in which to pay but because of you—I say, just because of you—I'm coming back here to-night, and if he hasn't got the money he'll have to get out! And a thousand curses—ten thousand curses —I say, a hundred thousand curses on you!

[With a glare that shrivels poor Cindy he stalks out of the shop, slamming the door behind him.]

CINDY [on the floor, disconsolately going over something on her fingers, mumbles]. That's a hundred and eleven thousand! Some curses! Now, why the blazes did I do that? Oh, gosh!

[A little sob escapes her. Then, as she sees that the fire is getting low, she puts a stick or two on it and kneels there on the hearth, staring wide-eyed into the flames. Now the little bell rings again, as Matinka enters through the Blue Door. He is a white-haired old gentleman, peering over brass-rimmed square spectacles. At the very first glance you may see that Matinka is quite as timid as Mr. I-Say is bold.]

MATINKA. Hello, there. Hello, Cindy. A fire?—that is a surprise. [Cindy goes and helps him with his tattered coat.] Where ever did you get the wood?

CINDY. The grocer's boy.

MATINKA. The grocer's boy gave you all that wood?

CINDY. Well, no. It was a trade. I showed him the knife trick and he wanted one—and, you see, I believe business is business. Brass tacks, I say, brass tacks. So I told him if he'd give me some firewood I'd let him have the knife. I didn't think you'd mind.

MATINKA. Of course not. But the wood was worth much more than the knife.

CINDY. That's what he said. So rather than have him think I'd cheat him I—threw in a kiss.

MATINKA. Cindy!

CINDY. Oh, it was just a little one— you know—none of that vamp stuff. Where have you been?

MATINKA. Next door to see Mrs. Dowdy.

CINDY. Now, it's no use your talking about that.

MATINKA. Cindy, dear, do let's be reasonable. She asked me to come up and talk to her again about you.

CINDY. I know—I know.

MATINKA. She has so many children she needs some one to take care of them. And she says you'd have very little to do.

CINDY. Now, you grab that by the horns, you can throw it better.

MATINKA. But she's got some money.

CINDY. What's that to us?

MATINKA. You see, Cindy—you see, I haven't any. And I'm afraid you'll have to go.

CINDY. You mean you're firing me?

MATINKA. Y—y—yes.

CINDY. Oh, bring that in Friday; it sounds fishy. You know you don't want me to go.

MATINKA. I don't want you to go, but we're so poor—

CINDY. I know—and we owe for the rent.

MATINKA. How do you know that?

CINDY. A little bird told me. Well, I wouldn't say exactly a *little* bird—but he was a *bird*, all right! I don't care what we ain't got—I know what we have got—and that's each other! You got as much chance to get rid of me as a snowball has in—

MATINKA. Cindy!

CINDY. Well, if you don't want me to swear, don't try to fire me again. You know what to-night is?

MATINKA. Why, no, I—

CINDY. Yes, you do. You know it's Christmas Eve.

MATINKA. Why, yes—so it is!

CINDY. I've watched the people going by all day with bundles of presents under their arms—and I made up my mind you'd have a present, too. [*She hands him the package wrapped in butcher's paper. He takes it gingerly.*] Merry Christmas! Open it—go on, open it!

MATINKA [*opens the package and then looks at her helplessly*]. Meat!

CINDY. That's what it is—a big piece of real meat!

MATINKA. Cindy!

CINDY. We didn't say nothin' to each other about to-morrow bein' Christmas because we hadn't any presents, but now we can talk about it because we've *got* one! You're goin' to put a nice big hunk of juicy meat under your belt!

MATINKA. How did you ever get it?

CINDY. The butcher's boy—for the rose that squirts water in your eye. And —oh, yes,—a kiss.

MATINKA. That wasn't nice!

CINDY. No, it was a bum kiss. He ain't no Romeo. But I did want the meat for a Christmas present—and now we're going to have a feast.

MATINKA. Cindy, you're just an angel. I couldn't get on without you.

CINDY. Of course you couldn't. But you won't have to because I'm never going to leave you. You're going to be my family and I'm going to take care of you.

MATINKA. It's a great responsibility. [*With a sigh, he sits.*]

CINDY. Not at all. It's easy when you get used to it. I've always had somebody to take care of—that's how I know. But you—you've been so long all alone—you never had no children—

MATINKA. Yes, I did, Cindy. I had a boy—a son that my poor wife and I loved—a golden-haired lad—

CINDY. You never told me.

MATINKA. I never spoke about it to folks much because it kind of hurts—here — [*He puts his hand to his heart.*] I guess I wasn't good enough for her. She ran away and took Danny with her. And then after a while I got word that she had died.

CINDY. And your boy—Danny?

MATINKA. I don't know. I never heard no more—it's nearly twenty years now. And sometimes I'm hoping—

CINDY. That he'll come back? Sure he will! And he'll bring a great fortune —and then you won't be poor any more and you won't have to work on dummy heads and disappearing tricks. Just sit around in your grand parlor all studded with pearls and diamonds, smoking tencent cigars and saving the swell bands for me. [*Matinka chuckles.*] There now —you're laughing. See, we're *having* a Merry Christmas, aren't we? And look— see what else I've got! [*She takes from her pocket a poor wisp of mistletoe.*] Mistletoe! See! You can kiss anybody if you've got one of these!

MATINKA. Who gave you that?

CINDY. I'd—I'd rather not tell.

[*She turns away from him and pokes at the fire.*]

MATINKA. Cindy, what's the matter? You're keeping something from me. You're blushing!

CINDY. I am not—it's the fire. [*She goes over to him.*] Will you promise you won't tell anybody?

MATINKA. Of course.

CINDY. Never?

MATINKA. Never.

CINDY. Swear it!

[*She kneels by his side.*]

MATINKA. On my honor.

CINDY. Cross your heart, too! [*Matinka very gravely crosses his heart, too.*] I'm—I'm in love.

[*She hides her head on his knee.*]

MATINKA. My poor little girl!

CINDY. He gave me this mistletoe and told me if I hung it up somewhere where we'd meet sometime—

MATINKA. He? He? Who is he? Do I know him?

CINDY. Oh, no. You've never met him —or any one like him. He's a King!

MATINKA. A King, Cindy? What are you saying?

CINDY. I tell you he's a King. A really truly honest-to-God King!

MATINKA. I can't believe—

CINDY. Oh, but it's true! He's a King with a purple and vermin robe and a golden crown on his head all studded with jewels of the rarest vintage—and he carries a specter in his hand!

MATINKA. But how—where—

CINDY. It was on Main Street—a great crowd of the populace was doing him homidge. He was there in his chariot—and the chariot was all precious stones, too.

MATINKA. Cindy, it's all so wonderful—

CINDY. Yes, it is. And he was giving away medicine that he said cost many thousands of dollars for just a few pennies—doing it for the sake of humanity —and I went along with the crowd and followed the chariot—and he sat there on his throne—and he saw me—and—do you believe in love at first sight!

MATINKA. It's all very strange.

CINDY. He called me to him—and he spoke to me.

MATINKA. The King—spoke to you?

CINDY. Just like I was anybody. And he asked me how I felt and I said, "Very well indeed, your Majesty," and he said, "That's too bad, because my Indian Sagraw Zodiac could cure you of anything." And I told him again that I didn't have anything—and he said of course if I didn't have anything he couldn't cure me! Then after the crowd had gone away he talked to me again and he asked me where I lived—and I told him about you—and the tricks—and the Great Vanishing Act—and he said maybe he'd come to see you and look at the trick; and I saw him again day before yesterday—and yesterday—and to-day he gave me this sprig of mistletoe and said he might come here to-night!

MATINKA. To-night! The King said he might come *here*?

CINDY. To look at the Vanishing Act. He said perhaps he could use it to amuse his subjects.

MATINKA [*as he rises and wanders about the room, greatly upset*]. Dear, dear—if he should come here I wouldn't know what to say or to do.

CINDY. Then I'll tell you. Just be yourself—and then when he finds out what a wonderful magician you are and that you were once the great Matinka— he'll make you Chief of his Court magicians or astrologers or something.

MATINKA. But you, Cindy—he ought not to see you that way. Maybe you could wear the gown that we made for the Vanishing Princess Act.

CINDY. Oh, that would be wonderful! —No, it wouldn't be right. I mustn't wear it. The King might not want to buy the trick if he saw the gown had been worn. And, anyway, I'd only have to tell him that I'd deceived him—that I wasn't really of royal blood.

MATINKA. I suppose that's true.

CINDY. But he mustn't see *you* this way. There surely won't be any harm in putting on your blue coat with the brass buttons so maybe he'll think you're a real astrologer or something.

MATINKA [*as he goes to the door*]. Yes, yes. I'll do it now. We don't want him to think we're poor.

CINDY. We don't want anybody to think we're poor—because we ain't.

MATINKA. If he thinks we are you just show him our Merry Christmas steak.

[*With a chuckle he goes out through the little tired door.*]

CINDY. I'll get supper ready. We'll have a feast fit for a king!

[*She lights two or three poor candles; then busies herself with the supper things. Once or twice she murmurs:* The King! *As she works she looks down at her stockings and observes a large ragged hole in one of them. She goes to Matinka's work bench and with a brushful of black paint daubs her leg to hide the hole. Through the store window the end of the Royal Chariot is seen. Mounted on the Chariot is the King himself, crowned and handsomely dressed, a flowing cape of royal purple over his shoulders. The King is speaking to his people. You can hear him quite clearly. It is all very strange—poor little Cinderella working by the fireplace—the snow gently falling outside—the lights in the windows of the houses across the way—and the crowd without, listening with rapt attention to the King's words.*]

THE KING. Come on, my good folks—listen to your friend, the great Medicine King! Come here among you to ease your pain—to alleviate suffering humanity! I have here the Pill that Will Cure every Ill; but before you go—I'll give you a show—at no great length—with a feat of strength—that will prove to you beyond the peradventure of a doubt the marvelous power one of those innocent-looking little pellets contains—the marvelous power that only one single pellet will bring to your King! I have here a bar of solid steel—examine,

please— [*He hands the steel bar to his people.*] Goliath and Samson together could not perform this feat of strength! And I get it all from just one of these pellets—which cure every ill that flesh is heir to. Observe, please—I swallow but one. If you did not see this with your own eyes you would doubt, and I should not blame you—the pill has done its work! It has brought strength, health and power to me! Observe closely— [*He bends the steel bar as though it were a piece of macaroni. The crowd is filled with awe.*] This pill, composed of Indian Sagraw and other secret ingredients, is a scientific compound working upon the bio-chemic system—each one of the twelve signs of the zodiac is represented in the human body by one of the twelve minerals, or cell-salts, in the blood. The cell-salt corresponding to the sign of the Sun is consumed more rapidly than the other minerals—hence a deficiency may arise which produces effects that we call disease.

Tell me the date of your birth and I will give you the birth-salt free—gratis —for nothing—with every bottle of my Sagraw Pill that Will, the price of which is one dime—ten cents—the smallest piece of silver coined by our beloved Uncle Sam.

The despondent and discouraged—all who are vacillating and unsuccessful—take my mighty and mysterious Indian Sagraw Zodiac Pill that Will and be cured forever! [*The King is rapidly selling his wonderful wares.*] Who wants the next bottle? Only a few more left—and the formula can never be duplicated. —Thank you—that's all—only ten cents—no, I couldn't take a cent more—I do this because I want to help humanity—here's your change—here's the last one—who'll take it?—thank you—sorry, I have no more. They're all gone!—Go now, my good people—and be happy.

[*The crowd has bought and gone. The King jumps down from his chariot and looks up at the sign above the Blue Door with the black hinges. He opens the door and the little Yellow Bell rings perhaps more happily than it has ever rung before. Cindy rises and bows very low.*]

CINDY. Your Majesty!

THE KING. Rise, Mistress Cindy. We

would greet thee in truly royal fashion. [*He takes her hand and, as she rises, kisses it.*] True to our promise we are here at the trysting place.

CINDY. I didn't think you'd come.

[*The King appears astounded at this remark for he replies in quite a loud voice.*]

THE KING. What? You doubted us when we had given our royal word?

CINDY. Oh, no—no, I didn't doubt you —only I didn't believe you— [*Then, very quickly.*] That is, I didn't believe you'd remember.

THE KING. Thou didst me but scant justice.

CINDY. I didst?

THE KING. Thou didst indeed! But, prithee give it no more thought. 'Tis forgiven.

CINDY. Prithee, I thankst thou!

THE KING. Pish tush! 'Tis nothing!

CINDY. 'Tis much — that thoust shouldst doest us so great an honor to visit our humble cot—with thy royalst presence. 'Twere good indeed. [*She goes to a chair and with her apron wipes the seat.*] Wouldst thoust sittest downst? We ain't got no thronest for thoust. But if thoust wouldn't mind—Holy Swiss cheese, I got to stop eating sugar—I'm getting too refined!—I beg your pardon, your Majesty, but if we could just talk regular talk maybe we'd know what we were talking about.

THE KING. Why, Cindy, I thought you liked it. Sure, it's a lot easier for me to be human. I thought you wanted me to play I was a real King.

CINDY. Oh, but you are—aren't you?

THE KING. Are you a princess of the royal blood?

CINDY. Don't kid the goldfish—it's been around the globe. Of course I'm not.

THE KING. Then no more am I a King. I'm just a medicine fakir who has been wand'ring 'round the world hoping to find somebody who would really believe in him.

CINDY. I believe in you!

THE KING. You do? Then my mission is fulfilled—my search is ended. And to-night—this Christmas Eve—I abdicate my throne. See! I doff my crown —never to wear it again!

[*He takes off his crown and his pur-*

ple robe, and there he is—a very nice young man!*]

CINDY. Oh, why did you do that?

THE KING. Because, Cindy dear, I have sold my last bottle of Sagraw—because I'm rich—richer than I ever dreamed—they say a sucker is born every minute, but mine came to me like shad —in roes—a million a month! And I've come home to find the poor lonely old man that you told me of—and to lay all my gold at his feet. [*From the robe he produces a great deal of money and many bags of gold.*] All this [*he waves his hand majestically toward the gold*] is for the lonely old man who's been waiting all these years.

CINDY. You're Danny!

THE KING. That's me.

CINDY. And I thought you were a King!

THE KING. Does it make any real difference to you, Cindy dear? Can't you like me just as well now that you know I'm only Danny?

CINDY. I don't know. You were such a grand King! But for Matinka's sake I'd a thousand times rather you were Danny.

THE KING. That's it! And I want to be Danny to you.

CINDY. Please don't talk so kind to me—I ain't sick!

THE KING. Call me Danny—go on, now.

CINDY. Danny.

THE KING. Great! Now do you suppose you could call me Danny darling?

CINDY. Oh, I'm sure I couldn't do that!

THE KING. Aw, try. It isn't so awfully hard to say if you don't think about it much—just remember I think you're the sweetest, prettiest, dearest, most adorable creature in the whole world. And I guess the most patient. Oh, Cindy, all the folks around here have told me what you've done for my dad—

CINDY. Tell them to use that apple sauce for dessert.

THE KING. Don't you suppose I've learned all about how you've worked to help take care of an old man—and how you've suffered—how poor you've both been—

CINDY. Don't rub it in, it's not liniment.

THE KING. And then I saw you—that day—and the minute I saw you I loved you, Cindy. And I planned to work till this very night, and finish selling my last bottle at this very door, and then come home—never to go away again.

CINDY. Are you married?

THE KING. I am not. I've waited for you. I want you to be my wife, Cindy. Now will you try to say Danny darling?

CINDY. Will I? Danny darling—oh, Danny darling!

[*The King is just about to gather her into his arms, and if he did the story would be over—but he doesn't. Happily for those who like the play—if there be any— Matinka's voice is heard.*]

MATINKA. Cindy!

[*It comes as rather a shock to the two young people for, strangely enough, at this precise moment they are thinking of nothing in the world but each other.*
Cindy guiltily jumps away from the King, and puts her finger to her lips with a warning "ssh."]

CINDY. Yes?

MATINKA. Is any one there with you? I've put on the old blue coat with the brass buttons!

CINDY. Don't tell him too suddenly who you are. He's not very strong.

THE KING. I know.

MATINKA [*as he enters in the beautiful blue coat with the brass buttons*]. Cindy, how do I look? Do you think the King— [*He sees that they are not alone.*] Oh, I beg your pardon.

CINDY [*in her very grandest manner*]. My lord, permit me to present Matinka, the Master of Magic. Matinka, the King.

[*The King steps forward and tenderly takes Matinka's hand. When he speaks it is in a rather strange voice.*]

THE KING. I'm very—very— [*there must be some dust in his throat!*] proud to meet you, sir.

MATINKA. The honor is mine, sir.

THE KING. This young lady has told me of a marvelous magic effect you have invented in the way of a Vanishing Act. I should like to buy it. Here's the money.

[*To Matinka's great astonishment he picks up the largest bag of gold and flings it upon the counter.*]

MATINKA. Buy it? But—but—you haven't seen it yet!

THE KING. That will come later. It has been fully described to me and I want it.

MATINKA. I should be very glad to have you buy it, sir. May I show it to you?

THE KING. If you like.

MATINKA. Then will you please sit there? [*The King sits.*] I call the effect "The Vanishing Princess." Come here, Cindy. You shall be the Princess-bride who fades away.

[*Matinka leads Cindy to the chair in the cabinet.*]

THE KING. If you please, sir, I hope you won't make her fade too far away.

CINDY. You may never see me again!

THE KING. Please don't say that!

MATINKA. As you see, she is hidden for the moment with this magic cloth. Now you may make a wish—and if it is a fair one it is very likely to come true.

THE KING [*and he says this very fervently*]. I *have* made a wish.

MATINKA [*picking up a lighted candle*]. Observe I wave this three times before the magic cloth. I pronounce the mystic, cabalistic "Abracadabra"—I throw aside the cloth and the young lady has disappeared.

[*Matinka suits his action to the word; he throws aside the cloth and sure as you live the chair is empty!*]

THE KING. Wonderful! Wonderful! But can you bring her back!

MATINKA. Oh, yes, if I choose.

THE KING. Then please do choose to bring her back at once.

[*Although this may seem a dreadful time to interrupt the story, the Blue Door with the black hinges is suddenly opened, the Yellow Bell once again complains, and Mr. I-Say enters the shop.*]

MR. I-SAY. Ah, there you are, Matinka! I say, there you are! I have called to talk over some very important business with you. I am not a man to mince words. I say, I don't mince things. I believe in laying my cards on the table, because business is business. That's what I always say. I say, business is business. Brass tacks, I say, brass tacks!

THE KING [*with his most courtly bow*].

You're quite right, sir. And I'm sure you won't mind waiting a moment or two until we've attended to another matter.

MR. I-SAY. You're a very polite young man—but I'm not such a fool as I look. I say, I'm not such a fool as I look. Your smooth talk does not deceive me. I don't know you, sir—and I've come for a very serious talk with Matinka. I've been grossly insulted here. I'll have no more patience with Matinka or that crazy child he keeps around this place. I'll have the law on both of them! And I've come to talk it over. I say, I've come to talk it over very seriously.

THE KING [with peculiar emphasis and a sidelong glance at Matinka]. While the gentleman is talking won't you ask him to sit down?

MATINKA. Of course—of course.

THE KING [pointing to the chair in the cabinet]. To sit down there. Your best chair, of course.

MATINKA. Oh—oh, yes. Please be seated.

[With a grunt or two, Mr. I-Say deposits himself in the chair of the cabinet. With a quick movement the King throws the magic cloth across the cabinet, picks up the candle and thrusts it into Matinka's trembling hand; he speaks in sharp, commanding tones.]

THE KING. Quick, now! Wave the candle and say the magic word! I have made a wish!

[Before old Matinka has time to think he has waved the candle—pronounced the fatal "Abracadabra." The King draws aside the magic cloth—and Mr. I-Say, thank goodness, has vanished!]

MATINKA. Oh, dear, dear! He's the new landlord! I must bring him back!

THE KING. No—no—don't do that. He must disappear forever. This invention of yours will make us all rich—no

one will ever again have to pay rent to a landlord!

MATINKA. But it doesn't seem right.

THE KING. To perdition with him! He's a heartless old villain and it's very fortunate that we can send him to oblivion where all villains should go.

[To stop Matinka, the King places his hand upon his arm. An almost imperceptible quiver goes through the old man. He looks queerly up into the boy's face.]

MATINKA. You'll pardon an old man, but I seem to feel that we have met before—that I know you. My eyes are dim, but— [His gaze travels over the boy; he looks down at the hand.] That ring!

THE KING. It was mother's. She placed it there before she died. She told me of my father and asked me to find him and seek his forgiveness.

[Matinka looks into the eyes of the King for a long time and then falls into his arms.]

MATINKA. Danny!

THE KING [as he hugs his father tight]. Dad!

MATINKA. My boy! Oh, my boy, you've come back to me!

THE KING. Yes, Dad, for always—to take care of you and Cindy—Cindy! Cindy!

[He throws aside the magic cloth and Cindy, in the beautiful gown of the Princess-bride, steps down from the cabinet.]

CINDY. Yeah! Look—I'm all dressed up like a salad!

[She takes the crown from the counter and places it on the King's head. From somewhere comes the sound of Christmas chimes and the melody of a wedding march is softly heard. The King and the Princess Cindy slowly walk to the arms of Matinka.]

[Curtain.]

THE DEATH OF NERO
A Play
By Herbert Gorman

CHARACTERS

NERO.
EPAPHRODITUS.
PHAON.
SPORUS.
A YOUNG GIRL.
A BOY.

THE DEATH OF NERO

A PLAY   BY HERBERT GORMAN

[The sparsely furnished outer room of the villa of Phaon at Baiae is empty. Yet a spirit of tension, of mysterious and monstrous things, chills the atmosphere and in spite of the many lamps which valiantly hold at bay the night there is a sense of shadows. The room shines with the bleak cold light of a setting pre-arranged by the gods for an abrupt finale. The low couch covered with a bearskin and the single curved chair crouch disconsolately, listening to the night as it pads about the villa, fumbling with soft horrible paws at the great center door now so securely barred against all ingress. Beside the door looms a thin marble pedestal upon which the bust of a bearded man stares with stony eyes into mystery. The door leading to the inner rooms is mantled with a red hanging, the one bright bit of color in this chilly austerity.

The silence is broken by the low sound of galloping horsemen which steadily mounts in violence until the shouts of the riders, the clang of their swords against stirrup-irons, and the rushing of hooves are manifestly passing the center door. The turmoil lessens in violence and dies away into a low rumble. At the height of the noise a Boy, young and dark-eyed and clad in a green tunic, thrusts aside the red hanging and runs over to the great door where he listens attentively. A young Girl, garmented in white, follows him, standing with her back against the hanging.]

BOY [*when the noise subsides*].   Is Rome on fire?
GIRL. Why should it be?
BOY.   I heard
The sound of racing horses in the dark
And muttering of voices and the clang
Of heavy swords against the stirrup-irons.

There was a man cried "By the gods!"
    and swore
That Rome was burning.
GIRL.   No, the city stands.
The Seven Hills remain unshaken. This
Is only the fever of your childish mind.
The city stands.
BOY.   I heard a dying horse
Scream in the roadway and the gates are
    splashed
With blood. The garden-wall is broken
    through
And all my flowers are trampled by
    strange feet.
GIRL. It does not matter now. Another year
And your bright garden will be new
    again.
The old things perish. Are the gateways
    locked?
BOY. Fastened and bolted for I feared
    the night.
It creeps about the house like some dark
    beast
And rustles at the windows and its
    eyes
Are like the eyes that came in every
    dream
When I lay sick and felt the lips of
    death
About my face.
GIRL. You must not talk of Death.
    [*She comes hastily to him and holds
    him tightly in her arms.*]
He is abroad this night. He rides on
    horses.
He walks the highways and he creeps
    through lanes
And knocks at many doors.
BOY.   He cannot break
The bolts upon our doors.
GIRL.   Poor fool, he breathes
With his thin icy breath out of the night
And our stout doors are thinner than
    thin mist.
    [*The low rumble of horses' hooves*

grows louder and stops before the door.]

Some one has stopped! Are all the doors with chains?

BOY. Close-fastened. Are you frightened?

GIRL. Yes, for night
Is horrible with monstrous things. The gates
Are splashed with blood!

BOY. You saw it, too! I know.
It was a horse that died; I heard it scream.

[*Suddenly there comes a loud pounding on the door. The Boy runs whimpering toward the inner room.*]

GIRL. Who's there? Who's there, I say!

A VOICE. Your master, Phaon.

[*The Girl runs to the center door and unbars it. It is flung open and Phaon enters, followed closely by Sporus and Epaphroditus supporting Nero. All of them are covered with dust from hard riding. The Emperor, a stout, coarse-featured man with disarranged red hair, is pale and covered with sweat.*]

PHAON [*to the Girl*]. Begone! Bring water!

[*She hurries out. The Boy bars the door and follows her.*]

Cæsar, you are safe.
My villa is quite hidden by the trees.

[*Nero is helped to the couch, where he lies gasping.*]

Will you have bread?

NERO [*shaking his head and fumbling with a huge emerald upon a golden chain through which he stares at Phaon*]. O, Rome! O, Rome! O, Rome!

SPORUS. You must be hungry.

NERO [*dropping the emerald*]. I will eat no more.
My stomach twists even to think of food.

[*He scrubs the perspiration from his face with his mantle.*]

Why do you stand about like gaping dogs
And hide your laughter in a mimic moan!
The city's lost. The Golden House is burned.
My jewels are gone. My throat is sore. My back
Is almost broken by that cursed horse.

Why was there not a litter? A litter with white mules?
Is this the state in which your Cæsar rides?
Bring me some scented pasties. No, some wine!
No, bring me water. Well, I will not eat.

EPAPHRODITUS. Your wits are wandering. Your litters, mules,
And Golden Houses are to dream about
For you will never know their ease again.
Here is your palace in this little room;
Here is your palace and your Mausoleum.

NERO [*staring at him through the emerald*].
I cannot laugh at your strange humors now.
My breath is short. I have a pain in the side.
Are you so joyous at disaster? Know,
And tremble at the knowledge, Rome is dead
For she abjures the holy torch of art.
Can we make Puteoli?

[*There is a dead silence.*]
Well? Well?

EPAPHRODITUS. You do not understand. Your brain is heavy
With too much life. We bring you here to die.
We bring you here to prove yourself a Cæsar.

NERO. I will not listen to this man. Good Phaon,
I never noticed you before and yet
You always were my friend. You never thrust
Hard words like swords against your Cæsar. Come,
And let us talk about to-morrow's games
And sunshine and the waking of this dream,
This nightmare that has almost killed me. Come.
To-morrow we will ride away from here;
But in a litter driven by white mules.
We'll make for Greece. We'll go to Egypt. Come,
And tell me what I want to hear. How soon
Can we depart out of this darkened place?
How soon can we take ship and live on oysters,
Great luscious morsels from the hidden bays?

To-morrow shall we go? Perhaps to-
night?
Can we make Puteoli?
EPAPHRODITUS. No! No! No!
Your way lies singly and the gods pre-
pare
The place. Your pathway no man living
knows.
It follows the vague devious ways of
death.
And you must travel it as Cæsar should.
NERO. But Puteoli—
EPAPHRODITUS. All the roads are filled
With running horsemen. Fire and sword
are swift.
The Roman, Galba, drives his Legions on
And seeks the head of Cæsar for his
spears.
The dark centurion at the cross-road saw
Your face before we rode upon him.
NERO. Gods!
I always feared dark men. They smell
of death;
There was a corpse before me in the sand
That had a broken nose and jellied eyes.
My horse was trampling on it ere I knew.
The gods betrayed me for the lightning-
flash
Made day about my face.
EPAPHRODITUS. You heard the talk,
How one said of us, "They are after
Nero,"
And then the other, "Is there any news?"
There's no escape from Galba but the
grave
If you would be the Roman that I'd have
you.
It is impossible to thread this maze
And Cæsar journeys with all dignity.
The black skiff touches on the river-bank,
The hoary oarsman waits.
SPORUS. All wait but Time.
NERO. Yea, death? The golden voice
must cease? No songs?
O, what an artist will be lost the world!
The tones that roused Achaia and
brought forth
Such thunders of applause in Antinum
And silenced all the golden odes of Na-
ples
Must be a legend? Are you mad to speak
Such things as would make Rome a
desert place?
EPAPHRODITUS. Would Galba suit
your purpose better?
[A pause.]
NERO. Ah!

You taunt me with misfortune. You are
one
Who follows me for gain.
EPAPHRODITUS. My gain is naught.
Ungenerous in death as well as life—
PHAON. The purple cloaks him still.
[The Girl enters with water.]
Why, here is water.
NERO. I am thirsty.
PHAON. Drink.
[Nero gulps down the water
eagerly.]
NERO. It is too warm. The water
should be cooled.
The winds are still ungenerous to me
And lacking in respect about my throat.
I think I have a cold. My chest is sore.
Good Sporus, can we make away by
dawn? I think
I could write something golden of this
night
And set it to soft notes that Greece
would bend
A willing ear to listen to.
SPORUS. You speak
In humor now. Be brave and be a king.
EPAPHRODITUS. Do you expect to live?
NERO [dashing the goblet on the
floor]. O gods, this man
Has murdered me already! Argument
About it and about!
EPAPHRODITUS. Do you not know
That you must kill yourself before the
dawn,
Before the Legions find you like a beast
Hard-driven to some dusty hiding-place?
[There is a pause through which
Nero breathes heavily.]
NERO. I think I know it. Yes, I know
it now.
Yes, yes, I know it!
[After a pause he speaks again.]
You'd all have me dead?
EPAPHRODITUS. Or Galba will. It is
not easy for
A Cæsar's neck to throttle in a fork
While what he was is beaten with sharp
rods
Until he breathes no more.
NERO [slowly]. Not easy—no.
[He turns to Sporus.]
I never could stand beating for my skin
Is softer than the breast of any woman.
To beat me! I, who smote the throb-
bing strings
Until the beasts grew quiet in their
dens,

Forgot their jungle-homes, and stood
like figures
Of frozen stone to hear my lifted song!
EPAPHRODITUS. Their music now is
humming of short swords
And thunder of hard iron. Cæsar, know
All music falters to that last discord
That is the end of breathing. You have
reached
The dizzy pinnacle of Time from whence
All roadways lead to silent Acheron.
NERO. This man is Death's own her-
ald. Sporus, Sporus,
The Theater wept with me when I wept
And laughed with me and thrilled when
my clear song
Climbed steadily to heaven. I was blest,
Thrice blest, in song and voice and subtle
art
Of honeyed strings.
EPAPHRODITUS. You must unlearn
this now
And understand the ways of death.
NERO. You bring
A graveyard breath to me. Good Spo-
rus, come
And weep with me about a bitter world.
SPORUS. My tears are for the world.
NERO. No hope? No way?
No swifter passage for me than cold
steel?
Am I not Cæsar? Bring me hemlock
brewed
Within a crystal cup. Make calm my
senses
With sleepy music that the voyage seem
A fading down still rivers. Sporus,
Phaon,
Epaphroditus, is there none of you
That will be generous?
PHAON. What do you mean?
NERO. Phaon, I have a jewel in my
breast,
A sardis stone cut by the cunning hand
Of some dead Ethiopian. It gleams
Like tigers' eyes at night. It shall be
yours.
It shall be yours if we make Puteoli.
I have green jewels from Smaragdus
Mons,
Carbuncles, sapphires, lapis-lazuli,
And beaten bars of gold from Egypt,
feathers
From crimson birds that sail beyond the
stars,
A silver sun-god come from Delphi, robes
And Gothic crowns and British slaves
and lutes

Inset with chrysoprase—
EPAPHRODITUS. All these are gone
And you have nothing but your body
now.
PHAON. If flight were possible do you
not think
I'd rather start you on your way than
see
The dark blood of a king upon my floors?
NERO. No way but this, indeed? Then
one of you
Draw forth a sword and lead me down
the way
My feet must travel.
SPORUS. Would our deaths make
smooth
Your lonely passage to the grave?
NERO. My heart
Is cold at killing such an artist. Earth
Would not forgive me easily.
EPAPHRODITUS. Oh, Gods,
I'll answer for the earth. The Senators
Have drawn an edict for your punish-
ment.
The Legions Galba leads would tear your
limbs
Apart and think the task a gift to earth.
NERO. Unworthy friend, your eager-
ness is such
That I must doubt your purpose.
EPAPHRODITUS. Doubt it not.
I served you always. You are Rome to
me.
PHAON. Is he not close to you in love?
NERO [throwing his cloak wholly
aside].
I knew
That never sun should shine on me
again,
For Time spoke to me in a hundred
voices
And prophecies and portents filled the
air.
Yet I was amorous of life and shook
The palsy from me, though the face of
Death
Was near me through the night, and bit-
terness
And long despair and longer tears were
quick
To warn me at all times. My voice was
such—
Well, I will say no more of it. My
friend,
Who only lives to see me die, has said
That he will answer for the world. Un-
kind!
Yet do I chide him not. Am I not calm?

These shaking hands shake but with
    expectation
And eagerness to plunge the little knife.
And yet, now that I speak of it, my
    courage
So like a mounting wave ebbs with the
    sea
And I am all undone. What! Must I
    die?
It takes a minute to establish this,
And minutes to a man about to die
Are each a blessed century of breath.
With many omens have the gods in-
    formed
Me of their ruthless purpose. Once I
    dreamed
Of steering a tall ship in sleep, and lo!
The rudder was dragged from me! Gods,
    gods, gods!
Why did they this? The rudder by a
    hand
Most slender was torn from me! Anice-
    tus
Came back into my mind . . . a horrid
    night. . . .
And Agrippina's glaring eyeballs, red
With furies from beyond the grave! Oh!
    Oh!

[He hides his head in a frenzy.]

SPORUS. This is a memory.

NERO [*hoarsely*]. Must I not be
A memory before another day?
Then, too, I dreamed I wandered in a
    way
Where pitchy darkness loomed on either
    side
And hands came from the murkiness and
    dragged
Me into choking mists wherein a shape
Laughed at me and it was Octavia!
I dreamed that I was covered with
    winged ants
Distilling poison into all my veins,
And that a Spanish horse I loved was
    changed
Into a hybrid beast. Its hinderparts
Were like an ape and yet its head gave
    forth
Most tuneful neighs.

PHAON. These dreams are over now.

NERO. So must I be before the golden
    day.
I never knew the day could be so fair
As now I see it in my mind. It shines
With color and the rivers flow and winds
Blow through my summer-gardens. Gold,
    all gold.

[He reverts suddenly to his visions.]

The Mausoleum doors were thrust apart
By hidden hands and many voices cried
Upon me, hailing, "Nero! Nero! Come!"
I knew those voices. There was Clau-
    dius,
Who perished through the flight of my
    ambition,
And young Britannicus and Seneca,
My teacher whom I slew for good advice,
Poppæa Sabina hailed, my slaughtered
    wife,
And all of them the voices of the dead!

EPAPHRODITUS. You must be brave
    and die.

NERO.   The grave is far
More terrible than life, for all I hated
Are waiting there for me. My Lares fell
Upon the Kalends ere the feast was set;
The key unto the Capitol was lost,
And Isidorus cursed me in the streets.
Were these not signs that I should make
    an end?
Locusto gave me poison in a box
Of gold but I was still afraid to die.
I called on Spiculus to strike me dead
But he had fled. Now Cæsar must be
    man
And make himself a god for later days.

*[He turns to Sporus and stretches
out his hand.]*

Give me your dagger, Sporus.

*[He takes a small dagger from Spo-
rus.]*

             Ah, so small?
This tiny bit of metal serves me so?
Why now, what strength lies in these
    lesser things!
A bit of bronze into the eye, a gnat
That's sucked into the windpipe or a
    drop
No larger than a jewel on the tongue
And all our days are part of history!
We live and die in little things and
    cringe
Before the shadow of a shadow.

SPORUS.   So!
What does it matter if the Time be
    short
If all our days are packed with great
    beginnings?
There is no grief except in finished
    things
And death may be the best adventure.

*[The drumming of horses' hooves
starts and grows steadily louder
to the end of the scene.]*

EPAPHRODITUS.   Hark!
Short swords are rattling on the high-
    ways. Shouts
Proclaim the Legions. Thrust the dag-
    ger home!
NERO [*placing the dagger to his
throat*].
How cold the tiny point upon my throat!
One thrust and I escape you all . . .
    and yet. . . .
Is there no way but this?
EPAPHRODITUS. No way but this.
SPORUS. Make haste! The hooves are
drumming on the highway!
PHAON. It will not hurt.
NERO [*pressing the point into his
throat*].
    It does! It does!
SPORUS [*striking Nero's arm and driv-
ing the dagger in*].
Strike home!
NERO [*sliding from the couch and
clawing at the dagger*].

Poppæa! Agrippina! Acte! Acte!
    [*He crashes to the floor.*]
PHAON. Now through the gardens!
    This way!
EPAPHRODITUS [*kicking the body of
Nero*].
Carrion dog!
    [*The three men flee through the door
    at the right. The roaring of
    hooves, now just without the
    center door, stops and an instant
    later a loud knocking resounds
    there. The young Girl enters
    from the right and runs to the
    door.*]
GIRL. There's no one here. My mas-
ter's gone away.
    [*As she stands fearfully at the door,
    the knocking continuing, the cur-
    tain falls.*]

    [*Curtain.*]

QUARE MEDICINE
A Comedy

By Paul Green

CHARACTERS

OLD MAN JERNIGAN.
HENRY JERNIGAN [*his son*].
MATTIE JERNIGAN [*Henry's wife*].
DOCTOR IMMANUEL [*a patent medicine vendor*].

PLACE: *Eastern North Carolina.*

TIME: *Several years ago at the close of a winter day.*

QUARE MEDICINE

A COMEDY   BY PAUL GREEN

[*The* SCENE *is the combined sitting
room and bedroom of the Jernigan house,
with a fireplace to the left, a sewing
machine to the right and a table in the
center of the room. The floor is carpeted with matting, and everything bris-
tles with tidy primness. A door is at
the center back and one at the left rear.
The window at the right center, neatly
curtained, shows a stretch of somber
fields filling up with the blue dusk of a
fading winter day.*
*The curtain rises on the empty room.
From another part of the house the voice
of a woman can be heard shrilly singing
"Rescue the perishing, care for the dying."
Presently the elder Jernigan, walking
with a stick, comes carefully in at the
rear door shivering with cold and carrying a mug in his hand. Below a mass of
white hair his face shines out like a
ruddy autumn apple, and his whole person suggests the toughness and dura-
bility of a dried hickory root. Halfway
across the room he stops and listens to
the singing.*]

JERNIGAN [*sharply imitating*]. "Rescue the perishing, care for the dying!"
[*He moves over to the fire and sets
his mug to warm; after which he
takes a bottle from the mantel,
pours out some medicine in a
spoon and swallows it. He sits
down and stretches his hands to
the blaze with a grunt of satisfaction. In a moment he feels the
cup and takes a long drink. The
woman's voice calls from off the
right.*]
VOICE. Father!
JERNIGAN [*starting*]. Ah-hah! What
is it?
VOICE [*nearer*]. Father—Fath—er!
JERNIGAN [*moving towards the door
at the left*]. What is it, Mattie?

VOICE. Supper's 'bout ready. Where's
Henry?
[*The singing begins again, fading towards the kitchen.*]
JERNIGAN. He's feeding up and'll be
here in a minnit.
[*He listens a moment and then reseats himself thoughtfully before
the fire. Presently there is a
heavy scraping of feet on the steps
outside and Henry Jernigan comes
timidly in at the rear. He is a
big awkward farmer of thirty or
more, hesitating and shy. He
takes his seat silently and wearily
in a rocking chair, being careful
not to touch the whitewashed
hearth with his feet. The old
man looks at him closely.*]
JERNIGAN. Tired out, ain't you?
Hyuh, try some o' this 'simmon beer, I
jest dreaned the barrel.
HENRY [*in a slow, fumbling voice*].
I don't want none o' that, I believe.
JERNIGAN. Uh-huh. [*They both lapse
into silence, staring before them. Presently the elder Jernigan peers through
the window at the winter sunset.*]
Gonna be cold, Henry, cold. Robins been
flying towards the south all day. [*Henry
says nothing.*] You're tireder'n common,
ain't you, Henry?
HENRY. Yeh. [*Lifelessly.*] Wore out,
wore out.
JERNIGAN [*taking his bottle from the
mantel*]. Hyuh, take this last dost of
Doctor 'Manuel's tonic. [*Henry shakes
his head.*] Well, I will then. [*He pours
out the last drop and swallows it.*] Doctor said he'd be by to-day. 'Bout night
and he ain't hyuh yit. You better git
him to give you something, ye better,
Henry, you're looking thin, thin.
HENRY. He ain't no doctor, he's a
humbug.
JERNIGAN. Lard help my life!

185

HENRY. Wonder that mess don't kill you—old branch water and chemicals he'd mixed up, I betcha. [*He sighs heavily, listening to the song in the kitchen.*] That old man's crazy with his poetry and talking and medicine!

JERNIGAN. Huh, not hardly. [*Solemnly.*] 'Taint body tired what ails ye, Henry, is it? [*After a moment he jerks his thumb in the direction of the song.*] Still singing, Henry. There it is.

HENRY. Yeh, I know.

JERNIGAN. Ah-hah, but folks will marry jest the same. She's worse'n ever, Henry. Good she is, religious good. Cooking and sewing and scrubbing and all fixed up fer to-night. Look over there on the machine at what she's got finished fer them there Hindoos or whatever they are. There's my coat I bought in Dunn five year back at Old Man Ransome Taylor's sale!

HENRY [*his eye traveling heavily about the room*]. What's she got on fer to-night?

JERNIGAN. Another one o' them there meetings. Old Mis' Pate and her gang's coming hyuh to sew fer the heathen and them that's starving over in the old world. [*Staring at him intently.*] This religious mess is gonna kill Mattie off ef you don't git up manhood enough to stop it. Sing and talk, sing and talk, Lord, I cain't stand it no more.

HENRY. I—I cain't— I ain't gonna putt my authority on nobody. She's her own boss.

JERNIGAN. Own boss! She's her own boss and our'n too. Well, ef you're scared of her, all right. They ain't no help fer it. [*He turns towards the fire, patting his foot forlornly on the floor.*] But, Henry, ye ain't gitting no fun out'n living, and right now's the time ye ort. And as fer me—I been wanting to talk— [*hitching up his chair*]—to you 'bout this. Why'n the name o' Old Scratch you don't up and putt down yer foot I cain't see. [*Henry says nothing.*] But ye won't. [*Half to himself.*] He ain't got no backbone, lets everybody run over him. [*He reaches for his cup and drains down the last of his beer in an angry gulp.*] Ye didn't git it from yer mammy ner from me, Henry. [*He mocks the singing in the kitchen.*] "Rescue the perishing—"

HENRY [*suddenly standing up*]. I cain't have no row with nobody, not with her nowhow, I tell you. [*At the door.*] I got to go part the cow and calf.

[*He slams the door behind him and the old man jumps in astonishment.*]

JERNIGAN. Dinged ef he didn't slam the door—hee, hee, hee. Good fer you, Henry, good fer you!

[*Mattie, a fair-faced young woman, comes in from the left, singing and carrying a stone churn in her arms. Despite her housewifely certainty of action, there is an indefinite feminine frailty about her.*]

MATTIE. What's good for Henry?

JERNIGAN [*hurrying in confusion to his chair*]. Nothing, Mattie, nothing at all.

[*She looks sharply at him a moment and then sets the churn by the hearth.*]

MATTIE. I'm putting the milk here to turn. I wisht you'd look at it every now and then and stir it with the dasher.

JERNIGAN. All right, Mattie, all right.

MATTIE. And mind, don't you spill none o' that old beer on the hearth.

JERNIGAN. I won't, Mattie, I won't.

MATTIE. What'd Henry go out for?

JERNIGAN. To git the calf away from the cow.

MATTIE [*the words piling out*]. I bet he didn't wipe his feet when he come in. And did you? [*Staring on the floor and following Henry's trail.*] No, he didn't—just look at the dirt, just look at it. [*She hurries into the room at the left and returns with a broomsedge broom.*] Here, sweep it up, Father. [*She pushes the broom into his hand.*] I've got to go back to my batter. [*She sticks her head out the door at the rear and calls.*] Henry—Hen—ry! Supper! [*She turns back into the room and old Jernigan falls to sweeping.*] Sweep it towards the hearth, towards the hearth, Father, and mind the milk, don't git it full of dust. [*She goes out singing, beginning where she left off.*]—"from sin and the grave."

JERNIGAN [*sweeping*]. Lard, Lard A'mighty, was ever martel man so persecuted! [*Leaning on his broom and musing.*] There he is—[*nodding his head to the right*]—pore soul, not at peace in his own household, going about like a man with the mulligrubs, cain't sleep, cain't eat, worried, worried down to the ground. And there she is—[*nodding to the left*]—reading the *Christian Herald* and hearing about dirt and disease and famine over in Azhy till she ain't fit to live with. Listen at her, listen at her, will you? What's to become of me, Old Moster only knows. What, to come to this, to this in my old age and me— [*thumping on his chest*]—yeh, me, old and with a crippled leg from marching in Furginny! [*He wipes his sleeve across his eyes and goes back to sweeping. Presently he stops and begins to muse again.*] Putts me to sweeping, she does, and churning and gitting up the eggs, and following old setting hens around. And she's had me at the wash-tub like an old woman, she has. Damn it! [*His voice sags over the oath.*] I ain't no woman. If Henry ain't got the grit to say something, I have. It's "Father do this, Father do that, Father —Father—Father!" But ding it all, she's a good girl. It's that drot'n old bell-cow of a Bella Pate and her gang what's got her wors'n she ever has been. I wisht a starm would come up and blow the whole shooting-match of 'em clean to Roosia or wherever it is. Then they'd git enough o' them there heathen, I reckon. But they ain't got no right to interfere with me, not a bit. [*He puts his hands into pockets and holds up a small tin box in his left hand and a plug of tobacco in his right.*] Here they come and set 'pon me about my tobacco. Chew chewing-gum, chewing-gum, they say, to save fer the heathen and to perfect my health. [*He rattles the tin box.*] And I've chewed that wad o' stuff till I cain't git rid of it in my sleep. Cain't wear it out, cain't by no means. I'm done of it, I am. Have to slip off and hide to chew my tobacco, and all in a land o' freedom. [*He stands thinking, then goes to the door at the left and calls.*] Mattie, air ye busy?

MATTIE [*from the kitchen*]. Yes, I've got my hands in the dough!

JERNIGAN. All right. [*He stealthily bites off a chew from his plug, drops his tin box back in his pocket and spits in the fire with grim happiness. Just as he is leaning to spit a second time, the door opens suddenly at the left rear, and Mattie comes in with a cloth. Old Jernigan draws back, and begins sweeping in a flurry of embarrassment. He calls out testily.*] Thought you was busy. Ain't I doing all right?

MATTIE. Sweep it clean, Father. I forgot this cloth for the churn. [*She raises the lid from the churn and stirs the contents around with the dasher.*] It's all right and ready, lacking just a bit, for churning. Don't you let it slosh on anything while you're a-churning it. [*She wraps the cloth around the handle of the dasher. The old man is sweeping and watching her out of the corner of his eye. While she is bent over she sees something on the hearth that attracts her attention. She rises up to her height and with a sharp note in her voice turns upon him.*] Mr. Jernigan—

JERNIGAN. Nah, nah, Mattie.

MATTIE. Signs don't lie, and there's signs of it there on my hearth. [*Working around the room and watching him furtively.*] Right here in my front room! Ain't you got your mouth full of tobacco right this minute? [*He shakes his head.*] Yes, you have, yes, you have. [*She stands looking at him as he sweeps.*] Father, why don't you say something, cain't you talk? [*He makes little movements of agony and finally chokes.*] Yes, yes, you are chewing right now. Spit it out, spit it out! Don't stand there and swallow that juice, it'll kill you. [*In desperation he runs to the fireplace and explodes into the fire, and stands coughing with a nauseated look on his face.*] I'll get you some water! [*She hurries out and reappears immediately with a glass of water and a battered wash-basin full of claying material.*] Here, drink it, and take this pan and rag and clay the hearth over. [*After drinking the water, he ruefully gets down on his knees and begins work. She goes to the sewing machine.*] Hurry and get it done, I got supper nearly cooked.

[*She sits down and begins sewing and singing "How firm a foundation—"*]

JERNIGAN [*indicating the garments*]. Air they fer the heathen?

MATTIE. They are that.

JERNIGAN [*timidly*]. Course you know best, I reckon. But how you know they wear britches over there?

MATTIE [*staring at him in amazement*]. Who ever heard of folks not wearing britches! You know they'd putt 'em in jail for such, if they didn't.

JERNIGAN [venturing]. I hearn they don't wear nothing over there but a string around their waist to tell where the middle is.

MATTIE [pedaling furiously]. You men don't care, of course, care 'bout nothing but your farming and your crops. Why, it's in the Christian Herald where the little children just go through the woods in big droves gnawing the bark off of the trees, they're so hungry. We've decided to give up our breakfast and send the cost of it to them.

JERNIGAN. That's why you didn't eat breakfast this morning. Well—you et a whole lot more fer dinner to make up fer it, didn't ye?

MATTIE [sharply and with a nervous note in her voice as she gets suddenly up from the machine and goes out]. Father, take all this mess out when you get done —that old 'simmon beer cup, and that old 'Manuel patent medicine bottle, and don't forget to carry the clay pan out.

[She goes out at the left. Her song is heard rising in the distance. Old Jernigan continues claying the hearth, muttering to himself. Henry comes in at the rear.]

HENRY [stretching his legs out carefully towards the fire]. What's the matter with the hearth now?

JERNIGAN [setting the pan in the corner by the wood-box]. Nothing, nothing, Henry. She thought she saw a speck on it some'r's.

HENRY. You must a-been chewing tobacco ag'in.

JERNIGAN. Well, why shouldn't I chew it?

HENRY. Yeh, yeh, I wisht you could in peace.

JERNIGAN. You'd be better off ef you'd go back to chewing.

HENRY. I know. But I promised her I'd quit and I have. Gits lonesome, though, plowing 'ithout it.

JERNIGAN. I used to chew it 'fore it quit raining in Africky or wherever it is and 'fore old Bella Pate brung her sanctified self around here, I did, and they was some joy in having a far then, and some reason for having a farplace, too. [Tapping on the andiron with his stick.] That's what it's made fer—to spet in.

HENRY [timidly and somewhat hope-fully]. Why don't you talk it out with Mattie? [Earnestly.] I wisht you would.

JERNIGAN. Durned ef I didn't come purty nigh telling her something a while ago. [He catches Henry by the arm.] Now look-a here, Henry, you'n me's got to do something. The thing for you to do is to walk down the road to-night and meet Mis' Pate and them folks and tell 'em they cain't come up here to carry on no prayer meeting and sewing business here. Tell 'em to go some'r's else. Tell 'em to go to hell!

HENRY [shrinking away]. I cain't do that, I cain't.

JERNIGAN. And tell 'em yer wife ain't gonna have nothing else to do with sich.

HENRY [quickly]. I tell you what, you do it.

JERNIGAN. I would in a minnit, Henry, but you're the head o' the house and you better, it's yer place to.

[Henry turns himself about before the fire.]

HENRY. Mebbe they won't come to-night, and before they meet another time mebbe we can figger on something to do.

JERNIGAN. Huh, they'll be hyuh, all right.

HENRY [staring off]. I hear they's mad dogs about. One bit at Dick Ryall's child this evening.

JERNIGAN [studying]. Well, that may break up the meeting, but I won't believe it till I see it, not me. Take more'n mad dogs to stop religion. You stand up to Mattie, I tell you, putt the britches on and wear 'em yourself. Lard, I cain't understand you. Why you let her impose on me in my old age the way you do I cain't see.

[He turns away and sits down in his armchair. Mattie comes in with a tin bucket in her hand.]

MATTIE. I've got to go across the fields to Mis' Ragland's a bit— [Suddenly stopping.] Henry, go right back out that door and wipe off your feet.

HENRY [mumbling]. I thought I cleaned my feet.

[He goes outside and is heard scraping his shoes on the edge of the porch.]

MATTIE. Sweep it up, Father. [He gets the broom and sweeps.] I got to borrow some soda from Mis' Ragland and she wanted me to bring her a jar o' jam.

HENRY [*coming back into the room*]. I'll go over there for you, Mattie.

MATTIE. No, I'll go, and you-all go on and git your supper. I've put the biscuits in the stove, and they'll be ready by the time you wash and get to the table. Now, Henry, don't let them biscuits burn.

[*She goes out.*]

JERNIGAN [*scornfully*]. Jest look at her—didn't have a bit o' business over there, jest wants to go over and see what old Nonie Ragland's got made up fer the heathen. Henry, you got to lay the law down, I tell you.

HENRY. Yeh, yeh.

JERNIGAN. Now, I'm gonna talk straight to you. Women is like mules and all dumb brutes, Henry, you got to break 'em 'fore they'll work.

HENRY. Nah, nah, I cain't do that.

[*There is a knock on the porch.*]

JERNIGAN. Who kin that be? [*Happily.*] That's my doctor, I betcha.

[*The knock is repeated at the door.*]

HENRY [*raising his voice in sudden irritability*]. Go on away! Go 'way!

JERNIGAN [*staring at him*]. What— Come in, come in! [*Doctor Immanuel comes in.*] I knowed it was you, Doctor, I knowed it was you.

[*The doctor is a man of medium height, about fifty years old, dressed in a cheap threadbare dark suit, celluloid collar and dark tie. His coat hangs low and nearly to the knees, clerical-like. Despite his cheap dress there is an indefinable air of distinction about him; something scholarly, something forlorn in his pale, clean-cut face and dark piercing eyes. He carries a well-worn medicine case in his hand. As he enters the door, he pulls off his derby hat, disclosing a huge mop of long black hair streaked with gray and resting like a bolster on his neck and shoulders.*]

DOCTOR [*in a deep level voice*]. Masters of this house, friends—

JERNIGAN [*pushing up a chair*]. Come right in, come right in and make yourself at home.

[*The doctor lays his hat on the bed at the right and puts his case in a chair. He moves in a sort of dreamlike, masklike manner, intent upon his business and paying little attention to the two men.*]

DOCTOR [*his voice moving in a level chant, half-singing as he opens his case*]. What can I do for you to-night? What can I do for you to-night? [*He takes out bottle after bottle, shakes it, squints at it towards the light, and replaces it, chanting as he does so.*]

As you all know, wherever I go,
My name is Immanuel,
I treat you well, I make you well,
Sound as the sweet church bell.

[*He turns suddenly on old Jernigan, who starts back in surprise.*] Now what is it, brother? What can I do for you?

JERNIGAN [*fetching his bottle*]. Another bottle. I just drunk the last.

HENRY [*growling*]. Another bottle of stump water, dishwater, rainwater.

DOCTOR [*holding up the bottle*]. Doctor Immanuel's Universal Remedy! Right it is and very fit. Distilled from secret weeds and herbs by mystic processes. Cures internal ailments, cuts, burns, bruises, is an antidote for poisons, can be taken internally or externally. For swelling in the joints, leg sores, sore throat, convulsions, dizziness, fits, and general disorders. [*The words roll from him in a flood. He turns towards old Jernigan and fixes him with his eyes, and suddenly sings out.*] What is your trouble, brother? Are you healed, better or— It's cold to-night, and ice on the pools in the lane.

JERNIGAN. In my knee, you remember, in my knee. [*He slaps his hand to it.*] I'm getting better, doctor, slowly, slowly.

DOCTOR [*holding his hand up in assurance*]. Slowly but surely, certainly, absolutely. Another bottle and you walk straight as any man.

As you all know, wherever I go,
My name is Immanuel.
I always make you well,
As any man will tell. . . .

[*His voice drops to a whisper and he hums under his breath, the while he is putting away the empty bottle and getting out another. He hands the bottle to old Jernigan.*] The price is one and a quarter now, brother. Prices have gone up, prices are going up. The demand exceeds the supply.

[*Again he chants.*]

I travel from morning till night
Curing and fixing things right.
From night until day
I'm on a-my way—

[*He begins placing his bottles back in his case.*]

Seeking the saddened sight—

[*Again he whirls upon the old man.*] Is the knee all that troubles you? Have you other troubles, diseases of the body or of the soul?

JERNIGAN [*shaking his head quickly*]. Nanh, nanh, I'm all right saving my knee.

DOCTOR [*picking up a small bottle and holding it lovingly up before him*]. Now here is a remedy, *the* remedy, the heart and soul of the matter, the help for the world's evils. Down in Egypt, the country of darkness, it was discovered. Dug out of the tombs of the powers of evil. Hid away they had it, but my agent discovered it, sent it to me, here it is. [*Reading.*] Dr. Immanuel's Egyptian Tonic.

[*Suddenly barking like an auctioneer, as Henry jumps in his chair.*]

Two dollars a bottle, two dollars,
Going at two dollars.
Are you weak and heavy laden,
Sore distressed, sad distressed?
It will cleanse of evil passion,
Restore you bowels of compassion,
Accidents, diseases chronic—

[*Suddenly shouting.*]

The marvelous Egyptian Tonic.

[*He sticks it out at old Jernigan.*]

Two dollars once, two dollars twice—
Going at two—

JERNIGAN [*backing away from him as he fumbles in his pocketbook for his money*]. Nanh, nanh, this bottle's enough. Here's yer dollar and a quarter. [*The doctor takes the money impersonally.*] Come up to the fire and warm yerself.

HENRY [*looking at old man Jernigan significantly*]. Annh-hanh, what'd I tell you? [*The doctor closes his case and goes to the bed for his hat. Henry calls to him bitterly.*] You better look out down in that creek for mad dogs.

DOCTOR [*turning back quickly but with dignity*]. Mad dogs?

HENRY. Yeh, dogs that are mad. Mad dogs. One of 'em bite you and you'll be madder'n you are now.

JERNIGAN. Yeh, you git bit and you'll foam at the mouth and gnaw bedposts and cut up terrible like Sarah Williams done 'fore she died. She run out in the yard and screamed, and they tried to ketch her but she tore off and lay down by the hedgerow and died biting her legs and arms and barking like a dog.

DOCTOR [*quickly taking a tiny package from his case*]. Doctor Immanuel's Mad Stone, good for all bites and poisons. Bring it near the afflicted spot and it seizes upon it—[*clapping it to the top of his hand*]—and sucks out the poison. Five dollars apiece, five dollars. [*Gazing at it fondly.*] This mysterious stone was taken from a bewitched deer, killed by the old prophet of the Cape Fear. [*Barking again.*] Five dollars apiece, five dollars, going at five dollars.

[*He stops and holds the stone out towards old Jernigan.*]

JERNIGAN. Nanh, nanh, I ain't run mad.

DOCTOR. Five dollars—five dollars once, five dollars twice—five dollars—

[*Suddenly he stops and stares at Henry as if perceiving something remarkable and strange about him. He mechanically wraps up the stone and drops it back in the case, never taking his eyes from the young man. He moves towards him and walks obliquely around him. Old Jernigan watches him with open mouth. As the doctor approaches, Henry turns and follows him suspiciously with his eyes.*]

HENRY. Hyuh, hyuh, what you up to?

[*The doctor continues to stalk him. He draws back dramatically and points a sharp finger at Henry.*]

DOCTOR [*grotesquely*]. Trouble!

JERNIGAN [*jumping and giggling nervously*]. Trouble, hee-hee!

HENRY [*staring at him*]. Trouble?

DOCTOR [*his words beginning to pour out in a roll*]. I see upon that brow suffering. My name is Immanuel. I am needed, needed here and now. [*Looking at him in anguish.*] You are weak and heavy laden. Tell me, speak forth your heart. I am come that ye might have rest from your suffering. Speak forth, thou unbeliever.

HENRY. Hyuh, hyuh, I ain't gonna have no monkey shines. [*With a touch of entreaty in his voice.*] Stop it now.

DOCTOR [*shaking his head mournfully*]. I must help you. I feel the call of pain. Speak forth your heart.

HENRY [*turning towards old Jernigan*]. What's he up to nohow?

JERNIGAN. Now, now, you needn't ax me.

[*There is a long silence while the doctor stares fixedly at Henry.*]

HENRY [*looking anxiously about the room and presently bursting out*]. I tell you to stop looking at me thataway!

DOCTOR. Trouble, trouble, suffering in the countenance of that face! [*Imploringly.*] Speak, speak, I have remedy for suffering. I can help and aid thee.

[*He clasps his hands and waits. Henry stirs uneasily in his chair and old Jernigan teeters nervously on his feet, beating his thighs with the back of his hands. At last old Jernigan explodes.*]

JERNIGAN. Well, you air in trouble, Henry! In a way ye're in the deepest sort of trouble. [*Muttering.*] Me too, and me too.

DOCTOR [*triumphantly*]. Ah—hah! Speak! Speak!

HENRY [*half in wrath and half in perplexed fear*]. Well, what'n the name of Old Scratch you want?

DOCTOR. Speak forth the evil that is possessing thee.

HENRY [*twisting about*]. You tell him, Pa, if they's any evil to be told.

JERNIGAN. Him and me's been seeing a right smart o' worry lately. We was talking about it before you come.

DOCTOR. I know, I perceive it.

JERNIGAN [*going on haltingly*]. As the scripture putts it, he's married to a wife.

[*He stops.*]

DOCTOR. One had his land, one had his yoke of oxen, another had his wife and could not come. As set forth in the gospel according to Luke.

JERNIGAN [*eagerly*]. That's it, doctor, his wife's tuk possession of everything hyuh.

HENRY. Now, now.

JERNIGAN. Well, she has. And that

there doctor kin help you, I done told you he could. [*He suddenly steps nimbly out into the room and sweeps it with his arms.*] Look-a there, will you? Look at that there h'a'th. Clean as a sheet. And the floor and everything. A speck o' dirt git in hyuh and it's skeered to death. [*Pointing to the sewing machine.*] And look over there at that there sewing. My good coat and britches gone fer good, all fer the heathen over the waters.

HENRY. You mought stop trying to tell everything.

JERNIGAN. Well, you tell it then.

HENRY. Go on then and say what you wush.

JERNIGAN. All right and I will as shore as you're born. That's jest it, doctor. She's plumb tuk with religion and sweeping and talking.

DOCTOR. Where is the lady of the house?

JERNIGAN. Off, off to see what Mis' Ragland's got fixed up fer the heathen.

DOCTOR. A common case, a common case. The man must stand up and be the master. The scripture tells as much.

JERNIGAN [*jubilantly*]. There you air, Henry, there you air. [*Jerking his thumb at Henry.*] But he won't, he won't, not him. He sets lak a wedge in the rain and takes it every bit. Big as a house he is and ain't got no backbone in him more'n a sack.

DOCTOR. Timid? Afraid? Lacking in manly courage?

HENRY [*wrathfully*]. Go on and have it your way!

DOCTOR. Doctor Immanuel will provide. He can cure.

JERNIGAN. You cure 'em both and I'll pay you. Fix it so's I kin chew my tobacco in peace and here's a five-dollar bill fer ye.

[*He pulls out his pocketbook.*]

DOCTOR. I shall cure them, I must cure them, I *will* cure them. Amen!

JERNIGAN. Do that and this here's your'n.

[*He flaps a bill in his hands. The doctor begins to pace up and down the room, pushing back his hair and mumbling to himself.*]

DOCTOR [*snapping*]. When will the lady of this house return?

HENRY. She just stepped acrost the field. But you needn't be planning none of your mess, I ain't gonna take no part in it.

DOCTOR. Mess! Mess! [*He resumes his walk.*]

JERNIGAN [*becoming excited*]. I dunno what you gonna do, Doctor, but I jest betcha you do it. [*Gleefully.*] I bet he does, Henry. Yeh, she'll be right back.

DOCTOR. No sooner said than done. [*Whirling.*] I can cure you both. I can bring peace and order into this distracted home. I can make a man of might out of you. I can make you a mighty man in Israel, both in deed and in word. I can bring back humility and love to the erring woman's heart. Yea, [*lifting up his voice*] I can prepare a proper helpmeet for you in your distress. [*Thundering and glaring.*] But—but—have you faith in my powers?

HENRY [*stammering*]. I dunno—I I dunno—Hah, crazy!

JERNIGAN [*ecstatically*]. Try to raise up yer faith, Henry. [*Grinding his hands in excitement.*] Hurry up, Henry, hurry up, she's gonna be back in a minute.

HENRY [*shaking his head weakly*]. I'm scared of all this business. How I know he won't kill me or something, or hurt her?

DOCTOR. Kill! Hurt! [*His jaw falling open in amazement.*] Alas, young man, your words are wild, wild and full of poison to my kindly heart. [*His tone suddenly changes to anger.*] Take your own benighted way then. I offer you peace, you choose strife. So be it.

[*Jernigan grasps Henry's arm in supplication.*]

JERNIGAN. Henry, Henry, try it, try it, boy!

DOCTOR [*raising a warning hand*]. But listen, before I depart over the creek: Behold, salvation is at hand and you refuse it.

JERNIGAN. Air ye crazy, Henry? There he is now going off.

HENRY [*beginning to show an unwilling interest under the doctor's spell*]. Well—

DOCTOR [*picking up his hat*]. I shall say no more.

JERNIGAN. Henry, Henry, don't let him go off like that there!

[*The doctor picks up his case and moves towards the door.*]

HENRY. Well, if you're shore you won't hurt me ner her, I mought—

DOCTOR [*apparently no longer interested in him*]. Well, good night and may you endure your punishment as befits a sufferer so blind.

[*He grasps the door knob.*]

JERNIGAN. Henry, Henry!

HENRY. Are you shore you won't hurt me?

DOCTOR. Faith! Have you faith?

HENRY [*standing up with sudden decision*]. Well, I'll try it then, by God! Where's your medicine? Bring it on.

[*With an amazingly agile bound the doctor springs back into the room.*]

DOCTOR. Saved! Saved! [*He opens his case and searches in its depths. Extracting two tiny bottles, he holds them up in his hands. Henry sits down again watching him with open mouth.*] Ah, here they are, Doctor Immanuel's Cure for the Unhappy Soul. The one is red, the other gray. The red is for the rich blood of manhood. Drink it and you become masterful, fearless, a tamer of the weaker sex. They will bow down to you, worship you, feed upon your words of wisdom as upon honeydew. Let the woman drink the gray and the man the red. He becomes the lord of his house and his goods. She becomes the meek and lowly helpmeet. There she sits by the fire silent, gentle and sweet. There he sits her master, her lord.

JERNIGAN [*his eyes shining*]. Listen at him, Henry, listen at him talk!

DOCTOR [*lifting up the red vial*]. I remember, I remember. I see in the past. It is a night of storm. The moon is sick and pale and wasting in the west. *The pale moon doth rain,* *The red moon doth blow,* *It bringeth water in its beak.* *The white moon doth neither rain nor snow.* I rise up in my dreams. Doctor Immanuel comes forth from his couch at the midnight hour, for now it is the time to seek for the cure of unhappy souls. Silently I go through the forest towards the appointed place. The rain and the wind they comfort me on my journey. I go forth alone in the forest, under the watchful heavens. The signs are right in the sky, it is the time of the bull, and the bull means life and more abundant life. [*He waves his hands before his face and treads up and down the room acting out his journey. Henry and old Jernigan stare at him as if mesmerized.*] I go by the elder bush in the pathless swamp, I touch the sorrel tree, and place my hand upon the bark of the smooth bay tree. I mount the hill and taste of the sweet sassafras and a bit of the bitter pine, and I, Doctor Immanuel, as the cocks begin to crow, come to the place of the silent old man and he waits for me. He has had his dream. Together we go towards the east, he with six dried sticks of the bloody mulberry and I with six of the nameless bush under our arms. We come where the young strong man died for love and his rich red blood ran into the ground. There we set the pot and build the fire. [*His voice takes on a hypnotic monotone and he moves back and forth in the room with the queer unreal steps of an automaton.*] And into the pot Doctor Immanuel casts his one and two and three. And likewise the silent one casts his one and two and three which shall not be named till time is done. The bottles are brought forth and filled. The silent old one to his home again which none but two can find. And Doctor Immanuel forth into the world to heal the distressed.

[*His voice dies away and he hums to himself.*]

HENRY [*breaking from the spell*]. Ain't he crazy right?

DOCTOR [*picking up the gray vial and throwing up his hand*]. And hark! [*He stands with his hand uplifted, and they wait. Presently he goes on.*] It is night, a night of peace. The farmer sleeps his toil away, and the stock rest in the stall. The seeds wait in the earth, in the warm ground. The poor bird sits in the hedgerow and the snake goes not forth to prey. And now the old moon sleeps in the new moon's arms, hanging in the heavens above the three dark pines. [*Again he falls to striding up and down the floor.*] Doctor Immanuel is forth from his couch. The signs are right. The virgin walks in the sky. He comes to the three dark pines and waits in prayer. And the three maids of the deep swamp minister unto him, they minister unto him. Out of the darkness they come with song and with dancing, their heads hanging low and their rings shining and their garments flashing silver and the flames of the

gold. [*He turns and stares at Henry who watches him groggily.*] From the mud of the turtle and the scaly snake they come, rising out of the deep night time, out of the mire and swampy slime, where the owl and the bat and the fever are. They rise, bringing the cure, the gray cure, the draught of humility, of peace. [*He stares at the gray vial and stands lost in thought. Presently he turns, his voice humming.*] Drink the red and be filled with life and power; drink the gray, become the meek and gentle of the earth. Doctor Immanuel has said his say!

[*He begins walking back and forth across the room. Henry and old Jernigan stare at him as if fascinated. Far off a woman's voice is heard singing. It draws nearer, and Mattie passes around the house singing "Rescue the Perishing," and goes into the kitchen.*]

HENRY [*swallowing hard*]. Hyuh, they's something quare!

JERNIGAN. He's gonna cure you, Henry. He is! Sink yer trust in him, Henry!

DOCTOR. Come, drink the drink! [*He closes his case and sets the two bottles on top of it.*] Call the lady of the house. She shall have the gray.

HENRY [*starting from his dream, sidling up to the bottles, and staring at them suspiciously*]. Mought be something in it, mought not. [*A queer unreal smile breaks over his face and he comes up to the doctor and stares at him intently.*] All right, dinged if I don't do it. Dinged if I don't!

[*Mattie's sharp insistent voice is heard in the kitchen.*]

MATTIE. Father! Fath—e—r! Henry! Henr—y!

JERNIGAN. Drink it, swallow it down, Henry! Cain't be no worse'n [*he turns and mocks Mattie*] "Father! Henry!" [*And singing.*] "Rescue the Perishing—" Go on, Henry.

[*Henry picks up the red vial, uncorks it and smells it.*]

HENRY. Hunh, it don't smell like nothing a-tall.

[*He sets it down and takes up the gray one and does likewise.*]

DOCTOR [*stopping in his walk and looking at him piercingly*]. Did the lady of the house come in?

JERNIGAN. Call her in, Henry.

HENRY [throwing his head about and beating himself as if trying to fight off the doctor's influence.] You call her, Pa.

[The door flies open at the left and Mattie springs in with a pan of burnt biscuits in her hands.]

MATTIE [in a shrill nervous voice]. Look what you've done, both of you. I told you not to let the biscuits burn. Now, time I cook some more it'll be too late before they all get here.

[Jernigan looks at Henry and Henry looks back at him.]

JERNIGAN [finally]. I thought Henry was looking after them biscuits.

HENRY [fumbling]. I didn't even think of 'em, Mattie.

MATTIE. I know, I know. That's just the way it is. That's just the way it is. That's always the way it is.

DOCTOR. Madam, lady of this house!

MATTIE [starting back]. Oh, I didn't see you. It's Dr. 'Manuel. Put some wood on the fire, Father. When'd you come, Doctor 'Manuel?

DOCTOR. Madam, when you appeared in the door we were in the midst of a most momentous question.

MATTIE. What'n the world is all this to-do about? You'll have to tell it quick, I've got to hurry and get supper. We are sewing here to-night—[with a weary, defiant look toward Henry and old Jernigan]—sewing for the heathen.

DOCTOR. Madam, after to-night you will not bother about the heathen. You have enough trouble in your own household. We are solving that momentous question.

MATTIE. What in the world is all this to-do about, I ask you?

DOCTOR [with high dignity]. Madam, behold the two bottles there. The one is red, the other gray. The red is for your husband, the gray for you.

MATTIE. Needn't think I'll drink any of your crazy mess.

DOCTOR. The husband will drink the red and take charge of his household. You will drink the gray and obey him in what he says hereafter.

MATTIE. The Lord help my life! [Turning to Henry.] Have you gone out'n your head same as him, to be taking on to such stuff?

HENRY [timidly]. Try and drink a little bit, Mattie. It won't hurt you! He says it's good for you.

MATTIE. The dog's foot!

HENRY [with a hint of determination in his voice]. He's done said if I drink that stuff you won't know me for another man. [Decisively.] And I've said I'll drink it.

DOCTOR. He's going to drink his and you're going to drink yours.

MATTIE. That I'm not. I've never heard of such. Henry Jernigan, you must be crazy to fool with him.

HENRY. Yes, I'm gonna do it. I'm plumb tired of sich a mess of things. I'm gonna change it or die a-trying.

[With a lunge he grabs one of the bottles and throws the contents down his throat.]

MATTIE. Henry, it'll poison you!

[Henry stands tasting with his lips. A foolish smile breaks over his face.]

HENRY. Why, it ain't no more'n—

[His eyes suddenly narrow and he walks back and forth across the room. The doctor moves around as if unconcerned. Suddenly Henry springs into the air with a yell. Old Jernigan starts back and falls over a chair.]

JERNIGAN. Lard, Lard, a-mercy!

MATTIE [running up to Henry]. Henry, Henry, honey, what is it?

HENRY [tearing wildly around the room and shrieking]. I'm pizened, pizened! Help, water, I'm afar inside.

[He doubles over in pain. Mattie pursues him, wringing her hands. All the while the doctor walks ecstatically and yet unconcerned around the room, carrying on his automaton-like actions and his monologue.]

DOCTOR [chanting].

As you all know, wherever I go,
My name is Immanuel.
I treat you well, I make you well,
As sound as the sweet church bell.
Down the road I travel,
Going in rain or shine,
Healing the sick and afflicted,
No medicine like unto mine.
This I tell who comes like Immanuel.

HENRY [falling into a chair and slobbering heavily at the mouth as he gasps]. Pizened! Pizened! Help, water!

[*Mattie throws her arms around his neck.*]

MATTIE. Run, Father, run and bring the bucket of water. [*The old man shoots into the kitchen and back like a streak. All the while Mattie is crooning over Henry and rubbing his face and forehead feverishly.*] Oh, darling, honey. What can I do?

[*She breaks into wild sobs.*]

JERNIGAN. Hyuh, hyuh, drink some water, Henry.

[*Henry springs out of his chair, knocking Mattie from him. He souses his head in the bucket and drinks, spits out great mouthfuls of water on the floor and empties the bucket over his head. Then he stamps the bucket to pieces, shrieking and yelling.*]

MATTIE. Run for the doctor, run for doctor!

DOCTOR. I am Doctor Immanuel at your service, madam. [*Mattie turns and glares at him a moment and slaps him in the face. Henry snatches up the broom and begins chasing the doctor around the room and beating him. The doctor makes an effort to get his case and hat as he is pursued, calling out.*] This is wrong, wrong!

[*He opens the door and flees into the night. Henry falls into a chair and rocks back and forth, groaning and moaning. Mattie comes sobbing up to him.*]

HENRY [*whirling and seizing Mattie by the throat*]. Who are you? I know: Mattie. You sew for the heathen and worry your husband's life out about dirt. Now in the grave they'll be plenty of dirt. And you sing, and you sing; and you talk and you talk. [*He grabs the remaining bottle and uncorks it.*] Drink this here bottle o' stuff.

MATTIE [*clenching her teeth and fighting back*]. I won't, I won't! It'll poison me, it'll kill me!

HENRY [*pulling open her mouth and pouring the contents in*]. Nunh—unh, I reckin it won't! [*She swallows and coughs and strangles, then drops to the floor crying. Henry strides about the room kicking the furniture and throwing out his shoulders and shouting.*] I'm a new man, a man o' might, a he-man in Israel! [*Turning upon Mattie.*] And

you have drunk the drink. You gonna be humble down, a helpmeet.

[*He drops back in his chair in a dying posture.*]

MATTIE. Oh, Henry, Henry, baby!

HENRY. When I'm gone, take care of Pa. Let him live in peace. Let him have his tobacco and spet in the far. [*Mattie crawls on her knees before him and lays her head in his lap, weeping.*]

MATTIE. Get the doctor, Father. Hitch up and go for the doctor.

[*Old Jernigan starts for the door. Henry jumps up and snatches him back.*]

HENRY. You ain't, you ain't. Let me die in peace.

[*There is the sound of a medley of voices outside. Women gabbling in excitement. Mattie climbs up to her feet and runs to the door.*]

MATTIE. Is that you, Mis' Della? Come here, come here quick. Henry's poisoned and he's a-dying.

[*The gabble and excitement outside increase. A voice replies from the yard.*]

VOICE. I'm coming, Mattie; I'm coming.

[*She is heard coming up on the steps. Henry gets up from his chair and begins to bark like a dog, blubbering and growling.*]

HENRY [*shrieking again.*] I been bit by a mad dog!

[*He barks.*]

VOICE. Lord a-mercy, he's run mad!

[*A low murmur of horror rises from the women outside, followed by shrieks and then the sound of running feet. Henry rushes out of the door barking and pursuing them.*]

MATTIE [*looking at old Jernigan through tears*]. He ain't been bit by no mad dog! Oh, Lord, that stuff's run him crazy!

JERNIGAN [*stuttering with excitement*]. Mebbe that's the way the pizen works. That doctor said he got it a quare way in the middle of the night and a storm on and a' old man helping him.

MATTIE. He's crazy. [*Wringing her hands.*] Why'd you let him give Henry that stuff? The mess I took wa'n't nothing, weak as water! [*She goes to the door calling piteously.*] Henry! Henry!

[*Old Jernigan comes up to the bottle she has dropped and looks at it.*]

JERNIGAN [*with a shout*]. He's tuk the wrong medicine, Mattie! He tuk that there gray stuff and you tuk the red!

MATTIE [*at the door*]. Henry, Henry! [*Henry comes back on the porch and gives a farewell bark. Mattie runs out and throws her arms around him. He flings her from him and strides into the room. His shoes are covered with mud. He goes to the fireplace and stamps it off on the hearth.*]

JERNIGAN [*running up to him excitedly*]. Hyuh, hyuh, you drunk that gray stuff. Look, look!

HENRY [*waving him off*]. It don't make no difference. 'Twa'n't nothing but water.

[*Mattie comes in and stares at him as he casually cleans his boot on the hearth.*]

MATTIE [*whimpering*]. What's happened, Henry? You seem—

HENRY. I been cured, that's what. The medicine done it. [*He gets up, looks around the room, goes over to the machine, gathers up the clothes for the heathen, picks out a coat and trousers and throws them at the old man*]. Here, there's your Ransom Taylor coat and britches. The heathen ain't gonna git 'em.

[*He wipes his shoes with the other garments and then calmly goes to his chair and sits down. Mattie has been looking on a moment and then with a glad cry of comprehension she falls on her knees by him and lays her head sobbing in his lap.*]

JERNIGAN [*dropping in his chair thunderstruck*]. Well, I be durned if I ever seed the beat!

[*He thinks a moment, and then bursts out in a low musical chuckle. His face spreads into a grin that breaks over his face in a thousand wrinkles. He cuts a caper on the floor, stopping now and then, trying to comprehend what has happened. Henry sits solemnly stroking Mattie's head. The door is cracked at the rear and Doctor Immanuel pokes his head in.*]

DOCTOR. Masters of this house—

HENRY [*turning and snarling*]. Hanh—Scat! [*He barks and the doctor slams the door. After a moment Henry calls to old Jernigan.*] Pa, go and tell him to come in and get his hat and case. [*Mattie's sobs gradually die away.*] Yeh, I know, pore child. I did scare you, didn't I?

[*Only a whimper from Mattie and a hugging of Henry's knees answer him.*]

JERNIGAN [*at the door*]. Come on in, Doctor, and git yer stuff. He ain't gonna hurt you.

[*The doctor comes gravely in and gets his case and hat.*]

HENRY. Pa, give him that five dollars.

JERNIGAN [*his sides shaking with enjoyment*]. Hyuh, hyuh, it is. You done it, Doc, same as you said you would.

HENRY. And you needn't come back. I don't need you! [*He lifts his head with decision written on his face.*] Lemme have a look at that plug of tobacco, Pa.

DOCTOR [*at the door*]. Remember that I am always at your service. Peace abide with you and this house always. I am on my way now to another patient, a mule sick at Brother Oaskins' house.

HENRY. That's all right, Doctor. You needn't bother about us. We ain't gonna need you no more. Are we, Mattie?

[*Mattie shakes her head.*]

DOCTOR [*going out*].

As you all know, wherever *I* go,
My name is Immanuel.

[*He closes the door and his chant dies away in the night.*]

HENRY. I said, Pa, I'd like a look at that tobacco.

MATTIE [*raising her head*]. Don't you spit on—

HENRY [*crushing her back on the floor*]. Nanh, nanh, I tell you I been cured. I'm boss. [*Breaking into a loud roaring laugh*]. Hooray! Hooray! I'm another man. I'm cured, I'm boss. Gimme that 'backer.

[*The old man hands it to him eagerly. Henry bites off an enormous chew and hands the plug back. Old Jernigan hesitates a moment and then also bites off a mouthful. A look of deep content comes over him. He snuggles into a chair*]

*and chews. Henry chews. They
look across at each other. Henry
signifies to the old man with a
motion of his hand that he spit
first. Old Jernigan, with signs,
refuses. Henry spits profusely
and loudly in the direction of the
fire. Old Jernigan does likewise.*]
JERNIGAN [*eyeing Henry slyly, as he
rolls his tobacco sweetly in his mouth*].
Hee—hee!
[*Mattie sits hugging Henry's knees.*]
HENRY [*nodding happily and wisely*].
Unh-hunh-yeh.
[*They sit, saying nothing. Presently
Henry looks over at the old man
and laughs suddenly and deeply.*]
JERNIGAN. What?
HENRY. I run them there women
right into the mudhole out there.
JERNIGAN [*beating his thigh gleefully*].
Hee-hee! Hee-hee!
HENRY. I shore did. [*They lapse into
silence. By this time Mattie has
somewhat raised her head and is
staring contemplatively by Henry's
chin into the fire.*]
JERNIGAN [*shivering a bit and stirring
the fire*]. Gonna be cold, Henry, cold.
HENRY. Yeh.
JERNIGAN. Robins been flying towards
the south all day.
[*They both lean towards the fire to
spit.*]
MATTIE [*softly*]. I got something to
tell you, Henry.
HENRY [*with a touch of condescen-
sion*]. Hah, all right, what is it?

MATTIE. Lean down your head and let
me whisper it.
[*She whispers something in his ear.*]
HENRY [*joyously*]. I'll declare, I'll
declare! Great goodness! [*Hugging
her to him.*] Honey, honey!
JERNIGAN. What is it? What is it?
HENRY [*bashfully, as he strokes Mat-
tie's head*]. She says there'll be—there'll
be four of us all in the spring.
JERNIGAN. Well, sir, well, sir, I been
'specting it— What you gonna name
him?
HENRY [*dropping his arms in horror*].
And here I been a beating you and banging you about! Lord, I'm the meanest
man in the world!
[*He lifts her up frantically*].
MATTIE. No, no, that's all right.
HENRY. And I went and choked you!
Let me help you to bed—right quick.
[*With a shower of tenderness he
helps her through the door at the
left. Old Jernigan stares after
them.*]
JERNIGAN. Well, well, ain't this a
come-off? [*He uncorks his new bottle of
medicine and takes a drink.*] That doctor shore— [*He suddenly jerks his
head up as if struck by a new thought,
and stands listening to Henry's mumbling in the other room.*] Ah, but
women is hard folks to get the best of.
[*Pondering.*] I wonder if she's a-fooling
him. [*He turns towards the door at the
left and calls.*] Henry, come hyuh a
minute!

[*Curtain.*]

JULIET AND ROMEO

A ROMANCE

BY HARRY WAGSTAFF GRIBBLE

CHARACTERS

RUTH OLIVER [*a rising dramatic star, playing Juliet*].
RICHARD JORDAN [*a rising leading man, playing Romeo*].
LESLIE P. LEGRANGE [*playing Friar Lawrence, and chorus*].
MRS. KANE [RUTH OLIVER'S *dresser*].
AN OLD MAN.

The action takes place within the four walls of a metropolitan theater where "Romeo and Juliet" is being played.

Characters and Parts Played	Presented by John Craig and Mary Young at B. F. Keith's Palace, Boston, Aug. 9, 1920	Presented by Lewis & Gordon at B. F. Keith's Palace Theatre, New York May 16, 1921	Nov. 2, 1925
RUTH OLIVER	Mary Young	Josephine Victor	Estelle Winwood
RICHARD JORDAN	Harry Wagstaff Gribble	Harry C. Power	Hugh Huntley
LESLIE P. LEGRANGE	Frederick Murray	William Barwald	Ernest Weber
MRS. KANE	Bertha Blanchard	Marion Dyer	Marie Falls
AN OLD MAN	Frank M. Readick	John F. Webber	Charles Scofield

JULIET AND ROMEO

A ROMANCE

BY HARRY WAGSTAFF GRIBBLE

AT RISE: [(Opening) Music—"Boc-chorini Minuet"—*Play while chorus speaks the following. Chorus enters center through drapes.*]

CHORUS. Good afternoon, or good evening, Mr. and Mrs. Audience. I shall ask you kindly to use your imagination for a while. You are not in this theater at all—you are in another theater and have been witnessing a performance of Shakespeare's immortal tragedy, "Romeo and Juliet," as played by those two rising young stars, Richard Jordan and Ruth Oliver. The performance is nearly over, in fact, Miss Oliver and Mr. Jordan are at this moment waiting on the stage for the curtain to rise upon the last scene—the famous Tomb Scene. Here is one thing you can do for us. When the curtain falls upon the tragic death of the young lovers, please applaud heartily and bring the actors before the curtain to make their bows. This is very important because—well, we will tell you why later. Please don't forget to applaud. [*He disappears.*]

[*Music changes to andante—Gounod. The curtains part, disclosing the Tomb Scene. Juliet is lying on the bier and Romeo is kneeling in front of it and slightly to left.*]

ROMEO. Ah, dear Juliet,
Why art thou yet so fair? shall I believe
That unsubstantial death is amorous,
And that the lean abhorred monster keeps
Thee here in dark to be his paramour?
For fear of that, I still will stay with thee.
   O, here
Will I set up my everlasting rest
And shake the yoke of inauspicious stars
From this world-wearied flesh. Eyes, look your last!

Arms, take your last embrace! and lips,
   O you
The doors of breath seal with a righteous kiss.
[*Taking the vial from his pocket.*]
Come, bitter conduct, come, unsavory guide!
Here's to my love! [*He drinks.*] O, true apothecary!
Thy drugs are quick. Thus with a kiss I die!
   [*He falls and dies in front of bier.*]
FRIAR LAWRENCE [*off stage right*].
Saint Francis be my speed! [*Enters.*]
How oft to-night
Have my old feet stumbled at graves.
   Who's there?
Romeo! O, pale! Ah, what an unkind hour
Is guilty of this lamentable chance!
[*Sets lantern down left. Juliet stirs.*]
The lady stirs.
   JULIET [*awaking*]. O, comfortable Friar! Where is my lord?
I do remember well where I should be
And there I am. Where is my Romeo?
   [*Noise within.*]
FRIAR LAWRENCE [*uncovers her*]. A greater power than we can contradict
Hath thwarted our intents. Come, come away.
Thy husband in thy bosom there lies dead.
Come; I'll dispose of thee
Among a sisterhood of holy nuns:
Stay not to question, for the watch is coming
Come, go, good Juliet, I dare stay no longer.
   JULIET. Go get thee hence for I will not away.
   [*Exit Friar Lawrence.*]
What's here? a cup, closed in my true love's hand
Poison, I see, hath been his timeless end.

O, churl! drank all, and left no friendly
  drop,
To help me after? I will kiss thy lips;
Haply some poison yet doth hang on
  them
To make me die with a restorative. [*She
  kisses him.*]
Thy lips are warm.
[*Off stage:* "*What ho, watch, this way.*"]
Yea noise? then I'll be brief. O happy
  dagger! [*Seizing Romeo's dagger.*]
This is thy sheath; [*stabs herself*] there
  rust and let me die.
  [*She falls across Romeo's body.*]

[*Curtain.*]

[*Romeo and Juliet come before the
curtain to take their bows. After the
first bow Romeo backs off and Juliet
takes as many bows as possible by herself. Music for bows—March—Gounod.*]
[*Friar Lawrence appears before curtains as chorus. Music as he speaks—
Allegro Maestoso. Gounod.*] Thank
you. Now we will tell you why we
asked you to applaud. Actors thrive
on applause. When they are hungry applause will feed them; despondent, applause will cheer them; dead, applause
can waken them. So to show you the
effect of your applause I shall take you
backstage and introduce you to Miss Oliver and Mr. Jordan, who play Romeo
and Juliet. This way, please—to the
left. Mind the sharp curve behind the
box. There are three stairs to the pass
door, don't bump your head on the scenery. We are now at Juliet's dressing-
room door. Mrs. Kane, her dresser, says
you may be seated and wait until Juliet
comes off the stage. You are a very good
audience and we thank you very much.
  [*He disappears. Curtains open disclosing Juliet's dressing room.
  Mrs. Kane is center—placing a
  white sheet on the floor.*]
JULIET [*entering from right*]. Oh, oh,
oh!
MRS. KANE. What's the matter, dear?
JULIET. Don't call me dear.
MRS. KANE. I beg your pardon, Miss
Oliver.
JULIET. The idea of his trying to
teach me my business.
MRS. KANE [*bringing kimono from up

left*]. Now, don't you think, Miss Oli-
ver, there is always something for each
of us to learn?
JULIET. Don't you try to teach me
my business. Oh, please help me with
this gown—I can't unhook it.
MRS. KANE. I beg your pardon—
there. You couldn't manage it because
it was pinned.
  [*Knock on door right.*]
JULIET. Don't answer it—go away.
VOICE [*off right*]. Miss Oliver—
JULIET. Oh!
VOICE. A package for Miss Oliver,
please.
JULIET. A what?
MRS. KANE. A package. I'll fetch it.
[*Goes to door and takes package—speaks
off stage.*] Thank you. [*Coming back.*]
It's a box of candy.
JULIET. What a silly little box. What
kind are they?
MRS. KANE [*looking at box*]. Choco-
lates.
JULIET. Chocolates! You may have
them.
MRS. KANE. Thank you.
JULIET. Set them down! Set them
down and help me.
MRS. KANE. Don't you want to see
whom they are from?
  [*Places box on dresser.*]
JULIET. Some silly man, I suppose.
MRS. KANE. Do you think all men
are silly?
JULIET. Yes, I do. All men!
MRS. KANE. I am afraid something
has happened to-night to upset you.
JULIET. Yes, that idiot Richard.
MRS. KANE. Richard?
JULIET. Yes—Richard, Richard, Rich-
ard!
MRS. KANE. Do you mean Mr. Jordan
who plays Romeo?
JULIET. Yes, Mr. Jordan who tries to
play Romeo.
MRS. KANE. Why, what could he have
done, I wonder?
JULIET. Think of it. He made a
scene on the stage after the curtain fell.
Said I took more curtain calls than he.
I'm supposed to. The management wants
me to. Besides, the audience wanted
me.
MRS. KANE. I shouldn't pay any at-
tention to him, Miss Oliver, he doesn't
mean it.
JULIET. He does—he's jealous.

MRS. KANE. As long as you're not jealous of him, it's all right.

JULIET. I jealous of him! Don't be silly.

MRS. KANE. If he were anybody you really cared about, it would be different.

JULIET. H'm! I wouldn't care about any man, as you put it.

MRS. KANE. Then all this gossip isn't true?

JULIET. What gossip? [*Changing shoes.*] Oh, you must have read those silly stories in the magazine sections of the Sunday papers. I suppose you saw one which said that Mr. Jordan and I were engaged, or was it married? Anyway, it doesn't matter because it's untrue. I don't give a snap of the fingers for him, do you hear, not a snap of the fingers. [*Knock on door right.*] Who is it?

ROMEO [*off stage*]. It's I.

JULIET. And who is I?

ROMEO [*off stage*]. Richard Jordan.

JULIET. Well, Richard Jordan, you can go away— [*Romeo enters—Juliet turns and sees him. She is in negligée.*] You can't come in.

ROMEO. I am in.

JULIET. Well, go out again!

ROMEO. Not until we have settled this argument you started on the stage.

JULIET. You started it.

ROMEO. I beg your pardon—I think you did.

JULIET. How?

ROMEO. By your unreasonable attitude.

JULIET. How can an attitude start an argument?

ROMEO. I'm not going to argue about that.

JULIET. I'm not going to argue about anything.

ROMEO. It's necessary to argue about this.

JULIET. I can't argue about any argument until I know what argument you are arguing about.

ROMEO. I should like to know something.

JULIET. It's time you did. Go away.

ROMEO [*subsides into chair right of screen*]. I should like to know which you consider the more important character—Romeo or Juliet?

JULIET. Juliet, of course.

ROMEO. Then why didn't Shakespeare call the play Juliet and Romeo?

JULIET. Why? Because in a title the important name always comes last. People say Romeo and JULIET—not R-O-M-E-O-and Juliet.

ROMEO. Oh, well, of course I have nothing more to say.

JULIET. You said a mouthful.

ROMEO. Who does the most work in the play?

JULIET. I do.

ROMEO. They always talk about Romeo.

JULIET. The way you play him, I don't wonder.

ROMEO. Romeo is the strongest part in Shakespeare.

JULIET. And Juliet is the most important.

MRS. KANE. Miss Oliver, if you don't mind, don't you think the parts are equally important?

ROMEO. Quite so, and therefore they should take equal honors and equal bows.

JULIET. Mrs. Kane was addressing me.

ROMEO. More than half the audience are women and they come to see Romeo.

JULIET. And the men pay because they love to see Juliet.

MRS. KANE. In Shakespeare's days they went to see the play.

ROMEO. You're right, Mrs. Kane. The play's the thing.

JULIET. Then what are you arguing about?

ROMEO. Just this. If I can't share at least equal honors with you I shall have to leave the company.

[*Rises and goes right.*]

JULIET. Very well.

ROMEO. Very well.

JULIET. Only before you leave perhaps you will try to play Romeo as he should be played—as you very nearly played him once.

ROMEO. Thank you. I'm glad I very nearly played him once. Perhaps you will tell me some of my faults.

[*Turns to her.*]

JULIET. Certainly. In the minuet you will kindly look at me—instead of at the ladies in the audience, and perhaps you will not tread on my toes.

ROMEO [*turns front*]. In the minuet we are standing side by side. How could I possibly tread on your toes?

JULIET. I don't know how you do it, I'm just asking you not to.

ROMEO. Anything more?

JULIET. Yes. [*Romeo turns to her.*] In the farewell scene you are supposed to gaze right into my eyes all the time like that— [*Romeo turns front in disgust.*] No, not like that—at the ladies in the audience— To-night you were so afraid of losing sight of them for one second that "the envious streaks were lacing the severing clouds of yonder east" behind you—while you were pointing to them—out among the ladies.

ROMEO. Any further suggestions?

JULIET. Yes—in the tomb scene I'm not really dead.

ROMEO. You don't say so.

JULIET. No, I'm not a real corpse, you know.

ROMEO. I didn't think you were.

JULIET. Then there seems no reason why you shouldn't actually kiss me.

ROMEO. No, no reason.

JULIET. Then will you please kiss me in the future, as you did on the first night when the critics were in front, and there weren't so many ladies?

ROMEO. Certainly. I'll give you a loud smack. It will probably get a howl but what the h——, oh, what difference does it make? By the way—at the end of the play when you die, would you make sure that you fall across my chest and not on the pit of my stomach? On several occasions when you have misjudged your fall, I have been unable to eat my supper.

JULIET. It's too bad about your supper—anything more?

ROMEO. Yes. [*Turns to her.*] Will you please provide your dresses with sufficient snap hooks. I prick the same finger each night in the same place. [*Puts his finger in his mouth.*] I fully anticipate blood poisoning.

JULIET. I'm sorry about your finger. Mrs. Kane—Mrs. Kane, put some snap hooks on my dress at once.

MRS. KANE [*crosses back of screen then down center*]. Snap hooks—pins, oh dear, dear, dear.

JULIET. Mrs. Kane!

MRS. KANE. Do you realize that you are playing the greatest tragedy ever written; a tragedy of love and youth and innocence and simplicity? And here you are arguing like—like two sophisticated old ladies.

JULIET. That will do, Mrs. Kane. When I want to discuss Shakespeare with you, I will tell you so.

MRS. KANE. Forgive me, Miss Oliver, I didn't mean to interfere. [*Crosses left and turns.*] But I can see you—

JULIET. Mrs. Kane, you can't be well—you can go home.

MRS. KANE. Yes, Miss Oliver. And before I go, I'll take this dress and sew on the snap hooks.

[*Exits left. Juliet sits left at dressing table.*]

ROMEO. Aren't you rather hard on her?

JULIET. Look here! I draw the line at you criticizing my behavior off stage. Go away.

ROMEO. Well, I'm supposed to take you to supper next door.

JULIET. I have an escort, thank you.

ROMEO. What?

JULIET. An escort.

ROMEO. You have a—oh, excuse me. [*Goes right; comes back.*] Well, I can't see any other course for me.

JULIET. Than what?

ROMEO. Giving in my notice on Saturday.

JULIET. Don't be absurd.

ROMEO. It's absurd to stay on under these conditions.

JULIET. Oh, very well, if you feel that way about it.

ROMEO. I do.

JULIET. I'm sure you'll have no difficulty at all in getting another engagement.

ROMEO. Oh, no. I know one or two people who will be crazy to have me.

JULIET. They certainly would be.

ROMEO. Thank you. Good night.

JULIET. Good night.

ROMEO [*hesitates. Juliet turns*]. Good night. [*Knock on door off stage.*] Yes?

OLD MAN [*enters from right*]. I beg pardon—is this Romeo's dressing room?

ROMEO. No, this is Miss Oliver's room—Juliet.

OLD MAN. But you are Romeo, aren't you?

ROMEO. Yes.

OLD MAN. I just wanted to shake your hand and congratulate you.

ROMEO. Thank you—thanks very much.

[*Turns and looks toward Juliet.*]

OLD MAN. Is—Juliet—here?

ROMEO. Yes.

OLD MAN. Could I—would she let me shake hands with her—do you think?

ROMEO. I don't know. You might try.

OLD MAN. Oh—

JULIET [*from behind the screen*]. Who is it, please?

OLD MAN. Only an old man. I just witnessed your performance from the front. And I sent you a little box of candy as a token of appreciation.

JULIET. Oh, yes—thank you. They were very good.

OLD MAN [*crossing to center*]. They were nothing. I half expected that you would give them away to your dresser or somebody, without opening them, as I have seen actresses do.

JULIET. Why, I wouldn't think of doing such a—

ROMEO [*giving her a look*]. Ahem!

OLD MAN. But I hoped you would be interested when you read the little inscription.

JULIET. Inscription—inscription?

OLD MAN. On the box.

JULIET. I'm sorry I didn't see the inscription. What did you say?

OLD MAN. I said—"To the new Juliet from a very old Romeo."

JULIET [*banteringly*]. And are you an old Romeo?

OLD MAN. Oh, yes! I played Romeo forty years ago to the Juliet of the great Panelli. I don't suppose you ever heard of her?

JULIET. Er—

ROMEO. Of course I've heard of Panelli.

JULIET. And so have I. May I ask your name?

OLD MAN. My name? Oh, you wouldn't know that—it doesn't matter. Such a sweet performance, Juliet.

JULIET. Thank you.

OLD MAN. And so very vivid. And Romeo, quite the best in many a long year. Ah, you are both in for a great success, and you have a great incentive for good work. You love each other.

JULIET. Ha!

OLD MAN. Oh, forgive me if it is idle gossip.

JULIET. It is just idle gossip, I assure you.

ROMEO. Quite idle.

OLD MAN. What a pity. May I tell you the few things I appreciated, especially, in your performance?

[*Takes program from his pocket.*]

JULIET. Please do. Won't you sit down?

OLD MAN [*offers her a chair and gets one for himself from behind the screen. Romeo offers a chair also. Juliet accepts the Old Man's chair and turns her back on Romeo. Romeo takes his chair upstage and leans on it. Old Man sits left of Juliet*]. Now let me see. Oh, yes—I thought you were so good in the minuet when you, Romeo, took Juliet's hand and danced with her. For a moment you looked straight ahead—at the audience.

JULIET. Ahaha!

OLD MAN. That was a little stroke of genius.

JULIET. What?

OLD MAN. Showing the young man's assurance of final conquest.

ROMEO. AHAHA!

OLD MAN. Most Romeos gaze right into Juliet's eyes all the time and we miss their facial expression.

JULIET. I can't bear an actor who gazes into my eyes all the time.

[*Romeo whistles.*]

OLD MAN [*to Romeo*]. And you were so graceful.

JULIET. What?

OLD MAN. I never before saw a Romeo who could dance. They generally tread on Juliet's toes.

JULIET. Mr. Jordan dances beautifully. [*Rubbing her toe.*]

OLD MAN. Then in the marriage scene. The way Romeo put his arm around your waist—it was so firmly and manly done. I have seen Romeos do it as if they were afraid Juliet might have a pin in her dress.

ROMEO. Miss Oliver never uses pins.

JULIET. No—always snap hooks.

OLD MAN. Then in your death scene. That wonderful tomb scene. The beautiful way you, Romeo, kissed Juliet.

JULIET. What?

OLD MAN. She was too sacred so he allowed his lips to rest only for a fleeting moment on yours.

JULIET. Oh, much less than that.

OLD MAN. And oh, Miss, when you stabbed yourself, the way you fell was so truly artistic. I have seen Juliets who, to vent their spite, appeared to select the part of Romeo's anatomy on which to fall.

ROMEO. So have I.

OLD MAN. But you did it so naturally forming a perfect cross.

JULIET. Thank you.

ROMEO. Perfect!

[*Turns his chair upstage.*]

OLD MAN. Well, that's all. I fear I have bored you both.

[*Rises.*]

JULIET. Oh, but I want to hear about Panelli, what became of her?

OLD MAN. She faded into obscurity, like me, only I wasn't a great artist.

ROMEO. I'm sure there are many who remember your Romeo.

OLD MAN. Not many, I'm afraid.

JULIET. Where are you acting now?

OLD MAN. I give Dickens' sketches at clubs, and then afterwards I try to sell my little poems. I won't even ask you to accept a copy because they're not good. People generally leave them behind on the table and then I—I gather them up and sell them again.

JULIET. How cruel of the managers not to have kept you in work! What could have held you back so?

OLD MAN. Jealousy.

ROMEO. Jealousy?

JULIET. Jealousy!

OLD MAN. Professional jealousy.

[*Looks exchanged between Romeo and Juliet.*]

JULIET. I don't understand.

OLD MAN. Panelli and I were both victims of this hideous vice. We were really in love with each other but jealousy killed our love. It all started with Romeo and Juliet. If we had stayed together we might have been the greatest stars of the day. Instead she lies in a pauper's grave somewhere and I, well, you know what I do—I collect the books and sell them again. [*Music—"Bocohorini Minuet".*] Well, I must toddle along. [*Crosses center between Romeo and Juliet.*] This has been a wonderful pleasure. Where does that music come from?

ROMEO. It's the "Bocohorini Minuet" —they are giving a supper party in honor of Miss Oliver.

OLD MAN. Do you know that the minuet you two children danced to is the same that Panelli and I—but what does it matter?

JULIET. Come and see me again sometime, won't you?

[*Kisses him on the cheek. Music stops gradually.*]

OLD MAN. If I come again—would you do that again?

JULIET. Of course I would.

OLD MAN. I'll come.

JULIET. And sometime you'll tell me about Panelli and her art.

OLD MAN. Perhaps I will.

JULIET. You see— [*Takes Old Man by the arm and goes left with him. Romeo follows them. Juliet gives him a look and he goes upstage.*] You see—if she failed, as you say she did, I should like to accomplish what she might have done; and I am sure you could help me. And perhaps she can see us and she will know that you have had a part in carrying on.

[*Mrs. Kane enters from left with Juliet's gown on her arm. Goes upstage and hangs it on hall-tree.*]

OLD MAN. What a sweet thought. Panelli! [*Mrs. Kane turns at this and slowly comes downstage. She is opposite the Old Man as he speaks the words "a great artist."*] Ah, she was a great artist—a great artist!

JULIET. I'm sure she was.

[*Old Man turns and becomes conscious of Mrs. Kane standing there. She seems like a specter to him. She approaches him slowly and then a gleam of recognition grows over his face.*]

OLD MAN. Panelli! Panelli!

MRS. KANE. John!!!

OLD MAN. I—thought—you—were—dead!

MRS. KANE. And I—you.

OLD MAN. I—guess—we—are—dead —both of us.

[*Turns upstage.*]

JULIET [*crosses to Mrs. Kane*]. You aren't really the great Panelli?

MRS. KANE. Not the great Panelli any more.

JULIET. But I abused you and scolded you because—

MRS. KANE. That's all right, dear— I beg your pardon, Miss Oliver.

JULIET. Please call me dear.

MRS. KANE [*stroking her hair*]. Dear—

JULIET. May I tell you that I think you are a great woman?

MRS. KANE. You are a great Juliet. [Crosses right.]

JULIET. Oh, I should like to think that to-night and here, after all these years you two could—

MRS. KANE. It's too late. Good night. [She goes out.]

[Old Man comes downstage to left of Juliet.]

JULIET. Go after her. It isn't too late—it can't be.

OLD MAN. Sometimes an old tune can't be recalled. [To Romeo.] I'm going to ask you to accept a copy of my little book—because it has been near my heart, and my heart beats for both of you—

ROMEO [taking the book]. Thank you.

OLD MAN. But I beg you—please—please don't read the poems.

[The Old Man goes out.]

ROMEO. Are you going to supper?

JULIET. Yes—No! And I'm not jealous—I'm not jealous, do you hear? And there's no similarity between the two cases.

ROMEO. Which two cases?

JULIET. Theirs and ours. She was in love with him but there's nothing silly like that about us. He was running after some other girl as they all do and she grew jealous of him and that's why they separated. [Sits.] My criticism of you is entirely impersonal.

ROMEO. I know that.

JULIET. No, you don't.

ROMEO. Of course I do. I know you have no personal feelings for me either way. The very idea is too absurd.

JULIET. Of course it is.

ROMEO. Of course it is. [Pauses.] Of course it is. Well, as you have an escort—

JULIET. What?

ROMEO. I said as you have an escort, an escort!

JULIET. Oh, yes.

ROMEO. I'll say good night.

JULIET. Good night.

ROMEO [hesitating at door]. Er—

JULIET [rising suddenly]. Yes?

[He leaves the room. Juliet is more peeved than ever. She throws the candy on the floor. Then she catches sight of a stick of grease-paint and writes on the pier glass. "JULIET AND ROMEO." She surveys this for a moment. Romeo returns, sneaks up behind the screen and catches sight of what she is doing. She erases the "JULIET AND" and adds "AND JULIET" after the "ROMEO." This she approves of, so she emphasizes it by kissing the "RO-MEO."]

ROMEO. Aha!

JULIET. Oh!

[Furious at being caught, Juliet seizes her wrap from the corner of the screen and runs to the door. The lights go out.]

THE STAGE AGAIN.
Music: Minuet.

[Mrs. Kane enters. She hears the music coming from next door. She starts to execute the steps of the Minuet. The Old Man enters and as she drops the curtsey he is standing opposite her in the pose of a courtly bow. Juliet enters at the same moment, comes between them and placing Mrs. Kane's arm in the Old Man's, says:]

JULIET. You see, it isn't too late, and the old tune has been recalled.

OLD MAN. Panelli!

MRS. KANE: John!

[They go off together, Juliet watching them. Romeo enters behind Juliet.]

ROMEO. Well?

JULIET. Well, aren't you going to take me to supper?

ROMEO. But you have an escort.

JULIET. Yes—you.

ROMEO. And in the future remember —Juliet comes first.

JULIET. No—in the future, Romeo comes first. They're playing the Minuet.

[Takes his hand to do the dance. They dance through the following dialogue.]

ROMEO. In the future, I'll try not to step on your toes.

JULIET. In the future, I'll try not to fall on your stomach.

[As they go upstage in the Minuet the Curtains come together.]

[Curtain.]

JACK AND JILL AND A FRIEND
A Comedy
By Cicely Hamilton

CHARACTERS

ROGER [*an unsuccessful painter*].
JACK [*a struggling author*].
JILL [*another struggling author*].
POSTMAN.

SCENE I: *Roger's studio, 9 P.M., Wednesday.*
SCENE II: *Roger's studio, 2 P.M., Thursday.*

Applications for permission to produce this play should be addressed to the author's
representatives, SAMUEL FRENCH, 25 WEST 45TH STREET, NEW YORK CITY.

JACK AND JILL AND A FRIEND

A COMEDY

By CICELY HAMILTON

[SCENE: *Roger's studio. Door (leading to street) center. Window left. Two doors right, one supposed to lead to bedroom, the other to kitchen-place. Easel; small table; canvases stacked on floor, etc. Stove left. Lay figure, if possible. As the curtain rises Jack is discovered. He is sitting staring thoughtfully before him, an unlit pipe in his mouth. After a moment's silence, Roger is heard calling off right through open door.*]

ROGER [*off*]. I say, Jack!

JACK [*rousing himself with a start*]. Yes, what is it?

ROGER [*off*]. Have you got the time?

JACK. Just on nine.

ROGER [*off*]. Only nine? Then I'm ready much too soon. Dancing isn't supposed to begin till ten.

JACK. Come along, and let's have a look at you.

ROGER [*off*]. Wait a minute. My belt's all cock-eye—I say!

JACK. Yes?

ROGER [*off*]. I don't seem to have any pockets. What did the Johnnies in the middle ages do with their handkerchiefs?

JACK. Don't suppose they had any.

ROGER [*off*]. I shall have to stuff mine down my neck—beastly inconvenient— [*He enters, dressed in medieval costume; strikes an attitude.*] What ho, varlet! What do I look like?

JACK. Nothing on earth—a penwiper.

ROGER. Go to, minion; try not to be funny. It is the worm of envy that prompteth thy feeble jest. I don't mind telling you that I'm rather pleased with the effect.

JACK. You would be.

ROGER. It strikes me as modest, but dashing. What are you going to do with yourself all the evening?

JACK. Jill said she'd come in for an hour if she could get her instalment off in time.

ROGER. I see. Still, with all respect to the lady of your heart, you can see Jill most evenings, and you might just as well have come to the dance to-night.

JACK. Can't afford.

ROGER. Oh, nonsense! If you're as broke as all that, you could have borrowed a quid or so.

JACK. I know I could—from *you*. But I didn't want to.

ROGER. Oh, well, if you're so beastly proud—

JACK. I've borrowed too much from you already.

ROGER. Rot, and Thomas rot!

JACK. I was just wondering when I should be able to stump up my share of the last two quarters' rent.

ROGER. When your ship comes in, dear boy; when your ship comes in. When editors begin falling over each other for your articles. When publishers grovel on their tummies in the hope that you will vouchsafe them a novel from your priceless pen. When you get five guineas a thousand words, instead of five shillings; in short, as I remarked just now, when your ship comes in. As it will.

JACK. I wish I was sure of that.

ROGER. Be sure of it. Buck up! Never say die! Try, try, try again. All things come round to him who waits. The copy books say it, so it must be true —and consequently I have hopes that, in the dim and distant future, I—even I— may some day sell a picture. You're always grousing about your failures, but what about mine? There's a stack of them in that corner, another over there. All beautiful, all unappreciated. My bedroom's lined with failures—nearly carpeted with 'em; and I don't know if you've noticed that they've lately begun

211

to overflow into the bathroom? And yet you tear your hair and grumble when you get a manuscript returned.

JACK. Well, it isn't exactly the same thing for you. You're not a Crœsus; but your painting doesn't mean your actual bread and butter. Even if people don't appreciate you, you don't have to do bad stuff against the grain to keep yourself alive; you can go on pegging away at work that you like—

ROGER. Oh, yes, I like my work. I'll go so far as to say that there are moments when I admire it. The trouble is that I can't get any one else to feel the same way about it.

JACK [bitterly]. You don't have to do as I do—write rubbish to keep yourself out of the workhouse. And then—

[He breaks off.]

ROGER. Yes?

JACK. I've got Jill.

ROGER. I shouldn't have thought that was anything to growl about. Aren't you jolly lucky to have her?

JACK. Do you suppose I don't know that? She's the one bit of luck I've ever had. But what I mean is that when you've got a girl—like Jill—it makes an awful difference about wanting to get on.

ROGER [kindly]. Of course it does. [Crosses to chair left.]

JACK. It makes me feel such a cad and a brute when I see her go struggling on—slaving her life out writing rubbishy serials for Pansy's Weekly and things like that—I want to tell her she can chuck it all and come to me—to give her a home of her own—so that she can look after it and be happy.

ROGER. Well, it'll come some day, old man. The luck's bound to turn in the end; and perhaps it will come with a rush. What makes you so down to-night?

JACK [after a pause.] I think it's because I—

ROGER. Well?

JACK [hesitates]. Swear you won't say anything.

ROGER. Of course not.

JACK. Not even to Jill—above all, not to Jill. Swear!

ROGER. I swear.

JACK. Well—I'm sort of hoping.

ROGER. What for?

JACK. For what you said just now—the luck that comes with a rush. It's a book I've written—a novel.

ROGER [doubtfully]. Oh! Think some one will take it?

JACK. You don't understand. It's a competition. Whittaker and Hunt have offered a prize for the best novel sent in to them anonymously—not less than eighty thousand words.

ROGER. And what's the prize? How much?

JACK. Two hundred and fifty pounds.

ROGER. Two hundred and fifty! Not bad!

JACK. And it wouldn't be only the actual money. If won, you'd make your name.

ROGER. And you think you've got a chance?

JACK. I know I have. It was announced in the papers last week that all the manuscripts had been returned, barring four. And mine hasn't come back; so it's one of the four.

ROGER. I say! And when will you know?

JACK. Any day—the decision is to be announced this week.

ROGER. Well, I wish you luck, old man—you know I do.

JACK. Thanks. If I could only—I get sick listening for every post. It will be brutal hard lines if I don't get it—after being so near. Brutal.

ROGER. Well, I suppose the other three poor devils are all feeling the same way about it?

JACK. But it would mean such an awful lot to me. I don't suppose it could mean so much to any one else. It's not so much myself I'm thinking of—it's Jill. It would mean a future for her as well as for me. We ought to be able to begin on that—with the start I should get— [Bell rings.]

ROGER. There is Jill.

JACK [going to door, center]. Remember, not a word—you've promised?

ROGER. Oh, solemnly.

JACK. If I've got to be disappointed I've got to be—but I don't want her— [He opens door. Enter Jill.]

JILL. Here I am, Jackie dear—Hullo, Roger!

ROGER. Greeting, fair damsel. What do you think of me?

JILL. Never have I beheld you more comical. Wish I was going with you. How soon are you off?

ROGER. Directly. Ten minutes more

and you and Jack can have the place to yourselves.

JILL. I suppose you've had your supper?

ROGER. At the chop house round the corner.

JACK. Haven't you?

JILL. Not a thing. My instalment for *Pansy's Weekly* had to go in to-night without fail, and I've been typing like mad to get it off in time. When I did finish the blessed thing I found I had neither milk nor butter nor anything else on the premises. So I came round here in hopes that you'd be able to stay the cravings of hunger.

ROGER [*going through door into kitchen; off*]. We've got bread and butter and milk; doesn't seem to be much else—we're relying on the char to bring us in breakfast. Jam? No—Jack cleaned the pot this morning. [*Comes back from kitchen.*]

JACK. That little grocer's round the corner keeps open till all hours. I daresay I can get something there—tongue or sardines.

JILL. You're an angel! Anything will do. And I'll put on the kettle and make myself some tea.

JACK. Righto! I'll be back in a minute. [*Exit Jack, center, then Jill into the kitchen.*]

JILL [*off*]. Roger!

ROGER. Yes?

JILL [*off*]. Is anything the matter with Jack?

ROGER. Not that I know of. Why? [*Sits.*]

JILL [*off*]. Don't you think he seems rather nervous and jumpy—the last day or two?

ROGER. Does he?

JILL [*coming out of kitchen*]. As if there was something on his mind.

ROGER. Oh, perhaps there is.

JILL. Has he said anything to you?

ROGER [*hastily*]. Oh, no—nothing.

JILL. You're sure?

ROGER. Quite sure—absolutely. How's the work getting on?

JILL. Same as usual. I've just turned out six thousand words of the most appalling rubbish ever written.

ROGER. The serial story?

JILL. Yes. It is wash, Roger.

ROGER. I expect you're unduly modest

about it. I don't read *Pansy's Weekly* myself—don't like the look of the outside cover—but I feel convinced that if I could only get over the cover, I should simply love your story. What's it about?

JILL. A viscount, a wicked actress, a millionaire, and a beautiful penniless maiden.

ROGER. And which does the beautiful maiden marry—the millionaire or the viscount?

JILL. Both. She's a perfect fool and the more I write about her the more I hate her. Sometimes I almost roll on the floor and curse *Pansy's Weekly*. How I shall bless the day when I can give the rag up—if it ever comes.

ROGER. Of course it will. Wait till Jack makes his fortune.

JILL. Dear old Jack! I wish he would make his fortune—and I wish I could make mine. I say, Roger—

ROGER. Yes?

JILL. If I tell you something, will you promise and vow not to say anything—even to Jack?

ROGER. Of course. Fire away!

JILL. It's a solemn promise, mind!

ROGER. Righto!

JILL. Well, there's just a chance that I may make my fortune.

ROGER. You don't say so!

JILL. Or if that's a rather exaggerated way of putting it that I may get a lift—a tremendous lift.

ROGER. How's that?

JILL. I don't know if you've heard about it, but a few months ago a firm of publishers offered a prize for the best novel sent in anonymously.

ROGER. Whittaker and Hunt?

JILL. Then you have heard?

ROGER. Yes—that is to say, some one was mentioning it to me just now—the other day; or perhaps I saw it in the paper.

JILL. It's a two hundred and fifty pound prize.

ROGER. Is it really?

JILL. And I've sent a story—the best thing I've ever done. And what makes it so deadly exciting is that all the competitors have had their manuscripts returned—except four.

ROGER. And you're one of the four?

JILL. I must be, mine hasn't come back—Oh, Roger, wish me luck!

ROGER. Of course I wish you luck. Naturally I do.

JILL. Think what it would mean—to Jack as well as to me. Two hundred and fifty pounds for us—and my name made as well. I should get better prices for my work—it would help us in every way.

ROGER. Oh, yes, I see that.

JILL. Oh, if only—if only—I can hardly sleep for thinking about it.

ROGER. And the announcement is to be made this week.

JILL. Oh, you know that?

ROGER [hastily]. I saw it in the paper.

JILL. This week. I might hear any moment. Whenever I hear the postman coming along the street I can hardly breathe for fear it's my book coming back.

ROGER. I don't wonder. It's enough to make any one feel jumpy.

JILL. Mind, you're not to say a word to any one—you've promised. If it comes off—if it only does—I want it to be a surprise to him—to take him off his dead old feet with joy. And if it doesn't, I've made up my mind not to tell him anything about it—to keep the disappointment to myself and not ever let him know. Here he is. [Enter Jack.] Well, what have you got for me?

JACK. Sardines and marmalade. Sorry I couldn't do better, but—

JILL. Don't apologize—I like 'em both and, just now, I could eat 'em if I didn't. I've got the kettle on and as soon as it boils I shall fall to.

ROGER. Make yourself at home. Jack, lay the table for the lady and ransack the larder. I regret to be unable to lend a hand in your domestic labors, as I am about to betake myself to the scene of revelry. [Puts on hat and coat.] What ho, varlet! My charger! In other words, I will don my hat and coat, adjourn to the corner and whistle for a taxi. [Exit Roger into bedroom.]

JILL. I wish you'd been going with him.

JACK. I wouldn't care for it a bit unless you were going too.

JILL. Dear old boy!

JACK. Have you put the kettle on?

JILL. Yes, but it will be a minute or two before it boils—I read your article in the Planet this morning. I liked it awfully.

JACK. Did you?

JILL. Anything wrong, Jack?

JACK. Wrong? No. Why?

JILL. I thought you looked a bit worried.

JACK. Oh, no, I'm not worried—at least, only the usual thing.

JILL. The usual thing?

JACK. I want to get on, and make money—for you.

JILL. Well, so you will—some day.

JACK. I want it now. Do you know we've been engaged nearly two years?

JILL. Do I know it? They've been the happiest two years of all my life.

JACK. That's all very well; but I sometimes ask myself if the time's ever coming when we can afford to be more than engaged.

JILL. Patience, boy; patience.

JACK. When you talk like that it makes me wonder if you care for me as much as I care for you.

JILL [tenderly]. Jackie, Jackie!

JACK. No, I didn't mean that really; but one gets so sick of being patient. I hate to think of you slaving away.

JILL. Oh, nonsense! It doesn't hurt any one to work—at least I know it doesn't hurt me. You mustn't worry about me so. Any one would think I was made of sugar! And you mustn't look on the dark side of things, Jackie. How do you know?—luck might come to us at any minute.

JACK. Yes—it might.

JILL. Wonderful things happen sometimes—quite unexpectedly—all of a sudden. People wake up and find themselves famous. And, think, when it comes, how splendid it will be—after all the waiting and the scraping and the struggling.

JACK. Yes. It would be all the more worth having eh?—because one had waited—

JILL. Rather!

JACK. To have got on—to have a name—to be able to write what you like—

JILL [laughing]. And to get your own price for it—

JACK. To have editors running after you—

JILL. And publishers—

JACK. Instead of getting your manuscripts flung back at you. And, best of all, to know I'd done something for you—made life easier—got a home for you.

That would be more than anything—that would be the best of all—that's what I want more than anything in the whole world. [*He holds her to him.*]

JILL [*softly*]. My kind, good boy! [*They stand silent for a moment, then she draws away from him, briskly.*] There's the kettle boiling. Go and make my tea, there's a darling and I'll cut the bread and butter. [*Exit Jack into kitchen.*]

[*Jill goes to table and takes up bread; then starts, puts it down and listens intently. The Postman's knock is heard faintly. She goes to window and peers out. The knock is heard nearer. She leaves window quickly and goes to door. Enter Jack with tea pot.*]

JACK. Hallo, where are you off to?

JILL [*confusedly*]. Only across the road—home—for a moment—to fetch something.

JACK. What is it—I'll get it.

JACK. Oh, no—I'd rather. It's only a letter—I just want to see—I'll be back. [*Exit hurriedly.*]

JACK [*calling to her*]. Be quick—supper's all ready. [*He begins to cut bread and butter.*]

[*As he is doing so, a Postman's double knock is heard at the door. He starts and stands absolutely still for a moment; then, with an effort, goes quickly to door, center, and opens it, showing Postman.*]

POSTMAN. Morrison?—Sign the receipt, please.

[*Jack does so, then shuts outer door; a moment's pause; after which Jack comes slowly back into the room, carrying a parcel. He comes down to the table, sets the parcel on it and stands staring at it for a second or two; then cuts the string and takes out a letter lying at the top of the parcel; reads it through, his face working, and finally sits with bent head, his eyes on the ground. Enter Roger.*]

ROGER [*in hat and coat over fancy dress*]. Hullo, what's the matter? Anything wrong?

JACK. Yes.

ROGER. What?

JACK. Oh, it's only—my manuscript's come back.

ROGER. Your manuscript? Which?

JACK. The one I was telling you about last night—from Whittaker and Hunt.

ROGER. The prize story?

JACK. Yes. I've lost the prize.

ROGER. I'm awfully sorry, old man.

JACK [*bursting out, after a momentary silence*]. It is hard luck—it's damned hard luck—after being so near it—and knowing I was so near! If only I hadn't known I was in the running! And now to get this [*looking at letter*] "—regret that the judges are unable to recommend it for the prize"—and, "will I kindly acknowledge receipt of manuscript?" Well, anyhow, the judges thought it good enough to keep till the last moment—and I'm hanged if I kindly acknowledge receipt of manuscript. They've registered the parcel, and what more do they want? I wish to heaven I'd never heard of their beastly competition!

ROGER. Oh, come, I shouldn't feel like that about it. I bet you've written a jolly good story—it must be jolly good, or it wouldn't have got into the last lap. So all you've got to do is to pack it up and send it somewhere else. Whittaker and Hunt aren't the only publishers on earth.

JACK. I've a good mind to burn it.

ROGER. Rot! You told me yourself it was the best thing you've ever done.

JACK. So it is—I wish I'd never written a line of it.

ROGER. Come, come—

JACK. I do. It's brought me nothing but disappointment. And I did put my back into it. I—well, I oughtn't to have been such a fool as to let myself hope. I ought to have known from the first that it was too much luck. But I went on hoping—because of Jill— It would have meant such an awful lot to her.

[*He breaks off and buries his face in his hands. Roger stands beside him, uncomfortably; then pats his shoulder. There is a loud and persistent rapping at the outer door.*]

ROGER. Hullo! Who's making all that noise?

JACK. Jill, I expect.

ROGER. Jill—what did she go out for? [*The knocking is heard again.*]

JACK [*giving his eyes a furtive dab*]. I don't know. You let her in.

[*Roger opens door, center, just as*

the knocking starts afresh, showing Jill outside.]

JILL [*excitedly*]. Roger, why didn't you come before? I thought you were going to leave me to knock the door down. [*She bursts into the room, followed by Roger.*] Jack! Where's my Jackie?

JACK. Here I am!

JILL. Oh, Jackie! I've got something to tell you—I don't know what you'll say and I don't know how to tell you—I feel as mad as a hatter—as mad as seven March hares! I don't think it can be true—I don't think it can be true—but it is! it is! it is! and I've got the letter! [*She dances round the room, waving a letter above her head.*]

JACK. What is it? What's the matter?

JILL. Nothing's the matter—the most heavenly luck in all the world! Roger knows all about it—I told him last night. Roger, I've won!

ROGER. You've won?

JILL. The prize! Mine's the best, out of I don't know how many hundreds. Look at Jackie—he doesn't know what we're talking about. Listen to this, Jackie—listen. [*Reading.*] "Dear Madam, I have pleasure in informing you that the judges have awarded the prize of two hundred and fifty pounds, under the conditions announced in the public press, to your novel, *Crown of Rue*. A check for the amount will be forwarded to you not later than Wednesday next. With sincere congratulations on your success, I remain, yours truly, Robert Grainger (for Whittaker and Hunt, Ltd.). P. S. If you can make it convenient to call here at any time between eleven and one during the next few days, I should much like to have a talk with you." Can you believe it? Can you believe it? Because I can't—and yet I know I do, all the time. What's more, I'm going to stand you two a dinner to-night—a real restaurant dinner—somewhere expensive! Only you'll have to lend me the money to pay for it, Roger—till I get my check.

ROGER. Of course—delighted.

JILL. Oh, Jackie, Jackie, think what it means! And he asks me to go and see him—Mr. Grainger. Don't you think that sounds as if he wanted more work from me? Say something. Aren't you surprised? I kept it from you on purpose. But I told Roger all about it, didn't I?

JACK [*constrained*]. Oh, you told Roger?

JILL. Yes, I didn't want you to—[*Jack does not answer. She looks from him to Roger.*] Roger—

ROGER. I say—I must be off. I'm awfully late. Best congratulations—I'm awfully glad! [*Exit Roger.*]

JILL. What is it, dear?

JACK. Oh—nothing.

JILL. There is something—aren't you glad for me?

JACK. Of course, I congratulate you.

JILL. Jackie! Tell me what it is—I want to know. Why are you so unkind? I was so happy—for your sake—for both of us. [*Jack is silent. Then he takes the parcel from the table and flings it savagely into a corner.*] What are you doing? What's that?

JACK. A manuscript.

JILL. But why?

JACK. Just come back. There's the letter that came with it. [*He hands letter.*] From Whittaker and Hunt.

JILL. Whittaker and Hunt? [*She reads letter.*] Oh!—you went in for it too?

JACK. Yes. Mine got into the last four. You've beaten me by a neck.

JILL [*going to him and putting her hand on his arm; gently*]. I'm sorry, dear. I'd rather you had won—I would indeed.

JACK [*looking away from her*]. Yes—in some ways it would have been better—in a good many ways. Of course I'm glad you're the lucky chap; but if I had come in winner, it might have made a lot of difference to us both.

JILL. What do you mean? I don't quite understand?

JACK. Well, you don't suppose I wanted the prize only for myself, do you? I'd planned—I thought we could have quite well started on the money—married! I meant to use it that way.

JILL. Well?

JACK. Well, I haven't got it. That's all.

JILL. But what difference does that make?

JACK [*sarcastically*]. What difference?

JILL. If you haven't got it, I have—Jackie, it's for us both.

JACK. It's very kind of you to say so, and I'm sure you mean it—

JILL. Of course I do.

JACK. But you can hardly expect me to look at the matter in that light.

JILL. I don't see why not. [*Jack shrugs his shoulders.*] Do you mean that you won't let me spend the money on—what we both want? On our home? [*She tries to put her arm around him. He draws away.*]

JACK. I'm sorry, but it's impossible.

JILL. Jackie! Why?

JACK [*doggedly*]. Impossible! A man doesn't sponge on the woman he's going to marry.

JILL. Sponge! You're upset, dear, and you don't see things quite straight. You're disappointed, and it's my fault. Don't make me sorrier than I am. If the money had been yours, you'd have looked upon it as half mine—you know you would. And I look upon it in just the same way. It's for you and me.

JACK. The situation is perfectly different.

JILL. No.

JACK. It is. I'm a man and you're a woman. It's my place to work and earn the same way. It's for you and me.

JILL. But if I can—

JACK. Oh, yes, you can. Apparently you're a good deal better at it than I am. You've pretty well made your name now, I suppose. You won't want me to help you.

JILL. And are you angry because I have made my name?

JACK. Angry? Oh, dear no! I was merely stating a fact. A woman who can stand on her own feet doesn't want a man to help her.

JILL. And you don't like to think I can stand on my own feet. You don't like to think I've got it in me to make a success on my own. The wife of a successful man—that's what you want me to be—but not a successful woman. You don't like to think I've got brains for anything better than *Pansy's Weekly*, and rubbish of that sort!

JACK [*sneeringly*]. Oh, if you imagine that a man falls in love with a girl because of her brains—

JILL. I'm not such a fool. But, whatever other men may do, I didn't imagine that you made it a condition of falling in love that the girl should have **no** brains at all. And if you think that I'll give up my brains—even for you, and to please you—you are very much mistaken. [*Sits.*] I've got just as much right as you have to work and win and struggle.

JACK. All right. Go ahead! If working and struggling satisfies you, I won't stand in your way. You're winning, right enough—you've beaten me at my own game.

JILL. And you can't forgive it! [*Jack is silent.*] That's what it amounts to—you can't forgive it. You wanted me to be your wife; but also, being your wife, you wanted to be able to look down on me. Now that you can't look down on me—now that you know I'm as good a man as you are—you don't want me any more.

JACK [*sneeringly*]. Oh, if you're beginning to give yourself airs already—on the strength of one success—

JILL. I'm not giving myself airs. I'm speaking the simple truth. You wanted me only when I was your inferior. You hate to think I'm as good as you.

JACK. Why don't you say better, at once? That would be the truth, too. You've beaten me in a fair fight and it's your turn to look down on me. I suppose your whole grievance is—

JILL. I haven't got a grievance. It's you—

JACK. I suppose your whole grievance is that you want to get rid of me—now you've had a bit of luck. Don't want to tie yourself to a poor devil you can give points and a licking to. Well, if that's the case, I'm not going to hold you to your word. You're perfectly free—free as air. And I daresay you're quite wise. A woman with a career before her oughtn't to marry—especially a man who can't do anything to help her—an inferior sort of chap who can't always manage to get along himself. It would be ridiculous to—to put anything in the way of your work—now you've had such a start. So we'll consider ourselves—friends. I'm sure that's what you want, even if you don't like to say so. And I hope you'll have the best of luck—and get on—and all that. I'm very sorry, but I have to go out now.

[*He fetches his hat and goes to the door. She is quite still till he reaches it.*]

JILL [*quietly*]. Jack!

JACK [*with his hand on the knob*]. Yes?

JILL. There's just one thing I should like to say to you before you go—if you have time.

JACK. All right. But don't be too long, please. I've got an appointment.

[*He stands with his back half turned towards her, still with his hand on the door. She is sitting and does not look at him.*]

JILL. Well, it's this—I suppose, when two people love each other they don't ever know exactly why. They make up reasons for themselves, of course; a man will think it is because the girl he cares for is beautiful or kind—but there are lots of women more beautiful and kinder that he never wants to turn his head to look at. And it's the same with the girl, if she really loves him. It's just that they want each other—and are drawn together; and when that happens, outside things don't matter at all. It's only themselves—each other. And that's my way with you. If you came to be a beggar and swept a crossing, I should still be glad of you—because you are Jack and I want you. And if you were the most successful man alive—with money and friends and all the world to play with—you would still be just Jackie

to me—because—that's how it is—and I hoped that was the way you cared for me.

[*There is a moment's silence, during which neither moves. Then Jack turns suddenly and kneels beside her, hiding his face in her lap.*]

JACK. Jill—I'm a brute—a brute!

JILL [*stroking his head*]. Oh, my darling, no!

JACK. I am—a jealous, ungenerous brute.

JILL. No, no, I was cruel. I oughtn't to have said what I did. And you mustn't think I don't understand. I know what your thoughts have been for me—how you've always planned to help me and give me everything. And now I'm asking you to do something more generous still—to take instead of to give. But it's you I want, my precious, not what you can do for me. You said just now that I could stand on my own feet. It's true, and I'm glad of it—but even though I stand on my own feet, Jackie, I still stretch out my arms to you.

[*She puts her arms around him as he kneels beside her, and he holds her closely.*]

[*Curtain.*]

THE DEMANDS OF SOCIETY

A COMEDY

BY OTTO ERICH HARTLEBEN

TRANSLATED FROM THE GERMAN BY HAROLD HARPER

CHARACTERS

RITA REVERA [*celebrated concert singer*].
FRIEDRICH STIERWALD [*head of Stierwald & Co., Rudolstadt*].
BERTHA [*Rita's maid*].

PLACE: *A large German watering place.*

TIME: *The Present.*

THE DEMANDS OF SOCIETY

A COMEDY   BY OTTO ERICH HARTLEBEN

[SCENE: *Rita's boudoir, small, tasteful, in the style of Louis XVI. At the back a wide double door leading into the hall. Left is another door, leading to the bedroom.*

Rita enters from the hall in ball dress, a gray silk cloak thrown over her shoulders. She has a parasol. She is singing.]

RITA. "Les envoyés du paradis
Sont les Mascottes, mes amis"—
[*Puts parasol on a table and pulls off her long gloves.*] Bertha! Bertha! [*Sings.*] Oh, Bertolina! Oh, Bertolina!

BERTHA [*enters, center*]. Madame?

RITA [*throws off cloak and goes to the mirror*]. I suppose the bell hasn't been fixed yet? I must sing for it before any one does any work, and just think what that costs! I sing enough for a whole benefit program!

BERTHA. The man hasn't fixed it yet.

RITA. Why hasn't he?

BERTHA. He couldn't come so early to-day.

RITA. As usual. He has no backbone, that man. [*Points to cloak.*] Brush it well—then in the bureau there. Look at the dust! And they call it a fresh-air resort. Any one call?

BERTHA. Yes, madame; the Count, and he—

RITA. I mean who *else?*

BERTHA. No one.

RITA. Bring me my wrapper. [*Bertha goes into bedroom, as Rita hums.*] How long did he wait?

BERTHA [*outside*]. Beg pardon?

RITA. How long did he wait?

BERTHA. Only one hour, madame.

RITA. He loves me no more! [*To Bertha.*] Why, he might have fixed the bell in that time.

BERTHA [*reënters.*] He had just come from the matinée, and wished to know

where madame had gone for coffee. Naturally, I didn't know.

RITA [*going into bedroom*]. Did he ask anything else?

BERTHA. No. He amused himself looking at the photographs.

RITA. Did he say he would call again to-day?

BERTHA. Oh, yes—at four.

RITA [*in doorway, looks at clock*]. Bother! It's half-past three now. Can't I even drink my coffee in peace! Quick, Bertha, get it ready.

[*Disappears into bedroom. Bertha picks up wraps, etc., and goes out, center. From the bedroom Rita is heard singing a plaintive melody.*

Enter Friedrich Stierwald. He is thirty, dressed in black. He comes in, center, followed by Bertha.]

BERTHA. I tell you, madame is indisposed.

FRIEDRICH. Tell madame I am just passing through town, and that I must see her on pressing business, very pressing business. Here. [*Gives his card and money.*]

BERTHA. Well, I'll give madame your card, though I hardly think she'll see you.

FRIEDRICH. Oh, I think she will! Take the card now—

BERTHA. You see. madame had a big charity matinée to-day—

FRIEDRICH. Yes, yes, I know. Ah! [*Rita is heard singing.*] She's all right! D'you hear that? Run along!

BERTHA [*still uncertain*]. Well—wait here a moment. [*Goes into bedroom.*] Madame!

RITA [*outside*]. Yes?

BERTHA. This gentleman—insists on speaking to you. He's just passing through town.

RITA. Help me into this first. Let

221

me see! Who—? Friedrich? Oh, I'll
be in directly.

BERTHA [*reënters and regards Friedrich
wonderingly*]. Madame begs you to wait
one moment.

[*Goes out center. Friedrich slowly
and cautiously takes in the room.
After a moment Rita enters in an
elaborate tea gown.*]

FRIEDRICH [*bowing formally*]. Madame! [*Rita gives him a half-amused,
half-disdainful glance.*] You—recognize
me, don't you?

RITA. I'm thunderstruck! *You* calling on *me!* But what about your strict
upbringing? [*Laughs.*] Have you no
sense of shame?

FRIEDRICH. Please, please, don't go on
like that. I have called on you to-day in
order to explain everything.

RITA. *You* here! I can't believe it.
Well, since you are, please sit down.
Now what can I do for you?

FRIEDRICH [*seriously*]. Fräulein Hattenbach, it is my earnest desire—

RITA. Pardon me for interrupting:
my name is Revera, Rita Revera.

FRIEDRICH. I am well aware that that
is the name you are now using, but to
me, an old friend of your family, you will
please drop this fantastic theater name.
For me, as always, you are a member of
the Hattenbach family, with whom I—

RITA [*staccato*]. With whom your
father is associated in business. I know.

FRIEDRICH. With whom I myself am
now in—

RITA. Indeed? But your father?

FRIEDRICH. If I had had the least
idea of your whereabouts, or even suspected what name you went under, I
should have sent you word of my father's
sudden and unexpected demise.

RITA [*pause*]. Ah! So he is dead. I
see; you are in mourning. When did it
happen?

FRIEDRICH. Six months ago. I have
been trying to find you ever since. So I
trust you will allow me to call you by
the name you were known by in our town.

RITA. Ridiculous! But do sit down.

FRIEDRICH [*still standing*]. I must
confess I had hardly expected this sort of
reception from you. I had thought that
after four or five years you would not
have received me with such—er—

RITA. Patience?

FRIEDRICH. No! Such self-assurance.

RITA [*angrily*]. What!

FRIEDRICH. I beg your pardon. Sorry
I said that.

RITA. Do you really expect me to take
you seriously? [*Sits.*] Well, what have
you to say to me?

FRIEDRICH. A great deal. [*Sits.*] But
—you are not feeling well to-day, I understand?

RITA. What makes you think that?

FRIEDRICH. Your maid told me.

RITA. A very clever girl. Now tell
me one thing: Do you plan to remain
long?

FRIEDRICH. With your permission, I
have so much on my heart.

RITA. So I thought. [*Calls out.*]
Bertha!—Would you believe it, I simply
can't get the people here to fix my electric bell!

[*Enter Bertha.*]

BERTHA. Madame?

RITA. When the Count calls, I am
seriously ill.

BERTHA. Yes, madame.

[*Goes.*]

RITA [*calling*]. What's become of the
coffee? I'm dying for it.

BERTHA [*outside*]. Coming at once,
madame.

FRIEDRICH. Did she say—the Count?

RITA. Yes. Awfully nice fellow—but
I don't want to see him now. What I
was going to say: I'm quite lost without
my bell. It's such a nice bell: all you
have to do is touch it lightly with the
tip of your finger and it rings like the
old Harry. Oh, I'm sorry, you wanted
to say something serious.

FRIEDRICH. I did. Now, Fräulein
Erna—

RITA. Erna?

FRIEDRICH. Erna.

RITA. Oh!

FRIEDRICH. Are you really in a serious frame of mind? Then listen to me,
and be assured that what I have to tell
you springs from a warm heart and the
purest of motives. During the years
since we last saw each other, I have
become a very earnest and solid man.
Possibly too serious for my age. But I
assure you, my feelings for you have
remained—young. Are you listening
to me, Erna?

RITA [*leaning back—with a sigh*]. I
am listening.

FRIEDRICH. And you know, Erna, from

my earliest youth—even before that—what great affection I had for you. You know that, don't you, Erna? [*She doesn't look at him.*] And how as a growing schoolboy I called you my fiancée, and could never imagine any one else as my beloved wife. You know that?

RITA [*eyes closed*]. Yes, I know.

FRIEDRICH. Then you are in a position to realize how terribly shocked and grieved I was when I discovered my father's interest in you. No, you can't realize it. I went through months of mental and spiritual agony. Ah, Fräulein Erna, we human beings are—are—

RITA. Yes, I know.

FRIEDRICH. So cramped and confined. How seldom is it given to one of us to live just as we want to live. Must we not always be considering other people, and—and the community in which we live?

RITA. *Must* we?

FRIEDRICH. Well, we *do*. And to think of my father! He was very willful. He built with his own energy and patience the great factory of which I am now the head.

RITA. Yes, he was a good business man.

FRIEDRICH. Wonderful. Even at the age of fifty-two, he was still—how shall I say it?

RITA. Wonderful.

FRIEDRICH. No; I mean, youthful, energetic—in the prime of life. He was a widower for fifteen years, and never away from his business. Finally, when it became firmly established, he began to think of shifting some of the responsibility to younger shoulders, and enjoying life.

RITA. In what way?

FRIEDRICH. He believed he had found in *your* youth a means of renewing his own.

RITA. That's just where you—oh, it's not worth discussing.

FRIEDRICH. You mean I should have taken a firm stand, and said to him: No, don't be an old fool! I am your son! Such happiness is for me, and not for you! No, Erna, I wouldn't do that.

RITA. I suppose not.

FRIEDRICH. I was only a salesman—and remember, I owed everything in the world to him. Under the circumstances, it was my sacred duty to say and do

nothing. That is what I did. I tried to forget you, to efface myself.

RITA. I seem to recall: you were very distant toward me. Most tactful of you—

FRIEDRICH. I thought—

[*Bertha comes in and serves coffee.*]

RITA [*to Friedrich*]. Coffee?

FRIEDRICH [*distraught*]. I thought—oh, I beg you pardon! No, thanks!

RITA. You don't mind if I drink some, while you go on?

FRIEDRICH. Please do.

RITA. You see, I'm used to it at this time. It is a duty—to my body. Go on.

[*Bertha goes out.*]

FRIEDRICH [*confused*]. I thought it my duty then to—to stifle my inclinations—

RITA. Oh! Don't lie about it! [*Gets up and walks to and fro.*] As though you didn't understand! Tell me what you used to think of me, when I kissed you?

FRIEDRICH [*rises*]. Oh, Erna, I—always—respected—

RITA. You're crazy! Raving mad! You're a puppy-dog, that's all.

FRIEDRICH [*after a pause*]. Don't—don't, Erna. You'll let me call you Erna, as I used to?

RITA. As you used to. [*Lightly.*] If you like.

FRIEDRICH. Oh, Erna!

RITA. Fritz! That sounds more like old times, doesn't it?

FRIEDRICH [*takes her hand*]. It does. You've lifted a heavy load from my heart. I'm glad; it makes it easier to tell you all I've come to say.

RITA. Have you so awfully much more to say?

FRIEDRICH. Tell me, Erna, how could you do this—leave home and go out into the wide world—

RITA. You ask that! Don't you *know*?

FRIEDRICH. Er—yes, I do. But, such an important step—so unusual. Though I must confess one thing; however wicked it must seem, the moment you left I felt a distinct sense of liberation.

RITA. Ah, that was your heroism.

FRIEDRICH. Don't misunderstand. I knew my father was thinking about you.

RITA. Please let's not say anything more about that.

FRIEDRICH. You're right—it was childish of me. Your poor father and mother! You ought to see them: they look ten years older. Your father's no longer good-natured, and his liking for—red wine—has become—er—almost a passion. Your mother is sickly; hardly ever leaves her room. They're both rather bitter toward their only child, who left them—

RITA. Have you come here on behalf of my parents?

FRIEDRICH. No. Why do you ask?

RITA. If you had, I should show you the door.

FRIEDRICH. Erna!

RITA. I have been through terrible struggles—debts, misery, and the rest. But now, the House of Hattenbach enjoys its former good reputation and as you would say, has successfully passed the crisis. So all's well with the world. Now please let's discuss something else.

FRIEDRICH. No, no, Erna. I don't like your tone; you insinuate—

RITA [*seriously*]. Your father was used to reckoning everything in the world on the basis of hard cash. Well, I, too, have learned to do that. Remember, he had my father under his thumb, but not me. I am free: I have made my own freedom, and I am my own mistress. [*Friedrich doesn't know what to say.*] Don't be distressed. Your father was the stronger then. Such is life.

FRIEDRICH. But he made you unhappy!

RITA. Who can say? At any rate I'm happy now.

FRIEDRICH. You call this happiness—living alone?

RITA. It's *my* happiness, because it means freedom. I love it, I am jealous of it: I made it myself.

FRIEDRICH. What sort of happiness can one have outside the family circle? It's—it's hardly respectable.

RITA [*laughs*]. Respectable! Thank heaven, I've escaped what you call respectability. Well, if you weren't sent here by my father, what *do* you want? What can I do for you?

FRIEDRICH. Erna! Why so hard?

RITA. I just suspected—that you wanted to take my freedom from me. How did you happen to come?

FRIEDRICH. That was rather difficult.

RITA. Rita Revera is hardly an unknown!

FRIEDRICH. Rita Revera! I should think not. I've seen the name often enough the past year or two—in the papers, on the billboards in Berlin, with letters three feet high! But how was I to know Rita Revera was you?

RITA. Why didn't you come to see me at the Wintergarten when you were in Berlin?

FRIEDRICH. I am not in the habit of frequenting such places.

RITA. I beg your pardon. I was forgetting your respectability.

FRIEDRICH. Please, my dear Erna, don't use that tone.

RITA. What tone?

FRIEDRICH. Erna, don't make it any harder for me. Well, I finally learned, through a registration bureau in Berlin that you were the celebrated Rita Revera. I was terribly shocked at the news, and grieved; I was on the point of giving up trying to see you at all. That meant the confirmation of my worst fears. You see, I thought you must surely be in good—well, I see you are as a matter of fact more than comfortably well off. And of course I was positive that you lived in a world absolutely apart from the world I lived in. I feared that we might not even understand each other.

RITA. D'you want me to tell you what your ideal was? What you had hoped to find me? A poor seamstress in an attic room, who had managed—oh, so respectably!—to struggle through four years of hunger and sorrow. Then you would have extended your knightly arm and the poor little dove, full of gratitude, would run to you and bury her head on your manly breast. Can you deny that that is what you dreamed?

FRIEDRICH. No. Is there anything wrong in dreaming that?

RITA. But how did it happen that in spite of your disappointment, you actually did come to see me?

FRIEDRICH. Thank Heaven, it was the memory of your childish laughter that thrilled my heart. I thought of the time when you loved me. Do you remember?

[*Rita looks at the floor.*]

[*Bertha enters, center, with a huge bouquet of roses.*]

BERTHA. From the Count, madame.

RITA [*jumps up*]. Roses! Beautiful dark roses! Here. [*Takes the bouquet and smells the roses.*] Did he leave any message?

[*Thrusts flowers under Friedrich's nose.*]

BERTHA. He didn't *say* anything—

FRIEDRICH [*turning away*]. No, thank you!

RITA [*without looking at him—to Bertha*]. Well?

BERTHA. He wrote something on the card.

RITA. Oh! [*Looks in the bouquet.*] Here it is! [*Pause.*] Very well. [*Bertha goes out.*] "Pour prendre congé." [*Sighs.*] So that's that.

FRIEDRICH. What's what?

RITA. Too bad. He leaves me before his education is half completed.

FRIEDRICH. What do you mean? I don't understand you at all.

RITA. Really too bad. Fatty degeneration of the brain is sure to set in now.

FRIEDRICH. Erna, answer me: What is your—er—relation to this Count?

RITA [*laughing*]. Does that concern you?

FRIEDRICH. Erna! This shall go no farther!

RITA. Don't you see it's all over anyway?

FRIEDRICH. It must be. You have got to put an end to this existence you are leading. You cannot go on.

RITA. You're truly extraordinary!

FRIEDRICH [*strutting to and fro*]. It's not respectable. I—I forbid you to go on. I—ask—you—I command—

RITA. Command?

FRIEDRICH. I command. Not on my own behalf, but on—on the grounds of common decency. I speak on behalf of society, do you understand? There are certain laws of decency which must be obeyed by every woman—

RITA. Must? Why?

FRIEDRICH. Why? Why? Good Heavens! Why, otherwise, everything simply —goes to smash.

RITA. What? Life?

FRIEDRICH. No: respectability.

RITA. Oh. Now I understand. I must be respectable—otherwise respectability goes to smash.

FRIEDRICH. Well, yes. That's simple enough, isn't it?

RITA. It is. Well, then, what must I do if I am to act on this command—or demand—of yours? I'm as curious as a

child; I'll listen to every word you tell me.

[*Sits down.*]

FRIEDRICH [*sits and takes her hand*]. Now it's this way, Erna dear. It's really very simple. You see, in Rudolstadt all the folks think you're living with relatives in England. Though you may never have been there—

RITA. But I have—I've sung there time and again.

FRIEDRICH. So much the better. You speak the language?

RITA. Well enough.

FRIEDRICH. And of course you know something about the country. Splendid. Oh, Erna, your father will be overjoyed. He told me himself. You know how sentimental he is.

RITA. So are they all!

FRIEDRICH. What?

RITA. Nothing. Please go on. So, I'm to go back home?

FRIEDRICH. Surely. Fortunately, none of the home folks have seen you on the stage. You simply *must* come back.

RITA. From England?

FRIEDRICH. Yes. The road is clear, and everything's settled. Your dear mother—she'll weep with joy—

RITA. Of course.

FRIEDRICH. Then when you've dropped the name of Rita Revera—they will be so glad!

RITA. Then they know?

FRIEDRICH. I wrote that. They'll be waiting for you with open arms. Erna, come with me. To-day. There's not a minute to lose. Who knows but some one from home may go to the theater here and recognize you!

RITA. No one from Rudolstadt would ever set foot inside a theater: they're too respectable—like you. But do go on. What next? Suppose I go home? What then?

FRIEDRICH. Why, you'll be in the bosom of your family, received in society, and—

RITA. And—

FRIEDRICH. And then—after you feel quite at home, and have forgotten this existence you are now leaving forever— as though nothing had happened—

RITA. But a great deal *did* happen.

FRIEDRICH. Erna dear. you mustn't think me such an awful philistine. Really, at bottom, I'm not quite so prejudiced as you imagine—word of honor. I—I am only too well aware of my own shortcomings, and I know something of life. I realize clearly that I can't expect you to put your whole career absolutely out of your—you see, so entirely—

RITA. Hm?

FRIEDRICH. And, naturally, I don't expect that during those years you have been—well, let us say—that is, I can scarcely demand—

RITA. Very wise of you.

FRIEDRICH. I mean: that is all buried and forgotten. Rita Revera is dead. Erna Hattenbach returns again to the bosom of her family.

RITA. Tableau! Very pretty. Then what? Do I start a young ladies' seminary?

FRIEDRICH. Erna! Can't you see what I have in mind? I—I—well, then, I should marry you, naturally. [*Rita just stares at him.*] Naturally! Why do you think I have been looking for you? Why am I here now? Oh, for the love of Heaven, Erna, don't stare that way!

RITA. Marry you! "Naturally"! Ha! [*Goes to piano, plays and sings.*] Farilon, farila, farilette—

FRIEDRICH [*rises*]. Erna! Stop that! It upsets me frightfully.

RITA. Upsets you? That wouldn't be nice. You're such a good man. Kiss me. [*Rises.*]

FRIEDRICH [*kissing her*]. My own Erna! I never knew you were so beautiful. Come, now, let's not lose another instant. [*She doesn't move an inch.*] Never mind packing—just come. [*Tries to make her leave with him.*] Tears!

RITA. Tears? Your grandmother! Rita Revera doesn't *use* tears!

FRIEDRICH. Erna, don't mention that name again. I insist.

RITA. You insist! I like that—you have the audacity to come here and think you can blot out four years of struggle and poverty and desperation by offering me a few little material comforts and middle-class happiness. Let me tell you, you know nothing about life, and still *less* about me! My name is Revera, and I'm marrying no moneygrubber from Rudolstadt!

FRIEDRICH. You mean—you're not sure?

RITA. Wait and see how sure I am. [*Going close to him.*] Do you know that often during those years of struggle I literally starved! Do you know that I've seen days when I was happy to have a single penny in my hand! Do you realize what it means to suffer physical and mental torture for the sake of a crust of dry bread! That's what my schooling has been. It was misery and want for me—or the other thing! At last do you understand how impossible, how cowardly, how stupid it would be for you to take me by the hand and lead me back among the philistines?

FRIEDRICH [*after a pause*]. No, I don't see that.

RITA [*gayly*]. I didn't think you would. Can you imagine me back there, afraid of every idiot I might see! Here I'm free, I have air and sunshine, and a clear conscience. No, no. D'you remember *Die Walküre?* [*Sings.*]

Greet Rudolstadt for me.
Greet my mother and my father,
And all the heroes—
To them I follow thee not!

Now you have your answer. [*Sits again at the piano.*]

FRIEDRICH. But *because* you have suffered so much I believe you are morally obligated to—abide by the—er—the proprieties—

RITA [*singing*]. Farilon, farila, farilette—

FRIEDRICH. What I cannot comprehend is your refusal of my offer of marriage. I offer you unconditionally an honorable position—

RITA. I have no use for an "honorable position." I don't like it.

FRIEDRICH. Am I then never to mean anything to you?

RITA. I don't say that.

FRIEDRICH. You—! But you said you'd marry no Rudolstadt moneygrubber?

RITA. I did.

FRIEDRICH. Well! You can't be so heartless, Erna! Why, oh, why did you kiss me? Ah, you must have been moved by the memory of those early days. You shed tears! Erna, come with me.

RITA. No.

FRIEDRICH [*rises*]. So I can't persuade you? You have nothing more to say?

RITA. Nothing.

FRIEDRICH. Think well.

RITA. I know what I'm doing.

FRIEDRICH. You are fully determined to remain here?

RITA. Exactly.

FRIEDRICH [*pauses, then quickly snatches his hat*]. Then—farewell!

[*Rushes off melodramatically—but into the bedroom!*]

RITA [*laughs*]. No, not there!

FRIEDRICH [*reënters, in confusion*]. I beg your pardon!

RITA. Poor old Fritz! What a terrible catastrophe! [*Points.*] That is the way out.

[*Fritz stands undecided. Starts to speak several times, but says nothing. .Rita starts to play. Friedrich comes toward her, as she sings:*]

. , , *Tach' d'en profiter, gross' bête!*

Farilon, farila, farilette!

[*Friedrich lays his hat on the table as she finishes.*]

RITA. Did you like that? I saw you smile.

FRIEDRICH [*kneels to her*]. Oh, Erna, you're the most wonderful creature in the world!

RITA. Then why run away? And if you are really in love with me, maybe some day—? You donkey!

FRIEDRICH. I'll stay, I'll stay, Erna, dear.

RITA. Call me Rita. You'll be good now?

FRIEDRICH. Rita! I'll be anything you say.

RITA [*kissing his forehead and smiling*]. Now explain to me all about your demands of society. You're adorable!

[*Curtain.*]

CREEDS
A PLAY
BY FRANCES HEALEY

CHARACTERS

SHEMSEDDIN [*a young Bedouin*].
NOUR [*his bride*].
HABSAH [*a servant*].
KHALIL [*Nour's uncle*].
GIRIES [*Khalil's son, betrothed to Nour*].

CREEDS

A PLAY   BY FRANCES HEALEY

[SCENE: *A roof-top in an Arab village east of the Bahr Lut. There is a parapet around the roof which, at the right, overlooks the village street. At the back a lower wall overlooks the garden, and at the center, a break in this wall shows the stairway leading to the garden below. The top of a fig tree can be seen, and beyond, the minaret of a mosque. Beyond the mosque is the desert, stretching to the sunrise. It is dawn. On the roof near the back are two mattresses, one empty. A figure is seen on the other. A second figure cowers in the shadow of the corner wall.*

When the curtain rises, Shemseddin is lying on a mattress at the back. Nour is dimly seen crouched near the corner of the parapet. Shemseddin moves and stretches out his hand.]

SHEMSEDDIN. Nour! [*No answer.*] Nour!

NOUR [*breathlessly, as if she had been crying or was in terror*]. My lord?

SHEMSEDDIN. Where art thou, my little dove? Why hast thou left me?

NOUR. I dreamed a fearful thing! I was afraid!

SHEMSEDDIN. Afraid? Thou? [*Rising and going to her.*]

NOUR. I thought my father's hands were hot on my shoulders. I heard his dagger drawn hissing from its sheath. I felt it cold and curved at my throat! O Shemseddin, Death has brushed me with the very hem of his garment!

SHEMSEDDIN. Not death. The desert wind moved thy veil, or this chain drew tight across thy throat.

NOUR. It was a fearful dream.

SHEMSEDDIN. Didst thou not leave thy father's house and thy bridegroom the night before thy wedding? Didst thou not come to me by the spring, alone? Allah, how we rode! But wast thou afraid?

NOUR. No. I was a child.

SHEMSEDDIN. A child, my gazelle? It was only as many nights ago as thou hast fingers on one hand! Wast thou afraid yesterday, when thine uncle passed so close to our hiding place that I could have killed him—and would not?

NOUR. I was not afraid for I was with thee. But, O my lord! His curses are a fearful memory! They are like vultures hovering above a dying man!

SHEMSEDDIN. See, beloved, it is almost the hour of prayer. First the call, then the sun and these shadows shall be driven from thy heart.

NOUR. O Shemseddin, my lord, I am afraid! I have sinned! I have brought shame on my father's gray hairs, sorrow to my mother's heart! I was their ewe lamb. They gave me clothes embroidered in colors—no maiden at the well was so gay as I! My bracelets of silver and my anklets of silver wire rang as I drew water from the well. I have repaid them with shame. I have sinned against my father and my mother. I have sinned against their god!

SHEMSEDDIN [*sternly*]. There is no god but Allah!

NOUR [*continuing*]. No woman of my race has done this. Not one. No woman of my race has married a Moslem. And I have done this shameful thing.

SHEMSEDDIN [*angrily*]. Shameful?

NOUR. O my lord, forgive me, forgive me! My heart is burned within me and dies like a little fire that has no fuel. It is dead like cold ashes on the ground.

SHEMSEDDIN. It is I that am shamed. If thou art Christian thou art naught of mine! Can the branch say to the trunk, "thou art cedar but I am fig"? The branch of the cedar is cedar. [*He goes to the back.*]

NOUR [*standing still and piteous in the same place*]. Alas, alas! Alas, my mother! [*Slowly, overwhelmed by the*

231

terror of the thought.] My mother has cursed me in her heart! She is childless in her old age! I am alone. Shemseddin! [*He does not answer.*] Shemseddin! [*She turns, frightened, and sees him standing back to her, facing the east.*] Shemseddin, my lord! I love thee! See, I am of thee! Listen, I love thee! There is no god— [*She draws herself up to repeat the creed but at that instant the muezzin rings out from the minaret. As the muezzin sings to the four points of the compass, the confession rings out sometimes loud, sometimes soft, always clear.*] Allahu akbar, Allahu akbar, Allahu akbar! Ashadú ana la ilahâ ill' Allah, wa Mohammedu rrasûl Allah! Hayya alas salâ!

[*The light in the east grows stronger. Shemseddin has prostrated himself on his cloak caught up from the bed, and facing southeast, prays. For a second Nour stands undecided, lifts her hands to her forehead in the first pose of prayer, then suddenly drops them, shuddering. She faces directly to the east, crosses herself slowly, kneeling and prostrating herself as the orthodox eastern Christians do. Shemseddin finishes his prayer and turns just as she rises. He catches her angrily by the shoulder.*]

SHEMSEDDIN.   Wallachi, art thou Christian?

NOUR [*stands limp in his grasp. Then with passionate intensity she raises her head and quivers erect*]. I am of thee. I am not Christian, I am not Moslem. I am of thee. Thou art my safety in danger, thou only art my rock—my spring in the desert! My strength and the song of my soul!

SHEMSEDDIN [*drawing her to him*]. The sun drives back the night and its fears. The smoke of the morning fires is blue above the roofs. And beyond, O my beloved, is the desert, where the winds are clean! Even from here one sees the desert, and beyond that sand lies more sand, far out in the desert where all things are clean.

[*They are silent for a moment while the dawn grows brighter.*]

NOUR. Yet thy desert is cruel! I love towns. The little shops with sweetmeats and silver bangles, the gay embroideries

from esh-Shams, the cunning leather work, red, and blue and yellow; the water trickling from the fountains and the maidens who come with jars of red clay high on their shoulders. I love to hear their bracelets tinkle against the stone as the water tinkles in the fountain; and the soft rush of wind in the palms! In thy desert the sun cleanses all, but O my lord, there are no shadows for rest!

SHEMSEDDIN.   Yet?

NOUR.   Yet I am of thee! I am of thy desert! Thou shalt be my shade, thou my tall palm, thou my cool spring in parched sands. I shall be content.

[*The city has gradually awakened and there are shouts of muleteers and camel-drivers, bursts of Arab song, cries of fruit and bread sellers in the streets. Shemseddin gathers up his cloak and puts it on.*]

SHEMSEDDIN. I will go buy thee dates and little figs of Tibé. And to-night we will leave the town. The camels are ready and we are safe. Thy uncle and thy betrothed have followed us thus far. All yesterday they were here in the streets, searching, asking, spying; but at nightfall they had gone. None knew of our presence save Amin and Habsah, and they have not betrayed us.

NOUR. Yet what does my fear tear me like pain! I dreamed—

SHEMSEDDIN. There is no fear in a lover's heart!

NOUR. My fear is for thee. My uncle's eyes see through stone. His ears could hear the beating of my heart behind stone walls!

SHEMSEDDIN. I am a wall around thee my dove! Thou art safe. Lo, the sun! I must go quickly!

NOUR. O leave me not! So great terror comes over me alone! Fear stalks round me and hems me in on every side, alone! I did not fear my uncle for I was with thee. But to-day—I shall die of fear—alone!

SHEMSEDDIN. Habsah shall come—

NOUR. I want thee, my lord!

SHEMSEDDIN. But now it is finished. Thine uncle has turned back from following us!

NOUR. It is not finished. My uncle is very crafty. He is a great hunter. He will follow a gazelle for days—a gazelle swifter than any horse. And because he knows the way of gazelles, and because he never tires—

SHEMSEDDIN. He will not follow us to-night. I saw him turn back towards Madaba!

NOUR. He cut the gazelle's throat, a little throat no bigger than mine.

SHEMSEDDIN. I know.

NOUR. O Shemseddin! Dost thou think it hurts when a man draws his dagger across such a little throat?

SHEMSEDDIN. It does not hurt, Nour. Only fear hurts.

NOUR. Yes, fear hurts. [As he starts to go.] O leave me not! Here we are safe! If my uncle should have returned to follow us! If even now he should be in the streets! If he should be there—now—watching for thee!

[For an instant Shemseddin hesitates. Then.]

SHEMSEDDIN. What is, is Allah's will. If He has willed that thine uncle follow, thine uncle will be here. If He has willed that in these streets thine uncle kill me—

NOUR. No, no!

SHEMSEDDIN. Who can struggle with Allah? [Less somberly.] But I hear the hot wind from my desert, singing, singing, and I think that to-night thou and I shall be far away—far, far from towns!

NOUR [with attempted bravery]. I shall laugh when thou comest back! I will dance for thee—I will sing—

SHEMSEDDIN. Now thou art indeed my wife. Stay here on the roof till I come. I will send Habsah to thee with food. But O Nour! Shame me not before her! Let her not see thy fear! Thou hast a bride's jewels! Laugh, sing, my bride! Let her see thee gay! [He hands her a little two-stringed guitar and she takes it dully.] Sing, Nour!

NOUR [tuning the strings]. I sing of thee, beloved. [Sings.]

Cruel is my love,
Cruel as the sun at noon;
But the sun goes to rest
In the west,
And my love comes to me
With the moon.

Still is my love
Still as the moonlight on the—
[Speaks.] Alas my lord, I have forgotten—

SHEMSEDDIN. It is no matter. Hab-

sah is coming. Farewell my dove, my gazelle!

[Nour hardly lets him go. His eyes rest on her till he disappears down the stairway. Nour runs to the garden parapet and peers over.]

NOUR. Farewell, my lord!

SHEMSEDDIN [off]. Farewell.

[Alone, Nour goes back to the guitar, takes it up and sings.]

NOUR.

Should any ask me on his form to dwell
Helpless I say, "He hath no parallel";
The lovers by the loved one all are slain,
No voice can answer from the dead again.

[Speaks.] If he should die! Alas, I am a stranger, and his desert is cruel! I am alone! I have left my mother—I have left my God!

[She hunts feverishly in the mattress covers, finding a Greek cross of silver.]

Alas, alas! Evil will come upon me for my sin! God will punish! For my sin I shall die!

[She hears Habsah coming up the stairs and thrusts the cross into her dress. She begins to prink and rearrange her jewels with the aid of the small mirror and comb fastened to the head of the guitar. Habsah comes with a tray which she sets on the floor beside Nour. She, too, squats beside her.]

HABSAH. Here is fresh bread.

NOUR. I am not hungry. First I will put on my jewels.

HABSAH. Thou hast come far, daughter?

NOUR. Very far.

HABSAH. Thou art a bride. Thy jewels are new.

NOUR. I am a bride. Never had another bride such a necklace. So heavy, so fine! See!

[She holds it out.]

HABSAH. Tch—tch! It is very fine. The favorite wife of Sheikh Suleiman himself has none so heavy!

NOUR. I wear it so. My husband is generous!

HABSAH. Ah-h-h-h, a bridegroom is always generous! Listen, daughter! Keep all he gives thee, for some day when thou art old, and bent, and thy hair is gray instead of red, and thine eyes are weak and watery from the tent-smoke, then a new bride will have the jewels—

NOUR. No!

HABSAH. Marloom! That is how men are! Why not? Our Prophet himself— on whom be peace—

NOUR. True, true. I had forgot.

HABSAH. Why remember what is of thy future? Only—the day comes. May it be far away! Thou goest to the desert to-morrow?

NOUR. To-night.

HABSAH. The desert is free. I was born in the Jowf and I miss it. Thou art town born?

NOUR. Yes. But listen! The cries are all silent! There is not a sound!

HABSAH. It is nothing. Here is the very edge of the desert, and sometimes the desert's own silence blows across us like its sirocco. Here is jasmine for thy hair. What pretty bracelets!

NOUR. They are very heavy!

HABSAH. They are heavy for thy little wrists. How soft thy fingers are! It will not last. The firewood is full of thorns, and thy fingers will be burned at the oven. The hands of Bedouin women are sore and cracked.

NOUR. My husband—

HABSAH. La, la! What do men know of such things? It is naught to them!

NOUR. Hark!

HABSAH. There is always shouting in the market place!

NOUR. No, no! Men are running.

HABSAH [listening and then speaking lightly]. They run like murderers from a corpse!

[Both women run to the street parapet and peer over.]

NOUR. Who are they? Shemseddin—

HABSAH. No, strangers.

NOUR [recognizing them with terror]. Run—fasten the gate!

[Habsah hurries down the stairway. There is the sound of scuffling from the garden below, and Habsah's voice crying "No!" Then two men run up the stairway and face Nour. A pause. Very slowly the older man advances. He speaks slowly as if trying to control his almost uncontrollable rage and shame.]

KHALIL. We have found thee, daughter of evil! [No answer.] Hast thou no shame to stand there, painted, decked with jewels—ah-h-h!

[He loosens the dagger at his belt and moves toward her. The younger man steps forward and lays his hand on the elder's arm.]

GIRIES. Peace, O my father! Nour is afraid—a frightened bird! She is trembling. Do not fear, my cousin!

KHALIL. She is a sinner!

GIRIES. Let me speak to her. [He goes toward her, both hands out.] O my love, come back with us. I love thee! Hast thou forgotten how we were betrothed as children? [Nour does not move.] Come back with us, Nour! Thy father's enemies mock him. They say, "Aha, his daughter ran away with a Mussulman!" O Nour! If thou couldest see how he is! [She shakes her head, the Arabic upward toss, and raises her hand as if to stop him, but does not speak.] Thy mother sits alone and mourns. She will not eat. O Nour, she will die!

KHALIL. Thou hast murdered thy father and mother!

[Nour hardens.]

GIRIES. Nay, my father! I pray thee! [To Nour.] Never has such shame come upon a house in our village! Never has a Christian fled with a Moslem! This, to thy father's house! Ah, Nour, come back to thy mother! Come back to thy God!

NOUR. She curses me?

GIRIES. She does not curse thee. She grieves.

NOUR. She does not eat?

GIRIES. She has not tasted food for five days and five nights.

NOUR. He is mocked? Ah yes—but she mourns?

GIRIES. Day and night, night and day she weeps.

NOUR. Alas, fear comes upon me—

GIRIES. Come back!

KHALIL. Time passes. Hurry.

GIRIES. Come back!

NOUR [in tears]. O my mother, my mother! Yes—yes! Take me back!

KHALIL. Art thou Moslem?

NOUR. No. I will go home. I will eat the bread of shame all the days of my life. God grant me few.

KHALIL. Art thou Christian?

NOUR. Yes. I have sinned, I have sinned. [She begins to strip off her jewelry.] Hurry, lest my mother die.

KAHLIL. Leave them on.

NOUR. No, they are his gifts. He will know—he will find them.

[*Lays them on mattress.*]

KHALIL. He? The dead care not for jewels!

NOUR. The dead?

[*She faces the men sharply.*]

GIRIES. Peace, my father!

NOUR. He is dead?

KHALIL. Thou art alone among strangers in a strange town. Quick, lest these Moslem dogs find their dead and we Christians all be killed!

NOUR. We Christians? Christian dogs! [*There is a murmur of voices from the street coming nearer and nearer till the end.*] What is, is Allah's will. I am not afraid. Only fear hurts. Allah is great. There is no—

KHALIL. Thou art Christian?

NOUR [*defiantly*]. No!

KHALIL. Thou art Moslem?

GIRIES. My father—Nour!

NOUR [*almost chanting, in exaltation*]. Allah is great! There is no God but Allah, and Mohammed— [*With one bound Khalil leaps to her and stabs her. Giries catches her as she falls and holds her on his knee. She half turns toward him*] is the Prophet— Ah, Shemseddin! I dreamed, O my love, I dreamed that thou hadst died! Thou hadst died—and I could not die! O my beloved, with thee I am not afraid—

[*She dies. Led by Habsah, the crowd has rushed through the garden and up the stairway.*]

KHALIL. Now, it is finished!

[*Curtain.*]

THE UNRULY MEMBER
A Play
By Crosby Heath

CHARACTERS

MICK MAGUIRE.
BRIDGET MAGUIRE [*his wife*].
NORAH [*their daughter*].
PATHEEN [*Norah's betrothed*].
THE INSURANCE MAN.

THE UNRULY MEMBER

A PLAY   BY CROSBY HEATH

[SCENE: *Living room in a house in Dublin. Mick is lying in bed. Bridget is showing the doctor out. He is just outside the door, and Bridget speaks at the door to him.*]

BRIDGET. God go with you, sir. Yes, yes, I will—ah! it is indeed. . . . [*Closes door and comes into the room.*]

MICK. What is he saying?

BRIDGET. You'll not wish to hear.

MICK. The man's a fool!

BRIDGET. He is that!

MICK. Is he saying I'm at me end?

BRIDGET [*nods*]. He says you'll not last out the week.

MICK. What day is it then?

BRIDGET. Thursday, it is.

MICK. Two days more, is it? The man's a damn fool! If I had me strength I'd be out of me bed an' afther him with a stick!

BRIDGET. Eight weeks you are lying there, weaker an' weaker each day.

MICK. It's against reason for a man to die that's got no disease.

BRIDGET. It's wasthin' away he says it is—

MICK. If I had the use of me legs, I'd waste him!

[*Enter Norah.*]

BRIDGET. Are ye back already? Where's Patheen?

NORAH. He's outside.

BRIDGET. You've not had time to go to the pictures.

NORAH. We turned back.

BRIDGET. You've been crying, Norah! What is it then? Your wedding only a week off, an' you coming in alone, an' crying?

NORAH. I don't know how to tell you. . . .

BRIDGET. Is it Patheen?

NORAH. It is an' it's not.

BRIDGET. You've not quarreled with that peaceable boy!

NORAH [*chokingly*]. No, it's not a quarrel, but he's . . . he's giving me up.

BRIDGET. What's this? An' the wedding a week off!

NORAH [*crying*]. It's not Patheen wants to give me up—it's his father—an' for that Maggie Finnigan.

MICK [*feebly*]. An' is it Maggie Finnigan they're putting above me own darlin'! Oh! if I had me strength and me stick!

BRIDGET. Leave them to me. A tongue'll do more work than a stick, anny day. Patheen indeed, to give you up! Where is he?

NORAH. He's outside, cryin'.

BRIDGET [*going to door*]. Patheen! Come away in with you. [*Enter Patheen.*] An' what's this Norah is telling me?

PATHEEN. Och! Mrs. Maguire sure, it's in the black bog I am with it all!

BRIDGET. Let me hear the story, an' I'll soon see how deep in the bog you are. Giving Norah up, indeed!

PATHEEN. Och! it breaks my heart, but what am I to do? It's my father driving me to better myself in marrying.

BRIDGET. The Saints save us! Betther yourself with Maggie Finnigan—her with a head on her would fire a hayrick, an' a squint that frightens the fowls when she's feeding them! Betther yourself, indeed?

PATHEEN. It's this way it is. Ould Finnigan has promised to give a ten-pound note with Maggie.

BRIDGET. She'd be dear at ten shillings! Have you no spirit, boy?

NORAH [*crying*]. Where's your handkerchief, Patheen?

[*He wipes his eyes, blows his nose, and continues to whimper.*]

PATHEEN. Me father says I can't wed a girl without a penny, when I can get ten pounds with another.

BRIDGET. Hear the gossoon! Are you

239

taking a ten-pound note to your bed, rather than warm flesh and blood?

PATHEEN. Ah! then, don't be hard on me! I've got nothing myself, you know well,' but the bed an' board me father gives me for helping him in the shop. An' he says he'll turn me off, if I won't take Maggie, an' get in another boy to help him. [*Crying.*] Och! I don't know what to do at all!

NORAH. It's not his fault, mother. He loves me as much as ever he did— don't you, Patheen?

[*Patheen nods, crying too hard to speak.*]

BRIDGET. If you had the spark of a man in you, Patheen, you'd go to the devil with Norah, sooner than rise to glory with Maggie Finnigan!

PATHEEN. An' so I would, Mrs. Maguire, an' thank God for it! Sure, I'd run to hell with both feet, if I had Norah by the hand!

BRIDGET. Well, I say again, Patheen, your father's a fool! And as for yourself . . . come then, bid Norah good-by, an' well you may cry over it, for it's losing love an' money you are with her.

PATHEEN. Money?

NORAH. Mother!

BRIDGET. Yes, money. You'd be getting twenty pounds with Norah, and you cast her off for a squint an' a ten-pound note! Of all fools there's none like a sensible man, such as your father.

PATHEEN. Oh! but sure, Mrs. Maguire, this is another thing . . . me father didn't know . . .

NORAH. Nor did I!

BRIDGET. Hould your tongue, Norah! [*To Patheen.*] An' why wouldn't your father have spoken to me about the money?

PATHEEN. Ah! then, how would he know you had it? Trade is so bad, an' work's not falling off the trees like it used to do—it's lit on the top branches an' it's mortal hard to bring it down. [*Looks towards the bed.*] An' himself lying on his bed this ten weeks—

MICK. Eight weeks it is, no more.

BRIDGET [*to Patheen*]. An' is that your father's business or mine, what happens to himself?

PATHEEN. I meant no harm. Och, Mrs. Maguire, shall I run an' tell me father about the money?

NORAH [*joyfully*]. Run as fast as ever you can, Patheen!

[*He starts to run to the door.*]

BRIDGET [*stopping him*]. An' have I said Norah'd bring you twenty pounds now, afther the ways she's been shamed?

NORAH. I don't mind being shamed, mother, if I marry Patheen! Ah! you will give us the money, won't you?

[*Kisses Bridget.*]

BRIDGET. Well . . . there's to be no more talk about Maggie.

PATHEEN. Indeed, no! Och! the cross-eyed crow! Whatever would I have done with her?

BRIDGET. Well, then, tell your father I'm giving you twenty pounds with Norah, an' if he'll look in upon me to-morrow, I'll let him see the money.

NORAH. Run, Patheen. I'll come with you.

BRIDGET. No, run you alone, my lad. Give Norah a kiss in the sight of God, an' away with you. She's staying with me. There's work for her.

[*Norah and Patheen embrace. Patheen goes out.*]

NORAH. Mother, where did you get the money?

BRIDGET. I've not got it—not a penny of it, but I'll have it to-morrow, an' you're to help me. Run now to the corner shop and fetch me a dozen good candles. And stop at the chemist's, and get me the smallest tin they have of white powder that the ladies would plaster their faces with. Make haste, then, for I've bigger errands for you.

[*Norah goes out.*]

MICK. For the love of Heaven, what is it you're up to?

BRIDGET. It's a big trick I'm going to try, an' it's you is to do the chief part of it. You know your life's insured for twenty pounds. I must have the money to-day.

MICK. To-day! But I'm lasthin' till Saturday!

BRIDGET. What's a couple of days, more or less, if it's to save your one child from shame? You big fool, you'd have married Maggie Finnigan's mother yourself, only I carried you off. Only for me you'd have had a red-headed rat for your daughter, instead of your own Norah!

MICK. 'Twas a good turn you did me.

But I can't die till I do, can I? An' I'm feeling a little stronger.

BRIDGET. Leave off thinking about feeling a little stronger! You're as weak as a drowned kitten! Of course you can't die till your time comes, but you can pretend to be gone, can't you, to get the insurance?

MICK. Is that your game? You were never one to turn your back on danger!

BRIDGET. Come now, I'll wash your face and cover you with a clean sheet.

[*She brings water, etc., washes his face; fetches clean sheet, takes off other covering, and covers his face and when all is finished Norah comes in.*]

NORAH. Och! What's the matter, Is father—

BRIDGET. Come here, now, till I tell you. The doctor was here early, and gave himself two days to last, and for love of you, he's consented to play a thrick on the doctor an' the Insurance, by pretending to be gone before his time. Hand me over the powder. Put the candles on the dresser. Run and find me nine empty bottles. [*Norah gets the bottles from a corner of the room.*] Now go to the doctor an' get your father's certificate. Say he went very sudden, just after the doctor had left him.

NORAH [*repeating*]. "He went very sudden, just after yourself had left him."

BRIDGET. The old fellow'll be after having his morning dram, and I'm thinking he'll give you the certificate, an' no questions asked. Mind you cry when you ask for it. And when you've got it, go on to the Insurance—it's in the next street, and ask for the money. Show the certificate an' sign annything they tell you.

NORAH. It's a big task you put on me, mother. An' what'll I do if the Insurance Man wants to come and see for himself.

BRIDGET. Let him come, if he will. I've no fear of him. Run, now and waste no time.

[*Norah goes out. Bridget sticks candles in the bottles.*]

MICK. What's that you're doing?

BRIDGET. I'm getting ready for your wake, for fear any one should come in.

MICK. I don't like it at all, at all!

BRIDGET. Whisha! An' isn't it a pleasure it'll be to you to enjoy your own wake, an' join in the food an' drink?

MICK. A drop of whisky now would do me no harm.

BRIDGET. Have you no sense! Am I to show a corpse with a red face, smelling of whisky to any may chance to come in? Here, now, let me prepare you.

[*She crosses his arms on his breast, and powders his face.*]

MICK [*sneezes*]. By the powers above, I'd sooner be a real corpse than a play-actor!

BRIDGET. What now! Play it out as I tell you, and you'll have a good dhrink the blessed minute it's at a safe end.

[*Drawing sheet over his face.*]

MICK. Woroo! You're smothering me!

BRIDGET. Breathe easy, an' you'll have no throuble.

[*She puts candles at foot and head of bed and lights them. Then she darkens the room.*]

MICK. For the love of Heaven, let me out for a minute.

[*Pulls sheet off his face.*]

BRIDGET. Don't fidget. Heaven help us! You've uncrossed your arms! Here, now, dhraw a long breath, and I'll settle you once more, an' mind ye never stir hand or foot should anny one come in.

MICK. I'm feared I'll betray you.

BRIDGET. Oh! you're doing fine. Think of the whisky. It won't be long now, please God, till I pour it out for you.

MICK. It'll put strength into me. Sure, I'm feeling a change for the better.

BRIDGET. Arrah! Don't talk nonsense!

[*Norah runs in breathless.*]

NORAH. Och! Mother, he's coming up. I ran ahead.

BRIDGET. Who is it, then?

NORAH. The Insurance Man!

BRIDGET. You've not got the money?

NORAH. He's bringing it with him. He wants to be sure, first. [*She goes to bed and turns back sheet.*] Och! What a lovely corpse!

BRIDGET [*rushes to bed and replaces sheet*]. Is it out of your seven senses you are, and the Insurance Man on the stair! Have you got the certificate?

NORAH. Here it is. The doctor was just going off to sleep, an' he wrote it out an' gave it to me. "God rest his soul," he says—Hark! There's steps outside.

BRIDGET [*whispering*]. Run into the back room. [*Norah goes into back room. Bridget falls upon her knees beside the bed. A knock is heard.*] Come in.

[*The Insurance Clerk enters.*]

MAN. I'm sorry to intrude . . . duty . . . you understand. . . . [*He puts his stick in a corner by the door.*]

BRIDGET [*rocking to and fro*]. Ochone! Ochone!

MAN. I'm sorry for you indeed. Loss . . . a husband . . . separation . . . you've been long married?

BRIDGET. Eighteen years. Ochone!

MAN. No one would think it to look at you.

BRIDGET. Sixteen, I was on my wedding day. Ochone!

MAN. I won't trouble you further. I've got the money in my pocket. [*Takes it out.*] If I could—would you allow me —a look, purely official . . .

BRIDGET [*rises and pulls down sheet*]. Och, Mick, how'll I'll go on living without you! Ochone!

MAN. What was his complaint?

BRIDGET. Sure, he never complained. A more peaceable man, with a quieter tongue never lived nor died.

MAN. I mean, what was his disease?

BRIDGET. Lord save us! Have you not read the doctor's certificate, a learned man like yourself?

MAN [*flurried*]. Yes, yes, of course. Very sad, very painful.

BRIDGET [*on her knees beside the bed*]. Ochone! Ochone! Ochone! Ochone!

MAN. Here, my poor woman. [*Gives her the money.*] God bless you!

[*Moves out, gently, leaving his stick behind.*]

BRIDGET [*calling softly*]. Norah! [*Norah comes in.*] Here's the money, an' heaven bless it.

NORAH. Och, mother! An' isn't it wonderful what talk'll do.

BRIDGET [*pulls sheet off Mick*]. There now! Feast your eyes on that! [*Shows money.*] Are you not the proud man to be giving twenty pounds with your daughter?

MICK. Sure your tongue's greased with the devil's own oil.

BRIDGET. I'll show you I'm a match for all Dublin when I'm defending my own!

NORAH. It's a mortal big thrick we've played. Please God we're not caught at long last!

BRIDGET. Have no fear. Come now an' help me get ready the dinner, an' a late dinner it is. How are you feeling, Mick asthore?

MICK. I've a wonderful feeling of feeling better. Hoist me up on the pillows a bit, an' for the Lord's sake, wipe the paste off me face.

BRIDGET [*wiping off powder*]. Well, it's done you good. Sure you're skin is looking more natural-like. [*Lifts him higher on pillows.*] Only the doctor ordered it for the weakness of your heart. I'd never have left you lie flat on your back all these weeks. You'll drink easier with your head up, and your throat free for the whisky to flow down it.

NORAH. I'd best put out the candles.

BRIDGET. Och! I clean forgot them. Put them out indeed. They'll do for the real wake when it comes.

[*Norah puts out candles and busies herself getting the meal ready.*]

MICK. I wonder will ye need them this while. I don't know was it the candles or the keening, but I'm feeling another man. I'm after moving my legs like as if I had the use of them again.

NORAH. Och! Father. Whatever'll we do if you get well? We've got your certificate.

BRIDGET. An' we've got the Insurance money.

MICK. An' what'll become of us at all if you have to give it back? Will it be jail for us?

BRIDGET. Sure we couldn't help it. It was a mistake like. You had a long fainting fit, an' I thought you were gone. Here! Here's the whisky.

MICK. Give me the glass in my own hands—och! It's only a dhrop. Fill it up!

BRIDGET. I'm afraid to give you too much for the first dhrink this eight weeks —you might go off in good earnest.

MICK [*drinks*]. Ah! That's the medicine. [*Looks at the food Norah is putting on table.*] A taste of that hambone would do me good.

NORAH. Will it hurt him, do you think, mother? Oh! I'm frightened with all this.

BRIDGET. You've no need to be frightened. We'll come to no harm while I'm able to use my tongue.

MICK. Where's my pipe? I'm feeling full of strength.

BRIDGET. It's full of spirits you are, an' that's twice the truth. [*To Norah.*] Get him his pipe.

NORAH. Shall I fill it for you, father? Wait till I find the tobacco. The room's so dark I can't see at all.

BRIDGET. Pull back the curtains. We're safe now.

[*Norah fills pipe and gives it to Mick.*]

MICK [*to Bridget*]. Give it the first dhraw, for luck.

[*Bridget lights pipe and gives a pull at it.*]

BRIDGET. I'm thinking of Patheen and his father. The ould man's face'll be a picture when I hold the money up before him.

NORAH. It'll give me a fine pull over them all. There's not another girl they could find would bring such a sum with her.

BRIDGET. We've got the power in our own hands now.

NORAH. Could we use it, do you think?

BRIDGET [*considering*]. Why wouldn't I say the money goes with you when the ould man promises to give Patheen his wages in shillings for the work he does?

NORAH. Over an' above the bed and bite for us both.

BRIDGET. I'll make that sure! Patheen's a good worker.

NORAH. An' he would be saving when he had wages to save. Sure the poor boy can't put by what he's not got. [*A knock.*] Och! holy Mother, what's coming to us?

MICK. Cover me up. Plasther me face! Och, we're done for!

[*Another knock and the Insurance Man enters.*]

MAN. My stick—I left—Good God! What's this I see!

MICK. It was a mistake it was, sir, sure it was indeed—

MAN. A mistake. I like that!

MICK. Ah then, don't be angry. It was the doctor fixed Saturday for me, and I thought—

BRIDGET. Keep quiet, Mick. Let me talk. [*Aside.*] Norah, machree, go and find Patheen and bring him back to the house, but don't come inside, the one or the other, till I call to you from the window. [*Norah goes out.*] Now, sir, I'll settle with you.

MAN. Settle with me! My good woman! I—I—well, there's no words for it! I—I come here in pursuance of duty, yes, ma'am, official duty, yes, ma'am, government duty—

BRIDGET. Just so, sir, and a poor figure the government cuts that puts authority on the likes of you.

MAN. What insolence!

BRIDGET. Oh! no, sir, there's no insolence meant. It's God's truth I'm speaking.

MAN. What do you mean?

MICK. Leave me a speak—

MAN. Yes, let him speak. It's a new experience, so it is, to be listening to a corpse.

MICK. It was in the middle of the wake, it was—

MAN. Wake! I believe you! And all the candles lighted. . . . Where are they? Am I drunk?

BRIDGET. No, you are not, sir, an' that's a mercy, for the other one was.

MICK. An' I come to, afther a faint . . .

MAN. Nonsense, nonsense!

BRIDGET. A long faint it was—

MAN. Oh! you're both in it. It was a put-up job to rob the Company.

BRIDGET. Och! no harm'll come to the Company.

MAN. You've cheated the Company, the Insurance Company, do you hear, out of a sum of twenty pounds! It's monstrous, monstrous!

BRIDGET. The Company'll not lose.

MAN. That's true, for I shall take back the money.

BRIDGET. Ah! I'm thinking you'll not do that.

MAN. I certainly shall. Give it over at once.

MICK. Oh! Lord save us!

BRIDGET [*offering whisky*]. Will you have a drop of whisky, sir? The doctor has often tasted it an' found it fine.

MAN. Drink your whisky! Monstrous, monstrous! You cheat the Company and then try to suborn their representative.

BRIDGET. It's easy seen what an education you have, sir.

MICK. It's like a book, his fine words.

BRIDGET. You wouldn't be married, sir? No, you're too young.

MAN. Of course, I'm married. What's that got to do with it?

BRIDGET. An' I'll make bold to say you married a wife without a penny—I can see it in your kind looks.

MAN. A girl without a penny! Not I! My wife brought me a neat little fortune—lucky for me, for I'm a bit too fond of backing winners, or I ought to say, losers! Marry a girl without a penny! Ha! Ha!

BRIDGET. Thrue for you. An' what man in his senses would!

MAN. I've got three children as well.

BRIDGET. God bless them all. I've but the one, sir—you saw her.

MAN. Yes, I saw her to my sorrow. She's not got your humbugging tongue—

BRIDGET. An' isn't one talking tongue in a house enough?

MAN. She's a pretty slip though.

BRIDGET. She's called the beauty of Dublin.

MAN. Really! I suppose you know the saying: "Beauty ne'er boiled a pot."

BRIDGET. What's that, sir? Are you putting it on me that Norah'd be an idle good-for-nothing? Why, it was herself baked the fine cake you've just tasted.

MAN. I've had no cake.

BRIDGET. May the Lord forgive me for a neglectful woman. [Goes and fetches cake.] Here, sir, try the skill of the creature. With her own hands she mixed it. Thick curds and two beautiful eggs is in it.

MAN. [eating]. I never tasted better.

BRIDGET. Ah! eat your fill. It'll may be the last cake from those hands.

MAN. Are you going to get her Insurance money, too?

BRIDGET. Would I insure the life of her and her but seventeen, and her wedding next week . . . but there, that's over, thanks to yourself.

MICK. Speak out, Biddy!

BRIDGET. Yes, though my tongue runs away with me to purgatory, I'll speak out.

MAN. The Bible says the tongue's an unruly member.

BRIDGET. And I've heard the priest tell of the tongues of men and of angels.

MAN. He never mentioned the tongues of women, did he?

BRIDGET [wheedlingly]. Ah! will you let me speak, sir? For it's at your door, my daughter's death lies, and I'd wish to give you the chance of saving her.

MAN. Just put that money where I can lay my hands on it and then you can explain what I've got to do with the girl's death. She was healthy enough an hour or two ago.

BRIDGET [puts money on dresser]. You have said it yourself, sir, no sensible man marries a wife without a portion. An' this is the way it is. Norah, her that you saw, sir, is marrying the most peaceable boy an' the most knowledgeable boy, in all Dublin. He's one that learning sticks to like a burr to your coat, an' that's the truth. He's not twenty, and he keeps his father's books, an' adds up figures would make you giddy.

MAN. What's all this blether to do with me?

BRIDGET. It's all to do with you, sir. Just be easy a minute an' I'll show you. It's Patheen's father, a sensible man like yourself, wants a portion with Norah, an' what with himself [points to Mick] being caught on the roof of the building in the big fire, an' carried down a ladder would frighten yourself to see the height of, och! An' him black in the face with the smoke that all but choked the life out of him—

MAN. Was it your husband the firemen rescued at the risk of their lives?

BRIDGET. Himself it was, sir, an' he's lying on that bed ever since, getting weaker and weaker each day, an' what with the doctor an' the medecines—

MAN. Not to mention the whisky and the candles!

BRIDGET. Ah! it's not a joking matter it is, for thanks to yourself I've not a penny to give with Norah, an' it's losing her husband she is by the same token. 'Twas this morning only the doctor told me Mick'd not last out the week—

MICK. Till Saturday he gave me. And whatever'll I do now, for I'm feeling stronger.

MAN [interested]. It's all this excitement has brought you back to life. You've been suffering from shock.

BRIDGET. A shock it was! An' my husband, being a man of feeling, with a warm heart in him, knowing his end so near, consented to—

MAN. To join in your trick. I never heard anything to equal it!

BRIDGET. Ah, sir, there was the twenty pounds so near, and it was to-night I had to have the money, or my daughter'd have been cast aside for a girl that was bringing cash with her. . . . Ah! what harm is it at all? The big Company'll never miss twenty pounds, and yourself well knows how to cover it up in the books.

MAN. Look here. No, this won't do!

BRIDGET. I mean no harm. Ah, sir, you've a father's heart—will you speak with the childer, sir, an' then say will you part them? [Calls from window.] Norah, come away in, an' Patheen with you.

MAN. Upon my soul—

BRIDGET. It'll cost you nothing, sir. [Norah and Patheen enter.] Here, Norah, here's the kindest friend you have in the world. An' you, Patheen, speak to the gentleman is saving you from Maggi Finnigan.

PATHEEN. Good-day to you, sir.

BRIDGET. You'll see what a lad he is. Why, he'll tell you the news in the paper an' you houlding it upside down.

PATHEEN. I have never to buy a paper, for I do be reading over people's shoulders in the tram.

MAN. A capital idea.

BRIDGET. Many's the penny he saves with his knowledgeable ways. Have you never a bit of news for us, Patheen?

PATHEEN. I had only time to read the big letters—it's Monkeybrand has won the race—

MAN [jumping up]. Monkeybrand! Hurra! I've won a hundred pounds. I backed him! The odds were ten to one against him!

BRIDGET. Ah! you're heaven's own darling.

NORAH. Mother, we met the doctor as we were coming in, an' he asked me was father feeling any more comfortable! He'd forgot the . . . .

BRIDGET. Hould your tongue, will you! Run now, darlin', with Patheen to the pictures. You'll get the late house.

[Norah and Patheen go out.]

MAN [excited]. A hundred pounds, by jove!

BRIDGET. And isn't it heaven's own hand is in it! You'll take twenty pounds off your winnings an' put it back into the Company—you'll have the full eighty pounds for yourself! And as for this—

[Takes paper from her pocket.]

MAN. What's that?

BRIDGET. The doctor's certificate. [Tears it up and throws pieces in the fire.] Oh! but heaven's had mercy on us all.

MICK. I'm feeling stronger.

BRIDGET. I'm frightened to think what the law would have put upon the doctor that gave the certificate without even coming to the house.

MAN. Now you've torn it up, you've no proof of your husband's death, and the Company—

BRIDGET. Do I want proof, and him alive this minute? Nor have you any proof to warrant your taking twenty pounds from the Company. But don't fret; sure no one knows it but me, an' the priest'll give you absolution for the sin you committed in handing over the Company's money without proper investigation.

MAN. Well, of all the . . . .

BRIDGET. God keep you, sir. You've meant well, and thried to do your duty, but another time, lay your hand on the corpse to see is it alive or dead. You'll leave me the money, sir.

[Puts it in her pocket.]

MAN. Well, upon my soul, you deserve it. I congratulate you on your day's work. [Goes to the door, and turns back as he reaches it.] Don't do it again!

[Takes stick and goes out.]

BRIDGET [at door calling after him]. Good-by, sir, may all the saints in heaven follow you! May all your sons marry money, an' all your daughters— [Closes door and comes back into the room.] It's luck we've had! Forty pounds I've won this day. Twenty pounds in my pocket and the Insurance still holding good!

MICK [as curtain descends]. I'm feeling stronger!

[Curtain.]

A LEAP-YEAR BRIDE

A COMEDY

BY LESLIE M. HICKSON

CHARACTERS

SALLY RAND.
ALFRED CHADWICK.
ALFRED BUNN.

A LEAP-YEAR BRIDE

A COMEDY

BY LESLIE M. HICKSON

[SCENE: *The outer office of the Reliable Automobile Company. In the rear is a glass door with the name of the company on the outside. On the left is a door with the name Mr. Johnson on it. On the left down front there is a flat desk having a placard on it with the name, "Alfred Chadwick," with desk chair left of it, and a straight chair at right of it. There is a similar desk having a placard with the name "Alfred Bunn." Right of the door in the rear is a small telephone switchboard and a typewriter table and chair facing right. A clock is over the entrance door set five minutes after nine. A hat tree stands in the upper left corner of the room and a water cooler in the upper right corner.*

AT RISE: *Sally Rand enters from the rear. She has some papers under her arm and in her hand a small bunch of flowers. She puts papers and flowers on the typewriter table, then crosses to upper left, glancing at the clock. She takes off her hat and coat and puts them on the hatrack. A buzzer rings. She crosses to left door, opens it and looks off.*]

SALLY [*talking into the other room*]. Yes, Mr. Johnson!

JOHNSON [*gruff voice off left*]. Has Chadwick come in yet?

SALLY. No, sir! Not yet!

JOHNSON. What time is it?

SALLY [*looking at the clock*]. It's—it's five minutes after nine, sir.

JOHNSON. Oh! Then my watch is wrong. When he comes in, tell him I want to see him.

SALLY. Yes, sir! I'll tell him just as soon as he comes in.

[*Closes door and crosses to her typewriter table. She picks up flowers, smells them and looks lovingly in the direction of Chadwick's desk.*

She takes a glass from a water cooler, rear right, puts the flowers and water in it and crosses to Chadwick's desk where she places the glass. She looks at the flowers critically, moves them a little, then looks at them with satisfaction. Her eyes fall upon the morning mail on his desk. She crosses right of desk, glances about the room, then picks it up and goes hastily through the letters. Finally she holds up a pink envelope, stares at it a moment, then drops it and the other letters on his desk again. She hastens over to the telephone switchboard, puts the receiver over her head and buzzes the phone.]

SALLY. Hello! Give me Canal 8102, please. [*After a moment of impatience.*] Hello! Maizie? That you? This is Sally! Listen, girlie! I done it! Uh-huh! I wrote him last night . . . the letter's on his desk now! [*With a deep sigh.*] Gee, I'm scared! Sure! I proposed to him! Uh-huh . . . that's the way I figured it! Leap year only comes once in four years and he can't do no worse than turn me down . . . and gosh, Maizie! Wouldn't it be wonderful if I was to be a leap-year bride? [*The switchboard starts buzzing.*] So long, dearie . . . I got a call! [*Her voice takes on a business-like tone.*] Hello! Reliable Automobile Company! You want to speak to a gentleman by the name of Alfred? Well . . . there's two of them here by that name. There's Alfred Bunn, and then there's Mr. Alfred Chadwick. . . . Oh, the heavy gentleman! That's Alfred Bunn. . . . He isn't in yet. . . . All right . . . I'll tell him! Good-by!

[*She pulls out the switch and takes the receiver off her head. Then she turns toward Chadwick's desk*

249

again, gazes at the flowers and sighs longingly. The entrance door at rear opens, Sally hastily turns to her desk and pretends to be busy with her work. Alfred Chadwick enters. He is a rather good-looking and well-dressed young man, but he has a sour expression on his face as though he had a lot of worries in life.]

CHADWICK [*shortly*]. Good morning, Miss Rand!

[*Crosses upper left, taking off coat and hat and hanging them up.*]

SALLY [*looking up and trying to repress her excitement*]. Oh! Good morning, Mr. Chadwick!

CHADWICK [*frowning at Sally as he crosses left of his desk*]. Have you finished those letters I gave you yesterday, Miss Rand?

SALLY [*uncomfortably*]. No, sir . . . not yet. . . .

CHADWICK. Say! I gave them to you yesterday *morning!* Hurry them up, will you?

[*He sits annoyed.*]

SALLY. Yes, sir. . . . [*Pause.*] Nice day, isn't it?

CHADWICK [*as he puts on horn-rimmed glasses and starts looking through his mail*]. Yeah!

SALLY [*romantically*]. We been having swell weather lately. Seems like you brought it with you when you came to work here!

CHADWICK [*coldly*]. You shouldn't say "swell" unless you are talking of something swollen.

SALLY. Oh, no, sir! I guess it sounded as if the weather was sore about something.

[*He picks up Sally's pink-enveloped letter.*]

CHADWICK. Hello! What's this? [*Sally rises to tiptoe out of the room. He throws the letter aside. Sally sits.*] Confound all this mail anyway! [*He glares at her angrily.*] I want to dictate some more letters, Miss Rand!

SALLY [*picking up her stenographer's pad and pencil. Crosses right of his desk*]. Oh, Mr. Chadwick! I just love to have you dictate to me!

[*Chadwick arranges his letters for dictation. As he does so, he knocks over the glass with the flowers, nearly spilling the water on himself.*]

CHADWICK. Say! Who put these flowers on my desk?

SALLY [*confusedly*]. I . . . I did, sir. . . .

CHADWICK [*looking at her in astonishment*]. Well! Thanks very much indeed. . . . [*Puts flowers on lower end of desk. Sally sits right of desk. He picks up a letter and starts dictating.*] This is to Mr. Edward Carey, 304 Monroe Avenue, City. Dear Sir:—In response to your letter of January the fifth, we are glad to know that your business has taken a great leap forward this year.

SALLY [*looking at Chadwick devotedly and not taking down a line*]. Oh, Mr. Chadwick! Them words of yours was so kind!

CHADWICK [*with a start*]. Eh?

SALLY. To appreciate my flowers shows you got a swell character. I mean a sore character—I mean—

CHADWICK [*angrily*]. I'll be sore in a minute.

SALLY [*hastily*]. I . . . I . . . in response to your letter of this leap-year . . . the . . . the . . . [*Looking at him helplessly.*] What was it?

CHADWICK [*angrily and rapidly*]. January the *fifth!* We are glad to know your business has taken a great leap forward this year. We shall be glad to coöperate with you along the lines you suggest. Have your representative get in touch with us immediately upon his arrival—[*Glaring at her.*] Have you got that?

SALLY [*who has been trying desperately to keep up with him*]. Yes, sir . . . yes, sir!

CHADWICK [*he looks at her for a moment as though he were contemplating doing her bodily harm. Then he picks up another letter*]. This is to Amos Smith, Spankahee Falls, Wisconsin. Dear Sir. . . .

SALLY. What kinda falls?

CHADWICK. S-p-a-n-k-a-h-double e! Spankahee Falls!

SALLY. Spankahe-he-he— [*Giggles.*] That sounds a little naughty, don't it?

CHADWICK [*enraged*]. My God! I mean Dear Sir:—Referring to your letter of October the third, we are unable to state whether there is any type of car to which it is practicable to attach *snow-plows*. However, we suggest that you get in touch with your nearest dealer in farming machinery. [*He looks up and finds Sally again gazing at him in blissful admiration.*] Miss Rand! Are you taking down this letter?

SALLY [*confused*]. No, sir! Yes, sir! What was that about goloshes?

CHADWICK. Goloshes?

SALLY. Maybe snow shoes.

CHADWICK. *Snow plows!* [*Rises enraged.*] Look here, Miss Rand! I've only been in this office two weeks and I don't want to start complaining about you, but really I've never seen such an inattentive stenographer as you! [*Pounding the letters on his desk.*] Look at these letters! Do you want me to write them out in long hand? I haven't got a day's work out of you since I've been here!

SALLY [*starting to sniffle*]. Oh! And I did *so* want to please you!

CHADWICK [*angrily*]. For heaven's sake, don't start to cry! What is the trouble, anyway? Do I make you nervous when I dictate? Don't you like to work for me?

SALLY [*looking at him fervently*]. Oh, Mr. Chadwick! I'd like to spend the rest of my life just working for *you!* [*Chadwick looks at her in astonishment. A buzzer rings. Sally grabs up her pad and pencil.*] The boss wants me. . . .

[*She exits left. Chadwick walks about the room angrily. He crosses upper center, right center, then left center. He notices the flowers. With a gesture of impatience he picks them up and looks about the room for a place to put them. He crosses right center to Bunn's desk and puts them there. Alfred Bunn enters from the rear door. Bunn is fat and wears very loud clothes. He has a plain but good-natured face which becomes quite attractive when he breaks into a good-natured smile. He is smoking a cigar with a gold band on it and seems in high spirits.*]

BUNN [*taking off his hat and greeting Chadwick*]. Hello, Alf! How's things? [*Crosses upper left, hangs up hat*].

CHADWICK. Hello, Alf! Rotten! [*Crosses to left of his desk, picks up index case.*]

BUNN [*crosses center*]. Say! Ain't this a swell day? [*Chadwick drops index case. Observing the flowers on his desk.*] Gosh! Has some one been sending bouquets to me? [*Crosses upper left corner of his desk. Holding up the flowers and looking at them.*] Who brought these in, Alf?

CHADWICK [*disgustedly*]. That swell girl. . . .

[*Sits.*]

[*excitedly*]. Who? Sally? Sally brought those flowers for *me!* [*He starts dancing about.*] Da-de-da-da-dee! Gol darn it, Alf! Ain't life a beautiful thing?

CHADWICK [*leans back in astonishment*]. Say! What's troubling you?

BUNN. Nothing, fel! Nothing! [*Puts flowers on his desk and crosses left center.*] But listen! Have you noticed anything peculiar about Sally since you've been here?

CHADWICK. For bone-headedness and general stupidity, I've never seen her equal!

BUNN [*happily*]. She's neglecting your work, fel?

CHADWICK. Neglecting it! She doesn't even do that much! How can the boss stand for such a girl?

BUNN [*triumphantly*]. He's bawling her out every day! Her mind's not on her work! Gol darn it, Alf! Ain't life a beautiful thing?

[*Dances to upper center.*]

CHADWICK [*looking at Bunn impatiently*]. Say, Bunn! Do you enjoy having a dumb-bell like that around?

BUNN [*crosses above of left center desk*]. Why, fel! Sally's a bright girl! She never used to be this way. The trouble with her is . . . she's in love!

CHADWICK. In love?

BUNN. Uh-huh! That's why she can't keep her mind on your work, fel. She's in love with *me!*

CHADWICK. For heaven's sake!

BUNN [*crosses upper right center*]. Of course! I realize there's no face a fellow loves like his own . . . [*turns*] and I might be prejudiced. . . . But just the other day she told me she could always see me coming from no matter how far away. . . . [*Putting his hands in his pockets and displaying a violently-colored checked vest and crosses left center then to center. Pointing to the flowers.*] And now she brings me flowers! She's gone, fel! She's gone! [*Crosses left center.*] And then, Alf! Haven't you noticed the way she's always looking at *you?*

CHADWICK. At me?

BUNN. Sure! You'd think she couldn't take her eyes off you. You'd think she was in love with *you!*

CHADWICK. What!

BUNN. Don't you see, fel? She's just trying to get a rise out of *me!* Gol darn it, Alf! Ain't life a beautiful thing?

[*Dances to upper center and center.*] CHADWICK [*rises*]. Look here, Bunn! The office is being disorganized by that girl's day dreaming! If you've got her this way by fooling her. . . .

BUNN [*indignantly*]. Fooling her? Wait a minute, fel! [*Crosses left center.*] I'm not fooling Sally!

CHADWICK. What do you call it then?

BUNN [*fervently*]. It's love, fel! That's what it is! [*Taking a solitaire diamond ring from his pocket.*] Why look, Alf! I even got the ring!

CHADWICK. What? You're engaged to that girl?

BUNN. Well not exactly, fel! No!

CHADWICK [*taking the ring*]. But . . . but you have an understanding with her. . . .

BUNN [*uneasily*]. No, Alf! No!

CHADWICK. Say! What have you got?

BUNN. I . . . I got the ring!

CHADWICK. Then you haven't said anything to her?

BUNN. Honest! I've tried a dozen times, but I simply haven't got the nerve. The subject seems too indelicate.

CHADWICK [*sarcastically*]. I see! So you're going to slip this ring on her finger while she's not looking . . . and then run away!

BUNN [*honestly*]. I thought of that, fel . . . [*Shaking his head.*] But I've got a better idea . . . and that's where *you* come in!

CHADWICK. Me?

BUNN. Uh-huh! You see, Alf, I figure it this way. You're the best friend I've got and I know you wouldn't mind doing a favor for me. So *you* ask her to marry me!

CHADWICK [*handing him back the ring and crosses below to desk right center*]. Here's your ring!

BUNN [*follows to desk right center*]. But listen, Alf! I'd do as much for you!

CHADWICK. You would! Say! This is your funeral. You can arrange with the undertaker yourself.

[*Crosses right and above to upper left corner of the desk.*] BUNN [*follows to right corner of the desk*]. But gol darn it! There couldn't be any harm in doing me a little favor like that! And honest, Alf! Can you have the heart to leave the poor girl around here, starving for love of me?

CHADWICK. No, I can't! So I'm going to ask the boss right now to fire her! [*Crosses left to door.*]

BUNN [*his jaw dropping*]. Ask the boss to . . . to fire—? [*Hastily.*] Wait a minute, fel! Listen to me! You're not going to get the boss to fire Sally. She's been working in this office for years and until a few weeks ago you couldn't have found a brighter or harder-working girl. The boss thinks a lot of Sally. If you go complaining about her, he's likely to get up on his ear and fire *you!*

CHADWICK [*crosses left of left center desk*]. Confound it! He might as well, if he won't fire that girl!

BUNN [*crosses upper right corner of left center desk*]. Well, Alf, if that's the way you feel, don't you see you can get rid of her if you'll only ask her to marry me?

CHADWICK. How do you mean?

BUNN. Why! If Sally'll marry me, I'm not going to let her work down here any more! If she's engaged to me, she quits her job to-day! Will you ask her, fel?

CHADWICK [*walking about agitatedly, he crosses upper left and then down left*]. Yes! No! Confound it, Bunn!

BUNN [*crosses down right corner of the desk*]. But, Alf! You don't have to ask her right out! You can just feel her out and see how she feels about it generally without mentioning any names! There couldn't be any harm in that?

CHADWICK. Alf! You're *sure* she's in love with you!

[*Crosses down center, glancing at flowers.*] BUNN. Fel! In my mind there isn't a question about it!

CHADWICK [*crosses down center to him*]. Here! Give me the ring!

BUNN [*handing him the ring*]. You'll do it, Alf?

CHADWICK [*taking the ring angrily*]. I'd do anything to get a real stenographer in here!

BUNN. Atta boy, Alf! [*Slapping him on the back overjoyed—Chadwick crosses left center.*] If you slip that ring on her finger. . . . [*Sally reënters from the door on left. She overhears Bunn's last remark and sees the ring in Chadwick's hand. Bunn and Chadwick turn to her with guilty looks. Chadwick hastily slips the ring in his vest pocket, while Bunn addresses her with a silly smile on his face.*] Why, Hell! hel . . . hello, Sally! How . . . how's things?

[*Crosses right of right center desk.*]

SALLY [*staring fixedly at Chadwick's vest pocket, she crosses above to center*]. The boss wants to see you, Mr. Bunn. . . .

BUNN [*grinning and shaking with agitation, he crosses above to left door*]. Does he? How . . . how's things? [*Indicating Chadwick.*] Mr. Chadwick wants to speak to you, Sally. He . . . he has something to . . . to say to you. . . . How's things!

[*Bunn grins at them foolishly, runs into door facing, and exits left.*]

SALLY [*crosses right center desk, leaves pad, then crosses left center*]. You . . . you got something to say to me, Mr. Chadwick?

CHADWICK. Why . . . yes. . . . [*Awkwardly.*] Sit down, won't you? [*Crosses below and left of desk—she pulls chair right of desk.*] The fact is, I . . . I'm going to ask you some very personal questions, if you don't mind?

SALLY. Oh, no, sir! I don't care *how* personal you get with me!

[*Sits with a sprawl.*]

CHADWICK. Well! That's fine! [*Feeling for his words.*] Er . . . to begin with . . . I . . . I suppose you get very lonesome at times?

SALLY. Mr. Chadwick! I get so lonesome sometimes I feel like going out on the street and grabbing the first man I see! And I wouldn't draw no color line! [*Eagerly.*] But why did you ask me that?

CHADWICK [*sits*]. Why! I thought perhaps if you were lonesome, you . . . you might want to be . . . be getting married one of these days. . . .

SALLY [*in a frightened, expectant voice*]. Wha . . . what do you mean?

CHADWICK. To be quite frank, there's a young man, Miss Rand. . . .

SALLY. Oh! Call me Sally, Alf!

[*Flops elbows on desk.*]

CHADWICK [*gulps*]. A young man whom you know very well. . . . He works in this office, to be more exact . . . so I don't suppose I have to mention his name. . . .

SALLY. Oh, no, sir! I *think* I understand!

[*Slips in chair.*]

CHADWICK. I hope you do. [*Rises.*] Well, he's very anxious to know how you feel about. . . .

SALLY. About getting married?

[*Straightens up.*]

CHADWICK. Yes! Because, you see, for some time he's been hiding something from you.

[*Fingers in pocket.*]

SALLY [*looking eagerly in the direction of Chadwick's vest pocket—leans forward*]. From *me*?

CHADWICK. Yes! He's been hiding a certain fact. . . .

SALLY [*disappointed, falls back*]. Oh! A fact. . . .

CHADWICK. The fact that he's very fond of you. . . .

SALLY [*springing up*]. Oh, Alf! You . . . he's very fond of me?

CHADWICK. Yes! He loves you very deeply and devotedly. . . .

SALLY. Oh, gee whillikins!

[*Wild gestures.*]

CHADWICK. And though he's been wanting to speak to you for a long time he hasn't dared. However, in spite of his silence he believes that you've realized his affliction. . . . I mean affection for you, and he's dared to hope that . . . that . . .

SALLY. Yes, Alf! Go on!

CHADWICK. That you reciprocate.

SALLY [*bewildered*]. Do what?

CHADWICK. Why, that you love him, too.

SALLY [*with all her heart*]. Oh, Alf! I do!

CHADWICK. Then, Sally, he wants to marry you!

SALLY. He . . . he wants to marry me? [*Pinching herself as she side steps to center.*] Oh, Alf! It ain't true!

CHADWICK [*taking the ring from his*

pocket]. To show how much he means it, he's bought this ring. . . .

[*Crosses center.*]

SALLY. For *me?*

CHADWICK [*putting it on her finger*]. Certainly! And I want to put it on your finger. . . .

SALLY [*gazing at the ring*]. I'm engaged! Oh, Scots! Great Scots!

[*Crosses below to down left center with hand to head.*]

CHADWICK [*crosses down center*]. Of course you know whom I am talking about.

SALLY [*crosses down center, throwing her arms around his neck*]. Oh, Alf! Don't keep it up any longer! I knew all along it was you!

CHADWICK [*aghast*]. What?

SALLY [*clinging to him, despite his efforts to free himself*]. I never seen such a bashful fellow! Alf, dear! Would you ever have done it if I hadn't proposed to you first? [*The buzzer rings.*] Oh, gosh! There's the boss! [*Circles for pad, then crosses below to right center, Chadwick crosses left center. She crosses above him, turns and leaps on his back.*] Oh, Alf! I couldn't half tell you in that letter how crazy I am about you!

[*Exits left. Chadwick reels and puts his hand to his head.*]

CHADWICK. Where am I! Where am I! [*He circles center. His eyes fall on the unopened letter on his desk.*] Letter? Proposed to me? [*Crosses left center and picks up the letter, opens it and reads*]: Dearest, darling Alf:—I know you will think this immodest and unmanly of me, but I can no longer conceal my lonely love for you. I know you are bashful and well-behaved and that you wouldn't like to get fresh with me and ask me to marry you, so I am taking advantage of this leap year to ask you to marry me. I am so used to being lonely and having no pleasure in life that I think I am well fitted to make you a good wife. Trusting you will give this your immediate consideration, I am yours, hopefully, Sally Rand.

[*Chadwick throws the letter on his desk and sits right of desk with an expression of utter dismay on his face.*]

BUNN [*enter left—crosses above to center—in a low, eager tone*]. Well, Alf! Did you speak to her?

CHADWICK [*as though coming out of a trance*]. Eh? Oh, yes! I spoke to her!

BUNN. *I* thought you did! She looked all flushed when she came into the boss's office! Did you fix it, fel?

CHADWICK. I'll say I did!

BUNN. What do you mean? What did she say?

CHADWICK [*rises, crosses center*]. Bunn! I hardly know how to tell you this . . . but there's a letter on my desk from her. . . .

BUNN. For me?

CHADWICK [*with a laugh*]. For *you!* [*Suddenly looking at the letter and then at Bunn again.*] Say! Wait a minute! [*Crosses left center, picks up the envelope of the letter, slips it in pocket. Then he takes the letter itself, folds it up and bends a corner of it over as though it were a note.*] It really isn't a letter. It's only a note.

BUNN. And for me?

CHADWICK [*crosses center and gives note*]. Yes, Alf! For you—for her "Dearest, darling Alf!"

BUNN. What's the matter with you? [*Taking the letter gingerly.*] What's in it anyway?

CHADWICK. Read it yourself and see! [*Crosses up left.*] She wrote it to you last night, Alf! She said you'd find your answer there!

BUNN. But . . . but where are you going? Where's the ring?

CHADWICK [*putting on his coat*]. The ring is on her finger! and I'm going to get out of here!

[*Crosses up to door.*]

BUNN [*excitedly crosses up left of Chadwick*]. Then she's accepted! What you been kidding me for? [*Joyously.*] By gosh, boy! If there's anything I can ever do for you . . . .

CHADWICK [*stopping at the door*]. Say! There's one thing you might do!

BUNN. What's that?

CHADWICK. Just mention the fact around here that I'm a *married man!*

[*He goes out, slamming the door angrily. Bunn looks after him for a moment in mild surprise. Then he opens the letter and crosses center reading.*]

BUNN. Dearest, darling Alf! I know you will think this immodest and unmanly of me, but I can no longer conceal my lonely love for you. . . . Da-de-da-

da-de! Ain't life a beautiful thing? [*Dances down right center, then starts to read again eagerly. Sally enters left. When she sees Bunn reading her letter she slams the door.*]

SALLY. Mr. Bunn!

BUNN [*romantically*]. Sally!

SALLY [*shuffily crosses back of left center desk, throws pad and pencil down.*] Where did *you* get that?

BUNN [*rapturously crosses center*]. *He* gave it to me!

SALLY. Oh! [*Crosses back of chair, right of desk.*]

BUNN. Oh, Sally! You really love your little Alf?

SALLY [*lowering her eyes*]. Ain't it wonderful?

BUNN. And you're wearing the ring! Oh, Sally! I don't know what to say!

SALLY [*holding up her hand proudly*]. Some sparkler! Gosh! I bet that diamond's *real!*

BUNN. Three carats! That cost a lot of money, girl!

SALLY. I wouldn't care if it cost thirty cents! It's from my Alf! [*Crosses right of the chair moving her arms.*]

BUNN [*throwing his arms around her*]. Oh, Sally!

SALLY [*pushing him center angrily*]. Don't do that! What'd *he* say?

BUNN. Who? The boss? Whata we care? I want to tell you, Sally, you're going to be the happiest little girl in this world!

SALLY. You bet I am! [*Crosses below chair and sits on edge of desk.*]

BUNN [*crosses left center*]. And, Sally! There'll be no more banging the typewriter for you from now on! You can spend the mornings buying clothes and the afternoons at the movies, and every evening little Alf and you'll be dining out at swell restaurants and seeing classy shows!

SALLY [*awed*]. Gosh! Did *he* tell you that? [*Rises on chair rungs.*]

BUNN. Who?

SALLY. Why, Mr. Chadwick . . . .

BUNN [*scornfully*]. No! These are my ideas! Why, Chadwick don't know how to treat his own wife!

SALLY [*gasping, slips off chair rung*]. His *wife!*

BUNN [*catches her and leaves her below chair*]. Yes! Didn't you know? He's a married man!

SALLY [*sits*]. A *married man?*

BUNN. Of course Alf's a good fellow, but his wife has to do all the housework and he hardly ever takes her to a show. [*Proudly, with hands in pockets.*] But that's not the way I do things, Sally! You're going to see how nice a fellow can really be, when *we* get married. . . . [*Circles center.*]

SALLY [*dazedly*]. When we get married, Mr. Bunn. . . .

BUNN [*his voice unsteady with emotion*]. When we get married, Sally! Gosh [*gesturing wildly*] but that's music to my ears! [*Crosses to her.*] I've been wanting to speak to you ever since I came to work in this office, but I didn't have the nerve. I don't know what I'd have done if good old Alf hadn't helped me out to-day!

SALLY [*finally understanding*]. Oh! He was proposing for *you!*

BUNN. Why sure!

SALLY [*holding up her hand and looking at him unhappily*]. I . . . I'm wearing your ring!

BUNN [*reassured*]. Of course you are! [*Sally bursts into tears. Bunn looks at her uneasily.*] Why, Sally! What you crying for?

SALLY [*sobbing*]. Oh, Alf! I'm . . . I'm . . . so . . . so . . . .

BUNN [*patting her shoulder*]. I know! Gosh! You women are funny things! The happier you are, the more you cry. There! There! Little Alf don't want to make you cry!

SALLY [*controlling herself*]. Oh, Alf! I won't cry any more. . . .

BUNN. Thata brave little girl! I want to make you laugh. [*Circles center.*]

SALLY. And you always did.

BUNN. And Sally! [*Crosses to her.*] You won't keep me waiting too long, will you? I'm so sick of eating my meals alone, and going home alone and sitting around alone. . . .

SALLY. Gee, Alf! You've got nothing on me!

BUNN. Then you'll make it soon, won't you?

SALLY. The way I feel now I've just

got to get married pretty soon! Oh, Alf!

[*Throwing her arms around his neck.*]

BUNN. Atta girl!

[*He hugs and kisses her. The buzzer rings.*]

SALLY [*disengaging herself with difficulty*]. The boss! [*Crosses above desk to left door and looks off—then crosses center.*] He wants you!

BUNN [*throwing his arms around her again*]. Oh, Sally!

SALLY. No! No! The boss!

[*In struggling, she gets right of him.*]

BUNN. Whata we care? Let him wait! [*He kisses her.*] And, Sally! To-night we'll have dinner together and talk things all over! We'll go to one of those swell Broadway places. . . . What do you say?

SALLY [*admiringly*]. Gosh, Alf! You are a sport, ain't you?

BUNN. You'll see to-night the kind of sport I am. And mind you, Sally! It'll always be that way!

[*A final hug.*]

SALLY. Oh, Alf!

BUNN [*crosses left*]. I'm not one of those birds that feeds a girl chicken à la king before he marries her and chicken hash afterwards! No siree!

[*He exits. Sally stands in the middle of the room staring after him. The telephone rings. She starts, crosses right to the switchboard and puts the receiver over head.*]

SALLY [*talking into the phone in a business-like way*]. Reliable Automobile Company! [*Changing her tone.*] Oh, hello, Maizie! That you? Yea, dearie! I'm a leap-year bride! But, my God, Maizie, you ought to see who to!

[*Curtain.*]

POTTERY
A Play
By Holland Hudson

CHARACTERS

The Interior Decorator.
The Voice.
Poseidon.
Triton.
Nereid.
Athenian.
Spartans.
Nymph.
Pan.
Silenus.

FOREWORD

This play is intended as a decorative diversion—a diverting decoration. The fact that some of it plays better than it reads calls for no other apology than that it was conceived for the theatre rather than the library.

In this decade it seems necessary to assure all and sundry that it contains no propaganda—neither direct nor indirect, objective nor subjective, and, in view of the fact that the fermented juice of the grape takes some part in the action, to assert flatly that this is neither a temperance tract nor a brief for alcohol—that it is nor more nor less than a clownish setting for a fragment of sheer beauty.

H. H.

POTTERY

A PLAY

By HOLLAND HUDSON

SCENE I

[*The action begins in a certain wing of the Metropolitan Museum, quite impossible of reproduction on any stage. Accordingly, we shall represent the museum by a black velvet curtain and indicate its collection of Grecian pottery by a single vase upon a pedestal, which a spotlight picks out as the curtain rises. Unless you know pottery, this exhibit may remind you somewhat of the jar you saw in that Philadelphia junk shop, save that the one you saw was in perfect condition. However, that one was brown, with green figures. This one is black, with a frieze of figures in terra cotta and the proportions, you know, aren't so bad. Once a young man named Keats—*

But at this moment a second spotlight illuminates a second figure, namely: The Interior Decorator. Let it be stated at the outset that he is only a prentice Interior Decorator and not a bad sort, personally. He is, for instance, still lacking in those elements of salesmanship which send the customer who wanted a lazy Susan home with a girandole. He also lacks, it is true, that obscure inner compulsion which might have created another positively bad painter instead of a merely mediocre Interior Decorator. Some abortive ghost of the divine afflatus perhaps, brings pad and pencil from his pocket. While he sketches we may observe that he is lean and gangling, pasty, nearsighted and bespectacled. We have no time to observe more for, after a peal of theatrical thunder and a flash of one hundred and ten volt lightning, out of the darkness booms a voice.]

THE VOICE. Hold! [*Quite a voice, indeed. Such a voice as you missed in the climax of the last Republocrat National Convention—and never miss anywhere else. A voice created for great open spaces—Buf-fa-lo, Chi-ca-go, O-ma-ha and points West—deep, sonorous, audible. By the time we have taken that in, the light is whisked from the vase to the owner of the voice. Our first thought is spoken by*]

THE INTERIOR DECORATOR. All right; I'll hold it. What's the answer—a movie, a new religion, a new brand of cigarettes, or a masquerade?

THE VOICE. I am the voice of Hellenic art.

[*He says it quite seriously, as in fact he says everything he is allowed to say. For all that, there may be something in what he says, for, save for the vigorous tints of his hair, eyes and mouth, his coloration suggests a pedigree by Pygmalion out of Galatea, with Phidias and Praxiteles somewhere along the line of descent. He is, in short, nor swart nor sunburned. His garment is better adapted to sculpture than to conquest. But we delay the conflict.*]

THE INTERIOR DECORATOR. Suppose you are. Why all the fireworks?

THE VOICE. Observe, rash mortal, the thunderbolts of omnipotent Zeus himself, before you desecrate the spirit of our ancient art!

[*More thunder and lightning.*]

THE INTERIOR DECORATOR. I had no such intention. On the contrary, I am merely an interior decorator. You Greeks always take so much for granted.

THE VOICE. I am not merely Greek, nor is the art of which I speak.

THE INTERIOR DECORATOR. Rhymes, too?

THE VOICE. The Greeks were mortal. They conquered, and were conquered. Ancient Hellas lived, and died. Modern Greece lives, and will die. Grecian art, the soul of ancient Hellas, is immortal, unconquerable. It has never died; it will

259

never die. It lives anew in every rebirth of the arts.

THE INTERIOR DECORATOR. All very true; all very obvious. I have heard all of this a number of times. Such sentiments have become the platitudes of every art school lecture. What do you expect *me* to do about it?

THE VOICE. You came here to steal—

THE INTERIOR DECORATOR [*interrupting*]. Oh, come now!

THE VOICE. —like Prometheus—

THE INTERIOR DECORATOR. That, of course, is something else again.

THE VOICE. —the beauty of this vase! To strew it along the highways—

THE INTERIOR DECORATOR [*interrupting*]. No such luck! I'll be fortunate if I get one customer to fall for the suggestion. You've no idea how hostile people are to new ideas in decoration, even when, as now, they are really very old ideas.

THE VOICE. Beauty is always new.

THE INTERIOR DECORATOR. Of course it is, and that's why there's so much hostility to extraordinary beauty everywhere. I daresay that when this vase was made it created quite a scandal.

THE VOICE. You wish the story of this vase?

THE INTERIOR DECORATOR. Why, I don't mind, if you know it.

THE VOICE. You shall have it.

[*He stalks slowly toward the proscenium.*]

THE INTERIOR DECORATOR [*strolling toward the other side of the arch*]. One might think me Aladdin and you the genie of the lamp—or, as it happens, the vase. By the way, what has happened to the vase?

[*He is answered by utter darkness and more thunder and lightning. But out of the darkness peals*]

THE VOICE. Si——lence!

THE INTERIOR DECORATOR. Have it your own way. I wasn't born with a megaphone voice.

[*Another peal of thunder is followed by a bit of orchestral sea music. The stage lights come on very gradually.*]

THE VOICE. Sing, goddess, the wrath of stout Poseidon, girdler of the earth, god of the dark hair, the ruinous wrath that brought on an Athenian warrior woes innumerable, and gave his body to be the prey of the sharp teeth of regret;

and so the counsel of the gods of sea and land wrought out its accomplishment from the day when strife first parted the stalwart Poseidon, god of waters, and the brave Athenian. Sing, muse—

[*Interrupted and abruptly bereft of his spotlight as hereinafter set forth.*]

SCENE II

[*The lights have now fully disclosed a terra cotta frieze consisting of Poseidon, a huge bearded man dressed in the skin of some sea animal, Triton, a younger edition of his superior deity, and a Nereid clad in diaphanous seaweed. Poseidon's great drapery lies at his feet, cunningly arranged to simulate a conventionalization of curling waves, black edging furnishing the necessary emphatic lines. The draperies of his companions are designed and disposed in like fashion. A terra cotta sun stands high in the sky, affixed to a movable strip of curtain. Triton blows on a conch, the blast of which interrupts the Chorus' travesty on the blind bard. The orchestra subsides and its music is replaced by devices imitating the sounds of inrolling waves and the rattle and roar of pebbles in the undertow. The group is motionless long enough to convey a static impression to the eye. Then Triton sounds the conch again.*]

THE VOICE. The great Poseidon, alone of all the gods, esteems most highly the nectar of his own resounding seas.

[*Poseidon nods, then turning to the Nereid, beckons. She fills a cup from an urn and hands it to him. He reaches for the cup. He stops.*]

Harken!

[*Sounds of battle are heard, the clash of swords, and, for good measure, a clap of thunder.*]

Harken, ye wise and powerful gods, to the clash of battle.

[*All three look toward the sound. Poseidon points to his mantle. Triton and the Nereid cloak him in it.*]

The gods assume the mantle of invisibility [*synchronizing their movements, they cloak themselves*] and go toward the conflict.

[*Poseidon lifts his trident and points*]

its prongs toward the battle. The lights fade out.]

[*The orchestra plunges into battle music which ends abruptly as the lights come on.*]

SCENE III

[*The sun is lower in the sky. In the center of the scene stands a beardless Athenian warrior in full armor, with sword and shield, giving battle to two swarthy, bearded Spartans, similarly equipped. At the moment of discovery they stand motionless with their swords crossed in midstroke. Poseidon appears.*]

THE VOICE. Invisible to mort.l eyes, the great sea god beholds the battle.

[*The battle resumes. The Spartans strike synchronously. The Athenian receives their blows upon his shield. The Athenian lunges at the Spartans. The Spartans, placing their shields edge to edge, stop his thrust.*]

THE VOICE. Since early morning has the Athenian, filled with valor, waged his lonely war against these overcoming odds. Woe, woe to Sparta, when its glory is so shrunken it must set two men against one!

[*The battle continues in this manner, the Athenian retreating a step at each blow. Poseidon approaches the conflict.*]

Behold the intervention of the invisible gods!

[*As the Spartans lift their swords Poseidon holds them aloft with his trident.*]

THE VOICE. Behold the valor of the Athenian warrior [*the Athenian dispatches both Spartans. Poseidon withdraws his trident. The Spartans fall*] who lifts to the unseen gods the sword of a conqueror!

[*The Athenian lifts his sword. Triton and the Nereid approach. The Athenian lowers his sword and sheathes it. Poseidon directs Triton and the Nereid to approach the Athenian. They do so. The Nereid removes his helmet. The Athenian, dismayed, snatches at his sword. Then, reassured, he sheathes it. Triton takes his shield.*]

The happy warrior recognizes the favor of the gods. Where the august gods lead, the warrior goes on winged feet.

[*A procession of triumph leaves the place, headed by the Nereid bearing the helmet and wound up by Poseidon, who points the way with his trident. The orchestra erupts a bit of the sort of music popularly supposed to indicate the sylvan, the vernal. This prelude produces three Nymphs, costumed in the current mode for nymphs, whose circlings bring them gradually to the dead Spartans. When these are discovered the rondo ceases abruptly. The Nymphs bend over the slain. Two of them lift up the shields. The third takes up both swords. The orchestra wails softly in minor key.*]

THE VOICE. Sing, goddess, of sharp swords, of shining shields and valorous hearts. These beloved of Sparta [*she kisses the sword hilts*] went forth one day [*she swings the swords*] in friendly fashion. [*She presents the hilts toward the spectator.*] They were attacked [*she presents the blades*] and defended themselves [*brandishes the swords, lowers the points*], but treachery overcame them and they were slain. [*Drops the swords.*] Peace to their ashes! [*Extends her arms over the bodies.*] And tears for their loss. [*She bows her head.*]

[*The orchestra bursts shrilly and dissonantly into some kappelmeister's version of the pipes of Pan. The traditional Pan executes his rondo before discovering the Nymphs. He stops short. The music stops.*]

THE VOICE. Horror chills the heart of the mighty god of woods and fields!

[*He motions the Nymphs aside. He sees the bodies.*]

[*Pan stoops over them.*]

THE VOICE. He calls upon the earth-shaking Zeus for aid against the enemy of Sparta.

[*He raises his arms aloft. He arms two Nymphs with the Spartan swords and sets them to guard the bodies, sending the third on an errand. The sun goes down. The moon rises. The absent Nymph returns, pointing whence she came. The orchestra obliges with*]

an uncertainly rendered Brindisi.
Silenus enters, bald and pot-bel-
lied, carrying a cup in his hand
and a skin of wine slung across
his back. He wears vine leaves
where his hair once grew.]

THE VOICE. The messenger brings Silenus, god of wine. Lo, the earth gods
conspire together.

[Pan siezes him by the scruff of the
neck and shows him the corpses.
Silenus hiccups and wags his head
sadly. Pan points after the Athenian. Silenus starts after him.]

Silenus goes in search of the Athenian
warrior.

[Pan summons the Nymphs. At his
direction they strip the Spartans
of their armor.]

Know ye, all friends of the ancient gods
of wood and field, that no man beloved
of him descends unto Hades. Now he
makes over these an incantation.

[Pan blows shrilly upon his pipes.
The Spartans rise, crowned with
new-budded horns and grown goat-
ish toward the ground. Nymphs
and Fauns leap into a brief bacchanal around the piping Pan.
The lights go out. The orchestra
takes up the melody of Pan's pipe
and doubles the time, playing
louder and faster, until, with a
peal of thunder, the light comes
on.]

SCENE IV

[The moon is now high. The Athenian enters, crowned with bays. He
follows closely upon Poseidon, Triton
and the Nereid, gazing rapt, the while,
at nothing.]

THE VOICE. All this while did the
Athenian warrior marvel exceedingly at
the high favor of the gods.

[He hears the call of a distant voice.
Now he stops, turns, and listens.
Silenus wabbles in and invites him
to drink. The Athenian accepts
the empty cup. Silenus fumbles
with the stopper of the wineskin.]

Great Poseidon bestows upon this mortal
the salty nectar of his sounding waters.

[At a signal from Poseidon Triton
fills the cup from his conch. The
Athenian lifts his cup ceremoni-

ously high in air. He spills a little on the ground. He drinks.
Grimacing, he spits out the salt
water.]

THE VOICE. Oh, rash mortal, thus to
reject the favor of the gods of ocean!
[Poseidon, offended, points the way with
his trident. The sea gods desert the
Athenian. The Nereid lingers.] He feels,
although he does not see the consequences
of his rash act.

[The Athenian turns and kicks Silenus. Silenus drops his vineskin
and waddles off, protecting his re-
treat with his hands. The Athenian regards the wineskin, thirst-
ily, glancing at his empty cup.
The Nereid, perceiving his intention, starts toward him. Poseidon
and Triton reappear. At Poseidon's direction Triton captures the
Nereid and carries her away.]

THE VOICE. Now bereft of all benefi-
cent divine protection, the Athenian falls
into the snare laid for him by the earth-
gods!

[The Athenian fills his cup from
the wineskin. He drinks. He
likes it. Another cupful. Another drink. Another cupful. Another drink. The orchestra now
offers the most alcoholic of Brindisi, a little presto as to tempo,
while the Athenian rises. He
smites his chest. He takes three
more drinks. He sits again. A
Nymph appears. He drinks to her.
A second Nymph is similarly greeted. And a third. Now comes Pan,
piping shrilly, followed by the
Fauns. The orchestra plays the
pipes of Pan and then Bacchanal.
The now inebriated Athenian rolls
to his feet. He attempts to pursue one Nymph, then another. The
Fauns get in his way. He wrestles
with them. At Pan's direction
they lead him back each time to
the wineskin for another drink.
The round becomes wilder and
madder. At length the Athenian
staggers. The music stops abruptly. A big drum continues a slow
rhythm. The dancers stop abruptly. The Athenian falls. The
dancers vanish. The lights go out.
The lights come on slowly.]

SCENE V

[*The sun slowly ascends.*]

THE VOICE. Lo, Aurora the rosy-fingered lifts the curtain of darkness from the Eastern sky.

> [*The Athenian lies unconscious. The orchestra wavers uncertainly between fragments of the Brindisi and some pastoral lyric, both turned sour by "modern" dissonances. He stirs uneasily. He puts his hand to his head. He raises his head. It hurts. He quickly lowers it. He struggles to a sitting position. He holds his head. He licks his lips. Wipes his mouth with the back of his hand. The music dies a sad death.*]

THE VOICE. Ai! Woe! Aie! Woe!

[*The Athenian looks about for water. Rises unsteadily, and finding himself dizzy, sits again, holding his head.*] But soon repentance wins back the favor of the gods.

> [*The Nereid appears with Triton and Poseidon. They thrill with pity at the parched throat and aching head of the Athenian warrior. She points to the Athenian. She describes his thirst. Poseidon nods. Triton hands her the vase of* SCENE II. *She lifts and tilts it.*]

THE VOICE. The god of all waters exerts his powers! [*Poseidon strikes the earth with his trident. A strip of gauze unrolls from vase to floor. Behind the scenes a mechanical imitation of running water. The Athenian hears the water.*]

THE VOICE. The nectar of mountain springs flows forth! [*The Athenian turns and sees it. Grovels toward it. He drinks from cupped hands and bathes his aching head. He drinks again. He rises a new man. He lifts his arms*]. Sweet and healing is the compassion of the gods. Give thanks, oh, warrior of Athens!

> [*A crash from the orchestra is followed by a peal of thunder, and the lights go out. The lights come up.*]

SCENE VI

[*Pan and his crew are grouped in a decorative frieze. At the first note from the orchestra, this static composition whirls into mad Bacchanal. Another crash and more thunder. The lights go out. The lights come up.*]

SCENE VII

THE INTERIOR DECORATOR [*is disclosed once more, alone, before the vase of the prologue. He appears to be unaware that he is alone, for he says:*] Yes, I like all that for myself. But it won't do at all for my customer. He made his money by running small boats out to the three-mile limit, and he would think that story was a personal reflection. Do you think that it— [*Suddenly he discovers The Voice has vanished.*] Now, what happened to him? I knew I shouldn't have taken that last drink!

[*Curtain.*]

A WORD TO THE DIRECTOR

The intelligent director will perceive at once that the essence of this piece is a pantomime in Hellenic decoration for the discerning, furbished with slapstick for the vaudeville habitué and subtitles for the cinema addict. By all means let the frieze assume all the beauty of which groups of human forms are capable. But in your zeal for beauty do not forget that in the theater of Greece clowns and clowning were beloved of many. Our contemporary audiences will forgive you much beauty if you will apportion enough laughter with it.

There is nothing esoteric about the settings or the stage direction. Everything essential is in the manuscript; left or right doesn't matter so that the action be visible and decorative—and continuous. The good actor does not hurry; but he doesn't DRAG. Let the action be static or dynamic, one or the other; clean-cut and brisk.

H. H.

THE LIAR AND THE UNICORN
A Comedy

By Babette Hughes

CHARACTERS

CHESTER COLLIS [*Clubman*].
WINIFRED ASHTON [*Debutante*].
GARETH LUCAS.

PLACE: *London.*

TIME: *The Present.*

Applications for permission to produce this play should be addressed to the author's representatives, SAMUEL FRENCH, 25 WEST 45TH STREET, NEW YORK CITY.

THE LIAR AND THE UNICORN

A Comedy

By Babette Hughes

[*The* Scene *represents the* Unicorn—*a fashionable men's club in St. James Street, London. The room has a spacious and cheerful appearance. At center back a wide doorway leads to the street; it is hung with curtains bearing on them the gilt image of a unicorn. Beside the doorway is a hatrack. At lower right is a chesterfield and a small table, having on it telephone and ash tray. Halfway down stage at the left are several easy chairs, a reading lamp, and a table on which is a whisky decanter and a siphon, also tall glasses. A fire burns in the fireplace at lower right. On the dark walls are vivid hunting prints.*

It is quarter past eight on an evening in October. As the curtain rises Gareth Lucas, jauntily twirling his stick, comes in through the doorway. He wears gray striped trousers, a frock coat and top hat; in his buttonhole is a pink rose. He is slightly diabolical in a debonair way. After looking about him he leans against the mantelpiece.

Chester Collis enters. He is a stolid young man wearing dinner clothes. Mechanically, he puts his hat on a peg of the hatrack and makes straight for an easy chair at left stage. On his way he glances casually, and without recognition, at Lucas. From a shelf beneath the table he takes a magazine which he settles down to.

Lucas wanders toward the doorway. From the hatrack he takes Collis' hat. After glancing inside the rim he returns it to its place. Disposing of his own hat and stick, he walks to the chair across the table from Collis, sits down and crosses his legs.]

Lucas. Cool weather we're having, isn't it?

Collis [*rather sharply*]. Yes.
[*He resumes reading.*]

Lucas. Ever since I hunted big game down in Africa, you know, I've lost my taste for this damnable London fog. Still, it's hardly ever this cold in July.

Collis. We're in October, I believe.

Lucas. Yes, I know. I was saying it was hardly ever this cool in July. I've been told it all depends on the Trade Winds. In fact Parliament is sitting now on a proposition to—by the way, did you ever hear about the Northern Horse Latitudes?

Collis. No.

Lucas. Very, very interesting! [*After several minutes.*] I wonder, Collis, if I might trouble you for a match.

Collis [*surprised to hear a stranger call him by name*]. No trouble.
[*Gets out box.*]

Lucas. Awful nuisance to go about asking for matches. Only yesterday I bought a box, too. Now I know where I left it—on the washstand when I was shaving—or in the medicine chest, I forget which. [*He lights a match, holding it to where a cigar might be. Not finding one between his lips, he laughs jovially.*] By Jove!
[*Collis grimly takes from his own pocket a cigar case which he opens and presents to Lucas. Lucas selects one and lights up. Then he blows out the match, pocketing Collis's match box.*]

Collis [*unlit cigar in mouth*]. How about a light? [*Lucas passes him his own burning cigar to light up with. Sarcastically.*] Thanks.

Lucas. I've always felt generously toward you, Collis. I hope you never thought it was otherwise after the little argument we had. Of course, a man can't always be certain to keep his temper. I may have spoken hastily but I wanted you to know I'm your friend through thick or thin.

267

COLLIS. I don't know what argument you're thinking of.

LUCAS. My dear Collis, you are a forgiving chap. But you can't take me in. Merely because we want to forget those things doesn't erase them from the sands of time. Only the waters of eternity can do that. I was feverish at the time, having only gotten back from Africa, or I never would have spoken as I did of the lady.

COLLIS. What lady?

LUCAS. The lady you were being seen with at the time. A blonde.

COLLIS. Winifred Ashton, you mean?

LUCAS. Certainly! Who else but she? Ah, my dear fellow, I see you do remember. Promise me, will you, from now on there will be no bad feeling between us. I thought at first you seemed a trifle cool.

COLLIS. I give you my word I remember no argument between us. I—

LUCAS. Shall we have a drink, to friendship and to Miss Ashton? [*He pours two large highballs, then rises and sings.*]

Here's to the maiden of bashful fifteen;
Here's to the widow of fifty;
Here's to the flaunting extravagant quean,
And here's to the housewife that's thrifty.

[*Chorus*]
Let the toast pass—
Drink to the lass,
I'll warrant she'll prove an excuse for the glass.

For let 'em be clumsy, or let 'em be slim,
Young or ancient, I care not a feather;
So fill a pint bumper quite up to the brim,
And let us e'en toast them together.

[*Chorus*] Let the toast pass, etc.
[*Lucas sits down abruptly.*]

COLLIS. Er—jolly song! Music hall?

LUCAS. No. Sheridan.

COLLIS. Oh!

LUCAS [*looking around*]. Jolly club. Not many members here this evening.

COLLIS. Dinner hour, that's why. I dined early. Thought I'd drop around and read until time for the theater. I've a ticket for Charlot's Revue.

LUCAS. You know, it's strange you should have spoken of Miss Ashton. She said she would meet me here this evening at eight-fifteen.

COLLIS. Meet you here! But, my dear fellow, you know ladies aren't allowed in the Unicorn. Why, they're expressly forbidden. I know because I myself raised the measure to keep them out. We don't want the Unicorn overrun with wives and fiancées.

LUCAS. You're behind the times, Collis, behind the times. Why only at the last election I proposed we have Thursday be ladies' night. You, yourself, voted for it, I believe. Really, old man, you have a rotten memory.

COLLIS. Well, I'm blowed!

LUCAS. Yes, Thursday night we let the fair sex in. To-day is Thursday, isn't it? Well, when this afternoon I glimpsed Miss Ashton at Lady Hencomb's lawn party I thought of Thursday being ladies' night, so I asked her here. Rather an exciting afternoon it was, too.

COLLIS. Yes, I heard so. My sister poured. She tells me about six o'clock Lady Hencomb discovered her pearls missing, that they searched every one present but one or two guests escaped. It will be a hard case for detectives. These lawn parties, you know what they are. Any one can merely walk in on them without an invitation, and no way to stop it. I call that carrying democracy too far. My sister has a fairly sharp eye. It seems she knew pretty nearly every one but a tall neat-looking fellow who disappeared before the search. I shouldn't be surprised if he was the thief. She says he had a diabolical look to him, and she's hardly ever wrong where character is concerned. I'm inclined to trust a woman's intuition in such matters.

LUCAS. Diabolical! I don't know. I think I should rather say devilishly attractive. But that's a fine distinction.

COLLIS. Then you noticed him too?

LUCAS. Who wouldn't have, my dear chap? A wolfhound among English bulls—that's what he was. Vastly entertaining, too, with his handkerchief tricks and whatnot. And when the Honorable Miss Peabody left—scrawny, chicken-breasted wench—he fetched half a dozen teaspoons, a silver creamer and no end of lace doilies from her muff. She swears she never let it go the whole time, and left in tears, thinking herself a kleptomaniac. Mightn't one almost forgive a chap of that sort for getting away with a pearl necklace?

COLLIS. What crust! By Jove, I almost envy a fellow like that. He must have no conscience whatsoever.

LUCAS. Rather not! He's all sorts of conscience. It's public opinion and a seat in the House he doesn't give a hang for. Let me tell you, Collis, no through-and-through Englishman ever lost his pudding-and-beef ideas of morality in time to get any fun from life. You've been nineteenth century since the Romans got driven out, and mid-Victorian from the day Alfred burned the cakes. That trickster fellow has mixed blood in him, and I'll wager he's damned glad of it.

COLLIS. Well, beef-and-pudding morality, as you call it, suits me. And I jolly well hope that pearl thief gets caught. I don't like his sort. Where would the British Empire be if we allowed thieves to go unpunished merely because they amuse one? Any man with a sense of property wouldn't think of making off with stolen goods. It's socialism, that's what it is. Rank socialism! The welfare of the Empire depends on its subjects having a strong sense of law and order. It's not the pearls I care about, or the fellow either; it's the principle of the thing. By jove, any one would think you sympathized with law-breakers. I don't like to hear a fellow talk that way, and you'd better not go about filling the heads of simple persons with your wild ideas. It's hitting at the heart of England and I don't like it.

LUCAS. I certainly shan't talk politics with Miss Ashton. And as for forcing my ideas on people, there's no danger. I'm positive an Englishman after the age of twelve is impervious to ideas.

COLLIS. To your sort, at least. I didn't know Miss Ashton had picked up with radicals. When I knew her she was a fine girl, absolutely English. I must say I'm disappointed in her. I always thought, for a girl, she had a good deal of common sense.

LUCAS. My dear Collis, here we are quarreling immediately after our vow of friendship. Shall we drink once more, this time to the British Empire?

[*He pours two highballs. Collis turns to his magazine. Through the doorway at back Winifred Ashton enters timidly. She is blonde and very insipid. She wears an evening cloak over a georgette dress of a pastel shade.*]

WINIFRED. Good evening!

LUCAS. So you've finally arrived! Drink with us to the British Empire, will you? A toast from so charming a lady will surely bring happiness to our King and country.

WINIFRED. Papa doesn't approve of my drinking, but perhaps I might have a sip from your glass.

LUCAS. Delightful! As many sips as you wish.

WINIFRED [*approaching Lucas*]. I shouldn't have been so late only papa was detained in leaving for the theater. Then when he had gone I had to dress and find a cab. Have you waited long?

LUCAS. Thirty or forty minutes—a mere trifle, I assure you. Are you ready for your sip?

[*Winifred takes the glass.*]

WINIFRED. To the British Empire.

[*She sips.*]

LUCAS [*draining the glass*]. It tasted indeed as though an angel had bathed in it. [*Collis also drinks. He has not turned nor Winifred seen him.*] Now let me introduce you to a friend of mine. Mr. Collis, Miss Ashton.

[*Collis rises stiffly.*]

WINIFRED [*drawing back*]. I am already acquainted with Mr. Collis.

[*She haughtily turns her back and walks toward the chesterfield at lower right.*]

LUCAS [*following her*]. So you know Collis? A fine chap!

WINIFRED [*sitting on the chesterfield*]. Mr. Collis and I are not speaking. I wish you wouldn't talk about him to me.

LUCAS. Your wish is law. We shall talk of nothing but your beautiful self.

WINIFRED. We don't have to talk about me.

LUCAS. Not talk about you? Would you spoil my evening entirely? Certainly we will talk of you, of your hair like honey, of your sapphire eyes, your rosebud lips, the slenderness of your ankles—

WINIFRED. Please! Don't you think —aren't we—it's foggy, isn't it, to-night?

LUCAS. It is.

[*With an adoring look into her eyes.*]

WINIFRED [*looking away*]. You know I thought papa would never leave. There I was, not able to dress until he had come to kiss me good night. You can't imagine how impatient I was. It was perfectly dreadful. But I'm here now.

LUCAS [taking her hand]. Yes, now you are here.

WINIFRED [putting both hands on her lap]. This afternoon I was just so surprised when you said you knew me, because you know I didn't remember you at all.

LUCAS. "Frailty, thy name is woman!" And so often as children we played in the same sand box. How well I remember you, little Winnie Ashton with her butter-colored curls. Sweet little Winnie.

WINIFRED. But my hair wasn't curly. I always wanted curly hair. It was straight and I wore it in pigtails down my back.

LUCAS. Down your back. But now it is curly. I'm sure you're mistaken about the pigtails. I'd swear they were curls; really, in my mind's eye I see curls.

WINIFRED. Well, perhaps you remember a time when I was going to a party. The governess used to curl my hair in rags before a party. But she wouldn't curl it every day because it is bad for the hair, it breaks it. [Feeling her hair.] Now of course I have a permanent wave.

LUCAS [solicitously]. Do you find it breaks the hairs?

WINIFRED. I'm afraid it does. But then they always grow out again, don't they?

LUCAS. I should think they might. Finger-nails do. So you didn't remember me this afternoon. That makes me feel very badly, Winifred.

WINIFRED. I don't want to make you feel badly. And it's not only you I don't remember, I often forget people.

LUCAS. I feel better to know that.

WINIFRED. I did notice you, even before you spoke to me. But papa being with me, I didn't dare to make any sign or return your smile. Papa is so strict. We were awfully lucky to get even a few words together, weren't we?

LUCAS. Do you think your father wouldn't approve of me?

WINIFRED. You won't be angry if I'm frank with you?

LUCAS. Be angry with you, my dear Winifred? Never!

WINIFRED. Well, then, I don't think he would approve of you. You see he

likes serious men—Mr. Collis, for instance. He likes men who talk politics and—well, they're never as handsome as you are. Even before I remembered you I thought you were terribly handsome.

LUCAS. Really? I suppose you know "handsome is as handsome does."

WINIFRED. That is what my governess used always to be telling me when I wanted my hair curled.

LUCAS. Your butter-colored hair. By the way, how forgetful I am. I asked you to have dinner with me, didn't I?

WINIFRED. I think you did. But it was so late before I left home that I had a cup of tea and a little cold ham. So I'm not very hungry. I hope you don't mind.

LUCAS. Why, my dear child, that is nothing at all. Tea and ham—that surely won't interfere with your appetite. Wait until you see the dinner I shall order for you.

WINIFRED. But really, I'm not very hungry.

LUCAS. Nonsense! You musn't humor yourself. [He takes from the table the telephone.] Haymarket 7349, please. The Pall Mall restaurant? I want a dinner sent around at once to the Unicorn Club, on St. James Street. Yes, dinner for two. . . . Let's see now [to Winifred], caviar canape, how is that, and green turtle soup?

WINIFRED. I think that will be nice. But don't ask me because really I like anything.

LUCAS. Not spinach, surely.

WINIFRED. I love spinach. It's so good for one.

LUCAS [into telephone]. Ready? All right: caviar canape, green turtle soup, hot—it must be hot—deviled broiled lobster, fillet of beef with mushrooms, frozen tomato salad, chestnut mousse, and coffee. Olives and salted nuts of course. Got it all? Good! Now for the wines. [To Winifred.] Have you any preference? [Into telephone.] First, a bottle of amontillado sherry. Sauterne with the lobster, two of champagne, and have you any Fine Champagne Cognac, vintage of 1851? Four guineas a bottle? Very well, send one. That's all, I think. [To Winifred.] Can you think of anything else?

WINIFRED [faintly]. No.

LUCAS [into telephone]. Very well.

Send it around at once, will you? The Unicorn! My name—Mr. Conrad Wallace. Thank you. [*Hangs up receiver and replaces telephone on table.*] There!

WINIFRED. How did you ever think up all those things to order?

LUCAS. Experience, my dear child, experience. In my day I have ordered many dinners. Well, we will soon dine. The Pall Mall is only a block or so away so we won't have too long to wait. Quick service, that's what I like them for.

WINIFRED. I have never known a man like you. And I've never before been in a gentlemen's club. You may think it silly of me but I didn't think ladies were allowed in them. This is a nice club, isn't it? Father belongs to the Conservative Club but I'm sure it can't be so nice as this one.

LUCAS. I asked you to come here because I thought it the nicest.

WINIFRED. Can you go to any club you like? Do you belong to them all?

LUCAS. Not all by any means. But I always manage to have a choice. It is so dull to be confined to one—the rooms and members get so tiresome.

WINIFRED. Father only belongs to one. I suppose he is old-fashioned.

LUCAS. No doubt. Tell me, this afternoon did you enjoy Lady Hencomb's tea?

WINIFRED. I'd almost forgotten about it. Doesn't it seem ages ago? It was lovely, wasn't it? except for poor Lady Hencomb losing her pearls. I felt so sorry for her. And then when they searched all the guests I was so frightened.

LUCAS. Why were you frightened?

WINIFRED. I don't know. Because every one was so serious, I suppose. And if the thief had been caught I would have been so sorry for him even though it is silly to be sorry for a thief.

LUCAS. It's not silly to be sorry for a thief. Sometimes they steal because they are hungry, or their children or grandmothers have no Christmas presents.

WINIFRED. I'm glad you think it's not silly because I can't help being sorry for people who go to prison. Papa says there are plenty of charities and poorhouses, they don't need to steal. But I guess they're too proud to take charity, don't you?

LUCAS. What a dear, generous little heart you have, Winifred!

WINIFRED. Everybody calls me Winnie.

LUCAS. What a dear, generous little heart you have, Winnie! A charming name—Winnie.

WINIFRED. Your name is Conrad, isn't it? Until I heard you say it when you were ordering dinner, I didn't know what it was. I like Conrad but I like Bobby even better. Bobby is such a cute name.

LUCAS. What a coincidence? Bobby is my middle name. All my best friends call me Bobby. Will you?

WINIFRED. I'd love to—Bobby. I'm so glad that is your name. Maybe I remember unconsciously from when we were children together that your name was Bobby.

LUCAS. That's what it is—unconscious memory. I wonder what the psychologists would say to that. It seems to me, Winnie, that childhood sweethearts should be allowed to hold hands. [*He takes her hands.*] Don't you like to hold hands?

WINIFRED. I love it. It makes me feel warm and nice all over. But men don't respect girls whose hands they hold. Men want girls to be reserved and dignified.

LUCAS. Only in England! Now let's pretend we're on the deck of a steamer bound for New Caledonia. Far beneath us the water ripples musically, white gulls are overhead in the silver glow of a harvest moon. You like boats, don't you?

WINIFRED. I've never been on a boat.

LUCAS [*looking at his watch*]. It is half after eight. Well, at that time on board ship the moon is just overhead and a southerly breeze scented with sea-violets ruffles one's hair. It is deliciously cool, even in October, so the hero slips his arm quietly about the slender waist of his beloved. [*Suits actions to words.*] At first she is rather reserved, then gradually a languor envelops her. The honey-colored curls touch the shoulder of her lover, her white eyelids droop and from the galley a watch calls eight or nine bells. The moon is dimmed by a cloud, the seagulls muffle their flight, and with indescribable tenderness the lover presses the lips of his beloved with his own.

[*Winifred jumps up.*]

WINIFRED. Oh! How dare you!

[*Collis, who has been dozing in his*

chair, leaps up at the cry. Winifred begins to weep.]

COLLIS. What's wrong there?

[*Coming toward the chesterfield.*]

WINIFRED [*tearfully*]. N-n-nothing.

[*She sits down again.*]

LUCAS [*brightly*]. I frightened the young lady by producing a mouse from my waistcoat. Shall we continue with the performance? Join us, Collis. [*Lucas, taking a red silk handkerchief from his pocket, causes it to disappear.*] A disappearing handkerchief—what could be more simple? Presto! [*He causes the handkerchief to reappear and become changed to a blue one.*] Merely a little parlor trick. [*Winifred watches with growing amazement. Collis with disgust goes back to his chair.*] Now are we happy again?

[*He wipes away her tears with the handkerchief.*]

WINIFRED. I think you're very rude. You shouldn't have kissed me.

LUCAS. It was in the story; you wouldn't have me ruin the story for a whim.

WINIFRED. I don't care about the story. I'm going home.

LUCAS. Very well, if you must. But first accept from me this rose.

[*From his buttonhole he takes the rose, which he holds out to her.*]

WINIFRED. I don't want a rose. I won't accept anything from you. You're not a gentleman.

LUCAS [*sadly*]. If you won't, you won't. The rose gives me no pleasure after you have refused it. Poor, doomed little flower, farewell!

[*He tosses the rose into the fireplace.*]

WINIFRED. The lovely rose! You're cruel and I hate you. [*She weeps.*] I I didn't want you to throw it away. It was so pretty.

LUCAS. You weep for the rose and have no thought of how cruel you are to me.

WINIFRED. It's wicked to destroy flowers, and it was such a pretty rose, so pink and sweet!

LUCAS. You refused it, but perhaps to make you happy I can find another. [*Taking a duplicate rose from his pocket.*] Will you accept this?

WINIFRED. Oh, thank you! I didn't

mean to be cross but I can't bear to see flowers mistreated.

[*Lucas pins the flower in her hair for her, then kisses her. This time she says nothing.*]

LUCAS. Exquisite! I long to quote Tennyson. "Queen rose of the rosebud garden of girls, Come hither, the dances are done." Apropos, isn't it?

WINIFRED. Yes, and so appropriate. I wish I could quote beautiful poems, but I'm so stupid. I never can think of the line I want.

LUCAS. My own predicament is so different! I never want the line I can think of, and since I never think of a line until I want it I never have time to want what I think of.

WINIFRED. I don't quite understand—but I think you're frightfully clever. [*Looking into a small mirror.*] Flowers are in so much better taste than jewels. I shall never ask my husband for diamond bracelets and pearls, only a bunch of violets occasionally, or forget-me-nots. I adore forget-me-nots. If Lady Hencomb had worn flowers rather than pearls to-day think how much trouble she would have been saved.

LUCAS. But how dull the world would be without trouble. No jewels: no robberies! No robberies: no thieves. No thieves: no Salvation Army. No Salvation Army: no street bands or reformed drunkards or good old melodramas. Have you ever passed a street corner when they were singing: "There may be flies on you, and there may be flies on me, but there ain't no flies on Jesus"? Have you?

WINIFRED. I don't think I have.

LUCAS. You must. [*After a minute.*] Jewels have always had a fatal fascination for me, pearls especially. Some men cannot resist gin, others have a weakness for whisky or dope or women. Well, pearls have been my downfall. Listen, Winifred, the story of my life is a strange and sad one. Do you want to hear it?

WINIFRED. If it's nothing you shouldn't tell. I wouldn't want you to tell me something you shouldn't.

LUCAS. My dear, sympathetic little friend, I knew I could rely upon you. This is it: when I was young, almost too young, my mother died. My mother,

Winifred, was very beautiful. I was left an orphan.

WINIFRED. Your father died too?

LUCAS. I can't say. Picture me as a sad little boy, only the hope of playing with you in the sandpile to cheer my lonely life. Often my large brown eyes would fill with tears. Then my aunt— one aunt was left me—dressed me in a little suit of white batiste.

WINIFRED. You must have looked cute.

LUCAS. I did. And she would say, "Bobby, here are two bob. Take them and go to the cinema." One day even that failed to cheer me. In desperation my aunt mixed for me a cocktail, a Martini, since that was my favorite. In it she dropped a small, pickled onion. I shall never forget how that little onion gleamed through the golden liquid. Then my aunt told me how Cleopatra, when she was sad, dropped into her glass of wine a lovely pearl, and was immediately made happy to see the pearl slowly dissolve. "Now, Bobby," my aunt said to me, "I want you to see the moral of this story. Cleopatra dissolved her sorrow with the pearl in wine." "But pickled onions don't dissolve," I said to my aunt. "Besides, this is a cocktail, not wine." Another person might have been baffled by my argument but my aunt was as clever as she was good. "God gave you an imagination," she said, "and you must use it. If your pearl will not dissolve, why, swallow it. With it you will swallow your sorrow." Realizing the wisdom of her suggestion, I drank my cocktail. At the bottom of the glass gleamed the small onion, more like a pearl than a pearl could be. The flavor was delicious, and from then on I was the happiest of little boys. Now, Winifred, you know why pearls fascinate me to this day.

WINIFRED. I think it was too bad of your aunt to give a cocktail to such a little boy.

LUCAS. We must not speak ill of those who have passed on.

WINIFRED. Your aunt is dead?

LUCAS. She died, too. But we must not allow it to sadden our lives. Did you notice, Winnie, at the garden party this afternoon, how fine Lady Hencomb's pearls were? A faint shade of rose, and perfectly matched, all forty-four of them.

WINIFRED. How do you know there were forty-four pearls?

LUCAS. A litle whim of mine, to know at sight how many pearls in a necklace. Very simple when you've got the knack.

WINIFRED. It seems to me you know a lot about Lady Hencomb's pearls. I should think you'd be more careful what you say considering they were stolen. A person, not knowing you well, might think you the thief.

LUCAS. I am the thief, my dear.

WINIFRED. I don't believe you.

LUCAS. Nevertheless it is true. I took the pearls from the neck of Lady Hencomb. They are in my pocket now.

WINIFRED. Why are you telling me? Do you think I won't go to the police? Because I will.

LUCAS. Would you send me to prison? I told you, Winifred, because you have made me want to reform. You have brought back memories of my childhood, of English ideals and honor. You make me realize what a depraved creature I have become.

WINIFRED. Not depraved.

LUCAS. Yes, depraved. I'm not fit to associate with a pure, sweet girl like yourself. Will you help me to reform, Winifred?

WINIFRED. What do you want me to do?

LUCAS. I want you to return the pearls so I can go into the world and turn over a new leaf. I may go to Canada or Australia, who knows? But wherever I go, with me I shall carry the thought of you and the desire to live a clean, wholesome life.

WINIFRED. Well, I'm willing to return the pearls if you really want to reform. Though I don't think you ought to have taken them in the first place.

LUCAS. We all do things we oughtn't. Be kind to me, Winifred. I mean to work my way to a new country, to endure hardship, hunger, cold, in order to make a man of myself.

WINIFRED. I wouldn't want you to be hungry. Perhaps you can get money by doing tricks for people.

LUCAS. No, that is a part of my old life, the life I am discarding. I want to starve and be cold.

WINIFRED. I can give you a little money if it will help. You'll have to buy new clothes, won't you? You can't work in those.

LUCAS. You think of everything. It's quite true I shall need coveralls. How much money have you?

WINIFRED. Three pounds. [*Taking money from her purse.*] Here is it. Will you promise not to steal ever again?

LUCAS. On my honor. Here they are —the pearls. I dare not look at them for fear they will fascinate me again, destroying my ambition. [*He drops the pearls into her purse which she closes. Lucas arises.*] Good-by, Winifred, and God bless you. [*He kisses her hand, goes swiftly to the door and takes hat and cane.*] Ah, the evening paper!

[*He brings it to the table by Collis, then leaves for good.*]

COLLIS [*startled into looking around just in time to see Lucas disappear*]. Er—cheerio!

[*He looks at his watch, yawns, and rises, preparatory to leaving for theater.*]

WINIFRED [*sobbing loudly as she flings herself on the chesterfield*]. Oh! Oh! Oh!

COLLIS [*drawing close*]. What is it? Winnie, what's wrong? Tell me!

WINIFRED. Keep away. Don't speak to me, don't dare. I hate you—oh, I'm so unhappy.

COLLIS [*rather perplexed, goes for his hat and cane, the newspaper he stuffs into a pocket*]. It's beyond me.

WINIFRED [*watching him from the corner of her eye*]. I'm so upset—oh, what shall I do? [*She powders her nose. Collis stands irresolutely at the doorway.*] My head's whirling—I feel so strange, as though I were going to faint. Why is it so dark? Oh, I can't see.

[*The last few words are very faint as her head droops gracefully to the cushions.*]

COLLIS [*approaching timidly*]. Is there anything I can do? [*Winifred pretends to being unconscious.*] Winifred! Winnie, do you hear me?

WINIFRED. Where am I? Come closer. [*Collis sits beside her. Immediately her head is against his arm.*] Chester, don't leave me alone. I'm so nervous.

COLLIS. Shall I take you home? You see I have a theater engagement and it's already quarter to nine.

WINIFRED. With a girl?

COLLIS. I'm through with women. You know that.

WINIFRED. Don't leave me, Chester. You can see I'm not well. Listen, the man who just left—you saw him?

COLLIS. I saw him making love to you.

WINIFRED. I had to let him, Chester. It was only a scheme on my part to get the pearls away from him.

COLLIS. Pearls! What pearls?

WINIFRED. Lady Hencomb's pearls. He was the thief, I knew this afternoon he was the thief so I got him here and forced him to give them up to me. They are in my handbag this very minute. So there!

COLLIS. Really?

WINIFRED. Do you think I'm prevaricating? This afternoon at the tea when no one was looking I saw him take them.

COLLIS. Why did you say nothing at the time?

WINIFRED. I didn't want him to go to prison. I thought I could reform him and I did. Now, Chester Collis, I'm going to call up Lady Hencomb so she won't worry any longer about her pearls, and you can go to your old theater.

COLLIS. Hang the theater! Do you know her number?

WINIFRED. Yes [*talking into the telephone*]. Mayfair 560. Is Lady Hencomb in? Lady Hencomb? This is Winifred Ashton speaking. I think I know where your string of pearls is. What? Really? I'm so glad. Yes, indeed. Good-by, Lady Hencomb. [*Hanging up receiver.*] I don't understand. She says the footman made off with them; only an hour ago they were found in his room.

COLLIS. She must be mistaken. Let me see the pearls.

WINIFRED [*taking them from her purse*]. You see I really have them.

COLLIS [*in reaching for them dislodges the paper. It falls open to the floor.*] What is this? A price tag—three shillings. Why, they can't be real pearls at all. But what would be the fellow's idea? [*Together they sit down despondently.*] It's all quite mysterious.

WINIFRED. He thought they were Lady Hencomb's pearls, I'm sure he did. Why, he was so serious and he wanted so badly to lead a clean life. [*Looking *down at the paper.*] Whose picture is that? [*Collis picks up the paper.*] It's Mr. Wallace, the man we're talking of. But why is his picture in the paper?

COLLIS [*reading*]. "Scion of old family disappears! Gareth Lucas not seen since he left home early yesterday morning. At the time he was dressed in gray striped trousers, frock coat and top hat. He is six feet tall, weighing approximately ten stone. According to statements made by his father, Sir Lucien Lucas, Mr. Gareth Lucas has been subject to occasional spells of forgetfulness since 1916 when he was shell-shocked. Similar spells have lasted from a week to ten days during which time the young man wandered about London acting with no apparent reason. Sir Lucien assures the public his son, during these periods, is not dangerous. He asks persons who believe they have seen Mr. Gareth to immediately report to him at his home, No. 16, Arlington St." [*Collis puts down the paper.*] Well—that's all!

WINIFRED [*picking up paper so as to gaze at picture*]. He is aristocratic looking; I was positive he wasn't a thief. But he didn't seem insane either.

COLLIS. He certainly acted with no apparent reason. But women don't seem to mind a little thing like that. If a man is handsome that's all that is necessary. And by the way, how could you possibly have seen him steal the pearls from Lady Hencomb as you say you did?

WINIFRED. I was mistaken, dear. After all, I'm only human. [*Nestling close to Collis.*] Don't be cross with me, Chester. I'm so upset.

[*Collis puts his arm about her.*]

COLLIS. Now the lunatic is gone, you're willing to look at me.

WINIFRED. Don't be silly. I would have looked at you sooner only I thought you didn't love me any longer. Do you, Chester?

COLLIS. Yes.

[*They embrace. At the door a knock is heard. Collis goes to find out the cause, and Winifred gazes sadly at Lucas's picture. She kisses it.*]

WINIFRED. He was so handsome. I think he was in love with me.

COLLIS [*entering*]. Three waiters are here from the Pall Mall Restaurant. They say a Mr. Wallace ordered dinner for two. Do you know anything about it?

WINIFRED. That's right, he did. I'd completely forgotten. But I'm not at all hungry—what shall we do?

COLLIS [*savagely*]. Pay for it—what else can we do? And the hell of it is I dined an hour ago. [*After a minute in the hallway.*] He wants ten guineas. I've only three with me. How much have you?

WINIFRED. I haven't any. I did have three pounds. [*She remembers her generosity.*] I gave it to Bobby—Mr. Wallace—Mr. Lucas, I mean.

COLLIS. I'll write them a check. [*Into hall.*] All right, bring on the banquet. I guess it's no harder to eat two dinners than to pay for two. [*He comes over to chesterfield. Suspiciously*] Winifred, what are you up to?

WINIFRED. I'm only cutting out this picture of Gareth Lucas. I mean to save it.

[*Curtain.*]

THE EVE IN EVELYN

A COMEDY

BY GLENN HUGHES

CHARACTERS

EVELYN PRICE [*an attractive girl of twenty*].
ROGER PRATT [*a young journalist*].
J. EDWARD PRICE [*Evelyn's father, a financier*].
MRS. PRICE.
SAM BRIGGS [*proprietor of Twin Falls Lodge*].

TIME: *The Present.*

Applications to produce this play should be addressed to the author's representatives, SAMUEL FRENCH, 25 WEST 45TH STREET, NEW YORK CITY.

THE EVE IN EVELYN

A COMEDY   BY GLENN HUGHES

[SCENE: *Twin Falls Lodge, a rustic inn thirty miles from a large city of the West. The setting represents the interior of Twin Falls Lodge—that is, the main lounging room. At the back are French windows, which open on to a low veranda. This is the only entrance from the outside, and is the one used by all arrivals at the Lodge. At stage left of the entrance is a small alcove containing a desk, a telephone, and the guest register. In the corner at upper left is a staircase leading to bedrooms above. At lower left is a door leading to the dining-room and kitchen. At lower right is a huge fireplace, with easy chairs and divan drawn around it. Victrola, library table, and other typical furnishings complete the room. The woodwork is rough, and is designed to give an effect of massiveness and rusticity. There is a large window in the right wall above the fireplace. From this window a view of the Falls is obtained.*

As the curtain rises, Sam Briggs, the fat and genial proprietor, is discovered sitting in his shirt sleeves before the fireplace, a newspaper on his lap, his eyes closed in sleep, his mouth drooping open. The lights in the room are rather subdued.

In a moment there are heard soft steps on the veranda, and then the French windows are opened, and Roger and Evelyn enter quietly. Roger carries a suitcase and a small traveling bag. He has his hat pulled down rather low over his eyes, and wears a rakish light overcoat. Evelyn wears a fur jacket and a small, pert hat. Roger is very nervous, Evelyn interested but not especially worried.]

EVELYN. Well, we've got this far.
ROGER. Sh! Not so loud!
EVELYN. Why? Aren't we safe now?

ROGER. Of course we're not.
[*He is irritated.*]
EVELYN. Well, put down those bags anyway. We're going to stay awhile.
ROGER. Maybe we are and maybe we aren't. Supposing—
EVELYN. Nonsense, Roger! Don't be such a 'fraid-cat. No one would have the faintest idea we were coming here.
ROGER. How do you know?
EVELYN. Because! For one thing, there are so many hundreds of places we *might* have gone that no one is going to be able to guess that we picked *this* one.
ROGER. But you *know* this is one of the most popular places. Everybody knows about it. And then it's got a falls.
EVELYN. Has it? I didn't see any falls. Where are they?
ROGER. Good Lord, Evelyn, use your head. The name of the place is Twin Falls Lodge. Naturally there would be a falls here.
EVELYN. Oh, I don't know. Lots of places don't live up to their names. If this one does, then there must be two falls around here.
ROGERS. Well, maybe there are. Anyway—
[*He puts down the bags.*]
EVELYN. Roger, why is it that honey-mooners always go to some falls or other? Is there any idea in it?
ROGER. I don't know. I never thought of it before. Maybe it's to give one of them a chance to bump himself off in case he's disappointed.
EVELYN. I wonder if that's it! [*She starts over toward the fireplace.*] Oh!
[*She utters a little scream as she sees Sam.*]
ROGER [*jumps*]. What is it?
EVELYN. A man!
[*She retreats toward Roger.*]
ROGER. Where?

EVELYN. There! In the chair!, Oh, I think he's dead.

ROGER [*trembling*]. No! No! Absurd!

EVELYN. He looked like it. His mouth was open, and he looked—

ROGER. For heaven's sake, Evelyn, keep still! He's only asleep.

EVELYN. Are you sure?

ROGER. Of course I'm sure.

EVELYN. Then why were you so frightened?

ROGER. I wasn't.

EVELYN. You certainly were. You shook like an asp.

ROGER. Not like an asp! Like an aspen!

EVELYN. What's the difference?

ROGER. An asp is a snake; an aspen is a tree.

EVELYN. Well, can't a snake shake?

ROGER. No, it can't!

EVELYN. Anyway, you shook.

ROGER. I did not. *You* were trembling, and naturally when you took hold of me your trembling made it seem as though I were trembling too.

EVELYN [*pointing to Sam*]. Who do you suppose he is—the proprietor?

ROGER. He looks as though he might be. I'll waken him.

EVELYN. I wish you would. He looks terrible that way.

ROGER. I will.

[*He starts toward Sam, but hesitates midway.*]

EVELYN. Go ahead. What's the matter?

ROGER [*putting his fingers to his lips and coming back to Evelyn*]. I was just thinking: suppose he has had word to look out for us. Suppose the police have telephoned and asked him to hold us. I'm sure your father has the whole police force after us by this time.

EVELYN. He was hot, all right. We shouldn't have called dad up and told him until to-morrow.

ROGER. I know, but I wanted to get it over with. I could never have spent tonight in peace with that hanging over my head.

EVELYN. It doesn't look to me as though you were going to be very peaceful as it is. You've got police on the brain.

ROGER. Your father dared me to leave town with you. That meant—

EVELYN. He'll try to find us all right. But anyway, we're married, aren't we, Roger?

[*She holds up her lips to be kissed.*]

ROGER. We are, Evelyn. [*He kisses her, but rather nervously.*] I hope your father doesn't annul the marriage.

EVELYN. He won't.

ROGER. He may. He can. You're only twenty.

EVELYN. He won't, if he doesn't find us until to-morrow.

ROGER [*embarrassed*]. I guess you're right, there. But he would if he found us to-night.

EVELYN. I suppose.

[*The telephone rings. They jump with fright.*]

ROGER. Good lord!

EVELYN [*whispering*]. Do you think . . . ?

[*It rings again, a long ring. Sam stirs and wakens and becomes slowly conscious.*]

ROGER. Sh!

[*Points to Sam. They move into the shadows at upper right. The telephone rings a third time, and Sam rises to answer it. He shuffles across the stage, rubbing his eyes and yawning as he goes. He does not see his guests, nor their luggage, which is at right of center, well back. He answers the phone.*]

SAM. Hello. Yes . . . What do you mean, slow? . . . Say, we never sleep. We're too busy . . . What's that? . . . You don't say! All right, I'll hold 'em for you . . . Nine o'clock? . . . Sure! Trust me! Right! Good-by!

[*He hangs up the receiver and starts back toward right. Roger and Evelyn have shown great anxiety over the telephone call. Now Sam's eye falls on the luggage. He stares at it for a moment in perplexity. Roger realizes that the moment has come. He takes a step toward center and addresses Sam in a quaking voice.*]

ROGER. They're mine. I just put them there.

SAM [*surprised to see his two guests*]. Well, well, when did you come in?

ROGER. Just now. You were—we didn't want to disturb you.

SAM [*expanding*]. That was kindhearted of you. Sorry I wasn't awake to welcome you.

EVELYN. That's quite all right. [*She comes forward a little.*] We weren't quite sure whether we were going to stay, anyway, so—

ROGER [*taking the cue*]. No; you see, we didn't know for sure just what sort of place we wanted, so we thought we'd stop and look around, and . . . .

SAM [*interrupting*]. I understand. You're looking for a room?

ROGER. Well, yes.

EVELYN. We wanted a rather large room, with a view. I suppose your rooms are quite small here.

SAM. Small? Not a bit of it. Fine big rooms. And every one with a dandy view, too. Can't beat the sight of the falls in the moonlight. Want to see a room now?

ROGER [*struggling to find a means of escape*]. Not right now, thanks. I think we'd better. . . .

[*Starts to pick up the luggage, and at the same time casts a meaning glance at Evelyn.*]

SAM [*taking the luggage from Roger*]. Let me take it. I'll put it upstairs, and you can come up and pick out your room after dinner. You must be hungry after that long ride from town. Just sit down and make yourselves comfortable for a few minutes. I'll be right with you.

[*He bustles upstairs with the luggage. Roger and Evelyn stand looking helplessly at each other for a moment.*]

ROGER [*pathetically*]. We're caught!

EVELYN. Why did you let him take the luggage? Now we've got to stay here.

ROGER. I couldn't help it. He took it out of my hands.

EVELYN. It was your luggage. You could have demanded it. You're a man.

ROGER. But I couldn't think of any excuse. Damn it!

EVELYN. Do you think that telephone call was about us?

ROGER. I suppose so! Confound it! Now we're in a mess. He'll hold us till the police come.

EVELYN. Well, think of something to do. Don't just stand and worry about it.

ROGER [*with sudden fire*]. I know! After he comes down I'll go upstairs and throw the luggage out the window. Then we can slip out, pick it up, get the car and beat it!

EVELYN. Good idea. But let's wait till after dinner.

ROGER. We don't dare. We'll be caught.

EVELYN. No, we won't. Didn't you hear him say nine o'clock? Over the telephone. If that had anything to do with us it means that whoever is coming for us won't be here before nine. It's only seven-thirty now. That gives us plenty of time for dinner, and I'm starved.

ROGER. I don't see how you can feel like eating at a time like this.

EVELYN. Well, I do. The more I think about it the hungrier I get. I hadn't realized it until the old fellow mentioned dinner.

ROGER. But dinner won't be ready. They always have to cook it especially in places like this. It will take too long.

EVELYN. We'll make them hurry. Meanwhile I wish I had an apple.

[*She crosses and sits down before the fire.*]

ROGER [*gazing after her in astonishment and disgust*]. An apple!

EVELYN [*rather tartly*]. Yes, an apple! A-p-p-l-e. You know—keeps the doctor away!

ROGER [*dazed*]. An apple! At a time like this! My God, Evelyn, how can you be so cool!

EVELYN [*facetiously*]. My God, Roger, how can you be such a fool!

ROGER [*incensed*]. At a time when our happiness is hanging on the brink of disaster, when any moment may bring ruin to both our lives, you sit down before the fire and long for an apple!

EVELYN. I like apples. They are good for one. If you had eaten more apples, Roger, your nerves would be better.

ROGER [*in exasperation*]. Is this a honeymoon? Or—or—

EVELYN [*warning him*]. Hush, dear, he is coming down!

[*Sam descends the stairs heavily.*]

EVELYN. Sit down, Roger. You're worn out.

ROGER. I don't want to sit down.

[*Drops sulkily into a chair.*]

SAM [*crossing to the fireplace*]. I'll

stir up this fire, then I'll see about dinner for you. [*He pokes the fire.*] How would some nice fried chicken do? With mashed potatoes and gravy, hot biscuits, salad, coffee, and fruit?

EVELYN. Oh, wonderful! Will you hurry with it, please?

SAM. Sure I'll hurry. Takes time, though. Can't hurry my cook too much. He ain't that kind.

ROGER. How long will it take?

SAM. Half an hour.

EVELYN. Oh, dear!

SAM. Well, maybe twenty-five minutes. I'll see what I can do.

[*Exits lower left.*]

EVELYN. Cheer up, Roger. It's going to be all right.

ROGER. I won't be able to eat.

EVELYN. Yes you will, when you see the chicken. But I still wish I had an apple to stave off hunger. Do you think it would be all right if I asked the old fellow for one?

ROGER [*in a haze*]. For a what?

EVELYN. For an apple.

ROGER. Still on that subject! No, for heaven's sake, don't ask him for an apple. It would be too childish. Haven't we ordered dinner? Can't you wait half an hour?

EVELYN [*in disgust*]. Roger, you're a prune!

ROGER. Your mind certainly runs to fruits.

EVELYN [*laughing, rises and crosses to him*]. *Poor Roger! He's so worried!* [*Kisses him on the top of the head.*] Do you love me?

ROGER. Well, I'm *here*, am I not?

EVELYN. I bet you wish you weren't. *Don't* you?

ROGER [*grudgingly*]. No. Don't be silly.

[*Reënter Sam at left. He goes up to the desk.*]

SAM. Now will you come and register, please?

ROGER [*rising*]. Oh, of course.

[*He looks at Evelyn, as though inquiring of her whether or not to sign his real name. She shrugs her shoulders noncommittally. He goes up to the desk.*]

SAM [*pointing to a blank space on the register and handing Roger a pen*]. Right there, if you don't mind.

[*Roger hesitates a moment then writes rapidly. He hands the pen back to Sam.*]

SAM [*after glancing at the signature*]. Thanks, Mr. Pratt.

ROGER [*embarrassed*]. By the way, I was going to tell you—that is, ask you, if you wouldn't mind—

SAM. I get you! Mum's the word! I'm used to this sort of thing.

[*He closes the register and puts it away.*]

ROGER [*lamely*]. Thanks.

SAM. Where's your car? I couldn't see it out front.

ROGER. No; I hid it down the road a way. You see I was afraid—

SAM. Sure, I see! That's all right.

ROGER [*not trusting Sam entirely*]. There haven't been any telephone calls for me, have there?

SAM. No; not a one.

ROGER. Oh—or—any *about* me? I mean, no one has said anything to you about *us?*

SAM [*suavely*]. Never heard of you till five minutes ago, when I found you standing here with your luggage.

ROGER [*relieved*]. That's good. Well, if any one *should* inquire for us, would you mind just—

SAM. I won't know a thing about you.

[*He smiles reassuringly.*]

ROGER [*laughing nervously*]. Thanks! That's fine! I— [*He hurries back to Evelyn, greatly relieved. To her.*] It's all right. I fixed it.

EVELYN. You're sure?

ROGER. Well, I think so. Unless . . . .

EVELYN. Unless what?

ROGER [*looking back at Sam, who is busy over some papers*]. Of course one can't ever be sure about human nature. Perhaps we had better clear out of here right after dinner. It might be safer.

EVELYN. I'm sure I'm willing. [*She rises and wanders up stage at right, and looks out window.*] Roger!

ROGER [*hurrying to her side*]. What's the matter?

EVELYN. The falls! Look! Just over there! And the moon is up! Aren't they beautiful!

ROGER. By jove, they are! We'll go out and see them after dinner.

SAM [*overhearing and coming toward them*]. How do you like my falls? Aren't they wonders?

EVELYN. There *are* two of them, Roger.

SAM. Absolutely. Twins they are, and dead ringers for each other.

ROGER. Later on we'll run out and look at them.

SAM. Sure. You want to be careful, though. The lookout platform's right on the edge. Don't get dizzy and fall off. It's five hundred feet to the bottom.

EVELYN. Oh! I wish we could go out now!

ROGER. Before dinner? No; there isn't time. Come on, we'll go upstairs and get clean.

EVELYN. That's a good idea.

SAM. I left the light on in the hall. Your room is number two.

ROGER. Right-o! Come on, Ev!

[*They run up the stairs. Sam moves down to the fireplace, pokes the fire and settles down in an easy chair. He picks up his newspaper again, tries to read, and begins to doze, when he is startled by the sound of a motor car drawing up in front of the entrance. The headlights flash across the windows, and the engine roars and then is shut off. Sam listens, rises, and goes to French windows. As he opens them, two heavy figures enter. They are Mr. and Mrs. Price. Mr. Price steps into the room quickly and looks around.*]

MR. PRICE. Seen anything of a young couple—elopers?

SAM. Why, if it isn't my old friend, J. Edward!

MR. PRICE [*looking at Sam and starting slightly*]. Hello, Sam. How are you?

SAM. So-so. Not as prosperous as I might be if those bonds you sold me had been any good.

MR. PRICE. Yes, yes! That was too bad. We'll talk that over some other time. I'm here looking for my daughter now.

SAM [*surprised*]. Your daughter? You mean she has eloped?

MR. PRICE. Yes, damn it! This afternoon, with a young whipper-snapper of a cub reporter. They telephoned me that they were married and were leaving town for a few days. I picked up their track; they headed in this direction. I got it from a boy at a filling station that

knows Pratt's car. I figure this is the sort of place that'd take their eye. Have you seen 'em?

SAM [*innocently*]. Say, I haven't been disturbed by a caller for so long I feel like Rip Van Winkle. I've been sitting by the fire taking a snooze. You woke me up.

MRS. PRICE. I knew it was a wild-goose chase, Edward. But you insisted.

MR. PRICE [*vehemently*]. Wild-goose chase your grandmother! I know what I'm doing. You don't care if your only daughter has made a damned fool of herself and us at the same time. You're willing to take this young ink-slinger as a son-in-law.

MRS. PRICE. Don't exaggerate, Edward. You know I did not favor their marrying. I didn't want to lose my little girl.

[*Her lip trembles and she begins to cry.*]

SAM. Come and sit down, won't you?

[*He leads Mrs. Price to a chair. She sinks into it, weeping.*]

MRS. PRICE. Oh, Evelyn, how could you do it! To break our hearts this way!

MR. PRICE [*to Sam*]. You hear that? You know what it means? It doesn't mean that she cares who the girl has married. She's crying because she got beat out of a church wedding.

MRS. PRICE [*sobbing*]. I am not!

MR. PRICE. You are, too. You said so not five minutes ago. All your plans were upset. That's what worries you. Now that they're married you don't want to do anything about it. Just sit at home and cry.

MRS. PRICE [*through her tears*]. They're married. What can we do? In the sight of God they're man and wife. All we can do is forgive.

MR. PRICE. Yes, we will! Not! We'll find them to-night and annul the marriage to-morrow.

SAM. You're pretty badly upset about this, J. Edward.

MR. PRICE. Who wouldn't be? Evelyn's our only child. That's the trouble; an only child. Spoiled! That's the real germ of the matter.

MRS. PRICE. Who spoiled her? I didn't.

MR. PRICE. We'll not argue that out again.

SAM. Where you going next?

MR. PRICE. Don't know. Any other lodges on this road?

SAM. Sure. A couple. Quite a ways from here, though.

MR. PRICE. Distance means nothing to me! My car covers the ground!

MRS. PRICE [whimpering]. I'm tired of covering ground.

MR. PRICE. C. n't help it. Every minute counts to-night.

MRS. PRICE. You won't find them. They're like needles in a haystack.

MR. PRICE. But they came this way. They're somewhere along this road, and this road is not a haystack.

MRS. PRICE. I don't feel well. I've a headache.

MR. PRICE. You'll get over that when you're back in the fresh air.

MRS. PRICE. I will not. I've had too much fresh air. That's why I've a headache. I want a cup of tea.

SAM [chivalrously]. A cup of tea? [He hesitates, looking significantly at the staircase.]

MRS. PRICE. A nice cup of tea would pick me up.

MR. PRICE. Then you'll be willing to go on, as soon as you've had your tea?

MRS. PRICE. Yes; I promise.

MR. PRICE. All right. Sam, can you get her some tea in a hurry?

SAM. Sure. I think there's hot water. [He goes off lower left.]

MR. PRICE [coming down and sitting beside his wife. He assumes a somewhat tender manner]. Now, Carrie, don't take on. We're both upset. I didn't mean to be cross.

MRS. PRICE [more upset than ever by this tenderness]. Oh, I'm so miserable!

MR. PRICE. Just keep quiet now for a minute, and steady your nerves.
[He puts his arm about her and they sit in silence.]

MR. PRICE [with sudden suspicion]. You don't suppose he could be hiding 'em, do you?

MRS. PRICE. What do you mean?

MR. PRICE. This is a big place—there's an upstairs. [Looks at stairway.] They might have talked him into hiding 'em. Sam don't like me any too well. By George, I'm going to investigate.
[He rises and starts toward stairs.

Enter Sam in time to intercept Mr. Price.]

SAM. Where you going, J. Edward?

MR. PRICE. Oh, I thought I'd run upstairs and have a wash. Get dirty driving, you know.

SAM. Sure. There's a washroom down here, though. Easier to get at. I'll show you.

MR. PRICE [hesitating]. Yeh? [Advances toward Sam.] Look here, Sam! You slipping anything over on me?

SAM. What do you mean? Thought you wanted to wash your hands.

MR. PRICE [glaring at him]. Who's upstairs?

SAM. Is there some one upstairs?

MR. PRICE. That's what I'm asking you. If you've hid those youngsters up there, by Jove, Illl . . . .
[The telephone bell rings.]

SAM. Just a minute, till I answer the phone. [Goes to phone and answers.] Hello. Yes, Twin Falls Lodge. Briggs speaking. . . . What's that? . . . Who? . . . Price? Yes; he's here. Want to talk to him? . . . Hold the line.

MR. PRICE. For me? It must be Murphy, Police Headquarters. I told him to call me here. [Goes to phone. Sam backs away and watches the stairs.] Hello! Murphy? . . . Yes, yes. . . . What! . . . The Golden Pheasant! . . . You're sure? . . . But great heavens! That's in the other direction! . . . Gray roadster? . . . That's right. . . . I will! . . . Thanks, Murphy! [Hangs up the receiver with a bang.] Damn! Damn! Damn!

MRS. PRICE. Edward! What is it?

MR. PRICE [raving as he comes downstage]. We're on the wrong track. Wait till I get back to that filling station. I'll wring the neck of that young devil. They had him fixed to steer us wrong. Murphy says they spotted Pratt's car heading for the Golden Pheasant.

SAM [whistles]. I should say you are on the wrong track. That's a long way from here.

MR. PRICE. I don't care how far it is. My car covers ground. We'll make it there in two hours. Come on, Carrie! No time to lose!

MRS. PRICE. But I haven't had my tea!

MR. PRICE. The devil with your tea! Think of your daughter!

MRS. PRICE. Oh, dear! When will this nightmare be over?

[*She rises.*]

SAM. Sorry, Mrs. Price, but I suppose under the circumstances. . . . You'll have to come back some other day for your cup of tea.

MR. PRICE. We're off! You'll see some fast driving now.

[*He starts toward the French windows. Mrs. Price starts meekly to follow him. Sam is ushering them out, an innocent expression covering his face. As Price reaches the windows, a voice comes from the upper landing of the staircase. It is Roger's.*]

ROGER [*above*]. Evelyn! I say, Evelyn!

[*The three persons below freeze instantly into complete immobility. A look of consternation spreads over Sam's countenance.*]

MR. PRICE. What the—

[*Roger comes bounding downstairs and almost into the arms of his parents-in-law.*]

ROGER. Evelyn! [*He sees who confront him.*] Oh!

[*Sam ducks into the office alcove as if fearing gunfire. Mr. Price leaps at Roger.*]

MR. PRICE. Aha! So here you are! You young cub—where's my daughter?

ROGER [*made pugnacious by the suddenness of the situation*]. I don't know. I'm looking for her.

MRS. PRICE. You don't mean she's lost!

MR. PRICE. It's another trick. He's hidden her.

ROGER [*shouting*]. I have not. But I suppose *you* have. Where is she? Are you kidnaping her and taking her back to town?

MRS. PRICE [*to Roger*]. We haven't even seen her!

MR. PRICE. Look here, Spratt, if you—

ROGER. My name is not Spratt! It's Pratt.

MR. PRICE. I'll call you anything I like. [*Seizes him by the shoulder.*] You stole my daughter, a young innocent girl. . . !

ROGER. She is not innocent! She's been to college! Take your hands off me or I'll have you arrested for assault.

MR. PRICE [*releasing him*]. Produce my daughter!

ROGER. Produce your grandmother! Do you think I'm a magician?

MRS. PRICE. But, Roger, wasn't Evelyn with you when you came here?

ROGER. Of course she was. Do you think I'd go on a honeymoon alone?

MR. PRICE. When did she disappear?

ROGER. About five minutes ago.

MR. PRICE. Didn't she say where she was going?

ROGER. No; she said she would be back in a minute. But she didn't come.

MRS. PRICE. She's probably in the bathroom.

ROGER. No, she isn't. I looked there. She isn't upstairs anywhere.

MR. PRICE. Could she have gone out any other way? Sam! Could she?

SAM [*coming down a bit timidly*]. There's a back stairs to the outside.

ROGER [*suddenly*]. I know! She went to look at the twins!

MRS. PRICE [*startled*]. The twins!

MR. PRICE. *Whose* twins?

ROGER. I mean the Twin Falls. There are two of them, you know.

MRS. PRICE [*relieved*]. Oh, that's different.

SAM. She shouldn't have gone out there alone. It's dangerous.

ROGER. Good Lord, perhaps she's fallen off the edge! Quick! Come on! I never thought of her having—

[*He starts for the door, the others following.*]

SAM. Hey! Just a minute. I'll lead this procession. You'll break your necks in the dark! All right now, come on!

[*Sam pulls Roger back, and takes the lead. Mr. and Mrs. Price follow him off back center. Roger goes out last. As he turns to close the door, Evelyn enters nonchalantly from lower left. She is eating a large apple. Roger sees her. The others have disappeared around the corner. He leaps back into the room.*]

ROGER. Evelyn! [*He flies to her and embraces her.*] Darling! You're safe!

EVELYN [*with a bite of apple impeding her speech*]. Why shouldn't I be safe? Are you crazy?

ROGER. I thought you had fallen into the falls!

EVELYN. Oh! I did look at them, from a safe distance. Then I came past the kitchen and asked the cook for an apple. I was starved. I thought I'd get it all eaten before you saw me. Are you cross?

ROGER. No; but listen. Your folks are here!

EVELYN [*pausing in the midst of another bite*]. What! [*Looks around.*] Where?

ROGER. They're looking for you. Just now they've gone to the Falls to see if you have fallen over the edge. I suggested it.

EVELYN [*laughing and choking*]. Oh, how gorgeous!

ROGER. Quick! What'll we do? They'll miss me and come back. Your dad is madder than a wet hen. He'll ruin us. We've got to jump!

EVELYN. Get the luggage! We'll beat it.

ROGER. Good! You run straight to the car! Remember where it is? Just around the curve. I'll go up and get the bags, come down the back stairs and join you at the car. [*Starts toward stairs.*] Where *are* those confounded back stairs?

EVELYN. At the end of the hall. Hurry!

ROGER. Hurry yourself! Beat it now! Better go through the kitchen!
[*Exit upstairs.*]

EVELYN. I will!
[*Taking another huge bite of apple she runs toward door at lower left, but suddenly thinks of something, and going up to the office alcove, seizes pen, ink and paper, scribbles a note, puts it in the crack of the French windows, then runs like mad out through the lower left door. It is only a moment before footsteps are heard on the veranda, and Mr. Price storms into the room. Evelyn's note flies to the floor at his entrance. He picks it up, reads it, crumples it in his hand, mutters an oath and dashes headlong up the stairs. In another moment Mrs. Price and Sam enter back center.*]

MRS. PRICE. It's very strange Roger didn't follow us. What could have happened?

SAM. I haven't any idea, ma'am. I thought he was coming right behind us.

MRS. PRICE. And *now* where on earth is *Edward?*
[*A banging of doors is heard from above.*]

SAM [*looking toward the ceiling*]. I should say he might be upstairs.

MRS. PRICE. Oh, I hope he isn't doing anything violent—to Roger, I mean. My poor little girl! If I only knew where she is! You don't think anything terrible has happened to her, do you, Mr. Briggs?

SAM. I can't say, ma'am, but my feeling is that she's safe somewhere.

MRS. PRICE. I'm so glad to hear you say that.
[*Mr. Price comes down the stairs, a defeated look on his face, the crumpled paper still in his hand.*]

SAM. Did you find him?

MR. PRICE. I found—no one—and nothing! Here, Carrie! [*Comes down and hands her the note.*] We've been tricked again. They're gone—
[*He sinks sadly into a chair.*]

MRS. PRICE [*reading the note aloud*]. Dearest Mother and Dad: Just heard you were here. I was out in the kitchen eating an apple. We are moving on. See you in a couple of days. Roger is a prune, but very nice. Your loving daughter, Evelyn.

MR. PRICE [*with a sudden renewal of rage*]. A prune! She admits it!

MRS. PRICE. Thank heaven she's safe!
[*She sighs.*]

MR. PRICE. First time I was ever beaten in my life. Goes hard with me.
[*He tries to look the martyr.*]

MRS. PRICE. There, there, Edward, you'll get used to Roger in time.

MR. PRICE. A prune for a son-in-law!
[*Rises angrily and advances on Sam.*] Sam, you're to blame for all this. You cooked up the whole deal. What about the telephone call from Murphy? You faked that!

SAM [*backing away*]. Me? You're crazy. You must think I'm a ventriloquist or something. All I did was ask you not to go upstairs. I admit that much. It is my duty to protect my guests.

MR. PRICE. And that business of falling into the falls? Who thought of that?

SAM. Not me. Your son-in-law

sprung that one. He's a bright boy. You ought to take him into your business, J. Edward. He might get to be as slick as you are at selling bum bonds.

MR. PRICE. Aw, lay off that business, Sam. I'll fix that up with you some day.

SAM. Yes, you will. I know you. I'll stay out of your way.

MRS. PRICE. Are you going to turn this into a business discussion, Edward? If you are through with the wild-goose chase, I should like to go home.

MR. PRICE. All right. We'll go. I give up. But it's a dirty trick.

[Starts toward door.]

SAM [ushering them out]. Come back again when you're not in such a hurry.

MR. PRICE [after handing his wife through the door]. Sam, you go to hell!

SAM [grinning]. Same to you, and many of 'em!

> The door slams. The motor is heard, then the klaxon, and the Prices are gone. Sam looks after them, returns to the fire, pokes it, sits down and resumes his reading of the newspaper. He yawns. Two figures appear on the veranda. They peek through the French windows, then open them cautiously. It is Roger and Evelyn. Roger sticks his head in.]

ROGER [in a loud whisper]. Have they gone?

[Sam starts up out of his seat.]

ROGER. Have they gone?

SAM. Oh, it's you. I thought you had gone. Come on in. The coast's clear.

[Enter Roger and Evelyn.]

ROGER. Where did they head for?

SAM. Home. They're tired out.

ROGER AND EVELYN. Hurrah!

SAM. How did you happen to come back?

EVELYN. It was the chicken.

SAM. What?

EVELYN. Yes. You see, I went through the kitchen, and the cook said our din-

ner was just ready. The chicken smelled heavenly! I couldn't bear to go away and leave it. So I made Roger wait around the corner until we heard the folks' car go down the road. And here we are. Can we have dinner now?

SAM. You sure can. How would you like to eat here by the fire? I'll bring in a table.

EVELYN. Oh, lovely!

ROGER. Good. I've recovered my appetite now. [To Sam.] You had me scared when we first got here. That telephone call. You said you'd hold them. We thought you meant us.

SAM. That? Oh, no; it wasn't about you. Just reservations for tables. Little party coming out at nine o'clock.

ROGER [laughing]. I see. Well, they won't bother us. We'll be out of the way by that time, won't we Evelyn?

EVELYN. Of course, dear.

SAM. Excuse me, and I'll have your dinner brought right in.

[Exit lower left.]

ROGER. Sit down, sweetheart. [Leads her to divan and sits down with her.] Isn't it heaven?

EVELYN. It is, Roger!

[They sigh contentedly.]

ROGER. Your apple nearly ruined things, though.

EVELYN [laughing]. Just like the garden of Eden. It was an apple that started all the trouble there, wasn't it? I'm like Eve.

ROGER. Well, silly, there's an Eve in Evelyn!

EVELYN. Why, so there is. [A pause.] I hope names don't mean too much!

ROGER. Why?

EVELYN. Stupid! Don't you realize where we're spending our honeymoon? The name of this place?

ROGER. Twin Falls— Oh! [He breaks off suddenly in embarrassment.] Oh, Evelyn! The good Lord forbid!

[Evelyn buries her head on his breast. He kisses her.]

[Quick Curtain.]

A COMEDY OF DANGER
A PLAY FOR BROADCASTING

BY RICHARD HUGHES

Reprinted from *A Rabbit and a Leg*, by Richard Hughes, by permission of and special arrangement with, ALFRED A. KNOPF, INC., authorized publishers.

CHARACTERS

JACK [*a young man*]
MARY [*a young woman*]   [*All English visitors*
MR. BAX [*an elderly man with a gruff voice and*   *to the mine*].
    rather a Johnsonian manner of speech]
VOICES [*a party of Welsh miners who say a few words and are heard singing off*].

The noises required include an explosion, the rush of water, footsteps, and the sound of a pick. There must be an echo, to give the effect of the tunnel.

A COMEDY OF DANGER

A PLAY FOR BROADCASTING

BY RICHARD HUGHES

[*The* SCENE *is a gallery in a Welsh mine.*]

MARY [*sharply*]. Hello! What's happened?

JACK. The lights have gone out!

MARY. Where are you?

JACK. Here.

[*Pause. Steps stumbling.*]

MARY. Where? I can't find you.

JACK. Here. I'm holding my hand out.

MARY. I can't find it.

JACK. Why, *here!*

[*Pause.*]

MARY [*startled*]. Oh! What's that?

JACK. It's all right; it's only me.

MARY. You did frighten me, touching me suddenly like that in the dark. I'd no idea you were so close.

JACK. Catch hold of my hand. Whatever happens, we mustn't lose each other.

MARY. That's better. But the lights! Why have they gone out?

JACK. I don't know. I suppose something has gone wrong with the dynamo. They'll turn them up again in a minute.

MARY. Oh, Jack, I hate the dark!

JACK. Cheer up, darling! It'll be all right in a minute or two.

MARY. It's so frightfully dark down here.

JACK. No wonder! There must be nearly a thousand feet of rock between us and the daylight. It's not surprising it's a bit dusky!

MARY. I didn't know there could be such utter blackness as this, ever. It's so dark, it's as if there never was such a thing as light anywhere. Oh, Jack, it's like being blind!

JACK. They'll turn the lights up again soon.

MARY. I wish we had never come down this beastly mine! I knew something would go wrong.

JACK. But it'll be all right, dear; it's only the lights.

MARY. Where are the others?

JACK. They're just on ahead, not far.

MARY. Suppose we get lost!

JACK. We can't get lost, Mary darling. The others will stand still, too, till the lights go up, and then we can easily overtake them. We've only got to wait patiently.

MARY. I wish you hadn't wanted to drop behind the others! Oh, Jack, I'm afraid of the dark.

JACK. My mistake. Buck up, Mary old girl; it'll soon be over. [*Pause.*] Listen!

[*Steps heard.*]

MARY. There's some one coming!

BAX [*distant, muttering*]. Of all the incompetent idiots, turning the lights off just when a party of visitors were seeing the place! Call this a coal mine! A damned, dark rabbit-hole I call it, a rotten rathole, a dratted, wet, smelly drain-pipe. The dithering fools!

MARY. It's Mr. Bax. . . . Hallo!

BAX. Hallo! Who's there? Of all the stupid, meddlesome idiots—

MARY. Oh, Mr. Bax, what's happened? Is it all right?

BAX. Is it all right, indeed! Leaving us suddenly in the dark like this!

MARY. But has there been an accident?

BAX. Goodness knows! I'd expect anything of a country like Wales! They've got a climate like the flood and a language like the Tower of Babel, and then they go and lure us into the bowels of the earth and turn the lights off! Wretched, incompetent— Their houses are full of cockroaches— Ugh!

JACK. Well, I suppose the only thing to do is to sit and wait for the lights to go up again.

MARY. There's no danger, is there?

291

BAX. No, young lady, there's no danger; but it's damned unpleasant!

MARY. Oh, I don't know; I'm beginning to think it's rather fun.

BAX. Well, if you can find any fun in breaking your shins in the dark—

MARY. Why, don't *you* call it fun, being in a pit disaster?

JACK [*quickly*]. But this isn't a disaster, it's only the lights—

MARY. Of course, silly! you don't think it would be fun if it was a *real* disaster, do you? But the lights going out *might* have meant a disaster, and think how thrilling it's going to be to talk about afterwards! I say, Jack!

JACK. Yes?

MARY. Let's pretend it's serious.

JACK. What do you mean?

MARY. Let's pretend it's a real disaster, and we're cooped up here for ever and will never be able to get out.

JACK. Don't joke about it.

MARY. Why not? There's no *real* danger, is there? Let's get all the thrills we can.

BAX. Well, of all the morbid— Young people nowadays . . . .

MARY. I love thrills. Let's pretend the roof has fallen in, and they can't get at us.

JACK [*uncomfortably*]. Very well; but what a baby you are! [*In mock solemnity*.] Here we are, my dear, buried alive!

MARY. Oh, Jack!

JACK. Alas, they will never find us!

MARY. Oh, *Jack!*

JACK. Well?

MARY. I'm so frightened!

JACK. What at?

MARY. About the roof having fallen in.

JACK. But it hasn't; it's only pretense.

MARY. Yes, but when I pretend it seems so real.

JACK. Then don't pretend.

MARY. But I want to pretend! I want to be frightened! Only hold my hand tight, won't you? Go on.

JACK. We shall suffocate, or starve, or both, my dear, in each other's arms.

MARY. Oh, Jack!

JACK. Even death shall not part us.

MARY. Oh, Jack, don't! It's too awful.

JACK. Our poor young lives cut so short!

MARY. Oh, don't, don't!

JACK. There'll be articles in all the newspapers.

MARY. Oh, I wish I could read them!

BAX. You can't have your funeral and watch it, young lady.

MARY. Oh, this is fun! I wouldn't have missed it for anything. Won't I make daddie's flesh creep! [*A distant explosion, with a long echo, swelling in volume*.] Oh!

JACK. Good God, Mary!

MARY. Oh, Jack! Jack, Jack, Jack, Jack, Jack!

JACK. Quiet, you little fool! Let go! you're throttling me! Let go of me!

MARY. Oooooh! [*Another explosion nearer, followed by the hiss of water*.] Oh, the dust! It's choking me! I can't breathe! Oh!

JACK. Stop screaming, you! How do you expect to be able to breathe if you're screaming all the breath out of your body? Quiet!

MARY. Oh, Jack!

JACK. Pull yourself together. We're all right; we're not hurt.

BAX. No, sir, we're not hurt. But listen! [*Water heard louder*.] Water.

JACK [*sotto voce*]. Shut up, you idiot. Don't let *her* hear!

MARY. What's that roaring?

JACK. It's only the echo.

MARY. Oh, Mr. Bax, can't we find the others?

BAX. I don't think we could, young lady: it wouldn't be much use to us if we did.

JACK [*quietly and sharply*]. Oh, good God! Good God! Good God!

BAX. They're no better off than we are.

MARY. Why, listen! that must be them! [*Voices heard singing:* "Ar hyd y Nos."] That must be the others. They can't be very far off. Let's call to them.

BAX. Sound carries a long way in a tunnel. But listen. [*More singing*.] Gad! those chaps have courage.

JACK. You're finding some good in the Welsh, then, after all?

[*The roar of water gets louder*.]

MARY. The echo's getting louder! Oh, Jack, it isn't an echo! It's *water!*

The mine's flooding! We'll be drowned! [*The voices sing a couple of lines of "Aberystwyth."*]

BAX. I wish I had the faith of those chaps, sir. It'd make dying easy.

MARY. Oh, Jack, I don't want to die yet! I won't, I won't, I won't.

BAX. It has got to come some time, young lady; isn't it better for it to happen now, in your lover's arms, both of you together? You don't know what might happen to you if you lived. Death might have parted you two, instead of which he's simply joining you closer together.

MARY. I want to live!

JACK. Shut up! You old fool, it's all very well to be stoical about death at your age, but we're young! We'd got all life before us.

BAX. Can't you keep quiet about it, then, you young jackanapes? Do you think I want to die, either? But it ain't good manners to talk about it. Where'd we be if we *all* started screaming about it, eh? Behave yourself, sir. But those chaps over there don't want to die, either, but they don't make a fuss about it; they sing hymns! If you and me don't feel like singing hymns, we can at least behave like gentlemen.

JACK. Behave like gentlemen, indeed! I tell you, it's all very well for an old chap like you, who'll die anyhow in a year or two, but it's different for us— we're young!

BAX. Well, if you want to make a scene, you shall have one, sir. D'you think it is any easier for the old to die than the young? I tell you it's harder, sir, harder! Life is like a trusted friend, he grows more precious as the years go by. What's your life to mine? A shadow, sir! Yours, twenty-odd years of imbecile childhood, lunatic youth; the rest a mere rosy presumption of the future. Mine, sixty solid years of solid, real living; no mere rosy dreams! Do you think it is as easy for me to leave my solid substance as you to leave your trumpery shadow?

JACK. What's your life worth to the world? Who's dependent on you? What good are you to any one?

BAX. And what good are you, young man?

JACK. One person is dependent on me, anyway.

BAX. You mean that you are loved by this young lady. If you both die, what loss is that to the world? Opposite quantities canceling out!

MARY. Oh, you beast! You cruel beast!

BAX. I must speak, madam, in common justice to my age, since that young cub has started the subject. The old are always being twitted with their unwillingness to die. Yet it is the most natural thing in the world that it should be the young, who haven't a notion what life really is, who should be ready to chuck it away for any footling reason that comes along.

JACK. Look here, instead of talking like this, let's *do* something; let's make some sort of an attempt at escape.

BAX. What do you propose to *do*, young man?

JACK. Why, look for some way out. We can't stay here and drown like rats in a cage.

BAX. If you start to walk, my boy, you'll start to run; and if you start to run, you'll get in a panic, and go mad in the dark. I'd rather die with my wits about me. I'd rather not die at all. Keeping still is the only thing for us, if we don't want to lose our heads. Remember, we're about a mile into the side of the hill. What earthly hope do you think there is of finding our way out?

MARY. Oh, the dark! I do hate the dark! I think I could go more easily if I could see light just once before it happened.

JACK. Here it comes! Listen! [*Rush of water quite close now.*]

BAX. Yes, it will be on us in another five minutes.

JACK. Pray heaven it finishes us off quickly.

MARY. Oh, *think* of dying somewhere out in the open, in the sunlight! Me able to see you, and you able to see me! What bliss it would be!

JACK. It's strange how little chaps wonder what will happen to them after death. One hardly thinks about it—yet I don't know. How thrilled we should be if we met a chap who really knew! In five minutes we're going to know ourselves, all three of us. [*Laughs unsteadily.*] I've always wanted to travel. Now I'm going to!

MARY. Oh, Jack, my poor dear!

JACK. Mary, do you know I'm beginning to feel as excited about it as a child going to the seaside for the first time. Aren't you?

MARY. Jack, how queer you are! I never looked at it like that.

JACK. Well, I wasn't in any hurry to die; but now it's coming, I feel sort of proud of myself, as if it was a very wonderful thing to manage to pull off.

MARY. Oh! Jack darling!

JACK. There's only one thing I'm sorry about.

MARY. What is it?

JACK [rather wildly]. I've forgotten the luggage!

MARY. Jack!

JACK. The train's coming, and there's no time to go back for it. [Laughs.] Who'll feed the parrot?

MARY. Jack!

BAX. Pull yourself together, sir. Keep control!

JACK. It's all right. Bax, I'm not going off my nut. I mean what I say. What do you think I've got to live for, besides myself and Mary? Why, my work! If it wasn't for that, Bax, I'd go to death without caring a tuppenny damn! I'd die just for the fun of the thing, to see what it felt like.

BAX [sarcastically]. I shouldn't worry about that if I was you: the world'll get on all right without you, never you fear! And what is your work?

JACK. I write. Poetry.

BAX. Good God! and you call that work!

MARY. Oh, Jack, the water's coming! It's over my feet! Oh!

JACK. Courage, darling.

MARY. Oh, Jack, I don't want to die! I hate it. I loathe it! I want to live.

JACK. Don't make it harder, dear; you don't think it's fun for me, you having to die?

MARY. Oh, Jack, it's awful! Only for an *hour* more! Oh, I do want to live another hour! Jack, there was something I wanted to say to you, and I can't remember it. . . . Oh, I must remember . . . it'll be too late soon. Oh, Jack!

JACK. Oh, God, can't I be allowed to finish my work!

BAX. Damn your work, sir! Do you think you're the only one dying before his time? I tell you, every man dies before his time, even if he lives till he's as old as Methuselah.

MARY. Oh, it's up to my knees!

JACK. Don't clutch at me like that, Mary; it won't do any good.

MARY. But the water—the current's washing me away—wooden thing!

JACK. Hold tight, then—got you tight!

MARY. Oh, if only I could see you!

JACK. Just think of all the things I had meant to do!

[Roars with laughter.]

BAX. Shut up about the things you had meant to do, you young cub! *Will* you realize we're all in the same boat, and it's as hard for me to die as you— or worse, by gad! A thousand times worse!

JACK. You hoary old sinner, can't you prepare to get out of the world instead of cursing at me!

MARY. Oh, Jack, let's pray.

JACK. Pray, if you like, Mary. I can't.

MARY. Oh! Jack, don't!

[A faint tapping is heard.]

BAX [hoarsely]. Help! help! I can't die, I won't die! I'm an old man—I won't, I won't, I won't!

JACK. Hold yourself in, you old coward!

MARY. Poor Mr. Bax! *I'm* quite calm now; I don't mind dying a bit.

JACK. Nor do I—now it's so close.

BAX. Help me! Help me! Help! Help!

MARY. It's no good, Mr. Bax; no one can possibly hear us. The only thing is to keep calm. It won't be long now.

BAX. Oh, help! Help! Help!

[Tapping a little louder.]

JACK. Tchk! What's that? Listen.

BAX. Help! Help!

JACK. Shut up, Bax; we want to listen.

[Tap, tap.]

MARY. It's up to my waist now, Jack.

JACK. My God! it's some one tapping. [Shouts.] We're here! Farther along!

MARY [calmly]. Is it? They'll find our bodies, that's all.

JACK. They'll find *us* if they're quick enough! [Shouts.] Farther along still. That's right.

MARY. They can't be quick enough. Besides, I don't want them to find me.

JACK. It's a strange thing, Mary, but, before, I looked on Death as a terrible thing; and now I am so nearly dead, I wouldn't come back to life for anything. There's such a lot to find out, the other side.

BAX. Help! Pick quicker, you fools, quicker! We're drowning.

JACK. Stop it, Bax; they won't be in time. Why can't you behave sensibly?

MARY. Jack darling, I'll never leave you.

[Quietly.]

BAX. How do you know they'll let you stay with him, you little fool? What do you know of death? I tell you death isn't Heaven and it isn't Hell. Death's dying, you young dolts. Death's being nothing—not even a breath of the wind or a mere drop of the rain; not even a dratted ghost clanking its chains on the staircase.

MARY. My soul's immortal, Mr. Bax; I know that.

BAX. Well, if your soul's immortal, is your mind immortal?

[Knocking grows louder.]

MARY. Oh, Jack, it's up to my chin! Help me!

JACK. Let me lift you in my arms, darling: then when it gets up to my chin, we'll die together.

MARY. Say it isn't true, what he has been saying.

JACK. No, darling, of course it's not true.

BAX. Hurry up, you dolts, you blockheads! Smash your way in! We're drowning, I tell you! drowning! Quick, quick!

MARY. Good-by, Jack, dear.

JACK. My God, they must be nearly through! God, this suspense! How much longer before we know whether we're going to live or die? I don't care which—but I do want to know!

BAX. Look! There's a light! A hole in the roof! Quick, quick!

[Sounds of strong blows, then of coal falling.]

JACK. They're through!

VOICES. Quick, below there! Catch on to the rope!

BAX. Quick! I'm an old man.

JACK. There's a girl here!

BAX [calmly]. By gad, Jack, a near shave! Come along, young lady: I've got the rope.

JACK. She's fainted.

BAX. Never mind; pass her up—she'll be all right. Well, she's had the thrill she wanted, all right! Give you something to write about, too, my boy. All right above there? Have you got her?

VOICES. Ri-ight. Now the next.

JACK. Up you go, quick, Mr. Bax. The water's still rising.

BAX. No, my boy, after you; you're more value in the world than I am.

JACK. Nonsense, sir! After you. You're an older man than I am. Quick, sir, or there won't be time!

BAX. You've got Mary to think of—now, Jack. Haul away above there!

JACK. No, no! Lower me! It's me you're hauling up, and it ought to be Bax!

VOICES. We'll have you up first; there's no tim to waste. Right?

JACK. I'm all right. Lower away again. Below there, Bax! Catch hold. Have you got it? [Pause.] Hi! [Pause.] Bax! Bax!— Good God, he's gone!

[Curtain.]

BLUE BLOOD
A PLAY
BY GEORGIA DOUGLAS JOHNSON

CHARACTERS

MAY BUSH
MRS. BUSH
JOHN TEMPLE
MRS. TEMPLE
RANDOLPH STRONG
These characters are negroes.
PLACE: *Georgia.*
TIME: *Shortly after Civil War.*

BLUE BLOOD

A PLAY

BY GEORGIA DOUGLAS JOHNSON

[SCENE: *Large kitchen and dining-room combined of frame cottage, showing one door leading into back yard. One other door (right side of room facing stage) leading into hall. One back window, neatly curtained. Steps on right side of room leading upstairs.*

Enter Randolph Strong with large bunch of white roses and a package. He places the package, unnoticed, on the table—still holding the roses.]

RANDOLPH STRONG. How is my dear Mother Bush?

MRS. BUSH. Feeling like a sixteen-year-old! That's right, you come right on back here with me. [*Notices roses.*] Oh! what pretty roses! Snow white!

RANDOLPH STRONG. Like um? Thought you would. . . . May likes this kind!

MRS. BUSH. She sho'ly do. Pore chile! She's turning her back on the best fellow in this town, when she turned you down. I knows a good man when I see one.

RANDOLPH STRONG. You are always kind to me, Mother Bush. I feel like the lost sheep to-night, the one hundredth one, out in the cold, separated by iron bars from the ninety and nine! Bah! what am I doing? The milk's spilt! [*Arranging flowers.*] Put these in here?

MRS. BUSH. Sure! My, but they look grand. There ain't many young doctors so handy-like!

RANDOLPH STRONG [*half to himself*]. The first time I saw her she wore a white rose in her hair. . . .

MRS. BUSH. Jest listen! May's plum blind! Oh! if she'd a only listened to me, she'd be marrying you to-night, instead of that stuck up John Temple. I never did believe in two "lights" marrying, nohow, it's onlucky. They're jest exactly the same color . . . hair . . . and eyes alike too. Now you . . . you is jest right for my May. "Dark should marry light." You'd be a perfect match.

RANDOLPH STRONG [*groans*]. Hold, hold for goodness sake! Why didn't you lend that little blind girl of yours your two good eyes?

MRS. BUSH. Humph! She wouldn't hear me. [*Goes up to him, speaking confidentially.*] 'Tween you and me, I shorely do wish she'd a said "yes" when you popped the question las' Christmas. I hates to see her tying up with this highfalutin' nothing. She'll re'lize some day that money ain't everything, and that a poor man's love is a whole sight better than a stiff-necked, good-looking dude.

RANDOLPH STRONG. It can't be helped now, Mother Bush. If she's happy, that's the main thing!

MRS. BUSH. But is she going to be happy . . . that's jest it!

RANDOLPH STRONG. Let us hope so! And yet, sometimes I think—do you know, Mother Bush, [*lowering his voice*] sometimes I think May cares for me.

MRS. BUSH [*confidently*]. Do you know, honey, somehow, sometimes I do too!

RANDOLPH STRONG [*excitedly*]. You do too!! Oh, if I could fully believe that—even now—at the last minute— [*Snaps his finger.*] Oh, what's the use? [*Constrainedly.*] Is everything ready?

MRS. BUSH. You bet! I'm all dressed under this apron. [*Swings it back and discloses a brilliant and much decorated gown. Then with a start.*] Lord save us! That Lyddie Smith ain't brought that my'nase dressing yet. Vowed she'd have it here by eight sharp, if she was alive. What time you got?

RANDOLPH STRONG [*looking at his watch*]. Eight thirty.

MRS. BUSH. Eight thirty? Good gracious!

299

RANDOLPH STRONG. I'll run over and get it for you.

MRS. BUSH. Oh yes, honey! Do hurry. Oh, what a son-in-law you would'a' made!

RANDOLPH STRONG. Good joke . . . but I can't laugh!

[*He goes. Mrs. Bush busies herself with the table arrangements and finally notices a package that had been left by Strong; she opens it and discloses a beautiful vase and reads aloud the card attached.*]

MRS. BUSH [*reading*]. For May and her husband, with best wishes for your happiness, Randolph. [*She sets it aside without saying a word—only wiping her eyes—thinks a while; shakes her head; picks up the vase again and calls toward the stairway:*] May! May! run down here a minute. I've got something to show you. [*Mrs. Bush polishes the vase with her apron and holds her head to one side looking at it admiringly. Enter May in negligee. Mrs. Bush—with vase held behind her:*] Not dressed yet? . . . Gracious! There . . . look . . . Randolph brought it!

MAY BUSH. Oh! . . . did he? [*Reads card.*] Randolph is a dear!

[*Fondles vase and looks sad.*]

MRS. BUSH. He brought these roses, too . . . said you liked this kind.

[*May Bush takes roses and buries her face in them, then thoughtfully changes them into Randolph's vase; looks at it with head one side, then breaks off one rose, fondles it, places it in her hair.*]

MRS. BUSH. May—May—are you happy?

MAY BUSH. Why—why—[*dashing something like a tear from her eye*] of course I am.

MRS. BUSH. Maybe you is . . . May . . . but, somehow, I don't feel satisfied.

MAY BUSH [*kisses her mother*]. Oh, Ma, everything is all right! Just wait until you see me dressed. [*Noise at door.*] Oh, somebody's coming in here!

[*May retreats partly up the stairway.*

Enter Mrs. Temple, talking. Voices and commotion heard as if coming from the front of the house, where heated argument is going on at front door, Mrs. Temple's muffled voice being heard. Hall kitchen door opens suddenly. Enter Mrs. Temple, excitedly.]

MRS. TEMPLE. Heavens! They tried to keep me from coming out here! The very idea of her talking that way to me—the groom's own mother! Who is that little upstart that let me in at the front door? I told her I was coming right out here in the kitchen, for even though we have not called on each other in the past, moving around—as you know—in somewhat different social circles, and, of course, not being thrown very closely together, yet *now*, at this particular time, Mrs. Bush, since our two children are determined to marry, I feel that my place to-night is right back here with you! [*Glancing upward, Mrs. Temple discovers May upon the stairway.*] Why, May, are you not dressed yet! You'll have to do better than that when you are Mrs. John Temple!

MRS. BUSH. Don't you worry 'bout May; she'll be ready. Where's John? Is he here?

MRS. TEMPLE. Sure—he brought me in his car, but the fellows captured him and said they were going to keep him out driving until the last minute. [*Again glancing upward toward May.*] Better hurry, May; you mustn't keep John waiting.

MAY BUSH [*slowly walking upstairs*]. Oh, John will get used to waiting on me.

[*Exit May.*]

MRS. TEMPLE [*to Mrs. Bush*]. What's this . . . chicken salad? Is it finished?

MRS. BUSH. No, it ain't. The my'nase ain't come yet. I sent Randolph for it. I jest got tired waiting on Lyddie Smith to fetch it.

MRS. TEMPLE. My gracious . . . give me the things and I'll make the dressing for you in a jiffy.

[*Mrs. Temple removes her white gloves and gets ready for her new rôle in the kitchen. Without waiting for Mrs. Bush's consent, she rapidly walks over to wooden peg on wall, takes down extra gingham apron and removes her hat and lightweight coat, hanging both upon the peg.*]

MRS. BUSH [*remonstratingly*]. I'm 'fraid you'll git yo'self spoiled doing kitchen work. Sich folks as you'd better go 'long in the parlor.

MRS. TEMPLE. Oh, no indeed. This

is my son's wedding and I'm here to do a mother's part. Besides—he is a Temple and everything must be right.

MRS. BUSH [*Takes materials for making the mayonnaise from kitchen safe and reluctantly places them before Mrs. Temple*]. You needn't worry 'bout this wedding bein' right. It's my daughter's wedding—and I'll see to that!

MRS. TEMPLE [*breaking and stirring eggs for the dressing*]. You'll have to admit that the girls will envy May marrying my boy John.

MRS. BUSH [*stopping her work suddenly, and with arms akimbo*]. Envy MAY!!! Envy MAY!!! They'd better envy JOHN!!! You don't know who May is; she's got blue blood in her veins.

MRS. TEMPLE [*laughing sarcastically*]. You amuse me. I'll admit May's sweet and pretty, but she is no match for John.

MRS. BUSH [*irately*]. She's not, eh? If I told you something about my May—who she is—you'd be struck dumb.

MRS. TEMPLE [*nervously stirring the mayonnaise, replies in a falsetto or raised tone, denoting sarcasm*]. Remarkable . . . but I am curious!

MRS. BUSH [*proudly*]. I bet you is—you'd fall flat if I told you who she is.

MRS. TEMPLE [*suspending the operation of the mayonnaise and curiously assuming a soft, confidential tone*]. Pray, Mrs. Bush, tell me then. Who is May?

MRS. BUSH. Who is May? Huh! [*Proudly tossing her head.*] Who is May? [*Lowering her voice, confidentially.*] Why . . . do you know Cap'n WINFIELD McCALLISTER, the biggest banker in this town, and who's got money 'vested in banks all over Georgia? That 'ristocrat uv 'ristocrats . . . that Peachtree Street blue blood—CAP'N McCALLISTER—don't you know him?

MRS. TEMPLE [*starts at the mention of the name but recovers herself in a moment*]. Y—e—s, I've heard of him.

MRS. BUSH [*like a shot out of a gun*]. Well, I'd have you to know—he's May's daddy!

MRS. TEMPLE [*agitatedly*]. W-h-y . . . I . . . I . . . I can't believe it!

MRS. BUSH [*flauntingly*]. Believe it or not, it's the bounden truth so help me God! Ain't you never seed him strut? Well, look at May. Walks jest like him —throws her head like him—an' she's got eyes, nose and mouth jest like him. She's his living image.

MRS. TEMPLE [*almost collapsing, speaking softly and excitedly*]. You . . . you terrify me. Mrs. Bush . . . Captain McCallister can't be May's father!

MRS. BUSH. Can't be May's father! Well, I reckon I ought to know who May's father is! Whut do you know 'bout it anyhow? Whut do you know 'bout Cap'n McCallister?

MRS. TEMPLE. Do you mean to tell—

MRS. BUSH [*interrupting*]. I mean jest whut I said. I'm telling you that my daughter—May Bush—has got the bluest blood in America in her veins. Jest put that in your pipe and smoke it! [*Mrs. Bush here proudly flaunts herself around the kitchen, talking half at Mrs. Temple and half to herself.*] Huh! Talkin' 'bout May not bein' a match fur John. I should say they don't come no finer than May, anywhere.

MRS. TEMPLE [*again collecting herself and speaking in a soft, strained, pleading voice*]. Mrs. Bush, Mrs. Bush, I have something to say to you and it must be said right now! Oh, where can I begin? Let me think—

MRS. BUSH. This ain't no time to think, I'm going to act! [*Takes mayonnaise from Mrs. Temple's apathetic hands.*] My chile's gotter get married and get married right. I . . .

MRS. TEMPLE [*breaking in*]. Please, please, be still a minute for heaven's sake! You'll drive me mad!

MRS. BUSH. Drive you mad! The devil I will. [*Abruptly runs and stands in a belligerent attitude in front of Mrs. Temple.*] Say, look here, Miss High-and-Mighty, what's you up to? Git out of here, you ain't going to start no trouble. here.

[*Tries to force Mrs. Temple toward the door.*]

MRS. TEMPLE [*breaking down in tears and reaching for Mrs. Bush's hands*]. Please, please, Mrs. Bush, you don't understand, and how can I tell you—what a day!

MRS. BUSH [*standing squarely in front of Mrs. Temple*]. Look here, is you crazy? or just a fool?

MRS. TEMPLE. Neither, Mrs. Bush, I'm just a broken-hearted mother and you must help me, help me, for May's sake, if not for mine!

MRS. BUSH. For May's sake! 'Splain yourself! This is a pretty come off. For May's sake.

[*Sarcastically.*]

MRS. TEMPLE. It's a long story, but I'll tell you in a few words. Oh, oh, how I've tried to forget it!

MRS. BUSH. Forget what! Look here, what time is it?

[*Mrs. Temple looks at her watch.*]

MRS. TEMPLE. A quarter of nine.

MRS. BUSH [*excitedly*]. Lord, woman, we ain't got no time fur story telling. I've got to hustle!

MRS. TEMPLE [*hysterically*]. You must hear me, you must, you must!

MRS. BUSH. Well, of all things, what *is* the matter with you?

MRS. TEMPLE. Be quiet, just one minute, and let me tell you.

MRS. BUSH. You'd better hurry up.

MRS. TEMPLE. Once . . . I taught a country school in Georgia. I was engaged to Paul Temple . . . I was only nineteen. I had worked hard to make enough to pay for my wedding things . . . it was going to be in the early fall—our wedding. I put my money in the bank. One day, in that bank, I met a man. He helped me. And then I see he wanted his pay for it. He kept on—kept writing to me. He didn't sign his letters, though. I wouldn't answer. I tried to keep away. One night he came to the place where I boarded. The woman where I boarded—she helped him—he bribed her. He came into my room—

MRS. BUSH. The dirty devil!

MRS. TEMPLE [*continuing her story*]. I cried out. There wasn't any one there that cared enough to help me, and you know yourself, Mrs. Bush, what little chance there is for women like us, in the South, to get justice or redress when these things happen!

MRS. BUSH. Sure, honey, I do know!

MRS. TEMPLE. Mother knew—there wasn't any use trying to punish him. She said I'd be the one . . . that would suffer.

MRS. BUSH. You done right . . . and whut your ma told you is the God's truth.

MRS. TEMPLE. I told Paul Temple—the one I was engaged to—the whole story, only I didn't tell him who. I knew he would have tried to kill him, and then they'd have killed him.

MRS. BUSH [*interrupting*]. That wuz good sense.

MRS. TEMPLE. He understood the whole thing—and he married me. He knew why I wouldn't tell him the man's name—not even when—when that man's son was born to me.

MRS. BUSH. You don't mean John?

MRS. TEMPLE. Yes . . . John. And his father . . . .

MRS. BUSH. Oh no . . . no . . . .

MRS. TEMPLE. Yes. [*With a groan.*] Winfield McCallister . . . is John's father, too.

MRS. BUSH [*clasping her hands excitedly*]. My God! My God! [*Whimpering, between sobs.*] Whut kin we do? Just think of my poor, dear chile, May, upstairs there—all dressed up jest lak a bride—'spectin' to git married—and all them people from everywhere—in the parlor—waiting for the seymoaney! Oh, whut kin we tell her . . . whut kin we tell them?

MRS. TEMPLE [*looking at watch. Gets up, walks up and down excitedly.*] Yes . . . we've got to think and act quickly! We can't tell the world why the children didn't marry . . . and cause a scandal. . . . I'd be ruined!

MRS. BUSH [*getting irate*]. So far as you is consarned . . . I ain't bothered, 'bout your being ruined. May'll be ruined if we don't tell. Why—folks'll all be saying John jilted her, and you can bet your sweet life I won't stand fur that. No siree! I don't keer who it hurts . . . I'm not agoin' see May suffer . . . not ef I kin help it!

MRS. TEMPLE [*bursting into tears*]. Oh! oh! we must do something!

[*Enter Randolph Strong, breathlessly, with mayonnaise dressing from Lyddie Smith's—placing large glass jar of mayonnaise on kitchen table.*]

RANDOLPH STRONG. Good evening, Mrs. Temple. I'm a little late, Mrs. Bush, but here's what you sent me for. [*He notices Mrs. Temple in tears.*] My, my, why, what's wrong?

MRS. BUSH. Randolph, my dear boy. . . .

RANDOLPH STRONG. What's the matter? What's happened since I left you awhile ago?

MRS. BUSH [*slowly and feelingly*]. Sump'n . . . sump'n turrible!

RANDOLPH STRONG. Has anything happened to May?

MRS. BUSH. Not only to her—to all of us!

RANDOLPH STRONG. All! Heavens!

MRS. BUSH. Listen, Randolph, and help us, for God's sake! May and John can't get married!

RANDOLPH STRONG [turning to Mrs. Temple]. Can't get married! Why?

MRS. TEMPLE. It's a long story. I've told—I've explained everything to Mrs. Bush. She—she understands.

RANDOLPH STRONG. You can trust me. I'm like one of the family. You both know that I have always cared for May.

MRS. BUSH [to Mrs. Temple]. Kin I tell him? [Mrs. Temple silently and tearfully nods her assent.] May mus' know it too—right away. Let's call her down. May! May! Oh, May! My dear chile come down here a minute—quick—right away! My poor chile . . . my poor chile!

MRS. TEMPLE. What a day! What a day!

MAY'S VOICE. Coming, Ma! [Enter May Bush, coming downstairs in her wedding gown.] Am I late? [Noting Randolph.] The roses are beautiful. See. [Points to one in her hair.]

MRS. BUSH. Randolph . . . Randolph remembered the kind you like, honey.

MAY BUSH [to Randolph]. Just like you!

RANDOLPH STRONG. How sweet of you to wear one!

MAY BUSH [proudly walking across room toward Mrs. Bush]. How do I look, Ma?

MRS. BUSH [tenderly kissing her daughter several times]. Beautiful, my darlin' [adding softly], poor chile!

MAY BUSH [walking toward and kissing Mrs. Temple]. How do you like me—my other mama?

MRS. TEMPLE. Charming—God protect you, my dear!

MAY BUSH [noticing the sad expression on the faces of both mothers]. My, you all look so sad; why so doleful? What is the matter with them, Randolph?

RANDOLPH STRONG. Why . . . I'm wounded, but smiling. The ladies . . .

MRS. BUSH [impatiently interrupting]. Oh, children—don't waste this precious time. We've called you together to tell you sump'n . . . [stuttering] we've got sump'n to tell you, and we got to tell you right now!

[Mrs. Bush draws May aside toward Mrs. Temple, hastily and cautiously locking kitchen hall door.]

MRS. BUSH [continuing]. Listen, May. Come here, come here, Randolph, for I feel that both of you are my children. May, you got to be strong—for if ever you needed wits, now's the time to use 'em. May God forgive me—and Mrs. Temple there, both of us—I just got to tell you 'bout it quick—for all them folks are in the parlor and if we don't do something quick, right now, this whole town will be rippin' us to pieces—all of us, you and me—Mrs. Temple—and—and—the las' one of us! There ain't time to tell you the whole story—but—May—my poor chile—I know you kin trus' your own, dear ma that far?

MAY BUSH [excitedly]. Yes, Ma, yes, but what is it?

MRS. BUSH. May, you and John can't marry—you jest can't marry!!

MAY BUSH [aghast]. Can't marry! Can't marry!

MRS. BUSH. No, never!

MAY BUSH. But why—why!

MRS. BUSH. Your father, and John's father—is—is—

MAY BUSH. You don't mean . . .

MRS. TEMPLE. Yes, May. John's father is your father.

MAY BUSH [wrings her hands]. Oh, I'd rather die—I'd rather die than face this . . . .

MRS. BUSH [crooning]. I know, honey . . . I know . . . God forgive me . . . God forgive that man. Oh, no . . . I don't want Him to forgive him.

MAY BUSH. Oh why, why did this have to happen to me—oh!! I wish I were dead!

RANDOLPH STRONG. May—don't say that. You mustn't say that.

MAY BUSH. I do. Oh, God—I've kept out of their clutches myself, but now it's through you, Ma, that they've got me anyway. Oh, what's the use . . .

RANDOLPH STRONG. May!

MAY BUSH. The whole world will be pointing at me . . .

MRS. BUSH. Ah, honey, honey, I'll be loving you . . . .

MAY BUSH. I wish I could die right now.

RANDOLPH STRONG. Will you listen to me, now, May?

MAY BUSH. Those people in there—they'll be laughing . . .

[*Knocking is heard.*]

MRS. TEMPLE. It's John. We can't let him come in here now. He mustn't know . . . .

MRS. BUSH. No. We can't let him know or he'll kill his own father. . . .

MRS. TEMPLE. What are you going to do, May?

MRS. BUSH. Yes, May—what are you going to do?

RANDOLPH STRONG. We are going to run away and get married, aren't we, May? Say yes, May—say yes!

MAY BUSH. John . . .

[*The knocking is heard again.*]

MRS. BUSH. Keep it from him. It's the black women that have got to protect their men from the white men by not telling on 'em.

MRS. TEMPLE. God knows that's the truth.

RANDOLPH STRONG. May! Come with me *now!*

MAY BUSH. Randolph—do you want me?

RANDOLPH STRONG. I want you like I've always wanted you.

MAY BUSH [*shyly*]. But—I don't love you.

RANDOLPH STRONG. You think you don't . . . .

MAY BUSH. Do you want me now?

RANDOLPH STRONG. I want you now.

MAY BUSH. Ma, oh, Ma!

MRS. BUSH [*in tears*]. Quick, darlin' —tell him.

MAY BUSH. My coat.

MRS. BUSH. I'll get your coat, honey.

MRS. TEMPLE. Here, May, take *my* coat!

MRS. BUSH. What we going to tell John—and all the people?

MAY BUSH. Tell 'em—Oh God, we can't tell 'em the—truth?

RANDOLPH STRONG. Mother Bush—just tell them the bride was stolen by Randolph Strong!

[*Strong puts the coat around her and they go out of the door, leaving the others staring at them.*]

[*Curtain.*]

DON JUAN'S CHRISTMAS EVE

A MIRACLE

BY HARRY KEMP

CHARACTERS

INNKEEPER.
TAPSTER.
A FRIAR.
ALESSANDRO [*a youth who has run away with his master's money*].
ROBERTO [*a middle-aged local peasant*].
SIGISMUND [*a thief and footpad*].
RODERICK [*a thief and footpad, Sigismund's companion*].
TADEO [*the half-wit stable boy*].
CHRISTOBAL DE MENDOZA [*the merchant from whom Alessandro has run away*].
TWO ALGUAZILS.
PAQUITA [*a courtesan*].
RICARDO [*her bully*].
DON JUAN.
DOÑA ESMERALDA [*a young married woman*].
JOSEPH [*an old peasant who has come as a pilgrim from far*].

TIME: *The Fourteenth Century.*

Applications for permission to present this play should be addressed to Mr. Harry Kemp, care BRENTANO'S, NEW YORK CITY.

Reprinted from *Boccaccio's Untold Tale and Other Plays,* published by BRENTANO'S, by special arrangement with the author and permission of the publishers.

DON JUAN'S CHRISTMAS EVE

A MIRACLE   By HARRY KEMP

[SCENE: *Interior of an inn in Spain.*]

INNKEEPER [*rubbing his hands cheerily and addressing Tapster*].
It is so cold the wind bites to the bone.
There will be small room in the inn to-night
For any who come late, and so we'll prosper.
In the kitchen every spit is turning
With roasts, and all the pots are bubbling over.
I think you'd better broach another cask
Of Malmsey.

TAPSTER.
Yes, good master.

INNKEEPER [*looking carefully about, in a lower voice*].
It will stand
A little mixing with some baser sort.

TAPSTER.
I am a tapster. Don't I know my trade?
[*Goes downstairs to cellar. Enter mendicant Friar.*]

FRIAR.
Have you lodging for a traveling friar?

INNKEEPER.
That is according to your purse, my friend.

FRIAR.
I live by charity, and do good deeds.

INNKEEPER [*callously*].
The only comfort I can give you, then,
Is a snack in the kitchen with the servants,
And a seat on a bench beside the fire—
That's good enough for any traveling friar.

FRIAR [*humbly*].
The God of all creation fared on less,
Ofttimes, when He walked up and down this world.
[*Enter Alessandro, a wild-looking youth. He seems agitated and furtive in his manner, in spite of his exterior boisterousness.*]

ALESSANDRO.
Ho, Innkeeper!
Give me the best in all your house to-night.

INNKEEPER.
Have you any money?

ALESSANDRO.
Enough to pay my way.

INNKEEPER.
Gold is the thing that counts, by night or day.
[*Enter Roberto, a middle-aged peasant, with a basket on his arm.*]

INNKEEPER [*to Roberto*].
What have you there?

ROBERTO.
Nice eggs, freshly laid,
Which my old woman gathered from the nests this morning.

INNKEEPER [*taking one of the eggs and holding it against the light*].
You lie! You've kept them by you for a week.
[*Holds egg to ear.*]
I almost hear the chick astir within.
[*The Tapster and Alessandro laugh.*]

ROBERTO [*protesting*].
I swear—
[*They carry on the rest of the conversation in dumb show, walking apart. The Tapster draws a flagon of wine for Alessandro, who seats himself at a table near the fire.*]

INNKEEPER [*coming up front again, followed by gesticulating peasant*].
That's all I'll give. Not a maravedi more.

ROBERTO [*as he takes money counted out in his palm*].
I will catch fire and brimstone from my wife.
Poor folk must live, as well as folk like you.

INNKEEPER [*bluffing*].
Take it or leave it; it's all one with me.

ROBERTO [*quickly*].
Then it's a bargain [*wheedling*] if
    you'll but throw in
A stoup of wine and a seat before the
    fire
Till I have armed myself against the
    cold.
    [*Innkeeper, contented with his bar-
    gain, makes a gesture to the Tap-
    ster, who brings over wine to Ro-
    berto, the peasant, as he painfully
    seats himself before the fire. En-
    ter Sigismund and Roderick. They
    bow familiarly to the Innkeeper,
    who seems well acquainted with
    them. Silently they seat them-
    selves apart from the others and
    order wine.*]
INNKEEPER [*ostentatiously, to Tapster*].
Give them the best, [*very low*] for
    travelers are their prey,
As they are ours.
SIGISMUND [*glancing stealthily about to
    observe who else is present; to Rod-
    erick*].
                    He hasn't come as yet!
RODERICK [*with meaning, leaning across
    to Innkeeper*].
Have you prepared the choicest room
    for him?
INNKEEPER [*coming over and addressing
    them in a low voice, nodding his
    head in the direction of Alessandro*].
Yonder's a youth beside the fire
Toasting his shins, just waiting to be
    plucked.
    [*They nod and laugh. Enter Tadeo,
    the stable boy.*]
TADEO [*to Sigismund and Roderick*].
Masters, your horses have been stalled
    and fed.
SIGISMUND [*reaching out his clasped
    hand to Tadeo*].
Here! Take these marevedi for your
    pains.
TADEO [*pocketing money and blowing on
    his hands*].
My thanks, kind sir. By all the saints,
    it is
The coldest winter night I've ever seen
To unhitch horses in, and panniered
    mules.
    [*A clatter, and a great calling of
    voices heard without.*]
INNKEEPER [*to Tadeo, who stands warm-
    ing himself, his hands spread out to
    fire*].

More guests! Tadeo, what are you
    doing there,
Lazing before the fire?
TADEO [*mumbling*].
                    My hands and fingers
Are stiff as ice from handling metal
    bits
And frozen harnesses—
INNKEEPER.
                    Fool, to your task!
Go, show them to the stables.
Take up your lantern. Go, or you shall
    lack
Your breakfast in the morning, and
    to-night
You shall sleep with the asses and the
    kine.
TADEO [*shivering; taking up his lantern
    again*].
I go, Master, I go. Pray work no ill
On Tadeo!
    [*He dodges grotesquely as the Inn-
    keeper fetches him a clout, and
    hastens out. Snow blows in at
    the door on the wind. All but the
    mendicant Friar laugh at the in-
    cident. Enter, after a space,
    Christobal de Mendoza and two
    Alguazils, or police officers, dis-
    guised as pilgrims.*]
DE MENDOZA [*to Innkeeper*].
Is there still room left in your inn for
    three?
INNKEEPER [*bowing low, in a quiet voice
    full of meaning*].
A multitude, with you, were welcome
    here,
Señor Christobal de Mendoza!
DE MENDOZA [*starting*].
                    How?
INNKEEPER [*quietly as before*].
You wore no beard when you were here
    before;
You had the best room in my hostelry.
She who was with you then was a poor
    maid,
Now known as Paquita, the courtesan!
DE MENDOZA [*looking about guiltily*].
Be quiet! Here is gold for silence,
    friend.
INNKEEPER.
There's no man in the world that better
    knows
The way to hold his tongue in secrecy
In such a case as this [*Pocketing gold
    slipped into his hand.*]
                    And now what's up?

DE MENDOZA.
A young man who was honest till
to-day
Has run off with my year's gain.
INNKEEPER.
What's his name?
DE MENDOZA.
Alessandro.
INNKEEPER [*winking to Sigismund and
Roderick and speaking in a loud
voice*].
There's no such fellow here.
[*While Alessandro crouches by the
fire, not perceiving what is going
on, the Innkeeper takes De Men-
doza aside.*]
INNKEEPER [*in a whisper*].
Yonder's the lad, sitting beside the fire.
But let us be in peace and quiet till
dawn. . .
I'll lock his door against him when he
retires.
[*De Mendoza beckons to the two Al-
guazils, who go off up the stairs
with him and the Innkeeper for
further conference.*]
SIGISMUND [*to Roderick, jerking his
thumb in the direction of the disappearing De Mendoza*].
Yon is the bird we'll pluck before the
day.
[*Enter Paquita, the courtesan, and
her man, Ricardo.*]
RODERICK [*to Sigismund, with a sweep
of the hand*].
And now the circle is well nigh complete:
A clear compendium of humanity. . . .
Thieves, merchants, innkeepers, pil-
grims, courtesans,
And even one priest, to strike God's
balance true!
SIGISMUND.
Stay, comrade, don't blaspheme!
[*The Friar says his beads and the
peasant mumbles a prayer and
crosses himself.*]
The Friar and the peasant overheard!
PAQUITA [*advancing to the two thieves
with mincing gait and rolling
eyes*].
Friends, where's the keeper of this inn?
RODERICK [*leering*].
Upstairs . . . where I will speak with
you anon.
PAQUITA [*affecting indignation*].
Why—you mistake! My husband here
will—

SIGISMUND.
Sweet girl, don't try to gull old friends
like us.
Keep those high manners for the laity.
PAQUITA [*coming over and recognizing
him*].
You, Sigismund? [*Lower.*] What is
afoot to-night?
SIGISMUND.
There's gold enough in sight, if that
is what
You mean.
RODERICK [*with an inclination of his
head*].
There's a young man there we meant to
lighten
Of stolen gold, but we'll be generous
And turn him over to your tender
heart.
He robbed his master, Señor de Men-
doza.
He boasted of the deed when he was
drunk
At a wayside inn, and so we followed
him.
But now we pass him by for bigger
game—
Mendoza himself, whom we will take
for ransom.
PAQUITA [*with affected unconcern*].
Mendoza? Why, I know him well.
RODERICK [*sarcastically*].
Aye, I'll warrant you do.
PAQUITA [*suddenly intense*].
When you get him in your power—say,
in the wood,
Or in some ruined castle, bound and
gagged—
As he lies helpless, let me prick him
lightly
With my poniard. That's the only
thing I ask,
For he it was who made a harlot of me.
SIGISMUND.
We're like to turn him over to your
vengeance
And lose his ransom and our lives as
well!
PAQUITA [*with a toss of the head, going
over to Alessandro*].
Shall we drink a stoup of wine to-
gether, lad?
ALESSANDRO.
As you wish, mistress! But how about
your friend?
[*Indicating Ricardo.*]
Won't he join us to the death of care?
RICARDO [*taking the proffered goblet*].

"A little wine for the stomach's sake,"
eh, Father?
[*Nudging the Priest.*]

PRIEST.
A little Scripture and a little wit!
[*Laughter. A violent knocking at
the door.*]

RICARDO.
Come in. Don't knock the house down.
[*Enter Don Juan and Doña Esmeralda, masked. Don Juan is an
elegant young nobleman, and Doña
Esmeralda is of refined appearance and of the same rank.*]

RODERICK.
Now here's a gallant, if there ever was
one!

SIGISMUND.
That is Don Juan Tenorio;
He is as ready with the rapier
As with a courtly, silken phrase. Don't
twit him.

DON JUAN [*to Esmeralda*].
This is the inn I spoke of, Esmeralda.
Its signboard reads: "The Tavern of
Three Ways."
It should be called "The Harborage of
Thieves";
For all that strikes at law and human
good
Finds shelter here. . . . It is just like
the world.

RODERICK [*to Sigismund*].
Who is this Juan that you tell about?

SIGISMUND.
Masked or unmasked, I'd know him
anywhere.
He is a bold, abandoned nobleman,
Sometimes, I think, the devil's very self.
The evil deed that he has not yet done
He has not thought of yet.

RODERICK.
I'll try him out,
Before the night wears far.

ESMERALDA [*looking about daintily*].
"The Harborage of Thieves"—how interesting!

DON JUAN.
You whispered me you wanted some-
thing new,
That the masque bored you. Speak a
little lower, though.
Thieves least of all
Like to be called by their right names.

ESMERALDA.
And you're quite sure we're safe?

DON JUAN.
With me . . . anywhere. . . .

I am a sort of universal man,
A student and a gallant and a bravo,
I know all people, and I dare all
things;
And I'm as ready with my rapier
As any cloud with rain. . . . Besides,
But put a bold face on, and all is well;
That is a method that goes every-
where.

ESMERALDA.
But my husband—?

DON JUAN [*laughing sardonically*].
They bore him home, thinking the
fumes of wine
Had overtaken him. It was a drug,
Only a harmless potion, that I poured
In his last glass, that made them call
his chair.
He need never know, the stupid fellow,
That you were here . . . as he need
never know
The mad, impassioned love that makes
us one.

ESMERALDA.
Need never know! I thought you
promised me—

DON JUAN.
Be not so hasty. He need never know
Until we both take ship to Italy . . .
when the time's ripe.
The brave man never looks for trouble,
But when it comes to him
He then receives it on his rapier's
point.

RODERICK [*to Sigismund*].
I think that your Don Juan's but a
boaster,
From his demeanor and the scattered
words
That I have caught from him.

SIGISMUND.
Do not mistake,
He's that rare kind
That barks and bites both. You would
best beware.

ALESSANDRO [*starting to his feet and
putting his hand to his pouch*].
I have been robbed!
[*To the Innkeeper, as he comes down
the stairs*].
Shut all the doors!
I have been robbed. . . . I think it was
this woman!
[*Points to Paquita.*]

INNKEEPER [*coming across to Alessandro,
with menacing intensity*].
If you've been robbed, it is but stolen
gold

Stolen again. My lad, I know your case.
Did you observe those three men garbed as pilgrims?
One was your master, Señor de Mendoza,
And two were Alguazils.

ALESSANDRO [*frightened*].
Hide me! Do not give me over to them.

INNKEEPER.
Very well. Sit quiet in your corner.
I hold no brief against mere robbery.
See that you hold none. . . . Wrap this cape around
Your shoulders. Pull this hat about your ears.
When all have gone to bed, I'll see you safe
Out at the door. But shout no more, "I'm robbed!"

DON JUAN [*coming up*].
What is the matter with the lad, Innkeeper?

INNKEEPER.
He's only a drunken fool seized with a fancy
That I've persuaded him out of.
[*Alessandro shrinks into the shadow. De Mendoza comes down the stairs with the two Alguazils.*]

DE MENDOZA [*to the Alguazils*].
The keeper of the inn advises best.

ALGUAZIL.
It is your money and not ours that's stolen.

INNKEEPER [*calling out through back door into kitchen*].
Set the table and bring in the roasts!
[*Two servants enter and arrange a long table in center of floor. Huge roasts are carried in, and baskets of bread. All the guests seat themselves, but Alessandro and the Friar go into the kitchen for their food. The Innkeeper acts as host. Enjoying their repast, the guests are brought into a momentary harmony by it.*]

INNKEEPER.
Fall to, good folk; let belly now be king.
There is no ill that good roast beef can't cure.
Ho, Tapster, fill their flagons—on the house!
[*The Tapster fills all the goblets.*]

DON JUAN [*rising*].
A toast to the king of Spain.

ALL.
Long may he live!

DON JUAN.
May every one here gain his heart's desire!
[*They all drink.*]

TADEO [*stumbling in*].
Masters, there is a wonderful star that hangs
Right over this place—a star I never saw before!
And a man has come with a woman, riding beasts
I never saw before, with funny humps
Upon their backs, and loose and slavering lips.

DON JUAN
Why, what damned farrago's this?

INNKEEPER [*to guests*].
Tadeo, my stable-boy's a poor half-wit,
And he is always seeing visions—so don't mind him.

TADEO.
There is an old man in poor peasant clothes;
And by him rides a beautiful young woman
Who looks as if she bore an unborn child—

INNKEEPER [*to Tadeo*].
Come, that's enough, my boy—you've talked enough.
Now hold your tongue and go into the kitchen.

TADEO [*as he goes*].
I put their strange, humped donkeys in the stable.
[*The mendicant Friar has come in with Tadeo's entrance and stands earnestly listening to what the latter has said. The door opens, and, framed in the night, stands a tall, erect old peasant, one possessed of a natural dignity that bespeaks self-respect and worth.*]

OLD PEASANT.
Have you room in the inn to-night for me
And for my wife—and child that's yet unborn?
We have come a long way. . . . We are weary.

INNKEEPER [*insolently, not liking the composure of the old man*].
There is no room in the inn for you or yours.

OLD PEASANT.
It is a cold night, and my wife is ill.

DON JUAN [*to Innkeeper, impulsively*].
Why, let the old man have my room
to-night.
[*To Doña Esmeralda.*]
We can post on unto another inn I
know of.

INNKEEPER.
What? Quarter a dirty peasant in a
tapestried room?

DON JUAN.
But his wife?

INNKEEPER.
You don't know these peasant women,
They're tough as cattle. . . . Old man,
You seem a stranger in this neighbor-
hood.

OLD PEASANT.
I am a stranger and a pilgrim.
My wife and I—

INNKEEPER [*brusquely*].
We have no time
For a long tale. What is your name?

OLD PEASANT.
Joseph they called me, where I lived
before.
[*The Friar crosses himself and
prays.*]

INNKEEPER.
Then, master Joseph, the only place I
have for you
Is the stable. . . . The mangers are
stuffed with hay
And warm. Take your wife there, and
close the door.

OLD PEASANT [*blessing them*].
The peace of God be on you all to-
night.
May God erase all evil from your
hearts
This holy time!
[*He goes.*]

DON JUAN.
He gave a benediction like a saint!

INNKEEPER [*a little smitten at heart,
calling out*].
Tadeo, follow that old man to the
stables;
Bring something to eat to him and his
wife.
Throw down some hay to make their
manger warm. . . .
I am not altogether a heartless man,
But gold is gold, as we must know, or
perish.
[*A curious hush falls over the group,
which is broken in a moment by
the wine passing around again.
Tadeo returns.*]

DON JUAN [*to Tadeo*].
Here, boy . . . here's a gold piece for
you. Is it cold?
Is it very cold out there where the old
man is?

TADEO.
It's perishing cold!

DON JUAN.
Take them this flagon of wine
To gladden their hearts with.
[*Tadeo goes out again, but in a moment he rushes in, pale and frightened. He still holds the flagon in
his hand. The wine spills about.*]

INNKEEPER [*furiously*].
Now what's wrong, idiot?

TADEO.
I am afraid. . . .

DON JUAN.
Did you not give the old man the wine
I sent?

TADEO [*in terror*].
I dare not go in there—in the
stable. . . .
Not for all the gold the king has!

INNKEEPER.
I'll flog you till you do, you moon-
struck fool!

DON JUAN [*staying the Innkeeper's arm*].
No, let him speak. What did you see
there, Tadeo?

TADEO.
The stable is all full of a bright flame
That does not burn, and all the cattle
kneel,
The oxen, and the asses.

ESMERALDA.
The lad's been reading story-books.

INNKEEPER.
He doesn't know one letter from
another.

DON JUAN.
It is an old folk-tale that, Christmas
eves,
At the midnight hour, all the cattle
kneel
In every stable in all Christendom
In poor brute honor to the birth of
Christ!
[*Singing is heard far off.*]

ESMERALDA [*crossing herself*].
Why, Heaven bless us,
We've half forgotten that it's Christ-
mas eve!
What else did you see there, lad?

TADEO.
I saw three old men
Kneeling beside a manger in which lay

A woman and a baby newly born;
And from them came the flame, the
   great, still flame,
That shone into my eyes and frightened
   me.

INNKEEPER [*snatching a lantern*].
Here—I'll go out and look into this
   thing.
   [*Just as he reaches the door, another
   knock is heard. The Innkeeper
   steps back, overcome by supersti-
   tious fear. A Christmas carol is
   heard.*]

DON JUAN.
What fools you all are, to let a poor
   lad's tale
Frighten you so! [*Jumping up, he
   flings open the door.*]
See, there was nothing at it but the
   wind!

RODERICK [*trembling*].
But we heard a knock. It was plain
   as speaking.
   [*Another knock.*]
There it is again!
   [*A third knock. that makes all the
   room shake, and seems to be at the
   door. Don Juan flings open the
   door again. A great gust of wind,
   riding white with snow, bursts in.*]

DON JUAN [*impressed, in spite of himself*].
It was a knock—and yet there's no
   one there!

PAQUITA [*breaking down and crying*].
Now God forgive me for my sins!

SIGISMUND [*bolstering up his courage*].
This is the strangest folly that I've
   ever seen.
   [*To Innkeeper.*]
Give me the lantern, craven; I'll go
   and see!
   [*There ensues a long pause after
   Sigismund has gone. Suddenly a
   motion as of a caravan is heard
   without. Bells like camel bells are
   heard tinkling. The tinkling and
   the soft, padded tread die off as*

*in the distance. Three great
knocks are heard. By this time
everybody from rich man to courtesan is grouped in huddled fear.
When the door bursts open of itself, letting in the snow again, no
one dares go to shut it. Presently
Sigismund staggers in.*]

SIGISMUND [*trying to pull a bold front*].
There is no light out there. It's dark
   and cold.
The animals and men are all asleep.

INNKEEPER.
But the stall—the stall where the old
   man slept—
This old man, Joseph, and his wife?

SIGISMUND.
I saw no old man with his wife. . . .

INNKEEPER.
You must have passed them by,
   then.
We heard the tread of beasts, as they
   departed.

SIGISMUND.
If they had been there, they could not
   have passed me by.

FRIAR [*coming forward*].
Oh, what a strange and evil world is
   this!
Blind are they, and they will not see
   —and, deaf,
They will not hear. . . .
           This was a miracle. . . .
Down on your knees and pray the
   merciful God
To cleanse the evil bursting in your
   hearts,
Thieves, murderers, and adulterers
   that you are!
Down on your knees!
   [*As if drawn by an invisible force,
   all the group fall on their knees.
   The Friar's lips move in prayer.*]

DON JUAN [*trying to overcome his genuine feeling*].
My knees bend, even if my mind says
   "no"!

        [*Curtain.*]

THE THRESHOLD
A Play
By Clarice Vallette McCauley

CHARACTERS

ELEANOR [*Mrs. Wadsworth's granddaughter*].
JAMES [*an old family servant*].
DOCTOR MARTIN [*the family physician*].
MRS. WADSWORTH [*Granny, and, the "Girl She Might Have Been"*].

TIME: *The Present.*

THE THRESHOLD

A Play   By Clarice Vallette McCauley

[PLACE: *The living room of the Wadsworth home. In the back wall, two French windows with a glimpse of the snow-covered garden beyond. In the left wall, one door at rear leading into reception hall; further down an open doorway (hung with drapery) into music room. In the right wall, opposite the hall door, another doorway hung with portieres. Below it is a fireplace. Between the doorway and fireplace stands a tall four-paneled screen, so set as to partly shut off the entrance from view. (Note: this room being much used by an invalid is provided with a screen to close off the draft from the open doorway. The placing of the screen is most important to the business.) At the right, set diagonally, a sofa. Near the fireplace (upper end) a small chair; at the lower end a low seat or stool. At the left, an armchair and small table. Between the door into hall and left window, a chair. The windows are hung with long draperies; the hour is that during sunset of a wintry day.*

When the curtain rises Eleanor is standing by the window, her back to the hall door, just slipping out of her coat and furs. She is a tall athletic looking girl who suggests the outdoors, but just at present she is rather pale and she starts nervously as James enters from the hall, carrying a plate with several letters on it.]

JAMES. Beg pardon, Miss Eleanor. I didn't know you'd got in. I'm sure sorry I startled you.

ELEANOR [*coming down and throwing coat on end of sofa*]. It's quite all right, James. I'm sorry to be so jumpy. Where's Granny?

JAMES [*putting tray of letters on table at rear*]. Mrs. Wadsworth's dozin' a bit, Miss, on de sleepin' porch.

ELEANOR. Sure she's done up well? It's cold to-day.

JAMES. Yes, Miss. I saw to it she had plenty of covers. 'Sides she gits de aft'rnoon sun—nice an' warm there now.

ELEANOR [*absent-mindedly examining the letters on the tray—yet suggesting that she would scarcely see one addressed to her if it were there*]. Mother go out?

JAMES. Yes, Miss. Your mother and Miss Car'line went out about an hour ago—said they wouldn't be back for dinner.

ELEANOR. I see. Well, I'm expecting the doctor any minute. When he comes will you show him in here, please. And you might take my coat and hat to my room.

JAMES. Yes, Miss. [*Near the screen he stops suddenly and says—half sheepishly and with a smile that at once establishes his utter devotion to Granny.*] Mebby I'd better go and see if Mrs. Wadsworth's all right and comfortable?

ELEANOR [*indulgently*]. Well—but don't disturb her, will you? And when she wakes—if she wants to come down stairs, come and let me know. I want to have a long talk with the doctor first, and I don't wish to be interrupted. [*Bell is heard ringing.*] There's the bell now. You'd better answer it, James. If it's any one else—I'm not at home.

JAMES [*leaving hat and coat on chair near door, and going into hall*]. Yes, Miss.

[*Left alone, Eleanor stands by the table; she doesn't move a muscle. At the sound of the Doctor's voice her strained expression relaxes a little.*]

DOCTOR [*heard outside*]. And how's James to-day?

JAMES. I'm feelin' right smart, sir.

DOCTOR. Miss Eleanor . . . .

JAMES. In the livin' room, sir.

317

DOCTOR [*entering*]. All right—I'll find her. B-r-r-r! It's cold to-day.

JAMES [*coming in after him, taking up coat and hat from chair, and crossing to door at right, through which he goes*]. Yes-sir! Yes-sir! It sure is.

[*The Doctor has entered bustlingly. He is a little man with silvery hair, a rosy face, and a child-like smile. He has left his coat and hat in the hall and is rubbing his hands briskly together as he goes straight to Eleanor.*]

DOCTOR. Well, here we are, Eleanor! I'm even better than my word—ten minutes ahead of time. What is it? Granny's heart again?

ELEANOR [*smiling apologetically—like a child ashamed of giving trouble*]. No; it's for me—this time.

DOCTOR. You? That's too bad. I thought you were looking a bit seedy. What seems to be the trouble, Eleanor?

ELEANOR. That's just what I don't know.

DOCTOR. Well, that's what we're going to make it our business to find out. Now then—

[*He goes to sofa and sits.*]

ELEANOR [*taking a light chair from near fireplace and placing it near him*]. You see—I hardly know how I'm ever going to make it clear to you.

DOCTOR. This sounds pretty serious. What have you been up to? Now, my dear, take your time; and remember only that I'm a pretty old man, and there isn't much in medicine that I haven't been up against at least once in my life.

ELEANOR [*sitting*]. It's not that sort of thing at all. I mean, it isn't medicine that I need. I seem to be well enough—was perfectly all right until this thing happened—and then—oh, I suppose it's just nerves.

DOCTOR. Hm—What are *you* doing with *nerves?* Not sleeping well?

ELEANOR. Hardly any—until four and five o'clock in the morning. But that's only because I think, and think, until—Doctor, how long have you known Granny?

DOCTOR. Granny? Let me see. . . . She first came to me as a patient the year before she adopted your father. What is he, now? about forty-five or six?

ELEANOR. Forty-six, last month. We celebrate the tenth—Granny never knew his birthday exactly. Was that before—or after her accident?

DOCTOR. Oh, after.

ELEANOR. Did she ever walk since you've known her?

DOCTOR. My, yes! For several years after the fractures were healed she got about with the aid of a cane. But it was always a great effort. I used to think that it was only her indomitable will that got her across the room at all. There was always considerable pain in her hip—and she never had a healthy spine—the two together did for her at last, though we managed to ward it off until your father and mother were in their teens. . . . Why do you ask all this, Eleanor?

ELEANOR. I'm going to tell you in a minute—but first . . . [*her voice trembles a bit and she controls her anxiety with an effort*] Doctor—I've never shown any signs of hysteria—or mental trouble of any kind, have I? [*As he stares at her in blank amazement, she repeats earnestly:*] Have I?

DOCTOR. Why, my dear girl! Quite the contrary—I've always thought till now. What nonsense is this? Now you come sit down here beside me—why, your hands are like ice! Now, let's have it! What's on your mind, Eleanor?

ELEANOR. I'll have to tell it my way—but you'll be patient, won't you? Two weeks ago last night I was left all alone in the house with Granny. That is—well, you know, we never count on the servants—one of the family always stays home with her—and it was my turn to stay. The others were going to the opera. I didn't *really* mind, only—well, it was "Butterfly" and of course I love it—and I suppose I was sort of mean—because I thought if my body did its duty and stayed home, it didn't much matter where my mind was. At any rate, as soon as the others were gone and Granny was settled for the night, I slipped down to the piano with the score. I was browsing through it, playing a bit here and there—oh, just touching the keys with the soft pedal on, when I felt that some one was coming down the stair. Sitting at the piano, you can see the whole stairway. I thought of course it was one of the maids, and looked up sort of casually—and there—at the head of the stairs—stood—

DOCTOR. Not your grandmother, Eleanor—surely!

ELEANOR. That's just it—I can't be *sure*—of anything.

DOCTOR. What do you mean?

ELEANOR. You remember I told you I was quite alone with Granny? Well—coming down the stairway—her hand on the rail—was a young girl.

DOCTOR. Your sister—back for something.

ELEANOR. Oh, no. Caroline is fair; this girl was dark—and very slight. She wore her hair in two funny little knobs over her ears—and two long curls over her shoulders. She had a little soft dress as pale as a moonbeam—and I could see the sheen on her slender ankles as she tripped down the stairs. . . . It was Granny.

DOCTOR. My dear girl!

ELEANOR. Oh, it was Granny! . . . Have you ever seen that daguerreotype of her that father has? No? Well, the dress was different—but the face and hair were the same. When she got to the foot of the stairs she looked straight at me—with her head tilted back, half-defiant, half-triumphant, and went on out the door.

DOCTOR. Out the door? The street door, you mean? Didn't you follow her?

ELEANOR. You see—she didn't open the door. She went *straight through it.* I was so dazed that perhaps it took me longer than I realized to get to the door and open it; but at any rate when I did there was no one in sight.

DOCTOR [*whose eyes have never left Eleanor's face*]. Certainly a very curious experience, Eleanor.

ELEANOR [*looking straight out with wide, distended eyes*]. There was a light snow on the steps—but there were no footprints.

DOCTOR [*quickly*]. Yet the others had passed that way . . . .

ELEANOR [*shaking her head, still in that dreamy, hypnotic tone*]. It hadn't started when they left—it had scarcely been snowing ten minutes—but there was *enough* to have shown *footprints.*

DOCTOR. My dear! [*There is a slight pause; then the Doctor reaches over and covers Eleanor's hand with his.*] Now, listen to me: you won't think I am making light of this, will you, because I'm far from doing that—but don't you think it's just possible that you were dreaming?

ELEANOR. No. I wasn't asleep. I could put my hands on the very chords I was playing when I heard the footsteps.

DOCTOR. But, Eleanor, you know as well as I do that all you have described could pass through the mind in just one moment's unconsciousness.

ELEANOR. I know—I know that. But you see, there's more to it.

DOCTOR. More? Oh! Well—go on.

ELEANOR. The moment I closed that door I knew that I must run straight up to Granny's room—although I didn't want to a bit—and was scared to death.

DOCTOR. Yes—of course! I can see that you *would* be.

ELEANOR. She was in one of those difficult faints of hers—you've seen her in them, and you know how alarming they are—and as it happened I was more alone than I had thought; for Susan had gone out and James was doing something to the furnace, and I didn't dare go for him, so I had to work over her by myself—and—[*She breaks down.*] Oh, I thought she wasn't coming out of it, at all!

DOCTOR. There — there — I know. Pretty rough on you, Eleanor, I must say. Small wonder you're unstrung.

ELEANOR. Oh, it isn't that—not the actual thing, I mean; it's what I can't understand that has unnerved me so. When she finally opened her eyes—she'd been moaning, you know, in that dreadful way people do—and she looked straight at me—just as the girl on the stairway did. You know that funny little short way she has of speaking—"Little minx!" she said—"I thought you had more sense. Too bad!" It was as though she was sorry—*to find herself still here.*

DOCTOR. Hm—and that was all?

ELEANOR. Yes—she's never referred to it. I can't tell what she remembers —or how much she's forgotten. But naturally, I can't forget it. I think of it all the time. Sometimes I almost see her—always laughing; and the other day when there couldn't be any one in Granny's room—I heard a young girl's voice—Oh, I'm afraid—

Doctor. What of, my child?

Eleanor. I don't know—it's so intangible—so uncanny—

Doctor. Eleanor, my dear—that's just the trouble. You can't fight a thing you can't put into words—that is, you can't fight it intelligently. Let's put it into words—and see how it looks. Come—you have plenty of courage—and a good brain. What do you make of it yourself?

Eleanor. Well, that's just it. Either it's an hallucination, in which case I suppose there is something wrong mentally with me, or—but that's the point, don't you see? If it's *not* an hallucination, and the fault is not in me, then what does it mean—about Granny? about *Life?*

Doctor. I don't know—but I can ease your mind of one thing, my child. If it's an hallucination—as you call it—there are two of us . . . *I've seen that girl, too!*

Eleanor. Doctor!

Doctor. Yes—just as you describe her; hair in two funny little knobs over her ears, and two soft curls over her shoulders—with mischievous, provoking eyes—and always dressed the same. She's stuck to one fashion pretty closely for the last forty years or so—as nearly as a mere man can judge.

Eleanor. You've been seeing her for the last forty years?

Doctor. About that; but until to-day—I've always thought—I had been dreaming.

Eleanor. But Doctor—is there any explanation—anything in science—

Doctor [*in deep thought*]. Pretty baffling, my dear—pretty baffling. [*Rousing himself, his manner becomes once more professional and reassuring.*] Of course, there are plenty of cases of dual personality, as you know—but they do not usually go about in dual bodies. [*He is treating it lightly for Eleanor's sake but his manner suggests that he is giving her only half his attention.*] Here we have a phenomenon that strains credulity to its uttermost—hm—and I'd always thought she was a dream.

Eleanor. What—what are you going to do?

Doctor. Nothing. What can we do? But I'm going to have a long talk with Granny—if she'll permit it.

Eleanor. You won't let her suspect? You know she's as sharp as a steel trap. She sees straight through you. I haven't dared say a word—for fear I'd say too much. And I've gotten the feeling somehow—that if she were surprised—if she were caught—out of herself, so to speak —there wouldn't be any more Granny.

Doctor. Yes—one does feel that way. Upon reflection, it wouldn't do to startle her—too dangerous—like waking a somnambulist. And then, as you say, she mightn't be able to—*get back.*

Eleanor. We all love her so! Mother and father couldn't adore her more if they were her own flesh and blood. [*There is a knock on the frame of the door right.*] Come in! [*James enters —just to the edge of the screen.*] Yes, James?

James. Mrs. Wadsworth's awake—and askin' for you.

Eleanor. Tell her I'll be right up. Will you come, Doctor?

James. Beg pardon, Miss Eleanor—she'd rather come down. She sure am a great ol' lady for her jokes—says she's 'fraid she ain't goin' to git her money's worth outen dat lift—lessen she uses it right smart often.

Eleanor [*laughing*]. The elevator father had put in—it's a great comfort to her. All right, James—I'll come with you. [*James goes out the way he came.*] You'll excuse me, Doctor? I'll be right back.

[*She follows James. Left alone, the Doctor walks thoughtfully up and down the room; comes mechanically to a halt at the window where he stands staring unseeingly at the setting sun. At the first sound of voices, however, he becomes alert—the professional man once more. He steps down to the armchair left, where he stands as though he had just risen. You hear voices before the speakers enter the room, Mrs. Wadsworth's being especially clear, with a high carrying quality that suggests mental aliveness.*]

Granny [*outside*]. I've been telling James, Eleanor, that he's getting exactly like an old hen—tiptoeing in and out all the time—

James [*chuckling*]. 'Deed I didn't,

Miss El'nor. I done just like you tole me—didn' disturb her noways.

[*The trio, though entering the room, are still unseen because of the position of the screen.*]

GRANNY. Oh, so! Eleanor encouraging you?—might have known it!

ELEANOR. Now, Granny.

[*The invalid chair is being rolled in —James behind it—Eleanor at right of it. The Doctor goes to meet them.*]

GRANNY. Squeaking in and out—in and out—Hello, Doctor! Glad you're here! I won't have it, James—mind! Get yourself a pair of sneakers if this is going to be a new fad of yours.

JAMES [*rolling chair carefully down to about center, his face a delightful mixture of solicitude and joy that the old lady is still able to scold*]. Yas'm, yas'm, Mrs. Wadsworth—I'll sure git 'em firs' thing in de mawnin'.

GRANNY. Hear that? Now—now— the chair will do very nicely right where it is—I tell you you fuss about just like an old hen. Go 'long with you! *Scat!* James!

JAMES. Yas'm, yas'm, Mrs. Wadsworth.

[*He goes out into hall, his face a broad grin. The Doctor and Eleanor look after him smiling. Granny is laughing. Sitting there in her invalid chair she seems intensely alive, although you are gradually aware that she never makes any movement of the lower part of her body, which is entirely concealed with soft blankets and afghans. She wears a loose silk robe with much fine lace at the throat and wrists, from which her delicate face stands out like a cameo. A cap of lavender and lace almost covers her hair, which she wears after the fashion of fifty years ago, parted in the middle with three little gray curls over each ear. She is slight—and oh, so frail—her head not nearly reaching the top of the chair— yet when she fixes you with her bright eyes you get the feeling of a tremendous personality. In her talk she has a way of clipping the personal pronoun out—as though she felt that life was short and*] there was still much to say—and breath mustn't be wasted in saying "I."]

GRANNY [*with a quick, birdlike jerk of her head backwards, indicating James*]. Isn't he a treat? They don't grow them like that any more. Wouldn't lose him for anything on the place! Couldn't fancy life without James to rag at. . . . Well? Been ordering a tonic for this girl, Doctor? Lord knows she needs it . . . nervous as a witch! . . . doesn't eat—doesn't sleep—

ELEANOR. Why, Granny! What can you know about my sleeping—you little fraud!

GRANNY. Notice how nicely she did that, Doctor? Not *old* fraud, you know, but just *little* fraud. There, run along, Eleanor, and get my smelling salts—will you?—on the porch, or in my room—just look, there's a dear.

ELEANOR. Why surely, Granny—I'll find them.

[*Goes off—right.*]

DOCTOR. Heart bad again, Mrs. Wadsworth?

GRANNY. No—no—nothing the matter with me, Doctor. Just a ruse—salts are in my bag. But there *is* something the matter with that child—and I know it. Never saw her quite so peaked before. Was going to have you called in myself to-day, only I found out she was doing it—thought I'd better not interfere. What's the matter with her? Worrying over me?

DOCTOR. What makes you think that, Mrs. Wadsworth?

GRANNY. Gave her a bad shock a couple of weeks ago—one of my heart attacks—must have been an unusually severe one—believe she thought I was going to die—she was looking like a ghost when I came to.

DOCTOR. There was—nothing else— that might have frightened her?

GRANNY. What else could there have been? Like to know what more was needed! Inexperienced girl—all alone with an old woman in a dead faint—expecting her to die on her hands any minute. What more would you want to scare the child out of a year's growth?

DOCTOR. Pretty bad—yes. Has your heart been worse than usual?

GRANNY. Can't say that it has. While I think of it, though, you might leave me some digitalis—almost out of it—can't afford to take any chances. Why, I'm just as chipper as I ever was—not a thing the matter with me—if only the children wouldn't fidget about me so! Eleanor's the worst—she and James. James is getting to be a regular old fool! Would you believe it? He actually came on that porch three times this afternoon, while I was dozing. Interrupts things so!

DOCTOR. Well, now—you oughtn't to complain of that. It isn't every one can command such devotion. Wanted to see if you were covered up, I suppose.

GRANNY. Nothing of the sort! You see, I've got a bad habit; hate to admit it—but I talk in my sleep. So they say —at least—doubt it myself, but I suppose I've got to take their word for it, though I notice they never can tell me what I say.

DOCTOR. Might be a symptom—rather important. Why have you never told me before? Have you—done it long?

GRANNY. How should I know? They say so, anyway—and it's true I've always dreamed a great deal. You see, I was such a lonely child—you knew I was an orphan, didn't you? Yes, of course, though I don't often speak of it before the children. I used to put myself to sleep with fairy tales about the wonderful home I had—and the adoring parents. I pretended that I was a great beauty—with wonderful talents. She was very real to me—that girl, but now that I think of it I don't believe that I ever *dreamed* of her until after I was married. Curious thing, that! After I had killed her—quite, quite dead, by marrying, you know—she began to come to me in my dreams; at first she only came to me when I was particularly heartbroken about something or other. I believe sometimes I actually relished being miserable all day—because I knew it would bring her at night. No wonder they say that women like to be unhappy.

DOCTOR. And did it?

GRANNY. Did it what?

DOCTOR. Bring her to you at night?

GRANNY. Always! She never deserted me but once. That was right after the accident. I think I must have frightened her away. I was so rebellious—so bitter —my nights were black pits of horror— and then I was always more or less un-

der drugs, you know—and when I wasn't, the pain—not only the physical—but the mental anguish of knowing that I had lost my baby in such a wicked, unnecessary way . . . .

DOCTOR. It was all pretty black, wasn't it?

GRANNY. Horrible! and never a tender memory left to sweeten the pain. Oh, don't let's talk about it! I thought she was dead, that girl, but she got back to me someway—I think you must have helped her. Oh, yes you did! That was the time I changed doctors. And then —I got the idea of adopting a little orphan kiddie as lonely as I had been. First John, then Carrie, wasn't she the darling baby?—so that John wouldn't be lonely. By that time I was pretty well confined to my bed—or my chair—my husband was dead—

[*Enter Eleanor with smelling salts —and a small daguerreotype case which she holds behind her back.*]

ELEANOR. Granny, I couldn't find yours so I brought mine—and something else. Look! Do you mind my showing it to the Doctor? I was telling him about it to-day.

GRANNY [*taking the daguerreotype from her hand*]. That? Why, wherever did you come across that?

ELEANOR. Why, it's father's—don't you remember? You gave it to him his first year at boarding school.

GRANNY. My—my—my! So I did!— and he's kept it ever since, eh? But that's not me!

ELEANOR. Why, Granny!

GRANNY [*returning case to Eleanor*]. No! That's the girl I might have been. [*As she tosses this phrase off lightly, casually, both Eleanor and the Doctor show that they have caught a glimmer of a clew which they would like to follow, but can't.*]

ELEANOR [*recovering first*]. Oh, Granny! That's just your funny way of talking. She must have been a darling girl, and I'm sure you looked just like her.

GRANNY. No, my dear—I was never like that in my life, but for one short evening—and an hour in the afternoon when I tried on the dress and was photographed. Show it to the Doctor.

[*Eleanor does so, her eyes questioning him.*] Would you know it, Doctor?

DOCTOR. I should know her anywhere. What an odd way of dressing the hair.

GRANNY. Like it?

DOCTOR. Adorable!

[*He crosses to the armchair, in which he sits, turning it slightly so that he faces Granny.*]

GRANNY. My own invention. . . . You see it was a play. I—little orphan Nellie—was taking part in a play! It was a great occasion—for besides that it was the school anniversary, it was being made particularly festive in my honor—and I—why, I was looking forward to finding what the world was like, with all the glamor of an engagement to a man whom I scarcely knew at all—and was therefore quite willing to believe a little tin god on wheels. Oh, it was a memorable night! Too memorable, as you can see, to bear repeating.

ELEANOR [*who, during the foregoing speech has brought a stool beside her grandmother's chair, and is now fondling her hand*]. What happened? What happened to you, Granny dear?

GRANNY. Oh, I was a success! too much of a one, perhaps. I must have thrown my smiles in all directions—and every one smiled back—just as you smile at a puppy when it wags its tail—that was all! But that would never do. Next day, the dress was laid away; for the god had spoken—"and all smiles stopped together."

ELEANOR. Oh, Granny! Grandfather?

GRANNY. Yes, my dear. Your grandfather was a very righteous and God-fearing man—one of the trustees of the orphan asylum—also he was fifty—and a little deaf.

ELEANOR. Oh, Granny!

GRANNY. Tut, tut, my dear! I knew I shouldn't be speaking of it. But you mustn't waste your sympathies on her—she was a wilful little chit, that girl.

ELEANOR. You could never have been that.

GRANNY. I had to be! Why, think a minute; how else could I have kept her alive with everything against her? I was like Aurora Leigh—of course, you don't know your "Aurora Leigh"—I'm sure I don't know what this generation is coming to; but you know it, Doctor, I'll be bound—how she stared at her reflection, "greatening before her in the looking glass, and said: 'The dogs are on us—*but we will not die!*'"

DOCTOR. You have a wonderful memory, Mrs. Wadsworth. No wonder one never thinks of you as growing old.

GRANNY. Old! I'm not old. I'm centuries younger than this child here. Presently you'll be saying like that young fop of Caroline's—

DOCTOR [*to Eleanor*]. What! Another beau?

GRANNY. —who wanted to say something very gallant—what was it, Eleanor?

ELEANOR. When he was introduced to Granny he said very elegantly: "Madame reminds me of some fragile, little, old Marquise—"

GRANNY. "Marquise?" said I—"well, maybe; *little*, I admit; *fragile*, I deplore; but *old! Merci bien! Je n'en vois pas l'occasion!*"

[*She bursts into a mischievous peal of laughter in which Eleanor joins.*]

ELEANOR. You should have seen him, Doctor. He was so embarrassed. Granny you *are* naughty.

GRANNY. 'Course I am. That's how I've kept out of heaven all this while. I have a feeling that the gates of the Beyond will never open except to the girl I was meant to be, when Granny's too tired to keep her alive.

ELEANOR. Granny! Now what do you mean by that exceedingly cryptic remark?

GRANNY. I'm sure I don't know, Puss. It just popped into my head—and said itself. You don't understand such impulses, Eleanor—because you're too old, but the Doctor here does—don't you?

DOCTOR. I think I'm beginning to understand a great many things that have puzzled me for years.

GRANNY. Another oracle, Eleanor! There's a pair of us. You see, my dear, I've been telling the doctor about this unfortunate habit of mine—

ELEANOR. Habit, Granny?

GRANNY. Yes. I really can't have you and Caroline taking turns at prowling into my rooms at all hours of the night, just because— [*she smiles*] I have pleasant dreams . . . .

ELEANOR. *Are* they pleasant dreams, Granny?

GRANNY. Oh, my dear! Such pleasant dreams. For in my dreams I am always young—and beloved—

ELEANOR. You're always *that*, Granny.

GRANNY. You darling! But then, you see, I can do all the things that I've never been able to encompass in all my life. I can swim, I can ride, I can dance, and I do all these things better and better the older I grow. Oh, that was the point! [*To the Doctor.*] That's what I started to talk to you about—don't you remember? I was telling the doctor, Eleanor, about this girl I dream of so much—how, at first she only came to me at rare intervals; but now—why bless you! I've only to close my eyes for five minutes, and cat-nap as I do a dozen times a day—and there she is. [*The Doctor and Eleanor exchange glances.*] Now, can you explain why that should be?

DOCTOR. I think I can.

GRANNY. Then for goodness' sake, let's have it. Only, no long medical terms; I can't abide them.

DOCTOR. I will use only one—and it's an easy one. Let's see what Eleanor here understands by the word "threshold."

ELEANOR. A threshold? Why—it's the—space between two rooms—or rather the entrance into a room—how should I say it?—the sill of a door, is that better? Isn't it funny how hard it is to define familiar words?

DOCTOR. The sill of a door—that will do for our purpose. . . . Well, you see, there is, at the entrance to the brain, what we in medicine call "the threshold" —in other words, the sill across which an idea or emotion must pass before it is translated into action. And as you will find the stone steps in any old cathedral worn away by the passing of many feet, so the constant passage of an idea wears away the threshold of the soul—making it increasingly easy for the emotion to step over, as it were.

GRANNY. That's a big thought, Doctor—a mighty big thought. You mean, then, that if you were to dally continuously with the thought of *theft*, let us say—

DOCTOR. It would presently become inevitable that you would have the *soul* of a thief—and extremely possible that the idea allowed to pass continuously over the threshold should presently be translated into action. Risky business— as you can see—this lowering of the threshold of the mind to anything but the noblest and best.

ELEANOR [*after a pause*]. You make me shiver, Doctor.

GRANNY [*who has been sitting absorbed in deepest thought, suddenly shakes herself free with a defiant little laugh*]. Well—you don't make *me* shiver —not a bit of it! Quite the contrary! I've always dreaded second childhood— now I'm going to look forward to it. So, if you see your Granny playing with a rattle some day, Eleanor, you'll know I'm only getting ready to be born again, and I hope to goodness that I'll make a better job of it than I did the last time!

ELEANOR. Granny! You irreverent little wretch!

GRANNY. Not *t* all! Irreverence never was further from my thoughts. Why, look at me! My soul's as young as yours, Eleanor—and my spirit could outreason both of you—yet poor old Granny's so tired, so tired. . . .

ELEANOR. We've talked you to death, Granny dear.

GRANNY. And made me miss most of the sunset!

ELEANOR. That's right! And Granny never likes to talk while the sun is setting. If you'll help me with her chair . . . .

[*This last to the Doctor.*]

GRANNY. It's too wonderful to spoil with idle chatter—though I can always stand [*she pats Eleanor's cheek fondly*] a little music at that time. [*They turn the chair and wheel it to back of room so that it stands diagonally facing the right-hand French window. Eleanor reaches for the screen.*] That's a dear child. Oh, you needn't mind the screen.

ELEANOR. Don't you want it, Granny? I thought maybe you might nap a few minutes.

GRANNY. Well—all right. Then you and the doctor can go right on talking —you won't disturb me one bit.

[*She gives her left hand to Eleanor, who raises it lovingly to her cheek.*]

DOCTOR. Don't you want your medicine first, Mrs. Wadsworth? it must be time.

GRANNY. No, darn your medicine! [*She offers her right hand apologetically* to the Doctor, and for a moment they stand so—the frail hands clasped on either side by the two who bend solicitously over her.] Just let—me rest—a bit.

[*The Doctor leaves her, going down to the left. Eleanor, however, stops for a moment to adjust a cover—to stop a second back of the chair, stooping over it—and to give the final little casual pull to the end of the screen—causing it to just overlap the chair, though it does not hide it; then she joins the Doctor.*]

ELEANOR. Doctor, I wish you'd do us a favor— [*Then in a quick undertone.*] I can't help 'being anxious— [*aloud again*] stay and have dinner with us tonight. Can you?

DOCTOR. I can—and will, if— [*looking at his watch*] you'll let me get off by eight. I was just thinking of inviting myself.

ELEANOR. That's dear of you. Just we three. Mother and Caroline are out —and father's likely to be detained. I think I'll tell Susan to have it a half hour earlier—better 'for Granny—and you won't be hurried. You'll excuse me, won't you?

DOCTOR. You know I'm quite at home here. Run right along.

[*Eleanor goes out lower door—left. The Doctor turns the armchair slightly, so that he, too, can see the sunset.*]

GRANNY [*after a pause*]. Doctor?

DOCTOR. Yes?

GRANNY. Eleanor gone?

DOCTOR. Just to speak to Susan, Mrs. Wadsworth. Do you want anything?

GRANNY [*sleepily*]. You *will*—give her—a tonic, won't you? She's looking so pale.

DOCTOR. Don't worry. I'll fix her up for you.

GRANNY. That's right. What would we do without you? [*From the room—left, comes the sound of a piano being played very softly. The music is from "Madame Butterfly."*] Ah! She's going to give us some music. Such a dear child!

DOCTOR. Very lovely. I think they must have endowed her with all your charm—when they named her after you.

GRANNY. Oh, no! She's much lovelier than ever I was. Besides, no one ever called *me* Eleanor—I used to wish they would—I was always—*just Nellie*—at the orphan asylum . . . .

[*A soft, sleepy sigh—then silence. The music plays on, very softly. The sunset glow deepens in the sky —darkness encroaches upon the room. The Doctor's body relaxes —his head is thrown back—his hands loosely gripping the arms of the chair. Once his head nods— there is no sound from Granny. Suddenly the Doctor's head and shoulders express a certain attention—as though to something outside himself. When he speaks his voice has a quality unlike his own —as of a man in a trance.*]

DOCTOR. You're in the room—you've come back—I can *feel* you. [*Pause.*] Why—don't you come to me?

A VOICE [*it is a voice as sweet as a silver bell—with a girl's shy laugh in it —yet on "horrid drugs" there is a sudden sharp reminder of "Granny."*] I can't —quite. It's your fault, I think. You've been doing your best to keep me away with your horrid drugs. Perhaps—if you called me by name—

DOCTOR. Nellie!

THE VOICE. Again!

DOCTOR. Nellie!

[*Facing the invalid chair, her head and shoulders aureoled in the rays of the setting sun, stands a young girl. As yet you get only her head and shoulders, because the chair screens her body.*]

NELLIE. You never knew me before! You're coming on, Benjamin!

DOCTOR. Nellie!

NELLIE. Such a quaint old-fashioned name—Benjamin. I suppose if I'd ever married you, I should have called you "Bennie." So preposterous for a famous doctor! [*With a low, mischievous laugh.*]. Oh, yes—I should have called you Bennie—I'm sure of it—even before company.

DOCTOR. Nellie—can't you come a little closer?

[*She steps down towards his chair— he does not move.*]

NELLIE. You would never let me come close before—you wouldn't believe in me.

You called me—"a dream." We might have been one all these years—if you hadn't been so stupid, Bennie.

DOCTOR [*still speaking in a hypnotic tone—with all emotions veiled*]. I didn't know—it was—YOU!

NELLIE. No—of course, you didn't. You couldn't be expected to recognize the "Girl-I-Might-Have-Been" in that poor wreck of bruised flesh and broken bones on a hospital bed. But she always knew you, Bennie—right from the first.

DOCTOR. Why—why didn't you tell me?

NELLIE. There wasn't anything to tell, my friend. Do you suppose I would have let you sadden your young life with the poor helpless wreck of me? I couldn't. You know, Bennie, when one really loves—it's like a title of nobility —and *noblesse oblige, mon ami.*

DOCTOR. But afterwards—didn't you ever see how lonely I was?

NELLIE. I tried to help. Think of all the pretty girls I used to have at the house—you wouldn't look at any of them.

DOCTOR. I was waiting for the girl that used to haunt my dreams.

NELLIE. And all the time she was right under your hand, my poor Bennie. But you weren't unhappy—were you? You were busy—useful—

DOCTOR. It was of you—I was thinking.

NELLIE. Of me? Oh, bless you, there never was a happier life than mine. The inner life is so much more real than anything that can happen in the flesh. Think of it! I have lived in this one frail shell all the wonderful girls of Shakespeare: Rosalind—Juliet—Miranda! I sang with Pippa one night or queened it with Colombe the next; and when I tired of them I tripped down a decade—or back a century—to browse in pastures new. I'm all the girls that ever yearned for love—or thrilled with fear at its approach; I'm all the girls that ever peeped at joy vicariously through the eyes of others happier than themselves. I am the girl that lies unborn in every youth's desire—that sleeps in every woman's heart—the Girl She Might Have Been!

DOCTOR. Why did you never speak before?

NELLIE. I couldn't—*before.* It isn't every day that one goes out like this— into the sunset.

DOCTOR. You're going?—you mean . . . .

NELLIE. Yes. Granny and the girl she might have been are going out into the sunset together. And you mustn't feel sad—above all, you mustn't cry. I shall wait for you—you won't be long, dear!

DOCTOR. Wait—wait for me—now!

NELLIE. I can't wait! I've gone over the threshold for the last time. Oh, don't—don't bring me back! I mightn't have the strength to cross again. Goodby, Benjamin . . . . Don't be long . . . .

[*She stands limned against the window, from which all light has now faded but the weird greenish afterglow that sometimes follows a winter sunset. Then, with a backward wave of the hand she appears to go straight through the window.*]

DOCTOR. Nellie—wait! Oh, Eleanor —my love!—Eleanor!

[*The music in the adjoining room stops with a sudden crash, and Eleanor comes in breathless.*]

ELEANOR. What is it, Doctor? You called me? Doctor! Doctor!

[*She leans over him—her hands on his shoulders—her face terrified. He is as though coming out of an hypnotic trance.*]

DOCTOR. Yes—yes—Eleanor. I'm—all right.

[*James enters from the hall. He has the appearance of having come on a sudden call, yet now that he is here stands mystified and abashed.*]

ELEANOR. James! What is it?

JAMES. Why—nothing, Miss. Just happened to think you might be . . . needing me, that's all. Shall I light up —now I'm here?

ELEANOR [*who can scarcely speak*]. Just the table lamp, please.

[*James switches on the table lamp between the windows, and tiptoes toward the window—right. He apparently sees nothing wrong with Granny's chair—though he gives it a passing glance as though to assure himself that all is well with her.*]

DOCTOR [*as James touches curtain*]. Don't touch that! Oh, yes, it's all right, but never mind the curtain, James. Is the window latched?

JAMES [*examining it*]. Yes, sir.

DOCTOR. That will do, then.

JAMES. Yes, sir.

[*Exits into hall.*]

DOCTOR. Now, Eleanor . . . .

[*He holds out his hand to her.*]

ELEANOR. Granny? She—she's—

DOCTOR. We will go and see—together.

[*Hand in hand they walk softly to Granny's chair. As the Doctor bends over the right side of it— raising one delicate white hand and pushing back the laces from the wrist to feel the pulse, Eleanor has with one movement folded back a section of the screen, and kneeling beside Granny looks into her face. Then, very tenderly, she takes her left hand and presses her lips to it with a little sob.*]

ELEANOR. Oh, Granny. . . .

DOCTOR. Don't weep for her, my dear . . .

ELEANOR. She's—dead?

DOCTOR. We won't think of it that way, Eleanor. She wouldn't want us to think of it that way. "The-Girl-She-Might-Have-Been" has only gone over the threshold—for the last time.

ELEANOR [*very softly—choking down her sobs*]. Oh, Granny! Granny dear!

[*Eleanor's eyes are fixed upon her grandmother's face, but the Doctor—although he holds her hand —stands looking out into the twilight—as*

The Curtain Falls.]

[NOTE: *Provided the actress who plays Granny has the gift of characterization, the technical problem of her change into the Girl does not present as many difficulties as might appear at a casual reading.*

In the first place she is, of course, completely underdressed. In place of a wig, the soft little fringe of white curls which show beneath her lacy cap may be attached to the edge of it so that one movement uncovers the hair. She should depend upon characterization, posture and the general pallor of old age, rather than on many lines, to get her effect.

To gain more time for the change—and also for another reason—Granny should leave the chair immediately after the line: "Just let me—rest a bit." Aside from the time gained the reason is this: from the moment the chair is left in position up by the window the audience will watch it, expecting something to happen. Any movement—and it is physically impossible to get out of a wheel chair without some movement—will, of course, destroy the illusion. Therefore, as Eleanor and the Doctor release Granny's hands they should be in such a position over the chair that they screen it on both sides, and it is while they are thus holding it steady that Granny slips from it to the shelter of the screen. Even then Eleanor lingers to tuck in the disarranged afghan and to pull the edge of the screen a little closer to the chair. She may take all the time she wishes to focus our thoughts upon the comfort of the person in the chair, for the play gains at this moment by a slowing up of the whole tempo.

This business is also a good place to begin the gradual dimming of the light in the room, but the Girl will profit by being played in a sort of rosy glow which may be gotten partly from the sunset through the window, reënforced by a fire on the hearth down right—which burns up more brightly as the room goes into shadow. The Girl should remain pretty well up stage and she should not come too near the doctor's chair—to play the scene down stage is to destroy the illusion.

The final disappearance is, of course, the producer's chief problem, for the window effect as described would require depth not often found on small stages; but by a rapid dimming of the back lighting from the time she goes to the window, she may be made to seem to fade out behind the chair and screen—which is almost as effective and not half so hard.

One thing more: it requires self-control on the part of the actress, but Granny should not attempt to reënter the chair until the Doctor and Eleanor are once more in position beside it, holding it and effectually concealing all movement— while they seem only to hesitate lest they disturb her peace.]

THE AVENUE
A Play

By Fenimore Merrill

CHARACTERS

THE BLONDE.
THE BRUNETTE.
THE TITIAN.
PAT.
MADAME GRADY.
ROSY.
LILY.
MRS. FITCH.
VAN VLIET.
BARLOW.
ELSIE PRICE.
MR. FITCH.

THE AVENUE was originally produced by The Washington Square Players, at the Comedy Theatre, New York, October 31, 1917.

THE AVENUE

A PLAY   By FENIMORE MERRILL

[*On Fifth Avenue, near the Cathedral,
is seen the brilliant show window of a
modiste's establishment with a broad
sidewalk running in front of it. At one
side is the shop door; at the other a
shadowy niche where two people might
stand unnoticed. All about is darkness.
It is six o'clock on a winter evening.
Over the show window is Madame
Grady's name in large letters. Behind
the glass are posed stiffly three gor-
geously clad wax figures—a blonde, a
titian, and a brunette. On a small stand
lies a magnificent sable wrap. Pat, a
red-cheeked boy in a smart uniform,
stands in position by the door. Motor
horns sound faintly, in the next street.
Madame Grady, a tightly corseted figure in black silk, parts the hangings at
the back of the show window and scans
the wax figures. She turns to call back
into the shop.*]

MADAME GRADY. Rosy! I want you
and Lily to come here and change these
forms, before you go. And get a move
on!

[*After a moment, Rosy and Lily,
two girls in black dresses, enter
the show window.*]

MADAME GRADY. It's after six. I
want to close up.

ROSY. Yes, Madame.

[*The two girls are at work on the
figures, rearranging draperies.*]

MADAME GRADY. Watch out how you
handle those forms—you'll break the
hands!

[*Mrs. Fitch enters, a portly figure
hurrying along, with the air of
one unused to walking. Pat opens
the door for her. She is greeted
by Madame Grady.*]

MRS. FITCH. O—!

MADAME GRADY. How do you do, Mrs.
Fitch!

MRS. FITCH. They made me leave my
car around the corner!

MADAME GRADY. What a shame!

MRS. FITCH. My gown—!

[*Pat closes the door, and the two
women disappear within. In the
show window, Rosy and Lily make
faces after them.*]

ROSY. Grouchy old pig!

LILY. An' the way she buffaloes that
poor old Mrs. Fitch!

ROSY. Keeps us every blooming night
after six, an' do you think she'll pay
extra—!

LILY. Can you beat it!

[*Rosy admiringly fingers the sable
wrap.*]

ROSY. Simple little trifle, what?

LILY. Ain't that the most gorgeous
fur!

ROSY. Lily Ryan, mark my words:
if I ever get a chance to sport anything
like that, I'm goin' t' grab it!

LILY. Well, some girls certainly has
a great time!

ROSY. Dance all night, sleep all morning, buy clothes all afternoon!

LILY. An' never hear an alarm-clock
in their lives.

ROSY [*striking an attitude*]. As fer
the subway! My deah, I nevah go neah
it; the air is *so* terrible!

LILY. Funny, ain't it? Us two run
around all day like a couple of mice in
a fish-globe—an' them plutes with not a
thing t' do till tomorra!

ROSY. If I had five hundred dollars—!

LILY. Ha—ha—hahaha!

ROSY. You can laugh! I'd buy a chic
outfit an' have one time!

LILY. Oh yes—an' jump off the bridge
in the morning!

[*Rosy catches sight of something in
the street outside and softly whistles.*]

ROSY. Shh!

LILY. What's the matter?

ROSY. Don't turn around!

LILY. Why not?

ROSY. Shut up!

[*The two girls affect to be very busy with the wax figures. Van Vliet and Barlow saunter in. Van Vliet is a good-looking, florid youth. Barlow's accent is faintly English.*]

VAN VLIET. Look who's here!

BARLOW. Rhine maidens!

[*They pause.*]

VAN VLIET. Let's fuss them!

BARLOW. You're so orthodox.

VAN VLIET. She's pretty.

BARLOW. Which one?

VAN VLIET. The little one. They both are!

BARLOW [*moving right*]. So they are. What of it?

VAN VLIET. Wait a minute, can't you!

BARLOW. Oh, break away!

VAN VLIET. Let's take them to dinner!

BARLOW. Good God, man—you might be from Oshkosh.

VAN VLIET. It's a great idea!

BARLOW. They'll chew gum for an appetizer, and finish off with toothpicks.

VAN VLIET. How'll I speak to them? [*Stepping to the window.*] Hi!

BARLOW. They won't go to dinner, you poor nut!

VAN VLIET. They look hungry.

BARLOW. It'll be perfectly dismal.

VAN VLIET. That little one likes me already—look at her blush!

BARLOW. We'll be seized for breach of promise or something.

VAN VLIET. Leave that to me!

BARLOW. Your inspirations always end the same way. Do come along!

[*Van Vliet takes out his notebook and pencil, and writes.*]

VAN VLIET. My inspirations always result in a good party.

BARLOW. You won't come?

VAN VLIET. Of course not.

BARLOW. Poor violet! Then I must stay and watch over you.

[*Van Vliet tears a leaf from the notebook, pokes Pat, and hands him a dollar.*]

VAN VLIET. Here, boy! Take this note to the young lady in the window; and do it quietly, see?

PAT. Yes, sir!

[*Pat furtively slips into the shop, throws the note into the window, and waits.*]

VAN VLIET. This is going to be good!

BARLOW. I detest cave men.

VAN VLIET. Signs of life!

BARLOW. My dear boy, you're over-supplied with the *joie de vivre*.

[*Rosy and Lily are reading the note, half afraid, but giggling. Van Vliet cheerfully pantomimes invitation to them, loudly whispering through the glass.*]

VAN VLIET. Food! Large time! We won't go home till morning!

BARLOW. And what do you propose to do if they accept?

VAN VLIET. Time enough to settle that after the frolic closes.

BARLOW. You sad wretch!

[*Rosy and Lily want to accept. Van Vliet grins at them, pointing to his watch.*]

VAN VLIET. What time? I say, what time?

[*The girls fearfully decide to say "Yes." Rosy speaks to Pat.*]

VAN VLIET. They're falling for it!

BARLOW. Serpent.

[*Pat comes out quickly, closing the door.*]

PAT. They can't get off right now, but they'll come later if you want.

BARLOW. Satan is foiled.

VAN VLIET. Foiled nothing.

BARLOW. Calm down; we'll go eat.

VAN VLIET. We'll go *drink*, and return later to take these fair creatures out on a binge! [*Nodding vigorously to the girls and pointing to his watch.*] We'll be back in half an hour!

[*Lily scents danger from inside the shop, and motions the boys away.*]

BARLOW [*amused*]. Wait—somebody's coming!

VAN VLIET. Come on, you poor icicle!

BARLOW. But I want to see the Madame bawl them out!

VAN VLIET. And spoil the party? You need a cocktail!

[*Van Vliet throws them kisses, and drags Barlow out. The girls in the show window clasp hands excitedly.*]

LILY. Oh—Rosy!

ROSY. Don't you "Oh Rosy" me!

Wasn't he good-looking? Us for that party!

LILY. Won't it be *fun!*

[*The girls fall to work. Mr. Fitch strolls along with Elsie Price. Massaged to a lobster pink, Mr. Fitch is crowded into snug clothes. Elsie Price is a stately vision. She pauses before the window.*]

ELSIE. Grady's! She's dressed three productions this season. Her things are lovely.

FITCH. I should hope so; they cost enough.

ELSIE. George, look at that sable!

FITCH. Luxury is the ruin of the American nation.

ELSIE. That's where I'm patriotic as the deuce. The sable is a love!

FITCH. Your love is too expensive. We've got to dine, or you'll be late for your performance.

ELSIE. George dear, you needn't fear. My understudy is quite too good-looking.

FITCH. Well, let's get away from this shop!

ELSIE. How can you! Grady's clothes are perfect.

FITCH. I ought to know: I've paid enough of her bills.

ELSIE [*laughing*]. Oh—does your wife go here?

FITCH [*gloomily*]. Yes.

ELSIE. George, I must have that sable!

FITCH. Nothing doing.

ELSIE. Yes, dear—it will be such a good joke!

FITCH. No, I tell you!

ELSIE. Now, George, you're going to be a good old sport and get me that fur, 'cause you love me and I love you and that sable isn't going to be any horrid old knife to cut our love in two.

FITCH. I can't afford it.

ELSIE. George, you know we've talked it all over. I've told you I think it's all right for you to charge the government all you can for your supplies. I'm sure Washington needs them enough! *But*— when you get off that can't afford it stuff, it doesn't go with *me.*

FITCH. That's all I'm good for—buy, buy, buy!

ELSIE. Whenever I wear it I'll think of you, dear—you and Mrs. Fitch.

FITCH. That'll do on Mrs. Fitch.

ELSIE. All right, darling; but you will get me the sable?

FITCH. You must think I'm the mint.

ELSIE. You are the mint in my julep!

FITCH [*plaintively*]. Elsie, I haven't got the money.

ELSIE. George Fitch, do you mean to stand there and tell me you're broke, when I know perfectly well you're making thousands of dollars a day over-charging the government for your silly old supplies! You ought to be ashamed!

FITCH. Elsie!

ELSIE. That's enough! I'm sorry I ever took any of your old presents.

FITCH. Now, Elsie—!

ELSIE. It isn't as though I were alone in the world. I have my friends!

FITCH. Oh, very well, go ahead!

ELSIE. Never mind!

FITCH. Order the furs in the morning. I'll mail you a check.

ELSIE. It doesn't matter. I don't mind freezing to death!

FITCH. I was only fooling, dear.

ELSIE. I don't care for your jokes.

FITCH. Won't you forgive me—?

ELSIE. I don't know. [*Glimpsing the sable.*] Maybe. I'll see.

FITCH. I didn't mean to be tight, Elsie.

ELSIE. I'll try to forget this, George.

[*The door is opened. Inside the shop, Madame Grady is bidding farewell to Mrs. Fitch.*]

MRS. FITCH'S VOICE. I am very much annoyed, Madame Grady, very—

MADAME GRADY'S VOICE. It's a disappointment to me, Mrs. Fitch. Your gown shall be delivered to-night, if I have to do it myself.

[*Panic-stricken, Fitch hustles Elsie to one side.*]

FITCH. My God—that's Mary!

ELSIE. You don't mean—?

FITCH. Yes. Get in there quick!

[*Fitch and Elsie make themselves small in the shadowed niche. Rosy, awestruck, watches everything; both girls pretend to be at work. Mrs. Fitch, like a ruffled hen, is followed soothingly by Madame Grady.*]

MRS. FITCH. If I hadn't ordered it in plenty of time there would be some excuse—

MADAME GRADY. There's a great deal

of fine hand work on that dress, Mrs. Fitch.

MRS. FITCH. Just send my car here—

MADAME GRADY. [to Pat]. Tell the chauffeur Mrs. Fitch is waiting.

[Pat runs out.]

MRS. FITCH. And I'm dining out! I shall be late—

MADAME GRADY. Darkness falls very early. It's not much after six.

MRS. FITCH. This cold is piercing—

MADAME GRADY. It's a shame you've been kept waiting, Mrs. Fitch.

MRS. FITCH. Personally, I don't mind your disappointing me, Madame Grady—

MADAME GRADY. I'm so sorry.

MRS. FITCH. It's my husband. Mr. Fitch always likes to see me in different things. For myself, I loathe clothes—

MADAME GRADY. But your taste is excellent!

MRS. FITCH. Still, I do insist on having things on time. There is no excuse for unpunctuality. I am never late myself, never! And I refuse to employ any one who can't be on the dot. I had to let my old chauffeur go because he would arrive five minutes after I ordered—

MADAME GRADY. I don't blame you!

MRS. FITCH. Busy as I am, I make a practice of being prompt. My husband says it's absurd to keep three motors but it's necessary, if one can't be kept waiting—

[Pat runs in.]

PAT. De chauffeur's had a scrap wid de corner cop, an' he'd be obliged if you'd just meet de machine in de nex' block!

MRS. FITCH. Heavens!

MADAME GRADY [to Pat]. Go and tell him to drive it here immediately.

MRS. FITCH. No, Madame Grady, I will meet the car around the corner. He may take me home to-night, for the last time!

[With the air of a Spartan, Mrs. Fitch walks out.]

MADAME GRADY. Good night, Mrs. Fitch. I'll send your gown right up.

[Mrs. Fitch disappears. Madame Grady shrugs her shoulders.]

MADAME GRADY. My God, I'm frozen.

[Madame Grady reënters the shop. When the door closes Fitch peers out, sees all safe, and emerges, Elsie follows, sulkily.]

FITCH. Wait a minute till the car's gone!

ELSIE. Afraid she'll catch you being a devil?

FITCH [apprehensively, looking off in the direction in which Mrs. Fitch has disappeared]. I'm not anxious to see her.

ELSIE. What a pretty picture you make!

FITCH. In a couple of minutes we'll go.

ELSIE. Oh, don't mind me!

[Fitch surveys her, exasperated.]

FITCH. Now what's wrong?

ELSIE. Nothing.

FITCH. Good Lord—haven't I just told you to get your damn fur?

ELSIE. Yes.

FITCH. Don't you want it?

ELSIE. I don't care.

FITCH. Well, I'll be—!

ELSIE. George, you know I always give a rotten performance if I have to stuff down dinner at the last moment. We're late now: how can you be so thoughtless? Do think of me some-times!

FITCH. You get the wrap to-morrow, my dear.

ELSIE. To-morrow—!

FITCH. And you'll promise to be a little nicer to poor old George, won't you?

ELSIE. To-morrow—I may be dead.

FITCH. Not a chance!

ELSIE. I could wear the sable for a shroud. [Brightening suddenly]. That would go well in the papers: "Elsie Price Dies—Buried in Costly Sables!"

FITCH. You'd never waste that much money.

ELSIE [dully]. But advertising always pays, George.

FITCH. Cheer up—we'll go to Sherry's and be in the swim.

ELSIE. In the swim—!

FITCH. Well, where'd you rather go?

ELSIE. I'm in the swim all right, in the middle of the current! I might as well be swept along.

FITCH. You bet!

ELSIE. "You can't fight the waters of bitterness!"

FITCH. Say, what's the matter?

ELSIE. Remember that line in my piece last year? "You can't fight the waters of bitterness!"

FITCH. And you were great in the part! Even the critics—!

ELSIE. I wasn't bad, for a fact. [*Taking his arm.*] Let's get some food. [*As they move on.*] Swept along— that's what I am! Swept along!

[*Fitch and Elsie go out.*]

ROSY [*solemnly*]. Do you know who that was?

LILY. Who?

ROSY. Elsie Price!!!

LILY. Is that right!

ROSY. She's playing at the Epic in "The Reward of Virtue."

LILY. Some class!

ROSY. The sweetest thing you ever saw! An' salary—*say*—they tell me she draws down a thousand per.

LILY. Golly!

ROSY. Elsie Price is my ideal, that's what she is.

LILY. She the one that was a mannequin before she went on the stage?

ROSY. Sure she was! They're the girls make money! an' gee—why shouldn't they? They got so many chances!

LILY. Never mind, honey—we're goin' t'have a swell time to-night ourselves.

ROSY. I tell you those boys were the real thing, Lily Ryan. I ask you, weren't they *class*? Why, believe me—!

[*Madame Grady's head parts the hangings at back of the show window.*]

MADAME GRADY. Do you girls think I'm conducting a rest cure? You've had half an hour for those forms!

ROSY. They're done, Madame.

MADAME GRADY. I should hope they are done! Hurry up now and finish Mrs. Fitch's gown. It's promised for to-night.

[*Rosy and Lily scurry by her and disappear into the shop. Seeing Madame Grady, Pat opens the door. She stands over him threateningly.*]

PAT. Can I go now?

MADAME GRADY. I'm not paying you four a week for a vacation. They've got packages for you to deliver.

PAT. I been here all day. I'm cold.

MADAME GRADY. You wait for Mrs. Fitch's box. It's got to go up town to-night.

[*Pat enters the shop. Madame Grady returns to the show window to give final touches to the wax figures.*]

MADAME GRADY. Can't get any work out of you girls to save my neck! I'll fire a few—then maybe the rest'll be worth something to me. Pour out money on rent for this hole, just because it's on the Avenue! *Spend* till I'm next thing to bankrupt, and I can't turn my back without somebody lying down on the job!

[*Madame Grady disappears into the shop. She can be heard storming at her assistants. Van Vliet and Barlow enter, in a riotous mood.*]

VAN VLIET. Stop me if I get noisy, old top!

BARLOW. What did I tell you? They're not here!

VAN VLIET. Where's the boy?

[*Van Vliet suddenly makes for the door. Barlow pulls him back.*]

BARLOW. Idiot! Do you want to gum the whole game? Wait and reconnoiter!

VAN VLIET. I won't wait: I'm hungry!

[*Pat staggers out of the shop with two great bundles.*]

BARLOW. The god's messenger!

[*Van Vliet grabs Pat.*]

VAN VLIET. Are they ready?

PAT. Say! Go easy on them packages!

VAN VLIET. You just snook in and tell the girls we're waiting, will you!

PAT. I gotta carry them boxes up town.

BARLOW. All right. Only just let them know we're here!

[*Pat looks back into the shop.*]

VAN VLIET. Go back and see. I'll give you another dollar!

PAT. You're the doctor! Hold on to them bundles!

[*Pat sneaks back into the shop, while the boys watch excitedly.*]

VAN VLIET. Look here, where'll we go to feed?

BARLOW. That depends on what kind of clothes they've got.

VAN VLIET. What do we care?

BARLOW. Are you anxious to be seen in some place where your friends are?

VAN VLIET. After three Manhattans I'd drag those two queens right up to the Colony Club!

BARLOW. Just what I'm afraid of.

[*Pat returns hastily.*]

PAT. They're comin'. Jiggers!

VAN VLIET [*giving him money*]. Here you are, kid!

PAT. T'anks, sport!

[*Pat shoulders his boxes and runs out.*]

BARLOW. Something tells me we shall regret this night's work!

VAN VLIET. We'll give them a run for their money!

BARLOW. *My* money, you mean.

[*Rosy and Lily, in street clothes, appear at the shop door. The two youths, all at once young and rather pleasing, take off their hats.*]

VAN VLIET. Hello!

ROSY. Hello yourself!

LILY. Don't let Madame Grady see us!

BARLOW. We thought maybe you'd —er—

VAN VLIET. Will you have dinner with us—and—

BARLOW. Go to a show or something?

LILY. We aren't introduced—

VAN VLIET. That's easy! His name's Bar; mine's Van.

BARLOW [*to Lily*]. What do they call you, when they feel awfully chummy?

LILY. Lily.

ROSY. An' I am known in Flatbush as Rosy.

VAN VLIET. That's over as easy as anything. So what about food?

ROSY. We don't care if we do.

BARLOW. I can see you and I are going to get along wonderfully. We have the same piquant sense of humor.

ROSY. Whatever that is!

BARLOW. We can see a joke.

ROSY. I should say I can, an' you're a new one on me!

VAN VLIET. He's all right, but he's not a self-starter.

LILY [*giggling with embarrassment*]. That's a good one, too!

[*Barlow and Rosy move to one side, talking.*]

VAN VLIET [*to Lily*]. Say, where do you want to eat?

LILY. Oh, I don't know—anywhere you say.

VAN VLIET. You know, I'm going to like you a lot.

LILY. You're terrible!

VAN VLIET. Do you think you'll like me?

[*Lily looks at him shyly.*]

LILY. Yes, I do.

VAN VLIET. What do you say we pick out some quiet place where we can—talk?

LILY. I'd love to!

ROSY. Say, how long are we going to stand here and vamp till ready!

BARLOW. Do you think you could stand me in a quiet place?

ROSY. Um—yes—with music in between.

BARLOW. Though you spurn me, yet do I adore you, Rosy. [*Offering his arm.*] Madame, will you walk?

ROSY [*seizing his arm*]. Come on, Algy! And maybe I'll let you hold my hand!

BARLOW [*taking her hand*]. Let's grab a taxi, Rosy! Sounds like a popular ballad, doesn't it!

[*Rosy runs out with Barlow.*]

VAN VLIET. Shall we ditch them?

LILY. Oh, I want to go with Rosy!

VAN VLIET. All right. But afterward—?

LILY. Oh—afterward—!

[*She laughs at him daringly, and runs out.*]

VAN VLIET. You little—! [*Laughing.*] Look here, Lily, you—!

[*He runs out after her. Their laughter is heard in the distance. There is silence followed by the sound of motor horns. After a space, the three wax figures slowly turn their heads and smile stiffly at one another.*]

THE BLONDE. It must be so dull—being real.

THE BRUNETTE. We do not represent reality: we are the ideal.

THE TITIAN. Which of them who gaze on us can accomplish our perfections?

THE BRUNETTE. Our faultless hair!

THE BLONDE. Our matchless flush!

THE TITIAN. Is there a woman as well dressed as we?

THE BRUNETTE. We are perfect.

THE BLONDE. We are envied.

THE BRUNETTE. We have succeeded where living women fail.

THE BLONDE. It is our reward for escaping humanity.

[*The Brunette glances off.*]

THE BRUNETTE. But they—feel.

THE TITIAN. They suffer.

THE BRUNETTE. They are not flawless.

THE TITIAN. For them there is the bill to pay.

THE BRUNETTE. For us—no to-morrow.

THE TITIAN. And no yesterday.

[*They resume their former poses.*]

THE BLONDE. We—we have no hearts!

[*The three figures seem to freeze into their former smiling immobility. Darkness.*]

[*Curtain.*]

THE RAZOR

A Drama

By Kichizo Nakamura

Translated by Yozan T. Iwaski and Glenn Hughes

CHARACTERS

Tamekichi Kimura [*a barber*].
Oshika [*his wife*].
Hayata Noguchi [*Secretary of the County Office*].
Keichi Sato [*Principal of the grade school*].
Kanshichi [*son of a rich merchant*].
Shusaku Okada [*Councillor in the Department of the Interior*].

Time: *The Present.*

Place: *A small village near Tokyo.*

THE RAZOR

A DRAMA   BY KICHIZO NAKAMURA

[*The stage setting represents the interior of a village barber shop. Three-fourths of the room is taken up by the zashiki—a raised platform about two feet high, covered with matting. In the center of the zashiki is a charcoal stove, upon which stand tea vessels. In the wall at the back of the zashiki are two sliding screens. The entrance from the street is through another sliding door, also in the back wall, but to the right of the zashiki. Two shabby mirrors hang on the right wall. Under them, on a shelf, are combs, brushes, perfumes, soap, etc. In the upper right corner is a washstand. Two light, movable barber chairs stand facing the mirrors. The atmosphere of the room is musty and stale. Dust lies everywhere. One bright-colored fan lying on the shelf is reflected in the mirror.*

Tamekichi is discovered in his white work jacket. He is busily engaged shaving a customer, and he appears much perturbed. His eyes flash nervously. Oshika sits on the zashiki by the charcoal stove, smoking a long Japanese pipe. She is about twenty-seven years of age, and has charming eyes. Her hair is dressed in cho-cho (butterfly) style. A few wisps of hair hang down across her pale white face.

Noguchi is sitting on the edge of the zashiki reading a newspaper. He is about twenty-five years of age. He wears nickel-rimmed glasses, and his hair is cut in a short pompadour. He is dressed in a hakama—a skirt-like garment made of coarse material.]

NOGUCHI. There will be a political speech at the Jyo-fuku Temple this afternoon, and to-night there is to be a reception. Well, he is a Representative in the House, and was appointed Councillor in the Cabinet. The newspapers are all talking about him, and so is every one in the village. It is a good thing that to-day is Sunday, so that a lot of people from neighboring towns will be able to come and hear him. It is certainly an honor for our village to have a great man like Mr. Okada.

OSHIKA. Isn't he quite a young man still—about the age of my husband?

NOGUCHI. Perhaps in his thirties. When he is forty he may be Governor or Commissioner, and when he is fifty, he will be a minister, I am sure.

OSHIKA. What! Is he really as great as that? What kind of looking man is he? I'd like to see him.

NOGUCHI [*laughing*]. Of course he is not handsome like an actor, but he has broad eyebrows, a tight mouth, and a dignified bearing. And then, he has piercing eyes—he sees through every one.

TAMEKICHI [*laughing sarcastically*]. He is related to a mind reader.

NOGUCHI. This is not a joke. Yesterday he came to the County Office to inquire about taxation, and after he left, the Chief and the Treasurer talked about him. "His eyes are fearful!" they said. "There is something striking about his eyes. But anyway, he is very democratic, or he wouldn't have come down to the County Office himself." They admired him very much.

TAMEKICHI. Huh! Democratic! He went there for his own convenience.

OSHIKA. My husband went to see him yesterday, but Mr. Okada was too busy to receive him. This made my husband angry, but in our position we can't help it.

NOGUCHI. That's right. Even I have not been able to talk with him yet. I've only caught sight of him.

TAMEKICHI [*working on his customer with the brush*]. Of course there is a difference between the Secretary of the County Office and a Councillor in the

341

Cabinet; but not between Shusaku and myself.

OSHIKA. You see, he and my husband were classmates in grade school. My husband graduated in first place, and Mr. Okada was second; so he thinks Okada is still his old-time friend. But the world doesn't go that way. I tell him not to think such things, or people will laugh at him. It really worries me.

TAMEKICHI. Which one of us will be laughed at—you or me?

NOGUCHI. The past is past. Now is now. If there is a difference between the Secretary of the County Office and a Councillor in the Cabinet, there is no relation at all between a village barber and a Cabinet Officer. Mr. Tamekichi's queerness goes too far. Maybe it is the weather.

[He takes up the newspaper again.]

OSHIKA. You are right! He is awfully disagreeable these days. Yesterday he tore up the newspapers that had the stories about Mr. Okada. He is crazy. I have to laugh at him.

TAMEKICHI. You talk too much nonsense.

[He glares at her, then takes the customer over to the washstand.]

NOGUCHI. Ha! Here is a two-column story: "Okada, Councillor, comes home covered with glory." It's in big type, too. Well, whether a man is good or bad, unless he is worth a headline in the paper, his life isn't worth living. For otherwise he is not sure whether he is dead or alive.

OSHIKA [smiling with meaning]. I got into the newspaper once.

NOGUCHI. Yes, yes. Over that suicide-pact. But you were young then.

OSHIKA. And now I am getting old.

NOGUCHI. No; I don't mean that. You are still beautiful. [He is confused.] Er . . . wasn't the man put in jail? You were lucky to get safely out of it.

OSHIKA. Yes, I am still alive, and am a barber's wife. No chance to get into the newspapers any more. It's better to keep out of the newspapers, anyway.

[Tamekichi has finished trimming the customer's hair, and now comes and sits on the edge of the zashiki. He lights his pipe. Kanshichi, the customer, joins them and smokes also. He wears a summer kimono, with a gray silk waistband.]

OSHIKA. Sit down, young master.

KANSHICHI. Thanks.

[He sits down.]

NOGUCHI [to Kanshichi]. Iseya-san, stay a while, and as soon as I get my hair trimmed, I'll get even with you at chess.

[He hurries to the barber chair and seats himself.]

KANSHICHI [to Tamekichi and Oshika]. You are busy?

OSHIKA. No, not exactly. Come up and have a cup of tea.

KANSHICHI. Don't bother about me.

OSHIKA. No bother at all. Won't you come up?

KANSHICHI [looking at Tamekichi, but speaking to Oshika]. You are sure it won't disturb you?

[He climbs gingerly up beside Oshika near the stove.]

OSHIKA. How is your wife? Is she getting better?

KANSHICHI. No; she is at her mother's; and I hope she doesn't come back. It is a terrible, lifelong burden to have a sick wife.

OSHIKA. It is a pity for you to say such things.

KANSHICHI. I can't help it.

NOGUCHI [laughs]. Ha, ha, ha! You infected your wife yourself, and now you are trying to get rid of her. You are heartless. It must be a miserable thing to be the wife of such a man.

OSHIKA. Yes, indeed! But all men are selfish. You are no exception.

NOGUCHI. Why, every one says Mr. Tamekichi is a loyal husband; but you seem discontented in spite of that.

OSHIKA. Of course I am.

[Tamekichi watches Kanshichi out of the corner of his eye.]

NOGUCHI. Say, Boss, when you finish your smoke, get my hair trimmed. I have to go to the Temple this afternoon and inspect the hall. I am very busy.

TAMEKICHI. You said just now you were going to play chess. Wait until I finish two or three more smokes. Don't get excited. I wasn't born to cut men's hair all the time.

NOGUCHI. But that's your business, so stop talking nonsense. If you expect to live by barbering, you have to pay attention to your customers.

TAMEKICHI. Yes, I live off my eight-cent customers. [*Sarcastically.*] Many thanks!

OSHIKA. Don't be foolish! Get his work done. Of course it doesn't matter so much if you talk that way to Mr. Noguchi, but just the same, it hurts business.

TAMEKICHI. I am getting tired of this business. I want to quit.

NOGUCHI. Oh, don't do that, Boss. You are the only barber in town. If you quit, every one will have to go to the next village.

OSHIKA. He talks that way all the time these days, and worries the life out of me. Young master, I wish you would speak to him about it.

KANSHICHI. Well, of course you have to work.

[*He drinks his tea.*]

TAMEKICHI. Yes, we have to work, and the young master has to loaf. It is a well-arranged world!

OSHIKA. Don't put it that way. The young master is rich and doesn't need to work. He has plenty of money; his employees work for him, so it is all right for him to play around. Our fate is quite different from his.

TAMEKICHI. Huh! Your fate is unlucky! I am sorry.

OSHIKA [*laughing*]. Perhaps my marriage was unlucky.

TAMEKICHI. If you had been redeemed by the young master, you would be a lady of the Iseya family, and wouldn't need to even speak to a barber like me. You were foolish, all right, to marry me. But as you were only a waitress in a tea house, your present position is quite appropriate, and you had better be content with it.

OSHIKA [*her face flushing with anger*]. Don't say such things before the young master, you fool!

TAMEKICHI [*cynically*]. The young master hasn't forgotten you, at any rate. He still comes to see you occasionally. You had better thank him for that.

KANSHICHI. I am going. Here is the money.

[*He throws a coin on the zashiki.*]

OSHIKA. Thanks . . . is it twenty sen? I'll get the change.

[*She rises.*]

KANSHICHI. Keep the change.

[*He gets down from the zashiki.*]

TAMEKICHI. Take your change. Here are twelve sen.

KANSHICHI. Never mind. I don't want it.

TAMEKICHI [*sternly*]. Yes you do. I have no reason to take more than the regular price.

[*Oshika hands twelve sen to Tamekichi, who holds it under Kanshichi's nose.*]

TAMEKICHI. Thanks!

[*Kanshichi takes the money and hurries out.*]

NOGUCHI. Boss, you are too outspoken.

TAMEKICHI [*looking after Kanshichi*]. Beast! [*With a backward look at Oshika.*] He's still thinking about her!

OSHIKA. Why are you so cross? We lose customers every day; and he is a very important one.

TAMEKICHI. Yes, important to you. But to me he is a sneak thief, who takes a barber shop for a tea house. Running after women—with his soft white face! There's not enough to him to pick up with chop-suey sticks. He eats, and produces nothing; but every one respects him because he is a rich man's son. It makes me laugh!

NOGUCHI [*growing serious*]. That's right; just as you say. That kind of fellow we call a "bad egg." [*He looks around cautiously.*] We must be careful not to talk too loud, though.

OSHIKA [*smilingly*]. And yet I hear you used to go around the tea houses with him, at his expense.

NOGUCHI [*confused*]. Well, of course, once or twice I went with him . . . for sociability. But I never made a fool of myself—for I have ambitions.

OSHIKA. Yes, I've heard for a long time that you were going to Tokyo to study. When are you really going to leave?

NOGUCHI. After I finish the correspondence course, I will study for a year or two more, and then take the examinations for the bar or the civil service. You can be sure I won't waste my whole life on this County Office Secretaryship. My superiors are always holding me down; and the only time I can show my importance is when I go to warn the delinquent taxpayers.

OSHIKA. That's just it. This spring you came here to warn us about paying our delinquent taxes, and you threatened to attach all our dishes and furniture and everything. You were quite a different person then; I was afraid of you.

NOGUCHI [*growing still more serious*]. I couldn't help performing my duty. At such times I am not myself. The power of our country's law takes possession of me; my natural feelings hide in some corner of my body, and I feel as though I had my hands on the pulse of other people. I enjoy seeing them suffer. But of course I am sorry afterwards, and am embarrassed when I see the same people again.

[*He scratches his head comically, and forces a laugh.*]

TAMEKICHI [*laughing cynically*]. Yes, just as you say—holding their pulse. I practice that every day. Only mine is more than their pulse—a vital point. Thus I hold the razor in my hand, and shave men's necks. One slash of the razor would stop their breathing. And when I think of that, it seems to me that all customers are trusting fools. They don't know anything of what I am thinking, and they trust their throats in my hands, without suspicion. They let me touch their naked flesh with my razor as freely as I like. No matter what noble faces they have, or how eminent they are, or how proud, I have hold of their necks, and it is in my power to kill or to let live, according to the motion of one finger. So, whenever I finish shaving a man, I feel that I have saved a life, and I laugh to myself.

OSHIKA. Oh my! You mustn't think and say such crazy things! There is something wrong with you. You had better go see a doctor.

NOGUCHI. Do you think such things while you are shaving people? That is terrible!

TAMEKICHI. In the beginning I did not. Then I was very cautious, and I tried to shave without hurting people, for the sake of my trade. But as I grew accustomed to it I got tired of doing the same thing every day, all day long. Finally I reached the point where I could stand it no longer. I wanted to cut somebody's throat, so that I could quit this place. And ever since then, this idea has nested in my head; when I shaved that youngster just now I thought I would thrust my razor into his throat.

OSHIKA. Oh! there is surely something the matter with him! What shall we do, Mr. Noguchi?

NOGUCHI. I can hardly trust him to shave me now. If I am killed here in the barber shop I can never rise in the world—and I have great ambitions.

[*He moves to another chair out of Tamekichi's reach.*]

TAMEKICHI [*with a contemptuous laugh*]. My craziness doesn't make me cut the throats of county officials. For I would have to pay with my own life for such a deed. You are not worth it, any more than that youngster was. But if he had done something to my wife, he would never have got out of here safely, I can tell you that.

NOGUCHI [*with a sigh of relief*]. If there is no cause, then, you will not kill any one.

TAMEKICHI. Well, if there were a cause, it would be only natural. Whenever I have finished shaving any one safely, I wonder why it is that the razor slides so smoothly over his face. If this point were to get just a little under the skin, it would cut the cheek bone, and the red blood would spurt out. Why does the razor always slide over the surface? Ha, ha, ha! I know. My hand has become a machine to trim people's hair and shave their faces. It is unbearable! I am still alive. And to prove I am alive, I would let the razor slip once. And yet, when I think it over calmly, something whispers to me that this would mean the exchange of my life.

OSHIKA. Mr. Noguchi! Why does he talk this way?

NOGUCHI. He has a rush of blood to the head. [*To Tamekichi.*] Say, Boss, you had better rest a little while.

TAMEKICHI. No. I am still considering my own life, so there is no danger. But if I found the right person, I would exchange my life, for to go on with this monotonous business until I am a bent old man—that is awful. But I never meet one who is worthy—only the County Commissioner, the Village Mayor, and the Postmaster. I couldn't cut their throats. . . . A month ago a Major came here to inspect the military drill, and he made a conceited remark about a country razor not being sharp enough. I thought of replying that if it wouldn't cut hair, it would cut bones; and I came near thrusting the razor into his throat. But I didn't do it; it seemed too foolish.

NOGUCHI. So the County Office was saved the trouble of settling that. It was a close call, though.

OSHIKA [with a deep sigh]. There is surely something the matter with him these days. Please, Mr. Noguchi, don't repeat these things to any one. We might lose trade.

TAMEKICHI. So much the better if we lose trade! I have other ideas. This isn't the only village the sun shines on. It's a wide world.

OSHIKA [soothingly]. Of course the world is wide, but this is our only way of making a living. We can't do anything else, no matter how hard we try.

NOGUCHI. What you say is probably right.

[He appears to think deeply. Sato, the School Principal, enters. He is about fifty years of age, with gray hair and whiskers. He wears an old-fashioned short frock coat, with silver chains on his vest.]

SATO. Good-day. Ah, Mr. Noguchi! You are waiting to be shaved, too?

NOGUCHI [very politely]. No; I am in no hurry. You first, Professor.

[Tamekichi nods to Sato.]

OSHIKA. Welcome, Professor. Please sit down.

SATO [speaking rapidly]. Thank you, thank you. Mr. Noguchi, you are first. No need for you to be so polite.

NOGUCHI. No . . . I . . . [Faltering.] You go first, Professor. . . .

TAMEKICHI [to Sato]. Pray, sit down.

SATO. Thank you. How is business? Good, as usual?

TAMEKICHI [heavily]. Yes.

SATO. Mr. Noguchi is very busy these days, too, I suppose, with all the receptions, lectures, and so forth?

NOGUCHI. Yes . . . no . . . just a little inspection this afternoon at the Temple. There are a lot of committees, so I am not very busy.

SATO. Is that so? Well, at any rate to-day is a very joyous occasion. It is an honor to our village and an honor to our school.

NOGUCHI. Yes, indeed. Last year we celebrated the twenty-fifth year of your service, and this year we do honor to

your pupil who has become a great man. So there is a double reason for rejoicing.

SATO. Indeed! It is a mutual pleasure. And Mr. Okada is as democratic as ever. He came to my house to see me last night, and we talked over old times. So to-day, as soon as I get shaved, I am going to repay his call. He leaves for Tokyo to-morrow evening. He is a very busy man.

NOGUCHI. Of course, as he is a high officer of the Central Government, time is important to him—even half a day.

SATO. That's right. And some day he will be a minister. Well, he showed signs of greatness even in his schooldays. He always stood first or second in his class—never lower.

NOGUCHI. It is all due to his school training, so you are responsible.

SATO. Thanks, thanks! At any rate, from my pupil develops a great man. I feel very proud. That is the reward of a divine mission.

TAMEKICHI. Say, Mr. Noguchi, you come over here and sit down. Let's start on you.

NOGUCHI. No. Professor, you first. Any time will do for me.

SATO. No, no, Mr. Noguchi! First come, first served.

NOGUCHI. Later will be all right for me. You first, Professor.

SATO. But that would not be right. I came later than you.

TAMEKICHI. I'll finish either of you.

NOGUCHI. Professor, you please!

SATO. No. Courtesy is courtesy.

TAMEKICHI [sharpening his razor]. Then, Mr. Noguchi, I will stop your breathing first.

NOGUCHI. Don't joke! I'm in no particular hurry to-day. My hair isn't too long, anyway.

TAMEKICHI. All right, then, Professor, I'll finish you.

SATO. Excuse me, Mr. Noguchi. [He crosses and sits in the chair. To Tamekichi.] You are working hard these days. That is fine.

TAMEKICHI. Not exactly fine. This miserable business. . . .

SATO. Why, one trade is no better than another. All that is necessary is for each man to do his best in his particular business.

NOGUCHI. That's right, Professor. Mr. Tamekichi has stayed with this business a long time now; if he only keeps it up a little longer he will be all right.

TAMEKICHI [*examining the razor blade*]. What shall I keep up?

[*He laughs loudly.*]

SATO. Every one has a divine work to do, and he must keep up that work.

TAMEKICHI. You told me that same thing twenty years ago, and I have kept it up until this day. But now I am tired of it.

SATO. Yes, after your graduation you wanted to go to Tokyo to continue your studies; but your father was worried, and he asked me to advise you to follow his trade. And I agreed with him; so here you are. Now, isn't that fine?

TAMEKICHI. But you didn't advise Shusaku to follow *his* father's trade, and become a farmer.

SATO. But Mr. Okada had plenty of money, so I agreed that he should study in Tokyo. And that is what made him the famous man he is to-day.

TAMEKICHI. If I had had the money, then, I would not be a barber now. So it is money that makes men great. Ha, ha, ha!

NOGUCHI. After all, that's just it.

SATO. Well, Mr. Tamekichi was very good in school, too. I thought about you a great deal. But if you had rushed off to Tokyo you would have gone astray.

TAMEKICHI. I did run away to Tokyo two or three times, but my father always came after me and dragged me back home. Since then I have been a good-for-nothing, and have gone from bad to worse. Oh, I have tried to get over the idea, but I can't forget it.

[*He resumes his shaving. Noguchi returns to the edge of the zashiki and talks with Oshika.*]

NOGUCHI [*whispering*]. You had better keep an eye on him, Oshika-san.

OSHIKA. Indeed I will.

[*She moves forward and watches Tamekichi as he works. He sighs occasionally.*]

SATO. My whiskers are too thick—better shave them off.

TAMEKICHI. All right.

SATO. I am getting a lot of gray hairs, too.

TAMEKICHI. You can't help your age. But if you talk too much, Professor, the razor may slip, and I can't tell where I will cut you.

SATO. All right. All right. You scold me every time, but you have a razor in your hand, so I must do what you say.

TAMEKICHI. Better keep quiet; otherwise I can't handle the razor.

SATO. All right. All right.

[*Tamekichi is now shaving around Sato's throat.*]

NOGUCHI [*in a low whisper*]. I am in a cold sweat. If he presses down with one finger, that will be the end. How helpless human life is!

OSHIKA [*turning to Noguchi*]. Sh-h! He will hear you! If he gets excited, no telling what will happen.

NOGUCHI [*lying down on the zashiki*]. How helpless we all are! We go on madly seeking fame, wealth, success; but the pressure of one finger can end everything—and our life accounts are settled. After one is thirty it is foolish to go to Tokyo to study. Ah-h-h-h!

[*He sighs.*]

OSHIKA. You are getting discouraged, Mr. Noguchi.

NOGUCHI [*excitedly*]. Without money one is powerless in the world!

OSHIKA. Yes, after all, it comes to that.

NOGUCHI. If he had the money, for instance, he might become Councillor too. You never can tell.

OSHIKA. Then I would be the Councillor's Lady! . . . But I have missed that destiny.

NOGUCHI. A woman can become famous without money. Her capital is a beautiful face and a fine body.

OSHIKA. If you look at it that way, then a man's capital is his arms.

NOGUCHI. Well, a man may have arms, but without money there is no hope for him these days. The times have made things that way. We can't help it. . . . [*He looks at Tamekichi.*] He is pretty near through. [*Muttering to himself.*] I am going out for a minute.

OSHIKA. What about your haircut?

NOGUCHI. After a while. I have something to do right now.—Excuse me, Professor.

[*He goes out hastily.*]

SATO [*coming back from the wash-*

stand, where Tamekichi has taken him.]
Ah! I look younger.

OSHIKA. Professor, you always look well.

SATO. There are many things for me to accomplish yet in life, so I must keep strong and healthy. By the way, give me a little perfume.

[*Tamekichi sprays him with perfume, then crosses to the zashiki. Oshika prepares some tea.*]

SATO. Has Mr. Noguchi gone? Oh, I am sorry I let myself be shaved first.

OSHIKA. No; he will be back soon.

SATO. Yes? [*He rubs his cheeks.*] I feel much better. When my whiskers grow I feel very strange; I can't tell whether it is my face or some one else's. But now it feels fine.

OSHIKA. Have a cup of tea.

[*She serves it.*]

SATO. Thanks, thanks. Here is the change. Good-by.

OSHIKA. Get your change, Professor.

SATO. No; never mind. Good-by.

OSHIKA [*following him*]. Thank you very much. [*She turns to Tamekichi.*] Tame-san, why don't you say "Thanks" or something? You are too rude.

TAMEKICHI [*blowing a cloud of smoke*]. No thanks necessary. That old duffer! If Shusaku was remarkable in school, so was I. I graduated in first place. Talking about "divine work," and hanging on by his teeth to this one job for twenty-five years without getting tired of it. A patient fool, that's all!

OSHIKA. But that is just why the Governor rewarded him—for his twenty-five years of patient service.

TAMEKICHI. Then I suppose I should wait for a reward from the County Chief when I have finished twenty-five years at the barbering business. Like hell!

OSHIKA. Don't lose your temper. That doesn't help matters.

TAMEKICHI. Well, I'm getting sick of this life, so it's only natural for me to lose my temper. In the first place those mirrors drive me mad. The same old dingy frames that were there in my father's time. And if I look in the mirror I see the faces of the men in the chair changing every day—but the man who stands beside the chair, in the white coat—his face never changes. It is the same man always. Three hundred and sixty-five days in the year, the same man

with the same hands, going back and forth in the same narrow room, repeating over and over the same stupid things without a blush. It is a glass prison! There is a man who cannot get out of it for his life; and I feel sorry for him, I pity him—but it is I, myself! I can't stand it!

[*He pulls his hair.*]

OSHIKA. Well—that is our fate; so after all, we must be content with the three meals a day we get out of it. There is no other way—no matter what you think—so you may as well change your mind and settle down to work.

TAMEKICHI. I do work, but what comes of it? I work all my life like this, and support you. That is well enough for you. But is that the object of my life? Damned nonsense! You may like it, but I tell you I don't!

OSHIKA. Well then, can you tell me any other way? I don't say I like to spend my whole life here, being supported by you. I don't say I am contented with that.

TAMEKICHI [*sarcastically*]. Yes, when I see you entertaining the customers, I have an idea you are getting tired of it.

OSHIKA. Just as you say, I do get tired. Your customers change, but mine is always the same.

TAMEKICHI [*looking at her suspiciously*]. You mean that I am your customer?

OSHIKA. Isn't my husband the only customer that I have now? It wasn't so before.

TAMEKICHI [*spitting out his words*]. Huh! In the tea house your customers changed every night. But nowadays your customer's face never changes. So that is why you say you are getting tired!

OSHIKA. You just got through saying that the man's face in the mirror never changed, so I was reminding you of my own case.

TAMEKICHI. What are you reminded of?

OSHIKA. Don't be angry. I am serious, too, and sometimes I think the same things that you do.

TAMEKICHI. Think what things?

OSHIKA [*half laughing*]. When I wake up in the middle of the night, the same man is always sleeping beside me—and how dreadful I feel! [*Tamekichi stares at her.*] Ha, ha, ha! Don't look at me like that—with that terrible expression! I don't mean that I hate you.

TAMEKICHI [*collapsing*]. Ah! Man cannot trust any one!

OSHIKA. Don't take it that way. You were talking about the mirror—I was talking the same way about my troubles. Every one has to stand something.

TAMEKICHI [*his voice trembling*]. That's why these young toughs hang around here—because you are so frivolous. Even that Noguchi can't be trusted. None of the customers can be trusted! That alone is enough to make me hate this business. I hate it! I'll smash that mirror!

[*He rushes across the room, Oshika following him and holding him by the arm.*]

OSHIKA. Don't lose your temper. If you break up everything, what will you do to-morrow? Can't you see we'll suffer for it?

TAMEKICHI. Let go! No matter how much we suffer—if we die, that will be the end of it. Let me go! Let me go!

OSHIKA [*clinging tightly to him*]. I don't want to die! If I wanted to die, I would have died a long time ago.

TAMEKICHI. With whom would you have died?

[*He turns and stares at her.*]

OSHIKA. With anybody. No matter who.

TAMEKICHI. You harlot! [*He strikes her on the face, and collapses in a chair.*] You said you loved me—but you lied!

OSHIKA [*scornfully*]. Think what you like.

TAMEKICHI [*gnashing his teeth*]. I was fooled—and by such a woman! Am I such a miserable creature as that?

OSHIKA. We are both miserable—you and I. We are a good match. That's what you get for losing your temper and crying. But there's no help for it.

[*Tamekichi grovels in his chair, his hands to his forehead. The door opens and Councillor Okada enters. He wears a frock coat and silk hat, with a gold chain on his breast. In his hand is a cigar, from which a cloud of smoke is rising.*]

OKADA [*smiling in salutation*]. Good-day.

OSHIKA [*bowing confusedly*]. Welcome.

[*Tamekichi rises and looks vacantly at Okada.*]

OKADA [*still smiling*]. It is I, Okada. It is a long time since we saw each other. I am sorry that last night when you called, I was busy with other guests.

TAMEKICHI [*his expression softening*]. Ah, Mr. Okada, you are welcome.

[*He nods his head. Oshika goes hurriedly to the zashiki and arranges the things upon it. In her embarrassment she places the old dirty cushions for Okada, instead of the clean ones.*]

OSHIKA. This way please, sir. Though everything is in bad shape.

TAMEKICHI. Please!

OKADA [*crossing in a dignified manner and sitting on the edge of the zashiki*]. Don't bother about me. I just came to pay my respects.

TAMEKICHI [*taking off his work jacket and sitting on the zashiki, facing Okada. Politely*]. I am very happy to see you in my humble place, and I offer you my congratulations.

[*He bows politely.*]

OKADA. Thanks. We haven't seen each other for a long time, but I am glad that you are getting along so well with your trade.

TAMEKICHI. No; everything is very bad—so bad that I am ashamed to have you see me.

OKADA. Nonsense, nonsense! All that can be asked of any one is that he do well with his own trade. There is no honor in being an official.

[*He puffs at his cigar.*]

TAMEKICHI [*with a bitter smile.*] But you are in an honorable position; while I am in such a miserable state that I am ashamed to talk with you. But I am thinking of quitting this business.

OKADA. Nonsense! Changing your trade wouldn't help matters any. You must be patient.

OSHIKA. That's right, sir, just as you say.

OKADA [*noticing her*]. Oh, I haven't spoken to you before, but I presume this is the wife of Tamekichi-san.

OSHIKA [*blushing*]. Yes, sir. I have

heard a great deal of you from Tame-kichi. It is very nice of you to remember us.

OKADA. Well, Tamekichi and I were good friends in our mischievous school days. I often think of those times.

OSHIKA. Anyway, it is a great honor for us to have you visit us.

OKADA. Well, I must admit that I didn't make a special trip here. I was seeing a friend nearby, and I thought I might as well drop in and get shaved.

[*Tamekichi looks at Okada, his eyes lighting up.*]

OSHIKA. Oh, is that so? Then—get to work, Tamekichi-san.

OKADA. No hurry. I have nothing to do until afternoon. When I came by the school building I noticed that the old black walls have been painted, but that the pasania tree hasn't changed at all.

TAMEKICHI [*coldly*]. Yes; some things change, and others do not.

OSHIKA [*laughing amiably, and speaking to Okada*]. Ha, ha, ha! You are the one who has changed most.

OKADA [*exultantly*]. I have not changed enough yet. I must break my cocoon two or three times more before I attain my desire.

OSHIKA [*flatteringly*]. Perhaps you will become a minister.

OKADA [*laughing loudly*]. Ah, you are flattering me! But a minister is nothing. Some one suggested not long ago that ministers should be appointed by throwing orange peelings into a crowd, and making ministers of those who are hit.

OSHIKA [*not knowing what to say*]. Er . . . ah. . . .

TAMEKICHI [*scornfully*]. It is not orange peelings that are thrown, but money. One who has money can become a Representative or anything else; but the one without money is—a barber.

OKADA [*seriously*]. Tamekichi talks as though he really were tired of his trade.

TAMEKICHI. Tired nothing! I should have been born in a rich family, and been given a good education. Of course in grade school it doesn't matter: there is no difference between the poor and the rich. The strong boy is the leader, and the weak one a follower; the good student wins first place, the lazy student comes last. There's no complaint on that score. And speaking of that pasania tree, Shusaku-san—I remember one time I picked acorns from it by standing on your back. It was a moonlit night.

OKADA [*reminiscently*]. Yes, yes. I remember that time. A bat flew out of a hole in the tree and frightened you so that you jumped down. I was frightened too, and tried to run, but stubbed my toe on a root, and fell on my nose, and made it bleed. I was thinking of that to-day. Ah, we were innocent in those days!

OSHIKA. My, my! Did such things really happen?

OKADA. It is very interesting to recall the days of our youth.

TAMEKICHI [*sighing*]. It makes me miserable. Mr. Okada has a future. Before me is darkness. I have lost my way. My hands and feet are bound.

OKADA. Why do you say such desperate things? If you work at your trade, isn't that satisfactory?

OSHIKA. There is a proper work for every one, according to his own ability.

OKADA. Quite right. If one can support a wife and child he is a real man, and has no reason to be ashamed.

TAMEKICHI [*laughing in self-contempt*]. I am sick of being "a real man"! Unless you become a great man or an utter fool, and can turn the world upside down, life isn't worth living. But to go on day after day with an existence as monotonous as a page of print, and not to be ashamed of it—that is not living at all. A man who does that is not a human being; he is a machine. I, myself, cannot tell sometimes whether I am using the clippers or the clippers are using me. It's a miserable thing!

NOGUCHI [*calls as he looks in at the door*]. Just a hair cut. I have shaved myself.

[*He enters, sees Okada, and is overcome with confusion. He bows embarrassedly.*]

TAMEKICHI. Only a hair cut, eh?

NOGUCHI. I am in no hurry.

TAMEKICHI. But you were first, so I will finish you up first. [*He puts on his work jacket and comes down to the barber chair To Okada.*] Just excuse me, will you?

OKADA. Yes, of course.

NOGUCHI. No! Mr. Okada; you,

please. Any time is all right for me. Er . . . this is an unusual place for me to meet you.

[*He bows rapidly and awkwardly.*]

OKADA. Go ahead, please. I am in no particular hurry.

TAMEKICHI. Mr. Noguchi has been waiting since this morning, so I will fix him up first. [*To Noguchi.*] It's strange that you shaved yourself. [*Sneeringly.*] No one would. . . .

OSHIKA. Do Mr. Okada first.

OKADA. It doesn't matter. [*To her.*] If I wait, I can talk with you.

OSHIKA. Perhaps he can come to your house later, and shave you there.

OKADA. No, no! Don't go to that trouble. When I was abroad I used to shave myself every morning, and since I got married, my wife shaves me. But my razor got dull and I sent it out to be sharpened. Then I came down here, and haven't shaved for two days, so I don't feel very well with my face so rough.

[*During this time Noguchi has seated himself in the barber chair. He leans back, and Tamekichi starts cutting his hair.*]

OSHIKA. So your wife shaves you? Is that so?

[*She smiles.*]

OKADA [*looking closely at Oshika*]. I have seen you somewhere. Have you ever been in Tokyo?

OSHIKA. Yes; about ten years ago. But I never met you before.

OKADA. What part of Tokyo were you in?

OSHIKA. . . . Er . . . well . . . just in an out-of-the-way corner . . . and for just a little while . . . I don't even remember very well.

OKADA. Is that so? Then it was my mistake. Some one that looked like you. Ha, ha, ha!

[*He laughs pleasantly.*]

OSHIKA. But Tokyo is a good city. It has changed a lot in ten years, I hear.

OKADA. It changes every day. Yes, Tokyo is the best city in Japan. Of course I'm not saying anything against my home town, but when I come here, I feel—cramped.

OSHIKA. That must be true. We would like to go to Tokyo to live. As long as you have to work hard anyway,

it would be better to work in Tokyo. We get tired of the life here.

OKADA [*in a familiar manner*]. Come to Tokyo. That will be better for you. Why, if I stayed here a week I would get so I couldn't stand it. Of course I shouldn't say this, for after all it is my own district, and my parents live here.

OSHIKA. I agree with you. [*Showing her dimples.*] I should like to work in your house.

OKADA. Ha, ha, ha! That is excellent! If you were not married, I would take you with me. But as you are, I can't very well do it.

[*Tamekichi is listening to them carefully.*]

NOGUCHI [*crying out*]. Ouch! Don't cut my ear off! Be careful, Boss!

TAMEKICHI. I barely touched it. That's nothing.

[*Okada, interested in Oshika, leans forward on the zashiki.*]

OSHIKA. That needn't make any difference. If you have a job for me, I'd like to go to Tokyo. So please don't think I'm joking. You find something for me to do there.

OKADA. Sure! My wife is sickly, and we need a housemaid; if you know of any one for the place, let me know. I'm not joking. You keep it in mind.

OSHIKA. You mean . . . your wife is really sickly?

OKADA. Yes; female trouble. She has been suffering for a year now, in and out of the hospital. It is very hard on me. A woman ought to be strong and healthy. You look as though you were.

[*He looks her over appraisingly.*]

OSHIKA. I am too poor to be sick; but really I am not very strong.

OKADA. Why, you are fleshy enough.

OSHIKA [*smiling*]. Maybe it is only fat. And besides, my color isn't good.

OKADA. Well, perhaps it is not so good where it is exposed, but in other places I imagine it is very good. There is no beauty in dark complexions, anyway. Ha, ha, ha!

[*He laughs loudly.*]

OSHIKA [*simpering*]. You are very naughty, sir! Don't you tease me. If you say things like that to young girls, they will believe you and follow you. Will you really hire me as a housemaid?

OKADA [*playing with his mustache*]. It is hard to manage with a married servant. But if you hear of any one else, let me know.

OSHIKA. I know of one. [*Fawningly.*] There are some ashes on your collar.

[*She leans over and brushes them off.*]

OKADA. Thank you. [*He looks over at Tamekichi, but speaks to Oshika.*] It will take him a little longer yet, and I am pretty busy this afternoon. Maybe you could shave me.

OSHIKA. I shave you? Oh, I never shave any one except Tamekichi.

OKADA. I'm not afraid of your cutting me.

OSHIKA. All right, then. Of course I won't shave you as well as your wife does.

OKADA [*laughs*]. But my wife hasn't shaved me for more than a year. [*He goes to the chair.*] Shall I sit in this chair?

[*Tamekichi looks askance at Oshika, and plies his scissors wildly. Oshika goes and puts the apron around Okada's neck.*]

OSHIKA. He is in a hurry, so I will shave him. Besides, he asked me to.

[*She sharpens the razor.*]

TAMEKICHI [*harshly*]. I'll be through in a minute.

OKADA. I will trouble your wife; then it won't be necessary for me to ask my old friend to shave me.

[*Tamekichi looks away displeased.*]

OSHIKA. You are going away to-morrow, sir?

OKADA. Yes; I expect to leave tomorrow afternoon. I am a pretty busy man.

OSHIKA. I am sure you must be. So much coming and going must be awfully hard on you. And to-day you have a lecture and a reception. You must be tired.

OKADA. I am tired. But for the sake of their hospitality I mustn't say so.

OSHIKA. The newspaper has something about you every day. We quarrel over who shall read it first.

OKADA. Ha, ha, ha! They are always exaggerating. The Tokyo paper attacks me, and says I am traveling on Government funds to boost our party. All that kind of nonsense. You know.

OSHIKA. When you get back to Tokyo will there be a reception for you?

OKADA. I'm afraid not. Ha, ha, ha! This time there will not be a reception. But the reporters will mob me at the station. It's an awful nuisance. And then they pad up their stories with lies! Especially the opposition papers. Oh, it bores me.

OSHIKA [*touching him with the razor*]. I can't do as well as your wife. I am only a beginner.

OKADA. That's fine; fine!

[*Oshika smilingly rubs Okada's cheeks with her fingers, and looks at him in the mirror. At the same time Tamekichi combs Noguchi's hair roughly, and stares at the others out of the corner of his eye.*]

OSHIKA. You have a very thick beard.

[*Tamekichi takes Noguchi to the washstand.*]

OSHIKA. You have such beautiful hair. How I envy you!

[*Okada is silent. Tamekichi nervously pours perfume on Noguchi.*]

OSHIKA. What a beautiful border of back hair you have! It is nice enough for a woman.

[*Okada is still silent. Noguchi returns to the zashiki, sees Okada in the mirror, and bows.*]

TAMEKICHI [*hastily sharpening his razor, his eyes changing color*]. Get out of the way, Oshika; I will shave him.

OSHIKA [*looking at him in surprise*]. Never mind. There is just a little more to do. [*In a lower tone.*] Besides, he has dropped off to sleep.

NOGUCHI. Oshika-san, you had better do the shaving. The Boss is wild. He cut my ear.

OSHIKA. Oh, that's too bad! There is something wrong with him, all right.

NOGUCHI. It's even dangerous to let him use the scissors. I was uneasy, I can tell you.

OSHIKA [*with a little laugh*]. Noguchi-san, you are too easily frightened.

TAMEKICHI [*finishes sharpening the razor, feels of its edge, and smiles maliciously*]. The razor is not going to use me; I am going to use it.

OSHIKA. Never mind. I will finish him. It is all done but the throat.

TAMEKICHI. Get out!

[*He glares at her.*]

OSHIKA. Never mind, I say! [*In a*

lower tone.] He is sleeping so nicely!

TAMEKICHI. Get out!

[*He takes her roughly by the arm and pulls her away.*]

OSHIKA. Don't be so rough! I am afraid he will wake up.

[*Tamekichi takes her place, and begins rubbing Okada's throat.*]

OKADA. Ah, you, Tamekichi? I was having a good sleep, and was dreaming.

TAMEKICHI [*coldly*]. Perhaps you were dreaming of great fame and power.

OKADA. Well, I dreamed that I got a telegram and returned to Tokyo. Then I was invited to a wonderful palace, where there was a great hall with walls of gold hung with red velvet. The floor was a checker board of black and white marble. It was something like a palace that I saw when I was abroad.

TAMEKICHI. Huh! I can't even dream of such things!

OKADA [*as if talking to himself*]. And there was a marble platform with three steps leading up to it, covered with a beautiful carpet. On the throne sat a queen wearing purple robes embroidered with gold. And it was very funny about the queen.

TAMEKICHI [*sarcastically*]. Eh? How, funny?

OKADA [*laughing*]. Yes; it was very funny. She resembled your wife! I never had such a funny dream. I am sorry I woke up.

[*Oshika smiles at Okada in the mirror.*]

TAMEKICHI. Huh! The queen resembled my wife, did she? That *is* funny!

[*He starts shaving Okada.*]

OSHIKA. You must be very careful. He is an important man.

TAMEKICHI [*turning upon her quickly*]. Who is important? You shut up!

OSHIKA. He's an important man, I say. Don't be as rough as you were on Mr. Noguchi.

TAMEKICHI. You make too much noise. Keep your mouth shut! [*He looks in the mirror and sees himself. Dramatically.*] There he is! The same as ever! Working in his prison as he always is. He is a prisoner in a white coat, that fellow! . . .

[*He remains staring at his reflection.*]

OKADA. What are you talking about?

TAMEKICHI. I see myself in the glass, and I am beginning to feel sad. That is what I am talking about.

OKADA. Well, what of it?

TAMEKICHI. Shusaku-san is dreaming of luxury, and of another man's wife in purple robes. While I stand beside him, shaving, and breathing the bad odors of other men. I can't stand it! I can't stand it!

OKADA. You are getting a little nervous.

TAMEKICHI. Now there are two figures reflected in the mirror. But when Shusaku-san goes away, I will be left here alone. Left here alone in this prison forever. I can't bear it!

OSHIKA [*coming over near him*]. What are you saying? You had better hurry and finish shaving him. He's a busy man.

TAMEKICHI. Chatterbox! You said you wanted to go away with him!

OSHIKA [*with a smile*]. Don't take that seriously. You are nothing but a big child.

OKADA. He seems awfully nervous. [*To Tamekichi.*] Why don't you hurry and finish with me?

TAMEKICHI [*growing excited*]. Yes! I will finish!—I hold the razor in this hand, and your throat in the other hand. Now I fear no man in the whole world. Even a Minister or a General would be helpless. There is no one more powerful than I. Until this moment I was slave to the razor, and was prisoner in the mirror; and I suffered and was afraid. Fool! I am still alive! And to-day I am master of the razor!

[*The blade flashes. Okada screams, and falls to the floor, the chair tumbling over with him.*]

OSHIKA. Oh-h-h-h! What have you done?

[*She screams.*]

NOGUCHI. At last he has done it! [*His voice trembles.*] And there will be no lecture or reception!

TAMEKICHI [*staring vacantly into space*]. Ha, ha! Ha, ha! It is my body that lies before me! [*He laughs madly.*] Behold! Justice!

[*He stands trembling—his face pale.*]

[*Curtain.*]

THE MARRIAGE OF LITTLE EVA

A Comedy

By Kenyon Nicholson

CHARACTERS

JIM THORNE [*who plays Uncle Tom*].
SADIE MONTROSE [*who plays Eliza*].
ALLEN PETTIBONE [*who plays Legree*].
HATTIE HALE [*who plays Little Eva*].
ORIOLE [*her daughter*].
WALLY WAMPLER [*proprietor of the troupe*].

SCENE: *The star dressing room of the Opera House, Ladoga, Indiana.*

TIME: *Just after the evening performance.*

THE MARRIAGE OF LITTLE EVA was first presented by the Community Players, Fond du Lac, Wisconsin, with the following cast:

JIM THORNE	*Walter Grimes.*
SADIE MONTROSE	*Melissa Joiner.*
ALLEN PETTIBONE	*Fred Hammond.*
HATTIE HALE	*Janet Farley.*
ORIOLE	*Betty Ann Mathews.*
WALLY WAMPLER	*B. F. Helmholz.*

THE MARRIAGE OF LITTLE EVA

A COMEDY

By KENYON NICHOLSON

[*It is a small triangular shaped room with a door, rear, leading to the wings. Along the right wall hangs a cracked mirror outlined in electric bulbs. Beneath the mirror is a shelf laden with various theatrical paraphernalia, including a battered make-up box. In the corner stands a wardrobe trunk, half open. Across its side is pasted the label: "Uncle Tom's Cabin Co." Down stage, left, is a screen which serves as a clothes rack. Before the screen stands a dilapidated sofa. The walls are whitewashed, and adorned with several faded lithographs of such past dramatic successes as "Peck's Bad Boy," "Lena Rivers," and "Eight Bells."*

As the curtain rises the exit march is heard emanating from the auditorium. The dressing room is empty save for a child of about eight who lies asleep on the sofa. It is Oriole, Hattie's daughter. In a moment Hattie Hale enters. Her small figure is draped in a flowing robe of white cheesecloth somewhat resembling a nightgown. To her back is fastened a pair of property angel's wings. She carries a gilded trumpet. She is Little Eva who has just been to heaven. Concerning Hattie's age there is considerable doubt. The provincial audiences who watch her sicken and die each night know nothing of the art of make-up. Hattie, however, does. Her eight-year-old daughter, coupled with the fact that this is her fifteenth season in the rôle of Eva, makes one suspect that Hattie is not far from thirty.]

HATTIE [*to her offspring*]. You awake, kid?

[*Receiving no answer Hattie sits down before the mirror and begins to remove her make-up. She is plainly elated over something, expressing herself somewhat inade-*

quately by humming off key. As she unhooks the angel's wings there comes a knock at the door.]

HATTIE. Who is it?

JIM [*off*]. It's me, Hat. Who'd you expect—one of the blood-hounds!

HATTIE. Oh, come on in, Jim.

[*Enters Jim Thorne. He is dressed as Uncle Tom, the faithful but much abused negro servitor. In spite of his senile make-up he seems rather young.*]

JIM [*beaming at Hattie*]. Well, how's my little blushing bride by now?

HATTIE [*rising*]. More in love with her Jim every minute.

JIM. That's the way I like to hear my Hattie talk!

HATTIE. Jim, why haven't you got out of your make-up? It always takes you so long.

JIM [*ecstatically*]. Why, Hat—I just had to come in and see you! You know, a while ago I stood out there in the wings while the transformation was on, and I'll say you looked like a *regular* angel!

HATTIE [*pleased*]. Honest, Jim?

JIM. On the level! Give us a kiss, Hat.

[*Hattie kisses him.*]

HATTIE. I'm crazy about you, Jim, honey bug!

[*In their embrace a black smudge from his Uncle Tom make-up has rubbed off on her cheek.*]

JIM. Ha! Now look at yourself. You're all black!

HATTIE. I don't care. . . .

JIM [*pointing to their reflections in the mirror*]. Look, Hat, at us there in the glass. See that great big ugly darkey hugging a little white girl?

HATTIE. Looks like a case for the Ku Kluxers, don't it?

JIM [*sitting*]. Hand me your make-up

355

towel, honey, and I'll fix it where I rubbed off on you. Here, sit on your Jim's knee, like a good little girl.

HATTIE [*imitating Little Eva*]. Yes, Uncle Tom.

JIM. You're not sorry for what you did this afternoon, Hat?

HATTIE [*slapping him playfully*]. Who can tell if they're going to like their husband after only five hours of being married to him!

JIM. I'm not tooting my own horn, understand, but I bet I'll make you a better husband than Wally would of.

HATTIE. Jim, I never thought serious of marrying Wally Wampler, and you know it!

JIM. Just the same, you kept me in hot water thinking you might.

HATTIE [*patting him*]. Wally's been awful good to Oriole and me. But he's not my kind of a man.

JIM. Who is your kind of a man, then?

HATTIE [*hugging him*]. You know who!

JIM. Well, you're sure my kind of a woman, sweetheart. And if Wally wasn't manager of this troupe, I'd of had you married to me while we was still playing Ohio—instead of just this afternoon.

HATTIE [*seriously*]. Jim, we got to quit being so scared of Wally. Just because he's boss and does the hiring and firing don't mean he can run us outside the theater.

JIM. I know, Hat, but it don't pay to get him down on you. Look at the way he razzed Maude and Freddie out of the show last season.

HATTIE. He wouldn't dare to let two good performers like us go, even if he wanted to. How much of a show do you think he'd have left?

JIM [*convinced*]. That's right, Hat. We're the backbone of this troupe.

HATTIE. He don't scare me with all his big talk and bluff.

JIM. Well, I've about made up my mind if it leaks out that we're married and he starts acting up, I'm going to stand right up to him and speak my mind.

HATTIE. It's the only way to handle these managers. They respect you for it.

JIM. Besides, honey, if he does give us notice for having got married, I guess we won't starve. You know we got that fruit farm my old man left me up there in Berrien County, Michigan, to fall back on.

HATTIE. Of course we have, Jim.

JIM. I can always make a living for you and Oriole up there—if I have to.

HATTIE. You know, Jim, I couldn't help thinking when we were standing there being married in that pretty little parsonage, how nice it would be if we was to go up to that farm right off, and settle down and have a home and everything, with you raising fruit.

JIM. It sure would be nice, honey. But remember, we're saving that for our old age.

HATTIE. Sometimes, Jim, I feel awfully old now. I don't feel easy any more, playing Eva. It's enough to make a dog sick when I get out there and pipe around. I don't want to be like Carrie Fountaine—die of old age in the part.

JIM. Don't let that fret you. You're still the prettiest, sweetest Eva I know anything about! [*She starts to embrace him.*] No, hon, don't kiss me again now. I just got you wiped off from last time.

HATTIE [*rising from his lap*]. Better run along and get into your street clothes; so's we can get on over to the car.

JIM. All right. I'll come back and we'll go across the street for a plate of ham and eggs . . . our wedding supper.

HATTIE. Heard yet what time we pull out to-night?

JIM. One of the crew was saying we'd get out of the yards by one.

HATTIE. I better wake up Oriole now, so's you won't have to carry her. You know how limp and cross she gets, poor kid.

JIM [*looking down at Oriole*]. Hope we can keep her from calling me Pop—at least around Wally.

HATTIE. If she gives us away I'll knock her block off. And I told her so, too!

[*There is a knock at the door.*]

ALLEN [*off*]. It's Al. Can I come in?

JIM. Sure, Al! Come ahead. . . .

[*Enters Allen Pettibone, who plays Legree with the company. He is wearing his street clothes, but an investigation would reveal grease paint still behind his ears. Without his villain's make-up he is a mild-mannered fellow—almost effeminate.*]

ALLEN [*cordially*]. Well, how are the love birds by this time?

HATTIE. Haven't scratched yet, have we, Jim?

JIM. Not so you could notice it!

ALLEN [*glancing at the sleeping Oriole*]. What'd the kid say, Hat, when you told her she had a new papa?

HATTIE. She just asked me for a piece of candy, and rolled over and went to sleep.

JIM. She's too young to realize what it means.

ALLEN. Well, I'll say she's got an A-1 daddy this time.

HATTIE. Thanks, Al. You and Sadie are the two best pals a woman ever had.

JIM. That goes for me, too, Al. And I want to thank you again for standing up with us. I hope I can do the same for you some time.

ALLEN. Glad to do it—glad to do it. . . .

JIM [*largely*]. Married life's the only life, believe me!

ALLEN. Sure Wally never got wind of what went on this afternoon?

HATTIE. So far as we know he hasn't. You heard that preacher promise he wouldn't give us away, didn't you?

ALLEN. I know, but I'd be breathing easier if we were on our way to the next stand. This is a mighty small burg, and such things as weddings get around mighty quick.

JIM. Nobody's going to run up to Wally and tell him—even if they do know it.

ALLEN. Well, here's hoping. Guess I'll be moving along down to the car. Pull out at one, you know.

[*As Allen opens the door Sadie Montrose enters. She is dowdy and middle-aged, looking more like a seamstress than an actress. However, she has been doing one-night stands practically all her life. And as Eliza, she has crossed the ice no less than five thousand times.*]

SADIE [*excitedly*]. Wally been in here yet?

JIM. Why, no—what's up?

HATTIE. Is he coming back stage?

SADIE. Dearie, I don't want to throw a scare into you, but I think he's wise.

ALLEN. You mean he knows they got married!

SADIE. I was out front just now signing an I.O.U., and he was fit to be tied about something.

JIM. What'd he say?

SADIE. All I heard was: "Those two've turned their last trick on me!"

HATTIE. That all?

ALLEN. What more do you expect?

SADIE. He kicked over a chair and yelled, "I'll teach 'em to make a monkey outa my show!"

ALLEN. My God!

HATTIE [*hoping against hope*]. You don't *know* he was talking about Jim and me, though.

SADIE. No, not sure. But I hurried back here to let you know, so in case it was you'd be ready.

JIM. That big bag of wind better not start anything around here.

ALLEN. Sadie, we better make ourselves scarce—just in case. . . .

SADIE. You're right, Al. We can't help you folks by mixing in. Shall I take Oriole with me?

HATTIE. No, she's still asleep. No need to get excited as I can see. I've watched these man-eating managers perform before!

SADIE. You know how mean Wally can be when he takes a notion!

HATTIE. They're all a bluff if you face them down.

ALLEN. Sadie and me will be outside waiting if you need us.

SADIE. Well, good luck, Hat, and don't say anything you'll be sorry for.

[*Allen and Sadie exeunt.*]

HATTIE. Now, Jim, you hustle along to your dressing room and get out of that make-up just as if nothing was going to happen.

JIM. What, and leave you here to face him alone?

HATTIE. I can handle him—I'd rather talk to him alone.

JIM. What if he begins to insult you?

HATTIE. Never you mind. I've been insulted by better managers than Wally Wampler. Go on, Jim—please!

JIM. I hate to have you fight it out with him.

HATTIE. Just leave him to me—I'm not scared. . . .

JIM. I'll be listening, hon, and if he

pulls any rough stuff just call. I'll come back and mop up the floor with him!

[*Jim goes out. Hattie sits before the mirror applying cold cream to her make-up. On the couch Oriole stirs, then sits up, rubs her eyes and whimpers. She is a typical stage child, anœmic and pimply.*]

HATTIE. It's all right, Baby, mamma's about ready. . . .

ORIOLE. Ain't it time to go down to the car, Mamma?

HATTIE. Don't say "ain't," Pet—we're going in just a minute now. . . . Lay down and rest some more.

[*Oriole obeys whiningly. Hattie removes her costume and gets into her street dress. She is thus engaged when there comes a knock at the door.*]

HATTIE [*cautiously*]. Come in.

[*Enters Wally Wampler, a pop-eyed, heavy-set man wearing a soiled suit of black and white checks. His hair looks too sleek not to be a toupee.*]

WALLY. H'lo, Hat.

HATTIE [*trying to be calm*]. How're you, Wally?

WALLY. S'prised to see me?

HATTIE. I sort of expected a visit from you, now you ask me.

WALLY. Somebody tip you off?

HATTIE. I'm not saying.

WALLY. What's all this I hear about you and Jim?

HATTIE. How should I know what you're hearing?

WALLY [*angrily*]. Aw, might as well can the stallin', Hat. I gotcha cold.

HATTIE. Have you?

WALLY. You know what I mean! About you and Jim gettin' married!

[*Wally's voice has risen so that Oriole is aroused. She begins to cry.*]

HATTIE. See what you did with your loud mouth! [*Tenderly.*] Go to sleep again, Oriole, sweetheart. . . . Mamma won't be long now.

ORIOLE. I want some candy, Mamma.

HATTIE. No, darling—not to-night.

ORIOLE. But, Mamma, I want some!

HATTIE. Hush, Oriole!

[*Oriole starts to cry again.*]

WALLY [*exasperated*]. For God's sake, give her some to shut her up!

HATTIE. Just one piece then, Pet. In the top of Mamma's trunk.

[*Oriole crosses to trunk and returns licking a large stick of molasses taffy.*]

WALLY [*getting back to the issue*]. Well, Hat, let's have it. What've you and Jim gotta say for yourself?

HATTIE. Nothing. We're not ashamed of it!

WALLY. Well, you oughta be! You sneak out to a preacher when my back's turned, like a coupla love-sick calves. . . !

HATTIE. Since when do we have to ask your permission?

WALLY. I never heard of anything to beat it, and I've had out a Tom show for the last twenty years.

HATTIE. What's the odds?

WALLY. Odds! I'll tell you the odds. How much business you s'pose we'll do, when we blow in a burg and it gets 'round to the customers that Tom and Eva are man and wife? Uncle Tom and Little Eva married! Damned if it's not immoral!

HATTIE [*sharply*]. I'll thank you not to curse before my child!

WALLY. It's enough to make a preacher swear.

HATTIE. I'll tell you what's wrong with you, Wally. You're just mad because I took Jim instead of you.

WALLY. You hate yourself, don't you?

HATTIE. I guess I can tell the truth when I see it. Why don't you be a good sport and leave Jim and me be?

[*There is a pause, during which Wally comes closer to her.*]

WALLY. I won't say I don't care a lot for you, Hat. And even now. . . .

HATTIE [*bristling*]. Don't forget I'm a married woman. . . !

WALLY. I can't forget you threw yourself away on a ham actor. I gave you credit for having more sense.

HATTIE. Take care how you talk about Jim, Wally Wampler!

[*Wally decides to take a new tack.*]

WALLY. Well, all I can say is, Hat, you're all washed up as far as your career is concerned.

HATTIE [*with a touch of pride*]. Jim and me don't have to act for a living. He's got a fruit farm up in Michigan.

WALLY. You two 'ud be a riot runnin' a fruit farm!

HATTIE. And I can always come back in the business if I get tired of it.

WALLY. They never come back. I seen what marryin' does for a performer. You begin eatin' too much, sleepin' too much, and before you know it you're fat. And in a coupla years' time you're sloppy and middle-age.

[*Hattie has crossed to the sofa and sits with her arm about her child, who is still effectively pacified by the taffy.*]

HATTIE. Haven't I earned a rest? Since I was twelve I've been living out of a trunk, playing under canvas, in town halls, skating-rinks and one-horse theaters like this—and eating in beaneries that wasn't fit for a hog. I'm sick of it. . . . I've earned a rest.

WALLY. All right, sister, hop to it! Only don't say I didn't warn you.

HATTIE. What I want worse than anything is a home; a place where I can spread out and do my own cooking and make my own beds, and do all those things that women are supposed to do.

WALLY. You'd sing a diff'rent tune after a year on a God-forsaken farm.

[*There is a knock at the door.*]

JIM [*off*]. About ready, Hat?

HATTIE [*rising*]. Come on in, Jim.

[*Jim enters, dressed in his street clothes. Wally looks him up and down contemptuously.*]

WALLY. I s'pose you feel quite proud of yourself for what you done this afternoon.

JIM. If you mean marrying Hat, I certainly am.

WALLY. Well, mebbe you won't feel so good when I tell you my wedding present to you is your notice.

HATTIE [*aghast*]. His notice! How do you figure that out?

WALLY. I ain't goin' to have a coupla honeymooners playin' Tom and Eva with *my* show. Not as long as I'm still in my right mind.

HATTIE. Wally, you're meaner'n I thought you was!

JIM. Well, I won't accept a notice, do you hear?

WALLY. Oh, you won't, won't you!

JIM. No! I resign. Now that I've got a wife I've made up my mind to leave the road anyway.

WALLY. Huh! It'll be an awful loss to the perfession!

HATTIE. Are you trying to pick a fight?

JIM. He can't bluff me. I don't have to take his lip. I got a fruit farm up in—

WALLY. Michigan. Yeh, I heard all about that!

HATTIE. You fire Jim Thorne and I go, too!

WALLY. You'll go right on playin' Eva, my fine lady—married or no married.

HATTIE. Oh, is that so!

WALLY. You forgot, I s'pose, I gotta season contract with you!

JIM. You can't hold her against her will.

WALLY. We'll see what the law says about that.

HATTIE [*frightenedly*]. You know you can't, Wally.

WALLY. Can't I? Say, you break your contract with me and I'll sue you. So help me I will!

HATTIE [*flaring up*]. Shame on you, Wally—coming between man and wife!

[*Jim sees that he is cornered and decides that it is best to conciliate.*]

JIM. Now, lookie here, Wally. No use getting all worked up about this thing. Let's reason it out.

WALLY. I'm willin' to lissen to reason. But Hat don't leave—that's final!

[*Oriole begins to whimper again.*]

ORIOLE. Ain't it time to go down to the car, Mamma?

HATTIE [*severely*]. One more crack out of you, Oriole, and I'll certainly spank you!

JIM. Wally, if I could produce an Eva to take Hat's place to work out the rest of her contract, will you let Hat go without making any trouble?

WALLY. What do you want to do—pick up some stage-struck jane and ring her in on me?

JIM. No, I'm on the level. I've got somebody in mind. Will you?

WALLY. I'll think about it. . . .

HATTIE. You better think hard, Wally. If I haven't my heart in my work I'm liable to crab the show.

JIM. Ssh, Hat! All right, Wally, here's what I'm offering you—Oriole.

WALLY. Oriole!

JIM. Why not give Oriole a shot at the part?

WALLY [*snorting*]. Say, you'd make a horse laugh!

JIM. You don't think she could handle it, do you? Well, you don't know.

WALLY. She couldn't touch it with a ten-foot pole!

HATTIE. That's all you know about it!

JIM. She's just the right age, got the voice, looks—everything.

WALLY. Did you ever hear of an eight-year-old kid playin' Eva? I ask you!

JIM. That's supposeᵈ to be her age in the script. It would be something novel and orginal.

HATTIE. Don't worry. Oriole could do it, but I don't know as I'd want her to.

JIM. It'd only be till your contract runs out. Besides, Sadie'll look out for her.

HATTIE [*to Oriole*]. What do you say, darling, to being an actress like Mamma?

ORIOLE. I don't wanta!

JIM. Sure you do, Baby!

HATTIE. Just think, Oriole, you'd get pretty lace dresses and ride in the pony cart every day in the parade!

ORIOLE [*only mildly interested*]. Could I have lots of candy—

JIM. Sure you could!

ORIOLE. Whenever I wanted it?

HATTIE. Maybe you could, Pet.

ORIOLE. Well, then, I'd like to be an actress, Mamma.

JIM [*triumphantly*]. Hear that, Wally! The kid says she *wants* to be an actress.

WALLY. Yeh, but that don't make her one!

JIM. Well, Oriole's got the goods. You tell him, Hat.

HATTIE. She knows Eva as well as I do—every if, and, and but.

JIM. She's learned it just standing in the wings, watching Hat work.

WALLY. You gotta show me—I'm from Missouri. . . .

JIM. Put her through the deathbed scene, Hat. Go on—show him we're right.

HATTIE. Oriole, be like Mamma. Start in where I say: "And is Heaven all full of gold streets and angels"—you remember.

ORIOLE. I don't feel like it, Mamma.

HATTIE. Oriole!

ORIOLE [*yawning*] I'm too sleepy. . . .

JIM. Do this nice for your Mamma, and I'll give you a pretty present when we get back to the car.

HATTIE [*going over to her daughter*]. Oriole, stretch out flat on the couch. Take little short breaths like Mamma showed you. Roll your eyes.

JIM. I'll feed her the cues, Hat.

WALLY [*sitting—interested in spite of himself*]. Well, I'm from Missouri. . . .

HATTIE. All right, Jim—start in.

[*Hattie stands by anxiously watching her daughter during the ensuing scene. Wally lights a cigar.*]

JIM [*assuming the rôle of Uncle Tom*]. "Dat's all dar in de good book, jes' like I tol' you, Little Eva."

ORIOLE [*in a high wavering voice*]. "And is Heaven all full of gold streets and angels, Uncle Tom?"

JIM [*kneeling by sofa*]. "Yes, Little Eva, angels wid big white wings and carryin' harps."

ORIOLE. "Will I have a harp when I go to Heaven, Uncle Tom?"

JIM [*business with handkerchief*]. "Don't talk dat way, Little Eva, yer breakin' my ole heart."

ORIOLE. "I hope you will always be a good man, Uncle Tom, and never do anything to vex your master. . . . Why is everything growing so dark, Uncle Tom? Is it evening. . . ? I can hear bells ringing afar off."

[*Uncle Tom is racked with sobs.*]

ORIOLE [*tremolo stop wide open.*] "Uncle Tom, I'm going far away. . . . I can hear the angels singing. Tell Topsy to be a good girl for my sake. Tell my mamma to kiss my papa good-by for me. Good-by, Uncle Tom. . . . Good-by. I will meet you all in Heaven. . . ."

[*Oriole sinks back upon her pillow.*]

JIM [*rising from his knees*]. What'd I tell you, Wally!

WALLY. By God, the kid's there! She made chills go up my back.

JIM. Sure puts new life in that old hokum, don't she?

HATTIE [*hugging Oriole*]. She's her mamma's precious, that's what she is!

WALLY [*to Oriole*]. Come here, kid, and give your Uncle Wally a big kiss.

ORIOLE. I don't wanta be kissed. I wanta go to bed!

HATTIE. Now is that a nice way to act?

WALLY. Kiss or no kiss, she's some swell little trouper.

JIM. Didn't we say she could do it?

WALLY. All right. You win.

JIM [eagerly]. And will you let her play out Hat's contract?

WALLY. Let her! Would I let Mary Pickford! Say, she'll knock 'em off their seats!

HATTIE. Funny, you never noticed it before to-night.

WALLY. Wait till we get her dolled up in your angel outfit. She'll make it a transformation scene worth lookin' at.

HATTIE [irrelevantly]. She eats too much candy.

JIM. It's in her blood to act. No more keep that youngun off the stage than fly.

WALLY. Hat, I'll bet she'll show you how the part oughta be played.

HATTIE [piqued]. Oh, I don't know about that. . . .

WALLY. Give her a week and she'll make you look like thirty cents.

HATTIE. Are you trying to tell me she can play Eva better than I can?

WALLY. Judgin' from the sample she handed us a while ago, I'd say she could.

HATTIE [wrathfully]. That's gratitude for you! Here, I've been slaving for you season after season in the part and now you say I'm a flop!

WALLY. Back up—I never said no such thing!

HATTIE. You did so! I can play Eva as well as anybody living!

JIM. Don't take him serious, Hat. He's just trying to get your goat.

HATTIE. If Oriole plays Eva, it'll be over my dead body!

[She flings herself on the sofa which Oriole has lately vacated, bursting into hysterical tears.]

JIM [going to her]. Brace up, Hat. . . . Wally didn't mean anything. . . .

WALLY [half to himself]. By God, if she ain't jealous of her own kid!

JIM. Come on, honey. . . . You're all nerves—let's get out in the air.

HATTIE [sobbing]. Leave me be!

[To add to the confusion, Oriole begins to cry out of sympathy.]

WALLY. Say, hire a hall! This ain't a funeral!

JIM [helplessly]. What can I do, Wally? It's a madhouse. . . !

WALLY [aside to Jim]. Take the kid outside. Leave Hat to me—I'll fix it up.

[Without another word Jim takes Oriole by the hand and leads her out of the room. As he goes out he casts a look at his weeping bride, shaking his head dejectedly.]

WALLY [after a moment]. Hat, come on—turn off the waterworks. [She continues to sob]. Hat!

HATTIE [sniffling]. What do you want?

WALLY [after another pause]. I've changed my mind—you and Jim can finish playin' out the season.

HATTIE. You was just kidding—about Oriole!

WALLY. Sure. . . . You know, Hat, Jim ain't the only one that's fell for you. . . .

HATTIE [a little ashamed of herself]. You understand, Wally, why I acted up when you wanted Oriole to take my place—

WALLY [largely]. Sure, I understand.

HATTIE. What kind of a mother would I be if I went off and left her to do my work for me?

[The Curtain Falls.]

THE BIRDCATCHER

A Play

By Seumas O'Brien

CHARACTERS

NELLIE AHERNE [*a young woman of twenty-one*].
THOMAS KENNEDY [*her uncle*].
SAM LOONEY [*a birdcatcher*].
DAN HOGAN [*a plumber*].
A POLICE CONSTABLE.

THE BIRDCATCHER

A PLAY   BY SEUMAS O'BRIEN

[SCENE: *Interior of a cottage in the south of Ireland. Nellie Aherne, a young woman of twenty-one, is seen packing a suit case. Thomas Kennedy, her uncle, an elderly man suffering from rheumatics comes from the next room. When Nellie sees him, she closes the suit case and tries to look unconcerned.*]

TOM. What are you doing, child?

NELLIE [*nonchalantly*]. Oh, nothing much, Uncle Tom.

TOM. One would think you were going on a summer vacation and the swallows already on their way home.

NELLIE. I'm just doing a little cleaning; that's all. Everything indoors gathers dust.

TOM. That's something I'm aware of, but there's no more dust on that bag of yours than you'd find in the eye of a hawk.

NELLIE. Oh, wisha, you're worse than any hawk yourself. 'Tis as bad to see too much as too little.

TOM. You're just like your mother, rest her soul. She'd have the last word and her own way in spite of any one. No wonder she sent your poor father to an early grave, and left you an orphan on my hands.

NELLIE. I thought you were very fond of my mother, Uncle Tom.

TOM. I was so. You couldn't help liking her. She was good nature itself, but the devil to live with.

[*Walks towards the fireplace.*]

NELLIE. What are you looking for?

TOM. My tobacco can.

NELLIE. Maybe you will find it in your own room.

TOM. In my own room! Will you ever learn to leave things in the one place?

[*Goes into room. While he is away Nellie hides the suit case behind the dresser.*]

NELLIE [*as he returns*]. Did you find your tobacco?

TOM. I did, strange to say. I have yet to find your equal for shifting things about. My bed and my armchair are never in the same place for two days at a stretch.

NELLIE. Don't I always do my very best to please you, Uncle Tom?

TOM. Maybe so, but it seems to me that everybody pleases themselves these days.

[*Draws a chair to the table, sits down and tries to open the can of tobacco.*]

NELLIE. Let me try.

[*Takes can from him, opens it after a struggle, but it falls and the contents spill on the floor.*]

TOM. God pity me this blessed day! I never can get anything done right that I don't do myself.

NELLIE [*picking up the tobacco*]. You shouldn't worry about little things. Accidents will happen.

TOM. Yes, always with people whose fingers are all thumbs.

NELLIE. Why do you say such things to me, Uncle Tom? You are becoming an awful crank.

TOM. Crank? Just think of it! Me the quietest man in the seven parishes, and the most afflicted man in the whole world to be called out of my name by my own niece. 'Tis about time you knew that I am never without a pain or an ache, and that Job himself had the life of a parish priest compared to me.

NELLIE. Some people don't know when they are well off.

TOM. What's that you said, young lady?

NELLIE [*annoyed*]. Hush now. I may not be a trouble to you much longer.

TOM. I'd like to know what you mean, young lady.

NELLIE [*surprised at what she said*].

Oh, nothing, Uncle Tom. When you are cross you always make me say foolish things.

TOM. But true things maybe. [*Affectionately.*] Nellie?

NELLIE. What is it, Uncle Tom?

TOM. You wouldn't think of leaving me, would you, Nellie? You mustn't forget that I have been a father and a mother to you since you were the height of my knee. I don't want to lose you now after all that I have done for you.

NELLIE. Whatever put such notions into your head? I have never been unmindful of all your kindness.

TOM. I hope not, child. [*Searches for matches in his pockets.*] Where have my matches disappeared to, I wonder?

NELLIE. I don't know, but I'll try to find some for you. [*Takes a box from the mantelshelf and hands it to him.*] Here you are.

TOM. Thanks. [*As he lights his pipe.*] There's something wrong with you lately, Nellie; and though you may not think so, I know what's the matter.

NELLIE [*with surprise*]. What is it?

TOM. Too many sweethearts you have. No wonder you can't remember where you put things. 'Tis thinking about them you do be instead of looking after me.

NELLIE. Too many sweethearts? I have only three, Uncle Tom. And one is in Australia at that.

TOM. And one a bigger fool than the other. Confused and bothered they have you. That's why all the return I get for my kindness is neglect.

NELLIE. The trouble with you is that you get too much attention. Have you no pity on me at all, or is it the way you have lost all your self-control to be carrying on as you are?

TOM. Self-control! Sure 'tis distracted I do be half the time from using the restraining hand on my poor self.

NELLIE. I don't want to offend you in any way, Uncle Tom, but I think it is only fair to let you know that I am getting a little tired of all your abuse.

TOM. Very well if you are. I know what I will do in future, and then there will be no occasion to chastise any one.

NELLIE. What will you do?

TOM. I'll keep the door closed, and won't let any of the poor angashores who came here to make love to you step over the threshold again. Too many admirers always spoil a young woman, not indeed that it takes a great deal to spoil the b. t of them.

NELLIE. What have you against my friends, Uncle Tom?

TOM. 'Twould take me a month of Sundays to tell you. To begin with I can't understand for the life of me, why a young girl like you should want to associate with her social inferiors.

NELLIE. What makes you think the people I mix with aren't as good as myself?

TOM. Isn't it a fact that Sam Looney, the most ardent claimant for your hand, is only a birdcatcher, and the other, Dan Hogan, is a plumber?

NELLIE. And what about it?

TOM. God only knows what the Australian is. A kangaroo catcher maybe, or a bandit of some kind for all we know.

NELLIE. What has a man's calling to do with one's affection? I'd rather share a crust with the man I love than live in a castle with the man I didn't.

TOM. Are you losing your senses, or maybe you never had any to lose?

NELLIE. I am not losing my senses.

TOM. Then you have no respect for the family you sprung from. I am ashamed of you, Nellie. You that had a father with a public house, and a horse and car of his own to have no higher notions than plumbing or birdcatching.

NELLIE. But I haven't told you who I am in love with, or whether I am in love at all or not.

TOM. Be said by me now, child, and if you are going to marry, take plenty of time and find some one who won't keep you in the kitchen all the days of your life. Anyway you are much too young yet to think of settling down.

NELLIE. A kitchen isn't the worst place to be in, Uncle Tom, and 'tis better to have some man to work for than no man at all.

[*Sam Looney enters. He has a birdcage with sprigs on it in one hand, and a paper bag with birds in it in the other.*]

SAM [*cheerfully*]. God bless all here.

NELLIE. And you too, Sam.

TOM [*looking scornfully at him*]. Here's one of the pests now. What the devil brings you here, I'd like to know?

SAM. I thought I was always welcome.

TOM. You surely have no small opinion of yourself. A decent man can't call his soul his own while he has enough of friends to pester the life out of him.

SAM. That's not a very charitable thing to say to an old friend, Tom.

TOM. Charitable! Who the hell do you think I am, St. Francis?

SAM. I hope your bark is worse than your bite at all events, and that you won't consider yourself too important to do me a favor.

TOM. What is it you want done now? All I do from daylight till dark is grant favors, and I'm getting tired.

SAM [handing him the birdcage]. Will you hide this cage and these few sprigs for me, and see that nothing happens the bird. He's the finest songster in the length and breadth of the land.

TOM. Why hide him?

SAM. This is the closed season, and I'm afraid I was seen sprigging linnets in the marsh beyond by a peeler. I want to give him the slip. It means a fine or imprisonment, maybe, if I'm caught.

TOM. Did he follow you?

SAM. I'm not sure, but I don't want to take any chances.

TOM. If there was a prize for the biggest fool since Adam ate the apple you'd get it. I hope you'll be caught or any one else that goes birdcatching either in or out of season.

SAM. What an unreasonable thing for a sensible man to say!

TOM. There's nothing unreasonable about it. I'd like to know how you'd feel if you were kept in a cage for the remainder of your days.

NELLIE. We are all kept in cages, but some of us are such fools we don't know it.

TOM. Some put themselves in them.

NELLIE. Why don't you do what Sam asks you to do? You always delight in scolding him, and he loves you just as much as I do.

TOM [taking cage]. All right, all right. I'll do what I'm told then. I'm more like a servant in my own house than anything else.
[Exit.]

NELLIE [to Sam]. Now, I don't want to scold you, Sam, but I am very angry just the same.

SAM. Why are you angry with me, Nellie?

NELLIE. Because you don't seem to have as much gumption as a crow. You were a great fool to put yourself in the power of the law by catching birds in the closed season. And you a lover of birds too! I don't know how you can excuse yourself at all.

SAM. I do.

NELLIE. I'd like to hear your defense.

SAM. It was to help another that I ran the risk of getting into a scrape myself. If we didn't help each other, Nellie, the world would very soon go to pieces.

NELLIE. Do I know the person you are so anxious to help?

SAM [smiling]. Indeed you do, Nellie.

NELLIE. A lady or a gentleman, Sam?

SAM. A gentleman.

NELLIE. I can't think who he can be.

SAM. 'Tis no less a person than Dan Hogan himself.

NELLIE. Dan Hogan the plumber who comes here?

SAM. The very one. He told me he was going to America, and said he would sail by the next boat if I could give him what he was short of the passage money.

NELLIE. How much did he say he wanted?

SAM. Five pounds. I have three that I saved, and in a little while I will have two more.

NELLIE [anxiously]. How are you going to get it, Sam?

SAM. From a Russian nobleman who is staying in Moore's Hotel. He promised me ten shillings each for four linnets and I have them now in this paper bag. I'll get the money as soon as they are delivered and as he leaves in the morning for Moscow no one will be a whit the wiser.

NELLIE [doubtfully]. What would a Russian nobleman want four linnets for, Sam?

SAM. A present for an Irish sweetheart he has away in the Caucasus Mountains. He came here to see the castle her father was born in.

NELLIE. But if the police find out, what then?

SAM. We can worry about that if I'm caught. Not another word about what I told you. I will leave by the back door to avoid being seen and return as soon as possible with the money. I'm to meet Dan Hogan here within half an hour.

NELLIE. Make haste then, Sam, and good luck to you.

SAM [as he leaves]. Everything will be all right, Nellie. I won't be long.

[A police constable looks over the half door.]

CONSTABLE. Good day, Miss Nellie.

NELLIE. Good day and good luck, Constable.

CONSTABLE. I suppose there's no objection to my coming in?

NELLIE. None whatever. We don't close the door on any one.

CONSTABLE. Thank you. [Walks in, sits down on a chair and mops his brow with a red handkerchief.] You don't seem to have very much company to-day.

NELLIE. The day is still young, Constable.

TOM [coming from the next room]. Who the devil have we now?

CONSTABLE. How are you, Tom?

TOM [annoyed]. A lot of trouble it gives you how I am.

CONSTABLE. You haven't changed a bit in all the years I know you. Surely you don't think it gives me any pleasure to know that you are in middling health. We all have our own troubles, Tom.

TOM. Wisha, in the name of God, what has a big fat slob like you to be troubled about?

CONSTABLE. Oh, 'tis enough for one man in the town to be always talking about himself and his complaints. I came here on official business and not to start an argument.

TOM. Official business?

CONSTABLE. Yes, I'm looking for the young man who came through your doorway a little while ago with a birdcage in his hand.

TOM. I'm afraid you are mistaken this time.

CONSTABLE. I am not, Tom. I tracked the offender from the marshes, and saw him enter here from the brow of the hill beyond.

TOM. Your imagination was always better than your eyesight, Constable. What kind of a man did you say he was?

CONSTABLE. He wasn't much of a man, but he had the look of a gom and the stride of a birdcatcher.

TOM. There was a great artist lost in you, Constable. Your observation is wonderful. Did he look like any of the boys of the neighborhood?

CONSTABLE. He did.

TOM. Which of them?

CONSTABLE. Sam Looney. I am ready to swear he was the gentleman I saw sprigging linnets and in private property too. You know of course what an offense like that means during the closed season. The law of the land must be obeyed.

TOM. Oh, to hell with you and the law! There were birds before the law and there will be birds after the law. 'Tis easily seen you haven't much to do. But I suppose you must find some excuse for drawing your wages at the end of the month. Any one who ever met Sam Looney knows he is too respectable to do anything out of the way.

CONSTABLE. Respectability and bird-catching are two different things, Tom. I have never seen a man with a spark of pride in him with a birdcage in his paw.

TOM. I don't feel a bit like discussing the merits or the demerits of the pastime. All I know is that Sam is not the man you want. He isn't the kind to put his neck in a halter; for he hasn't courage enough to be either a scamp or a hero.

CONSTABLE. Are you quite sure he didn't come in here?

TOM. Didn't you get your answer already? You ought to know that I wouldn't harbor a lawbreaker no more than you would yourself.

CONSTABLE [rising]. Well, I've got to find the transgressor wherever he has gone to; and when I do there will be one less of his kind at large for some time to come.

TOM. Don't let your generosity run away with you whatever you'll do. More have been ruined by their hearts than their heads.

CONSTABLE [as he leaves]. Don't squander your advice, Tom. You will need it all for yourself. Good day to you both.

TOM AND NELLIE [together]. Good day.

TOM [to Nellie]. Now you see what happens when you have anything to do with those beneath you. It always involves one in trouble.

NELLIE. It isn't fair to say that Sam is beneath me, Uncle Tom. Money after all is only a superficial distinction. You should never allow your feelings to interfere with your judgment.

TOM. If you had a grain of judgment you wouldn't be dividing your affection between two poor creatures who haven't the makings of a man between them. And besides 'tis morally wrong. No young woman should allow a young man to get too fond of her unless she intends to return his affection.

NELLIE. If people like me I can't help it.

TOM. But you shouldn't be too friendly with them. Anyway 'tis better not to encourage or marry those we love. We keep our dreams all the longer.

[*Enter Dan Hogan, a swaggering young man of twenty-four.*]

DAN. God bless the good people of the house.

TOM. Wisha, may the devil take you! What brings you here again? You're like the cockroaches, there's no getting rid of you.

DAN. Is it possible that you are not glad to see me? If you're not then I'm glad to see you.

TOM. How long have I become a source of attraction?

DAN. I always like to have a talk with you, Tom.

TOM. And why may I ask?

DAN. Because you are so different from the other caubogues around here.

TOM. Other caubogues, did you say?

DAN. That was what I said, but maybe 'tisn't what I meant. I don't always express myself very clearly.

TOM. I don't know how a damn fool like you could.

DAN. I didn't mean to cast a reflection on you, Tom. I was only referring to the others. They haven't either a good or a bad word to say about any one but you have more to say than one would want to listen to.

TOM. Is it me or yourself you are trying to compliment, I'd like to know?

DAN. You, of course, Tom.

TOM. 'Tis a good job you're not trying to make a living as a commercial traveler, young man.

NELLIE. Don't be so cranky, Uncle Tom. Dan is a little embarrassed, and you are only making him worse.

TOM [*thoughtfully*]. I suppose 'tisn't fair to be too hard on those who are naturally stupid. [*To Dan.*] I can't

see for the life of me what you want coming here at all for.

DAN. If you were a young man on your first legs wouldn't you want to see a girl like Nellie?

TOM. When I was a young man I waited for the girls to come after me.

DAN. That's why you are an old bachelor to-day.

TOM. If you had any sense in that empty head of yours, you would know that you are not good enough for Nellie.

DAN. 'Tis better that the woman should be a little more refined than the man, of course, but even at that I don't see what's wrong with me.

TOM. Of course you don't. What future have you that you should entertain serious intentions of any young girl, especially a well handed, thrifty girl like my niece?

DAN [*proudly*]. I have an estate.

TOM. What?

DAN. An estate. Dr. Johnson says "He who has a trade has an estate," and I have a trade.

TOM. The idea of a poor plumber who never learned to wipe a joint to have such opinions. What you call a trade is nothing more than a poor excuse for making a living.

DAN. You don't know what you're talking about. Plumbing is the first and last of trades. Only for the members of my profession, all the Americans would freeze to death in winter, and wouldn't be able to wash themselves in the summer. And moreover I want you to know that it was one of us invented the bath tub, the greatest boon to humanity since the discovery of soap and bad language.

TOM. You talk with all the assurance of a man of knowledge or a man of wealth.

DAN. Knowledge is sometimes a handicap, and if I haven't wealth, I have what's more valuable.

TOM. What's that? Presumption, I suppose.

DAN. No, Tom, health, youth, and a desire for adventure.

TOM. It is true that we only enjoy making fools of ourselves when we are young, but I hate to think of all the trouble you will cause before you'll be gray.

DAN. Well, I am not likely to cause you any more uneasiness at all events.

TOM. Maybe with God's help you are going to leave us?

DAN. I am, Tom.

TOM. It sounds too good to be true. It will be the happiest day of my life when I'll see you going down the road for the last time.

DAN. It always pleases me when I can give others a little pleasure; especially an old friend like you, Tom.

TOM. Where are you going to?

DAN. Where would any enterprising young man be going to but the States?

TOM. How are you going to get there, may I ask? Walk maybe?

DAN. No, Tom. I have my passage money all but five pounds. If I could raise that much now, I could get away from here to-day. A boat leaves Cobh to-morrow.

TOM. Do you mean to tell me that if you had five pounds now, you would clear out, not bother Nellie any more with your attentions, and leave us all in peace and quietness?

DAN. That trifling sum is all that stands between me and a glorious future.

TOM. I can spare five pounds. You can send it back to me when you can spare it; though that may be never. 'Tis but little faith I ever had in talkers like you.

DAN. Not only will I send back whatever you will loan me but twice as much so that you can drink my health with the rest of the boys when it comes.

TOM. When it comes! That's what they all say. I suppose you'd like to have the money now?

DAN. There's no time like the present.

TOM [as he goes for the money to the next room]. You're not as foolish as you look, young man.

[Exit.]

NELLIE [to Dan]. You will be the death of me with the dreadful things you are doing; taking money from poor Uncle Tom, Sam and any one else that will give it to you.

DAN. Hold your tongue and don't spoil my chances. A man at his wit's end will do many a queer thing. I might as well have some of the old man's money as the doctors, and they not doing him a ha'porth of good. But think of the grand time he will have abusing me.

NELLIE. And don't you mind?

DAN. Devil a bit. 'Tis the silent ones I'm always afraid of.

NELLIE. He will never forgive you.

DAN. And even if he don't? He will enjoy having a grievance. There's only a few more years in him anyway, and 'twould be a pity to deprive him of having a good time. You should never take a grumbling man seriously.

TOM [from the door of his room]. Nellie, where are the keys of my chest of drawers?

NELLIE. I don't know, Uncle Tom.

TOM. Come here and help me find them.

NELLIE. I will in a minute.

TOM. Come now if you please.

NELLIE. All right.

[As she leaves Sam Looney enters.]

SAM. I'm glad you're here, Dan. Are you waiting long?

DAN. Not very long, Sam. What kind of news have you for me?

SAM. Good news, Dan.

DAN. You sold the linnets to the nobleman, I hope?

SAM. I did.

DAN. That's fine. Have you the money?

SAM. Yes, I have.

DAN. The whole five pounds?

SAM. Every penny of it. [Handing notes.] Here you are, Dan. One, two, three, four, five.

DAN [taking the money]. God bless you, Sam. I hope you are not leaving yourself short.

SAM. Oh, don't bother about me. Money isn't everything.

DAN. 'Tis the thing that stands in the way of most people's happiness, Sam. However, I'll refund it all and great deal more to you as soon as I'll get a job on the other side of the Atlantic.

SAM. You don't seem to think much of crossing the ocean, Dan.

DAN. Why should I? We must keep traveling whether we like it or not, only some are content to keep going around in circles. Are you never tempted to pull up your anchor, so to speak, go adrift and see all the wonders of the world?

SAM. I'm tempted sometimes. But it takes great courage to go where there are only strange faces, and never again hear the song of the birds you love maybe. I wouldn't want to wake up in the morning and find myself in a place where I couldn't hear the birds singing.

DAN. Surely you don't want to remain here all your lifetime listening to the birds? I don't believe you were ever a half a mile from a haystack, Sam.

SAM. I love this place, Dan, and I want to be here in the spring, when everything that's alive rejoices, and I want to be here in the summer when the air is thick with fragrance. And I want to be here in the autumn when the corn ripens and every tree is laden with fruit, and above all I want to be here in the winter.

DAN. In the winter?

SAM. Yes, when the landscape is covered with snow.

DAN. How can you enjoy yourself then?

SAM. I can come here in the evenings, and sit with Tom and Nellie by the fireside.

DAN. But won't you get tired from listening to old Tom and his lamentations?

SAM. I won't mind so long as Nellie is beside me.

DAN. But what about Nellie? Keeping house for a cranky, selfish old man, and having nothing to look forward to but you for a husband isn't much of a prospect for any one.

SAM. I'm very fond of her, Dan. I don't know what I'd do with myself if she wasn't here.

DAN. You're a queer man. I suppose it wouldn't do if we were all alike. If 'twas for fun the world was made, there must be fools as well as wise people. 'Twill be all the same anyway when the penny is on our eye. However, while we are here, we might as well enjoy ourselves, and make the most of everything.

SAM. I hope you will have lots of good luck when you go away and find a girl who will make every day like Sunday for you.

DAN. I probably will, Sam. God always looks after me.

[*Nellie comes from the next room. Tom appears at the door and calls Dan.*]

DAN [*as he leaves*]. You will excuse me a moment, Sam.

SAM. Certainly.

[*Exit Dan.*]

NELLIE. Welcome back, Sam. Did you sell the birds?

SAM. I did, Nellie, and I gave the money to Dan.

NELLIE. It was very good of you, Sam.

SAM. Dan will be better off in a foreign country and we'll be better off, too. We can have more time to talk to each other. This time to-morrow he'll be riding the breakers, and watching the screeching seagulls from the prow of a ship and she racing like the wind itself across the wide ocean.

NELLIE. A wonder you never thought of going away, Sam.

SAM. I never want to leave you, Nellie.

[*Puts his arm around her and tries to kiss her.*]

NELLIE [*drawing away from him*]. You mustn't do that any more, Sam.

SAM [*surprised*]. Why, Nellie?

NELLIE. You mustn't; that's all.

SAM. But, Nellie, you are the only girl I ever kissed or ever want to kiss. Is it anything bad you have heard about me?

NELLIE. No, Sam. I have never heard anything bad about you.

SAM. And you never will. And what's more you will never find any one who will love you half as much as I do.

[*Dan and Tom come from the next room.*]

DAN. I won't forget your great kindness when the money will begin to come my way. Needless to say, I am sorry to leave you all, but the best of friends must part. Life is made up of comings and goings. 'Tis a mistake to stay in any place longer than you are wanted, and if I had any sense I'd have gone away long ago.

TOM. Some people don't wake up until they are about to die, but better late than never.

SAM. Aren't you afraid of being lonesome at all, Dan?

DAN. Even if I am, what can I do about it? An Irishman would be lonesome in heaven.

TOM. Dan is doing the right thing at last by going away. Why should he stay here with the old people who have lived their lives, and are waiting for the call to the other world?

DAN. I nearly always do the right

thing. I don't think I could make a mistake if I tried.

TOM. Your modesty will never be the cause of your downfall at all events.

DAN [walking towards the door]. I hope it won't rain to-day.

[Goes outside and looks up at the sky. Nellie follows him.]

SAM. Isn't it a grand thing that we are getting rid of him so easily? I'll be able to get along without the few pounds I lent him.

TOM. Did he borrow from you, too?

SAM. He did. But I was glad to be able to oblige him under the circumstances. 'Twas on his account that I went sprigging linnets so that I could sell them and make up the amount he wanted.

TOM. That fellow has all the low instincts of the aristocracy. He knows how to get others to work for him for nothing.

SAM. I don't care so long as he keeps away. I was afraid he was going to hang around forever and take Nellie away from me, maybe.

TOM. Take her from you! But what about me? I couldn't do without her now that my joints are getting stiffer and stiffer, every day. All young people are selfish, and women are like birds. Unless you keep them in a cage, so to speak, you can never be sure of them for five minutes. A jackeen like Dan Hogan would only put roving and marriageable ideas into her head, and she might run off some fine morning, and I'd never see her again. That would be the end of my happiness.

SAM. And mine, too. Nellie will be a great wife and she that can make from your cap to your stockings.

[Dan and Nellie enter.]

DAN [looking at his watch]. Time is slipping and I must be on my way. [Shaking hands.] Good-by, Nellie, good-by, Tom, and good-by, Sam. I hope to find you all hale and hearty when I'll come back on my first visit. God bless and protect you all.

TOM. We can go as far as the end of the road with you.

DAN. That will be fine. I'm sorry you are not coming all the ways with me.

SAM. You'll be better off without us.

[All leave but Nellie. She stands at the door.]

TOM. Aren't you coming with us, Nellie?

NELLIE. No, Uncle Tom. I'll stay here. I have too much to do to-day.

TOM. Can't you do whatever you have to do as well to-morrow?

NELLIE. I'm afraid not, Uncle Tom. Run on now and don't bother about me.

TOM. Very well.

[When they disappear she closes the door, puts on her hat and coat and opens the window, takes the suit case from behind the dresser, looks around sadly, wipes her eyes, and leaves by the back door. After a short silence loud knocking is heard on the front door.]

TOM [without]. Nellie, Nellie, Nellie, why don't you open the door?

[Knocking continues.]

SAM [looking through the window]. Nellie, open the door quick. Uncle Tom was taken bad on the road, and had to return. [Anxiously.] Nellie, Nellie, Nellie. Where are you at all? 'Tis Sam is calling. Why don't you heed me?

[He crawls through the window, looks around, and when he doesn't see her he opens the door and lets Tom in.]

TOM. I was a fool to walk so far.

SAM [helping him to a chair]. Sit down, Tom, and you'll be all right in a minute.

TOM [sits down and looks around]. In the name of God, where's that niece of mine? Nellie, Nellie, Nellie!

SAM. I don't know what has become of her at all. I can't understand why the door was closed.

TOM. See if you can find a suit case behind the dresser?

SAM [searching]. I can't find a trace of it, Tom.

TOM. Was the door leading to the fields open when you came through the window?

SAM. It was, Tom.

TOM. Then the bird has flown.

[Curtain.]

THE MOON OF THE CARIBBEES
A Play
By Eugene O'Neill

CHARACTERS

YANK
DRISCOLL
OLSON
DAVIS } [*seamen of the British tramp steamer, Glencairn*].
COCKY,
SMITTY
PAUL
LAMPS [*the lamptrimmer*].
CHIPS [*the carpenter*].
OLD TOM [*the donkeyman*].
BIG FRANK
DICK } [*firemen on the Glencairn*].
MAX
PADDY
BELLA
SUSIE } [*West Indian negresses*].
VIOLET
PEARL
THE FIRST MATE.
Two other seamen—SCOTTY *and* IVAN—
and several other members of the stokehole-engine-room crew.

Reprinted from *The Moon of the Caribbees and Six Other Plays of the Sea*, through the courtesy of Mr. Eugene O'Neill and BONI & LIVERIGHT, INC., the publishers of the book. Application for permission to perform this play should be addressed to BONI & LIVERIGHT, INC., 61 WEST 48TH STREET, NEW YORK CITY.

THE MOON OF THE CARIBBEES

A PLAY   By EUGENE O'NEILL

[SCENE: *A forward section of the main deck of the British tramp steamer* Glencairn, *at anchor off an island in the West Indies. The full moon, halfway up the sky, throws a clear light on the deck. The sea is calm and the ship motionless.*

On the left two of the derrick booms of the foremast just out at an angle of forty-five degrees, black against the sky. In the rear the dark outline of the port bulwark is sharply defined against a distant strip of coral beach, white in the moonlight, fringed with coco palms whose tops rise clear of the horizon. On the right is the forecastle with an open doorway in the center leading to the seamen's and firemen's compartments. On either side of the doorway are two closed doors opening on the quarters of the Bo'sun, the ship's carpenter, the messroom steward, and the donkeyman—what might be called the petty officers of the ship. Near each bulwark there is also a short stairway, like a section of fire escape, leading up to the forecastle head (the top of the forecastle)—the edge of which can be seen on the right.

In the center of the deck and occupying most of the space, is the large, raised square of the number one hatch, covered with canvas, battened down for the night.

A melancholy negro chant, faint and far-off, drifts crooning, over the water.

Most of the seamen and firemen are reclining or sitting on the hatch. Paul is leaning against the port bulwark, the upper part of his stocky figure outlined against the sky. Smitty and Cocky are sitting on the edge of the forecastle head with their legs dangling over. Nearly all are smoking pipes or cigarettes. The majority are dressed in patched suits of dungaree. Quite a few are in their bare feet and some of them, especially the firemen, have nothing on but a pair of pants and an undershirt. A good many wear caps.

There is the low murmur of different conversations going on in the separate groups as the curtain rises. This is followed by a sudden silence in which the singing from the land can be plainly heard.]

DRISCOLL [*a powerfully built Irishman who is sitting on the edge of the hatch, front—irritably*]. Will ye listen to them naygurs? I wonder now, do they call that keenin' a song?

SMITTY [*a young Englishman with a blond mustache. He is sitting on the forecastle head looking out over the water with his chin supported on his hands*]. It doesn't make a chap feel very cheerful, does it?

[*He sighs.*]

COCKY [*a wizened runt of a man with a straggling gray mustache—slapping Smitty on the back*]. Cheero, ole dear! Down't be ser dawhn in the marf, Duke. She loves yer.

SMITTY [*gloomily*]. Shut up, Cocky!

[*He turns away from Cocky and falls to dreaming again, staring toward the spot on shore where the singing seems to come from.*]

BIG FRANK [*a huge fireman sprawled out on the right of the hatch—waving a hand toward the land*]. They bury somebody—py chiminy Christmas, I tink so from way it sound.

YANK [*a rather good-looking rough who is sitting beside Driscoll*]. What d'yuh mean, bury? They don't plant 'em down here, Dutchy. They eat 'em to save fun'ral expenses. I guess this guy went down the wrong way an' they got indigestion.

COCKY. Indigestion! Ho yus, not 'arf! Down't yer know as them blokes 'as two stomachs like a bleedin' camel?

DAVIS [*a short, dark man seated on the right of hatch*]. An' you seen the two, I s'pect, ain't you?

375

COCKY [*scornfully*]. Down't be showin' yer igerance be tryin' to make a mock o' me what has seen more o' the world than yeself ever will.

MAX [*a Swedish fireman—from the rear of hatch*]. Spin dat yarn, Cocky.

COCKY. It's Gawd's troof, what I tole yer. I 'eard it from a bloke what was captured pris'ner by 'em in the Solomon Islands. Shipped wiv 'im one voyage. 'Twas a rare treat to 'ear 'im tell what 'appened to 'im among 'em. [*Musingly.*] 'E was a funny bird, 'e was—'ailed from Mile End, 'e did.

DRISCOLL [*with a snort*]. Another lyin' Cockney, the loike av yourself!

LAMPS [*a fat Swede who is sitting on a camp stool in front of his door talking with Chips*]. Where you meet up with him, Cocky?

CHIPS [*a lanky Scotchman—derisively*]. In New Guinea, I'll lay my oath!

COCKY [*defiantly*]. Yus! It *was* in New Guinea, time I was shipwrecked there.

[*There is a perfect storm of groans and laughter at this speech.*]

YANK [*getting up*]. Yuh know what we said yuh'd get if yuh sprung any of that lyin' New Guinea dope on us again, don't yuh? Close that trap if yuh don't want a duckin' over the side.

COCKY. Ow, I was on'y tryin' to edicate yer a bit.

[*He sinks into dignified silence.*]

YANK [*nodding toward the shore*]. Don't yuh know this is the West Indies, yuh crazy nut? There ain't no cannibals here. They're only common niggers.

DRISCOLL [*irritably*]. Whativir they are, the divil take their cryin'. It's enough to give a man the jigs listenin' to 'em.

YANK [*with a grin*]. What's the matter, Drisc? Yuh're as sore as a boil about somethin'.

DRISCOLL. I'm dyin' wid impatience to have a dhrink; an' that blarsted bumboat naygur woman took her oath she'd bring back rum enough for the lot av us whin she came back on board to-night.

BIG FRANK [*overhearing this—in a loud eager voice*]. You say the bumboat voman vill bring booze?

DRISCOLL [*sarcastically*]. That's right —tell the Old Man about ut, an' the Mate, too. [*All of the crew have edged*

nearer to Driscoll and are listening to the conversation with an air of suppressed excitement. Driscoll lowers his voice impressively and addresses them all.] She said she cud snake ut on board in the bottoms av thim baskets av fruit they're goin' to bring wid 'em to sell to us for'ard.

THE DONKEYMAN [*an old gray-headed man with a kindly, wrinkled face. He is sitting on a camp stool in front of his door, right front.*] She'll be bringin' some black women with her this time— or times have changed since I put in here last.

DRISCOLL. She said she wud—two or three—more, maybe, I dunno.

[*This announcement is received with great enthusiasm by all hands.*]

COCKY. Wot a bloody lark!

OLSON. Py yingo, we have one hell of a time!

DRISCOLL [*warningly*]. Remimber ye must be quiet about ut, ye scuts—wid the dhrink, I mane—ivin if the bo'sun is ashore. The Old Man ordered her to bring no booze on board or he wudn't buy a thing off av her for the ship.

PADDY [*a squat, ugly Liverpool Irishman*]. To the divil wid him!

BIG FRANK [*turning on him*]. Shud up, you tamn fool, Paddy! You vant make trouble? [*To Driscoll.*] You und me, ve keep dem quiet, Drisc.

DRISCOLL. Right ye are, Dutchy. I'll split the skull av the first wan av ye starts to foight.

[*Three bells are heard striking.*]

DAVIS. Three bells. When's she comin', Drisc?

DRISCOLL. She'll be here any minute now, surely. [*To Paul, who has returned to his position by the bulwark after hearing Driscoll's news.*] D'you see 'em comin', Paul?

PAUL. I don't see anything like bumboat.

[*They all set themselves to wait, lighting pipes, cigarettes, and making themselves comfortable. There is a silence broken only by the mournful singing of the negroes on shore.*]

SMITTY [*slowly—with a trace of melancholy*]. I wish they'd stop that song. It makes you think of—well—things you ought to forget. Rummy go, what?

COCKY [*slapping him on the back*].

Cheero, ole love! We'll be 'avin our rum
in arf a mo', Duke.

[*He comes down to the deck, leaving
Smitty alone on the forecastle
head.*]

BIG FRANK. Sing something, Drisc.
Den ve don't hear dot yelling.

DAVIS. Give us a chanty, Drisc.

PADDY. Wan all av us knows.

MAX. We all sing in on chorus.

OLSON. "Rio Grande," Drisc.

BIG FRANK. No, ve don't know dot.
Sing "Viskey Johnny."

CHIPS. "Flyin' Cloud."

COCKY. Now! Guv us "Maid o' Am-
sterdam."

LAMPS. "Santa Anna" iss good one.

DRISCOLL. Shut your mouths, all av
you. [*Scornfully.*] A chanty is ut ye
want? I'll bet me whole pay day there's
no wan in the crowd 'ceptin' Yank here,
an' Ollie, an' meself, an' Lamps an'
Cocky, maybe, wud be sailors enough to
know the main from the mizzen on a
windjammer. Ye've heard the names av
chanties but divil a note av the tune or
a loine av the words do ye know. There's
hardly a rale deep-water sailor lift on
the seas, more's the pity.

YANK. Give us "Blow The Man
Down." We all know some of that. [*A
chorus of assenting voices:* Yes!—
Righto!—Let 'er drive! Start 'er, Drisc!
etc.*]

DRISCOLL. Come in then, all av ye.
[*He sings:*]

As I was a-roamin' down Paradise
    Street—

ALL. Wa-a-ay, blow the man down!

DRISCOLL. As I was a-roamin' down
    Paradise Street—

ALL. Give us some time to blow the
    man down!

CHORUS

Blow the man down, boys, oh, blow
    the man down!
  Wa-a-ay, blow the man down!
As I was a-roamin' down Paradise
    Street—
  Give us some time to blow the
    man down!

DRISCOLL. A pretty young maiden I
chanced for to meet.

ALL. Wa-a-ay, blow the man down!

DRISCOLL. A pretty young maiden I
chanced for to meet.

ALL. Give us some time to blow the
man down!

CHORUS

Blow the man down, boys, oh, blow
    the man down!
  Wa-a-ay, blow the man down!
A pretty young maiden I chanced
    for to meet.
  Give us some time to blow the
    man down!

PAUL [*just as Driscoll is clearing his
throat preparatory to starting the next
verse*]. Hay, Drisc! Here she come, I
tink. Some bumboat comin' dis way.
[*They all rush to the side and look
toward the land.*]

YANK. There's five or six of them in
it—and they paddle like skirts.

DRISCOLL [*wildly elated*]. Hurroo,
ye scuts! 'Tis thim right enough.
[*He does a few jig steps on the
deck.*]

OLSON [*after a pause during which all
are watching the approaching boat*]. Py
yingo, I see six in boat, yes, sir.

DAVIS. I kin make out the baskets.
See 'em there amidships?

BIG FRANK. Vot kind booze dey bring
—viskey?

DRISCOLL. Rum, foine West Indy rum
wid a kick in ut loike a mule's hoind leg.

LAMPS. Maybe she don't bring any;
maybe skipper scare her.

DRISCOLL. Don't be throwin' cold
water, Lamps. I'll skin her black hoide
off av her if she goes back on her worrd.

YANK. Here they come. Listen to 'em
gigglin'. [*Calling.*] Oh, you kiddo!
[*The sound of women's voices can be
heard talking and laughing.*]

DRISCOLL [*Calling.*] Is ut you, Mrs.
Old Black Joe?

A WOMAN'S VOICE. Ullo, Mike!
[*There is loud feminine laughter at
    this retort.*]

DRISCOLL. Shake a leg an' come
aboard thin.

THE WOMAN'S VOICE. We're a comin'.

DRISCOLL. Come on, Yank. You an'
me'd best be goin' to give 'em a hand
wid their truck. 'Twill put 'em in good
spirits.

COCKY [*as they start off left*]. Ho,
you ain't 'arf a fox, Drisc. Down't drink
it all afore we sees it.

DRISCOLL [*over his shoulder*]. You'll

be havin' yours, me sonny bye, don't fret. [*He and Yank go off left.*]

COCKY [*licking his lips*]. Gawd blimey, I can do wiv a wet.

DAVIS. Me, too!

CHIPS. I'll bet there ain't none of us'll let any go to waste.

BIG FRANK. I could trink a whole barrel mineself, py chimminy Christmas!

COCKY. I 'opes all the gels ain't as bloomin' ugly as 'er. Looked like a bloody organ-grinder's monkey, she did. Gawd, I couldn't put up wiv the likes of 'er!

PADDY. Ye'll be lucky if any of thim looks at ye, ye squint-eyed runt.

COCKY [*angrily*]. Ho, yus? You ain't no bleedin' beauty prize yeself, me man. A 'airy ape, I calls yer.

PADDY [*walking toward him—truculently*]. Whot's thot? Say ut again if ye dare.

COCKY [*his hand on his sheath knife —snarling*]. 'Airy ape! That's wot I says!

[*Paddy tries to reach him but the others keep them apart.*]

BIG FRANK [*pushing Paddy back*]. Vot's the matter mit you, Paddy? Don't you hear vat Driscoll say—no fighting?

PADDY [*grumblingly*]. I don't take no back talk from that deck-scrubbin' shrimp.

COCKY. Blarsted coal-puncher! [*Driscoll appears wearing a broad grin of satisfaction. The fight is immediately forgotten by the crowd who gather around him with exclamations of eager curiosity. How is it, Drisc? Any luck? Vot she bring, Drisc? Where's the gels? etc.*]

DRISCOLL [*with an apprehensive glance back at the bridge*]. Not so loud, for the love av hivin! [*The clamor dies down.*] Yis, she has ut wid her. She'll be here in a minute wid a pint bottle or two for each wan av ye—three shillin's a bottle. So don't be impashunt.

COCKY [*indignantly*]. Three bob! The bloody cow!

SMITTY [*with an ironic smile*]. Grand larceny, by God!

[*They all turn and look up at him, surprised to hear him speak.*]

OLSON. Py yingo, we don't pay so much.

BIG FRANK. Tamn black tief!

PADDY. We'll take ut away from her and give her nothin'.

THE CROWD [*growling*]. Dirty thief! Dot's right! Give her nothin'! Not a bloomin' 'apenny! etc.

DRISCOLL [*grinning*]. Ye can take ut or lave ut, me sonny byes. [*He casts a glance in the direction of the bridge and then reaches inside his shirt and pulls out a pint bottle.*] 'Tis foine rum, the rale stuff. [*He drinks.*] I slipped this wan out av wan av the baskets whin they wasn't lookin'. [*He hands the bottle to Olson who is nearest him.*] Here ye are, Ollie. Take a small sup an' pass ut to the nixt. 'Tisn't much but 'twill serve to take the black taste out av your mouth if ye go aisy wid ut. An' there's buckets more av ut comin'.

[*The bottle passes from hand to hand, each man taking a sip and smacking his lips with a deep "Aa-ah" of satisfaction.*]

DAVIS. Where's she now, Drisc?

DRISCOLL. Up havin' a worrd wid the skipper, makin' arrangements about the money, I s'pose.

DAVIS. An' where's the other gels?

DRISCOLL. Wid her. There's foive av thim she took aboard—two swate little slips av things, near as white as you an' me are, for that gray-whiskered auld fool, an' the mates—an' the engineers too, maybe. The rist av thim'll be comin' for'ard whin she comes.

COCKY. 'E ain't 'arf a funny ole bird, the skipper. Gawd blimey! 'Member when we sailed from 'ome 'ow 'e stands on the bridge lookin' like a bloody ole sky pilot. An' 'is missus dawn on the bloomin' dock 'owlin' fit to kill 'erself! An' 'is kids 'owlin' an' wavin' their 'andkerchiefs? [*With great moral indignation.*] An' 'ere 'e is makin' up to a bleedin' nigger! There's a captain for yer! Gawd blimey! Bloodÿ crab, I calls 'im!

DRISCOLL. Shut up, ye insect! Sure, it's not you should be talkin', an' you wid a woman an' childer weepin' for ye in iviry divil's port in the wide worrld, if we can believe your own tale av ut.

COCKY [*still indignantly*]. I ain't no bloomin' captain. I ain't. I ain't got no missus—reg'lar married, I means. I ain't—

BIG FRANK [*putting a huge paw over Cocky's mouth*]. You ain't going talk so much, you hear? [*Cocky wriggles away from him.*] Say, Drisc, how ve pay dis voman for booze? Ve ain't got no cash.

DRISCOLL. It's aisy enough. Each girl'll have a slip av paper wid her an' whin you buy anythin' you write ut down and the price beside ut and sign your name. If ye can't write have some one who can do ut for ye. An' rimimber this: Whin ye buy a bottle av dhrink or [with a wink] somethin' else forbid, ye must write down tobaccy or fruit or somethin' the loike av that. Whin she laves the skipper'll pay what's owin' on the paper an' take ut out av your pay. Is ut clear to ye now?

ALL. Yes—Clear as day—Aw right, Drisc—Righto—Sure. etc.

DRISCOLL. An' don't forgit what I said about bein' quiet wid the dhrink, or the Mate'll be down on our necks an' spile the fun.

[A chorus of assent.]

DAVIS [looking aft]. Ain't this them comin'?

[They all look in that direction. The silly laughter of a woman is heard.]

DRISCOLL. Look at Yank, wud ye, wid his arrm around the middle av wan av thim. That lad's not wastin' any toime.

[The four women enter from the left, giggling and whispering to each other. The first three carry baskets on their heads. The youngest and best-looking comes last. Yank has his arm about her waist and is carrying her basket in his other hand. All four are distinct negro types. They wear light-colored, loose-fitting clothes and have bright bandana hand-kerchiefs on their heads. They put down their baskets on the hatch and sit down beside them. The men crowd around, grinning.]

BELLA [she is the oldest, stoutest, and homeliest of the four—grinning back at them]. 'Ullo, boys.

THE OTHER GIRLS. 'Ullo, boys.

THE MEN. Hello, yourself—Evenin'—Hello—How are you? etc.

BELLA [genially]. Hope you had a nice voyage. My name's Bella, this here's Susie, yander's Violet, and her there [pointing to the girl with Yank] is Pearl. Now we all knows each other.

PADDY [roughly]. Never mind the girls. Where's the dhrink?

BELLA [tartly]. You're a hawg, ain't you? Don't talk so loud or you don't git any—you nor no man. Think I wants the ole captain to put me off the ship, do you?

YANK. Yes, nix on hollerin', you! D'yuh wanta queer all of us?

BELLA [casting a quick glance over her shoulder]. Here! Some of you big strapping boys sit back of us on the hatch there so's them officers can't see what we're doin'. [Driscoll and several of the others sit and stand in back of the girls on the hatch. Bella turns to Driscoll.] Did you tell 'em they gotter sign for what they git—and how to sign?

DRISCOLL. I did—what's your name again—oh, yis—Bella, darlin'.

BELLA. Then it's all right; but you boys has gotter go inside the fo'castle when you gits your bottle. No dhrinkin' out here on deck. I ain't takin' no chances. [An impatient murmur of assent goes up from the crowd.] Ain't that right, Mike?

DRISCOLL. Right as rain, darlin'. [Big Frank leans over and says something to him in a low voice. Driscoll laughs and slaps his thighs.] Listen, Bella, I've somethin' to ask ye for my little friend here who's bashful. Ut has to do wid the ladies so I'd best be whis-perin' ut to ye meself to kape them from blushin'.

[He leans over and asks her a question.]

BELLA [firmly]. Four shillin's.

DRISCOLL [laughing]. D'you hear that, all av ye? Four shillin's ut is.

PADDY [angrily]. To hell wid this talkin'. I want a dhrink.

BELLA. Is everything all right, Mike?

DRISCOLL [after a look back at the bridge]. Sure. Let her droive!

BELLA. All right, girls. [The girls reach down in their baskets in under the fruit which is on top and each pulls out a pint bottle. Four of the men crowd up and take the bottles.] Fetch a light, Lamps, that's a good boy. [Lamps goes to his room and returns with a candle. This is passed from one girl to another as the men sign the sheets of paper for their bottles.] Don't you boys forget to mark down cigarettes or tobacco or fruit, remember! Three shillin's is the price. Take it into the fo'castle. For Gawd's sake, don't stand out here drinkin' in the moonlight.

[*The four go into the forecastle. Four more take their place. Paddy plants himself in front of Pearl who is sitting by Yank with his arm still around her.*]

PADDY [*gruffly*]. Gimme thot!

[*She holds out a bottle which he snatches from her hand. He turns to go away.*]

YANK [*sharply*]. Here, you! Where d'yuh get that stuff? You ain't signed for that yet.

PADDY [*sullenly*]. I can't write me name.

YANK. Then I'll write it for yuh. [*He takes the paper from Pearl and writes.*] There ain't goin' to be no welchin' on little Bright Eyes here—not when I'm around, see? Ain't I right, kiddo?

PEARL [*with a grin*]. Yes, suh.

BELLA [*seeing all four are served*]. Take it into the fo'castle, boys. [*Paddy defiantly raises his bottle and gulps down a drink in the full moonlight. Bella sees him.*] Look at 'im! Look at the dirty swine! [*Paddy slouches into the forecastle.*] Wants to git me in trouble. That settles it! We all got to git inside, boys, where we won't git caught. Come on, girls.

[*The girls pick up their baskets and follow Bella. Yank and Pearl are the last to reach the doorway. She lingers behind him, her eyes fixed on Smitty, who is still sitting on the forecastle head, his chin on his hands, staring off into vacancy.*]

PEARL [*waving a hand to attract his attention*]. Come ahn in, pretty boy. Ah likes you.

SMITTY [*coldly*]. Yes; I want to buy a bottle, please.

[*He goes down the steps and follows her into the forecastle. No one remains on deck but the Donkeyman, who sits smoking his pipe in front of his door. There is the subdued babble of voices from the crowd inside but the mournful cadence of the song from the shore can again be faintly heard. Smitty reappears and closes the door to the forecastle after him. He shudders and shakes his shoulders as if flinging off something*]

which disgusted him. Then he lifts the bottle which is in his hand to his lips and gulps down a long drink. The Donkeyman watches him impassively. Smitty sits down on the hatch facing him. Now that the closed door has shut off nearly all the noise the singing from shore comes clearly over the moonlit water.]

SMITTY [*listening to it for a moment*]. Damn that song of theirs. [*He takes another big drink.*] What do you say, Donk?

THE DONKEYMAN [*quietly*]. Seems nice an' sleepy-like.

SMITTY [*with a hard laugh*]. Sleepy! If I listened to it long—sober—I'd never go to sleep.

THE DONKEYMAN. 'Tain't sich bad music, is it? Sounds kinder pretty to me—low an' mournful—same as listenin' to the organ outside o' church of a Sunday.

SMITTY [*with a touch of impatience*]. I didn't mean it was bad music. It isn't. It's the beastly memories the damn thing brings up—for some reason.

[*He takes another pull at the bottle.*]

THE DONKEYMAN. Ever hear it before?

SMITTY. No; never in my life. It's just a something about the rotten thing which makes me think of—well—oh, the devil!

[*He forces a laugh.*]

THE DONKEYMAN [*spitting placidly*]. Queer things, mem'ries. I ain't never been bothered much by 'em.

SMITTY [*looking at him fixedly for a moment—with quiet scorn*]. No, you wouldn't be.

THE DONKEYMAN. Not that I ain't had my share o' things goin' wrong; but I puts 'em out o' me mind, like, an' fergets 'em.

SMITTY. But suppose you couldn't put them out of your mind? Suppose they haunted you when you were awake and when you were asleep—what then?

THE DONKEYMAN [*quietly*]. I'd git drunk, same's you're doin'.

SMITTY [*with a harsh laugh*]. Good advice. [*He takes another drink. He is beginning to show the effects of the liquor. His face is flushed and he talks rather wildly.*] We're poor little lambs

who have lost our way, eh, Donk?
Damned from here to eternity, what?
God have mercy on such as we! True,
isn't it, Donk?

THE DONKEYMAN. Maybe; I dunno.
[*After a slight pause.*] Whatever set
you goin' to sea? You ain't made for it.

SMITTY [*laughing wildly*]. My old
friend in the bottle here, Donk.

THE DONKEYMAN. I done my share o'
drinkin' in my time. [*Regretfully.*]
Them was good times, those days. Can't
hold up under drink no more. Doctor
told me I'd got to stop or die. [*He spits
contentedly.*] So I stops.

SMITTY [*with a foolish smile*]. Then
I'll drink one for you. Here's your
health, old top!
[*He drinks.*]

THE DONKEYMAN [*after a pause*].
S'pose there's a gel mixed up in it some
place, ain't there?

SMITTY [*stiffly*]. What makes you
think so?

THE DONKEYMAN. Always is when a
man lets music bother 'im. [*After a few
puffs at his pipe.*] An' she said she
threw you over 'cause you was drunk;
an' you said you was drunk 'cause she
threw you over. [*He spits leisurely.*]
Queer thing, love, ain't it?

SMITTY [*rising to his feet with
drunken dignity*]. I'll trouble you not
to pry into my affairs, Donkeyman.

THE DONKEYMAN [*unmoved*]. That's
everybody's affair, what I said. I been
through it many's the time. [*Genially.*]
I always hit 'em a whack on the ear an'
went out and got drunker'n ever. When
I come home again they always had
somethin' special nice cooked fur me to
eat. [*Puffing at his pipe.*] That's the
on'y way to fix 'em when they gits on
their high horse. I don't s'pose you ever
tried that?

SMITTY [*pompously*]. Gentlemen don't
hit women.

THE DONKEYMAN [*placidly*]. No;
that's why they has mem'ries when they
hears music.

[*Smitty does not deign to reply to
this but sinks into a scornful silence. Davis and the girl Violet
come out of the forecastle and
close the door behind them. He is
staggering a bit and she is laughing shrilly.*]

DAVIS [*turning to the left*]. This way,
Rose, or Pansy, or Jessamine, or black
Tulip, or Violet, or whatever the hell
flower your name is. No one'll see us
back here.
[*They go off left.*]

THE DONKEYMAN. There's love at first
sight for you—an' plenty more o' the
same in the fo'c's'tle. No mem'ries jined
with that.

SMITTY [*really repelled*]. Shut up,
Donk. You're disgusting.
[*He takes a long drink.*]

THE DONKEYMAN [*philosophically*].
All depends on how you was brung up,
I s'pose.

[*Pearl comes out of the forecastle.
There is a roar of voices from inside. She shuts the door behind
her, sees Smitty on the hatch, and
comes over and sits beside him and
puts her arm over his shoulder.*]

THE DONKEYMAN [*chuckling*]. There's
love for you, Duke.

PEARL [*patting Smitty's face with her
hand*]. 'Ullo, pretty boy. [*Smitty
pushes her hand away coldly.*] What
you doin' out here all alone by yourself?

SMITTY [*with a twisted grin*]. Thinking and—[*he indicates the bottle in his
hand*]—drinking to stop thinking.
[*He drinks and laughs maudlinly.
The bottle is three-quarters
empty.*]

PEARL. You oughtn't drink so much,
pretty boy. Don' you know dat? You
have big, big headache come mawnin'.

SMITTY [*dryly*]. Indeed?

PEARL. That's true. Ah knows what
Ah say. [*Cooingly.*] Why you run
'way from me, pretty boy? Ah likes
you. Ah don' like them other fellahs.
They act too rough. You ain't rough.
You're a genelman. Ah knows. Ah can
tell a genelman fah's Ah can see 'im.

SMITTY. Thank you for the compliment; but you're wrong, you see. I'm
merely—a ranker. [*He adds bitterly.*]
And a rotter.

PEARL [*patting his arm*]. No, you
ain't. Ah knows better. You're a genelman. [*Insinuatingly.*] Ah wouldn't
have nothin' to do with them other men,
but [*she smiles at him enticingly*] you
is diff'rent. [*He pushes her away from
him disgustedly. She pouts.*] Don't
you like me, pretty boy?

SMITTY [*a bit ashamed*]. I beg your

pardon. I didn't mean to be rude, you know, really. [*His politeness is drunkenly exaggerated.*] I'm a bit off color.

PEARL [*brightening up*]. Den you do like me—little ways?

SMITTY [*carelessly*]. Yes, yes, why shouldn't I? [*He suddenly laughs wildly and puts his arm around her waist and presses her to him.*] Why not?

[*He pulls his arm back quickly with a shudder of disgust, and takes a drink. Pearl looks at him curiously, puzzled by his strange actions. The door from the forecastle is kicked open and Yank comes out. The uproar of shouting, laughing and singing voices has increased in violence. Yank staggers over toward Smitty and Pearl.*]

YANK [*blinking at them*]. What the hell—oh, it's you, Smitty the Duke. I was goin' to turn one loose on the jaw of any guy'd cop my dame, but seein' it's you— [*Sentimentally.*] Pals is pals and any pal of mine c'n have anythin' I got, see? [*Holding out his hand.*] Shake, Duke. [*Smitty takes his hand and he pumps it up and down.*] You'n' me's fren's. Ain't I right?

SMITTY. Right it is, Yank. But you're wrong about this girl. She isn't with me. She was just going back to the fo'c's'tle to you.

[*Pearl looks at him with hatred gathering in her eyes.*]

YANK. Tha' right?

SMITTY. On my word!

YANK [*grabbing her arm*]. Come on then, you, Pearl! Le's have a drink with the bunch.

[*He pulls her to the entrance where she shakes off his hand long enough to turn on Smitty furiously.*]

PEARL. You swine! You can go to hell!

[*She goes in the forecastle, slamming the door.*]

THE DONKEYMAN [*spitting calmly*]. There's love for you. They're all the same—white, brown, yeller 'n' black. A whack on the ear's the only thing'll learn 'em.

[*Smitty makes no reply but laughs harshly and takes another drink; then sits staring before him, the almost empty bottle tightly*

clutched in one hand. There is an increase in volume of the muffled clamor from the forecastle and a moment later the door is thrown open and the whole mob, led by Driscoll, pours out on deck. All of them are very drunk and several of them carry bottles in their hands. Bella is the only one of the women who is absolutely sober. She tries in vain to keep the men quiet. Pearl drinks from Yank's bottle every moment or so, laughing shrilly, and leaning against Yank, whose arm is about her waist. Paul comes out last carrying an accordion. He staggers over and stands on top of the hatch, his instrument under his arm.*]

DRISCOLL. Play us a dance, ye square-head swab!—a rale, godforsaken son av a turkey trot wid guts to ut.

YANK. Straight from the old Barbary Coast in Frisco!

PAUL. I don't know. I try.

[*He commences tuning up.*]

YANK. Attaboy! Let 'er rip!

[*Davis and Violet come back and join the crowd. The Donkeyman looks on them all with a detached, indulgent air. Smitty stares before him and does not seem to know there is any one on deck but himself.*]

BIG FRANK. Dance? I don't dance. I trink!

[*He suits the action to the word and roars with meaningless laughter.*]

DRISCOLL. Git out av the way thin, ye big hulk, an' give us some room.

[*Big Frank sits down on the hatch, right. All of the others who are not going to dance either follow his example or lean against the port bulwark.*]

BELLA [*on the verge of tears at her inability to keep them in the forecastle or make them be quiet now they are out*]. For Gawd's sake, boys, don't shout so loud! Want to git me in trouble?

DRISCOLL [*grabbing her*]. Dance wid me, me cannibal queen.

[*Some one drops a bottle on deck and it smashes.*]

BELLA [*hysterically*]. There they

goes! There they goes! Captain'll hear that! Oh, my Lawd!

DRISCOLL. Be damned to him! Here's the music! Off ye go!

[*Paul starts playing "You Great Big Beautiful Doll" with a note left out every now and then. The four couples commence dancing— a jerk-shouldered version of the old Turkey Trot as it was done in the sailor-town dives, made more grotesque by the fact that all the couples are drunk and keep lurching into each other every moment. Two of the men start dancing together, intentionally bumping into the others. Yank and Pearl come around in front of Smitty and, as they pass him, Pearl slaps him across the side of the face with all her might, and laughs viciously. He jumps to his feet with his fists clenched but sees who hit him and sits down again smiling bitterly. Yank laughs boisterously.*]

YANK. Wow! Some wallop! One on you, Duke.

DRISCOLL [*hurling his cap at Paul*]. Faster, ye toad!

[*Paul makes frantic efforts to speed up and the music suffers in the process.*]

BELLA [*puffing*]. Let me go. I'm wore out with you steppin' on my toes, you clumsy Mick.

[*She struggles but Driscoll holds her tight.*]

DRISCOLL. God blarst you for havin' such big feet, thin. Aisy, aisy, Mrs. Old Black Joe! 'Tis dancin'll take the blubber off ye.

[*He whirls her around the deck by main force. Cocky, with Susie, is dancing near the hatch, right, when Paddy, who is sitting on the edge with Big Frank, sticks his foot out and the wavering couple stumble over it and fall flat on the deck. A roar of laughter goes up. Cocky rises to his feet, his face livid with rage, and springs at Paddy, who promptly knocks him down. Driscoll hits Paddy and Big Frank hits Driscoll. In a flash a wholesale fight has broken out and the deck is a surg-*

ing crowd of drink-maddened men hitting out at each other indiscriminately, although the general idea seems to be a battle between seamen and firemen. The women shriek and take refuge on top of the hatch, where they huddle in a frightened group. Finally there is the flash of a knife held high in the moonlight and a loud yell of pain.]

DAVIS [*somewhere in the crowd*]. Here's the mate comin'! Let's git out o' this!

[*There is a general rush for the forecastle. In a moment there is no one left on deck but the little group of women on the hatch; Smitty, still dazedly rubbing his cheek; The Donkeyman quietly smoking on his stool; and Yank and Driscoll, their faces battered up considerably, their undershirts in shreds, bending over the still form of Paddy, which lies stretched out on the deck between them. In the silence the mournful chant from the shore creeps slowly out to the ship.*]

DRISCOLL [*quickly—in a low voice*]. Who knoifed him?

YANK [*stupidly*]. I didn't see it. How do I know? Cocky, I'll bet.

[*The First Mate enters from the left. He is a tall, strongly-built man.*]

THE MATE [*angrily*]. What's all this noise about? [*He sees the man lying on the deck dressed in a plain blue uniform.*] Hello! What's this?

[*He bends down on one knee beside Paddy.*]

DRISCOLL [*stammering*]. All av us— was in a bit av a harmless foight, sir— an'—I dunno—

[*The Mate rolls Paddy over and sees a knife wound on his shoulder.*]

THE MATE. Knifed, by God. [*He takes an electric flash from his pocket and examines the cut.*] Lucky it's only a flesh wound. He must have hit his head on deck when he fell. That's what knocked him out. This is only a scratch. Take him aft and I'll bandage him up.

DRISCOLL. Yis, sor.

[*They take Paddy by the shoulders and feet and carry him off left.*]

The Mate looks up and sees the women on the hatch for the first time.]

THE MATE [*surprised*]. Hello! [*He walks over to them.*] Go to the cabin and get your money and clear off. If I had my way, you'd never— [*His foot hits a bottle. He stoops down and picks it up and smells of it.*] Rum, by God! So that's the trouble! I thought their breaths smelled damn queer. [*To the women, harshly.*] You needn't go to the skipper for any money. You won't get any. That'll teach you to smuggle rum on a ship and start a riot.

BELLA. But, Mister—

THE MATE [*sternly*]. You know the agreement—rum—no money.

BELLA [*indignantly*]. Honest to Gawd, Mister, I never brung no—

THE MATE [*fiercely*]. You're a liar! And none of your lip or I'll make a complaint ashore to-morrow and have you locked up.

BELLA [*subdued*]. Please, Mister—

THE MATE. Clear out of this, now! Not another word out of you! Tumble over the side damn quick! The two others are waiting for you. Hop, now!

[*They walk quickly—almost run— off to the left. The Mate follows them, nodding to The Donkeyman, and ignoring the oblivious Smitty.*

There is absolute silence on the ship for a few moments. The melancholy song of the negroes drifts crooning over the water. Smitty listens to it intently for a time; then sighs heavily, a sigh that is half a sob.]

SMITTY. God!

[*He drinks the last drop in the bottle and throws it behind him on the hatch.*]

THE DONKEYMAN [*spitting tranquilly*]. More mem'ries? [*Smitty does not answer him. The ship's bell tolls four bells. The Donkeyman knocks out his pipe.*] I think I'll turn in. [*He opens the door to his cabin, but turns to look at Smitty—kindly.*] You can't hear it in the fo'c's'tle—the music, I mean—an' there'll likely be more drink in there, too. Good night.

[*He goes in and shuts the door.*]

SMITTY. Good night, Donk.

[*He gets wearily to his feet and walks with bowed shoulders, staggering a bit, to the forecastle entrance and goes in. There is silence for a second or so, broken only by the haunted, saddened voice of that brooding music, faint and far-off, like the mood of the moonlight made audible.*]

[*The Curtain Falls.*]

WIND O' THE MOORS
A Derbyshire Play

By L. du Garde Peach

CHARACTERS

ANNA.
OLD GREGSON [*her grandfather*].
MICHAEL [*a gamekeeper*].

WIND O' THE MOORS

A DERBYSHIRE PLAY

BY L. DU GARDE PEACH

[SCENE: *A small room, barely furnished, in a cottage in the midst of wild moors. The walls are white, discolored with age and dust, with oak beams in the plaster and across the ceiling. On the right is the great open fireplace, with guns over it, etc., and above it an old high-backed oak chair. A fire is burning. In the middle of the back wall is the window, with red curtains drawn across it, and to the left of it a door. A further door to an inner room is above the fireplace—in the same wall. Other chairs and a settle are about the room, and a table is in the middle. A cupboard, with plate rack, small table, etc., is in the left wall. Sheepskins, bits of harness, an old coat, crocks, sticks, and an odd sampler or so, hang on the walls. The place is lit by a pair of candles in brass candlesticks on the mantelshelf and another on the table. The wind howls throughout, and rain showers patter at intervals against the window panes. Anna is looking out of the cottage door. She pushes it to, as though struggling against the wind. Then she turns to her grandfather. She speaks loudly to him; he is deaf.*]

ANNA. There's a great wind out on t' moor to-night. Aren't ye goin' to your bed, Granfer? It's gone by ten.

OLD GREGSON. Is it wind as ye say?

ANNA. Can't ye hear it?

OLD GREGSON. It's i' my bones as I con feel it. It's wi' t' shakin' o' th' 'ouse as I con feel it—shakin' under my feet as I sit. It's a great wind to-night, ye say?

ANNA. Ay.

OLD GREGSON. Great, like th' wind as took away t' th' end bracken stack four year gone?

ANNA. Ay, I doubt it. It's blowin' like it never were to.

OLD GREGSON [*to himself*]. I thowt I were gone then, but I come through wi' it. . . .

ANNA. Aren't ye goin' to your bed, Granfer?

OLD GREGSON. Bed is it as ye say, lass?

ANNA. Ay, it's gone by ten.

OLD GREGSON. No, I'm non goin' t' my bed. Hear t' wind—i' all t' th' moor hollows—down by t' quarry end, an' ower by t' stones.

ANNA. Ye'd best go.

OLD GREGSON [*half rising from his chair*]. D'ye know what th' wind's come for? It's come for me—me lass. It's last neet as I've getten. D'ye think I'm goin' to my bed? It's i' here as I know it. It were i' a great wind as my father were took—it were i' th' greatest wind as th' country e'er knew as my granfer were took. Ye know t' winds when ye live your days out on t' moor.

ANNA. Dunna talk so, Granfer.

OLD GREGSON. I thowt it were come four year agone. But it's to-neet—last neet as I've getten.

ANNA [*hiding her face in her hands*]. Granfer.

OLD GREGSON. Ay, ay. Who'll care for thee when t' th' old mon's took? Lass, I'd a wish to 'a seen thee wed wi' Michael afore I went.

ANNA [*flashing out*]. That ye'll ne'er see. I wouldna wed wi' him if he were t' last mon left to me.

OLD GREGSON. Ye used to think kind o' him, Anna.

ANNA. I hate him—dunna speak o' him.

[*The wind moans loudly outside, and the door rattles. Anna crosses to it.*]

OLD GREGSON. Hark at it, lass. Ay, ye can mek door fast, but it'll be t' same. It's mony a great wind as I've been out

387

i' on t' moor. An' I allus knew as it were t' wind as ud tek me at th' last.

ANNA. Granfer, ye'd best go. Ye'll be better i' t' morning.

OLD GREGSON. I'st see no morning. I know it, I tell ye—I know it deep down i' t' bones o' me. It mun be great f' t' be took i' a great wind. Wi' all t' storm clouds round ye, an' t' peewits tumblin' an' cryin', same as I've seen 'em many a while. It's a great life as I've had. Mon an' boy I've lived here, workin' on t' moor for my bread. I've had great days, when there seemed nowt as I could put my hand to an' non do better'n another. I were strongest mon o' all these parts. There wasna one as 'd stand up to me and wrestle, or run agen me. No, non even Michael could a' done it when I were myself. And t' times as I've had at th' singin's wi' th' gypsies o' evenin's o' th' road edge. There werena one o' them as could sing wi' me, though I've non sung these twenty years.

ANNA. They do say as ye sang beautiful, Granfer. I've heard 'em down at th' village.

OLD GREGSON. Do they, lass, do they?

ANNA. Ay, they say that when ye sang o' evenin's it were t' sweetest singin' as any one e'er heard. They say that all t' folks used to come round, an' there'd be great gatherin's at fair times. An' they say as fine folks 'ud come out o' their carriages round th' fire edge, an' mebbe stay a while.

OLD GREGSON. Ay, it's true as they say. I were a great singer. An' they've non forgotten down i' th' village, though there's none now as e'er heard me when I were young. They're all gone—an' i' th' mornin' I'll be gone an' all.

ANNA. Nay, Granfer.

OLD GREGSON. Ay, lass. Heark to it. Scratchin' at door bottom like a dog as ye've shut out i' t' yard. Heark at it round by t' tor top. [*He half rises and looks toward the door, then sinks back into his chair.*] An' do they talk o' t' wrestlin'?

ANNA. Ay. I've heard 'em many a while. They say as ye threw Tom Worton—him as was th' greatest wrestler i' t' country.

OLD GREGSON. Ay, I did, I did. I mind it as if it werena no more nor last week.

ANNA. Ye mun 'a bin a fine great man, Granfer.

OLD GREGSON. Ay, sixty year back.

ANNA. An' they still talkin' o' t' things as ye used do. It's a grand thing f' t' be one as folks talks on for sixty year.

OLD GREGSON. What's a few songs an' a man thrown? They'll leave talkin', an' all t' fine life as I've had'll be forgot, an' t' great man as I was. There's non one left as heard th' songs nor felt strength o' my arms. An' then I'st be nowt but owd Gregson as lived up on t' moor top. An' then they'll go, an' their children, an' there'll be none as remembers me no more. I'st be nowt but a cut name o' a' old stone down yonder. An' folks'll read it, an' they'll say—who were Gregson—an' there'll be none as'll be able to tell 'em o' all t' great life as I've had.

[*A knocking comes at the door. The old man does not hear it, but sinks slowly back into his chair, huddled together, hearing and seeing nothing. Anna goes to the door. The wind is moaning.*]

ANNA. Who's that knockin' so late?

MAN'S VOICE. Oppen t' door.

ANNA. Michael. Is that you, Michael?

MICHAEL. Ay—oppen t' door.

ANNA. I shall not oppen to ye.

MICHAEL. Oppen i' charity, Anna. I'm wet wi' t' rain an' cold wi' t' wind. It's a charity as I'm askin' ye.

ANNA. What is it you're wantin' i' your black heart?

MICHAEL. Anna. Gie me shelter an' a fire corner.

[*Anna suddenly draws herself up rigid, her back against the door and her arms outspread as though to bar entrance. Her right hand touches the ax hanging on the wall, and she draws in a quick breath. Then she turns slowly and stares at the old man.*]

ANNA. Michael, are ye there?

MICHAEL. Ay—oppen t' me.

ANNA. I' a minute, Michael—I mon speak wi' Granfer—bide a minute.

MICHAEL. It's wet i' the rain an' cold i' the wind.

ANNA. Ay, ay—bide a minute.

[*Anna goes stealthily across to the old man and stands behind him.*]

ANNA [*laying her hand on his shoulder to rouse him*]. Granfer.

OLD GREGSON [*rousing up*]. All t' thought o' me an' life o' me gone—What is it, lass?

ANNA. Th' folks are talkin' o' ye down i' t' village, Granfer.

OLD GREGSON. Ay, lass, ay.

ANNA. They're talkin' o' t' strongest and greatest man o' t' countryside—

OLD GREGSON [*raising himself in his chair*]. Strongest and greatest—sixty year ago. Soon forgot when th' old man's gone—to-neet—

ANNA. Granfer. Will ye do that as'll make 'em ne'er forget? Will ye do that for me as'll make 'em talk o' ye all time as t' greatest and strongest man o' t' countryside, as'll make 'em make songs about ye as children'll sing i' hundreds o' years?

OLD GREGSON. Lass, lass—what is. it as ye're meanin'?

ANNA. Will ye do it, Granfer?

OLD GREGSON. For 'undreds o' years—

ANNA. Will ye do it, Granfer—?

OLD GREGSON. To be allus remembered—talked on—when I'm churchyard mold a 'undred years—

ANNA. Will ye do it, Granfer?

OLD GREGSON. What is it? What are ye meanin'?

ANNA. Will ye kill Michael, Granfer?

OLD GREGSON. Kill—Michael?

ANNA. Kill him, kill him—

OLD GREGSON. Kill Michael—friend as comes an' sits by t' fireside wi' me—lass—lass—what's—

ANNA. Ay—friend as sits by t' fire corner. Kill him, Granfer.

OLD GREGSON. Why—what's come to ye—

ANNA. I hate him—I hate him. [*Passionately.*] Kill him, Granfer.

OLD GREGSON. Kill—Michael—whyfore mun I—kill him—him as was courtin' ye—?

ANNA. Mun I tell you—what they whisper i' th' village—what they point at me—me—with their fingers i' the village—. That Michael's made a light thing o' me—o' me. Granfer, kill him, kill him. [*Her voice suddenly becomes coaxing, and she caresses the Old Man with her hands.*] They'll ne'er forget ye, Granfer—it'll be t' great thing o' your life, Granfer—they'll tell o' i' by

t' fireside, Granfer—they'll make ballads o' it—they'll—

OLD GREGSON [*gripping his stick and half rising*]. Is it true as ye say—?

ANNA. Ay—it's as true as—Granfer—kill him—this night. Granfer—

[*Michael knocks again on the door. Anna is on her knees at her grandfather's side. She turns to the door with a snake-like movement.*]

MICHAEL. Will ye no oppen, Anna—?

ANNA. Bide a while, Michael—

MICHAEL. Anna, I've summut f' t' show ye.

ANNA. I'll see what ye an f' t' show me, Michael. Bide a minute.

OLD GREGSON [*sitting straight up and staring straight in front of him*]. My grand-darter—child o' my little Anna. [*He raises his hands with his fingers spread and tense like claws.*] I'll choke wicked life out o' him. I'll—[*He lets his hands drop again.*] I'm an old man—day o' my strength is gone—I've near ninety years o' my shoulders—

ANNA. It's non, Granfer. Hark to t' wind—t' wind o' your last night, Granfer, as ye say—men's strength comes back to 'em o' their last nights, Granfer—great men, like you, Granfer—hard to it—

OLD GREGSON [*standing up*]. Ay—th' wind—an' t' strength comin' i' my arms—I've lived strong—. Lass, where is he—where's Michael—?

ANNA. Here, Granfer—here at door. [*Michael knocks again at the door. Anna crosses as before.*]

ANNA. Ay, Michael—I'll oppen t' ye. [*She comes back quickly to her grandfather.*] Granfer—wi' t' great ax—he'll come in an' bide a while—when he goes out o' t' door—follow him on to t' moor.

OLD GREGSON. Oppen t' door to him—I'll kill him—kill him as he stands there—i' t' door—

ANNA. No, Granfer—out on t' moor. I canna see it, Granfer—on t' moor—I've had his kisses o' my lips—I've had—[*She suddenly covers her face with her hands.*]—out on t' moor, Granfer.

OLD GREGSON. Oppen to him.

ANNA [*whispering*]. On t' moor, Granfer.

OLD GREGSON. Oppen to him.

[*He sinks back into his seat with*

his eyes glittering and his hands clenching and unclenching. Anna stands tense a moment drawing in a deep breath, then goes across to the door and opens it. Michael enters. He is a dark, handsome young giant, dressed as a game-keeper, and carrying a gun. He is very wet and crosses at once to the fire, leaning the gun against the door post.]

MICHAEL. I'm wet wi' ye keepin' me, Anna.

ANNA. Ay.

MICHAEL. Ye've a grand way wi' a man at your door, askin' shelter o' a night as 'd make ye oppen to a dog.

ANNA. Ay—t' a dog. The like o' you is less than dogs.

MICHAEL. Fine talk for a head game-keeper as is a guest i' your house— Granfer.

ANNA. Head gamekeeper they call you—every one knows the game you keep—breaking young girls' hearts— that's the game you keep.

MICHAEL. Keep your tongue civil— or you'll be sorry.

ANNA. Ha. Keep my tongue civil. I'm t' have my life ruined—I'm t' have folks pointin' and whisperin' at me on account of you—an' I'm to keep my tongue civil.

MICHAEL. I can't help what folks does—ye should ha' kept yesel' apart fro' folks.

ANNA. Ay, I should—I should ha' kept myself apart fro' you—wi' your devil's ways—

MICHAEL. Curse the rain for sendin' me in to a tongue like yours.

ANNA. Ay, ye can curse the rain— hark at it—hark at wind. Ye can go out i' it if ye've a mind—or ye can stay an' hear what I've a mind—from t' lips as ye've kissed—

MICHAEL. Ye'd have me out i' it gettin' death i' my bones as soon as— as ye'd 'a kissed me six months back— ye've a lovin' heart i' ye, Anna.

ANNA. No, Michael—I would not have ye get death i' ye bones from t' rain this night—

MICHAEL. Hopin' t' live an' see me 'anged, 'appen. Ha, it's a kind thought o' ye, Anna. I' t' meantime, Granfer, will ye ask this dutiful granddarter o' yours if she's a mind t' give a guest in your house a drop to keep the cold out, an' a bite to keep the body up—

ANNA. He doesna' hear ye—but ye shall have what ye want.

MICHAEL. That's kind o' ye now. What's matter wi' Granfer? He looks strange like to-night. [*Raising his voice.*] What is it, Granfer—what's amiss wi' ye to-night?

[*Anna busies herself with getting beer and something to eat out of a cupboard on the left behind the door. She places it on the table in the center of the stage.*]

OLD GREGSON. Reach me down yon Bible, Michael. [*Michael hands him a large family Bible from the mantel-shelf.*] Hark to t' wind. Hark to it i' t' quarry, an' among t' trees ower t' th' tor top—

MICHAEL. Ay, it's blowin' strong to-night. It's carried away a couple o' barns, an' scattered one o' t' lane end ricks already—it'll be worse before mornin' an' all—

OLD GREGSON. Afore mornin'. I shanna see t' mornin'.

MICHAEL. What's come to him, Anna?

ANNA. A strange fancy—a reet strange fancy.

[*She laughs wildly.*]

MICHAEL. What is it you're laugh-ing at?

ANNA. 'Appen th' wind—scatterin' th' ricks—all over t' country side afore mornin'.

MICHAEL. What's amiss wi' ye both to-night?

OLD GREGSON [*turning over the pages of the Bible*]. Th' wicked shall perish off th' face o' th' earth.

MICHAEL. We'll hope so, Granfer. There'll be more room for us few honest ones as is left.

ANNA. Honest ones— Come to your bit o' supper.

MICHAEL. An' may it choke me, eh?

[*He sits left of table.*]

ANNA. There's 'appen worse ways o' dyin' than chokin', Michael.

OLD GREGSON. Young man, i' t' pride o' your strength—

MICHAEL. It's a grand welcome I get —atween t' two o' ye.

ANNA. An' it's a grand welcome as ye deserve from t' maid as ye've wronged.

MICHAEL. Wronged—what are ye

talkin' o' wronged—I ne'er wronged you
—it were you as wronged me—wi' your
—wi' your great eyes an' your soft ways
—an' your red lips—as've blasted life
o' many a man.

ANNA. Ye lie, Michael. Ye know as
no man e'er touched me but you.

MICHAEL. An't more fool you—

ANNA. Ay, ye can say that. It needs
a man t' say that. [*She sits at the back
of the table and rests her chin on her
hands, watching him.*] You're a grand
man, Michael—aren't ye?

MICHAEL. I s't make a grand supper,
wi' you sittin' there hopin' as every bite
I take'll choke me.

ANNA. I've a mind to sit an' watch
ye, Michael.

MICHAEL. Ye're welcome.

ANNA. Ay—you're a grand man.
It'd take a deal more than a maid's
spoiled life f' t' spoil your supper.

MICHAEL. I doubt it would.

[*Pause.*]

ANNA. They say men as is goin' to
be hung eats good breakfasts.

MICHAEL. Ha. Ye've a grand for-
givin' spirit, Anna.

OLD GREGSON. An eye f'r an eye, an'
a tooth f'r a tooth.

MICHAEL. Granfer an' all, seemin'ly.

[*Pause.*]

ANNA. Are ye ne'er afraid, Michael,
when ye're out on t' moors as th' hills'll
fall in an' crush t' life out o' ye?

MICHAEL. I can't say as I am.

OLD GREGSON. Gie me my glasses,
Anna.

[*She gets up and gives him a pair
of glasses, which he puts on. She
then arranges a candle so that
the light falls on the book in his
hands. He commences to read
in a muttered monotone, very
slowly.*]

MICHAEL. Granfer's took sudden to
his Bible, a'n't he?

[*Anna comes and stands behind the
table watching him.*]

ANNA. An' non th' only one as'd be
t' better for it.

MICHAEL. What's amiss wi' him?

ANNA. Granfer's an owd man.

MICHAEL. Ay—I doubt he's non so
long for this world.

ANNA. An' he has reet strange
fancies, Michael—like old men has. He
thinks as when t' great wind comes

there's allus some as has t' die. Are
ye afraid o' dyin', Michael?

MICHAEL. It seems make grand
thinkin' for ye, Anna—me dyin'.

ANNA. Ay, it does.

[*Pause. Anna picks up the bread
knife to cut him another piece of
bread. He sees the knife in her
hand and jumps to his feet, catching her wrist.*]

MICHAEL. Put down yon knife.

ANNA [*laughing hysterically*]. Ye're
a fine great man, Michael. Afraid o' a
lass as is goin' t' cut a bit o' bread
for ye.

MICHAEL. There's no trustin' a wild
cat like o' you. Ye'd stick a knife i' a
man as soon as—soon as kiss him.

ANNA. Ye'd best take care, Michael.

MICHAEL. Ay—I meant t' take care.

ANNA. Will ye 'an your bit o' bread
—brave man?

MICHAEL [*surlily turning away and
kicking his chair up to the table*]. No,
I want no more o' your bread.

[*He goes across to the window, and
looks out, drawing aside the short
red curtain. The wind is still
moaning and howling outside,
and every now and then the rain
patters in driving showers against
the panes.*]

ANNA. Ye said, Michael, when ye were
outside door there, as ye'd somethin' t'
show me. I doubt it were lyin' talk—

[*Michael turns quickly and comes
to the table.*]

MICHAEL. Lyin' talk—what d'ye call
that?

[*He throws a paper on the table.
Anna picks it up slowly.*]

ANNA. What is it?

MICHAEL. Oppen it an' read it.

[*She opens out the paper and stares
at it.*]

ANNA. It's got my name on it—an'
—Michael—an' yours. What is it,
Michael?

MICHAEL. Can't ye see what it is?

ANNA. It's—Michael—it's for us to
be wed—

MICHAEL. Seems so.

ANNA. Michael. [*She goes close up
to him with the paper in her hand.*]
D'ye mean it so? D'ye mean ye're goin'
t' marry me?

MICHAEL. Seems so.

ANNA. What's made ye change—

sudden? Michael—do ye—do ye—still —love me—Michael—

MICHAEL [turning away]. Seems so.

ANNA [suddenly standing tense]. Tell me.

MICHAEL. I allus meant to marry ye —spite of what ye said— An'—

ANNA. Ye'd a strange way o' showing it. Ay—

MICHAEL. An' then a week or so back Sir John said—

ANNA [suddenly breaking forth]. Ah — . . . Sir John said— Sir John said as he'd heard o' your ways. Sir John said as he wouldn't have his head keeper spoken of i' that way. He said as it were a scandal. Oh, I know what Sir John said. An' now ye come sneakin' t' marry me, so's not to be turned off fro' your job. Ye're a grand man, Michael—a grand man. Ye allus meant to marry me—ay—after Sir John's told ye ye'd be turned off if ye didna. D'ye think I'd marry ye now. . . . Take th' bit o' paper as ye thought'd buy your job for ye.

[She throws the paper on the floor.]

MICHAEL. Anna—are ye mad—?

ANNA. I've a value now it seems— non just a girl t' be thrown away when ye've done wi' her.

MICHAEL. Anna—it's not that. I— I—want ye to marry me—

ANNA. Ye lie, Michael.

MICHAEL. Six months ago—

ANNA. Ay—six months ago ye hadna left me t' be pointed at an' whispered at i' th' streets. Six months ago I was somethin' to ye—though I'd no job tacked on to my back. On'y six months ago.

MICHAEL. Anna, have ye forgot—?

ANNA. Nay, I've forgot nothin'. It's you that's forgot. [Michael stands biting his lips. Anna stands looking at him, panting.] Forgot. All t' love as I give ye. Men's hateful. I thought so that ye loved me. An' ye threw me off —an' come creepin' back t' me— . . . Michael . . . [She speaks slowly, hesitatingly and coaxingly.] Say it's non on'y because o' Sir John—I'll believe ye if ye'll say it. . . . Think o' all t' love as we had, Michael. Ye havena forgot that—ye canna have forgot that— Ye havna forgot the summer evenin's as we had, out on t' moors, wi' all t' heather smellin' so sweet an' we so happy. An' all t' dear things as ye used to say to me. Ye meant 'em then, Michael. T' feel o' me i' your arms, an' all t' kisses as ye had o' my lips—Michael, ye havna forgot—ye do love me still. Michael, it's non on'y because o' Sir John—say it isna— Michael, say it isna . . .

MICHAEL. Anna—I—

ANNA. Michael—ye do love me—ye must—ye can't have forgot—everythin'. See—I'm as young as I was then. Ye used to say I was beautiful. I'm th' same now. Michael, don't ye want me now?

[He suddenly becomes overpowered and clasps her tightly in his arms.]

MICHAEL. Anna—I do—I do. I want your kisses agen. Give 'em me. Anna —Anna—

ANNA. Ah. . . .

[They kiss passionately. Old Gregson rises slowly to his feet, dropping his Bible and spectacles on to the floor. He is muttering to himself. They do not notice him.]

OLD GREGSON. Th' hand o' th' Lord.

[He crosses to the door, takes the ax from left of it, and slips quietly out, closing the door behind him.]

ANNA. Michael, it's goin' t' be like it was again, isn't it?

MICHAEL. Ay—

ANNA. Kiss me again, Michael.

[He seems to hesitate a moment. Then he kisses her, but not quite so ardently as before.]

ANNA. Tell me as ye love me, Michael.

MICHAEL. I love ye, Anna—there— Wind's dropped, an' t' rain's by. I must go, Anna.

ANNA. Ye leave me happy, Michael. I could cry wi' t' happiness that's i' me.

[She drops into the chair left of the table and buries her face in her hands. Michael looks at her hesitatingly a moment, then shrugs his shoulders and leans over and kisses her. She looks up happily.]

ANNA. Ye'll come to me to-morrow, Michael?

MICHAEL. Ay—I'll come up to-morrow.

[She gets up and takes him to the

door. *He takes his hat from the peg and picks up his gun. She suddenly leaves him and runs to the cupboard.*]

ANNA. Ye'll 'an a nip of granfer's whisky afore ye go. Michael.

MICHAEL. Ay, thank ye.

[*She goes to pour it out. He sees the paper on the floor, picks it up and looks from it to Anna and back again. Then he shrugs his shoulders again.*]

MICHAEL. Well, it might ha' bin worse.

[*Anna comes to him and gives him the whisky. They can neither of them see from where they stand that Old Gregson is no longer by the fire because of the old high wooden back and side pieces of the chair. Anna has quite forgotten in her happiness what has passed earlier.*]

MICHAEL [*speaking carelessly over his shoulder*]. Good night, Granfer.

ANNA. He doesna hear ye. Fallen asleep over his Bible, I doubt. [*She takes the glass from him.*] Good night, Michael.

MICHAEL. Good night.

[*He kisses her hurriedly and goes out. She follows him to the door, and watches him a moment. Then she waves her hand, shuts the door, and turns back into the room. She goes and puts the glass down on the side table, and then stands musing a moment. Then she turns and comes down to the old chair, speaking quite quietly and happily.*]

ANNA. Grandfer, Grandfer. . . .

[*She suddenly realizes that he is not there. She looks round, dazed. Then she suddenly runs out through the door to the inner room and is heard calling wildly outside. Then she rushes into the room again, and stops short as she realizes that the ax is no longer by the door. She gives a*

strangled shriek, with the back of her hand up to her mouth—she seems to be biting into the flesh. Then the latch of the door is raised and the door begins slowly to open. Anna retreats backwards, as though hypnotized by the opening door, until she is crouching on the extreme right below the fire. There she watches as Old Gregson comes into the doorway. He seems to have grown bigger and stronger since he went out. He is no longer a senile old man. When he speaks his voice is full and clear, and the ballad music of his youth is in his words. His eyes flash, and his face is hard and firm. He throws the ax on to the floor with a crash.*]

OLD GREGSON. Blood o' a man. Blood o' a man. He were a strong man i' t' pride o' his strength. He come towards me. Ower t' heather. An' I felt strength comin' into me. I stood up afore him an' raised great ax above my head—same as I could forty year back. An' I saw i' his eyes as he were a bad man—an' afraid. An' I let great ax fall o' his head. Wi' all t' strength o' my arms. An' he fell ont' ground. A strong man i' t' pride o' his strength. Afore a' owd man. Wi' many a year o' his head. An' folks'll tell o' t' way as he died. An' t' way as owd Gregson died. For many a year. They'll tell t' tale round fires o' winter neets. An' they'll sing songs o' t' great strength as come to me from t' days when I were young. [*The wind has been rising all through the above, and is now howling loudly round the cottage. The Old Man raises his hand and listens.*] There's th' wind. It's come for me. Wi' t' black clouds racin', an' t' peewits tumblin'. Out on t' moor—

[*He turns and goes out. The wind rises to a shriek, and the door is banged violently to.*]

[*Curtain.*]

ESCAPE
A Play

By Theodore Pratt

CHARACTERS

JOHN WINWOOD.
MARY [*his daughter*].
HUGH [*his son*].
WALTER PEMBROKE.
JIM HILDER.
A YOUNG MAN.
A BOY.
A GIRL.
A MAN.

ESCAPE

A PLAY   BY THEODORE PRATT

[*The* SCENE *shows both the living room and the business establishment of John Winwood and his son and daughter. The small, dingy living room is at left, and the little confectionery store is at right, with a partition separating them. There is a door in this partition in which are hung faded, green draperies.*

In the living room there is a door at rear, right, which leads to rooms on the second floor; there is a second door at left, leading both to the yard in back of the establishment and to the basement. There is a table in the center of the room on which are a cover, papers, and a small lamp. Several chairs are about the table, while there is a comfortable armchair to the left of it. At rear there is a dark old sideboard. To the right of this is a stand upon which is placed the telephone. In the store there is a door at right leading to the street, on either side of which are windows hidden at the bottom for some feet by white curtains. At rear, left, there is a counter containing candy and stationery. At rear, right, so that there is an opening between, there is a smaller counter containing cigars and cigarettes. There are shelves at the rear wall upon which are supplies of candy boxes, stationery, toys, etc. A small green table with chairs stands at right near the door.

The time is about three-thirty in the afternoon of a spring day. Mary Winwood is seated behind the cigar counter in the store, gazing out into the street. Mary is a pretty girl of twenty-two. She is well-formed in a good-looking way and has dark brown hair. She looks listlessly out at the things passing in the street with an air of resigned melancholy. After a moment she buries her face in her hands, then looks up in a tired way. A young man enters from

397

right in the store and goes to the cigar counter.]

YOUNG MAN. Package of Lucky Strikes. [*He puts his hand in his pocket for money. Mary reaches behind her on the shelf for cigarettes and places them on the counter on which the Young Man flips a coin. Mary makes change and gives it to him.*] Got any matches?

[*As he opens the package of cigarettes Mary gives him a paper of matches; he lights cigarette and goes out at right. Mary continues to look out of the window.*

John Winwood enters from rear in the living room. Winwood is an old man on the verge of actual feebleness. He is considerably shrunk in body, with graying hair and a somewhat stooped appearance, and he is not very spry either physically or mentally. He goes slowly to the armchair, where he sits, puts on his spectacles and begins to read a paper which he has taken from the table.]

WINWOOD [*sighing comfortably*]. Uh ... well ... [*He mumbles a few sentences out of his newspaper, then lowers it and looks right.*] Mary! [*A pause. Mary gives no evidence of hearing him.*] Mary!

MARY. Yes, father.

WINWOOD. Ain't that some one in the store? Didn't I hear some one come in?

MARY. No, father; no one is here, now.

WINWOOD. They've got to be waited on. We've got to give good service!

MARY. There's no one here, father.

WINWOOD. Oh, well! I thought I heard somebody. I was almost sure I did. [*Thinks a moment. Mary is si-*

lent.] Mary, my hearin' ain't as good as it used t' be.

MARY [*without looking around*]. Why, of course it is, father.

WINWOOD [*dubiously*]. No; it ain't now. Huh-m. . . . [*Starts again to read his newspaper; puts it down.*] Mary!

MARY. Yes?

WINWOOD. Where's Hugh, Mary?

MARY. He's in the basement getting up the new candy, father.

WINWOOD. I was just wondering. It always gives me a start when I don't know where you'n Hugh are, Mary. I ain't satisfied unless you're both around. You know how I mean it, Mary.

MARY. Yes.

[*Winwood sits back and thinks slowly for a moment. During these times there is a deadly pall of dullness about his establishment, unrealized by him, but felt acutely by his children. Winwood puts down his paper, adjusts his spectacles and sits up as though he had a very important idea.*]

WINWOOD. Mary. Oh, Mary, come here.

MARY [*looks left, then leaves her chair and walks to door in the partition*]. Yes, father.

WINWOOD. Mary, I've got something I'm goin' to tell you'n Hugh to-day.

MARY. What is that, father?

[*She seems to know what it is and does not welcome it. She goes near the old man and then stands to left of table.*]

WINWOOD [*pleased with his thoughts*]. It's June, Mary.

MARY. Yes; it is.

WINWOOD. It's near the end of the month. Now, ain't that right, is it, Mary?

MARY. Yes, father, that's right. It's the twenty-fifth.

WINWOOD. Well, do you know what's goin' to happen on the first of the month?

[*He chuckles over his secret plans.*]

MARY. What is going to happen, father?

WINWOOD. Ah-ho! Mary, something that's goin' to give you'n Hugh things you want.

MARY [*expectantly*]. Oh, father! You—you don't mean—?

WINWOOD. I mean I've got a surprise for both of you.

MARY [*realizing that he does not mean her father will give his children their freedom*]. Oh! It's the—contracts again, isn't it?

WINWOOD. Yes, Mary, it's the contracts. But there's goin' to be something more in them this time. Something more, Mary.

MARY. Something more, father?

WINWOOD. You know I think a lot of those contracts; I do, Mary. It makes it so I hire you'n Hugh on a regular business basis. I never wanted you to feel I was forcing you to work in the store. So by giving you regular papers it's put it on kind of a business basis. Now ain't that so, Mary?

MARY. Why, yes, father.

WINWOOD. I'm proud because I can do that. It makes it so it's sort of— sort of free, for you'n Hugh, don't it? [*Mary does not answer, but looks away.*] You've been a good daughter, an' Hugh's been a good boy. That's what makes it so nice to give you my surprise, Mary.

MARY. Yes.

WINWOOD. Where's Hugh, Mary?

MARY. He's getting up the new candy, father.

WINWOOD. Well, I want to tell you both something. It's kind of special, so you go call him, Mary.

MARY [*going to door at left and calling*]. Hugh! Oh, Hugh!

[*Winwood seems very pleased with what he is going to tell them.*]

HUGH [*his voice comes from off, below*]. Ye-es?

MARY. Come up, will you? Father wants to see us.

HUGH [*off*]. Just a minute!

MARY [*returning right*]. He's coming in a minute, father.

[*There is a silence between father and daughter in which there is a strain felt only by Mary. Winwood seems to be thinking of something. He finally speaks.*]

WINWOOD. Mary, there's something— well, there's something I wanted to say to you, alone. [*Mary looks at him.*] It's about Walter Pembroke again, Mary.

MARY. Oh, father!

WINWOOD. It must be said, Mary.

First off, though, I want to say that I don't hold anything against him, as I've always said. I think Walter's a fine, up-standin' boy. But I don't think you should be goin' out with him any more. One thing is, he's got a little money, an' we ain't much, Mary. Then you're too young to get married.

MARY. But I promised you a year ago I wouldn't. My promise was to last until—the first of next month.

WINWOOD. Then your promise is up this week, Mary. An' I want you to make it over again.

MARY. For—for another year?

WINWOOD. Yes, Mary.

MARY. Oh, father!

WINWOOD. It ain't much, it ain't so much, Mary. Only a year. After then we'll see.

MARY. Oh—I can't.

WINWOOD [turning to her]. You ain't promised him already, Mary?

MARY. No. But I—I might want to, you see. And then—

WINWOOD. Mary, you'n Hugh 're all I have. You're both close to me—I need you, both of you. Not only in the store, but—but all inside me, Mary.

MARY [going to him]. Oh, yes, father; I understand. [Turns from him.] But I can't promise what you ask.

WINWOOD. You must; you must promise it!

MARY [after a moment]. Father, if I decided I wanted Walter, and a home with him—and—and children, nothing in the whole world could stop me!

WINWOOD. Mary! You—you don't mean that—I know you don't. [Hugh has entered at left, his arms laden with candy boxes. Hugh is two years older than his sister; medium-sized and well-filled out, with regular but not handsome, features. He is at present without coat or vest, and he wears a white shirt. Winwood sees him.] Well, Mary, we'll see—we'll see later.

HUGH [looking at them]. Well, hello! What's this nothing in the whole world could stop you from doing, Sis?

MARY [making signs to Hugh not to continue the subject]. Father and I were just talking, Hugh.

HUGH. Oh. [He goes to the table and deposits his boxes there tempo-rarily.] You say you wanted to see both of us, Dad?

WINWOOD [brightening again]. Yes; yup! I've got something of a surprise for you both. I wanted you here together so's I could tell you.
[He gets up, for this occasion is important.]

HUGH. Well, Dad, here we are.
[Hugh and Mary look at him.]

WINWOOD. I just told Mary how proud I am of the legal papers we've had between us. I've given them to you'n her every year. It makes it sort of a business proposition. Well, it's the first of July soon an' I'm drawin' up new contracts for you.

HUGH. Yes, Dad, I know.

WINWOOD [pleased with what he is saying to them]. But that ain't all. That ain't all! For the past three years Mary's got fifteen dollars a week as her own money, an' you've got twenty, Hugh. That's what's always been in the papers. Well, now, what d'you suppose is goin' to be in the new ones? [He looks at them as if he were about to explode a bomb in the room.] Mary, you're goin' t' get twenty dollars a week, an' Hugh, you're goin' t' get twenty-five! Well, now, what d'you think of that?

MARY. Oh!
[There is a short pause. Hugh seems to be thinking of something else.]

HUGH. Well, that's fine, Dad—certainly fine. I guess Mary and I—well, we never expected it.

WINWOOD. Ah-ho! I guess that's sort of a surprise to you, eh? Mary, what d'you say?

MARY. Why, father, it's—it's fine. Yes. And you'll have the new contracts in—in five days?

WINWOOD. Yup. In five days. Just think what you can do with five dollars more a week, Mary. Why, you can put it in the bank an' have a fortune in no time. Or you might want to buy things for your hope chest in a few more years.

MARY. Yes—my hope chest.

WINWOOD. Maybe you'd just want to put it in the bank an' save it?

MARY. Yes, father. That's probably what I'll do. And it's—it's good of you. [Two small children, a boy and a little girl, have entered the store. Mary sees

them.] There's some one in the store.
I'll go.

[*She goes right into the store.*]

WINWOOD. Well, I'm glad you both
appreciate it. [*He sits and picks up his
newspaper again.*] You'n Mary've always been good to your old dad. Don't
know what I'd do without you, I don't.

[*He becomes engrossed in his newspaper and forgets Hugh, who is
at rear of the room walking about
and thinking. In the store the
two children, who are mere tots
with pennies clutched in their
small fists, investigate the candy
counter through the glass. The
Boy gravely does the ordering.*]

THE BOY [*pointing*]. A cent's worth
of those, 'n a cent's worth of those. . . .

THE GIRL. Oo! Lookit! Oo!

THE BOY. 'N one more cent's worth
of that. [*He takes his lady friend's
coins and counts their combined re-
sources.*] Two cents' worth of those.

THE GIRL. Lookit! Oo! Oo!

THE BOY. 'N another cent's worth of
that.

[*Mary fills a small bag with candy.
The Boy hands over payment with
due portentousness.*]

MARY. And here's a lollypop for each
of you. There!

THE BOY. Oh, thanks! [*To his mini-
ature bit of femininity.*] All-day sucker!

THE GIRL. Oo! Oo!

[*They go out at right, the lady
friend of the young man giving
vent to her perpetual wonder until they disappear. Mary watches
them go, then is listless again.
She looks toward the room at left
and sits behind the counter staring out into the street. Winwood
in the living room shuffles his
paper, looks around and sees that
Hugh is still there.*]

WINWOOD. Hughie! I didn't know
you stayed here. My hearin' ain't as
good as it used to be, boy.

HUGH. Why, of course it is, Dad.
[*He seems to be wavering between two
ends of a decision.*] But you see I
stayed to—well, Dad, you see it's this
way: I—

WINWOOD. What is it, Hugh? Maybe
you want to thank me for my surprise?

HUGH. Why, yes, of course, and I do,
but I—I—well. . . .

WINWOOD. What you thinkin' of,
Hugh?

HUGH. I'm thinking that—no, no,
I'm not! Nothing!

[*He suddenly picks up his boxes
from the table and goes with them
into the store.*]

WINWOOD [*looking at him and saying
a poor joke*]. Guess he's thinkin' of the
girls, an' doin' that, he ain't so happy.
Oh, well!

[*Mary glances at Hugh as he enters
the store and begins to arrange
the boxes on a shelf. They are
silent. Winwood in the living
room mumbles over his newspaper
and in a moment takes out his
pipe, fills and lights it and begins
to smoke in a satisfied way.*]

HUGH [*piling the candy boxes*]. This
is the fourth year he's given us—contracts, isn't it?

MARY. Yes, the fourth year.

[*There is a pause. Hugh works and
Mary stares out of the windows.*]

HUGH. What time is it, Sis?

MARY [*looking at her wrist watch*].
A quarter to four.

HUGH [*stops his work, looks about*].
Hm-m . . . . [*He meditatively continues
at the candy boxes.*] The contracts
havn't been a bad idea, though, have
they, Sis?

MARY. No, they haven't been a bad
idea. But— [*Turning to him.*] Oh,
Hugh, it's made me feel as if I were tied
down to something! I know how father
values them, and I do, too—for his sake.
But it's made me feel as if I *have* to
stay in the store. With all the world
out there, a world neither of us has ever
really seen, we are forced to stay here!
All my life, all my youth, I've been here.
Oh, Hugh, sometimes I feel like a caged
thing, like a bird who wants freedom,
light, space!

HUGH [*again stopping his work*].
Yes, Sis, I've felt a good deal that way,
too. Both of us are the greatest thing in
Dad's life—but I can't go on here for-
ever. I want to do things of my own!
I've got things to do! Here—well, I . . . .

MARY. We're like two things that
want to get away, Hugh, like animals
in the zoo. Do you remember how we
used to watch them in their cages, pacing up and down, always looking for a
way out? Some of them were old—it

didn't matter so much about them. But the young ones! They wanted to escape, to get out, to do things, to live!

HUGH. Some day—soon, Sis, one of us will be going away from here. Then the other one will have to stay with Dad.

MARY. I wonder—I wonder which of us it will be who goes away?

HUGH. I—you can't tell, Sis.

MARY. Hugh, he wants me to promise not to see Walter for a year.

HUGH. He does!

MARY. That's what we were talking about when you came in.

HUGH. What are you going to do?

MARY. I don't know! I suppose I'll agree to it and—and not even see him! But—oh, Hugh, I can't do that, I can't, I can't!

HUGH. Sis!

[The door at right opens and Jim Hilder enters. Hilder is a slow-moving, genial man of middle age. He is already in the stage when solid comfort is located in a game of checkers and a congenial pipe with his friend, John Winwood.]

HILDER. Hello, Mary.

MARY. Hello, Mr. Hilder.

HILDER. Nice day it is out to-day. 'Afternoon, there, Hugh.

HUGH. Hello, Mr. Hilder.

HILDER. I see you're both busy as bees. You're a good pair of kids to have. Now I've got some! [Looking toward the living room.] I suppose that father of yours—

WINWOOD [who has by now heard him]. That you just come in, Jim?

HILDER. Yep, John, it's me. [To Mary and Hugh, as he goes left.] Just listen to that. And now he'll tell me his hearing ain't as good as it used to be. [Mary and Hugh watch him go into living room.] Well, John, how's to-day treating you?

WINWOOD [getting up to greet his visitor]. Pretty good, Jim, pretty good. Only my hearin' ain't as good as it used t'be.

HILDER. Go on! You've said that for the past ten years, and your ears ain't changed in that time.

WINWOOD. Well, now, you know it seems t'me they have.

HILDER. Why ain't you out puttering in that garden of yours, to-day?

WINWOOD. I was out there all morning, Jim. You come out now an' look at my patch of corn. It ain't much y'know. but it's way up for June.

HILDER. I'd like to see it.

HUGH [in the store]. Well, I've finished this pile.

WINWOOD. Mary'll come with us. [Calls.] Mary! Oh, Mary!

MARY. Yes, father?

WINWOOD. Come out with Mr. Hilder'n me to see the corn.

MARY [getting up and starting left]. All right.

[She goes into the living room. Hugh watches her.]

WINWOOD [as Mary joins them]. Course, this patch ain't much, Jim. [They go left.] But I nursed it along early, so it must be 'way ahead of anything in town. . . .

[They go out at left. When they have gone, Hugh, who has been watching them, looks out the front windows of the store for a possible customer. He goes left, stops, and thinks. He makes a decision after a moment, then goes swiftly into the living room to the telephone.]

HUGH [in a low voice]. Operator, Main three o one nine—yes! [He looks off left while waiting for the number.] Hello—Helen? Will you be ready? . . . Good! We'll go this time; I've finally decided—I can't keep on any longer. I'm buried; we'd both be buried all our lives —Mary can take care of things . . . yes . . . my bag's ready; I'll be right over . . . we can get the four-fifteen. Yes, Helen—yes! Soon . . . good-by!

[Hugh puts down the telephone and goes out the door at rear. In a moment he reappears, now with a hat on his head and putting on his coat. He carries a small suitcase. He looks about again and then walks quickly into the store, where he exits at right. Mary enters from left. She stands by a chair in the living room and thinks rather pensively. Walter Pembroke enters from right in the store. Pembroke is about twenty-seven and is tall and fair. He sees Mary through the open doorway.]

PEMBROKE. Mary!

MARY [*looking right*]. Walter. . . .
[*She goes to him.*]

PEMBROKE. I've come to tell you some good news, Mary. The Company has offered me the opening as district manager in Buffalo. I've wired my acceptance.

MARY. Walter! That's fine!

PEMBROKE. And it'll be finer, Mary, if you'll do what I want you to do.

MARY. Oh, Walter!

PEMBROKE [*taking her hands*]. It's just the time for us, now, Mary. You told me last week you wouldn't marry me only because you had to stay in the store with your father.

MARY. He doesn't want me even to see you for a year, Walter.

PEMBROKE. He wants you to do that?

MARY. Yes.

PEMBROKE. Well, I understand how he feels, but it's unfair, Mary. Why should we waste these years? Hugh can take care of the store, and this contract he gives you runs out this week, doesn't it? The store doesn't need both you and Hugh.

MARY. But he does, Walter.

PEMBROKE. And you—do you need me, Mary?

MARY. Oh, yes!

PEMBROKE. Then let's go away, now! We'll drive up to Buffalo in the car and we can get married on the way.

MARY. I—I want to!

PEMBROKE. Then do it, Mary. Up there with a new job on my hands, I'll want you, I'll need you. You'll be forever buried here. Hugh is capable of running the store alone. Mary, come!

MARY [*looking at him*]. Yes—yes, Walter, I will!

PEMBROKE. Mary! [*They kiss.*] Now, get your things; don't bother to take much—we can buy whatever you need. I'll wait here.

MARY [*gladly; now happy*]. Walter—yes!

[*Mary goes into the living room and out at rear, right. Pembroke paces about in the store. Winwood and Jim Hilder enter from left in living room. Pembroke sees them and stands in the store so that they do not know he is there.*]

WINWOOD [*completing something he has been saying*]. . . . you bet they're a fine pair of kids, Jim. Why, if it wasn't for them I guess there wouldn't be anything for me.

HILDER. You've held them pretty close, John.

WINWOOD. Ye-es.

HILDER. Some day they've got to go away from here and out in the world.

WINWOOD. But not yet, Jim—not yet!

HILDER [*casually suggestive*]. Well, I'll just beat you a game, John. I've got time for just one.

WINWOOD. Huh-ho! You'll beat me a game, will you? You'll beat me a game? Maybe you will, an' maybe you won't.

[*He goes to the sideboard and gets the checker board. They sit at the table and arrange the game.*]

HILDER. Let me have the reds. I guess you remember what happened last time I had them, don't you?

WINWOOD. I remember! But just you wait! I ain't goin' to be beat like that, again. You move first, Jim.

[*Hilder moves, Winwood moves, followed after a moment of thought by Hilder moving a second time. The game progresses. Pembroke glances in at them and waits for Mary.*]

HILDER [*making a move*]. Got you in a hole!

WINWOOD. Hu-m. . . . [*Moves; takes a man.*] Not so much! Not so much! . . . y'know, as I said before, it's great comfort to have Mary'n Hugh. I can sit here an' not worry about the store at all—you move, Jim.

HILDER [*moving*]. Yep. They're good kids.

WINWOOD. I told them what I was goin' to do for them next year an' they seemed mighty pleased about it.

HILDER. I guess they would be, John.

WINWOOD. Yes, sir, I don't know what I'd do without either one of 'em! They're just all I've got, Jim.

HILDER. And they're sure a lot to have.

[*They ponder over the checker board. Mary, with a hat on and carrying a bag and coat, appears in the doorway at rear. She sees her father and Hilder, and disappears. When she comes back into view she no longer carries the bag, she*]

*has taken her hat off and carries
it and the coat so that the two
men cannot see them. She enters
the room and Winwood sees her.
Pembroke in the store watches
them.*]

WINWOOD [*looking about*]. Where's
Hugh, Mary?

MARY. Why, father—he's bringing up
more candy, I suppose.

WINWOOD [*turning back*]. I was just
wondering.

[*Mary starts to go into the store;
she stops, makes as if to speak to
her father, decides not to, and goes
in to Pembroke, who meets her.*]

MARY [*in a half whisper*]. I had to
leave my bag!

PEMBROKE. That's all right; we'll
get the things you want. Come, Mary!

MARY [*with a last glance toward the
living room*]. Yes!

[*They go out at right.*]

WINWOOD. I'm always thinkin' of
them two, Jim. I guess maybe I'm an
old fool, but with two like Mary'n Hugh,
it'd make anybody proud.

HILDER. I guess it would, John. I
take your man.

WINWOOD. Hm-m. . . . They're all
I've got so I don't mind bein' kind of
stuck-up about 'em. Don't know what
I'd do without either one. . . .

[*The game progresses and Hilder
takes a number of Winwood's
checkers.*]

HILDER. Now you've got two left,
John. If I take them you'll be licked.

WINWOOD. Two, just like Mary'n
Hugh. But you're not goin' to take 'em,
Jim; nobody's goin' to take 'em.

HILDER. Nobody but me, John!

[*He takes the checkers and gets up
to go.*]

WINWOOD. Huh! Well, now! That
was funny! Huh—that's all you got
time for, Jim?

HILDER. Yep. I've got to make sure
that kid of mine got the new lumber over
to the Morley place. Mine don't stick so
close to their old man as yours do, John.

WINWOOD. No. No, now.

HILDER [*going*]. So long, John. See
you to-morrow.

WINWOOD. Good-by, Jim.

[*Hilder goes out. In the store he is
surprised not to see Mary, but
thinks she has stepped out for a
minute, and then exits. In a
moment a customer, a man, enters
the store and stands at the cigar
counter to be waited on. No one
comes. He gets impatient and
knocks on the glass with a coin.
Winwood looks through and sees
him. The man raps again.*]

WINWOOD [*calling*]. Mary! Oh, Mary,
there's somebody in the store. Don't you
see him?

[*There is no answer.*]

THE MAN. I'll have to be waited on
or I won't trade here!

WINWOOD. Mary! There's a man to be
waited on. We've got to give good
service. [*Mary is not there to answer.
To the man.*] Just a minute—somebody'll be right in. [*To himself.*]
That's funny—she must of stepped out
a minute. [*He rises slowly to his feet
and calls to off left where he believes
Hugh to be.*] Hugh! Oh, Hugh!
[*There is no answer.*] There's a customer an' Mary's out. Come up an' wait
on him. [*The Man raps impatiently
again.*] Hugh! Hugh! Why don't he
answer, now? Where'd he go? [*He goes
off left to investigate. The Man in the
store goes out in disgust. Winwood can
be heard off left calling Hugh. He reenters, baffled.*] He ain't there. He
ain't there, now. [*He goes to doorway
leading to the store.*] Mary, you there?
Mary! [*He sees she is not there, becomes agitated, and goes to the door at
rear of the living room where he discovers Mary's bag.*] I don't see where
they'd go to. . . . [*Picking up the bag.*]
Mary! Mary. She—she—Hugh. . . .
[*He senses that something is terrifically
wrong. Clutching the bag he goes to a
chair and sits.*] He-he—I don't see—
Hugh! Uh; he-he—why—you've—you've
—I knew it'd come some day, but not
now, not now—they've gone! Hugh—
an' Mary— 're gone! I'm all alone.
Alone! Hugh . . . Mary . . . Mary. . . .

[*The Curtain Falls.*]

BROTHERS
A Play

By Abraham Reisin

Translated from the Yiddish by Etta Block

CHARACTERS

Glickman ⎫
Bas ⎪
Hurwitz ⎬ [*new arrivals in town*].
Berman ⎭

Hannah [*a comrade*].
First Peddler.
Second Peddler.
Third Peddler.
Fourth Peddler.

BROTHERS

A PLAY   By ABRAHAM REISIN

[SCENE: *A room off a long corridor on the fourth floor. Near the east wall stands a small table without folding-leaves. A tea machine lies neglectedly under the table; near the table stands a chair with a broken arm; the arm lies orphaned on the floor near it. A broken iron bedstead stands near the north wall. It is not made up. The quilt drags near it on the ground, exposing a coarse, straw mattress, out of which protrudes a handful of straw. Over the bed, upon the wall, hangs a shabby hat and an old, worn, short coat. Upon the rise of curtain and for a short while thereafter the scene remains unoccupied. Behind the scene the voices of Glickman and Bas are heard. The door opens and they stumble into the room.*]

GLICKMAN [*twenty-seven years old; tall and spare; shabbily dressed in an old outfit and soiled collar*]. There you have it! He's out, too. When it doesn't go, it doesn't go, that's all.

BAS [*of medium build; wears a blue shirt; has long, black hair and wears glasses, out of which look two angry black eyes*]. So, that's your magnate! [*Examining the bed.*] A fine magnate!

GLICKMAN. I didn't represent him as a capitalist. I only said that at times he gets a few rubles from home. Maybe he got some to-day.

BAS. And if he did get it, he's probably spent it long ago.

GLICKMAN. You think every one is made in your image. But what's the use? He is not here. Come.

BAS. No, I can't go any further. I haven't any strength left. I'm going to lie down on that bed and lie there till my soul goes out.

[*He stretches himself out on the bed.*]

GLICKMAN. You're a fool. One mustn't give up. I tell you we're bound

to get some money to-day. I feel in me a certain power—strength!

BAS. I don't need anything. I'll just lie here and. . . . If only we had a cigarette. You have none—perhaps a partly smoked one?

GLICKMAN. I must have about me somewhere one partly smoked. I want a smoke, too, badly. We'll divide it. Let's see, have you a match?

[*Finds a cigarette in his pocket and takes it out.*]

BAS. A match? I think I have. [*Still lying down, he takes a match-box out of his pocket and opens it.*] Only one! Careful, now.

GLICKMAN [*examining it thoughtfully*]. The match is a good one apparently. [*He carefully strikes the match, holding the butt of the cigarette in his mouth; he watches the match to see whether it will burn.*] Now—now—no. Will it go out? No.

BAS. Hurry.

GLICKMAN [*carrying the bit of fire to his mouth quickly. Presently a tail of smoke issues*]. Done!

BAS. Well, thank God it smokes. You smoke and leave a few whiffs for me.

GLICKMAN. I'll leave some, I'll leave some.

[*He takes several long draws and hands the rest to Bas. Bas gazes at it grudgingly, miserly, makes a wry face and puts it to his mouth.*]

BAS. If I had something about me just now that would destroy the whole town I'd do it—willy nilly!

GLICKMAN [*musingly*]. And if I had something to sell this minute to get a good dinner, I'd do it. What, for instance, could I sell? [*Looks through his pockets and pulls out an old purse.*] What do you think, Bas, could one get for it?

407

BAS [*looks it over from where he lies*]. You can throw it away.

GLICKMAN. It once cost a half ruble.

BAS. Once—once you were worth more, too!

GLICKMAN. Yes, once. Never mind, I'm not done yet. Somehow, I feel that life is still before me—that all this is just a—prelude. What matters it if the prelude does trifle a bit?

BAS. Your whole life will be a sort of prelude. You will never quite grasp the root of life itself and your future will be a constant search for pupils and —a dinner.

GLICKMAN. As to that we shall see. [*From the court is heard the cry of a peddler.*] If only there were something to sell.

[*The cry is repeated.*]

BAS. What have you to sell—your soul? Who'd buy it? It's already soiled.

GLICKMAN [*he glances up at the wall and sees the coat*]. Why should I sell my soul when there hangs right before me here a fairly good little coat? [*Feels of the coat.*] Yes, not at all a bad little coat.

BAS [*shocked*]. Is it yours, then?

GLICKMAN. You're a fool. Mine?! The peddler's in the yard and we're in here—so it's ours.

BAS. True, I am a bit of an anarchist, that you know. But there are nicer ways. . . . [*The peddler continues his call: "Peddler, peddler." Glickman runs out into the court. Bas remains alone. He stands up. After a bit Glickman returns with the peddler—a man about fifty years old. He wears a long, well-worn coat and high boots.*]

PEDDLER. Well, let's have a look at your wares. What have you?

GLICKMAN [*takes the coat off the wall*]. Here, this coat. I would like to sell it.

PEDDLER [*takes the coat and turns it over on all sides*]. An old little coat. It's got a few holes already. . . .

GLICKMAN. Where?

PEDDLER. Where, you ask? Don't you see? Have you anything else, old shoes, pants?

GLICKMAN. Just what you see. More, I haven't. Well, what do you give for it?

BAS [*groaning*]. What a man can come to!

PEDDLER [*examining the lining*]. The lining is already rotten. What can one give for such a coat? I mean—what can one offer. . . . How much do you want?

GLICKMAN. You buy constantly. You must know better.

PEDDLER. I think . . . what do you mean, I know better? It's your goods so you must set your price.

GLICKMAN. Yes, that's true, my goods . . . .

BAS [*getting anxious*]. Well, make it quicker.

GLICKMAN [*blurts out*]. Two ruble.

[*Peddler glares angrily at him, takes his sack under his arm and prepares to leave.*]

GLICKMAN [*anxious*]. Well, how much will you give? You can say at least.

PEDDLER [*softens and comes back*]. I'll sell you such coats myself for fifteen kopecks apiece—at least a hundred of them.

GLICKMAN [*angrily*]. I don't deal in coats. Say what you'll give.

[*Peddler again takes the coat and examines it.*]

BAS. Oh, I don't feel right about this business.

PEDDLER. A half ruble.

GLICKMAN [*hurriedly*]. Take it. It's really given away, but let a man make a living.

BAS [*quietly to Glickman*]. You're a rare one!

GLICKMAN. Keep still. [*Peddler examines the coat once more, turning it over again and again on all sides; Glickman, impatiently.*] Well, mister, make it quicker.

BAS. He's backing out.

PEDDLER. Backing out is not business. I'm not backing out, but rich from it I won't get, either. [*Takes out of his pocket a small purse, scratches about in it with his fingers, and finally takes out a silver ruble.*] Have you change—a half ruble?

GLICKMAN. No.

BAS. If we only had a half ruble!

GLICKMAN [*treads on his toe*]. Shut up.

PEDDLER. What's to be done? I'll have to go out and get it changed.

GLICKMAN [*again anxiously*]. Haven't you smaller change?

PEDDLER. No, I only have a few rubles.

GLICKMAN. Well, let's go down to the store together and change it.

BAS. Come back quickly.

GLICKMAN. In a minute.

PEDDLER [*throwing the sack over his shoulder and the coat under his arm*]. Come.

GLICKMAN [*hesitating*]. Put it inside, please—the coat into the sack.

PEDDLER. You want it in the sack? Let it be in the sack.

[*Throws the coat into the sack. Both go out.*]

BAS [*he strides back and forth across the room. Steps and voices are heard in the corridor. Hurwitz enters, followed by another peddler. He stands still on seeing Bas, who is pale, agitated and embarrassed*]. Your friend, Glickman, brought me here. My name is Bas.

HURWITZ [*also agitated*]. Delighted. Sit down. [*To the peddler.*] I'll show it to you right away. [*Goes to the wall.*] Where's the coat? [*He looks at Bas, who laughs hysterically.*] What are you laughing at?

PEDDLER. Well, I haven't time.

[*Steps are heard in the corridor. Glickman enters.*]

HURWITZ. Where were you?

GLICKMAN. Down to the store. Bought some cigarettes.

PEDDLER. Well, what's going to be? Are you going to show me the coat or not?

HURWITZ. Right away, right away. [*To Glickman.*] A peculiar thing. When I went away I left the coat hanging on the wall. I saw it there myself. Now, it's not there.

[*He looks at Bas.*]

GLICKMAN. Well, whose fault is it? When you go out you should lock the door.

BAS [*to Glickman*]. You ugly creature!

PEDDLER. Then it seems I came for nothing.

HURWITZ. Please excuse me, mister. What can I do? It must have just been stolen. Hard luck!

PEDDLER. The cheek of him! Drags me—drags me all the way from the other street, and what—where—stolen!

GLICKMAN. Here, mister, is a ten-piece for you and go in health.

PEDDLER [*taking the coin gladly*]. Thanks. It would seem there'll be bread here to-day. [*Sighs.*] Eh, eh, hard times.

[*He goes.*]

HURWITZ [*sitting down on the bed*]. What times! One shouldn't be able to borrow a kerbel. [*To Glickman.*] Tell me, have you nothing toward a meal at least?

GLICKMAN. What do you mean—I have nothing? Just now I'm rich. I've three whole gulden in my pocket.

HURWITZ. How far will it go for three?

[*Looking at Bas.*]

GLICKMAN. Ett! It'll be enough. We'll make a feast at home and it will come cheaper. Who will go and bring the eats?

BAS. Give me the money, I'll bring it.

GLICKMAN. Here you are. [*Handing him several coins.*] Buy two pounds of bread.

BAS. Will that be enough?

HURWITZ. Of course, not enough. I'm as hungry as a dog.

GLICKMAN. Well, buy three pounds of bread, a good herring—but a good one! Tea and sugar for a few kopecks and cigarettes, and if you have any money left buy a bit of good cheese.

BAS. We'll see.

[*Goes.*]

HURWITZ. It seems like a punishment from God. I wanted to sell the coat though it wasn't mine. It belonged to Berman.

GLICKMAN. How do you come by Berman's coat?

HURWITZ. He slept here with me last night. He had no other place to go to. It was a heavy coat and the day was warm so he went out in his light jacket, which he usually wore under his heavy coat.

GLICKMAN. Well, never mind, just now the weather is warm.

HURWITZ. Yes, but still I am sorry. How could I possibly come to want to sell his coat! In great need one forgets even the first principles of honesty. But he's taking long, that friend of yours—what's his name?

GLICKMAN. His name is Bas, but he's

a splendid fellow—somewhat inclined to anarchism, as is usual with a person who hasn't eaten for three days.

[*Steps are heard in the corridor.*]

HURWITZ. Here he comes. I'm fearfully hungry.

GLICKMAN. No, it isn't he. Those are not his footsteps.

[*Berman enters with a third peddler, dressed like the first one, but slightly older; he carries a sack in his hand; over the other arm hangs a pair of rubbers.*]

BERMAN [*to Hurwitz, after looking at the wall over the bed*]. Have you seen my coat?

HURWITZ [*stammering*]. The coat— the coat? I don't know, either. I was looking for it, too.

PEDDLER. Well, make it quicker, I haven't any time to waste.

BERMAN. Yes, yes.

HURWITZ. What do you need the coat for?

GLICKMAN. I suppose to sell it, can't you see?

PEDDLER. Well, what's going to be?

BERMAN. I can't understand it. . . .

[*Shrugging his shoulders.*]

BAS [*both arms filled with paper parcels. He is struck by the expression on the faces about him: with an angry, significant glance at Glickman, he throws the parcels upon the table*]. Here, eat.

GLICKMAN. And you?

BAS [*angrily*]. I don't want to eat. [*Calling Glickman aside.*] Listen, if you don't confess that you sold the coat I'll not eat.

GLICKMAN. Good! [*Turning to the others.*] The coat—I sold. I know you won't be displeased.

HURWITZ. Fool, why didn't you say so before?

BERMAN. Sold? I should worry. Quite the contrary. I was only breaking my head to know what could have become of the thing.

PEDDLER. Well, who is going to pay me for my trip?

GLICKMAN [*to Bas*]. Maybe you've a few kopecks left? Give it to him.

BAS. Not a groschen.

GLICKMAN. I hope you won't mind, mister. Maybe you can use this hat? [*Offering him the hat on the wall.*]

HURWITZ. Yes, let him have the hat. I won't wear it any more.

PEDDLER [*examines the hat and lays it down again*]. I can't use the hat. It is worth nothing to me.

GLICKMAN. Well, how can we help it? [*To the others.*] Brothers, let's eat. Bas is a dandy, he's bought a lot of stuff.

HURWITZ [*to the peddler*]. Perhaps you would like to dine with us?

PEDDLER [*a little embarrassed*]. I guess—what harm can there be—I would really like to take a scrap of herring.

GLICKMAN. Ah, so be it. Sit down, mister.

BAS. Perhaps you would like to wash your hands?

HURWITZ. Wait, I'll bring water.

[*He runs out into the corridor with a tin kettle and comes back with it filled; the peddler washes his hands from the kettle, the water running onto the floor. He makes the blessing—"Raise thy hands . . . ," wipes his hands with the tail of his coat and cuts off a slice of bread and a piece of the herring. All eat.*]

GLICKMAN [*chewing*]. Well, I didn't do so badly.

HURWITZ. Very well—no one's complaining.

BERMAN. I, certainly not.

BAS. I, for one, am against such proceedings. To steal, yes, but not that way. There are other ways.

PEDDLER [*wiping his whiskers and preparing to leave*]. Very likely young people! Good herring! Listen, brothers, I buy second-hand stuff from the rich, but I tell you, one should only deal with such as you.

GLICKMAN. See, and Bas here is dissatisfied with us!

BERMAN. Yes, upon my word, it's a comedy. The only pity is now I'll have to wear my light coat and at night it is really a bit chilly.

PEDDLER. Oh, never mind. Young men don't freeze. Once, when I was a young bachelor I went about a whole winter through in a summer coat and if one is destined to live—you see, in spite of everything.

[*Steps are heard in the corridor.*]

HURWITZ. Who is it this time?

GLICKMAN [*running to the door*]. Another peddler, I suppose.

BAS. A peddler would have no business here now. The property is already disposed of!

[*Hannah, a girl of about twenty, runs in. She has a rather masculine face, flat bust and deep voice.*]

HANNAH. As I live, they're really eating! Gluttons, leave a bite for me! [*Grabs the rest of the bread.*] Not enough! [*Snatches a piece of bread out of Glickman's hand.*] Why have you eaten everything up?

PEDDLER. He, he! The poor girl wants something to eat, too.

HANNAH. Who is this man? Are you trying to make a radical of him, perhaps?

BAS. He's a peddler. Perhaps *you* have something to sell?

HANNAH. To sell? As I live! We should *sell* him something. Would you buy a ring?

PEDDLER. Ah, why not? I buy everything.

GLICKMAN. Now we *will* live, as I'm a Jew!

HANNAH [*removes from her finger a little ring*]. What will you give, mister, for this?

PEDDLER [*examining it closely*]. A half ruble.

HANNAH. Show us the money! [*Peddler counts out ten copper coins, examines the ring once again.*] It's really not worth that much.

GLICKMAN. It's worth it, mister, it's worth it.

HURWITZ. A question whether it's worth it. A genuine Nahrlin!

HANNAH. A present from my grandmother.

PEDDLER. Let it be from your grandfather.

HANNAH. Now, we'll feast all over again.

GLICKMAN. Maybe some one else has something to sell? Don't be bashful, brothers.

PEDDLER. On the contrary, hunt up something.

HURWITZ. I have nothing at all.

BERMAN. I, certainly not.

BAS. I—nothing—unless it be my soul.

HANNAH. Paupers! Proletarians!

[*To peddler.*] Come along, mister, do you buy rubbers?

PEDDLER [*boastfully*]. I told you I buy everything.

HANNAH. Then come along. I live just opposite. I have a pair of rubbers that I still have from home. At home, there's often much mud. Here, I don't need them. Here, it's dry.

PEDDLER. Of course, here one doesn't need rubbers. Who wears rubbers here, except, perhaps, a lunatic?

BAS. Why do you buy them, then?

PEDDLER. I mean—I told you, didn't I—I buy everything.

HANNAH. Come along then.

GLICKMAN. But come right back. Leave the half ruble here with us.

HANNAH. I'll come right back.

[*Peddler and Hannah go.*]

GLICKMAN. A mighty fine thing, as I live, Hannah should turn up with a ring and a pair of rubbers.

BAS. What else have you to sell!

[*Out in the courtyard is heard the cry of still another peddler.*]

GLICKMAN [*with a glowing face*]. Oh, I have such a fortunate idea!

BAS. What is it?

HURWITZ. Yes, what?

GLICKMAN [*looking at the bed*]. Why, for instance, do we need the bed?

HURWITZ. Why? To sleep in, of course.

GLICKMAN. The aristocrat! He must sleep in a bed! And to sleep upon the floor you're too delicate!

BERMAN. He knows what he's talking about. The bed is worth at least sixty kopecks.

HURWITZ [*reluctantly*]. For my part—let her be sold.

GLICKMAN. Of course. She's too narrow for three, anyway, and on the floor four, at least, can sleep comfortably.

BERMAN. He's right, as I live!

HURWITZ [*giving way entirely*]. Well, call in the peddler.

GLICKMAN. Let me.

[*He goes out.*]

BAS. I regard you all as abnormal beings, brothers.

HURWITZ. The whole world is abnormal!

BAS. Yes—yes.

[*Pause. Glickman's voice is heard on the stairs: "I'll show you a*

bed." *The gruff voice of the peddler: "A bed? Let it be a bed. Everything is merchandise."*
GLICKMAN. Here is the bed.
[*Indicating the bed. The peddler is a very old man with spectacles. He examines the bed closely.*]

PEDDLER. The bed is worth nothing. [*All become suddenly depressed.*] Have you nothing else to sell?
GLICKMAN. Nothing at all.
[*Peddler goes away.*]

[*Curtain.*]

THE CHIP WOMAN'S FORTUNE
A Play
By Willis Richardson

CHARACTERS

SILAS GREEN [*a store porter*].
LIZA [*his wife*].
EMMA [*their daughter*].
AUNT NANCY [*the chip woman*].
JIM [*her son*].
TWO OTHER MEN.

THE CHIP WOMAN'S FORTUNE

A PLAY

BY WILLIS RICHARDSON

[*The* Scene *is the very plain dining room of a poor colored family. The floor is without covering and the walls are without pictures. In the center of the floor is a rectangular table near which are a couple of chairs. In the rear wall is a fireplace where a low fire is burning, and at the left sits Liza in a low rocker. She is wrapped from shoulders to ankles in blankets; for she is just up from a spell of sickness. At the right of the fireplace in the rear wall is a window.*

A door is at the right side leading to the other rooms and through to the back yard. Another door at the left leads to the front of the house. A Victrola is at the left side. There is a deep silence as Liza sits gazing into the fire. She looks at the little clock on the mantle, then looks towards the right and calls.]

Liza [*calling*]. Emma! Emma!
[*Presently Aunt Nancy appears at the right. Every one of us has seen her kind—those old women who go about the streets with baskets picking up chips of wood and lumps of coal, or searching the trash cans for whatever they can find. Such is Aunt Nancy. She is old and her back is bent on account of constant stooping. She is wearing a bonnet which partly hides her black, wrinkled face, and has a shawl thrown over her shoulders.*]

Aunt Nancy. You callin' Emma, Miss Liza?

Liza. Yes'm, Aunt Nancy. You seen her?

Aunt Nancy. No'm, ah ain't seen her.

Liza. Ah wonder where she is? Ah want her to go to the store for me.

Aunt Nancy. Ah don't know where she is. Ah ain't seen her for the last two hours, but ah reckon she'll drop in in a minute or two. How you feelin' now?

Liza. Ah'm feelin' pretty good. The medicine you give me last night must be doin' me good.

Aunt Nancy. Ah don't reckon you need no more medicine to-day.

Liza. Ah reckon not. How you feelin'? Seems like ah ought to be askin' you that instead o' you askin' me.

Aunt Nancy. Ah'm feelin' right sharp for a old woman. To tell the truth, ah ain't felt better since the day ah got married. Ah'm 'spectin' somethin'.

Liza. You 'spectin' somethin'?

Aunt Nancy. Yes'm.

Liza. What?

Aunt Nancy. Can't tell you that, Miss Liza; but maybe you'll find out before the day's gone.

Liza. Is it anything good?

Aunt Nancy. Didn't ah tell you ah ain't felt better since the day ah got married?

Liza. Ah'm glad somethin' good's happenin' to somebody. Ain't nothin' good happenin' to me.

Aunt Nancy. You gettin' better, ain't you?

Liza. Yes'm, ah'm gettin' better.

Aunt Nancy. That sure is good; and besides, you're young yet, lot o' good things can happen to you before you die.

Liza. Ah hope so.

Aunt Nancy [*going close to her*]. Lemme look in your eye. [*After looking into her eyes.*] Your eyes is startin' to shine. You'll be gettin' all right pretty soon.
[*She whispers something into Liza's ear.*]

Liza [*blushing*]. Oh, no'm, Aunt Nancy!

Aunt Nancy [*laughing*]. That's all right, you wait. Ah likes to see a woman's eyes shinin'. It shows she's got some life in her. Ah don't like to see no woman with dead eyes, 'specially a young woman. Ah likes to see 'em pert.

Liza. You ain't by yourself. Everybody likes to see a young woman pert.

Aunt Nancy. Ah was goin' in the woods to dig you some roots, but ah reckon ah'll wait till to-morrow.

Liza. To-morrow'll be all right, Aunt Nancy; you don't have to go to-day.

Aunt Nancy. Ah'll go now and sit out on the back steps in the sun and think. Ah like to sit in the sun and think.

Liza. Think about what?

Aunt Nancy. Ah got somethin' to think about.

Liza. What?

Aunt Nancy. Ah can't tell you everythin'. It ain't good to tell everythin' you think about, you know. 'Spose everybody told all their thoughts?

Liza. That wouldn't never do.

Aunt Nancy. 'Deed it wouldn't never do. Everythin' ud be upside down with other people knowin' what you was thinkin' about.

[*She starts out.*]

Liza. If you see Emma out there send her in to me.

Aunt Nancy. All right, ah will. [*Looking towards the right.*] Here comes Emma now.

[*Emma enters. She is a pretty brown girl of eighteen.*]

Emma. You want me, Ma?

Liza. Yes, ah want you. Where you been?

Emma. Upstairs.

Liza. Upstairs doin' what?

Emma. Combin' ma hair.

Liza. Combin' your hair this time o' day? You combed your hair once this mornin'. What you comb it again for?

Emma. Ah wanted it combed.

Liza. You wasn't always so fond o' combin' your hair. What's comin' off?

Emma. Nothin'.

Liza [*looking at her closely*]. Come here, gal. [*Emma comes nearer.*] Ah believe before God you been puttin' powder on your face. Is you been puttin' powder on your face? [*Emma does not answer.*] Where'd you get that powder from?

Emma. Ah bought it.

Liza. Bought it with what? [*Emma is silent.*] Don't you hear me talkin' to you? Bought it with what?

Emma. Bought it with some change Pa gave me.

Liza. Wipe it off! Wipe it right off! And don't put no more on. Leave it up there and ah'll use it when ah get on ma feet. You're too young to be powderin'.

Aunt Nancy [*who still stands near*]. Let the gal alone. You was young like her once. She ain't goin' to be that young but once.

Liza. She don't have to paint herself up like a billboard just because she's young. [*To Emma.*] Get the basket. Ah want you to go to the store for me.

[*Emma goes back out.*]

Aunt Nancy. Ah'll be out on the back steps if you want me.

Liza. All right'm, ah hope ah won't need you.

[*Aunt Nancy goes out and Liza sits rocking until Emma returns.*]

Liza [*as Emma returns with the basket*]. There's somethin' mighty funny goin' on around here, you primpin' and Aunt Nancy thinkin'. Ah reckon we're going to have a thunderstorm.

Emma. Ain't nothin' funny goin' on.

Liza. What you doin' plasterin' your face up and combin' your hair if somethin' funny ain't goin' on? You know you ain't never combed your hair twice the same day in your life if it wasn't Sunday.

Emma [*trying to change the subject*]. What did you say get from the store?

Liza. Get some potatoes and some cakes. Some o' the little ones your Pa likes so.

Emma. Is that all?

Liza. Yes, that's all. Look here, did Aunt Nancy take you in the woods and show you how to dig them roots yesterday?

Emma. Yes'm, she showed me, but ah don't remember much.

Liza. Why don't you? You ain't got your mind on no boy, is you?

Emma. No'm. She says she's goin' to show me all over again so ah'll know how to find 'em for you when she's gone.

LIZA. Aunt Nancy ain't goin' nowhere.

EMMA. Ah hope she won't; but if she does ah'll be sorry. She's so good ah love her.

LIZA. 'Deed she is good; and you can't help from lovin' her; ain't no way in the world to help from lovin' people that do good by you.

EMMA. And Aunt Nancy's certainly done good by us.

LIZA. Nobody knows that like ah do.

EMMA [starting out]. Ah'm goin' now.

LIZA. Wait a minute. Start this Victrola off before you go, and go out the back way, it's nearer.

EMMA [adjusting the needle]. When we goin' to get some new records, Ma?

LIZA. New records? You better wait till the Victrola gets paid for. You got a plenty o' records.

EMMA. But they're all old.

LIZA. That's all right, you can keep on usin' 'em. You ought to be glad to get bread to eat and let new records alone.

[Emma starts the machine and goes towards the right.]

LIZA. Don't stay long.

EMMA. No'm, ah'll be right back.

[Liza is listening to the Victrola when Silas enters from the outside. He is a man of five and forty, wearing the uniform of a store porter. As he enters Liza looks up at him in surprise.]

LIZA. Why, Silas, what you doin' home?

SILAS [throwing his cap down and moving to the table]. They sent me home.

LIZA. Not discharged?

SILAS [not in the best of spirits]. No, ah ain't discharged, but it's almost as bad; ah'm furloughed for a couple o' days without pay.

LIZA. Furloughed for what?

SILAS [motioning towards the Victrola]. It's on account o' that old Victrola. Seems like it's bringin' us more trouble than it's worth.

LIZA. What's the Victrola got to do with your job?

SILAS. It's just like everything else. When a man's got trouble o' one kind seems like everything goes wrong.

LIZA. That ain't tellin' me nothin'.

SILAS. Well, you know we ain't paid nothin' on that Victrola since the first payment, don't you?

LIZA. Yes, ah know that; but you been promisin'.

SILAS. That's the trouble. Ah been doin' a lot o' promisin' and no payin'.

LIZA [impatiently]. Well, what else? You just as well tell me all of it at once. Ah don't feel like askin' a million questions.

SILAS. The man said he was goin' to send here and get the thing if we didn't pay this month, didn't he?

LIZA. Yes.

SILAS. Well, you know we ain't been able to pay, so he's goin' to send after it.

LIZA. Goin' to take it away?

SILAS. Yes.

LIZA [half in sarcasm and half in petulance]. So that's why you got furloughed, is it? 'Cause they goin' to take the Victrola away.

SILAS. No, that ain't it exactly.

LIZA. Ah see you ain't told me. What is it exactly?

SILAS. The manager o' that music place is a friend o' ma boss; and this mornin' while ah was sweepin' off the front pavement he passed by me going in the store. When he seen me he stopped and looked at me hard, then he went in. Ah thought trouble was comin' when ah seen him look at me so hard. After he came out the boss called me in and told me they was goin' to send after that Victrola; and then he says: "Go home and stay a few days and maybe you'll learn how to pay your debts." So here ah am.

LIZA. Ah'll be mighty sorry to lose that Victrola; but if it can't be helped, it can't be helped.

SILAS. No, it can't be helped, but that ain't the worst of it. If ah don't pay and they take it away, when ah go back the boss'll always have his eyes on me, and ah bet it won't be long before ah'll be losin' ma job.

LIZA. What you goin' to do?

SILAS. Ah'll do anything to save ma job.

LIZA. Ah know you'd like to pay and keep the Victrola; but ah don't see where you goin' to get the fifty dollars from.

SILAS. Ah know one thing.

LIZA. What?

SILAS [*determined*]. Aunt Nancy's got to start to payin' for her room and board.

LIZA [*surprised*]. Aunt Nancy!

SILAS. Yes; we can't keep her around here as high as everything is.

LIZA [*earnestly*]. But, look what she done for me. She brought me from flat o' ma back. Ah had one foot in the grave before she come here. And look at me now; ah'm almost on ma feet.

SILAS. Ah can't help it. Ah know she done a whole lot for us, but ah can't keep things goin' if she don't pay.

LIZA. She helps along. She picks up chips, and pieces o' wood and lumps o' coal on the street. That keeps you from havin' to buy 'em.

SILAS. Everything you sayin' is true, but she's either got to give us some money for stayin' here or she's got to go.

LIZA [*much concerned*]. If she goes who's goin' to nurse me? Who's goin' in the woods and get the roots to make ma medicine?

SILAS. If that old woman didn't have money ah wouldn't say nothin'.

LIZA [*not understanding*]. If she didn't have what?

SILAS. If she didn't have money; but ah know she's got money.

LIZA [*angrily*]. Where in the devil would Aunt Nancy get any money from?

SILAS. Ain't no use to get mad about it. Ah know what ah'm sayin'.

LIZA. How do you know she's got money?

SILAS. Ah know because ah been watchin' her for the last week or so.

LIZA. You been watchin' her, is you? Well, what did you find out?

SILAS. Ah found out that people passin' in the street give her money every day.

LIZA. You ain't talkin' about a cent or two that anybody might give a old woman, is you?

SILAS. No. Every day ah see people givin' her dimes and nickels and quarters. And it ain't no longer than yesterday that ah seen two rich lookin' men give her greenbacks.

LIZA. Ah ain't never seen her with no money.

SILAS. Ah knows you ain't. She hides it.

LIZA. Hides it where?

SILAS. In the back yard. Ah know the very place.

LIZA. Did you see her hide it there?

SILAS. No, ah didn't see her hide it there, but every time ah go out there by that spot she comes right behind me.

LIZA. Ah hope you ain't mean enough to try to take her money if she's got any.

SILAS. No, ah ain't been tryin' to take it. Ah just wanted to see what she had there. Ah tried it time and again, and every time ah went by that place she'd come right up.

LIZA. Why didn't you wait till she went away?

SILAS. Ah done that twice; but every time ah went out there she come right back just like somethin' drawed her back. Once ah went out there with a spade and up she comes and stands right on the spot. Ah told her ah wanted to dig a hole for a post and she said, "Please don't dig it right here, Mr. Silas; ah got somethin' planted here." Now you know if anybody had anythin' planted they wouldn't go and stand right on the spot.

LIZA [*after a moment's thought*]. Well, whether she's got money or not, ah don't think you ought to put her out after what she's done for us.

SILAS. That's the only way ah know we can get by.

LIZA. That won't make it the right thing to do. A lot o' people get by by doin' the wrong thing. Ah know Emma won't like it.

SILAS. It's got to happen just the same if she don't hand out some money. Where's Emma?

LIZA. She went after somethin' for dinner.

SILAS. When she comes in tell her what ah said. 'Course, the old woman might get open hearted and let us have fifty dollars or so; then we won't have no trouble at all and ah can go back to work to-morrow.

LIZA. Maybe she'll let us have that much if she's got it, but ah don't believe she's got that much.

SILAS [*determined*]. Somethin's got to be done. [*As he starts out.*] Ah reckon ah better change these clothes so they'll be clean when ah do go back.

[*He goes out, leaving Liza gazing into the fire. Presently Emma returns with the basket on her arm.*]

LIZA. Ah got a lot o' sad news for you, Emma.

EMMA [*a little frightened at her mother's tone, resting the basket on the table and gazing at her*]. What's the matter? Anything bad happened?

LIZA. They're goin' to take the Victrola away.

EMMA [*surprised*]. The Victrola! Who's goin' to take it away?

LIZA. The men from the store's comin' because we ain't been makin' no payments.

EMMA. Does pa know about it?

LIZA. Yes, he told me.

EMMA. He been here?

LIZA. He's here now. They sent him home from work because we ain't been makin' no payments.

EMMA [*fearfully*]. He ain't discharged?

LIZA. He ain't discharged, but he's furloughed and that's just as bad.

EMMA. You mean they're goin' to let him go back?

LIZA. Yes, they'd let him go back to-day if he could make a good payment on that Victrola; but he reckons he'll have to stay out two or three days as it is.

EMMA. Ah'm mighty sorry they put him off, and ah'm mighty sorry we can't keep that machine. Hearin' that thing was about the only pleasure ah had.

LIZA. That ain't the worst yet.

EMMA. What, somethin' else?

LIZA. Your pa says if Aunt Nancy don't pay some money for stayin' here she's got to go.

EMMA. Where's Aunt Nancy goin' to get any money from?

LIZA. He says he's seen people give her money almost every day; and she's got it buried in the back yard.

EMMA. If she's got any money at all it's just a few cents; but ah don't believe she's got none.

SILAS [*entering just in time to hear what Emma says. He is now wearing overalls*]. Yes, she is got money, too; and she'll either have to pay some or get out.

EMMA [*turning to him*]. Ah don't see nothin' fair in that. She picks up chips, she brings you wood and coal, and

she nurses ma. What more do you want?

SILAS [*sitting at the right of the table*]. If she'll give me a few dollars or let me borrow a few dollars maybe ah can go back to ma job to-morrow.

EMMA. If you put her out ah believe ma'll go right back to bed, 'cause there won't be nobody that'll know what to do for her. So ah don't see nothin' you'll gain by puttin' her out.

SILAS. If she'll let us have the money—

EMMA. If she's got any money it's just a little she's savin' for her son.

SILAS [*surprised*]. Her son! Ah didn't know she had a son.

EMMA. Yes, seh, she's got a son.

SILAS. Where's he? Ah ain't heard nothin' about him.

EMMA. He's been in the pen all the time, but ah reckon he's out now.

SILAS. In the pen?

EMMA. Yes, seh.

SILAS [*still puzzled*]. And she's savin' money for him?

EMMA. Ah reckon that's what she's savin' it for if she's got any.

SILAS [*in disgust*]. Well, for God's sake! Savin' money for a jailbird!

EMMA.. She says she wants him to have a few cents to keep him till he can get a job.

SILAS. Did she tell you all this?

EMMA. Yes, seh. Ah wrote a letter for her the other day.

SILAS [*turning to his wife*]. Did you know anything about this, Liza?

LIZA. No, this is the first time ah've heard a word about it.

SILAS [*to Emma*]. Why didn't you say somethin' about it?

EMMA. You always told me to tend to ma own business. Ah didn't want to be tellin' her business around.

SILAS. It's all right to tend to your own business; but it ain't all right to keep secrets from your parents when it concerns 'em. You say her son's out now?

EMMA. He was to be out yesterday. She's lookin' for him to come here to-day.

SILAS. What was he sent up for?

EMMA. Ah don't know, seh; somethin' about a woman, ah believe.

SILAS. He means to come here, does he?

EMMA. Yes, seh.

SILAS. You hear that, Liza?

LIZA. Yes, and ah ain't particular about havin' no jailbird comin' here neither.

SILAS. Ah reckon ah just as well talk to her now as any other time. Was she out there when you came in, Emma?

EMMA. Yes, seh, she was sittin' out on the back steps; but she got up when ah came in and started off.

SILAS. Well, go tell her to come here.

EMMA [starting out]. Ah'll have to catch her 'cause ah reckon she's gone.

SILAS. Just go out and stand by that middle clothes prop and she'll come in sight. Ah've already tried it a lot o' times maself.

[Emma goes out.]

SILAS. Liza, ah want you to understand ah'm not actin' this way 'cause ah mean to be hardhearted. Ah've just got to get out o' this trouble.

LIZA [discouraged]. Ah'm sorry everythin' turned out like this, 'cause ah reckon ah'll have to go back to bed if she goes.

SILAS. Don't say that. The Lord couldn't be that hard on us.

LIZA. Ah hope you're right; goodness knows ah do.

SILAS. If ah can get her to do us this favor before the men come after that Victrola, everythin'll be all right.

[There is a pause while they ponder over their situation.]

SILAS. And even if she will agree to help us, Liza; ah'm tired o' this kind o' life. Ah'm sick o' livin' from hand to mouth.

LIZA. Ah reckon we ought to be thankful to be livin' any kind o' way with all the trouble we had. Some people gets along better'n we do, but a whole lot o' others don't get along as good. Ah only got one consolation besides believin' in the Lord.

SILAS. What's that?

LIZA. That things ain't always been like this, and that they might not always be like this.

SILAS. Ah hope not. [He listens.] Here they come.

LIZA. Now, don't be hard on her, Silas. You know she's been mighty good to us.

SILAS. Ah ain't goin' to be hard on her. Ah'm goin' to be as fair as ah can.

[Emma enters, followed by Aunt Nancy.]

AUNT NANCY [coming to the table and speaking to Silas]. You want to see me, seh?

SILAS [kindly]. Yes, Aunt Nancy, ah want to talk to you. Get her a chair so she can sit down, Emma.

[Aunt Nancy looks around for a chair. Emma brings her one and she sits at the right of the table.]

SILAS. The first thing ah want to do, Aunt Nancy, is to thank you for all the good things you done for us. And then ah want to tell you that we're in trouble.

AUNT NANCY. You all in trouble, Mister Silas?

SILAS. Yes'm, the men'll be here today after the Victrola, and ah'm put off from work a few days 'cause ah didn't pay for it.

AUNT NANCY. Ah'm mighty sorry for that.

SILAS. And you know you been stayin' here with us for six months or more and we ain't been chargin' you a thing.

AUNT NANCY. No, and ah wouldn't a been able to pay nothin' nohow.

SILAS. Now ah'm askin' if you'll pay us for stayin' or let us borrow a few dollars from you?

AUNT NANCY [with a long face]. 'Deed the Lord knows ah can't pay nothin', Mister Silas. Ah ain't got nothin' for maself.

SILAS. But we know you got money hid out there in the back yard.

AUNT NANCY [frankly]. Ah got a little money out there; but that ain't for me, that's for ma child.

SILAS [feigning surprise]. You didn't tell us you had no child.

AUNT NANCY. Ah reckon you'd call him a man, but ah call him ma child. He's grown.

SILAS. Where is he?

AUNT NANCY. Ah reckon he's on his way here now.

SILAS [still pretending ignorance]. Ah don't see what a old woman like you wants to be savin' money for a grown son for. He ought to be workin' and takin' care o' you. Ain't he workin'?

AUNT NANCY. He's been locked up.

SILAS. In jail?

AUNT NANCY. In the pen.

SILAS. That's so much the worse. You ought'n be savin' money to give to a common jailbird.

AUNT NANCY [offended]. He ain't no jailbird, Mister Silas; don't call him that. He's ma son.

SILAS. He ought to be shamed o' hisself for not workin' and takin' care o' you.

AUNT NANCY. That used to be the way when ah was comin' up. When the children used to get grown they used to take care o' the old folks; but now it's difference. The old folks has to take care o' the children.

SILAS. Ah wouldn't never look out for no grown son.

AUNT NANCY. Ah reckon you wouldn't. Fathers never was like mothers and never will be.

SILAS. And specially if he went to the pen.

AUNT NANCY. Goin' to the pen ain't nothin'. Some o' the best men in the world's been to the pen. It ain't the goin' to the pen that counts, it's what you go there for. Once it used to be a big disgrace to be locked up; but the people in them days forgot that the Lord was locked up. No, seh, it ain't the bein' locked up, it's what you locked up for. If the Lord had a got locked up for stealin' somethin' or killin' somebody do you think people would be praisin' him now like they do?

SILAS. Ah know they wouldn'; but what did your son get locked up for?

AUNT NANCY. He got locked up about a woman, but he done what any other man might a done. He was goin' with a woman what he thought was crooked, but she was crooked. He run up on her one night when another man was handlin' her kinder rough and beat the man up—he beat the man up bad. Then he found out the woman was crooked and he lost his head and beat her up, too. That's the worst part of it.

SILAS [doubtfully]. And they sent him to the pen for that, did they?

AUNT NANCY. Yes, seh. The man he beat up was one o' these big fellers what went to church every Sunday, and looked so clean and nice in his biled shirts and white collars and fine clothes all through the week days, but in the night he trailed in the gutter. He used his influence and put up a job on Jim that sent him to the pen.

SILAS. Ah don't mean to hurt your feelin's, Aunt Nancy, but your boy can't be much if he beat a woman up.

LIZA [who has been listening closely]. 'Deed he can't.

AUNT NANCY [hanging her head]. That's the worse part of it. Ah didn't mind him beatin' the man, but ah never did care much for a man that would hit a woman—no man but ma own son. [Looking up.] And you know a mother can't help that.

SILAS. Ah always did think some mothers were too kindhearted.

AUNT NANCY. No, they ain't. Mothers ain't half as kindhearted as God is. If God was hard as some people is, everybody in this world would be farin' mighty hard. You know there ain't no man perfect, and no woman neither.

SILAS. Ah reckon you must be right there. But the main reason ah sent for you was to ask you if you wouldn't let us have a little money; and if you can't do that we'll be in a hole sure enough.

AUNT NANCY. Ah wish ah could. Ah'd be willin' to do anything in the world for you, but he comes first, you know.

SILAS. Do you reckon he'll let us have it?

AUNT NANCY. Ah don't know; he's mighty kindhearted. He's takin' a mighty long time to come, too.

[There is a loud knocking on the outside door.]

AUNT NANCY [starting to rise]. Ah reckon that's him now.

LIZA. Don't get up, Aunt Nancy; Emma'll let him in.

[Emma goes out.]

SILAS [to Aunt Nancy]. Why don't you take your bonnet off? You don't want to look like you ain't at home.

AUNT NANCY. Never mind, ah'll keep it on. We won't be here long, ah reckon.

EMMA [returning]. It's the men after the Victrola.

[Silas hastens out.]

AUNT NANCY [sighing]. Oh, Lord, ah thought that was Jim. Ah wonder why he don't come?

LIZA. Don't worry, Aunt Nancy; it ain't late.

EMMA. Ah reckon he might be lookin' for the place.

AUNT NANCY. But you put this number in the letter, didn't you?

EMMA. Yes'm, ah put it in.

SILAS [*returning*]. Ah don't know why ah done it, but ah told 'em to wait a few minutes.

[*He sits.*]

AUNT NANCY. Ah don't know, Jim might come.

[*There is another knock on the door.*]

SILAS [*rising*]. Ah wonder what they want now?

[*He goes out again.*]

AUNT NANCY. That might be Jim.

LIZA. Ah hope it is.

[*Silas returns, followed by Jim. When Aunt Nancy sees who it is she flies to him. Jim opens his arms and draws her to him.*]

AUNT NANCY [*holding him off and looking at him*]. Is it you sure enough, Jim?

JIM [*smiling*]. Yes'm, it's me.

AUNT NANCY. Come over here.

[*She draws him over to the table and we have an opportunity to get a good view of him. He is a man of thirty, standing over six feet in height and large in proportion. He is wearing a blue shirt with a collar attached and a dark suit.*]

AUNT NANCY. These is the people ah been stayin' with all the winter, Jim. [*She names each one in her way of introduction.*] This is Mr. Silas, Jim.

JIM [*smiling*]. Glad to meet you, Mr. Silas.

AUNT NANCY. That is Miss Liza.

JIM [*bowing to Liza*]. Pleased to meet you, Miss Liza.

AUNT NANCY. This is Emma. [*Jim and Emma smile at each other as they bow.*] These people been mighty good to me, Jim.

JIM [*speaking to them all*]. Ah'm glad to hear that and ah thank you all for it.

LIZA. We ain't been half as good to her as she's been to us.

EMMA. 'Deed we ain't.

AUNT NANCY. Ah ain't done nothin' that no good woman wouldn't 'a' done. Jim knows me.

JIM. Ah know her well, too.

AUNT NANCY. What made you take so long to get here, Jim?

JIM. Well, ah hung around a little while—

AUNT NANCY. Now, Jim, you know you ain't got no business hangin' around when ah'm waitin' for you.

JIM. And even when ah got here ah wasn't sure this was the right place 'cause ah seen two men hangin' around out front and they looked kinder like bootleggers.

SILAS. Them's the men what come to take the Victrola away. Ah just asked 'em to wait a minute till ah tried to borrow some money from your ma. You see the winter's been so hard ah ain't been able to pay nothin' on it, so the man sent them to take it away.

JIM [*turning to his mother*]. You say these people been good to you, ma?

AUNT NANCY. Yes, they been mighty good to me.

JIM [*reaching into his pocket*]. Ah've got fifteen dollars. You can have that if it'll do you any good.

[*He gives it to Silas.*]

SILAS [*taking the money*]. Thanks for that. Maybe some o' these days—

[*The two men who have been waiting outside enter.*]

FIRST MAN. Ah'm sorry, but we can't wait all day; we got to get back to the store.

JIM [*to Silas*]. How much do you owe on it?

SILAS. Fifty dollars.

JIM. Fifteen dollars won't do much good then, will it?

SILAS. Well, it'll help. Ah been tryin' to borrow it from your ma.

SECOND MAN [*roughly*]. Come on, Dan, let's take it; they ain't got nothin'.

SILAS [*as they take hold of the Victrola*]. Wait a minute.

JIM [*again turning to his mother*]. You got any money, ma?

AUNT NANCY. Ah got a little ah been savin' for you.

JIM. How much?

AUNT NANCY [*who is not very good at figures*]. Ah don't know, but ah reckon it's enough. Ah'll get it.

[*She rises and goes out right.*]

SECOND MAN [*impatiently*]. Come on, Dan, this is all a bluff.

[*They take the Victrola towards the door.*]

JIM [*getting in the doorway*]. There ain't nobody or nothin' goin' out o' here till she comes back.

[*Jim is such a large man and so nearly fills the doorway that the two men stop and reconsider their plan. They decide to wait.*]

JIM. Ah don't mean no harm to nobody and ah wouldn't hurt a hair in nobody's head; but when ah say wait, ah mean wait.

FIRST MAN. But you see, mister, we been waitin' a long time already.

JIM. Well, you won't have to wait much longer. She'll be back in a minute.

[*Here Aunt Nancy returns with a rather dirty box which she puts on the table and opens. All gaze into it.*]

AUNT NANCY [*pouring its contents on the table*]. This is yours, Jim; ah been savin' it for you ever since you went away.

JIM [*staring at the money*]. All this for me?

AUNT NANCY. Yes, and you can do anything you want to do with it.

JIM [*pushing half the money to Silas*]. Here, take this; maybe it'll be enough.

[*Judging from the expression on Aunt Nancy's face, Jim is giving away too much.*]

SILAS [*drawing the money to him*]. 'Deed it will be enough. [*He counts the money for the men.*] Here's your fifty dollars.

[*The First Man takes the money and with the aid of the other man pushes the Victrola back to its place. Having done this they start out.*]

JIM [*to Silas*]. You better get a receipt for that.

SILAS [*to the men*]. Hey! Wait a minute! [*The men stop.*] Gimme a receipt for that money.

[*The First Man takes a receipt book from his pocket and writes a receipt for Silas. They go out.*]

SILAS [*looking at the receipt*]. That's better. [*Indicating the money left on the table.*] Ah reckon you better take this back, Jim.

JIM. No, you keep it. You all been good to ma, and ain't nothin' ah got too good for you and ain't nothin' ah can do ah wouldn't do for you.

LIZA. She's done a whole lot more for us than we could ever do for her.

AUNT NANCY. Ah'd 'a' give you that money before, Mr. Silas, but ah was savin' it for Jim, and ah just didn't have the heart to give it away.

SILAS. That's all right, Auntie; ah 'preciate it just as much as if you had given it to me when ah first asked you.

AUNT NANCY [*taking her basket*]. Well, Jim, ah reckon we better be goin'.

LIZA [*in surprise*]. Goin'! Where you goin'?

AUNT NANCY. Goin' to get a place to stay.

JIM. Then ah'm goin' to look for a job.

LIZA. But ah thought you was goin' to stay here with us.

AUNT NANCY. You ain't got no room for both of us, child.

SILAS [*shifting the chairs around*]. Yes'm, we is. We'll make room.

JIM. No, seh, ah don't want you to cramp yourself on ma account. It won't take us long to find another place.

LIZA. But how'll ah get on, Aunt Nancy, with you gone?

AUNT NANCY. Ah won't be far away. Ah'll come in and look after you every mornin', child.

LIZA. Ah'm mighty sorry you goin'; and ah want to thank you again for what you done for us.

AUNT NANCY [*standing near the door with Jim*]. Maybe we'll ask you all to do us a favor sometime.

SILAS. And we'll be mighty glad to do it.

AUNT NANCY. Well, good day till tomorrow.

SILAS, LIZA, EMMA. Good day.

JIM. Good day to all.

SILAS, LIZA, EMMA. Good day.

[*Aunt Nancy and Jim go out.*]

EMMA [*who has been quite silent*]. Ah'm sorry she's gone.

LIZA. You must be mighty sorry he's gone, too, by the way you looked at him.

SILAS. 'Deed she must be. She looked at him like her life depended on it.

LIZA. To tell the truth about the thing, ah'm mighty sorry she's gone, too. She's certain'y goin' to be a loss to me.

SILAS. But she says she's goin' to come around every day to look after you.

LIZA. Yes, but that ain't like stayin' here.

SILAS. Well, there ain't nothin' ah can do.

EMMA. Ah reckon you're mighty glad you didn't put her out.

SILAS. Ah am, ah'm mighty glad.

LIZA. She got us out o' trouble, all right.

EMMA. 'Deed she did.

SILAS. Ah got to go and get ma clothes on and go and see about ma job.

LIZA. She saved your job, too, ah'm thinkin'.

SILAS. You bet your life she did.

[*He goes out right.*]

[*Curtain.*]

THE VEIL
A Belgian Play

By Georges Rodenbach
Translated from the French by Harold Harper

CHARACTERS

JEAN.
THE DOCTOR.
SISTER GUDULE.
BARBARA.

SCENE: *A room in Jean's home, Bruges.*
TIME: *The present.*

THE VEIL

A Belgian Play   By Georges Rodenbach

[*A vast dining room with a high ceiling. Long curtains hang in ample folds over the two windows. Against the wall stands an old oak clock. There are three doors: one at the back, opening upon a corridor leading to the street; one at the left, to the garden; one at the right, to the bedrooms. This last stands open during the entire play. At the center is a table, set for two. A fire is burning in the fireplace.*

As the curtain rises, the faint tinkling of a near-by church bell is heard.]

BARBARA [*as she finishes setting the table*]. Is that all? Let me see: glasses, mats, the lamp. Yes, and the carafe with its laughing water! I don't know what ails me to-day! I am so weary of everything. And the everlasting bell, and the rain against the windows. Really, I cannot imagine what is wrong. I seem always to be somewhere else. Everything is changed. Ah, the house looks different. How sad is a house where some one lies sick!—especially when one is near a church—with its bell! My poor mistress! [*The bell starts ringing.*] She lies motionless in her bed, like a stranger. How dreary it all is. And now I must bow down before the authority of the nun, Sister Gudule, who nurses her, so carefully. Ah, how I loved the house before that unearthly nun came with her cold voice, which flows as from the frigid lips of a statue!

[*Sister Gudule appears in the doorway on the left with a huge bouquet of chrysanthemums.*]

BARBARA [*aside*]. Sister Gudule!

THE SISTER. Barbara? Give me a vase. I hurried out and gathered these flowers; they seemed so lonely—like orphans.

BARBARA. What will Monsieur Jean say?

THE SISTER. I have not so much gathered them as taken them to me for protection: they seemed to suffer, poor flowers! And now, here under the lamp, they make a halo, brightening the table. One may love flowers; even those who have taken the veil may enjoy this harmless passion. [*She looks ecstatically at the flowers.*] These are the last survivors of the garden, these autumn chrysanthemums—so sad, so fragile, golden-hued, like the gold of an age-old crown—the crown of dead and faded summer, flowers of the old age of the year!

BARBARA. Are you so fond of them?

THE SISTER. Is it not right that I should succor them before they fall into decay, these short-lived, late-blooming flowers? It is a way for us to mother something.

BARBARA. In your convent do you ever regret the world you left?

THE SISTER. No! Our Order is not a very severe one. Our vows put us, as it were, behind a glass through which we can see the world, and yet not be of it.

BARBARA. I shouldn't have wanted to be a nun, and live in the convent, because of the rule, which is hard on a woman, even of my age, that requires her to cut off her hair. One's faith must be strong to do that! Because our hair—is a part of us. I should feel as if I were no longer alive if my hair were taken from me—as they take hair from the dead.

THE SISTER. I should willingly have given *my* hair! But you know our Order does not require eternal vows; we are spared that. Under the headdress, shaped like the Holy Spirit in the semblance of a dove, we keep our hair.

BARBARA. Indeed! And have you kept all your flowing tresses?

THE SISTER. Yes, all, though they are

427

useless. We do not renounce them alto-gether, we only exile them, as it were.

BARBARA [coming to the Sister]. Sis-ter, we are forgetting the patient, who may wake any moment. Don't you think it wise to brighten her room with lights?

THE SISTER. Yes, the old are afraid of darkness. They are like children.

BARBARA. And besides its warm com-fort, it almost seems as if the light laid a restraining hand on death.

THE SISTER. Death is not stopped by so little! It comes to us all. It follows us step by step and casts over the life of to-day the shadow of to-morrow. Do you really think a little light can tame it? But I shall reassure her and light the lamps.

[The Sister goes out.]

BARBARA. She always gets the better of me with that heavenly voice of hers! But I don't think it right for her to treat me like a peasant. She is really a coquette, behind all her religious ways, and in spite of the beads she tells off with her hands of ivory! I wonder if they have bouquets in the convent? Her talk about the flowers just now shocked me as much as if I were to find a sachet among a nun's robes. [The hour strikes from the old church tower.] There! Seven o'clock. The master! I recognize his step on the stairs.

[Jean enters from the back, shiver-ing.]

JEAN. It's good to be back again, and feel the soft warmth of the fire. What nasty November weather! [To Bar-bara.] How is my aunt?

BARBARA. Asleep. You mustn't wake her.

JEAN. And Sister Gudule?

BARBARA. Is with her.

JEAN. Tell her supper is ready. [Barbara goes out.] Everything seems to smile upon me here. [He catches sight of the chrysanthemums on the ta-ble.] A bouquet! But it is sad, and it gives no perfume. An autumn bou-quet, sad like this house! It was doubt-less Sister Gudule who gathered these; she tries to make it cheerful here. How good she is! But how she troubles me! She conceals that hair of hers—no one knows the color!

[Enter Sister Gudule. Barbara brings in the supper from another door.]

THE SISTER. Monsieur Jean! Good evening.

JEAN. Good evening, Sister. I wished to see my aunt, but I did not dare: Barbara told me she was asleep.

THE SISTER. She is resting. She had better be left alone.

JEAN. Poor aunt! She was so good to me when I was young! My heart is sick to see her lying ill, helpless in the face of death, which is not far off. There are times, such as this, when I feel I am truly her child! Let us have supper.

[They go toward the table.]

THE SISTER. Like a pagan? With-out even a small prayer? Just a sign of the cross, to please me? I don't want to feel I am supping with a stranger.

JEAN [seating himself and making the sign of the cross]. If you wish it.

THE SISTER. When people are living together, it is best that they resemble each other a little.

[Barbara, having served, goes out.]

JEAN. Life is strange. To think of our being together here, you and I! We have no hearth of our own, and we shall never have one, yet our life here is a little like that of man and wife. It makes me happy to call you "Sister."

THE SISTER. I am a sister to you—in our Holy Mother the Church.

JEAN. But there is something besides: you are a friend, almost a real sister, a sister found after a long absence, one who speaks to me of playthings we had when we were children together.

THE SISTER. Yet what a slender chance it was that brought our two lives together for an instant! [She notices Jean shivering.] You are trembling!

JEAN. I am cold. Why do you talk of going away? We shan't have to think of that for some time; why not forget? I have become used to living here with you. I cannot stay alone; you have made everything sweeter by your pres-ence. You, a nun, and I, a disillusioned, silent man, coming from the very ex-tremes of life, without having known each other! Even now, we are stran-gers. We have come together, and brought our lonely lives with us, to watch at the bedside of my aunt, speak-ing in subdued whispers, like brother and sister—or man and wife. Yet I know nothing of you.

THE SISTER. You know enough.

JEAN. There is mystery behind those great up-raised eyes of yours!

THE SISTER. They are the mirror of Jesus.

JEAN. A cold mirror! I am afraid when I see myself in it. Cold as that hood that clasps tight your flowing hair. Why such mystery about your hair? Why hide it under a hood, where I can form no notion of its fair waviness? Are your tresses black, auburn, brown? It troubles me not to know; sometimes I imagine them dark, sometimes light. . . .

THE SISTER. They are hidden from view, forever.

JEAN. But tell me, at least. It is an absurd obsession. Tell me—tell me only the color.

THE SISTER. I do not know the color. When I dress it is faint daylight, and when I undress, it is the same.

JEAN. Tell me! I do not wish to see them, I wish only to know. Settle the mystery.

THE SISTER. My hair is a mystery to myself. I seem to remember long ago what it was like, but it must have changed. . . . What difference can it make to you?

JEAN. Tell me; that will not force you to break your vows.

THE SISTER [rising from the table]. No. Christ Himself is the only one who knows: He alone may know.

[She goes and sits down near the fireplace, working at her embroidery.]

JEAN. You are indeed strict in your faith. You ought not to renounce so much. God has no wish for that. Does one bury a rose in the snow? And how calm you always are! You fear nothing but the devil. And how disinterested you are! You give up even your name. Each nun calls herself after some saint.

THE SISTER. As if we were already in the sacred precincts of Paradise.

JEAN. As if you were already dead!

THE SISTER. Or in heaven!

JEAN. Do you never regret leaving the world? Do you never want children? Are you not in continual mourning for them?

THE SISTER. Jesus is our husband, and if this robe we wear is black, it is in order that our souls may shine the more brightly.

JEAN. So I shall learn nothing? You are unkind. Yet—tell me the secret that haunts me, and I shall not trouble you again. Is it auburn?

THE SISTER. Please! I don't know why—unless it be what I feel—I don't know why what you ask me seems evil! It is like the beginning of sin.

[At this moment the door-bell rings, awakening the echoes in the sleeping house.]

JEAN [suddenly aroused]. The bell! Sister, did you hear? Ah, we were too happy. That bell breaks the enchantment.

THE SISTER. You are mistaken. The bell did not ring. There is no one. Who would come at this hour?

BARBARA [opening the door at the back]. The doctor, Monsieur.

JEAN [surprised]. Now? [To Barbara.] Ask him to come in. [Barbara goes out.] Why this evening? I tell you that bell marks the end of my happiness, Sister.

[Barbara ushers in the Doctor, and then leaves the room.]

JEAN [rising to greet him]. Doctor!

THE DOCTOR. Good evening, friend. Are you surprised? I was passing by, and I wished to come in for a moment and see the patient.

JEAN [nervously]. Is she worse?

THE DOCTOR. Oh, no: she is making a courageous struggle. [Affecting an air of indifference.] Terrible winter weather.

THE SISTER [rises and walks slowly to the bedroom door]. I shall tell Madame.

[She goes out.]

THE DOCTOR [sarcastically]. What a stately manner!

JEAN. She is decidedly Gothic—like a saint who has stepped out of a stained-glass window.

THE DOCTOR. She is exquisite. So the two of you live in this quiet old place as in a convent; you, practically a monk, and she, the best of her Order. Truly charming!

JEAN. I feel less alone now. She brings a ray of light, a voice in the silence . . . .

THE DOCTOR. Take care! When the danger is charming, one is only too soon enthralled . . . .

JEAN. No! Women have never troubled me except as beings moving about in some far-off bluish dreamland; the moment I approach, the charm is gone. Perhaps the city, the church bell, these convents, this mysticism in the air, are to blame!

THE DOCTOR. Yes, but the flesh is weak.

JEAN. The city is dead, and the city is like me. The stagnant water in the canals—I feel it in my heart. Other cities sparkle with brilliancy, tire one, excite; this one I love as in a dream. Here I love with my brain: a gesture, the sound of a voice, a woman's hair, a curve of the body. The moment that mere nothing which excited me has gone, the woman ceases to interest me. I loved only what my dream added to the reality.

THE DOCTOR. Exactly. And here with the Sister, you are dreaming that you have your own little home. You eat together, and you cannot help being reminded of married people. . . .

JEAN. Don't say such things!

THE DOCTOR. And to yourselves you seem like two children.

JEAN [slightly irritated]. Don't! To laugh at us when I ask you to be silent! You are sacrilegious.

DOCTOR. An innocent joke. Well—I shall go now and see the patient.

[He goes out.]

JEAN. Yes, I do feel less alone. Sister Gudule is a woman! Do I love her? What is love? When does one know one loves? May it last! Oh, may it last!

[Enter The Sister from the bedroom.]

JEAN [anxiously]. Well?

THE SISTER. She is worse. The pulse is abnormal. Her mind is wandering. And there are other bad symptoms.

JEAN [agitated]. Is it—the end?

THE SISTER. We must resign ourselves to the Will of the Almighty.

JEAN [sobbing]. The end! Poor aunt! She was so good to me. . . . She gave up her whole life to me—she was a mother to me. I remember the first time she took my hand and took me to Mass. I was very small . . . .

[The bell outside begins ringing again.]

THE SISTER. Monsieur Jean, God watches over us, and who knows? He gives us other interests, other affections in life.

JEAN. I feel it in my heart—the end is not far off.

THE SISTER. You must not give up hope.

JEAN. That bell! It cuts to my heart!

THE SISTER. Let us pray. The parish church bell will carry our prayers to heaven.

JEAN. I cannot! My God!

THE SISTER. Why not pray—just a little—Monsieur? To say one's rosaries and burn candles can do no harm. [The bell stops ringing.] The patient is not yet at the gate of death, but death is our lot on earth: we go sooner or later. People love, live together, and separate. The candlestick holds two candles; two people live in the same house, and hardly have they come to love one another before they must go—each his way.

JEAN [looks at her in astonishment after these last words]. Go? True. It all happened so quickly. How—separate?

THE SISTER [going to him and taking his hand affectionately in hers]. Each shall be merely the absent one to the other. We shall see less and less of each other; grow old, and live only in the past; and finally—forget.

JEAN [in great agitation]. No! You will not forget me! Beneath what you say, I understand at last! I feel it in your hands! You are sad at the thought of having to leave!

THE SISTER [withdrawing her hand]. I do not understand you!

JEAN. You felt that you could not leave me alone. In spite of yourself, an ineffably sweet secret has escaped from the depths of your heart. . . .

THE SISTER [startled]. What do you mean?

JEAN [embarrassed, as he sees his mistake]. Nothing, Sister, nothing. I said—

THE SISTER. I feel tired. I must rest. Barbara will take my place at Madame's bedside, and watch until midnight. Good evening, Monsieur!

[She goes out.]

JEAN. Yes, I love her. Does she love me? Or did she only pity me? Two deaths! One is inevitable, is like the disappearance of the moon behind a cloud of mist. But the other I can prevent—if the Sister is willing! She *will* pity me! She must stay! I need her, I want her! The priests can release her from her vows. She will be my belovéd, my saintly wife. I shall decorate her hair with another, a more beautiful hood, a hood of flowers! And all this happened because of her white hood, like a bird, of her robe concealing that body of hers that is scarcely of the earth, of my not knowing the color of her hair. This is how love crept into my heart. And that sweet voice of hers, soft and light as her hood! [*Cries of alarm and hurried footsteps are heard in the next room.*] What is that?

A VOICE [*in the other room*]. Monsieur Jean!

JEAN. Some one calling me—
[*Sister Gudule appears on the threshold of the door. She has apparently just awakened, for she is without her hood, and her hair streams over her shoulders and down her back.*]

THE SISTER [*in terror*]. It is I!

JEAN. You! Her hair!

THE SISTER. Quick! I was asleep! Barbara is calling. Madame is dying!

JEAN. Is she dead?

BARBARA [*at the bedroom door, greatly agitated*]. Help! Come quick!

THE SISTER [*embarrassed*]. I am not yet dressed—

JEAN. Dead!
[*He goes hurriedly into the bedroom.*]

THE SISTER [*turning to Barbara*]. Let us say the Pater, to help her to the gate of heaven. [*They kneel and repeat together:*] Our father which art in heaven, hallowed be thy name. Thy kingdom come. Thy will be done in earth, as it is in heaven. Give us this day our daily bread. And forgive us our debts, as we forgive our debtors. And lead us not into temptation, but deliver us from evil: For thine is the kingdom,

and the power, and the glory, for ever. Amen.
[*Jean reënters. The Sister goes out.*]

JEAN. I closed her eyes—they gazed vacantly into the distance. She looked so old! I joined her hands. She did not suffer. She loved me so! Now I am alone!

BARBARA. Who will bury her? Who will wrap her in the winding sheet?

JEAN. Ask the Sister. [*Barbara goes out.*] It is over. Now begins my loneliness. [*The bell begins to ring again.*] The bell! Yes, yes, begin again! Weep, weep, shed your tears for two deaths! I have seen Sister Gudule, revealed to me as a woman—without her nun's hood. Her loosed tresses! My love, born of mystery, dies the moment I learn the secret. The Sister is no longer herself. I see her as she is, and she is not what I dreamed she was. She has lost her halo. It is all over: I knew too much. Love must have a secret to nourish it.
[*Barbara reënters, followed a moment after by the Sister. The latter now wears her hood, and her arms are crossed over her breast, as she clasps about her the mantle which nuns wear out of doors.*]

THE SISTER. I am sorry to leave, Monsieur Jean, but it is the rule of our Order. We do not watch by the body; we take care only of the living. I shall leave you now. Two novices will come from the convent for the funeral.

JEAN [*resigned*]. If you must go—

THE SISTER. Good-bye, Monsieur, I shall pray for you.

JEAN. Thank you, Sister. [*He stands thinking for an instant.*] Just—Sister! Good-bye.
[*Jean gives a gesture of despair and turns to the room where the dead woman rests.*]

[*Curtain.*]

BUMBLEPUPPY
A Comedy of Climate
By John William Rogers, Jr.

CHARACTERS

ANDREW BUGG [*around fifty*].
HAMLET PRINNEL [*nineteen*].
GENTRY DAVENPORT [*around fifty*].

TIME: *The Present.*

BUMBLEPUPPY

A COMEDY OF CLIMATE   BY JOHN WILLIAM ROGERS, JR.

[SCENE: *A small clump of shade trees not far from the Prinnel farmhouse in one of the older states of the South.*

Between two tree trunks which are on the left is hung an ancient and somewhat ragged hammock. Against a third trunk which is to the right, an old cane-bottomed chair leans propped on its two hind legs. In the center of the stage, at a carefully measured distance between the chair and the hammock stands a weather stained table on which have been placed—obviously with further regard as to equidistance—two lumps of sugar. A third chair stands somewhere back of the table.

Beyond the immediate shade of the three trees, there is every evidence of the glare and heat of a sweltering mid-afternoon in July.

Andrew Bugg, an elongated, somewhat ancient, rural individual, is discovered leaning back in the chair which is against the tree, a large palm leaf fan in his hand. He is coatless and collarless. His trousers are held up by a venerable pair of suspenders and his shirt is the worse for at least two days' perspiration and dusty roads. It being Wednesday, a three-day growth of beard is on his face. On the ground beside him lie his large straw hat and an empty mail pouch.

Opposite Andrew in the hammock sprawls Hamlet Prinnel in overalls and a blue shirt. He also holds a palm leaf fan. Hamlet, who at nineteen is a good-natured, somewhat appealing youth, will be a shambling, colorless, middle-aged farmer at thirty, unless something quite unexpected happens to him.

As the curtain rises, somewhere in the foliage a locust is droning his hot weather zuree-zuree-zuree-z-z-z, and both men seem just on the point of being overcome by the languor of the afternoon, when Hamlet, using a minimum of effort, lifts his head enough to regard the lump *of sugar nearest him. He yawns and speaks disgustedly.*]

HAMLET. Them flies ain't never comin'.

ANDREW. Give 'em time. Give 'em time.

HAMLET [*sinking back into the hammock*]. T'ain't hardly worth fifty cents to keep awake so long.

ANDREW [*scornfully*]. I never did think you had no sportin' blood in you.

HAMLET. Oh, I'll keep awake all right. . . . You watch your own lump of sugar.

ANDREW. I'm a watchin' it. I'm a watchin' it. [*As if to prove it, he fans his sugar with a long sweep of his palm leaf.*] I was a bumblepuppy champeen 'fore you was taller'n a hog's back.

HAMLET. Bumblepuppy air a funny game.

ANDREW [*a little sensitive*]. What air funny about it?

HAMLET. Folks a settin' waitin' for flies to come and light on two lumps of sugar.

ANDREW. Ain't no funnier than folks just *a settin'*, I reckon, and a heap er folks I knows does a lot er that.

HAMLET. Yeah. Settin' do seem to be popular.

ANDREW. Playin' bumblepuppy, you can't never tell when you might win fifty cents. [*Scornfully.*] You can set all day and all you'll do is wear out the seat er your pants.

HAMLET [*yawning again*]. Uh-huh.

[*Hamlet drowses lying on his back. Somewhere in the branches above, the locust begins his song again and is answered by another in the distance. Andrew looks out into the burning glare and mops his face with a large handkerchief.*

ANDREW [*sighing deeply*]. Whoopee.

It's hotter'n Mis' Pharaoh's cook-stove. [*He is just about to settle back in his chair when he notices something flying over the table. He becomes alert, looks quickly at Hamlet to make sure he is drowsing, and uses his fan very gently to drive the quarry from his own sugar toward Hamlet's. On his face is written that beatific consciousness of being alive which comes to sportsmen in supreme moments of the chase. His movements are convulsive with excitement. He looks over at Hamlet, then stands up pointing at the latter's lump of sugar, shouting triumphantly.*]

ANDREW. He's done lit on your sugar first. Gimme your fifty cents.

[*Hamlet, startled by Andrew, almost falls out of the hammock. Then after an examination of his sugar, he turns away deliberately, with disgust, and starts getting back into the hammock.*]

HAMLET. Shucks, t'ain't nuthin' but a gnat. [*Scowling at Andrew.*] Gnats don't count. Shoo. Shoo. [*He drives the insect away with his fan.*] What you want to get a feller out of a hammock fer nothin' fer?

ANDREW [*setting himself back in his chair*]. You thought I had you that time. [*Cheerfully.*] I ain't seen you move so fast sense a hen had teeth. . . . Say, Ham, if a snail in a well thirty feet deep crawls up three feet every day and falls back two feet every night, how long will it take him to . . .

HAMLET. Aw, come on, Mr. Bugg, this ain't weather for brain work. [*With admiration.*] You always *was* a bird dog, though, for that there higher mathymatics.

ANDREW [*modestly*]. Well, mental arithmetic is just kinder my natural mental recreation—same as some folks likes to set and look through a Sears-Roebuck catalogue.

[*Andrew's attention is suddenly attracted by something off stage to the right. Hamlet sees him looking at something.*]

HAMLET. What's a matter?

ANDREW [*while looking*]. Folks a stoppin' at your front gate. You're a goin' ter have company.

HAMLET [*lying back in the hammock comfortably and stretching his arms*]. I ain't. Comin' to see mom, I reckon. [*Making a slight effort to see, without taking the trouble to raise himself up.*] Who is it? I can't see.

ANDREW [*still looking*]. Looks like Maria Abernathy's Ford. . . . They're a gittin' out all right. [*Impressed.*] She's got Gentry Davenport with her.

HAMLET. Gentry Davenport? [*Interested, he sits up and looks.*] Yeah, that's him. He come to see mamma last week, the day after he got here. . . . They both busted out cryin' soon as they had a good look at each other.

ANDREW. Cryin'?

HAMLET. Yeah. Mom was a bridesmaid or *somethin'* when he was married to his wife, and she's dead now.

ANDREW. Myrtle Horn, she was. I used ter kinder buzz around Myrt a little myself.

HAMLET. Mr. Davenport ain't been back here since they left when they was married. Him and mom was talkin' it all over.

ANDREW. Your ma and Myrt used to be powerful close friends.

HAMLET. They was cousins.

ANDREW. When I used to go courtin' the gals, you never seen one er them without lookin' for t'other. . . . Myrt's been dead quite a spell now.

HAMLET. But Mr. Davenport didn't never marry again. He said to mom it was just like she'd went yesterday.

ANDREW. There's them as is one woman men, and others—well, as ain't so particular. Personally, I 'low I always would be a *marryin'* man.

HAMLET. Newt White said that Mr. Davenport owns four thousand acres of the best apple country in Oregon, and he's got at least fifty thousand dollars coolin' in the bank.

ANDREW. It's a pity Myrt didn't never have no children. All that money and ain't no tellin' what's to become of it. . . . It's a dog-goned mixed up world anyhow. Here I am—eleven children and no money.

HAMLET. Reckon what he'll do with it?

ANDREW. Dunno. Wish he'd give me thirty-nine dollars and fifteen cents. I been a owin' on groceries at Kimbrough's store fer six months. A side er bacon at my house don't last no longer than a loaf of bread. . . . It do look like I have got the out-eatin'-est family in three counties.

HAMLET [*fanning away a bee from his sugar.*] Shoo. It's a bee.

ANDREW [*fighting at the bee which has flown over to his sugar*]. Git away. Git away, durn you. [*Aggrieved.*] Sence Scena Mulberry tuk to keepin' bees, it's got so you can't have a comfortable game er bumblepuppy in ten miles, 'thout bein' pestered to death. Shoo. . . . Say, young feller, if you're a playin' bumblepuppy with me you lie back in that hammock where you belong and stop inchin' up. How 'm I gonner get that four bits out er your pocket an' you a crowdin' your sugar like a settin' hen?

HAMLET [*lying back in the hammock*]. All right.

[*He looks toward the house, a little doubtfully.*]

ANDREW. I don't suppose you want ter quit and go up to the house along er the company.

HAMLET [*hesitating*]. I reckon they ain't studyin' me.

ANDREW. Yep. We ought to finish this game. It would be a pity to stop without somebody winnin'—after we've worked this hard.

HAMLET [*a bit confessionally*]. You know, Mr. Bugg, sometimes I think I'd like to go off to some fer place like—like Oregon—like Mr. Davenport done when he was young. Don't nothin' ever seem to happen around here.

ANDREW. Well, the bollweevil gits worse.

HAMLET [*wistfully*]. To us, I mean. It would be a heap er fun to go off and do somethin'—like Mr. Davenport. Looks like the folks that goes away from here has it all over us that stays.

ANDREW. Oh, I don't know. There was Bazzie Grimes. He went all the way to St. Louis and caught the pneumonia and died. He might have done as well as that if he'd stayed home.

HAMLET [*almost dreamily*]. I'd like to see Oregon. . . . Mr. Davenport says he's got an apple orchard more'n a mile square. That must be a pretty sight—all in bloom.

ANDREW. It must be a heap er work to pick all them apples.

HAMLET. He says in Oregon—

ANDREW [*interrupting*]. You know, Ham, Gentry Davenport was lucky; his pa died and left his ma with a mortgaged farm that couldn't nobody make a livin' on nohow.

HAMLET. You call that luck?

ANDREW. Yep. It was plain luck, I tell you. T'warn't nothin' fer Gentry ter do after the bank sold the farm to pay off the mortgage, but to light out all together. Now, if his pa had left him just an everyday onery farm—the kind my Cousin Plutarch Pittard's been a starvin' on fer thirty years, he'd be adown here settin' on it to-day, wonderin' where he was goin' ter find enough money to put a new roof on the spring house. . . . Bein' tied to a little pore land have caused a heap er folks a lot er trouble.

HAMLET. Mr. Bugg, with your way of figurin' out things, you'd orter be a rich man.

ANDREW [*holding out his hand in protest*]. Naw, sir. I figured it warn't worth while. Now, my chillun is goin' to have a chance equal to anybody. They ain't goin' to have nothin' to hold 'em down.

[*Andrew abruptly gets up and dropping his fan apparently tries to kill a fly between the palms of his hands. After one or two passes, he finally crushes it.*]

HAMLET. Hey, what you a doin'? How we ever goin' to finish this game, and you a killin' off all the ammunition?

ANDREW [*seriously, holding out his hand to which the body of the fly has clung, for Hamlet to see*]. Twarn't nothin' but one er them yaller tassel flies, Ham. [*He flecks the fly away with his forefinger.*] I know some folks counts 'em [*contemptuously*], but I never could take no comfort in a game er bumblepuppy with tassel flies. A tassel fly ain't got near as much sense as one er these here little black cur flies. Look how much easier they is to kill. I always says, if you're playin' tassel flies—count me out. [*Encouragingly, as he settles back in his chair and picks up his fan again.*] I seen a black fly a scoutin' around up there just now. He's already done gone up to your house to tell some er his friends. He'll be bringin' 'em back with him in a few minutes.

HAMLET [*resentfully*]. I'll bet they're all off somewhere, havin' a nap.

ANDREW. Well, there's one thing to be said fer this climate, Ham. Those of us that gits to hell is more'n likely to feel at home.

HAMLET. Mr. Davenport say it don't never git hot in Oregon.

ANDREW. Yep, but I reckon the winters is powerful cold. I'd rather sweat a little than be froze ter death. . . . [*Andrew and Hamlet begin to be slightly more active with their fans in guarding their sugar, as though the flies had begun to gather around it.*] You know I used to go to school with Gentry Davenport. He was a little spindle-legged feller—always had his big toe tied up in a rag. He was everlastin'ly stubbin' his toe. His voice had a way er slippin' up where it didn't belong, and he always seemed to be tryin' to hide behind something. God-a-mighty, how he's changed. I was at the station the other mornin' a waitin' fer the mail, when he come in on number four. He walks over to the porch er Kimbrough's store, a steppin' like a race horse and all curried up in a blue suit and a collar and tie, like a prize mule at a fair. . . . Hello, Androo, he say, a holdin' out his hand to me. I thought he was one er them St. Louis drummers a tryin' to be democratic fer business reasons.

HAMLET. Show nuff.

[*He fans away a persistent fly from his sugar.*]

ANDREW. Newt White and Dalo Wilkes was a settin' there, too, but didn't none of us know him, he was that pepped up.

HAMLET. He do have a mighty active air about him.

ANDREW. What might call too active, if you ask me . . . without meanin' no disrespect to Gentry, it always makes me kinder nervous to see a man bustin' with too much energy.

HAMLET [*sympathetically*]. It ain't comfortable.

ANDREW. It's a sign his nerves is inflamed. It's unhealthy.

HAMLET. I always had a feelin' it must be somethin' like that.

ANDREW. I reckon Gentry can't help it. . . . There warn't nobody to meet him at the station the day he come in —that there telegraph office in town had fergot to telephone out to Maria Abernathy and tell her he was a comin'. I carried him down ter her house as I come on with the mail.

HAMLET [*fanning his sugar*]. Shoo. 'Tain't nothin' but another bee.

ANDREW. Course, he wanted to hear about everything. [*Speaking as though it were a surprising fact.*] You know when you come to figure it up, there's been a heap er changes in this country in the last twenty years. . . . He didn't know about the lumber mill Tracy Minor and Abe Pittard had built back er Pigeon Roost, and he hadn't heard nothin' at all about the big fire when Uncle Charlie Taylor's store and the gin burned down, at the station. . . . I guess you was too young to remember that.

HAMLET. I kinder recollect.

ANDREW. Gentry was mighty interested in hearing about you. He said when Myrt got a letter from your ma tellin' that you was comin' into this world, she was that excited, it might have been a baby of her own. He wanted to know what kind of a feller you was. I told him that, personally, you seemed a pretty good sort, but it was the gals around here who was show-nuff enthusiastic about you.

HAMLET. Aw, come on, Mr. Bugg. . . . Quit yer hurrahin' me.

[*Both men become interested in defending their sugar from the flies. From the right enters Gentry Davenport, neatly dressed in a dark blue suit and panama. When he takes off his hat, which he does as soon as he gets into the shade of the trees, one sees that he is grizzle-haired, with the healthy, ruddy tan complexion of a man who has long been active out of doors. His movements are quick, and suggest vitality and impulsiveness. His collar is a bit too high and worries him a little now and then, so that while his appearance is decent enough—one feels he is very probably wearing his Sunday clothes and is slightly conscious of them.*]

GENTRY. Hello, Andrew—afternoon, Hamlet.

ANDREW and HAMLET [*together*].
ANDREW. Howdy, Mr. Davenport.

HAMLET. Evenin', Gen.

HAMLET. We was just a talkin' about you.

[*Andrew and Hamlet wield their fans against the flies.*]

ANDREW. We seen you drive up with Maria.

GENTRY. Why—what's this— As I live — bumblepuppy. [*Amused.*] I haven't thought of bumblepuppy in twenty years. You still play it around here, do you?

ANDREW [*dryly*]. Some on us do. . . . Shoo.

GENTRY. You still wet the lump of sugar and wait for the flies, eh?

[*He laughs heartily.*]

HAMLET [*pointing to the chair back of the table*]. Take a chair, Mr. Davenport.

GENTRY [*sitting down*]. Well, that'll be something to tell them about when I get back to Oregon—bumblepuppy.

[*He laughs.*]

ANDREW. You want ter get in the game?

GENTRY [*protesting good-naturedly*]. No, I guess I haven't got time. What's the stakes?

ANDREW. Fifty cents.

GENTRY. Well . . . you are getting reckless around here. It used to be a quarter in my day.

ANDREW. Waal, everything costs more these days. You used to could get a shave fer ten cents.

GENTRY. Did you ever play golf, Andrew?

ANDREW [*turning his head slowly and regarding Gentry*]. Golf? What's that?

HAMLET. Cow pasture pool. You've heerd of cow pasture pool, ain't you?

ANDREW. One er them new fangled games, I reckon. But I 'low it ain't no better than the rest. I've played 'em all in my time—parchesi, flinch, ping-pong, horse shoes, checkers, croquet— My gals is just mailed off a coupon fer one er them Chinee games—Ma's Wrong, er somethin'. But I tell 'em 'tain't no sense in sendin' off. There ain't no game suits this climate like bumblepuppy.

HAMLET. Mr. Bugg is kinder partial.

ANDREW. Naw, sir. Sugar ain't hard to get and I ain't never seen flies no rarity. [*Fanning.*] Shoo. A man can't afford to wear hisself out in this climate. He'll git all pulled down by the hot weather if he do.

GENTRY [*turning to Hamlet with an air of becoming serious*]. I suppose you are going to be a farmer like your father, Hamlet?

HAMLET [*sitting up in the hammock. He speaks with a slightly embarrassed little laugh*]. Essir. I reckon so.

GENTRY [*despite a slightly pompous verbiage, there is a kindly, simple sincerity about him which makes him sympathetic*]. Well, I've always been partial to the land myself. A man can do well on a farm, if he works hard and keeps his fence corners clean. I've done pretty well. I had to work hard, too—but I'm not sorry. The farm—any kind of a farm—is no place for a boy that doesn't want to work. He might just as well go to the city and have done with it.

HAMLET [*in the little nervous laugh*]. Essir.

GENTRY. We've got some mighty bright boys out our way. Hard workers, too. Some of them are going to be rich men. [*Andrew yawns and makes a "ho-hum" sound. Gentry turns to him.*] What?

ANDREW [*quickly, with a guilty innocence*]. I didn't say nothin'.

GENTRY [*turning again to Hamlet*]. But you know, Hamlet, I don't think those Oregon boys are any better than our boys here. I've been gone a long time, but I never have forgotten that I grew up a boy in these hills around Pigeon Roost Creek. I've always loved these old rocky, red hills, poor as some of 'em are for making a living. I suppose what really makes me love them so are the people. They're my people and they were Myrtle's, and I don't believe at heart there are a finer, nobler set of men and women on God's Green Footstool. The folks out in Oregon . . . .

[*Andrew begins to fan vigorously; Hamlet's attention is also distracted by the flies and he busies himself defending his sugar.*]

ANDREW [*to Hamlet as they fan*]. Lay back—none er your inchin' on me.

[*Hamlet lies back in the hammock and for the next few moments they engage busily in the game. Gentry is obviously annoyed with the interruption of his fine sentiments, but the players are too occupied to notice him. He looks from one to the other, purses his lips, and apparently swallows down an irritation. Then with an assumed patience, he waits for them to pay attention to him again. Eventually, the flies give the combatants a respite and Hamlet turns to Gentry.*]

HAMLET. You was sayin' somethin', Mr. Davenport?

GENTRY [*still slightly ruffled*]. Well, I . . . .

ANDREW. Keep right on talkin'. It don't bother us, and the flies don't mind.

HAMLET. About Oregon?

GENTRY [*with dignity, after a slight hesitation*]. Well, I was about to say . . . . [*Andrew fans again.*] There's a great future for a young man out in Oregon. Plenty of room, and plenty of room to grow. [*Andrew fans again, Gentry is annoyed, but continues, speaking meaningly with a glance at Andrew.*] And there's a different spirit, too. If I was a young man to-day, I'd go to Oregon. But, of course, every young man can't just pick up and leave . . . . [*Forgetting his irritation in his interest in what he has to say.*] For a long time, Hamlet, I've been thinking. A farmer has time to do a lot of thinking, if he's a mind to. That's one of the compensations which comes to the man who lives in the country. He isn't hurried along in a senseless mad rush. He has time to think.

ANDREW [*interested*]. I does a heap er studyin' about things myself. I reckon that's why I never did move into town—I'm kinder philosophical. I come near movin' into Addle Junction, though, once. Sorter wish I had.

GENTRY [*to Hamlet*]. It was always my dream before Myrtle went, that I might have a son . . . . I could almost picture him—fine stalwart boy—having a lot of things about him I didn't . . . . But I don't let my mind dwell on that sort of thing. I've always had the feeling it was sinful for a man to let his thoughts go flying in the face of Providence.

ANDREW. Thoughts is pretty skittish

things. Tryin' to drive 'em down this road and that is worse than herdin' a lot er young colts.

GENTRY [*not unkindly, but a little pointedly*]. Those that do all they're put into this world to do, don't have time to let their thoughts go wanderin' off like a lot of young colts.

ANDREW [*fanning*]. Shoo.

GENTRY. When I have thoughts that aren't practical, I try to find an inspiration in them for deeds that are. I began doing that a long time ago, Hamlet, and I found it paid. . . . Our young men have got to dream dreams and see visions, but dreaming and seeing aren't enough.

HAMLET [*with the laugh*]. No, sir.

GENTRY. There's doing.

HAMLET [*with the laugh*]. Essir.

GENTRY. Providence put a lot of young people in this world. If they aren't my sons, they are other people's, and I know what a helping hand means from the lack of one in my own time. It seemed to me—well—I'll explain a little more first. I've been thinking a good deal about Pigeon Roost lately. Somehow as a man gets along his thoughts seem to turn back . . . .

HAMLET [*fanning*]. Shoo.

GENTRY. Somewhere back in those hills, I said to myself, there's a young fellow . . . .

[*Andrew has begun to fan vigorously and grow excited in the game.*]

ANDREW. Hep.

HAMLET [*countering him*]. Oh, no, you don't.

[*The players again forget all about Gentry, who rises angrily and paces the ground indignantly glaring at the game.*]

ANDREW [*as the fanning slows down*]. Waal, that was a real pert roun'. Flies round here just as lively as they ever was, Gentry. You know folks devils a lot about flies, and they is a nuisance, but summertime without flies would be mighty queer. . . . You was a sayin' something, Gentry.

GENTRY [*shaking off his irritation and trying to take a tolerant view of things*]. Oh, well, I guess I'm the one that's changed. I won't say now that I've come back here I've found everything like I'd painted it in my imagination. But, then, looking at things through the eyes of youth and twenty years . . . . : It's another case where a man must be practical and not . . . .

[*Hamlet and Andrew, who have been listening to Gentry with one eye on their sugar, start fanning again and once more forget Gentry. This is too much for him and he loses all control.*]

GENTRY [*bursting out*]. Oh, hell!

ANDREW [*turning slowly*]. What'd you say?

[*Having exploded, after a moment's hesitation, Gentry seems to change his intentions. He loses all his resentment and answers amiably.*]

GENTRY. It's a hot day, isn't it? [*He mops his brow with his handkerchief.*] Well, I expect I had better be getting back up to the house. Maria will be waiting for me. I just came down here to tell you folks good-by. I'm going back to Oregon to-morrow.

[*Hamlet and Andrew both stop the game a moment, surprised.*]

HAMLET. To-morrow?

ANDREW. Why, you ain't stayin' long to have come so fer.

GENTRY. Well, I've got to get back to my farm. It's home out there now, you know. I just wanted to get back here a little while and see all the folks that were left—look over the old stamping ground. [*He starts over to shake hands with Hamlet, who begins to struggle out of the hammock.*] No, don't get up. I'd hate to disturb your bumblepuppy. You finish your game. [*Shaking his hand.*] Good-by, Hamlet, my boy. Come out to Oregon and make me a visit some time. Bring your wife, it'll make a nice wedding trip. [*He turns to Andrew and goes over to him, shaking hands.*] So long, Andrew. Take good care of yourself. I'm going to tell them out in Oregon what a bumblepuppy champion you are. [*Suddenly.*] Look out—there's a fly lighting on your sugar now.

[*Andrew, startled, turns to defend his sugar and Gentry makes a quick exit calling "Good-by." The bumblepuppy play becomes lively, reaching a climax.*]

HAMLET. Whoa! Keep down in your chair there. Hold steady. . . . It's too

late. Hey, hey, stop—stop. He's already on it.

ANDREW [*jumping up and slinging his fan down, like an irate golf player does his club*]. Oh, mad-dog backward.

HAMLET [*getting out of the hammock*]. I won fair. Where's your money?

[*He holds out his hand. Andrew hesitates a moment, looks uncertain, then reluctantly puts his hand into his pocket, carefully drawing out some change which he examines looking down sideways.*]

ANDREW [*speaking at last, with resignation*]. Well, Ham, here's fifteen cents. [*Positively.*] I had four nickels. There must be a hole in this here pocket. [*He turns the pocket inside out to discover it whole, then puts it back and reluctantly offers the fifteen cents to Hamlet.*] Here, I'll just owe you thirty-five.

HAMLET [*good-naturedly*]. Any time, Mr. Bugg.

ANDREW [*picking up his hat and the mail bag*]. I ain't gettin' no younger standin' here. I reckon I better be movin' on. [*Hospitably.*] Come go home with me.

HAMLET [*equally hospitably*]. I can't. You come go home with me.

ANDREW. Much obleeged. [*He is starting to go when he looks off stage and stops a moment.*] Yonder goes Maria and Gentry. [*Rather suddenly.*] Did it strike you Gentry wanted to say somethin' while he was down here that he didn't never get out? 'Peared to me he talked kinder jumpy-like . . . . You know, I thought . . . . [*Shaking his head meditatively.*] No, I reckon I'm wrong. I guess that's just a way folks has er talkin' out in Oregon.

HAMLET [*who is also looking in the direction of the departing visitors*]. Gee, I was a goin' out to Oregon . . . . [*The two pause a moment, gazing off stage.*] Oh, shucks.

[*He turns back from looking off the road.*]

ANDREW [*consulting a large Ingersoll watch on a leather thong*]. Quarter to five.

HAMLET. Is that all? [*Yawning.*] I got time for a good sleep afore supper.

ANDREW [*exiting*]. So long.

HAMLET. So long. [*Calling after him.*] Play you another game of bumblepuppy some day.

[*He stretches himself and makes sleepy noises in a kind of a yawn, then gets into the hammock and composes himself for a nap. Above in the foliage, the locust takes up his song more droningly than ever — zureeee-zureeee-zureee-z-z-zz. The hot afternoon sun has turned into a ruddy gold. The curtains come together slowly, just as a faint reassuring, peaceful snore is heard from Hamlet.*]

[*Curtain.*]

THE THIRD ANGLE

A Comedy

By Florence Ryerson

CHARACTERS

JERROLD PAIGE [*an artist*].
ANNE PAIGE [*his wife*].
CLARABELLE BRENT [*completing the triangle*].

THE THIRD ANGLE

A COMEDY   By FLORENCE RYERSON

[*The curtain rises on Jerrold's studio. It is a delightful room, with a fireplace and mantel to the right. Before the fire is a roomy couch, a table, chair, droplight and telephone.*

At the upper left a north light and clutter of painting gear, lower left a street door. Center back, French windows give into the garden.

Jerrold is painting from a lay figure dressed in a gorgeous evening wrap and seated upon a raised platform. He is about thirty, dressed in a painting smock and tousled hair. He pauses to rearrange the drapery.]

JERRY [*muttering*]. Little more to the left . . . mm . . . mm . . . no . . . not like that . . . there . . . better . . . .
[*Returns to picture whistling. Anne enters through the French windows, her hands full of flowers. She is in the late twenties, a person of delightful and humorous curves. She is wearing a very simple frock of linen. She crosses the room and begins to arrange the flowers in vase at right. She is humming as Jerry whistles.*]

JERRY. What you doing that for?

ANNE. I thought the place needed some flowers. There was a pink envelope in your morning's mail, Jerry. I hadn't been married a month before I learned a pink envelope at breakfast meant a lady to tea.

JERRY. Huh! What does a lavender one mean?

ANNE. That you're going out to dinner!

JERRY. Well . . . you're wrong this time . . . no one's coming.

ANNE. Why, Jerry, that's too bad . . . did her husband get back?

JERRY. Whose husband?

ANNE. The tea-lady's.

JERRY. No . . . at least . . . well . . . anyway, she isn't coming.

ANNE. You're *sure?* Well—in that case I'll just call the bishop.
[*Starts for phone and picks up book.*]

JERRY. Here . . . hold on . . . *what* bishop?

ANNE. Bishop Wilson, dear . . . you know, the fat, pink, Episcopal one. He wants to talk about a portrait.

JERRY. Hang it all, Anne, I don't want to paint him.

ANNE. But, dear, you paint such nice bishops!

JERRY. I don't care. I've done four this year and I'm *sick* of bishops. I won't do any more. I told you so when I finished that skinny one. I won't, I tell you—I won't!

ANNE [*coming behind him soothingly*]. Yes, dear. You're getting on nicely with the picture, aren't you? And you only started last week. When does she sit again?

JERRY. To-morrow. I'm just blocking in the cape to-day.

ANNE [*counting on fingers*]. Let me see . . . one, two, three . . . I suppose you'll finish by next week . . . that means you can start the bishop on Friday.

JERRY. I told you I wouldn't paint the bishop!

ANNE. Oh, yes, you will, Jerry. We need the money. This business of painting only pretty women is all right, but I've found it isn't the women who pay and pay . . . it's bishops!

JERRY [*throwing down his paints*]. Oh!

ANNE. And, then, bishops are so restful. No husbands to worry over, no love letters to get back . . . Jerry . . . I don't remember your ever writing love letters to a bishop. While the women you paint. . . .

445

JERRY. Hang it all! You don't have to keep reminding me! I'm through with them all!

ANNE. Yes, dear, I know you are . . . I've cancelled checks to prove it.

JERRY. Oh! How do you expect me to paint when you go on nagging me like that?

ANNE. I'm not nagging.

JERRY. Yes you are . . . nagging about checks and women and letters. It makes me nervous . . . you know it does. It upsets me . . . it gives me cold chills!

[*He walks the floor.*]

ANNE. Jerry. Look at me!

JERRY [*fiercely*]. I won't.

ANNE. Jerry . . . You've been writing letters again!

JERRY. I haven't . . . at least, only one . . . on my word . . . [*In sudden thought.*] Anyway . . . it's none of your business. I gave you my word after that Fontenelle affair that I wouldn't and here you are . . . just like a woman . . . doubting my word again!

ANNE. But if you'd just forget how to write, dear. If you'd just develop writer's cramp . . . or housemaid's knee or something. When you feel an attack of love letters coming on, can't you take a long breath and say to yourself, "Do right and fear no man, don't write and fear no woman"?

JERRY. Hang it all! I wish you would keep still! I can't *stand* it!

ANNE. Yes, dear. Is it Clarabelle Brent?

JERRY [*startled*]. How'd you know?

ANNE. Well, you painted her last, didn't you? Let me see . . . I suppose you've reached the South Sea stage?

JERRY [*starts*]. What do you mean?

ANNE [*busily straightening out room*]. You're such a comfort, Jerry. You've got your system perfected so I can always tell just where you are in your love making. When you're sketching her in, you discover she's different from any woman you ever knew. When you start on the background you find out I've never really understood you . . . and by the time you've finished the picture you've reached the South Sea stage, with the "faint, elusive fragrance of jasmine in the moonlight."

JERRY [*sarcastically*]. *Then* what do I do?

ANNE. You start another picture. Did you ask Clarabelle to elope with you . . . to walk out hand in hand to some magical isle in the South Seas where a man's a man . . .

JERRY [*furiously*]. Look here! You read that letter!

ANNE. No, dear. But I've a whole collection of your letters I bought and paid for. Well . . . is she going?

JERRY. Is *who* going?

ANNE. Clarabelle. Is she going to the South Seas?

JERRY [*shortly*]. No!

ANNE. Jerry! She didn't turn you down!

JERRY. She didn't answer my letter . . . and I wrote it last week.

ANNE. Why, the nasty little cat! I don't blame you for being nervous . . . and after you've started a picture of some one else, too! Only . . . are you cross because you think she's turned you down, or because you're afraid she won't?

JERRY. Oh . . . for heaven's sake! *Keep still!* I don't want to talk about her . . . I don't want to see her . . . I don't want to hear of her again . . .

ANNE. But, Jerry . . . if Clarabelle . . .

JERRY. Clarabelle! Clarabelle! I tell you, I'm through with Clarabelle! [*The phone rings and he picks it up.*] Hello . . . hello . . . oh . . . Clarabelle!

ANNE. Ha!

[*She chuckles.*]

JERRY. No! No! . . . I said no . . . you mustn't . . . not now! I said not now! But, Clara . . . but, *Clara* . . . but *Clara* . . . but CLARA . . . hello . . . hello . . . Central! [*To Anne.*] She's rung off.

ANNE. I don't blame her . . . the way you talked!

JERRY. But, hang it all . . . she's just around the corner . . . she's coming here!

ANNE. Well . . . why shouldn't she? If you're going to elope you've got to start from somewhere.

JERRY [*almost frothing at the mouth*]. Elope! Elope! I tell you, I don't want to elope! I don't like her type! She's got black hair . . . I'm sick of black hair! She's intense . . . I detest intense women. She's misunderstood by her husband . . . I loathe wives that are misunderstood by their husbands. [*Bell rings.*] There . . . she's here now . . . look here . . . you've got to stay and meet her. Don't you dare leave me alone!

ANNE. Wait a minute, Jerry. Are you going to paint the bishop?

JERRY. No! I'm not going to paint the bishop.

[*Bell rings.*]

ANNE. Jerry, listen to me. I'm tired of straightening things out for you. I'm tired of getting bishops for you and playing the third angle in your triangle. I'm tired of it and I'm through . . . do you understand . . . through! You can hunt up your own bishops and manage your own affairs. . . . I won't help . . .

[*Bell rings.*]

JERRY. Anne . . . please . . . just this once . . . I can't be left alone. . . .

ANNE [*at garden door*]. No . . . I'm going to the house . . . you can fight it out alone. But . . . [*she looks back*] if you change your mind about the bishop . . . ring the bell and I'll come. There . . . go let her in, and, Jerry [*at door*] give her my love and regrets!

[*She exits. Jerry attempts to follow her, but finds the door held from the other side. The street door opens and Clarabelle enters.*]

CLARABELLE [*Clarabelle, as Jerry has said, is dark and intense. She is entirely swathed in sentimentality. Never in her whole life has she been quite natural*]. Jerrold! I've been ringing and ringing . . .

JERRY [*against French windows*]. Have you? . . . I . . . I didn't hear. . . .

CLARA. What does it matter? At last I am here . . . with you! [*Holds out her hands. He takes them nervously.*] You may kiss them.

JERRY. Thanks! Thanks, awfully. But . . . you . . . you oughtn't to have come without warning. . . .

CLARA. When I got your letter I tried to write, but I tore it up. I wrote five . . . ten answers; but Jerrold . . . every one of them was "No."

JERRY [*in relief*]. Oh! Then it's all right.

CLARA. Yes, dear. . . . I changed my mind! [*Jerry jumps in horror.*] This morning. Do you know what day it is, Jerry?

JERRY. No. It isn't your birthday, is it?

CLARA. It's the first of the month. The bills came in and Augustus . . . oh, I won't spoil this moment by telling you the things that brute said at breakfast! [*Holds out hands.*] Jerrold . . . I have left him forever . . . I am yours!

JERRY [*backing off*]. No! Wait . . . wait. I must say something first. Clarabelle, when I wrote that letter I was mad . . . I didn't realize what I was asking. Now I have come to my senses. I can't let you sacrifice yourself like this. I can't! [*Stands up nobly.*] Clarabelle! I give you up!

CLARA [*almost in tears*]. Jerrold! I adore you! I knew you were fine, but I never knew . . . I never dreamed you could be as fine as this! But you shan't . . . I am willing to give up everything . . .

JERRY. No! No!

CLARA. My husband . . my friends. . . .

JERRY. It is asking too much!

CLARA. I am glad to go!

JERRY. I can't let you do it.

CLARA. I insist.

JERRY [*still noble*]. I refuse!

CLARA [*crossing to him*]. Jerrold! I won't go back now. . . . [*He retreats against wall and desperately rings bell.*] What are you doing?

JERRY. I . . . I'm ringing for—the bishop.

CLARA. Bishop? What bishop?

JERRY [*mopping his forehead*]. I mean my wife! You must meet her.

CLARA. Jerrold! I see. You are going to tell her now!

JERRY. Tell her?

CLARA. About us. She must know before any one, even before Augustus.

JERRY. You mean . . . you want *me* to tell her about . . . about our . . . .

CLARA. Had you rather *I* did it?

JERRY. No . . . no . . . I don't want that . . . oh, good Lord! Here she comes.

[*Anne enters with a sewing basket. She is humming "Just a Little Love, A Little Kiss." The whole effect of her is Pollyannish in the extreme.*]

ANNE. Did you call me, Jerry? Oh . . . don't you look nice and cozy . . .

with the fire and everything. I'll just close the curtains and make it more homey. [*Draws curtains.*] I do love an open fire. [*Comes down facing Clarabelle.*] And this . . . I suppose this is Miss Williams?

JERRY. Williams!

CLARA. Williams! My name isn't Williams!

ANNE. Oh . . . isn't it? Wait . . . don't tell me . . . let me guess! Black hair and blue eyes . . . I know! It's Genevieve Harlow, of course.

JERRY. Anne? Are you . . . are you *crazy?* This is Mrs. Brent!

ANNE. Brent? Brent? The name is vaguely familiar . . . oh, yes . . . didn't Jerry paint you once?

CLARA. Of course!

ANNE. I beg your pardon. I'm fearfully stupid about names. I don't often come into the studio and meet Jerry's ladies . . . so I can't always keep track. Won't you sit down? There . . . that's a comfortable chair . . . a cushion for her back, Jerry. . . .

CLARA. Mrs. Paige . . . before I sit down I want to explain. . . .

ANNE. Oh . . . no explanation is necessary! While we talk I think I'll just mend one of those cushions. I noticed it was burned after Miss Barton left. Jerry . . . next time you sit on the floor with Miss Barton you *must* pay some attention . . . you scorched the whole corner off.

CLARA. Barton . . . what Miss Barton?

ANNE. Just one of Jerry's little friends. Not that it really matters, about the cushion, I mean. Jerry's studio cushions always get worn out so quickly . . . perhaps you've noticed it, Miss Bush?

CLARA. Bush . . . my name isn't Bush!

ANNE. Oh . . . I beg your pardon . . . there *was* a Miss Bush.

JERRY. Anne . . . I simply won't have this!

ANNE. Yes, dear . . . you might get a hassock for Mrs. Trent.

CLARA. Brent . . . Mrs. Paige . . . *Brent!*

ANNE. How stupid . . . Mrs. Trent was blonde, of course.

CLARA. Mrs. Paige . . . while we're here together we feel there is something

we should tell you . . . something you must know. . . .

JERRY [*hastily*]. No . . . not now!

ANNE. Jerry . . . you mustn't interrupt like that . . . really you mustn't!

CLARA. We feel the time has come for telling you. . . .

ANNE. Are you sure it has come? Sometimes if you wait there's nothing to tell. If you take my advice, Mrs. Barlow . . .

CLARA. My name is *not* Barlow.

ANNE. Oh . . . how absurd! You see, the one before the last was named Barlow.

CLARA. The one before the last *what?*

ANNE. The next to the last lady Jerry wanted to elope with. He wanted to go to China with her. Every one was painting China that year . . . I don't mean crockery, of course. He wanted to go to Pekin and draw Mah Jongs or something. That was before O'Brien's book came out and he saw Gilda Gray dance. Now it's the South Seas. He simply aches to go down there and shoot batiks. In Samoa—it *was* Samoa you were telling Miss Dowling about, wasn't it, Jerry? . . . Why, Jerry . . . you haven't gotten that hassock for Mrs. Bents . . .

CLARA [*a trifle wearily*]. Brent, not Bents . . .

ANNE. Oh, yes . . . of course . . . but there *was* a Miss Bents . . .

JERRY [*dumping hassock*]. There!

ANNE. Under her feet, Jerry . . . and poke up the fire . . . it's quite chilly to-day . . . have you noticed it?

CLARA. Mrs. Paige . . . you are trying to prevent my talking and it's no use. . . . I am determined to have my say.

JERRY. Oh!

[*He drops the poker on Clara's foot and crosses right.*]

ANNE. Jerry . . . where are you going?

JERRY. Out for a minute . . . I . . . I forgot something. . . .

ANNE. Jerry . . . you come back and sit down . . . no, not there . . . you're sitting in your paints . . . look, dear . . . on the back of your coat . . . you'll find a rag in the table drawer. . . .

JERRY. Oh, damn!

ANNE [*to Clarabelle*]. I can't think what's gotten into Jerry to-day, he seems so nervous, I never saw him like this before. Now with that Fontenelle woman he was really enthusiastic. . . . I remember he did most of the talking . . . dear, dear . . . I really thought I was losing him that time. . . .

CLARA. Fontenelle . . . what Fontenelle? Not the dancer?

ANNE. Why . . . didn't he ever tell you about her? She was a lovely thing and so sympathetic, "with a husband who didn't understand her nature." Jerry . . . do show Mrs. Brent the letters you wrote Mrs. Fontenelle . . . perfect works of art, my dear—absolute works of art—and I had to pay Old Masters' prices for them, too—but they were worth it—especially the one about the faint, elusive fragrance of jasmine in the moonlight. . . . Do get it for her, Jerry . . . they're in the bottom drawer. . . .

JERRY. I'll be damned if I do!

CLARA [almost in tears]. Stop! I won't have you trampling on our sacred feelings! I can see what you are trying to do . . . you are trying to frighten me . . . but you can't! I know Jerry has loved other women. He says compared to me they are like candles in the sun. I understand him as you never have. You are simply crushing his soul. Your mind can't rise above dollars and cents while his floats in regions beyond . . . beyond . . .

ANNE [helpfully]. Yes? Beyond what?

CLARA. There . . . that's just the kind of thing I mean!

JERRY. Wait. You mustn't talk like that. She may not understand me, but she's always meant well.

ANNE. Jerry . . . come here! [He approaches.] Did you tell Mrs. . . . Mrs. Brent that I was crushing your soul?

JERRY. Well . . . not exactly. . . .

ANNE. That I kept your genius from floating . . .

JERRY. No . . . that is . . .

ANNE. That I was ruining your life?

CLARA. You are! I know it!

ANNE. I'm talking to Jerry.

JERRY. Well . . . hang it all! You are cross about the bills!

ANNE. But I mean well! Jerry . . . that settles it.

JERRY. What do you mean?

ANNE. I mean that I'm through being the third angle . . . my dear . . . I'm going to give you up!

CLARA. Ah! That's fine . . . that's noble!

JERRY. But I won't be given up!

ANNE [with concealed humor]. Hush, Jerry! This is my great hour . . . I won't have you spoiling it! I shall give you over into her hands . . . I shall step out of your life now . . . this moment. . . .

[She starts for door.]

JERRY. Here . . . wait a minute!

CLARA. Where are you going?

ANNE [still noble]. Now that I know, I can't bear to stand between you another minute. [Hands basket to Clarabelle.] Here . . . I leave this for you . . . I shan't need it any more. You'll find Jerry's shirts in the mending-drawer by the sewing table. There are buttons off all of them . . . and oh, yes . . . speaking of laundresses . . . Mrs. Flannerty left last week with the silver . . . you'll have to get another. . . .

CLARA. Mrs. Paige . . . I didn't mean you to do anything like this—so suddenly. . . .

ANNE. It's the only way. The sooner the break the better . . . I couldn't bear to stay around another hour crushing his life and meaning well. [Starts for door and pauses.] Oh, yes . . . I forgot the vacuum cleaner . . . it's in the broom closet and the tube's broken. You'll have to use it every day because Jerry's so careless with ashes . . . and his winter flannels are in the highboy. See that he puts them on in November, or he gets all sniffly, and colds make him cross. . . .

JERRY [thundering]. Anne!

ANNE. Oh, yes, they do, dear—and hay fever, too—but that's in the spring. I hope to goodness you'll be able to understand him when he has hay fever . . . I never could. . . .

JERRY. Look here! Are you going to stop this drivel?

ANNE. Hush, Jerry . . . don't spoil the beauty of this moment. . . . I want to remember it always . . . [She crosses and kisses him on the forehead.] Forgive these tears!

[Pulls handkerchief from bag.]

CLARA [greatly affected]. My dear!

ANNE. Oh, look! I almost forgot!

CLARA. What?

ANNE. Jerry's checkbook! And he's overdrawn again . . . you'll have to go down and fix it. Here [*opens it*] he's added instead of subtracting . . . seventy-five dollars. [*To Jerry.*] That bracelet for Miss Stratton, dear . . . . [*To Clara.*] But never mind . . . you needn't bother, because after to-day he won't need a checkbook, all the money is mine. I won't crush his genius with it any more. . . .

[*She really seems to be going this time.*]

CLARA. Wait! You can't go . . . don't you see I can't be left here alone with Jerrold. . . .

ANNE. But that's what you wanted.

CLARA. No . . . no . . . there's some awful mistake . . . I never thought of staying here with him . . . really, I didn't . . . don't . . . don't go . . .

[*Clings to her.*]

JERRY [*clinging on other side*]. Anne . . . you can't . . .

ANNE. Well . . . if you'd really rather I stayed . . .

CLARA. Much . . . much rather . . .

ANNE. Perhaps it would be better if you both went.

CLARA. Went?

JERRY [*startled*]. Went where?

ANNE. Hand in hand to the South Seas.

JERRY. But, hang it all . . . I don't want to go!

CLARA. I . . . I can't . . . why . . . my clothes . . . I haven't any clothes. . . .

ANNE. You don't need any clothes. They just wear hula hulas made of grass, and there's lots and lots of grass. Wait a minute, here's a paper . . . I'll look up the ships. There ought to be one going to-night . . . the tenth page . . . *Empress of China* . . . *H. H. Effington* . . . *Pacific Mail* . . .

JERRY [*to Clara*]. I won't, d'you hear? I won't . . . you can't make me!

CLARA. Ugh! You brute . . . do you think I'd go with you now? With your Bartons and Trents and Fontenelles? Not if you were the last man on earth!

JERRY. Well . . . you got us into this . . . now get us out!

CLARA. I got us . . . I . . . I . . . .

ANNE. And the *Manchu* . . . um . . . oh, yes . . . the *Canton* . . . that's it . . . sailing, sailing . . . oh, this is splendid! It's sailing to-night! [*Looks*

at watch.] You've got just time to make it comfortably if you hurry. I'll phone for reservations. . . .

[*Starts to phone.*]

JERRY. ANNE!

CLARA. Wait!

ANNE. But I don't dare wait! You'll lose the boat!

CLARA. But I want to lose it! Don't you see . . . there's my husband. I haven't really thought about him. He loves me and his heart is weak. Who would break it to Augustus?

JERRY [*delighted*]. Yes, who would break it to Augustus?

ANNE. Don't you worry . . . I'll break it to Augustus.

CLARA. You!

JERRY. *You!*

ANNE [*taking up phone*]. What's his number?

CLARA. Now? You're going to phone him *now?*

ANNE. I'll be careful of his heart!

CLARA. No! No!

ANNE. Perhaps he won't care, after all.

CLARA. Won't care! Oh . . . how can you! Of course, he'll care . . . he . . . he'll come right over here and shoot Jerrold . . . that's what he'll do . . . he'll shoot Jerrold. . . .

ANNE. Why should he? I'm not shooting you!

CLARA [*almost in tears*]. No, you're not. And I . . . I don't know . . . I don't like the way you're acting. I don't like it at all!

ANNE. Do you *want* me to shoot you?

CLARA. No!

ANNE. Then what's your husband's number?

CLARA. I won't tell you!

ANNE [*picking up the telephone book*]. I can look it up.

JERRY [*snatching book*]. I'll be damned if you do!

ANNE [*through phone*]. Information, please. Information? What is the number of Mr. Augustus Brent . . . the office number?

CLARA. Stop her! Oh . . . if you were a man you'd stop her!

JERRY. I can't stop her . . . when she once begins nobody can stop her!

ANNE. Faber 8742. Thank you. Faber 8742. [*Through phone to Central.*] Faber 8742.

CLARA. No . . . no . . . don't you dare call him!

ANNE. Hello . . . Faber 8742? Hello . . . is Mr. Brent there? Thank you . . .

JERRY. This has got to stop . . . I say it has *got* to stop!

CLARA. I don't want to go. I don't . . . I don't! I hate your husband . . . hate him!

ANNE. Hello . . . Mr. Brent . . . This is Mrs. Paige speaking . . . Mrs. Jerrold Paige. . . .

CLARA. No! You shan't! you shan't . . . [*Snatches phone.*] Gus! Gus! Is that you? I . . . I want to meet you for dinner. I said for dinner, right away . . . I'll come down and we'll go somewhere . . . anywhere . . . just you and I . . . yes, dear . . . yes . . . good-by . . . good-by. [*Hangs up and turns defiantly.*] There . . . I'm going . . . don't try to stop me . . . or I'll fight . . . I will! I never want to see you nor your precious husband again . . .

never . . . never . . . never!

[*She starts for door.*]

ANNE. Wait . . . just a moment. . . . You've a letter from Jerrold . . . about jasmine, and the moonlight . . . I'd like it for our collection. . . .

CLARA [*dragging letter out from her dress*]. There . . . take it! Take it! [*She tears it in shreds and throws the scraps on the floor.*] Take it!

[*She exits violently through door, right.*]

ANNE. Good-by . . . good-by [*Crosses to phone.*] Central . . . Oh, Central, give me Faber 6432.

JERRY. My God! You're not calling her husband?

ANNE. Faber 6432. Her husband? Oh, no, dear . . . [*Through phone.*] May I speak to Bishop Wilson? Thank you. [*To Jerry.*] It's time that you painted a bishop.

[*Curtain.*]

MORAL COURAGE
(THE GRAVITY OF LIFE)

A PLAY

BY FELIX SALTEN

CHARACTERS

HUGO [*Baron of Neustift*].
DR. CONRAD HOPFNER.
EMILY [*Hopfner's wife*].
A MAN SERVANT.

MORAL COURAGE

(THE GRAVITY OF LIFE)

A PLAY   BY FELIX SALTEN

[SCENE: *A sitting room in an old castle-like country-house, in the neighborhood of the town. Gunracks, bookcases, a large writing table, comfortable sofas. Big family portraits. A chimney-piece, on which a French clock stands with a fairly clearly visible dialplate. Right and left doors. In the middle, glass doors which open on to a veranda. From these outwards few steps into the garden.*
Man Servant ushers in Conrad and Emily.]

SERVANT. The master will be here immediately.

CONRAD. What? Is my brother-in-law not at home?

SERVANT. Oh, yes, Doctor.

CONRAD [*to Emily*]. Well, how do you like that? He lets us wait.

EMILY [*to Servant*]. Where *is* my brother, Alois?

SERVANT. Master's gone to the stables.

CONRAD [*with a snort of laughter*]. Hau! to the stables. . . .

EMILY. Thanks, Alois, thanks.
[*Servant bows and goes.*]

CONRAD. That, again, is exactly like your brother—he simply isn't in, when we come.

EMILY. Yes, but he certainly doesn't mean anything by it.

CONRAD. I never said he did, dear Emily. Kindly do not twist my words.

EMILY. But . . . .

CONRAD. No—I merely remarked it's exactly like your brother.

EMILY. He's sure to be back soon. After all it's only a trifle.

CONRAD. Trifles are often very eloquent; trifles are apt to be symptomatic; what would you think, if I, as a physician, were in the habit of overlooking trifles?

EMILY. That's something quite different.

CONRAD. My dear Emily, it is not different. Disease and character are diagnosed through symptoms. It is a remarkable fact; I am generally understood by you well enough, but whenever we speak of your brother . . . .

EMILY. Because you are always too severe on Hugo

CONRAD. Too severe? I wish my severity had been of some use in earlier days when I was still wasting my time in educating your brother.

EMILY. Yes, you . . . . You ought not to judge every one by your standard.

CONRAD. Look at the way your brother behaves: he knows how precious my time is, he knows how many patients I must leave in the lurch to come out here. This, too, should be borne in mind, when I am asked to pay a professional visit, I must be . . . hau! it's not the first time the better man's been kept waiting. And he goes to the stables!

EMILY. Well, I am delighted he has gone to the stables, it shows his illness can't be so very bad.

CONRAD. That may be. But I am bound to say that for a long time I have been uneasy about him.

EMILY. Good heavens, do you believe that Hugo is seriously ill?

CONRAD. I didn't say so. At any rate he is spoiled, through and through: he summons me for a cold which any little jobber could cure.

EMILY. Surely you don't think the worse of him for valuing you so highly as a doctor?

CONRAD. Hugo—value any one! Well, if he did, it wouldn't be a feeling he need be ashamed of. He'd be in no bad company in valuing me.

455

EMILY. On the contrary, in the very best.

CONRAD [pleased]. You think so? Eh? in good company. At least I hope he'll never get into worse.

[Hugo comes over the veranda through the glass doors.]

EMILY. Here he is.

HUGO. What? You, too, Emily. That is jolly. I am delighted. How do, Conrad? Fancy your coming out too, Emily!

EMILY. Your letter made me anxious.

HUGO. Oh . . . without reason, without reason. I believe there's practically nothing wrong with me.

CONRAD [to Emily]. What was I this very moment saying?

HUGO. Ah? You thought so too, did you?

CONRAD. You are perfectly aware how limited my time is and it would have been perhaps more considerate of you to have come to me. It's a long way out here.

HUGO. More considerate . . . ?

CONRAD. To my many patients, at any rate.

HUGO. Ah, yes. . . . But I don't know: the town gets on my nerves. It smells so vilely, now in the spring, especially, and I am very sensitive to smells.

CONRAD. Because the town smells vilely, as you say—for a reason like that, I must—you are always the same.

HUGO. Am I? I do hope not. It is disgusting to be always the same.

CONRAD. Disgusting . . . ?

HUGO. Tedious and therefore disgusting.

CONRAD [irritated]. Pardon . . . .

HUGO [interrupting]. Everything, everything. If what I have said annoys you, I take it all back. In the first place I really do not know whether I am right; then I do not attach the very slightest importance to being right and finally I would give the world not to quarrel with you again about a theory.

EMILY. Yes. Don't quarrel. Conrad only means really that he has so much to do.

HUGO. Of course, Kid dear, of course. Conrad must not be angry with me either. I know how he is plagued. It won't do him any harm to waste two hours in the country on such a beautiful spring afternoon. Be good for you, too. Besides to me, a consulting room is dreadful. Post-offices, railway stations, consulting rooms, there are no other places where you cease so entirely to be your own self and feel so acutely that you are a thing in the hand of another.

EMILY. Yes, but why ever do you keep standing there with . . . that shooting thing? What is the matter?

HUGO. Oh, this. [Lays the revolver on table.] It's about Diana.

EMILY. Diana, you haven't . . . ?

HUGO. It's too sad. The poor dog. Only think for eight days she's been whining; can't live, can't die, lies there in the stables huddled up in the straw, and suffers—suffers. Early this morning the vet came. He thought there was nothing for it. It may last long; it may end soon. In either case there's nothing to be done.

EMILY. And so you shot her?

HUGO. No, I didn't. I wanted. . . . But when I went in to her, she tried to hide from me—for the first time, mind you . . . the little beggar, so keen on me, too . . . she crept right into the corner and stopped whimpering.

EMILY. Oh, poor, dear Diana.

HUGO. Yes, stopped whimpering, as though she wanted to conceal her pain from me. And when I stooped over her, she wanted to get away, away . . . past me—and her whole face full of dread—she seemed to scent death in my hand—

[Emily goes up.]

CONRAD. Ridiculous!

HUGO. No. I know the little beggar too well.

CONRAD. Sentimentality.

HUGO. Senti— [Controls himself.] Oh! as you like. Anyhow I couldn't shoot and came back, a bit depressed, almost . . . condemned.

CONRAD. Better say, like a condemned murderer.

HUGO. Yes, that is the word.

CONRAD. Immense! Instead of finishing the business and simply liberating the creature from its pain.

HUGO. Liberating . . . all respect to liberating, but too often it requires the nerves of a butcher.

CONRAD. I may take it you have not called me here on account of your sick dog.

HUGO. You may. It would have been a good idea, saved the situation perhaps, but it never came into my head. However, if you could bring yourself to it . . . you probably understand the matter better than the vet.

CONRAD. You know I have no liking for such jokes.

HUGO. Or for jokes of any kind. I happen, though, to have spoken in earnest.

CONRAD. Then I am bound to say . . . that I, as a working physician, feel such words to be frivolous.

HUGO. So you have no right to any opinion on the matter.

EMILY. Oh, dear! your old quarrel. [*Goes up.*]

HUGO. I do not quarrel. It is the simplest thing in the world. To me the rage for work is incomprehensible: to you my—doing nothing. Good. So you work—and I do not. Everything is in perfect order. If the position were reversed, then it *would* be most painful. If I stood in your place, and you in mine.

CONRAD. Never would I be in your position.

[*Emily down to table.*]

HUGO. Excellent. Nor I in yours. We have every reason to love one another.

CONRAD. It is sad to have any one talk like you.

HUGO. But why? I am only frank, and, I believe, not improper. It would be the most shocking thing if I were obliged to work; every moment I should be conscious of my limitations. If I had a goal, I should be for ever doubting whether I should reach it and that would worry me, would make me restless.

CONRAD. Thank God I am a man who works, who works hard. I am a man who has a goal—none too mean as you were good enough to allow—who has a profession which I don't carry out so badly. There is one theory and one only: it is, that a man must be of some use in the world.

HUGO. No, that is the cardinal mistake. I have never been of the slightest use, and I am entirely without misgivings about it. There is no question of *duty*—in being of use. Some people are so of their own free will. Very nice of

them, too, if they show special gifts for the job. I possess none, and do not obtrude my mediocrity. The majority of men do so because they *desire* to do by means of usefulness, precisely what I *can* do without it—to live.

CONRAD. No, no. That's no proposition: that sounds to me like the silliness of an undeveloped boy.

HUGO. You may always consider me a boy, but you must try and not forget that you are now no longer my tutor.

CONRAD. How charming of you! To remind me I was a private tutor. [*Goes up.*]

HUGO. Oh, no! I merely remind you that you are one no longer.

CONRAD. You think you can crush me by saying that. You can't. I'm proud of it. Yes, I was a private tutor. It adds to my honor and you are the last person who ought to throw it in my teeth.

EMILY. Hugo meant nothing of that kind.

HUGO. I am extremely sorry if I . . . . Good God, you know how far I am from thinking such a thing!

CONRAD. But in this connection . . . .

HUGO. Enough! Enough! I don't want to argue.

CONRAD [*haughtily*]. Nor do I. We had better come to the point. You wanted my professional advice. [*Emily goes right.*]

HUGO. Yes, I wanted to ask you to examine me.

CONRAD. You'd better leave us, Emily.

HUGO. No, no—we can go in here, into my room. I should prefer it.

CONRAD. Just as you like.

HUGO. It wasn't clever of me to argue with you, as I did just now.

CONRAD. Why not clever?

HUGO. Because I have an idea you are not feeling kindly towards me at the moment. And I like a doctor to inspect me with kindness. I always like a doctor to love me a little.

CONRAD. Nonsense. As a doctor, I am a doctor, and know nothing of animosity.

EMILY. Hugo, you surely do not doubt Conrad's affection for you.

HUGO. Affection? Sometimes I'm not so very sure about it.

CONRAD. Perhaps now you wouldn't mind telling me what is the matter with you.

HUGO. I have a feeling of tiredness. A strange oppression. And I'm conscious of my body, which I used not to be. Especially of my lungs. [*Goes up.*]

EMILY. Hugo, you're not in pain?

HUGO. No, not in pain exactly . . . it's like a nuisance one keeps noticing in one's body. It doesn't hurt: it's only a sensation, like sadness.

CONRAD. There is nothing to be inferred from that. You watch yourself too closely because you are too self-absorbed and have nothing else to do.

HUGO. Really, I'd much rather you'd leave that alone.

CONRAD. What do you mean?

HUGO. I'd so much rather have a little more doctor and a little less school master.

CONRAD. I must ask you to . . . .

HUGO. Pardon. It is obviously part of my condition, to be irritable, impatient . . . .

CONRAD [*interrupts*]. We'll lose no time, then. Come and be examined. [*Crosses left to door.*]

HUGO [*delaying*]. I am wondering if you'd be capable of telling me . . . ?

CONRAD. Telling you what?

HUGO. Supposing, for instance . . . supposing it were something very serious . . . .

EMILY. Conrad certainly couldn't.

CONRAD. Why not? A doctor is often brought into such a predicament.

HUGO. Really! You can speak out . . . such a thing?

EMILY. I don't think, Hugo, you could ever have been a doctor.

HUGO. And if I were past all help, would you tell me that?

CONRAD [*already by the door, leaning against it*]. Perhaps you'd like me not to tell you the truth and . . . .

HUGO [*quickly*]. Of course . . . don't worry about that . . . it only occurred to me . . . . [*To Emily.*] This week's papers are on the table. [*Crosses right with Emily.*]

EMILY. Oh, thanks. I want to look at all the dear old things here. I shall like to be alone. [*Hugo goes with Conrad through the doors, left. Emily alone,*

walks all round the room, looks at the pictures on the wall, picks up a little vase, then a picture, smooths the antimacassars on an easy chair, sits on a little sofa near the easy chair, and looks round the room, taking it all in. Servant comes through the garden door.]

EMILY. What is it?

SERVANT. The master's not here?

EMILY. No. You see he's not. He's in there. [*Servant bows, and makes towards door, left.*]

EMILY. What do you want? You mustn't disturb my brother now.

SERVANT. It's only about Diana . . . over there in the stables . . . we can't do anything more for her . . . I think she'll be gone soon.

EMILY [*with feeling*]. Poor little beast!

SERVANT. The master instructed me to call him.

EMILY. Well, you can't now . . . wait . . . I'll just run there myself with you. [*Servant up right. Servant opens the garden door, lets Emily out and follows her. Pause. Conrad and Hugo enter.*]

HUGO. Emily . . . she's not here!

CONRAD. I am glad she's not.

HUGO [*turning quickly round*]. Is what you've got to say so bad then? You look so gloomy, you . . . .

CONRAD [*stands sharply erect, steps back from Hugo, claps one hand on the other*]. You yourself are to blame. . . . It is my firm conviction that you are to blame.

HUGO [*putting on his coat again*]. What am I to blame for?

CONRAD [*emphatically*]. That matters have come to such a pitch.

HUGO [*hiding his terror*]. My dear good man, I know that in any case you would give me the blame whatever happens.

CONRAD [*to him*]. You don't believe me? Of course you have never believed me. I've always told you your way of life spelt ruin.

HUGO [*becoming pale*]. You mean it's all up with . . . . [*Conrad is silent.*]

HUGO [*with a forced smile*]. And

. . . may I ask how long you think it may go on?

[*Takes hold of chair.*]

CONRAD [*resisting*]. Difficult to say. [*Conrad is silent, with difficulty.*]

HUGO [*still smiling*]. A year . . . ? Less than that . . . six months—

CONRAD. About. [*With immediate regret.*] That's to say, one can't be exact.

[*Sinks in chair.*]

HUGO [*expressionlessly*]. Six months . . . [*sits down*] then . . . done with . . . done with for good and all . . . . Let's see, we're now in June . . . in December.

CONRAD. Don't figure it out like that. My dear Hugo, it's not the time now for reproaches, but it might all have been so very different.

HUGO. Leave off preaching to me . . . now at any rate.

CONRAD. It is my firm conviction . . .

HUGO [*as though alone*]. Over there in the stables lies my dear old dog and worries herself with this dying and fights . . . and now I am as she is. . . . Just now I wanted [*lifts the revolver from the table and lays it down again*] to end her misery. Who is coming to free me from all the pother that is waiting for me?

CONRAD. Calm yourself.

HUGO [*waking up, looks at him*]. Oh, that word stinks of you. I must die, but I must be "calm." [*Suddenly screams out.*] Ah . . . ah . . . I can't endure it . . . I can't endure it . . . horror is choking me . . .

[*Gets up for a moment.*]

CONRAD. Be a man, Hugo!

HUGO [*beside himself*]. Yes, yes . . . please, there . . . the glass of water. . . .

CONRAD [*hands it him*]. Here—here. Pull yourself together, Hugo. A man must bear everything.

HUGO [*like a child*]. Everything—?

CONRAD. Everything. Believe me.

HUGO [*raving*]. I shan't bear this! No—not this! To know, to know! Always to be feeling the months—the days—gradually to be moving nearer to an open grave.

[*He bursts out sobbing.*]

CONRAD. Hugo, crying! How can you cry?

HUGO. To have nothing in front of you . . . nothing but that. Oh, I want to live, I want to live. Conrad, save me! save me! I don't want to die, I don't want to die—I can't die!

[*Kneels.*]

CONRAD. I'll do everything—everything. Rest assured of that. I—don't cry, Hugo. You are still the same as you always were, still like a mere boy, and ask not to die just as though it were an imposition and I could let you off it.

HUGO. I entreat you. I'll do everything . . . everything you wish. . . . I'm so afraid, so afraid.

CONRAD. Afraid? Naturally, but one must not give way to fear, you understand.

HUGO [*crying*]. To die—to die. . . .

CONRAD. God! it's not so certain as all that—not yet, I tell you. But the fact remains a man must be able to look death in the face, every moment he must be able to. Take me for example—I am ready any moment that fate likes to call me.

HUGO [*looking full at him*]. Any moment . . . you are ready?

[*Gets up.*]

CONRAD. Certainly I am. A respectable man is careful to keep his self-control.

HUGO. I've got my self-control.

CONRAD. Now look here. You mustn't think about it any more. You mustn't think about it, do you understand. You must be—cold-blooded.

HUGO [*with hidden meaning*]. I am cold-blooded.

CONRAD. I'm glad. [*Away down left.*] With proper will-power, every thought can be driven away as it comes. Thoughts can be turned away, like beggars from the door.

HUGO. I can't turn beggars from the door.

CONRAD. I am only speaking now of thoughts. The door is shut—slam and they are gone.

HUGO. Can you do that?

CONRAD. I can. It needs training, but it works. I tell you this, will-power and self-control—all *that* is acquired in the fight for existence, in daily renewed work.

EMILY [*through the glass door*]. Oh —have you done . . . ?

HUGO [*terribly upset by her entry, cries out*]. No, no, we're not nearly done. Go . . . please go!

EMILY. Hugo! . . . what's the matter . . . ? Conrad . . . ?

HUGO [*catching her up, impatiently*]. Later, later, Emily . . . . [*Quickly to Conrad.*] I suppose I may ask you to say nothing now?

CONRAD [*quieting*]. Exactly as you please.

EMILY. All this makes me so afraid.

HUGO [*distressed*]. Afraid . . . ? Why? It's nothing . . . really it's nothing . . . but please, dear, go! . . . Go now . . . into the garden . . . or into the billiardroom.

CONRAD. Go, Emily, we will call you in a little while.

EMILY. But . . . I'd rather stop with you . . .

HUGO [*loudly*]. You can't stop *here* now. [*Looking at Conrad, very markedly.*] I have a word to say to your husband—quite alone.

CONRAD. You see . . . Hugo can't now . . . .

HUGO. I'll call you . . . afterwards. . . .

[*He takes her to the door.*]

EMILY [*already half outside. . . .* Soon?

HUGO. I don't know . . . perhaps soon! [*Shuts the door behind her.*] There! [*Turns the key.*] And there!

CONRAD. Why do you lock the door?

HUGO [*after a moment's pause surprises him with the question*]. Why did you tell me—that?

CONRAD. What?

HUGO [*in a trenchant voice, full of suppressed fury*]. Why did you tell me —that?

CONRAD. You're no longer a child . . . but I'm sorry I did now . . . if I'd realized it, I should have been silent.

HUGO. Do you know why you were unable to be silent? Why you told me? [*Short pause.*] Out of conceit and hatred.

CONRAD. What have you got into your head now?

HUGO. Out of conceit, because you are a little, mean man, choked by the filth of his own vulgarity—and because it turned your head to hold another man's fate in your hand. . . .

CONRAD [*as though struck by a heavy blow*]. You're mad . . . you're . . . .

HUGO [*cutting short his answer*]. And out of hatred. Because you have always hated and envied me in a mean, low, crawling way. [*Movement from Conrad.*] Yes! Crawling! For you are utterly beneath me, and have always known that you were beneath me, and have struggled against it, bitten against it— from the time when I was a little boy and you were my tutor.

CONRAD. I beneath you? [*Laughing.*] You allude to your rank, I take it.

HUGO. No—or rather, yes, I do mean my rank! For you felt yourself far beneath this rank, and so you set yourself to whine against this rank every instant and to belittle it and to mock at it. Socially, humanly, spiritually you are beneath me and you hate me for it; for this reason you have always hated me. I realize it now for the first time—at this very moment. A great light flashes out, and all the years that lie behind me are illumined by it. Now I see how you've crept about here, as my enemy, as the enemy of us all, crept about with the soul of a lackey, trying to acquire our distinction. It's all so plain to me now, so devilish plain. Your trumpery speeches about your personal strength, by which you've worked your way up, these speeches you've always dinned into our ears, thrown them at us, as the mob used to throw dirt at a royal carriage. Still must I be listening to all that you've become, without fostering care, without help, without encouragement, all by your own efforts . . . still must I be listening to this impudent conceit, which ignores every bounty, every kindness it has received. [*Turns left.*]

CONRAD [*interrupting.*]. I protest . . . .

HUGO. As often as you've prattled this muck about your personal strength, I've felt sick, and I've been ashamed *for* you . . . yes, for *you*. Have you ever uttered one word about all the help, all the encouragement, all the protection which my father took care that you got? But how often have you proclaimed, right in my father's face, how far you had gone and how no one had helped you? And I still see him, my father, and the way he listened to you, with a smile. Oh! he never spoke a word about it, he was merely silent and merely smiled . . . but these are things which pass above your understanding.

CONRAD. You dare to say all this to me? To me who have had the best intentions. . . .

HUGO. Your best intentions! I know now what you have very likely never put to yourself in so many words—what you, through insensibility or through cowardice, have never cared to own—what you have just heard so clearly from my lips . . . that you are our enemy, have always been our enemy.

CONRAD. And your sister has become my wife.

[Goes up.]

HUGO [hastily]. She has become your prey! You had to get her. As satisfaction for the fact that you had crept about here and been humble: she, Emily, was your first claim to any position. . . . Oh, I see it all now through and through, spread out before me—and you . . . you I can open wide as though I had found the key to your being.

CONRAD [in the endeavor to establish his worth]. I have no desire to be abused by you here. What I was bound to disclose to you, is certainly hard to bear. But that you on that account should attack me unwarrantably like this, and try your utmost to wound my feelings—such conduct shows what kind of man you are. I have seen simple fellows from the people, who did not pucker up their lips to a whimper, when they were brought face to face with the inevitable. . . . But you . . . you must have some one to vent your spite on now. I will not be abused by you.

[Turns to the garden doors.]

HUGO [quick as lightning seizing the revolver, calling him back]. Stop. You remain here, I tell you, you remain here.

CONRAD [remains standing, notices the revolver in Hugo's hand, is indignant]. What does this worn-out farce with the revolver mean? . . . Put it down. Yes! That's the last wisdom of such young gentlemen as you, when they've frittered away their lives . . . a bullet through the brains . . . stylish! [Commanding.] Put the revolver down, you . . . ! Even if you really had the pluck and wanted to . . . which I very much doubt . . . it's undignified to play the clown with it.

HUGO. You are making a mistake, my good friend. It's not a question of my life—not at this moment. It's a question of yours. If you take one step farther, I shall shoot you!

CONRAD [turning to Hugo with a jerk]. Have you gone mad?

HUGO. Not in the least degree. But you must permit me to beg you to be seated.

CONRAD [ironical]. You'll be very much disappointed if you think you can frighten me.

HUGO. So much the better. It will be extraordinarily useful to me, if you're not a bit frightened of me now. For now I want you to give me one more lecture.

[Sits down.]

CONRAD. You must observe that I treat you with every consideration. I forgot that you were a man who had not the moral courage to look your destiny in the face.

[Sits.]

HUGO. No. I do not possess that courage . . . worse than that, I do not believe in the existence of that courage.

CONRAD. Thank God, it exists for all that. In a life of toil and of duty it is acquired.

HUGO. You say so—unfortunately that does not help me. You must prove it to me. That is the lecture which you must give me, and I think, considering that you are my old tutor, it is only my due.

CONRAD [understands a different meaning, is flattered, and speaks in a slightly friendlier voice]. If you feel sincere promptings towards earnestness, I will gladly help you to follow them up.

HUGO. Thank you. And I have never been so full of earnestness as now. . . . [With emphasis.] You shall now show me how to die.

CONRAD [uncertain]. Show you . . . ?

HUGO [dwelling on each word, almost solemnly, as a death sentence is spoken]. You will never leave this room alive, do you understand, Conrad! When the finger of that clock points to the hour, that is to say in five minutes, I shall shoot you.

CONRAD [after a moment]. Do you want to make me afraid? I've already told you that you can't frighten me.

HUGO. I have already told you, I am glad of it. I do not want to make you afraid, that would be quite contrary to my intention. Now you must teach me how to look death in the face. You must show me that you, as a man who has controlled his destiny, who is always ready are possessed of moral courage.

CONRAD [hastily]. This is not the proper time for a joke.

HUGO. No. It is not. And I am not joking.

CONRAD [uncomfortable]. An end to this! . . . I shall call Emily.

HUGO [stern]. Don't move—or you are a dead man.

CONRAD [quails]. I believe you really intend . . .

HUGO [gay]. You've got it at last! [Changes again to the relentless, stone-hard voice.] You have still five minutes to live . . . as I have still six months to live . . . [As though explaining.] You are suddenly and incurably ill, you see, my dear Conrad, you must pass away. [Throws chair away.] If you move, if you shout, if you make the slightest attempt to escape, you die that very second. Such is the nature of your complaint. You must take care of yourself in order that you may get the full time. [Noticing Conrad's glance towards the door.] Don't hope. I tell you, don't hope! If any one came unexpectedly you would be lost beyond all recovery. I shall kill you at the least noise I hear, quicker than any one could open the door.

CONRAD [horrified]. What do you want from me?

HUGO [stone-cold]. To see how strong you are, how brave you are—to be shamed by you and then myself to become strong by your example and to gain courage.

CONRAD [trying to control himself]. I have as much courage, I think, as a man can have. And I can meet any fate with resolution—

HUGO. Excellent, Conrad! Proceed, proceed!

CONRAD. But do you believe that I will resign myself to letting a boy like you, a half-grown, worthless boy, stand over me and decide on my fate?

HUGO. That is illogical. A slate can fall from a roof and kill, a gnat can sting and be fate. I am not more insignificant than a slate or a gnat.

CONRAD [in growing disgust]. Let us talk sensibly together.

HUGO. I am ready for every topic—so long as there is time for it. Don't forget that!

CONRAD. Admitting that you really would carry out . . .

HUGO. I'll carry it out . . . never fear.

CONRAD [helpless]. Think of yourself, think of the consequences it would have for you—of the punishment . . .

HUGO [rises, straightening himself]. Who can punish me? And with what can I be punished . . . with death . . .? I am already condemned to death. Don't you see, don't you even see yet that you have raised me high above all that human law can hinder or permit? Don't you see that I am free, quite free . . .? Don't you understand where you have driven me? To the very edge of existence! On this uttermost, narrow ledge I stand, right over the abyss . . . I stand there and no man's arm can reach me any more! You have torn me away from all that can strike terror into a man. I am delivered from earthly justice. I am mightier than any man in the world. Who can overtake me now with punishment? Who with threatening? And here I stand . . . with you . . . beyond life, beyond law, quite alone with you, and I've got the power to thrust you down first, to give myself the pleasure of this spectacle.

[Conrad gets up.]

CONRAD. If you want to frighten me . . . if you want to pay me out . . . I've had enough of it.

HUGO [unapproachable]. I do not want to frighten you; I do not want to pay you out. I want to learn from you! Show me how to look death in the face. Show me the moral courage, which you have meant at such pains to recommend to me.

CONRAD [in ever-increasing nervousness]. Hugo, for God's sake . . . I may have been mistaken . . . it's even quite likely that I am mistaken . . . that can happen to the best doctor. . . .

HUGO [crushingly]. So much the worse; nevertheless you did not hesitate to . . . .

CONRAD [broken down by fresh fear]. It was silly of me, I allow.

HUGO. Ah—? You, too, for once have been silly—but only when it concerns others . . .

CONRAD. You can get well . . . you will get well . . . I'll make every effort . . .

HUGO. You are too anxious about me. It's no good. Time flies. You must think of yourself. I take it you have a few preparations to make, and I expect you to make them with perfect coolness and composure. I am waiting; and I assure you that I shall never forget this sight during the remainder of my life.

[*Conrad gets up.*]

CONRAD. It's a murder . . . a low murder! . . .

HUGO. You, too, committed a murder . . . a low murder.

CONRAD [*his fear breaks out, he screams*]. Help . . . help . . .

HUGO [*his revolver raised and pointed*]. Stop. Don't imagine you can escape!

CONRAD [*sobbing*]. On my knees I entreat you—have mercy on me! . . . have mercy!

[*Falls on his knees.*]

HUGO. You had none on me—just now. Never have you had mercy on me —I can remember no single instance when you have ever shown mercy to me.

CONRAD [*gets up, half crazy*]. What am I to say . . .? What am I to say . . .?

[*He retreats behind the writing table from Hugo, who only looks at him.*]

HUGO [*sits table*]. Nothing [*With a long look.*], or perhaps just the *one* thing that lies in the depths of your soul.

[*Conrad stares at him in silence.*]

HUGO [*sternly*]. Only two minutes are left.

CONRAD [*with a loud cry*]. You cur!

HUGO [*pleased as at something expected and inviting more*]. Yes . . .?

CONRAD [*beside himself, shrieking, with broken voice*]. You cur! . . . How I hate you! . . . Yes, you were right, you were quite right . . . I hate you. I have always hated you . . . you proud, insolent lout! [*With sincerity.*] How I have always hated that imper-

turbable pride, in you, in your father, in you all . . .! I spit at you, you and your insolence and your conceit, yes, I spit at you. I have always spat at you. I'm glad you know it, damn you!

HUGO [*almost triumphant, overpowering Conrad's shriek*]. Ah, that's right, that comes from the bottom of your soul.

CONRAD [*continuing to rave*]. Yes, that comes from the bottom of my soul. It comes from all the years during which I have been silent.

HUGO [*joyful*]. There, now! That is the first honest word I have ever heard from you.

CONRAD [*breathless*]. Wait! I'll tell you some more truths, you wretched creature, I'll tell you how you've got to die . . .

HUGO [*struck, a quick step forward*]. No!

CONRAD [*with a last effort*]. Yes! Oh, it won't be easy; much harder than my death . . . if you murder me now . . . much harder. Slowly . . . the cold . . . will creep up and up . . . you'll know you're done for . . . you'll be stifled.

HUGO [*bitterly*]. Be quiet.

CONRAD. Stifled . . . Stifled . . .

HUGO. I'll blow your brains out as the clock strikes five—

[*The clock on the mantelpiece strikes loudly and solemnly four.*]

HUGO [*raises the revolver*]. Your end has come—

CONRAD [*in thin speech—indistinctly*]. Help . . . . Help . . . aaah! [*Falls fainting in a chair in front of the writing table.*]

HUGO [*slowly lets the revolver drop, throws it with a little jerk on to the writing table, looks at Conrad*]. That's just about what I sized it up at . . . this moral courage.

[*Smooths his eyes and forehead, as though he wanted to wipe something out, pulls himself together, takes up a cigarette from writing table, lights it and goes slowly out at the garden door.*]

[*Curtain.*]

THE GIANTS' STAIR
A Play
By Wilbur Daniel Steele

CHARACTERS

Mrs. Weatherburn.
Til [*her sister*].
Bane [*the Sheriff*].
The Man at the Door.

THE GIANTS' STAIR

A PLAY   BY WILBUR DANIEL STEELE

[PLACE: *A farm at the upper end of a mountain valley, "The Giants' Stair," which descends by easy alluvial benches from amongst the high southern buttresses of The Footstool.*

TIME: *Late November of the present: an evening when, the false autumnal summer having come to a close, winter gathers its forces for the initial assault. A storm of wind and rain invests the shell of the farmhouse with a note insistent, mournful, and menacing, and from moment to moment, in a wilder onslaught, rocks the edifice on its foundations as if with its next to tear it from its granite bed and hurl it bounding and crashing down the terraced floor of the gorge.*

SCENE: *The farmhouse kitchen, a gaunt, high-studded, white-plastered room, modified by forlorn attempts at cheer in touches of colored muslin at the windows, one on either side of the central door, and by a pink crêpe-paper shade which warms the light of the kerosene lamp on the table at the left. A door at the right leads into the woodshed; above it, on pegs, rests a double-barreled shotgun. The kitchen range, flanked by cupboards, is at the extreme right; at the extreme left an ordinary wall telephone, the kind with a crank.*

At the rising of the curtain there are discovered Mrs. Weatherburn and her sister, Til. Mrs. Weatherburn, a large-formed, soft-footed woman, has been manipulating the dampers of the range. When she lifts one of the lids the new wood, kindling with a pent roar, as if some of the outer gale had got down the chimney and into the stillness of the house, casts up a ruddy light and reveals the face bent over it, a face fleshy and unlined, the lips set together solidly but without strain, the eyes widely placed and so serene of expression as almost to beget a doubt of them—as if their very bovine tranquillity might be suspected to hide depths of ardor or passion or bitterness which would seem too silly in the scheme of existence of a mountain farm. *Brooding into the heat, her hand, still holding the stove lid, poised as if it has forgotten what it is about, she remains standing so for a moment, her back to her sister, seated by the table across the room.*

Til is physically almost the counterpart of the other, large, putty-fleshed, and colorless. Beyond this outer aspect the likeness fails. Til is what would be called in Oriental countries "inspired." She sits motionless under the pink glow, her hands, pallid, puffy, inert-looking, folded loosely in her lap; her eyes staring fixedly ahead of her at nothing at all. She speaks in a high-pitched, unaccented tone.]

TIL. This is another of them nights, Abbie. Hark, Abbie! Hark to that tempest! It's one of them nights again.

MRS. WEATHERBURN [*idly*]. What nights, Til?

TIL. One of them nights when the giants comes up the stairs to go on the mountain. Makin' a noise on the stairs.

MRS. WEATHERBURN. Goin' *down*, I should say, Til. The wind's from *up*.

TIL. No, giants goes against the wind. Don't you know that?

MRS. WEATHERBURN [*replacing the stove lid noisily, as if to put an end to that sort of talk, and glancing at the clock above the door*]. Mercy livin', Til, look the time it is. Past seven, and supper not yet gettin', say nothing of laid. [*Taking down a saucepan from behind the stove and peering into it for dust.*] It's a queer, funny thing. When John was here—

TIL. When John was alive—

MRS. WEATHERBURN. When John was here, I'd have give him a piece of my

467

mind for bein' ten minutes late of six for supper; and yet now here it's *me* that's dawdlin'—lazin' and dawdlin' till all hours—now't John's away—

TIL. Now't John's dead—now't he's dead and gone for a ghost—ghost in the trees—'long with the dead giants' ghosts —troopin' through the trees! Hark to that wind, Abbie! [*In the instant of silence following, the telephone bell begins to ring. With each prolonged, shrill iteration Til pronounces a name, like a child repeating in sing-song rote the rule of three. Ring!*] Banes'! [*Ring!*] Tolleys'! [*Ring!*] Jetherses'! [*Ring!*] Whites'! Mis' White's, Abbie. Somebody wantin' Mis' White's. Who could it be wantin' Mis' White's?

[*Rising suddenly and softly, she steps to the instrument, lifts the receiver from the hook with furtive care, and puts it to her ear.*]

MRS. WEATHERBURN. Don't, Til! [*More hopelessly.*] Don't do that, Til!

[*Til, on whose face the blankness has given way to a look of animation at once eager, willful, and sly, only puts her hand over the mouthpiece for answer, and continues listening.*]

TIL. It's Mis' Jethers, talkin' with Mis' White. Mis' Jethers says Jethers is havin' trouble with his growth again. She says the Pros'cutor was by to-day, and what can the Pros'cutor be snoopin' 'round this neighborhood for—unless it's about— Oh! [*She jerks the receiver from her ear.*] Oh!

[*She looks at it with an expression of malignance, wounded, bewildered.*]

MRS. WEATHERBURN. For Heaven sake, Til! What—

[*Til replaces the receiver with a vicious click, and as abruptly goes droopy and appealing, tears in her eyes.*]

TIL. They says I was *list'nin'*. They says that. Says somebody was snoopin' in, and they'd warrant the somebody wa'n't a million miles from the Weatherburn place. Abbie!

MRS. WEATHERBURN [*crossing to put an arm about her sister's shoulders*]. There! Don't you take on! Come, Til, you set down in your chair again. That's a good girl! [*Having pushed and petted Til into place, she turns to the phone,*

takes the receiver, and after a moment's listening speaks into it.*] Yes, here's "somebody" again, May White. Yes, "snoopin'," Clara Jethers. Only 'tain't the same "somebody," happens. Yes, it was Til. My Til. And all I wanted to say was, I think two *ladies*, such as you, would consider 'emselves in pretty business, mindin' *Til!* Mindin' and mockin' such a one as *Til!* That's all. Oh, no, no, I didn't mean to be snappy, Clara. No, nor to you either, May. Only— No, I don't want you should think— How? Yes, 'tis. Blowin' furies up here. Yes, perfect cats and dogs. How? The road bridge! [*To Til.*] Clara Jethers says the brook's so swole down her way that their hay bridge has gone out and the road bridge like to any minute. [*To phone.*] Don't tell me! Yes, I knew 'twas swellin', even up this far. When I was out to the chickens I hear it roarin' down to the meadow bottom. Dear —dear! I guess we sha'n't look to have many callers to-night, 't any rate. More likely to be callin' ourselves down your ways, house and all. [*Hastily, to the agitated Til.*] No, Til; no; that was only jokin'. No danger of *that*, I guess. [*To phone.*] I was speakin' to Til. Yes, good night to both of you; good night. [*Replacing the receiver, she moves away toward the range, but halts before reaching it, and stands with her head lifted, harkening to the scream of the elements without. After a moment she speaks to herself.*] I wish John was here to-night.

TIL [*apprehensively*]. Don't say that! Not with *this*—*these!* They might hear you—and send him.

[*Mrs. Weatherburn makes no rejoinder. As if taking herself in hand, she glances at the clock, tidies her apron, and is continuing toward the stove when a knock on the door brings her again to a halt, wheeling, startled. Til, rising, open-mouthed, wide-eyed, stares from her sister to the door and to her sister again. As Mrs. Weatherburn, shaking off her momentary irresolution, starts forward, Til brings her up again with a whispering "Abbie!" The knock is repeated, and immediately then the door opens and Bane comes in. Bane is a stocky, hard-fleshed, red-complexioned fellow in middle age, a farmer out of a line of farmers; a man, one would say, without imagination. His cowhide boots are muddy and his short overcoat sodden with water, as is the hostler's cap which he takes off as he closes the door behind him and blinks into the unaccustomed light.*]

TIL [*with almost a sob of relief*]. Why, it's—it's only Sheriff Bane!

BANE [*peering from one to the other, noting their attitudes*]. So, Til! And who'd ye 'magine I would be? [*Turning to Mrs. Weatherburn.*] And you! You're not still hopin', Mis' Weatherburn! Or—*mistrustin'*!

MRS. WEATHERBURN [*controlling a gesture of impatience*]. It was only you give us a start—to think of any livin' mortal being out to-night—

TIL. Along with *them* as *ain't.*

BANE [*ignoring her; to Mrs. Weatherburn*]. Make certain I shouldn't've been if I'd know. It wa'n't anything like so bad when I start. I been up the mountain all afternoon on the lookout for them two young steers of mine, the red ones, that's been strayed since Tuesday night. You ain't see 'em, I suppose? Well, then, when it come on so all-creation bad, and I see the light in your window—

MRS. WEATHERBURN. And quite right you was, Bane. Look at you—drownded! Take off that overcoat and draw up to the stove.

BANE [*looking down at himself*]. No, thank ye; my boots are too messed. I'll just take a chair by the door here a spell if ye don't mind.

[*Removing his coat, he hangs it over the chair back; then seats himself, his boots planted solidly apart, his cap hanging between his knees.*]

TIL [*gazing into space*]. What did them red steers of yourn die of?

BANE. *Die* of! They ain't died of anything I know of. Why?

TIL. I only thought 'twas queer a body'd be searchin' anything *livin'*—up this mountain here—to-night. Did you hear any of 'em round about you?

BANE. Any what? The steers?

TIL. The giants. Comin' up the stairs.

BANE. Giants! I *declare* for the woman! Th' ain't no such things as giants *alive!*

TIL. No, they're all dead now—long ago, long ago. And then them other dead things—passin' up through the trees and the long grass and the bushes —troopin' up—

BANE [*furiously, to Mrs. Weatherburn*]. What's she about? What's all this darnation foolishness about, anyhow?

MRS. WEATHERBURN. Nothin', Bane. Don't mind Til. It's like she's got it into her mind it'd be hard for anything mortal to get up the road to-night. We had a phone the bridge to Jetherses' is like to go out any minute. You'll hardly get home to-night, I'm afraid, will you?

BANE. Don't look it. I'll set here, if ye don't mind.

MRS. WEATHERBURN. Land, no! But you ain't et! No more've we. I'll put some eggs on directly—

BANE. I've et. Before I start—

MRS. WEATHERBURN. But I thought you was on the mountain all after—

BANE [*hastily*]. I—that's what I was goin' to say—only—only ye wouldn't leave me finish. Before I start *down*, I was goin' to say, havin' take a snack along in a paper. See?

MRS. WEATHERBURN. Oh! [*And after a perceptible pause.*] Well, you don't mind if we have ourn, Til and me? I was just gettin' at it—

BANE [*doggedly*]. No. But *I've* et.

[*Mrs. Weatherburn takes up the saucepan from the stove and, again peering into it, again falls into reverie.*]

TIL [*reseated, her eyes blank*]. The first step in the stairs is Banes'. The next step is Tolleys'. Big, huge steps in the dark. It's feelin' for 'em with their feet in the dark makes the din. [*Mrs. Weatherburn, still brooding into the saucepan, has shifted nearer to Bane. Til continues*]. The next step after Tilleys' is Jetherses'. That's a higher one. Some stumbles there.

MRS. WEATHERBURN [*in a resolute undertone*]. Bane, there's one thing I'd like if you'd make clear. When you come in you says to me: "Still hopin'?" and by that I take it you mean still hopin' it might be my husband come back. But it's what you says next I

want explained. "Or *mistrustin'!*"
Why'd you say, "Or *mistrustin'*"?

BANE [*confused*]. What'd I mean?
Land! I never meant—it was more like
a—a joke. Only—

MRS. WEATHERBURN. Only *what*,
Bane?

BANE. Nothin! Only— [*straightening his shoulders and looking significantly about him.*] You been bright'nin'
things up a bit since John was—was
gone—eh? Them window curtains makes
a difference now, don't they? John
Weatherburn was never much on decoration, was he? And that there pink
lamp shade. Makes the room a sight
cheerier, don't it, though? And then
the telephone. A telephone's a comfort,
'specially to the women folks, what with
their gossipin' and egg prices and howdy-do's. I'm glad for you you got the
phone in at last, after all these years
it's been up the valley clean to your next
door neighbor's. John was never much
for contraptions, was he? 'Specially
when they cut into the money. John
was insured, wa'n't he?

MRS. WEATHERBURN [*in a level tone,
facing him squarely*]. Is there anything
in this valley, stick, stone, or straw
stack, *ain't* insured, and insured as
high's ever the agent'll let you?

BANE [*keenly*]. Why'd you say "straw
stack"?

MRS. WEATHERBURN. Why shouldn't
I say "straw stack"?

TIL. And then the next step is
Whites', where the walls comes closer
t'gether. And there's the brook to crost
again, the roarin' brook, tumblin' and
roarin' and takin' the bridges out in the
dark—

MRS. WEATHERBURN. Bane, you never
come here to-night *about steers!*

BANE [*rubbing a hand down over his
lips*]. Well, as a matter of fact—
[*Blowing out his lips.*] Set down, Mrs.
Weatherburn.

MRS. WEATHERBURN. Thank you, I'll
stand.

BANE [*blowing out his lips again*].
Was a Mr. Cantpole by to-day?

MRS. WEATHERBURN. That's the Pros'-
cutor from over Twinshead way, ain't
it?

BANE. Yes, Cantpole happens to be
Prosecutin' Attorney; that's him.

MRS. WEATHERBURN. Yes, he was by

What's more, you know well enough he
was by. Look here, Bane, speak out!
Is it about—John?

BANE. About John—I'm afraid.
About John's—vanishin'.

TIL [*in the same dreaming tone*].
About John's dyin'. About John's dyin'
o' murder in the dark.

BANE [*wheeling in his chair*]. And
how'd *you* know he was murdered, Til
Jessup? *How'd* you come to know?

TIL [*shaken out of her reverie; dismayed*]. How'd I know? Why—why—
I'll tell you how—I hear Mis' Jethers
sayin' 's much—day before yesterday,
'twas—to Mis' Tolley—or leastways to
Mame Tolley—Mis' Tolley bein' to
Twinshead. Mis' Tolley's always to
Twinshead Thursdays, ain't she? That's
her day to Twins— [*The phone rings.
Til counts.*] Banes'! Tolleys'! There's
for Mis' Tolley's now. Wonder who could
be—

[*She half rises with a yearning
glance toward the instrument;
then, remembering herself, casts
an abashed eye in the direction of
the visitor and relapses. The
Sheriff passes his hand again over
his face and returns his attention
to Mrs. Weatherburn.*]

BANE. I trust you'll believe me, Mis'
Weatherburn, when I tell ye 'tain't of
my own wish I'm here to-night.

MRS. WEATHERBURN. No, I s'pose not.
But hark'nin' to all the gossip that's
round—

BANE. No, 'tain't no question of gossip sent me. It's Cantpole. I shouldn't
've moved of myself, same as J *ain't*
moved before—

MRS. WEATHERBURN. Yes, I've give
you credit for a deal of sense—till now.
I says to myself, there's one man in
the valley's got sense enough to know
John must've just gone away a spell,
somewheres—

BANE. No, Mis' Weatherburn, 'twa'n't
that. For that wouldn't be *sense*. Don't
think I blind myself. What manner of
sense would there be tryin' to believe a
man like John Weatherburn, a solid
church-goin' man with a good farm and
a bank account, and a fam'ly—that a
man like that'd be changin' all of a
sudden, one special night, and skippin'
for it, no word to nobody and never hear
of again? That's too much!

MRS. WEATHERBURN. There's queer things happens in the world.

TIL. There's queer things happens in the world.

BANE. No, no, 'tain't that. [*He looks down at his cap, which he wrings between his fingers.*] 'Tain't that. It's something—[*Putting the palm of his hand on the crown of his head.*]—something here. Something settin' heavy, and sorrowful, like a weight. Mr. Cantpole never lived in this valley. I have. I've lived neighbors with you folks; you've been to dinner to my house, and me to yourn. I've know John Weatherburn since him and I was boys. Boy and man I've known him. Why, I was the last person to see him alive—the last that'll confess to it, anyhow. When he leave me that night, there at the bars of my top pasture—when I see him walkin' away in the dusk of that ev'nin' —if I had think—if I'd been able to know what was in store— Oh, dear! It sets heavy, Mis' Weatherburn. It's set so heavy on me I ain't been myself. The farm work's suffered; nothin' tended, nothin' done. And here's the Pros'cutor all the while: "When ye goin' to act, Sheriff?" And me settin' there to home, thinkin', thinkin': "Sorrow has come on that fam'ly up there. If I, Edwin Bane, was willin'ly to set out to add to that sorrow—" But to-day, when Cantpole was by, there wa'n't no "When ye goin' to act?" This time 'twas: "*Act!*"

MRS. WEATHERBURN. So, you acted! [*Holding up the saucepan, she peers into it for the last time. She takes it to the stove, fills it from the teakettle, and sets it on. She glances toward Til. Then, picking up the wood basket:*] Til, would you mind gettin' me in some wood? That's a good girl! And wait! Take along this candle— [*Lighting a candle end for Til as she takes the basket.*] For I want some good sticks this awful night. Good, medium-small, square sticks. Mind! Pick 'em careful, won't you, Til? That's a good girl! [*Ushering her out and closing the door behind her, she stands with her back against it, facing the Sheriff in his chair.*] So, Bane, you acted! You come to accuse me of murderin' John!

BANE [*reddening*]. Not so fast! Not so fast!

MRS. WEATHERBURN. You come here to accuse me of murderin' John!

BANE. Not so fast. [*Rising and casting his eyes about.*] I come here, at Cantpole's orders, simply to—to have a look around. That's all. That John's gun up there? [*Taking down the weapon and balancing it thoughtfully across tis palms.*] H'm'm'm! Good gun. [*Sniffing at the muzzle.*] D'you ever try shootin' this gun, Mis' Weatherburn?

MRS. WEATHERBURN. No, I never shot that gun.

BANE. Sure o' that, ain't ye? [*The door is attempted from the other side. Mrs. Weatherburn props her back more desperately against it, calling over her shoulder.*]

MRS. WEATHERBURN. Better wood'n that, Til! Better wood'n that! [*To Bane.*] What do you mean, Bane?

BANE. I just mean—I was just wonderin'—if 'twa'n't you— [*With a quick movement he "breaks" the breech, pulls out one of the shells, notes that it is empty, and, lifting the weapon to point to the light, squints through the barrel.*] Just wonderin', Mis' Weatherburn, if 'twa'n't you, who 'twas.

MRS. WEATHERBURN [*after a moment's hesitation*]. I'll tell you who 'twas. It was my husband himself. I rec'lect now. 'Twas the day before he—left. I rec'lect him comin' in with that gun, sayin' as how he'd had a shot at some quail up in the stone pasture. But he'd missed.

BANE. I don't doubt your word, Mis' Weatherburn, nor your rec'lection. Your husband may've shot this gun that day. All I want to say is [*Holding up the shell.*] he never shot *this load!*

MRS. WEATHERBURN. Why?

BANE. If your husband—or any other man—was to've shot this load, he'd've cleaned the gun after him. No man that'd shot his gun would leave it grimed and pittin' up like this. No, sir! He'd go to work and have his rod and rag out; that's what he'd do. [*His voice lifting.*] He'd give it a thorough cleanin', he would! [*Still higher.*] He'd set up all night cleanin' of it! [*With a vehemence almost of ecstasy.*] Cleanin' of it and cleanin' of it till it shine like the Gates of Heaven, he would!

MRS. WEATHERBURN [*abandoning the*

door to advance upon him]. Bane, you gi'me that ca'tridge and that gun. They're my prop'ty, not yourn.

BANE [*thrusting the shell into a pocket*]. No, sir! Sorry, but I guess I'll want to hang onto these articles a spell. Sorry!

MRS. WEATHERBURN [*deliberately*]. Bane, what would you do if I was to tell you '*twas* me shot that gun?

BANE. Shouldn't b'lieve ye.

MRS. WEATHERBURN. Bane, what are you *at?*

BANE ["*hefting*" *the weapon thoughtfully*]. H'm'm. You and John been gettin' on well together these past few months? I don't know's I take much stock in gossip, but they do say John wa'n't always the easiest man on earth to get on with—to home. Good man— savin' man—but temp'ry—they say. And of course there's women with tempers, too—

MRS. WEATHERBURN. I sha'n't stand here harkin' to you—

BANE. Wimen with tempers, too. 'Specially out on lonesome farms—'thout telephones nor gossip nor sociability nor nothin'—tryin' to the temper that is. 'Specially after it's been goin' on some years—draggin' on—always the same— workin' on the mind and temper. 'Specially with a man to do with—a sober man—a savin' man—but—

MRS. WEATHERBURN. Bane, them ain't your words! Them ain't your ideas!

BANE. Grant it. They ain't mine. They're the Pros'cutor's.

MRS. WEATHERBURN [*starting forward again*]. You gi'me—that—gun!

BANE [*warding her off with his free hand*]. Sha'n't! [*The door to the woodshed opens. Til enters and stands regarding them stupidly, the candle in one hand, in the other the basket of wood. Bane, with an inspiration.*] Look here, don't let's bicker over the gun. Let's leave Til decide. Here, Til, take it! [*As he extends the weapon toward her Til recoils, letting the candle and basket go. A screech of repugnance escapes her lips.*] What's wrong, Til? It's a good gun, ain't it?

TIL. Don't want it!

[*Recoiling another step.*]

BANE. Why?

TIL. Kills things! Murders things!

All manner o' livin' things it murders and kills!

BANE. *Then why'd you shoot it that time?*

TIL [*falling into the trap*]. I—I don't know. I—I feel like I wanted to —to *horrify* myself! Want to hear it *bang!* To—*horrify* myself!

BANE. And what did you shoot *at*, Til?

TIL. Nothin'. Leastways nothin' but giants and ghosts and the like.

BANE. In the dark?

TIL. In the dark.

[*Bane, appearing satisfied, returns to his seat, and, propping the weapon beside him, rubs his hand over his face.*]

MRS. WEATHERBURN. Ed Bane, if you pretend to think Til knows what she's sayin'—

BANE [*blowing his lips*]. I don't pretend to think, one way nor t'other. That's other folks' business. All I say is, don't be s'prized! When John's body comes to be found one of these days, hid in the bushes somewheres or 'nunder somebody's straw stack—I say—don't be s'prized if his head's found half blow off in the back with a charge of bird shot. Mark what I say, and don't be s'prized. That's all.

MRS. WEATHERBURN. Set down, Til. [*Til obeys with a kind of bewildered docility. Mrs. Weatherburn picks up the wood basket, deposits it by the stove, takes two or three sticks, and lays them in the fire. All her movements have grown lethargic. She recovers the candle from the floor and restores it to the shelf, and afterward stands staring dully at it. She starts to speak.*] Bane!

[*The telephone rings.*]

TIL [*as before*]. Banes'—Tolleys'— Jetherses'—Whites'—Us! *Us*, Abbie! Should I—?

[*Half rising.*]

MRS. WEATHERBURN. Set down, Til. [*She crosses the floor, still moving with the same appearance of apathy, and takes the receiver.*] Yes, hullo! Yes, it's Abbie. Yes, what's wantin, Marion? [*To Bane.*] It's to your house, Bane; your sister speakin'. Would you want to— [*Back to the phone again, with a* [*Queer, new, tight note.*] How? *How?* [*She listens, standing curiously rigid, her face empty, almost stupid. After a space she takes the receiver from her ear, studies the rubber contrivance for a blank moment, replaces it on its hook, and drifts back to the stove. She starts to take up the saucepan, but desists in the act. She turns slowly to face the others.]* It's him.

BANE. Not—*John!*

MRS. WEATHERBURN. John.

TIL. Not—*livin'!*

MRS. WEATHERBURN. In the flesh.

TIL. No. [*Shaking her head solemnly.*] No, no, no.

BANE. John! Well, of all things! And me here, then, all for nothin'! But how come? Where's he to? Not to *my* house? Did Marion—

MRS. WEATHERBURN [*speaking in a distrait monotone*]. 'Twas your hired man, Eggar, see him, Marion says. She says Eggar was up to the pasture just now, lookin' to get the gray colt in out of all this storm. He had a lantern with him, lookin' everywheres for the colt. He think he see somethin' movin' along the road, and, thinkin' mebby 'twas the colt had got out, he climb the fence there near Tolley's straw stacks—

BANE. Where?

MRS. WEATHERBURN. —by Tolley's turn where his straw stacks are—

TIL. Mebby he's been 'nunder Tolley's straw stacks. Seems I've hear somebody sayin' he might be 'nunder somebody's straw stack—

BANE. Nothin'. Go on!

MRS. WEATHERBURN. —where his straw stacks are, and then he see 'twa'n't the colt after all. 'Twas a man. Walkin' along, Eggar says, matter o' fact, his hat pull down and his shoulders hunched and his hands in his pockets, in the rain. Eggar give him good ev'nin', Marion says, and when the man give him no answer Eggar throw the light in his face, and he couldn't b'lieve his eyes first, when he see 'twas John. Marion says he speak to him again—ast him where he come from, and then ast him if he hadn't best stop in a spell till the rain let up, but John never says a word, 'cordin' to Eggar, but comes on up along the road like a—a deaf man—

TIL [*musing*]. —dead man—

MRS. WEATHERBURN. He look wore out, Eggar says.

TIL. Wore out. No wonder. Wore out.

BANE. Well, I vow! Of all things!

MRS. WEATHERBURN [*glancing around her with a numbed air.*] I s'pose I better put on somethin' hot to eat, if he's comin'.

BANE. I shouldn't worry. He may be *comin'*, all right, but I doubt he'll *reach*, a night like this. It's too much for mortal man, the way the brook's swole, and the wind—

TIL [*absorbed*]. He'll reach. John'll reach. But he won't want for nothin' to eat, John won't.

MRS. WEATHERBURN. I s'pose I better put on somethin' hot. Le'me see, le'me see.

[*Wandering to the cupboard by the stove, she prods amongst its contents with aimless fingers. She examines the state of the fire. She takes three plates from a shelf and carries them to the table. Depositing them under the pink lampshade, she suddenly relapses into a chair. After a moment she drops her arms on the table, buries her face in them, and begins to weep without sound. Til remains oblivious to all this, her head lifted, attentive to the outer gale.*]

TIL. Hark to 'em! Hark to 'em come, makin' a moan and a drone and a racket on the stairs o' the mountain! All the things that's dead! The old things that's dead, like the giants! And the new things that's dead! Comin' against the wind! Hark!

BANE. Pester the woman! [*Turning his uncomfortable attention.*] Come, come, Mis' Weatherburn!

TIL. Hark to 'em troopin' through the long wet grass. Hark to 'em swishin' through the trees.

BANE [*jumping up with an exasperated clatter*]. Pester the crazy— [*Moving toward Mrs. Weatherburn, laying a hand on her shoulder.*] Come now, Mis' Weatherburn! Come! I know it's a good deal of a shock to ye—happy shock, of course—but a shock, all the same. But you've had your cry now, ain't ye? Now's the time to smile. Ain't ye glad John's turned out alive, after all? Eh? Ain't ye glad?

MRS. WEATHERBURN [*lifting her head and speaking with a curious vehemence*],

Am I glad? If you was to know *how glad!*

BANE. There! That's better! It's but natural a woman should be glad havin' her husband back again, safe and sound.

MRS. WEATHERBURN. 'Tain't that, Bane. [*With a quick glance at Til.*] Til, I know what I'll put on for supper. You rec'lect that fowl I got hung for Sunday out in the shed? You go bring it in for me.

TIL. He won't want it.

MRS. WEATHERBURN [*sharply*]. Til, you do as I say!

TIL [*sullenly, rising*]. Don't like the dark. There's things.

MRS. WEATHERBURN. Don't be a scared cat. Here! [*Getting up and lighting the candle for her.*] Take this, then the dark won't be there. That's a good girl.

[*She stands facing Bane, as Til goes out and the door closes behind her. After a moment he speaks.*]

BANE. What you mean, " 'Tain't that!"? Ain't you glad to have John back?

MRS. WEATHERBURN. John's comin' or goin'—'specially after he's laid *this* on us to bear through—his comin' or goin' ain't apt to affect my happiness one way or t'other. That's what I mean, Bane.

BANE. You do speak out, don't ye? But you says you was glad he was—

MRS. WEATHERBURN. Alive! To *know* it. More glad and relieved than I can—

BANE. I see now! Then after all, 'twas about—

MRS. WEATHERBURN. Yes.

BANE. —about Til! You wa'n't so sure's you made out, about Til. About that gun, and shootin' at ghosts, and all that.

MRS. WEATHERBURN [*giving way to the revulsion of relief; wringing her hands*]. I tell you true I didn't know *what* to think. Oh, if you'd had the bringin' up of that poor creature! If you'd had the worry of her and the shieldin' of her! and knowin' every minute you never know an atom of what was next in her poor wild brain! Oh, if you had! And then I was away that night, too; most an hour I was away, down to Mis' Jethers's. And then there's another thing. Til's fond of me. She's

like a dog. I b'lieve she'd do *anything*—

BANE. Yes, go on. And mebby there was some special reason—mebby you and John'd had words or somethin'—

MRS. WEATHERBURN. We'd had words that day. John was his worst that day. Over my wantin' the phone. John lay a hand on me for the first time.

BANE. And Til see him?

MRS. WEATHERBURN. Til see him. Oh, if you'd had that thought weighin' on your brain, week after week! Oh, you'd know why I was glad!

BANE [*blowing out his lips, thoughtfully*]. I'm glad you been frank, Mis' Weatherburn. I'm glad you've tell me these things. I shan't forget—and I hope *you* won't forget—

MRS. WEATHERBURN. Sssh! [*The woodshed door bursts open; Til enters in haste, glancing nervously over her shoulder, the extinguished candle in her hand.*] What's wrong, Til? Where's the fowl?

TIL. There's things. They blow my candle out.

MRS. WEATHERBURN. *Til!* Where's that fowl?

TIL [*sulkily, still peering behind*]. He won't want it. Where's the use o' spoilin' earthly victuals— [*The telephone rings. Her facile attention runs to it.*] Banes'—Tolleys'—Jetherses'— Whites'—*Us!* Abbie! They've see him again!

[*She starts sidling toward the instrument, half scared, half furtive, as if hoping she may reach it first. Mrs. Weatherburn passes her and takes the receiver.*]

MRS. WEATHERBURN. Yes, it's me, Mattie. How? Speak louder. Yes, I hear now. Yes, I tell you I hear. [*She continues attentive. The hush in the room grows long.*] Yes, I'm list'nin'. He wa'n't himself, you say.

TIL. Abbie!

BANE. Be quiet, Til!

MRS. WEATHERBURN. Yes, Mattie, yes, I've hear it all. Much obliged, Mattie.

[*Replacing the receiver, she half turns and stands staring at the door.*]

TIL. *Abbie!*

MRS. WEATHERBURN [*as to herself*]. What's ailin' of him? There's something queer.

TIL. Abbie, for *mercy* sake, say somethin'! Where was it—to Tolleys' this time?

MRS. WEATHERBURN. Yes, to Tolleys'. He's been by. 'Twas Tolley himself see him. He was comin' back from havin' a last look at the road bridge—that's gone and carry out now after all—Tolley was, when he met him. Mis' Tolley says Tolley got home in a sweat, as if he'd see a ghost.

TIL. Yes. See a ghost.

MRS. WEATHERBURN. Seems Tolley speak to him before he see who he was. He says to him: "Best stop back, mister; the bridge is gone out above." Then, gettin' no answer, Tolley look closer and see who 'twas he was speakin' to. Tolley was so laid out for a minute he didn't know which end up. Then he think of the bridge again, and "John," he says, "if you *are* John Weatherburn, 's you seem to be, you best come back to my house along with me." But by that John was gone on up the road and disappeared.

BANE. And the bridge out, ahead of him!

MRS. WEATHERBURN [*with the new thought*]. Mercy angels! he'll walk straight in—

BANE. No, but he'll see—

MRS. WEATHERBURN. —and be drowned!

TIL. Ha-ha-ha-ha—

[*Her laugh rises shrill, tenuous, ironic, queer.*]

BANE. Pester you! Quit!

MRS. WEATHERBURN [*staring into the pink light*]. What's ailin' of him? Where's his senses gone? Where's he been to? What's he done? What makes him come on, come on, keep comin' on, never sayin' a word to no one, just comin' on, comin' on through the soakin' night? What is it—drivin' him?

TIL. Ha-ha-ha-ha-ha—

BANE [*in a fury*]. Gol pester you! If you don't quit that! What makes ye keep laughin' that crazy way?

TIL. It's the horror! It's the horror gettin' into my throat!

BANE. Horror? Horror o' what?

TIL. Him! Comin'! Comin' up the wind! Drove! Comin' up the road, comin' up the field, up the cowyard, up the steps, comin' in the door there, takin' off his hat there, settin' down in his chair there 'thout a word, with his back to us all, so's we'll have to see the back of his head there, half blow off, and straws stickin' into it—

BANE [*shouting*]. Straws? Where from?

TIL. From Tolley's stacks. Didn't you say he come from Tolley's straw stacks? I hear you say a while back—

BANE. Mis' Weatherburn, mark that! I call on ye to make note of that! I'll ast ye to rec'lect that!

MRS. WEATHERBURN. What on earth you talkin' of—

[*The phone rings. Til's voice drones in a note of fascination.*]

TIL. —Banes'—Tolleys'—Jetherses'—Whites'—*Us!*

MRS. WEATHERBURN [*who has the receiver with the last signal*]. Yes, me! [*After an instant she puts out a hand to the wall to steady her. She turns to the others, still holding the receiver to her ear.*] They've found his—body.

BANE. Where? [*Blanching.*] I—I demand you tell me *where?*

MRS. WEATHERBURN [*in the phone*]. Where? In the brook? No? [*Turning again.*] No, not in the brook. This side. This is to Jetherses' now. Joe Jethers see the body lyin' on its back in the mud down by their gate. He come back for Ed. [*At a signaling flutter in the receiver.*] Yes, Clara? How? Gone! You didn't say—*gone?* [*She hangs up the receiver and slowly turns.*] When Joe and Ed get back to the gate, 'twas gone. So it couldn't have been his bod—; he couldn't've been *dead.* He must've just swounded there a minute—like's not—

TIL [*in the same eery note*]. Ha-ha-ha-ha—

BANE [*choking*]. I'll kill ye, Til Jessup! I'll strangle ye 'f you don't leave off that— Here! Where ye goin' *now?* [*As Til moves, or, rather, seems to be pulled toward the door.*] Til, if you open that door, I vow— Quit it! Mis' Weatherburn, make her quit it, the crazy, ravin' thing! [*Til lifts the latch with a trancelike deliberation, pulls open the door, and stands on the sill, framed by the darkness, cringing and hugging her body with her fleshy arms.*] I vow! That's the end!

MRS. WEATHERBURN. What you carryin' on so for, Til?

TIL [*peering into the night*]. To *horrify* myself. I got to look. To *horrify* me. I see him! [*Crouching a little.*] Black as pitch it is, and yet I see him. 'Nunder the trees he is; 'nunder the meadow rise he is, and yet I see him— comin' on—comin' on up the road toward Whites'.

[*She crouches yet a little lower. The backwash of the wind in the house's lee lifts the strings of her unkempt hair.*]

BANE [*almost in a whisper*]. That's the end! That's enough!

TIL. Comin' on, comin' on. He's up the hill to Whites' now. He's under the aspen trees, up by the lower gate to Whites' now. Comin' on under the aspen trees. In the black dark there, in under the aspen trees at the bend; in under the drippin' aspen trees. The dead eyes shinin' pale in his head, pale as ashes in his blowed-out head—shinin' pale in the drippin' dark in under the aspen trees. You'd think he'd drag his feet, but he don't drag his feet. His feet's not on the ground. Inches above the ground his feet is, and he comes on floatin' against the wind, sailin' against the black wind and rain. Not against the wind! Betwixt the wind! Betwixt the flakes of the wind! Comin' on out— out from in under the aspen trees—

BANE [*who has been closing on her, step by rigid step*]. That's the end! [*Grasping her arm roughly, he drags her within the room and slams the door. He stands with his right hand spread against it; with his left he shakes an ecstatic finger in her face.*] Just for that, Til Jessup—to learn ye, Til Jessup—for that—I—here *and* now—I arrest ye, Til Jessup, in the name of the law—I arrest ye for the murder of John Partley Weatherburn on the night of—

MRS. WEATHERBURN. Edward *Bane*, you crazy? What you sayin'? And him comin' there in the flesh!

BANE [*flinging around on her*]. 'Tain't so! All a trick! What'd ye *think* the Pros'cutor'd been by to every house in the valley to-day for? All a trick o' Cantpole's doin'! *Pre*'ranged, every mite of it! *Re*hearsed, every word of it! The whole livin' thing's a big goll-danged *trick!* There! Don't ye

b'lieve me? Me? That was with him when he 'ranged it? [*Still receiving no answer of word or gesture from the suddenly quiet woman, he returns his attention to his prisoner, whose wrist he shakes.*] You hear me, Til? I arrest ye for the murder. Moreover, I arrest ye for goin' to work and concealin' the corpse—by your own confession, mind ye—in some one or 'nother of Tolley's straw stacks—where I and the Pros'-cutor'll have a look in the mornin'—

MRS. WEATHERBURN [*bewildered, appealing*]. Bane, that ain't right! 'Tain't true! You're just—just twistin' the poor child's words about—that's what you're doin'—to your own ends.

BANE [*wheeling*]. Own ends? Own ends, ye say? I'll ask ye to weigh your words, Mis' Weatherburn. I vow! Next thing you'll be accusin' *me* of—of—most anything! Accusin' *me*, the Sheriff o' Twinskill County! Of—most anything!

[*Til stands as though untouched by all this, inert, entranced, staring at the door as if its panels were no barrier to her occult vision.*]

TIL. Comin' on swifter now, he is. Comin' on, comin' on. He's been by Whites' now, and they've see him. Mis' White's see him; in the light from the porch she see him. Now she's goin' back through the hall, white's a sheet. Now she's goin' acrost the dinin' room. Now she's to the telephone— [*Til's head swings irresistibly in the direction of the phone. As irresistibly the others' gazes follow. The bell begins to ring.*] Banes'— [*She glances at Mrs. Weatherburn, who does not move.*] Tolleys'— Jetherses'— [*Throwing off the Sheriff's hand, she runs to the instrument and puts the receiver to her ear.*] Yes? Yes? Quick, Mis' White! Yes? Quick—

[*Bane is upon her. Wresting the receiver from her hand, he thrusts her aside.*]

BANE [*in the phone*]. Who's there? Hullo! Hullo! Who's there? It's me, Bane — Sheriff Bane — me speakin'. What? Yes, I hear! What? Hullo! Hullo! Dang it, they're gone again! [*Rattling the hook.*] Hullo! *Goll* dang the thing! [*With a sudden malignant fury he strikes the instrument from the wall, so that it hangs swaying from one* screw, the wires broken.] There now, dang ye! Ring, will ye! Go on and ring! Ring! [*Turning around with a hand to his head, his eyes fall on Til, back at the door again, holding it wide, staring out.*] Goll dang ye, Til!

TIL. He's on the farm now. I hear the gate just now. In the roar and moan of the wind I hear the gate. [*Lifting her voice to a nerve-struck scream.*] John! John!

MRS. WEATHERBURN. Oh, *Til!*

BANE [*advancing*]. Oh, "*Til*"? I'll "*Til*" her! I'll "*Til*" the crazy! [*Dragging her back, he casts her violently on the floor. He slams the door with a force sufficient to carry away the latch, which falls in a clatter of bits about his feet.*]

MRS. WEATHERBURN. You broke the latch!

TIL [*from the floor*]. You broke the latch. Now you *can't* keep it shut.

BANE [*deep in his throat*]. *I* guess I can! *I* guess I can! [*He stands facing it, his two hands spread against it, his feet propped out solidly behind. Silence follows, the clock-tick silence of the room enclosed in the outer shell of storm. Bane remains propped and motionless, breathing heavily. Mrs. Weatherburn sinks into a chair and holds her hands crossed on her breast. Til, still on the floor to one side of the door, holds her head erect and attentive.*]

TIL [*after a time*]. That's the other gate. The near one.

BANE [*his breath rasping*]. I never hear a thing! [*The hush runs on again for seconds.*]

TIL. You hear that, then? On the gravel? He's come out of the wind now. He's got his feet on the ground now. Hear that?

BANE. No! No! No! [*Another moment.*]

TIL. On the step. There. Standin'. Standin' still. [*The hush returns. After a space of it a voice becomes audible, racked, thin, almost falsetto. It is the voice of Bane, to the door.*]

BANE. Go 'way! Go 'way, I tell ye! [*Beating the panel.*] Go 'way!

TIL. He ain't gone. Still standin'.

BANE [*after a moment, putting his lips nearer the wood*]. I'll tell ye somethin' there! Ye listenin'? I'll tell ye somethin'. I got a gun here. It's your own gun, John, and it's loaded with bird shot. Right here to my hand I got it. [*Removing one hand cautiously from the door, he gropes out blindly to the right, where the shotgun rests against the wall beside the chair.*] Right here I got it, John! [*Finding he cannot reach it, he takes his other hand from the door, and is about to take the furtive, necessary step, when the door begins to swing inward, slowly. A cackle emerges from Til's open mouth; a kind of high, tight, tittering of the palate. Bane flings himself against the door again, slamming it tight.*] No, ye don't! No, ye don't! [*A summons sounds on the panels, a muffled knock as of a soft glove.*]

BANE [*screeching in his throat*]. No, ye won't! Ye can't! Ye can't touch me, John Weatherburn! No, sir. 'Twan't my fault! 'Twa'n't! Ye oughtn't've called me a liar, there by the gate! Not with a gun in my hand! Ye oughtn't've dare strike me! Not when I had a gun in my hand! Ye ought've known me better'n that, John! Your own fault, John! 'Twa'n't m-i-n-e——

VOICE FROM WITHOUT. Open the door, Bane! Open, I tell you!

MRS. WEATHERBURN [*wondering*]. That's never the voice of John. [*Bane, wilting and letting go the door, relapses into the chair and claps both his hands over his eyes.*]

BANE. It's Cantpole. Thank God! it's only Cantpole, after all.

TIL [*from the floor*]. John's went and bring the Pros'cutor along. [*The door swings open. Mr. Cantpole enters, removing his soft hat and shaking out the wet. He looks at Mrs. Weatherburn, still seated in her chair.*]

CANTPOLE. Good evening, Mrs. Weatherburn. I just dropped up from Mr. White's place—as by *arrangement* with Mr. Bane. [*He peers around the door at the figure huddled in the chair there.*]

So, Sheriff? Just as well I came, eh? What's all this I hear? Good *Lord!* What's *that?*

> [*As from the tail of his eye he perceives something scuttling past him on the floor and out of the door.*]

MRS. WEATHERBURN. That's only Til. Til, where you goin' to?

TIL [*lost in the darkness without*]. To—*horrify* myself! [*And fainter, still further off.*] John! John!

[*The Curtain Falls.*]

THE DANCE BELOW

A Satirical Drama

By Hudson Strode and Larry Hornthal

CHARACTERS

JOHN BATES [*the C. P. O.*].
PAUL KNOX [*the Poet*].
AGNES [*the Girl*].

THE DANCE BELOW, under the title THE JIG, was first produced on the evening
of May the ninth by the Birmingham Little Theatre at Birmingham, Alabama, as
a 1927 prize play under the direction of Bernard Szold, and simultaneously the
same night the play was presented by The Blackfriar Players at the University of
Alabama under the direction of Mr. Strode.
The original cast at the University of Alabama was as follows:

THE C.P.O.	*Bruce Robertson.*
THE POET	*Bryant Sells.*
THE GIRL	*Charlcie Hedge.*

THE DANCE BELOW

A SATIRICAL DRAMA　By HUDSON STRODE AND LARRY HORNTHAL

[*The* SCENE *is a bare looking room in Hell. The walls are a dingy gray, and on either side of a blackened door in the center of the back wall two windows give out on a gray monotonous landscape with perhaps a dead black tree or two rearing up in the distance. There is another door towards the back of the right wall, and right center there is a bare table with two chairs. Down front left center there is a stiff wooden bench. There are two other plain chairs in the room. It is about four-thirty in the afternoon. The air is very still. An unfriendly pale green light seems to haunt the faces of the actors who move more or less noiselessly as if wearing rubber soles.*

When the curtain rises Paul Knox, lost in thought, is seated on the bench leaning forward smoking a pipe. On earth Paul has been a poet and the audience guesses the fact at once by his yellow and slightly wavy hair, his melancholy blue-gray eyes and the prematurely old expression about his face when his features are in repose. He is dressed in light gray flannel trousers and his soft white shirt is open at the throat. There is something delicately fine and yet sculptural in the chiseling of his features.

John Bates stands at the center door looking out expectantly. He is a tall, thickset, red-blooded brunet who in life was a Chief Petty Officer in the navy, and in Hell he still wears his blue uniform with a sailor's swagger and all the high spirits of his prime thirty years. Bates, puffing on a cigarette, glances towards Knox and then back again out the door.]

BATES [*speaking finally in a deep voice*]. Not a sign of anybody yet.

[*Knox shifts his position, but does not reply. Bates regards him for a moment and then comes to the bench and slaps him affectionately on the shoulder.*]

BATES. Cheer up, old man, you look like you were waiting for a funeral, instead of your wife. What are you so glum about? Ever since you heard that your wife was coming you've looked worried—unhappy—like you were afraid to see her. You were crazy about her, weren't you?

KNOX. Yes, yes, of course, mad about her. I, I loved her too much, perhaps. I loved her more than life—more than my poetry [*smiles*], more than my hope of salvation—more than anything—but—

BATES. But what?

KNOX. I never felt sure that I made her happy. And I tried hard—I did everything I could. Sometimes, maybe for just a single moment I felt that she was mine entirely, and then a strange look would come into her eyes—as if she wished—oh, I don't know what. And I went on groping—but I never felt sure.

BATES. Aw, I bet it was just your imagination.

KNOX. Perhaps . . . .

BATES. Maybe you were too easy on her—always giving in to her. . . . Some women like rough treatment—and when they do I believe in giving it to 'em. *Rough.*

[*Bates moves to chair nearest center, emphasizing his roughness by putting his foot on it.*]

KNOX [*smiles*]. No, Agnes was too sensitive for that. [*Changes.*] You know, another thing that worries me terribly is wondering how she is going to stand this place. It isn't very beautiful down here. Don't you suppose you could get some flowers—or something to brighten it up?

481

BATES. Well, of all idiots—flowers in Hell. That *is* a good one.

[*Bates laughs.*]

KNOX. Well, we *should* do *something* to make it sort of beautiful for Agnes.

BATES. Say, you forget this isn't an afternoon tea. We're here to pay for our sins like the Good Book says.

KNOX. Sins? No, mistakes, maybe. [*Smiles.*] Like planting turnips in a flower bed when the seeds look alike.

BATES. There you go again—flowers! Quit dreaming, can't you? What do you want me to do? Pin a *Welcome to Our Happy Home* sign over the door?

KNOX. No—just sort of make her happy. You're so light hearted. Maybe you can make her laugh—that helps sometimes.

BATES. Say, you forget I'm expecting company, too. *My* girl will probably arrive about the same time as yours. I'll have a job myself getting her adjusted.

KNOX. Oh, I did forget. I'm sorry. [*With a friendly smile.*] But we'll have to see lots of each other just the same. I wonder which one of them will get here first?

BATES. Well, you got the news about your Agnes before I heard my Aggie had kicked off, so—I don't know. [*A new thought.*] Say, it's funny our girls having mighty near the same names.

KNOX. Yes, isn't it? I—I hope they like each other.

BATES. They probably won't. Women never do.

KNOX [*looks out of the window at the grayness*]. I do wish there was just one beautiful sunset for her. [*Sadly.*] But how do I know she would like it? I gave her sunsets up on earth and—and she cried. [*Changes.*] Did your Aggie love pretty things?

BATES. Yes, she liked 'em all right. She—

KNOX [*enthusiastically*]. Was she lovely and still—like a bird before it sings?

BATES [*doubtfully agreeing*]. Well, kinda—but not for long. [*Pompously.*] She sure did love me. I remember one one night before the fleet shipped south . . . .

KNOX. Was it moonlight—or just pale silver stars?

BATES. *Nah.* It was dark. The dock was full of coal dust.

KNOX [*slowly*]. Agnes would have to have stars.

BATES. My girl Aggie didn't want any stars—nor anything but me. She loved me like Hell.

KNOX. I loved Agnes like—Heaven. I tried to make it for her too.

BATES. Yeh, I know. Queer they don't understand—trying don't always work.

KNOX. No, I suppose not. Anyhow I kept trying to give her all the beauty and color I could.

BATES. They like the dark sometimes. Aggie liked the coal dust. She said it made things more human-like—or something like that. She'll like it down here all right with me!

KNOX. I'm afraid my Agnes won't. She wasn't like that. She couldn't have stood ugly things. That's why she's coming down here to-day. I wasn't there to show her how lovely things were. That's why she took to drugs. This place—if there was only one beautiful thing! [*His face lightens.*] I know. I have a jasmine flower she gave me when we were first in love. I've kept it dried in a book. Anything is better than nothing.

> [*Knox goes out, putting his pipe in his pocket. Bates, smiling at Knox's sentimentalism, sits down on the bench with his legs thrust out on it—hums. A timid knock is heard. Bates starts up joyously—he hesitates—throws down cigarette butt and steps on it; then walks behind bench and adjusts his collar and hair. The knock is repeated. The door opens slowly. A thin, dark-eyed, dark-haired girl about twenty-five years of age enters. There are circles beneath her eyes. Her skin is ivory white, her lips crimson. She wears a dark dress with a string of black beads about her neck. She is half afraid—timid.*]

BATES [*holding out his arms to her and uttering a cry of delight*]. Aggie! [*The girl turns, sees him and rushes into his arms.*]

AGNES. John!

[*Her voice is low, passionate, perhaps a bit husky. A long embrace. They draw apart. He holds her at arms' length. They embrace again. She strokes his hair and face and utters a little sob of joy. She staggers slightly. He catches her.*]

BATES. Why, Aggie—?

AGNES [*passes her hand across her brow*]. It's all right. I'm just a little faint. I—I didn't know just what it would all be like down here—I'm so tired—and I—I'm overcome with joy at seeing you. Oh, John, this is too wonderful!

[*She throws her arms about him again.*]

BATES. My own Aggie. [*He draws her to him and pats her shoulder.*] Gee, but I'm glad to see you.

[*He starts to lead her toward center of stage. She begins to look about her.*]

AGNES. And this is Hell! Why, it doesn't look at all the way I had expected. It looks a lot like earth. [*Radiant and almost hysterical.*] And, John, I have you! I have you! It isn't Hell at all. They've sent me to Heaven. [*He kisses her hands. She begins to laugh.*] John, they've sent us to Heaven. [*She laughs and laughs triumphantly.*] Why, what are you looking so serious about?

BATES [*worried*]. I've seen people tricked down here before. They think it's one way, and they learn it's another. They think they've escaped, and they get caught. Hell plays a cat and mouse game sometimes.

AGNES [*cheerfully*]. Don't be silly. What can happen? We're together— and— [*She draws away suspiciously. Whispers.*] You don't love some one else?

BATES. Of course not.

AGNES. Then forget it. Oh, John, I'm so happy. [*She catches him around the neck again.*] It's Heaven, John, it's Heaven. We're alone. [*Seductively.*] dead—and alone in Hell. *He's* gone to Heaven. Nothing can happen. We're just you and I, John. [*She reaches for his mouth. A singing is heard from the next room, a bar or two from Mario's last aria in "La Tosca." Agnes steps back terrified, straining to listen. Whispers distractedly.*] What—what—is— it?

BATES. Why, what's the matter?

AGNES [*her hands moving wildly, whispers*]. That voice—that tune—he used to sing it to me—when he was unhappy. [*Louder.*] John, it's his ghost!

BATES [*soothing her, smiling*]. Oh, it's nothing. Just a pal of mine. He's wonderful—you'll be crazy about him. He's a *poet* and everything.

AGNES [*terrified*]. A poet! I knew it —Oh, my God! what are we going to do?

[*She moves quickly left.*]

BATES [*slowly following her*]. You don't mean—

AGNES. Yes—my husband.

[*Bates turns away in horrified astonishment and mutters "cat and mouse" as Knox enters with book. Knox is surprised and delighted to see Agnes.*]

KNOX. Oh, my darling, you've come. I'm so happy to see you. [*He takes her tenderly in his arms and kisses her brow. She smiles wanly.*] I know you're tired. I'm so sorry I didn't meet you—but I didn't know which route you were coming by. [*He starts to lead her to the bench, when he remembers Bates.*] Oh, Agnes, this is my friend, John Bates. He's a trump. Really, it would have been unbearable here without him. John, my wife.

BATES [*strained*]. How do you do.

AGNES [*strained*]. I'm very pleased.

[*Knox and Agnes sit down on bench.*]

KNOX. Yes, Bates has been a life saver. He's great fun. One of those sailor fellows who keeps you laughing all the time. By the way, he's expecting some one too. *His* girl.

AGNES. Really! How splendid.

KNOX. Yes, isn't it. We shall all have some happy times together. Bring up a chair close to us, Bates.

[*Bates sits astride a chair, center stage.*]

KNOX. Tell us about your trip, dear. Was it very tiring?

AGNES. Rather. But it was interesting. Strange. The scenery was so different. New. I was tired of that on earth. But tell me about yourself. What do you do down here?

BATES. Mostly work.

AGNES. What sort of work?

KNOX. Awful work! Digging graves for mangled illusions. Ugh. It's terrible.

BATES. It's not as terrible as mine. Picture me making little hooks out of pins to catch weak souls. Me with these paws! When night comes, I'm dead tired messing with the blooming things.

KNOX. Don't let's talk about work, John. Tell Agnes what you saw the other day. [*Enthusiastically.*] She'll like that!

[*He catches her hand, holds it tenderly.*]

BATES. It wasn't much. I saw a kid come down the street that leads to the Museum of Dead Dreams. Some men were laying a road of oyster shells—dirty things. The kid picked them up and washed them, and built a castle. A right pretty little place.

AGNES. A child down here?

BATES. She didn't stay. It was a mistake.

AGNES. And the castle?

BATES. Oh, the men kicked that down, of course.

KNOX. Such a pity. [*Musingly.*] Yet, beauty is always beauty—even in the dust. I have seen dead hopes that shone like phosphorus in dark water. [*At the word water the girl looks at Bates and sighs. Knox hears her, and brightens his tone.*] You must be hungry, dear. We'll have some tea. I'll get it at once. Bates, you tell Agnes some of your stories while I'm preparing it. Tell her that joke about the artist who came down here looking for new landscapes.

[*Knox leaves.*]

BATES [*rising and coming close to her and speaking in a low voice*]. So that's him? The one you sent to the country for his health? He died out there, didn't he?

AGNES [*dully*]. Yes.

BATES. And they sent you here, for fooling him?

AGNES. Yes—that and the dope. But I wanted to come, anyhow.

BATES. Wanted to? Wanted to come *here*?

AGNES. Yes. You remember you used to say "I love you like . . ."?

BATES [*bitterly*]. Hell?

AGNES [*looking off*]. It was easy to take dope, and go down. It's great!

You go way down out of people's way. You sink where they won't bother you any more.

BATES. Do you still take it?

AGNES. Yes, sometimes—in the late afternoon—when I am tired. [*She takes from her pocket a tiny silver container, like a lipstick holder.*] See? [*Gazing at it thoughtfully.*] Dope is sweet when it leads to . . . .

BATES [*bitterly*]. Hell?

AGNES [*looking up at him*]. No—you. [*She replaces the container. Bates leans forward—remembers—then stops—*]

BATES. What about Knox?

AGNES. I've never really loved him, John—never wanted him as I have you.

BATES. Why, he's ten times as good as I am. He's a gentleman and got a college education and everything—a heart of gold, too, and he loves you, Aggie. His face has brightened up so since you came.

AGNES. He *is* wonderful. Why didn't I love him? It's queer. . . .

BATES [*thoughtfully*]. You'll *have* to love him now.

AGNES. Why do you say that?

BATES. It's the only decent thing to do.

AGNES. I can't—I love you, John. You know it. I'm going to live with you.

BATES [*looks at her miserably*]. No. You're his.

AGNES [*jumping up*]. I'm not—not *now.* I came down here for you! I knew you—*needed* me. He doesn't. He has his roses—his sunsets!

[*She looks out of the window. The sky is gray.*]

AGNES [*slowly*]. Oh, I forgot—there aren't any—here.

BATES [*dully*]. Yes, that's why you've got to stay with him.

AGNES [*pleadingly*]. I can't. I can't do it. Why, it will be forever—for eternity. I'm going to stay with you!

BATES [*with a twisted smile*]. Oh, no, you're not.

AGNES [*wonderingly*]. John?

BATES. Not after what he told me.

AGNES [*anxiously*]. What did he tell you? What?

BATES. That he loved you like—Heaven. [*Agnes droops.*] Didn't you love him at all?

AGNES [*slowly*]. I did love him—in a

way—but, oh, John, not like you. Don't you remember?

BATES [*rising impatiently*]. Sure; I remember everything.

AGNES [*leaning toward him*]. Down on the docks—no stars—nothing—just us—dark—Oh, why didn't he go to Heaven where he belongs? When he died out there in the country I thought we'd got rid of him. Why didn't he go to Heaven? [*Loud and rebellious.*] Why did he have to come down here and *spoil* things?

BATES. He had to. It was part of the Jig.

AGNES. The Jig? What's that?

BATES. That's what Knox calls it. Us and life and eternity all mixed up.

AGNES. Is that why he's down here?

BATES. That's my opinion, but the higher authorities said he wasn't quite good enough for Heaven. I think he made 'em jealous.

AGNES. Jealous? How?

BATES. Oh, all the time worshiping Greek gods who don't have morals. He just out and said they were more beautiful. No wonder they sent him down here. He should have known better. [*Changing his tone.*] I guess they didn't do so bad, though. They sent you to him.

AGNES [*almost stridently*]. To him! No. I tell you no. I thought I was coming to you. I won't stand it. I've gone through enough up on *earth*. My conscience eating into me like poison, burning me like vitriol, scratching lines and smudging shadows into my face.

BATES. Well, the dope didn't help things any either.

AGNES [*softly*]. Ah, the dope. It brought me peace and sweet dreams of you, John—and—it was always there as a symbol of escape. [*Slowly and subtly significantly towards the audience.*] An overdose can kill so easily, John. We must run away. I can't bear to look into Paul's eyes again. They torture me. They are so trusting—so—so accusing in their pale innocence. I can't face him. You must take me away. Now. Quick, before he comes back, John.

[*Pleading and commanding, she stands close to him.*]

BATES [*stands stolidly, right front, but his face is working. He shakes his head negatively*]. It wouldn't be right. He's my pal, Aggie.

AGNES [*coaxingly*]. Oh, John, it will mean so much less suffering in the end. He's bound to find out sooner or later. Let's go quietly—quickly—now! I tell you I can't face his eyes—and I came down to Hell for you, John—I'd do anything—for you—I'd go through anything for you. I'm the only one you've ever really loved! We're not responsible for our love. The moment I saw you, John, I knew there was no use fighting against it. [*Slowly, pleadingly.*] And you said I was a magnet drawing you. [*Faster.*] We didn't ask each other questions. I didn't care *who* you were or *what* you were. I only knew we wanted each other, John. We were meant for each other. You can't desert me now. You've got to take me away. [*She leans against him seductively and moves her fingers up his arm.*] Please, John—don't you remember those nights down on the dock—the warm darkness—no stars—just the rhythmic beating of the waves, John—and the throbbing of our hearts. [*She has slipped her arm about his neck and has her mouth close to his ear. He begins to weaken. Plaintively.*] You will take me, John— [*Low.*] You will—take me? Yes? You will? You will?

BATES [*like a man submitting to a power beyond his control*]. Yes. [*He gathers her passionately to him and kisses her.*] Come, let's go quick.

[*They start out.*]

KNOX [*calling from the other room*]. I haven't forgotten you. Tea's almost ready. I'm coming right away.

[*Bates starts and draws away from Agnes, coming down to left front, struck by a grim recollection.*]

AGNES. Why, what is it? Quick. Let's go before he comes.

BATES [*miserably and dismally resigned*]. I forgot— [*He shakes his head slowly.*] There's no place to go—that's part of the punishment—You're fixed—You can't run off—anywhere—in Hell! [*He throws himself onto the bench as if giving up. Agnes stands center stage rooted with horror at the thought, and whispers with a ghastly expression on her face.*] Fixed!

[*Knox enters bearing tray with tea*

pot, cups, biscuits, etc., and sets the tray down on the table.]

KNOX. Not very dainty, I'm afraid, Agnes, dear, but rigorous simplicity is the keynote in this place. Now that you've come, however, dear, we can expect something really attractive. [*He looks toward Bates, who sits facing audience.*] Eh, Bates? Oh, bring a chair over. Suppose you sit here, Agnes. [*He pulls out chair at table for her so that she will be seated between them, facing audience. Knox is at Agnes' right. Bates at her left.*] I'm sorry *your* friend hasn't come, Bates. I wonder what's delayed her.

BATES. I dunno. Maybe they found they had made a mistake—and sent her on to Heaven. They say it's just a toss up whether some folks go to Heaven or Hell, anyhow. Hah, think of the angels throwing up a golden coin, and calling "Heads, Heaven; tails, Hell!" ha, ha!

AGNES [*shuddering*]. Please!

BATES. Oh, sorry, I'm sure, mam.

KNOX. Did he tell you that joke, Agnes?

AGNES. What joke?—oh, about the mix-up—the Jig?

KNOX. No, about the artist.

AGNES. No, we got—to talking about the Jig—and [*Suddenly looking at Knox who isn't at the moment looking at her.*] What *is* the explanation of it all, Paul? Surely you know *now*.

KNOX [*looking very serious. The atmosphere becomes tense—unearthly—still*]. No, that's the frightening thing. A year has gone by and we know nothing yet. There are, of course, rumors afloat. But there's really been no explanation.

BATES [*frightened by the unknown, his voice low*]. Yeh, that's the biggest Hell—not knowing anything—if they would just tell us. A man can stand anything—if he knows.

AGNES [*slowly in a low strained voice*]. How long are we in for?

KNOX. They say eternity.

AGNES. How long is eternity?

KNOX. Another riddle. Perhaps æons and æons of years. [*Agnes' face works unhappily.*] Sometimes an eternity is in one kiss. A brief dream may be an eternity, or a guilty thought.

BATES [*grimly and defiantly*]. It's forever and ever and there's no way out. That's what it is.

[*He rises and walks to other side of the room and pulls out a cigarette. Agnes has become more and more nervous.*]

BATES [*calling back as he lights his cigarette*]. It's the crazy people that are the lucky ones.

KNOX. But even they have bad dreams. Haven't you heard them scream?

[*A little cry from Agnes as she moves restlessly.*]

KNOX. Oh, my dear, forgive us for talking of gruesome things. And our tea is getting cold. Will you pour it? And, oh, I had forgotten. [*He gets dried jasmine from the book.*] Look!

AGNES [*pauses in pouring the tea*]. What is it?

KNOX. The little flower you gave me when we were first in love. [*He stands behind her lovingly. She fingers it tremblingly. She and Bates steal a miserable glance at each other.*] Remember?

AGNES. Oh, oh, yes. How sweet of you to keep it.

[*He leans over to look into her face. She turns her head.*]

KNOX. Look at me, dear.

AGNES [*putting him off*]. Just a moment. [*Reaching for her hand bag.*] I must look a fright. I haven't even powdered my nose.

[*She fumbles in the bag. Knox gently places his hand over the vanity.*]

KNOX. You don't need that. Look at me, dear. I haven't really had a good look at you since you came.

[*He tenderly tries to draw her face toward him. She shivers.*]

AGNES. It's so cold in here, Paul.

KNOX. I'll close the window.

[*He goes to the window.*]

[*Agnes, in a fit of nervous trembling, takes out the silver container with the dope and with a look of desperation on her face shakes the whole contents into Knox's cup. Then she begins to powder her nose. The men return to their places. Agnes looks at Knox with growing dread. Bates returns to the table and takes up his tea cup.*]

KNOX [*trying to be cheerful, stirring his tea*]. You see it isn't so bad down here—things are much the same as in life. There is just no color here. A great drabness sobers everything. You'll get used to it. [*He drinks.*] You have to make adjustments. You can't *change* anything—it's too late for that. But you can get used to doing without things —without the perfume of life—like this poor little jasmine flower—But how sweet are the dried memories it symbolizes! [*Here he finishes his tea.*] It all depends on how you take it here. Do you remember Hamlet's line: There's nothing either good or bad but thinking makes it so?

[*Agnes has become more and more nervous.*]

AGNES [*half rising*]. Paul, the tea is so strong—will you get some hot water?

KNOX. Why, certainly, dear—I forgot.

[*He goes out. Agnes rises and begins to breathe hard. She walks down left, making inarticulate noises and places the back of her hand over her mouth as if to stifle some emotional agony.*]

BATES. Why, what's the matter?

AGNES. I—I—Oh, my God—

BATES [*following her. Both of them are down stage*]. For Heaven's sake, what's the matter with you! You look ill.

AGNES. John, I couldn't stand it any longer—I couldn't face eternity. And I gave him the dope—all of it—I sent him out of the room on purpose. I—I've killed him—and I couldn't bear to see him die.

BATES [*astonished, backing away from her*]. You gave him all the dope. You —you've killed him! [*With rising bitterness he comes toward her and grasping her by the shoulder roughly he wheels her about to face him.*] The God Almighty nerve of it. [*Contemptuously.*] *You* killing a man like *him.* I won't stand for it, I tell you. [*He catches her by the throat.*] *You* killing *him!*

[*He shakes her violently and forces her to her knees.*]

AGNES [*calling out*]. I couldn't stand his eyes I tell you. [*Screaming.*] John don't *kill* me!

[*At the word "kill" he throws her to the floor. Her beads break and scatter. He laughs as once again he grimly recollects.*]

BATES. Kill you! What a pair of fools we are. *I* can't kill *you.* You're already dead—*You* can't kill Knox— *He's* already dead. *You're* dead. *I'm* dead. We are *all* dead. You can't die but once. That's part of the Jig. [*Bitterly.*] WE'RE FIXED!

[*Agnes is on the floor gasping. She looks up towards the audience horrified at the inevitability of the situation. Knox enters.*]

KNOX. Why, what's up?

[*He hastily puts the hot water on the table and comes behind the two as Bates stoops and begins searching for the lost beads. Agnes rises.*]

BATES. Your wife broke her beads.

[*Bates rises.*]

KNOX [*laughs*]. Broke her beads? Why, I thought something terrible had happened. I thought she screamed. Agnes was always breaking her beads up on earth. [*Bates rises as Knox stoops down between them.*] If this doesn't seem too funny—down here—looking on the floor for beads. [*He looks up towards audience.*] Isn't it amazing how much like the earth this place is? Hell is just life over again. Isn't it?

AGNES [*facing audience bitterly and utterly broken*]. Exactly.

BATES [*smiling grimly, facing audience*]. Exactly.

KNOX [*dreamily*]. Exactly.

[*Curtain.*]

A BUDAPEST SALESMAN SHOULD NOT READ FRENCH ILLUSTRATED MAGAZINES

A Comedy

By Béla Szenes

CHARACTERS

ARTHUR KONDOR.
MRS. KONDOR.
MARY [*a maid*].
THE PRIVATE SECRETARY TO THE PRESIDENT OF THE FRENCH REPUBLIC.
THE BRITISH AMBASSADOR.
THE TURKISH AMBASSADOR.
FIRST GENERAL.
SECOND GENERAL.
JEAN [*a valet*].
THE PRINCESS.
THE PRINCE.
TWO DUELING SECONDS.

TIME: *The Present.*

A BUDAPEST SALESMAN SHOULD NOT READ FRENCH ILLUSTRATED MAGAZINES

A COMEDY

By BÉLA SZENES

[SCENE: *The modest suburban apartment of the Budapest salesman, Arthur Kondor.*]

SCENE I

MRS. KONDOR [*a pretty young woman, sits beside a table crying*]. Half-past five . . . .

MARY. Do stop crying, ma'am, I'm sure nothing has happened to Mr. Kondor.

MRS. KONDOR. He always was home by four o'clock of a Sunday. My poor, dear, darling husband. It must have been a tramway accident.

MARY [*at the window*]. Oh, ma'am, there is the master. I can see him coming.

MRS. KONDOR [*in a different voice*]. Oh, so this is the time the wretch comes home!

MARY. He is reading some paper; that is why he walks so slowly.

MRS. KONDOR [*wipes her eyes*]. Here I am crying my eyes out like the fool I am, while he has plenty of time to read the paper in the street. Well, I'll show him what's what.

[*She sits in a corner of the room, takes up some needlework and awaits her husband with rigidly severe features.*]

MARY [*trying to say something*]. Please, ma'am . . . .

MRS. KONDOR [*snappily*]. You had better get out to the kitchen.

MARY [*offended*]. Yes'm.

[*Exits.*]

KONDOR [*enters, carrying a number of the French illustrated magazine "L'Illustration" in his hand. He greets his wife pleasantly*]. How do, darling.

MRS. KONDOR [*rigidly*]. Good evening.

KONDOR [*accepting the situation*]. Good evening? Very well, then, good evening.

[*He sits down beside the table, calmly spreads out his paper, begins to read.*]

MRS. KONDOR. It is half-past six.

KONDOR [*serene*]. Five minutes past.

MRS. KONDOR. Is that all you have to say?

KONDOR. Well, what else should I say?

MRS. KONDOR. I have only one Sunday afternoon in the whole week.

KONDOR. As far as I know, I haven't got two, either.

MRS. KONDOR. But I am not in the habit of spending that Sunday afternoon at the Salesmen's Club, as you are.

KONDOR [*with the utmost calm*]. You know quite well that I am not a member at the Tokey Club.

MRS. KONDOR. Sure, it was Révész who dragged you up to that horrid club again.

KONDOR. Sure.

[*He calmly continues his reading.*]

MRS. KONDOR. Of course. Révész again. I knew it all along. If Révész chooses to tell you to jump into the river, you'll jump into the river.

KONDOR. That is not probable.

MRS. KONDOR [*working herself into a fury*]. And if Révész chose to tell you to pitch your wife into the river, you'd pitch your wife into the river.

KONDOR. That's a question worth considering.

MRS. KONDOR. Révész, Révész, it's Révész all the time. . . .

KONDOR. My dear, leave Révész alone. Can't you see I am reading?

MRS. KONDOR. What paper is that?

KONDOR. A French paper. It is called [*Pronouncing in English.*] Lilustrashon.

491

MRS KONDOR. Since when are you in the habit of reading French papers?

KONDOR. Since four o'clock this afternoon.

MRS. KONDOR. Have you brought it from the club?

KONDOR. That's it.

MRS. KONDOR. How can you have taken one of the club's newspapers?

KONDOR. I walked into the reading room. There on the table it lay. What sort of a magazine is this? I asked the boy. A French magazine, he said. *L'Illustration*. He pronounced it in that funny way. I suppose he can't spell properly. What is the use of a French paper here, I asked myself. Who on earth can read French in this place? So I just brought it home with me.

MRS. KONDOR. Why, can you perhaps read French?

KONDOR. I am going to keep it for little Paul. As soon as he can go to school, I'll have him taught French—so why shouldn't there be a French paper in the house—what?

MRS. KONDOR. So you mean to show off to your son about it, eh?

KONDOR. Of course. A child looks up to his parents in quite a different way if he sees them reading French papers.

MRS. KONDOR. But considering your son is still in long clothes, you can safely put that paper away.

KONDOR [*quietly goes on reading*]. Why should I put it away?

MRS. KONDOR. Your son won't need it before he is six.

KONDOR. Well, I will just about have finished reading it by that time.

MRS. KONDOR. You want to read that paper for six years?

KONDOR. Reading French is not as easy as you think.

MRS. KONDOR. Especially for a person who can't read at all.

KONDOR. Easy, my dear, easy. As a matter of fact, I was always considered a very good reader. [*Reads, pronouncing English fashion.*] Monsieur le Président dans sa maison—you see, there is nothing the matter with my reading.

MRS. KONDOR. Well, and what does that mean?

KONDOR. Well, I am not quite positive about that. But I can understand a good deal—especially if I read the pictures that match.

MRS. KONDOR. I suppose you will say that you speak French perfectly, next.

KONDOR [*growing irritable*]. I could hardly learn French perfectly well since four o'clock this afternoon, could I? It's good enough if I've learnt as much as is needed for everyday use. Here is this picture, for instance—here they put under it: Le Président—you see that's French, but I understand quite *well* what it means.

MRS. KONDOR. Very clever of you. Of course it means the president. I suppose that is the President of the French Republic.

KONDOR. You see, dear, you are beginning to understand a bit of French, too. One must only work with a will and one is sure to succeed. [*Contemplating the pictures enviously.*] Just to look at these pictures makes a fellow's heart ache. That's Life, that is! Not the sort of life we lead. The president! Le Président! Wouldn't it be fine if my picture were printed in there! But what on earth could they put under it? Le Arthur Kondor. Le salesman. [*He walks across to the sofa, goes on turning the pages of the magazine, then stretches himself on the sofa.*] That president chap is worth looking at, he's got such swell clothes on. [*Yawns.*] Goodness, but I'm sleepy.

MRS. KONDOR. Seems to me you are mostly sleepy.

KONDOR [*jovially*]. Well, my dear, can't I be sleepy even by day? [*Continues fingering the magazine.*] What a first-rate silk hat that president's got on! Looks as if he was just come from a wedding. This woman with the flowers that is standing by him is his wife. The president, Le Président, has just come home from the presidency and his wife receives him in their home. She doesn't receive him a bit like my wife receives me.

MRS. KONDOR. Why didn't you see you were born a president of the French Republic, then?

KONDOR. You bet if I had been asked before my birth what I wanted to be, I should have said I had rather be anything but commercial traveler to Fisher and Company's in Budapest. [*Goes on enjoying the pictures.*] Le Président! White-robed virgins stand behind his wife. That's what I call a reception. When I come home, I am received by Mary.

MRS. KONDOR. So you would like to be president of the French Republic.

KONDOR. Well, I should be content to be a vice-president, even. [*Turns the pages of the magazine.*] Or this other picture, [*Spelling slowly.*] Le Général. [*Vastly pleased with himself.*] Le Général—you see, I know what that means, too.

MRS. KONDOR. Le Général, the General. I expect it's some famous French general.

KONDOR. You see, I'm teaching you quite a bit of French. [*Studies the picture.*] Le Général. A General. If I could ever be a General like that chap, I'd give five years—of the life of my boss.

MRS. KONDOR. Now you want to be a general. But I remember a time when you were happy to be flat-footed.

KONDOR. I'm not. I only was.

MRS. KONDOR. If you were, you are still.

KONDOR. That's your mistake. Who'll be such a fool as to be flat-footed in times of peace? And what if I am? A General rides on horseback, anyway. [*Contemplates the picture.*] Le Général. And what a lot of decorations he's got dangling on his coat. If ever I had such proud crosses ornamenting my breast . . .

MRS. KONDOR [*laughs ironically*]. Your breast?

KONDOR. Why? What is the matter with my breast? My breast is as good as the breast of Krauss, whom your mother wanted you to marry.

MRS. KONDOR. Pray, what has Krauss to do with it?

KONDOR. I don't like personal remarks. They always come from your mother. But your mother would speak in a different vein if . . .

MRS. KONDOR. If what?

KONDOR. If I once would come home on horseback. And I could make things hum a bit at Fisher and Company's, too, if I once rode into the old shop at the head of my troops. And wouldn't the boss sit up if I walked into the office with the decorations upon my proud breast and asked for a raise.

MRS. KONDOR. I thought you meant to remain a General. What's the good of a raise, then? I suppose you don't mean to remain with the firm?

KONDOR [*reproachfully*]. It is all your fault if I am still with them, anyway.

MRS. KONDOR. You never told me you wanted to be a commander-in-chief.

KONDOR. I could have been bank manager ages ago.

MRS. KONDOR. A bank manager isn't a general.

KONDOR [*getting more and more sleepy*]. A man's a manager, then he advances to general manager, if all goes well, why shouldn't he, in time, be general altogether?

MRS. KONDOR. Get to sleep. That will be better for you. You are sleepy enough, anyway.

KONDOR [*continues looking at the illustrations*]. Races at Auteuil! What a picture! What perfect gentlemen walking all over the place! And just look at the way that fellow is riding. I am sure that must be a count. And what a lovely woman he is walking with. Sure that must be a princess. If the prince should hear about it, a nice mess she'll be in.

MRS. KONDOR. How do you know she isn't his wife?

KONDOR. This isn't the first time I see a husband and wife walking beside each other. Bit of a difference. I say, darling, do cover me up with a shawl. . . . I'm that sleepy. . . .

[*She covers him.*]

KONDOR. A count . . . If I were a count . . . And the princess would walk into Fisher and Company's to see me . . . [*Half asleep.*] The princess . . .

[*He has fallen asleep.*]

[*Mrs. Kondor carefully arranges the shawl, takes the magazine from his hand.*]

MARY [*enters*]. Please'm . . .

MRS. KONDOR. Sh-sh, your master is asleep.

[*Kondor mutters in his sleep.*]

MARY. See, ma'am, how uneasily he sleeps.

MRS. KONDOR. Sh-sh, Mary.

MARY [*bending over him, surprised*]. I suppose he is dreaming. What can he be dreaming about?

MRS. KONDOR. Sh-sh, Mary!

[*From the moment that Mary has entered the room, the scene has gradually become darker. As the last words are spoken it is entirely dark. Now it slowly grows light, the room is flooded with a curious kind of rose-colored light, which shows that the scenes that follow are pictures in a dream.*]

SCENE II

[*Kondor asleep on the sofa.*]

SECRETARY [*an elaborately elegant young man in evening dress, his shirt-front covered with decorations, shakes him awake*]. Mr. President . . . Mr. President . . .

KONDOR [*startled*]. What is it?

SECRETARY. Mr. President . . .

KONDOR [*sitting up*]. Who are you?

SECRETARY [*bowing obsequiously*]. A thousand pardons that I dared to disturb your afternoon repose . . .

KONDOR. "Repose" . . . that sounds well . . . he's a man with education . . .

SECRETARY. But I was obliged to disturb your repose . . .

KONDOR [*likes the sound of the word*]. "Repose" . . .

SECRETARY. . . . as the British and Turkish Ambassadors have been waiting for you for over a quarter of an hour.

KONDOR. Waiting for whom?

SECRETARY. For you, Mr. President.

KONDOR [*looking around*]. There is no one else in the room, the fellow is speaking to me. Won't you tell me, please . . . [*Standing up.*] but I beg your pardon . . . [*Introducing himself.*] my name is Kondor. May I know to whom I have the pleasure of speaking?

SECRETARY. Oh, Mr. President, you are pleased to make fun again.

KONDOR. Mr. President! Say, where on earth am I president?

SECRETARY. Will you allow me, Mr. President, a humble remark?

KONDOR. Why not? [*Aside.*] Why on earth does that fellow keep bowing?

SECRETARY. Allow me, Mr. President, as secretary who has the honor of being allowed to work on your staff, to express my admiration of the fact that in the midst of your numerous daily cares you have not lost your sense of humor—you are always full of fun and jokes.

KONDOR. Why, man, I couldn't be first commercial traveler to Fisher and Company's otherwise, could I?

SECRETARY. You are joking again, Mr. President. Who would believe that the President of the French Republic is, in spite of his daily cares, so full of fun?

KONDOR. Who is?

SECRETARY. The President of the French Republic.

KONDOR. Who is that?

SECRETARY. You, Mr. President.

KONDOR. I?

SECRETARY. Of course.

KONDOR. That's different. [*Walking up and down.*] That's different. Say . . .

[*Suddenly stops.*]

SECRETARY [*bowing*]. Mr. President . . . ?

KONDOR [*composed*]. Or, rather, don't say anything. In the end I'll wake up, anyway.

SECRETARY. You were saying, Mr. President . . . ?

KONDOR. Nothing, Mr. Secretary. So you say I am the President of the French Republic?

SECRETARY. Certainly, sir.

KONDOR [*quite resigned*]. Very well. I have dreamed worse things before this.

SECRETARY. Will you allow me, Mr. President, to give a brief sketch of our program for this afternoon?

KONDOR. Do, Mr. Secretary. Why not? Sketch away, if you like.

SECRETARY. You will first receive the British Ambassador, sir.

KONDOR. Very well.

SECRETARY. And the Turkish Ambassador.

KONDOR. I don't mind if I do.

SECRETARY. Or would you prefer not to receive the Turkish Ambassador?

KONDOR. Why shouldn't I? I have nothing against him.

SECRETARY. So you wish to receive him as well?

KONDOR [*with dignity*]. I wish to.

SECRETARY. So you will deign to receive the British and Turkish Ambassadors.

KONDOR. If you think I ought, I don't mind receiving a few smaller ones as well. Best to get it over.

SECRETARY. The audience is only going to be a formal one. You will kindly address a few polite remarks to their excellencies. . . .

KONDOR. All right, I'll address.

SECRETARY. It would create a good impression if you would address the British Ambassador in English, as you, Mr. President, happen to speak English as well as you speak French.

KONDOR. Just as well, you are right there.

[*Knocking heard at the door.*]

SECRETARY. There they are already. [*The door opens, enter two Ambassadors in full gala dress.*] Mr. President, Their Excellencies, the British and the Turkish Ambassadors.

[*The Ambassadors come forward, bow. Kondor bows clumsily.*]

SECRETARY. Mr. President, allow me to introduce Lord Hemendex, the British Ambassador.

BRITISH AMBASSADOR [*stepping forward*]. My name is Lord Hemendex.

KONDOR. Your name sounds familiar, your Lordship. Pleased to see you.

[*Shakes hands.*]

BRITISH AMBASSADOR. The pleasure is all mine.

SECRETARY [*solemnly*]. Mr. President, may I introduce Löwinger Pasha, the Turkish Ambassador.

TURKISH AMBASSADOR. My name is Löwinger Pasha.

KONDOR. What a very Turkish-sounding name. My name is Kondor.

TURKISH AMBASSADOR. Glad to meet you.

KONDOR. How do you do.

[*Friendly handshake. The Ambassadors stand stiffly at attention.*]

SECRETARY. Your Excellencies, His Excellency the President will now address to you a few words in the language of your own countries. If you please, Mr. President. English first.

KONDOR [*scratches his head*]. That's easier said than done. [*Stepping forward, aside.*] A good thing I know a few words of English. [*To the British Ambassador.*] Beefsteak, rumpsteak, howdoyoudo, goal, London!

[*British Ambassador bows profoundly.*]

KONDOR [*relieved*]. That went better than I expected. But what shall I say in Turkish? [*His face brightens up.*] Got it! [*Starts singing a popular music-hall ditty.*] Kemal, Kemal, Kemal!

[*Turkish Ambassador, profound bow.*]

SECRETARY. And now, Mr. Ambassador, pray be kind enough to transmit the kind regards of his Excellency the President of the French Republic to his Majesty the King of Great Britain.

KONDOR [*interrupting him*] . . . hoping that your honored firm will keep up the pleasant connection with our firm, as in the past, also in the future.

BRITISH AMBASSADOR [*bowing*]. Very well, Mr. President.

[*Knocking heard at door.*]

SECRETARY. Her Excellency, the wife of the President is starting for the opera. I beg your pardon, your Excellencies, but His Excellency the President wishes to speak to his wife.

[*Ambassadors bow and exeunt.*]

KONDOR [*politely*]. I hope soon to have the pleasure again, gentlemen. [*Calling after them at the door.*] Should you be in need of any articles in textiles, you can always find me at Fisher and Company's.

[*Enter Mrs. Kondor in an elegant opera wrap.*]

SECRETARY. The Presidentess!

KONDOR. I wonder now who that is going to be?

MRS. KONDOR. Arthur, I am off to the Opera.

KONDOR [*taken by surprise*]. Oh, I say! What a frock. [*Goes up to his wife and embraces her.*] I swear I will always have you dress like that—in my dreams.

MRS. KONDOR. I shall expect you in my box. If we have the gala box on the grand tier at our disposal, why should I not be there? Ta-ta, dearest. [*She floats away like a vision, but stops a moment at the door.*] Arthur, I am going on before you with mother.

KONDOR. What? Is your mother here, too? It's no good—a man can never be perfectly happy, not even in his dreams.

MRS. KONDOR [*affectionately*]. What a lucky woman I am to be the wife of the President of the French Republic! Au revoir, dearest.

KONDOR. Le au revoir. [*Mrs. Kondor has gone.*] Mr. Secretary, can I dictate a letter to you?

SECRETARY. Certainly, Mr. President.

KONDOR. Please write, Mr. Secretary:

Messrs. Fisher and Company, Textile Merchants, Budapest. Dear Sirs: With reference to the time I spent in your service at veritably dog's wages, I have the honor to inform you that I am now, thank the Lord, in an excellent situation in Paris. Concerning the advance of 150,000 crowns which you have made me, I have given orders to the Treasury for the return of the said sum to your address. Yours truly, Arthur Kondor, President of the French Republic.

SECRETARY [*finishes typing the letter, repeats*]. . . . Republic.

KONDOR [*sitting down on the sofa*]. So there! And now I should like to get a little rest.

SECRETARY [*stupefied*]. Rest? But you cannot be serious. Our program for to-day has still got some seventy items.

KONDOR. Leave me alone. I am tired, I want to rest.

SECRETARY [*reading from a list*]. Next on the program is an audience to the Minister of Commerce.

KONDOR. That is of no importance.

SECRETARY. Audience to the Naval Minister. The Papal Nuntius also wishes to pay his respects.

KONDOR [*astonished, sitting up on the sofa*]. Who did you say?

SECRETARY. The Papal Nuntius. The delegate of His Holiness the Pope.

KONDOR. Aren't you making a mistake?

SECRETARY. I am not, Mr. President. Next . . .

KONDOR. Wait a bit, Mr. Secretary. What do you think, does this Nuntius know that I . . . er . . .

SECRETARY. What, Mr. President?

KONDOR [*aside*]. It seems *he* does not know, either. Is the fellow blind?

SECRETARY [*reading mechanically*]. At five o'clock, you are to open the Apiary Exhibition; at half-past five, awarding of Academy prizes; at six, seeing off the King of England; at quarter-past six, visit to the Futurist exhibition; at half-past six, survey of the State Horse Stud. At seven, reception of the Shah of Persia; at seven-ten, unveiling of the Memorial; after a quarter-past seven, current affairs . . . .

KONDOR. Nice of you to have left a little time for those, too.

SECRETARY. At eight, reception in the small drawing room; at half-past, visit at the Opera House, it being a Wagner gala night.

KONDOR. Anything but that.

[*The stage is getting dark.*]

SECRETARY. But, Mr. President! Our program! Duty! The French Republic!

KONDOR [*his voice diminishing in force*]. I won't go, I won't go, I won't go . . .

[*The stage is entirely dark.*]

SCENE III

[*Kondor asleep. A general in full gala uniform, his breast covered with decorations, endeavors to shake him awake.*]

GENERAL. Mr. Field Marshal!

KONDOR [*continuing as at end of last scene*]. I won't go, let me sleep, let me sleep. I'm so tired!

GENERAL. Mr. Field Marshal! Wake up!

KONDOR [*waking up*]. Where am I?

GENERAL. At the Headquarters of the French Army.

KONDOR. Nice snug little place I've got to again. [*Lying down again.*] If I ever wake again, I'll tear that Lilustrashon to pieces.

GENERAL. Sir, the British-French War has broken out.

KONDOR. Well, and what if it has?

GENERAL. You are destined to lead the French troops.

KONDOR [*furiously*]. You wait until I do. [*Gets up from the sofa.*] A fellow hasn't got a moment's peace—but serves me right, a Budapest salesman should not read French illustrated papers. [*Motioning to a helmet lying on the table.*] What is that?

GENERAL. Your helmet, Mr. Field Marshal.

KONDOR. Helmet? [*Tries it on before the glass.*] Not half bad. See, if I'd walk up to my club with this on my head and pinned a few of those danglers on my coat the head waiter would behave quite differently, I'm sure. [*The General spreads a map on the table.*] What are you doing?

GENERAL. The map of the theater of war.

KONDOR. You can leave that here, at any rate. It will be a nice toy for my little boy. But why do you stick such a lot of little flags on it?

GENERAL. Mr. Field Marshal, please

decide where I shall place this flag—that will be the place where we will first attack the enemy. The place where we will stick this flag shall be made level with the ground.

KONDOR. Stop!

[*Rushes to the map.*]

GENERAL. What are you looking for, sir?

KONDOR [*bending over the map*]. Budapest. Here we are! Ninety-three Eagle Street. Fisher and Company. [*Triumphantly sticking in the flag.*] I'll teach them what's what! Giving Jones a bigger rise than they have given me, what? Level with the ground!

[*Without, the roar of cannon.*]

KONDOR [*startled*]. What's that?

GENERAL. Cannon, sir. [*Enthusiastically.*] The battle has begun.

KONDOR [*frightened out of his wits*]. And you mean to say you can hear it as far as this?

GENERAL. As we are within gun range . . . .

KONDOR [*hurries to the farthest side of stage*]. Even if I stand here?

GENERAL. Undoubtedly.

[*Firing again.*]

KONDOR [*getting more and more nervous*]. There it goes again. [*Wringing his hands.*] I had a good, secure berth in Budapest, whatever did I get myself in such a mess for?

GENERAL. Mr. Field Marshal, buckle on your sword.

KONDOR. Leave me alone. I am not a child to play with a sword.

[*Firing heard again.*]

KONDOR [*nervously*]. Go and tell them to stop that hammering, it gets on my nerves.

[*Firing.*]

SECOND GENERAL [*rushes on the scene, panting*]. Mr. Field Marshal!

KONDOR. What's that? Another chap? What's going on here? A fancy dress ball?

SECOND GENERAL [*still out of breath*]. Sir—I have just come from the front. The soldiers want to see their leader.

KONDOR. Meaning me?

SECOND GENERAL. Yes. The only thing that can save us now is your personal appearance in the firing line.

KONDOR. Then you are lost.

SECOND GENERAL. Sir, you refuse to go to the front at the head of your troops?

KONDOR. Not just now. Another time.

FIRST GENERAL. But as Commander-in-Chief . . . .

KONDOR. Leave me alone. Anyway, I am unfit for service. I am a sick man.

[*Sits on the sofa.*]

FIRST GENERAL. But, sir, you are strong and healthy.

KONDOR. In times of peace. But not in war times.

SECOND GENERAL. From head to foot, there is nothing whatever the matter with you, sir.

KONDOR. But the foot, man, the foot! With such a flat foot one cannot possibly fight at the front. I have a medical certificate to that effect.

FIRST GENERAL. But you will ride on horseback. You will fling yourself into the saddle . . . .

KONDOR. Fling myself? I am not in the habit of flinging myself. I don't even fling myself into the subway, still less into a saddle. If you wish to fling yourselves, you may go on ahead.

FIRST GENERAL. Sir, when our country, when France is at stake, you cannot be afraid to risk a life?

KONDOR. Not even of risking two. You are both welcome to go to the front.

SECOND GENERAL. You undertook to command our troops. You undertook . . . .

KONDOR [*interrupting*]. I only undertook office work. I am a man with a family, I have got a wife dependent on me. [*Aside.*] Good thing I remembered that. Yes, I have a wife and she would never allow me to rush into certain death.

MRS. KONDOR [*enters*]. What is it, darling? What is it all about?

FIRST GENERAL. Madam, your husband refuses to visit his faithful soldiers at the front.

MRS. KONDOR. What is this I hear, Arthur?

KONDOR [*aside to her*]. Say you don't allow me to go. Say it will be your death if I go to the front.

MRS. KONDOR. No, Arthur, I can never say such a thing. Duty comes first.

KONDOR [*taken aback*]. Bertha, you want to send me to my early death?

MRS. KONDOR. Yes, Arthur, the

French Army expects you to do your duty and you must go!

KONDOR [*calls after her*]. You wait, Bertha, you shall have to account for this—when I wake up! [*Turning back.*] And now, you leave me alone, you two, because I am not going.

GENERALS. But, Mr. Field Marshal . . . !

[*Firing without.*]

KONDOR [*stops both ears and shouts*]. I'm not going, I'm not going.

[*The scene gets darker, finally grows quite dark.*]

SCENE IV

JEAN [*a valet, tries to wake the sleeping Kondor*]. Your Lordship! Your Lordship!

KONDOR. What is the matter again?

JEAN. Your Lordship, your bath is ready, kindly walk into the bathroom.

KONDOR. Into what?

JEAN. You gave orders that in future a bath should be prepared for you twice a day.

KONDOR. I couldn't possibly have said that. Twice a day! I said a month, perhaps, not a day. And I did not say twice!

JEAN. Does Your Lordship wish to drive out in the automobile or in the carriage?

KONDOR. Automobile. [*Aside.*] If I have the choice, I may as well choose the automobile.

JEAN. Which car shall I order?

KONDOR. Why, are there several?

[*A bell rings.*]

KONDOR. Go, Jean, my boy, and see who it is. [*With sudden alarm.*] But if it is anybody in uniform, don't let them in.

[*Jean goes out and in a moment returns excitedly.*]

JEAN. Your lordship, a lady! A closely-veiled lady!

KONDOR. Don't let her come in! You never can tell—it may be my mother-in-law!

JEAN. One can see through the veil that it is a beautiful young lady.

KONDOR. Well, and didn't you ask her who she is?

JEAN. I asked, but she did not answer.

KONDOR. Then it is not my mother-in-law. Show the lady in, Jean.

[*Jean exits, Kondor arranges his tie before the glass.*]

PRINCESS [*entering*]. Count!

KONDOR [*bowing*]. Madam!

PRINCESS. Don't you know me?

KONDOR. I can't deny . . . .

PRINCESS [*raising her veil*]. And like this?

KONDOR. Ah! You look familiar. [*Reflectively.*]

PRINCESS. You may have seen my picture in *L'Illustration*.

KONDOR. That's it.

PRINCESS. My name is of no importance. The chief thing is that I am a princess. You cannot expect more than that.

KONDOR. Certainly not more. But I couldn't do it at less. Princess, pray be seated.

PRINCESS. Thank you, Count. But may I first take off my hat?

KONDOR. Certainly. [*Aside.*] This dream is improving.

PRINCESS. The rest—later.

KONDOR. Why wait? Take off the rest, too. The sooner the better.

PRINCESS. Count, you are too eager. Why are you in such a hurry?

KONDOR. With my luck, I am sure to wake up before anything has had time to happen.

PRINCESS. Let us sit down first, Count, and talk. Where do you think we met for the first time?

KONDOR. Not in Budapest, at Fisher and Company's?

PRINCESS. On the Paris race-course.

KONDOR. You don't say so? And what was I doing there?

PRINCESS. What you were doing? You rode.

KONDOR. Did I?

PRINCESS. You had the finest horse. But the horse felt that it had never carried such a horseman yet.

KONDOR. I should think it hadn't.

PRINCESS. The more restive the horse got, the more calmly you sat in the saddle. The spectators were in a fever of expectation. A crowd of thousands was yelling: Hurrah for Count Kondor! Hurrah! The ladies of the aristocracy had eyes for no one but you and I resolved to visit this Hungarian peer in his home, even if my husband should kill me for it.

KONDOR [*in a different voice*]. Your husband?!

PRINCESS [*in a conversational tone*]. I had to tell you this, my dear. And now, if you wish it . . .

[*Beginning to undress.*]

KONDOR [*protesting*]. Pardon me . . .

PRINCESS. What's that? You were in such a hurry just now!

KONDOR. Just a moment, please . . . You were speaking of your husband?

PRINCESS. Yes, my husband, the Prince . . . that wild beast . . .

KONDOR [*stuttering*]. Wild beast . . . ?

PRINCESS. Yes, he is terrible.

KONDOR. Wild beast?

PRINCESS. You know, the Prince is one of those men who only feel happy in the fencing-room, with a sword in his hand, or in Africa, shooting lions.

KONDOR [*hopefully*]. And at present, I hope, he is in Africa?

PRINCESS. No, he is in town at present—but that has really no importance for you.

KONDOR. Well, I shouldn't say that exactly.

[*Bell rings sharply.*]

PRINCESS [*with a scream*]. Good Lord! That is my husband ringing the bell. I know his ring. Every time he catches me in the act, he rings like that. I am perfectly sure of it. If this wild beast finds me here he will kill me. For Heaven's sake, where is the back door?

KONDOR. If there were one, you bet I should have gone out by it before this.

PRINCESS. I hope you know your duty and you will tell him you seduced me after having dragged me here against my will.

KONDOR. Who did? How dare you say such a thing to my face? Oh!

PRINCE [*storming in*]. Ha!

KONDOR [*motioning to the Princess*]. It's all her fault.

PRINCE [*in a blood-curdling voice*]. Be quiet, Count! My wife here, in your house! Undoubtedly this is a case of "in flagrante."

KONDOR [*wiping the perspiration from his brow*]. Wish I were waking up.

PRINCE. I hope, Count, you know your duty. Good morning.

[*Exits.*]

PRINCESS. Good-by, Count. The prince is going to kill you in duel. Tell me, what flowers do you prefer on your grave? Forget-me-nots or lilies of the valley?

KONDOR. I should prefer a box of cigars. Never fear, Princess, he won't hurt me. I am going to Budapest by the afternoon express.

PRINCESS. Adieu, Count. When you arrive in a better world, remember . . . .

KONDOR [*utterly unnerved*]. Please don't speak to me of a better world. And I won't undertake to run any errands for you.

[*Lies down on the sofa, with back to the Princess.*]

PRINCESS. Well, good-by, then, Count. [*Bell rings.*] There are your seconds already.

[*Exit the Princess. A minute afterwards enter two gentlemen dressed in black.*]

KONDOR. Good Heavens, are these already the undertaker's men? What do you want? I am still alive!

FIRST GENTLEMAN. My dear fellow, we must be going.

SECOND GENTLEMAN. My friend, it is time for us to start. In five minutes, you are to meet the Prince—we decided on pistols. If a man wants to be a Count, he must be prepared to fulfill the social duties of his station.

KONDOR. Im not going . . . I'm not going . . . I'm not going . . . I don't want to die so young . . . .

[*It has gradually grown quite dark.*]

SCENE V

[*The stage is again in full light, Kondor asleep on the sofa. Mrs. Kondor sitting by the table, reading "L'Illustration."*]

MARY [*comes in, a newspaper in her hand. Stops near the sofa*]. Master is still asleep. . . . How he grumbles in his sleep! Sure, he is dreaming something bad. . . .

MRS. KONDOR [*goes up to her husband, rouses him*]. Arthur! Arthur!

KONDOR. I don't want to die. I want to live. . . . Who is it? . . .

MRS. KONDOR. Arthur, it's I.

KONDOR [*glaring at her*]. You had the heart to send me to the front and you dare come before my eyes?

MRS. KONDOR. Arthur, what have you been dreaming about?

KONDOR [*rubbing his eyes*]. Awful things. . . . And this last part, with the undertaker's men, this was the worst! [*Wipes his forehead.*] Phew, I'm hot! [*Gets up from the sofa.*] But it serves me right. A Budapest salesman shouldn't read French illustrated papers. Where is that magazine? I want to throw it in the fire.

MRS. KONDOR. Don't, Arthur, . . . While you slept . . . I looked at the pictures a bit . . . [*Sits on the sofa, sighs.*] What beautiful dresses there are in that magazine . . . what hats . . . what frocks . . . what women . . . [*Lies down on the sofa.*] If I could lead a life like those women do. . . .

[*Yawns.*]

KONDOR. Gee!—now she's caught the infection from that silly paper. . . . Put a shawl on your mistress's feet, Mary . . . There . . . [*Sympathetically.*] She is al-

ready asleep . . . [*Sees the paper in the servant's hand.*] What is that paper?

MARY. The *Budapest Daily News.*

KONDOR. Give it me. And this [*handing her the French magazine*]—take this and throw it into the fire.

[*Mary exits.*]

KONDOR [*alone, sits at table, reads the paper*]. Tramway catastrophe on Üllöi Street. . . . A fight on Gizella Square . . . Murder in Rose Street. . . . [*Contentedly.*] How different this is . . . a fellow feels more at home.

[*Mrs. Kondor, who has been sleeping restlessly, groans in her sleep.*]

KONDOR [*looks at the sleeping woman with sympathy, but also with a little malice*]. Poor thing, I suppose she is just now talking to the British Ambassador. . . .

[*Curtain.*]

THE LETTERS

A COMEDY

BY FRANK G. TOMPKINS

CHARACTERS

KENT [*the editor of a literary magazine*].
DAWSON [*who controls the stock in the company*].
ASHE [*a poet*].
KIMBALL [*a critic*].
ROYCE [*the husband of Mrs. Compton-Royce (the
American novelist who does not appear)*]

Reprinted from the Appleton Little Theater Plays by permission of the author and publishers.

THE LETTERS

A COMEDY   BY FRANK G. TOMPKINS

[SCENE: *One of the suite of offices be-longing to the editors of a very literary magazine. There is a door into the hall and another into an inner office. In the center of the back wall is a fireplace and above it the portrait of a woman with a brilliant, proud, cynical face, a strong face, all surface and quite unreadable. In front of the fireplace stands a long table with several chairs. Somewhere in the room is a desk so placed that its oc-cupant is not visible to people entering from the outside. There is a bowl of roses on the desk and a small man is seated before it. This is Mr. Royce, the husband of the woman in the portrait. At the door of the inner room, just going out, is a slim, polished gentleman of cultured appearance. He is the very lit-erary editor of the magazine, Kent by name.*]

KENT. I wonder, Royce, if you are quite generous in this matter. Aren't you considering just yourself? Your wife's wishes might be different, [*He glances at the portrait.*] if she were here to choose.

ROYCE. That's exactly what I'm do-ing, Kent. I am considering myself. So long as Martha was living we both con-sidered her; now I'm going to have one thing as I want it. Of course, Martha wanted those letters published, but I don't. At least, I'm going to find out something about them first.

KENT [*with disapproval in his tone*]. But why is it necessary to call in a—rabble, to sit in council on what surely concerns only Mrs. Compton-Royce, and yourself, and—the man to whom she wrote the letters? How many have you summoned to—your literary inquest?

ROYCE. Only three. The poet, Ken-yon Ashe; Kimball, the critic; and Daw-son. That's all.

KENT. A motley crew, isn't it? Do you know, Royce, you put me in rather a peculiar position. A poet whose poems I always reject, a critic who calls me very unpleasant names, and the owner of my magazine, who insists on proceeds first and literature second. It's a little trying for me, isn't it? You mustn't ask me to do more than sit back and listen.

ROYCE. Sit back and listen? Nothing of the sort! I sit back and listen; you lead the discussion.

KENT. I refuse.

ROYCE. Then I refuse to let the let-ters be published. That's final. I re-fuse.

KENT. I wish I had your wife's secret of managing you, my dear Royce.

ROYCE. It died with her, thank God! I manage myself now. You know how I devoted my life to Martha and her genius, but this thing concerns me, and unless Martha is too much for me still, I'm going to have my way. And oh, Kent, I don't want these men to know who I am unless it's necessary. Do you mind? You'll get a much freer expres-sion of their opinion, if they don't know that the husband of the complete letter writer—no disrespect, my dear—is in their midst.

[*He nods casually to the portrait.*]

KENT. I don't approve. But if you want it that way, you must be ready to take what they say without offense. Will you send them in when they come?

[*He goes into the inner office.*]

[*Royce places a little silver vase, that would hold one flower, under the portrait and goes back to his desk, where he is not visible from the outside door.*]

[*The door opens and Kenyon Ashe enters. He has a white rose in his hand. As soon as he sees that no*

*one is there, he puts his rose in
the vase on the mantel. He
strikes an attitude before the portrait in a half humorous way.*]

ASHE. A tribute to you, my dear!
From one genius to another. [*He looks
at the portrait more closely.*] No, my
dear lady, I don't like your smile. It's
too superior, too knowing. My dear
Mrs. Royce, come to think of it, there
are too many clever women and too
many stupid men in your incomparable
novels, to make men trust you quite.
I don't feel just sure of you. If I didn't
have your letters here in my pocket,
[*Slaps himself.*] I'd wonder just what
that smile means. I wonder—No, I'll
keep this rose myself.

[*He puts it in his buttonhole.*]

ROYCE [*clearing his throat*]. Mr.
Kent is in the inner office. He wants to
see you, I think.

ASHE. Great guns, man! Why don't
you scare a fellow to death! Are you
hired to hide behind that desk to trap
criminals? You make a man realize that
he must have looked rather silly.

ROYCE. Silly! I don't know. I won't
pretend that I didn't hear you; but I
will promise you that it didn't interest
me in the least.

ASHE. Hold on, my dear man, don't
make me feel any smaller. I shan't ask
you not to tell, because I hope you will.
Mention me in your memoirs, and we'll
call it square. Every little mention
helps. Don't apologize.

[*He goes into the inner room.
The outer door opens and Dawson
and Kimball come in together.*]

KIMBALL. . . . call attention to the
fact that all the critics are wrong about
her. They harp always on her brilliant
intellect and on her cold, disinterested
analysis of women. But I contend that
beneath the surface of those very books
there ran a deep emotional undercur-
rent, powerful but controlled—controlled
by an iron will. I feel it in all her
books, and I have personal reasons for
believing that my judgment will be veri-
fied by outside evidence.

[*He puts his hand on his pocket.*]

DAWSON. You're right, Kimball, absolutely right! But what beats me is,
how did you know it?

KIMBALL. Oh, one gets a nose for

those things. Of course some critics
never do but—

[*He takes out his rose and starts
for the vase.*]

DAWSON. I say, Kimball, have you
brought a rose too?

KIMBALL. TOO? Have you brought
one?

DAWSON. No, but I ordered a bunch
of them sent over this morning. Say,
I'd like to know how you knew about
the roses. Does she mention them anywhere in her books? I don't remember
it. I suppose that's your critical nose
too?

KIMBALL. Knew about them? Who
else— Look here, I'd like to know how
you knew—

ROYCE. Mr. Kent is waiting for you
gentlemen in the inner office.

DAWSON. Oh, yes, Kent to be sure.
Kimball, you've got a surprise coming—
later. Hello, are those my roses?

ROYCE. No doubt they are. They
came this morning. [*To Kimball.*]
Would you like to add yours to the collection?

KIMBALL. No, thank you. I'll put
mine here. [*He puts his rose in the
small vase.*] It has a greater signifi-
cance than—that hothouse you have
there.

DAWSON. I don't understand—

KENT [*from the inner door*]. How are
you, Dawson? Kimball, will you fellows come in here? Or no, Ashe and I
will join you at the long table. [*They
enter.*] Will you sit down? Here's a
chair, Dawson.

DAWSON. Take the head of the table
yourself, Kent. It's your party. And
tell us what we're here for.

[*Kent has the head of the table.
Dawson and Kimball are on his
left, and Ashe on his right at the
sides of the table but far enough
back in their chairs so that they
are all visible. Royce goes to
inner office.*]

KENT. I shan't waste your time with
preliminaries. It's a question for your
judgment. You've been chosen to make
a rather delicate decision—a poet, a
critic, a publisher. You know how the
public looks on the publication of an
artist's letters after his death. [*Dawson coughs, Ashe feels of his pocket, and*

Kimball merely turns to give closer attention and scowls.] This is a question of letters.

ASHE. They buy them like hot cakes and then give the publishers hell for publishing them.

KENT. We have reason to believe that there are such letters from one of the most interesting women in American literature—

KIMBALL. Mrs. Compton-Royce.

KENT. Exactly. A series of letters of the most private character. In fact—

ASHE. Love letters. Why *do* they do it?

KENT. Yes. Love letters.

DAWSON. But she was a married woman, wasn't she? I thought— Doesn't that—?

KIMBALL. Certainly she was. But can't you allow something to genius? Besides who was Royce? Did anybody ever see him?

ASHE. I saw him once, long ago. He was a pale little affair trotting around in the wake of a blazing comet of a woman. How far did this—correspondence go? Have you any idea?

KENT. It was purely a correspondence. They never met. But it is not a literary dialogue, and it is *not* platonic. In fact, the letters must have been of the most frankly passionate character.

DAWSON. That makes it different again. Just the kind the public likes to read and just the kind they'll blame us for giving them a chance to read.

ASHE. May I ask how you are so sure of the existence of these letters? Has the man given any hint?

KENT. Certainly not. I hope he's a gentleman.

KIMBALL. Then granting that you know what you're talking about, what makes you think he'll give them up?

KENT. I'm not at all sure of it. But I think if you men decide that the letters ought to be published, they will be forthcoming. It rests with you. Of course, we all know the arguments against their publication. They are private and their author is helpless to protect herself now. It was bad enough in the case of the Browning letters. You know what the world thought of that. And *they* were written from a woman to her husband. These are not.

DAWSON. But they *will* sell. How they will sell!

KENT [*stiffly*]. I trust we can leave their salability out of the question. But there is a more valid reason for their publication. Mrs. Compton-Royce belonged to the public in the larger sense. Just as Whitman did. It's a question whether such genius doesn't sacrifice its right to privacy in return for the idolatry the public gives.

KIMBALL. That's not it, Kent. There's the larger question of the psychology of genius, which demands their publication. If Mrs. Compton-Royce had one personality for her books and another for her private life, we have a right to know that. Her work is an incomplete revelation. Her work plus her life is a complete work of art. That's the way I put it. And so little is known of Mrs. Royce's life. Literally nothing. Her letters are public property. The man who holds them ought to have the sanction of all of us for their publication, and even our encouragement—our backing.

KENT. How do you feel about it, Ashe?

ASHE.. Kimball's right. Lucky beggar to have his name go down in literary history linked with hers, unless he's such a nonenity that it'll swamp him.

DAWSON. Do you think, Kent, that we can use them in the magazine? The circulation would go up in leaps and bounds.

KENT. Don't put it that way, Dawson. If I didn't understand you and Ashe better, I should be distressed by the motives you profess. However, the principle is right.

DAWSON. Right? Now you're talking. We owe it to the public. Eh, Ashe?

ASHE. I say, go ahead.

KIMBALL. By all means.

KENT. I believe then we are agreed — It seems to be your best judgment— all of you—?

DAWSON [*throwing them in the center of the table*]. Well, here are your letters.

[*They all start back.*]

ASHE. The letters! Dawson, do you mean to tell me—

KIMBALL. Are *those* from Mrs. Royce?

DAWSON. Certainly. Those letters are from Mrs. Royce. Mrs. Compton—hyphen—Royce, and they are written to me.

KENT. But Dawson, we don't mean business letters—

DAWSON. No more do I, my dear fellow. Business letters! Not much! They deserve every adjective you applied to them, and then some.

[*They are all silent a moment, gazing at Dawson, who faces them belligerently.*]

ASHE [*in a tone of protest*]. Dawson, do you mean that those are the letters Kent was talking about?

[*Every word is emphasized, slowly, incredulously.*]

DAWSON. I do.

ASHE. But they can't be, Dawson. Then, [*Suddenly changing his tone.*] what about these?

[*He throws down his pack.*]

DAWSON. What? Say that again, Ashe. Those? But mine are love letters!

ASHE. You couldn't call these anything else. Mrs. Compton-Royce wrote them and she wrote them to *me*. These are the letters Kent was referring to, aren't they, Kent?

[*Kent has risen and stands by the mantel with his back to them.*]

DAWSON. Don't talk nonsense, Ashe. [*Suddenly convinced.*] Is *that* why you were wearing a white rose? What the devil—? Look here, Kimball, what about your rose? You had a rose.

KIMBALL. I did. I *had* a rose, and —there are my letters. I needn't say a word about them. You've described them exactly.

ASHE. I say, Kimball.

DAWSON. It isn't a joke, Kimball.

KIMBALL. I'm inclined to differ with you there.

DAWSON [*like a peevish child*]. But mine are love letters, I told you. She wrote them to me. She couldn't have written love letters to you too. Are you sure?

ASHE [*giving his a shove into the center of the table*]. Love letters.

KIMBALL [*doing the same*]. Love letters. Make a nice little triangle, don't they? A new version. My God, what a woman! Say, this thing has gone far enough! I decline to be—

DAWSON. Wait, Kimball, there's some mistake. It was my letters you meant, wasn't it, Kent? Kent, wasn't it mine?

[*Pathetically, pleading.*]

KENT [*turning to face them*]. No, Dawson, it wasn't. The whole affair has taken such an unexpected turn, I don't know what to say. Well. [*He takes them from his pocket.*] There are the letters I was talking about.

ASHE [*rises and shakes his fist at the picture*]. You fiend! You vampire! Devil-woman!

KIMBALL. Sit down, Ashe, you don't need to make a fool of yourself. She's tended to that nicely for us.

DAWSON [*querulously*]. But I don't see what she would do it for? There isn't any sense in it! I can't understand it.

KIMBALL. Do it for? For her own amusement.

ASHE. I don't care a hang what she did it for. She *did* it.

DAWSON. Well, I guess we haven't got any letters to publish.

ASHE. We've got too many letters to publish.

KIMBALL. *Haven't* we? If the rest of you are soft enough to have any scruples now, I haven't. There isn't any question of our right to publish anything she wrote, now. We have the right. The question is which set—

DAWSON. I believe you. You've hit it, Kimball. I think my set would sell.

ASHE. So would mine. And I say, fellows, think what it would mean to me. Why, it would make my stuff.

KIMBALL. Make your own stuff, Ashe. I say—

KENT. Listen, please, a moment. Of course, Mrs. Compton-Royce has no rights in the matter now, but haven't we any dignity ourselves? This mustn't get out. Never! And you men mustn't print one scrap of what she wrote.

DAWSON. Oh, I say, Kent, destroy all this? Think what it's worth as literature, if you don't care about the money. I'm not proud of my letters; I'm pretty sore about it. Truth is, I felt pretty puffed up. Still, I don't feel like throwing away such good material.

KIMBALL. No doubt they'd sell better if we printed the warmest extracts from all of them. A sort of anthology. A lovely garland to hand the deceased lady. And let the public in on the whole story.

KENT. There is one set of these letters that won't ever be printed, gentlemen. They are mine to do with as I please, and I please to do—this.

[*He throws them into the grate.*]

KIMBALL. Kent! You've thrown away a literary curiosity.

ASHE. Mine too, Kent. I'd counted on it, but I don't want to go down to posterity as the butt of a tasteless joke.

[*He adds his to Kent's.*]

DAWSON [*doubtfully*]. If you fellows think that is the thing to do—but I don't want to.

KIMBALL. Hold on, Dawson. I'm going to keep mine. This thing needs more study. I'm not going to let foolish pique cheat me out of first-hand material of incalculable value. I'm willing to put aside my personal feelings and make it a subject for a biographical criticism that will be unique.

DAWSON. If Kent don't use them, will you let me back your book? I suppose you wouldn't want my letters too?

KENT. You mustn't do this. Kimball, think!

KIMBALL. I've thought, Kent. That's where I differ from you. Your scruples aren't thought, they're childish pride.

KENT. Dawson, *you* don't want—

DAWSON. I'm with Kimball, old man. We're going to publish those letters, and neither you nor Mrs. Compton-Royce can stop us, so cut it out—

KENT. How about Mr. Royce? [*He steps to the inner door.*] Royce, I want you to talk to these men. [*Enter Royce.*] This is Ashe, Kimball, and Dawson. Gentlemen, this is Royce.

ROYCE. Reading from left to right, I suppose, in the orthodox fashion. Who had the letters?

KENT. Royce, I don't know how much you knew or how much you've heard. You chose these men, and they all had letters. Of course there must be some explanation. There weren't any symptoms of mental—?

ROYCE. Not a bit of it, Kent. I wish I could give you that comfort, but her mind was never clearer. She was working on "Intercepted Visions" not an hour

before she died, and the last sentence is as clear as a bell. No, she did it knowingly and with malice-aforethought, if she did it. The question is, what are you going to do about it?

DAWSON. We're going to publish.

ROYCE. Publish! Surely not! It'll only make you all ridiculous.

KENT. You see, Royce, there are my letters in the grate and Ashe's too. Excuse the pun. But Dawson and Kimball feel differently about it. We all feel pretty much ill-used, but I confess I don't get their point of view when it comes to publishing.

ROYCE. But even two sets of letters! Aren't two sets of letters from one woman rather ridiculous? I don't ask anything for her or for myself. We deserve anything you choose. But think of yourselves!

DAWSON. Look here, Royce, I hadn't thought quite what a rotten deal this was—is for you. Honestly, I hadn't. I don't like to use any fellow that way. Royce, you can have 'em back. Here.

ROYCE. Dawson, you're white, damned white. I knew it the minute you came in. And Kent and Ashe, too. And now, Kimball, you.

KIMBALL. I keep the letters.

ROYCE. U-um. I don't know just how to deal with a man like you, Kimball.

KIMBALL. I don't believe you do. You see I carry my brains in my head and not—under my waistcoat pocket. I *keep* the letters. Incidentally, there's only one set now, and there's nothing absurd about one set. I keep 'em.

ROYCE. Do you know, Kimball, I don't believe you do.

KIMBALL. Go ahead.

ROYCE. Not when you know who wrote them.

KIMBALL. Well, hurry, my good man. If Mrs. Compton-Royce didn't write them, who *did?*

ROYCE. I did.

KENT AND ASHE. *You* wrote them?

DAWSON. Royce, what are you saying?

KIMBALL. Keep cool, gentlemen. Don't let him trick you like that. He never wrote them. I know better. By all the internal evidence only a woman could have written those letters, **and** only one woman at that, the woman who wrote "Inhibitions." It is as unmistakable as the imprint of the human thumb. Any critical intelligence in America to-day would vouch for that. Well, Royce?

ROYCE. I don't know—I'm afraid you're right. Look here, Kimball, will you recognize that testimony that damages the witness is strong testimony? Testimony that he doesn't want to give because it incriminates him and makes him a cad and a bounder and a fellow that decent men don't want to associate with? That's the best testimony, isn't it?

KIMBALL. It's good. Go on.

ROYCE. Well listen, then. I'd rather die than tell you this, but I want those letters. You'll never speak to me again and I value your opinion and I'd like your respect, but I can't have it and have those letters. Do you remember when Martha—when Mrs. Royce used to write articles for the sociological journals, revolutionary stuff, clear headed, unemotional stuff with not much imagination in it. Years ago it was, when she was just out of college. Would you have predicted then that she could ever write those novels? Would you, Kimball?

KIMBALL. No, I wouldn't. I fact, I didn't.

ROYCE. Well, you were right; she couldn't. She didn't. We were married shortly after, in 1900. Do you remember when *The Awakened Galatea* was published?

KIMBALL. 1902. It's a date in American literature.

ROYCE. Well, doesn't that mean something to you?

KIMBALL. It does. It means that for some reason—pardon me if I seem rude—some reason that I can't fathom, you awakened the Galatea in Miss Compton and she became the thinker plus the woman.

ROYCE. It means nothing of the sort. She never woke up. She was always a passionless intellect, a regular Herbert Spencer of a woman. If she hadn't married me, she would have been a third-rate essayist to her dying day.

KIMBALL. I can admit that and still not credit—

ROYCE. But you *must* see; she never wrote those books alone. I wrote them too.

KENT. Oh, I say, Royce, don't ask me to believe—

ASHE. Balderdash, why man alive—

KIMBALL. Leave this to me, can't you? See here, Royce, those books aren't put together that way. There isn't a patch of reasoning and then a patch of womanly sentiment. It's all one thing—

ROYCE. Of course, it is. We didn't do it that way. Martha thought it out and outlined the idea, but she never got any grip on the characters till I made them live for her. Hers were just puppets. And she couldn't keep them alive after she once got them started. Her mind was abstract; mine is concrete. When she wanted to know what her women would think or do, she'd ask me. I knew. I'm ashamed to tell you, but I *knew*. Who went over every word she'd done with painstaking care to see where she'd slipped in spite of her coaching? I did. I typed them all too and if the puppets had gone dead, I started them living again. She could think and she could construct a work that was architecture, but I had to keep it human and individual. You'll find it all in her notes. She had inexorable logic but she didn't understand people, men or women. Do you remember *The Book of the Four Masters?*

KIMBALL. If you did that, you are guilty of her biggest fiasco.

ROYCE. I didn't. That's the point. I was sick when she wrote it. I begged her to put it off till I could help. But she was too self-confident. She learned her lesson. She never forgot it and she never underestimated my help after that. Alone, we were both third-raters. Together we did some of the best work —you've said so yourself, Kimball— that's been done in America.

ASHE. But how comes it, Royce, that you understood women so well yourself —women as well as men?

ROYCE. Oh, I don't know. I suppose I have a woman's intuitions. Some men have. Fiona McLeod had. I've always understood them. They don't like it, except Martha, and she hadn't a woman's mind. I understand woman's way of thinking. It isn't like a man's thinking. It doesn't pass for logic with men. But it's just as logical—once you get the hang of it, and somehow I have the hang of it. Martha hadn't. They're after such different things in life— women are. You can't see how it is, un- less—well, unless you can. Isn't that woman's logic for you?

ASHE. Yes, I can. I see. It's like that with me sometimes. Royce, you're right. Your way of going at this is a woman's way.

ROYCE. I'm sorry if it is. But it's the only way I can see.

KENT. But haven't you made the let- ters invaluable by your very confession?

DAWSON. There's our literary find! A positive scoop! Hooray! Great stuff! The man and the woman doing the novels together. It's great! Do you expect Kimball to give them up now?

ROYCE. I do. He's a gentleman.

KIMBALL. A gentleman? I'm not. Nothing of the sort. I'm a critic. But you must know what we think of you. I have no more compunction about publishing *your* letters than I had about hers. Less. You're a literary freak if what you say is true, and as a man you don't merit a moment's considera- tion.

ROYCE. I know that. I knew that before I told you. But—

KIMBALL. What did you do it for?

ROYCE. For our last book, *Intercept- ed Visions.* You were all in it. We couldn't make you come alive. You were all wrong in her book. She couldn't realize you, and somehow neither could I. I didn't understand any of you. She kept worrying about you, and asking me if we must give it up. Finally I got you. You answered our letters and I had what I wanted. I'm sorry and I'm ashamed, but you weren't real people to either one of us. You were copy, characters that we wanted to make real, and we would have dissected your hearts out to get what we wanted to fill our pattern. We'd have used ourselves and each other and the most sacred things in the world just that way to get what we wanted. Nothing else mattered and we never ex- pected to know any of you. Since the

book is gone and I've come to know Kent, I hate myself for it—but I'd do it again, and so would Martha if she were here. And Kent and Ashe and Dawson have been so much finer than I thought they could be—

KIMBALL. How about me? I'm just what you thought I was. Those docu- ments are literary history. I'd do any- thing for the truth of literary criticism. I'd sacrifice you just as readily as you sacrificed me. I hold a bomb in my hand and I'm afraid I'm going to touch it off.

ROYCE. It'll explode us both. Kim- ball, I hate to do it but if you publish those letters as mine or hers I shall have my answer.

KIMBALL. What?

ROYCE. I will publish your answers. They're literary material too.

KIMBALL. Well, what of it?

ROYCE. Your love letters to me. Can you stand that? The fool, the dupe you'll look! If your devotion to criti- cism is as great as that, come on. Let the whole world read the burning epis- tles you wrote to a prosaic, dried up, little middle-aged man—

KIMBALL. Take your damned let- ters! They burn my fingers. I'm through with the whole rotten business.

ROYCE. Thank you. Now, gentlemen, I have what I had to have. At a very heavy cost to me. I know you'll never any of you want to see me again. I'm sorry. I didn't know a man could be as good a friend as you were, Kent. I suppose, Kent, you couldn't—

[*He holds out his hand tentatively, wistfully.*]

KENT. I'm sorry too, but I guess you'll have to give us a chance to get over it first. You treated us pretty shabbily, you know—

ROYCE. I know. Good-by, then.

KENT. Good-by.

[*He starts for the inner office. Dawson goes without a word, only a curt nod.*]

ASHE. It's been very interesting, old man, but not—very elevating. Come on, Kimball.

KIMBALL. Wait a minute. About the white roses. They weren't her favorite flowers?

ROYCE. No, she hated them.

KIMBALL. What did she like?

ROYCE [*ironically*]. Musk.

[*Kimball and Ashe go out and Kent closes the door of the inner office. Royce gets his coat and hat. Suddenly he faces the picture.*]

ROYCE. You fiend, how could you? You conscienceless—devil! Look what you made me do! Here, take your white roses, and your shoddy romances. I wish—I wish—I wish I'd thrashed you.

[*Curtain.*]

(3)